HISTORICAL ATLAS OF CANADA

HISTORICAL ATLAS OF CANADA

Volume III

Addressing the Twentieth Century

1891–1961

Donald Kerr
EDITOR

Deryck W. Holdsworth
EDITOR

Susan L. Laskin
ASSISTANT EDITOR

Geoffrey J. Matthews
CARTOGRAPHER/DESIGNER

UNIVERSITY OF TORONTO PRESS

Toronto Buffalo London

For Alexandre, Dyan, Félix, Jean-Philippe,
Jennifer, Lily, Mathew, Michael, Peter, and Stewart
and for the young people of the twenty-first century

© University of Toronto Press 1990
Toronto Buffalo London
Printed in Canada

ISBN 0-8020-3448-9

Cet ouvrage est également disponible en langue française
aux Presses de l'Université de Montréal.

Canadian Cataloguing in Publication Data

Main entry under title:

Historical atlas of Canada

Partial contents: v. 3. Addressing the twentieth century, 1891–1961 /
Donald Kerr, Deryck W. Holdsworth [editors].
Includes bibliographical references.
ISBN 0-8020-3448-9 (v. 3).
1. Canada – Historical geography – Maps.
I. Matthews, Geoffrey J., 1932–
G1116.S1H58 1987   911'.71   C87-094228-X

The research, cartography, and publication of
volume III of the *Historical Atlas of Canada*
have been funded by the
Social Sciences and Humanities Research Council of Canada.

Contents

Canada 1891–1961: An Overview

1

CANADA IN 1891

Marvin McInnis, Peter J. Usher (native land use)

2

TERRITORIAL EVOLUTION

Norman L. Nicholson, Robert Galois (BC), Michael Staveley
(Nfld)

3

ECONOMIC GROWTH

Marvin McInnis

4

POPULATION COMPOSITION

Donald Cartwright, Murdo MacPherson

PART ONE
THE GREAT TRANSFORMATION
1891–1929

National Economic Patterns

Regional Dimensions of the Production System

Canadian Society during the Great Transformation

38
ORGANIZED LABOUR

Gregory S. Kealey, Douglas Cruikshank

Maps
Units of the One Big Union, 1919
Affiliates of the All-Canadian Congress of Labour, 1927
National and Catholic Unions in Québec, 1921–1922
Graphs
Union Membership by Province, 1911–1920, 1921–1930
Union Membership by Industry, 1914–1930
Union Membership by Affiliation, 1911–1930
Trades and Labor Congress of Canada and Alternate Union
    Centres, 1891–1930
Railway Unions, 1911–1929
Bricklayers and Masons International Union of America,
    1890–1906
Development of Mining Unions, 1890–1930
Metal-Trades Councils, 1911–1927
National and Catholic Unions, Québec, 1913–1930
Labour Politics, 1897–1932: Federal Elections; Provincial
    Elections; Results by Province

39
STRIKES

Gregory S. Kealey, Douglas Cruikshank

Maps
Striker Days, May, June, and July 1919
Strikes with Collective Violence, 1891–1930
Strikes with Military Intervention, 1891–1930
Graphs
Strike Issues, 1891–1930
Strike Settlement Methods, 1891–1930
Strike Results, 1891–1930
Strikes in May, June, and July 1919
Frequency, Size, and Duration of Strikes, 1891–1930
Strikes with Collective Violence, 1891–1930: By Decade; By
    Industry

PART TWO
CRISIS AND RESPONSE
1929–1961

The Great Depression

40
ECONOMIC CRISIS

Elizabeth Bloomfield, Gerald Bloomfield, Deryck W. Holdsworth,
Murdo MacPherson

Maps
Manufacturing Employment in Central Canada: 1929–1933;
    1933–1937
Employment Index, 1926–1939
The Gold Mining Boom, 1926–1939
Abitibi Power and Paper Company: Newsprint Capacity,
    1932, and Mill Closures
Graphs
Index of International Incomes, 1929–1939
National Income, Selected Sectors, 1926–1939
Employment Index, Selected Sectors, 1926–1939
Selected Exports, 1926–1939
Money Supply, 1913–1961
Gross Domestic Investment, 1926–1939
Mineral Production, 1926–1940
Canadian Newsprint, 1920–1940
Manufacturing Employment by Region, 1929–1937
Motor-Vehicle and Railway-Car Production, 1926–1940

41
THE IMPACT OF THE DEPRESSION ON PEOPLE

Murdo MacPherson, Deryck W. Holdsworth (trekking)

Maps
The Trek in Search of Work
Relief Recipients by Province, 1930–1940
Graphs
The Unemployed and Relief, 1926–1940
Occupational Classification of Workers on Relief, 1935
Monthly Relief Budgets, Family of Five, Montréal, 1936
Monthly Food Allowances, Family of Five, Selected Cities,
    1936
Deportations, 1903–1960
Price and Wage Indices, 1926–1940
Wage Rate and Purchasing Power, 1926–1940
Table
Relief Budget for One Week for a Family of Five, Montréal,
    1932
Illustration
'Riding the Rails'

The Second World War and the Post-War Period

Donors

Throughout the history of this project major funding has come from the Social Sciences and Humanities Research Council of Canada. More recently, additional support has come from several corporate and public bodies, without whose help we could not have continued. Of these, the Bank of Montreal has been the most generous of corporate sponsors. The Executive Committee of the *Historical Atlas of Canada* and the Editorial Board of this volume join in acknowledging with deep gratitude the contributions of these donors.

Social Sciences and Humanities Research Council of Canada

Department of the Secretary of State of Canada

Government of Ontario
Ministry of Colleges and Universities
Ministry of Culture and Communications
Ministry of Education
Ministry of Intergovernmental Affairs

The Birks Family Foundation
Imperial Oil Limited
George Cedric Metcalfe Charitable Foundation
Royal Canadian Geographical Society

CGC Foundation
Harlequin Enterprises Limited
Molson Companies Donations Fund
The Toronto Star
University Arts Women's Club

We also wish to acknowledge with thanks the many individuals who have encouraged us by making donations to the *Historical Atlas of Canada* and who have thus helped to bring this volume to publication.

BANK OF MONTREAL

Mapmaking and nation-building are inextricably linked. As routes were charted through the Canadian wilderness, traders and settlers soon followed, and new territories were established.

Like Canada's first mapmakers, our predecessors at the Bank of Montreal once stood on the threshold of a vast frontier. They too played a leading role in charting the nation's economic development.

Those early bankers pioneered our financial system by providing Canada's first currency and first foreign exchange operations. They financed canals, roads, and bridges and helped build the Canadian Pacific Railway. In this century, the Bank of Montreal has provided funds for a great variety of resource projects in Canada's mining, forestry, and hydroelectric power industries.

It is with special pride, then, that the Bank supports the *Historical Atlas of Canada*. By revisiting the paths we have journeyed as a nation, this important work reminds us of the debt we owe to those who came before us, and our responsibility to those who will follow us.

M.W. Barrett, Chairman

Foreword

I

Maps are a vital part of our cultural heritage. There is an apt description of their power to communicate in G.B. Greenough's presidential address to the Royal Geographical Society, London, in 1840: 'Words following words in long succession, however ably selected ... can never convey so distinct an idea of the visible forms of the earth as the first glance at a good map ... In the extent and variety of its resources, in rapidity of utterance, in the copiousness and completeness of information it communicates, in precision, conciseness, perspicuity, in the hold it has upon the memory, in vividness of imagery, in convenience of reference, in portability, in the happy combination of so many and such useful qualities, a map has no rival.' What Greenough was describing were essentially topographic maps. Modern thematic maps such as those presented in the *Historical Atlas of Canada* can communicate even more powerfully. They require more than a 'first glance,' but their intensive study returns rich rewards.

The *Historical Atlas of Canada* by definition focuses on the Canadian past, but it does not concentrate exclusively on political, military, or administrative events as such atlases have traditionally done; rather it depicts cartographically Canada's social, economic, and cultural evolution. Through the mapping of the character and structure of our society, our patterns of livelihood, our transformation of the landscape, through glimpses into the lives of ordinary people, the *Atlas* provides clear insights into our past. It interprets the events and patterns of the Canadian historical experience in innovative ways that will be of value to both scholars and interested general readers. It serves too as an authoritative reference work for all readers.

The research needed to produce the plates in these volumes was necessarily cross-disciplinary. Scholars from many disciplines, including archaeology, cartography, demography, economics, ethnology, historical geography, geography, geology, history, and sociology, and from one end of Canada to the other have generously shared their knowledge and skills to ensure that the maps and elaborative texts make a national and a scholarly contribution to Canadian studies. In order to fulfil their utilitarian function of communicating ideas, maps must also be aesthetically pleasing. From the beginning this work has demanded cartographic ingenuity and imaginative map design. The creative cartographic designs of Geoffrey Matthews have striking visual impact and the plates in these volumes prove that an atlas can be a beautiful work of art as well as a scholarly reference tool.

Financing this complex, lengthy, trans-national enterprise has been a daunting problem but the *Atlas* has had substantive encouragement from every quarter. The Social Sciences and Humanities Research Council of Canada (SSHRCC) generously maintained virtually all the research costs for the three volumes over a nine-year period, and in addition provided a large portion of the cartographic and publication costs. Only through the SSHRCC's funding was it possible to organize and mount this monumental undertaking. For the Council's commitment all of us who have worked on these volumes – scholars, researchers, and cartographers alike – are most deeply grateful.

When the SSHRCC's Major Editorial Grant came to a close in 1988, shortly after the publication of volume I, further help was sought from the Secretary of State of Canada through the good offices of one of our co-ordinating editors, Jean-Pierre Wallot. His efforts, combined with numerous letters of support from academic colleagues across the country, persuaded the then Secretary of State the Honourable Lucien Bouchard to investigate means of finding financing to complete the work. James E. Page, then Director of Canadian Studies in the Office of the Secretary of State, was appointed to this task. The *Atlas* gratefully acknowledges Mr Page's diplomacy on our behalf, including the raising of some financial support from the Office of the Secretary of State itself. He organized a commitment from the Breakthrough campaign of the University of Toronto, along with additional funding through a grant from four departments of the Government of Ontario: Ministry of Colleges and Universities, Ministry of Culture and Communications, Ministry of Education, and Ministry of Inter-governmental Affairs. This was the first of five annual grants from the Government of Ontario for the period 1988–1993.

The *Atlas* also wishes to record the vigorous efforts of Geoffrey Dean, a special consultant, who contacted various departments of the Government of Ontario on our behalf. Mr Dean was instrumental as well in negotiating much needed business and corporate sponsorship of the *Atlas*. For example, Imperial Oil Limited purchased the artwork for three plates for its archives.

Bell Canada, Ontario Region, most generously produced a videotape describing the nature and production of the plates in volume I for distribution to school boards in Ontario and presented a copy of the volume to each Ontario secondary school.

The benevolent work of the Breakthrough Campaign of the University of Toronto, which committed itself to raising over one-half of the outstanding funds needed to complete the project, has been crucial. We are grateful to Gordon C. Cressy, Vice-President, Development and University Relations, to Mary Alice Stuart, National Chairman of Breakthrough, and to other staff members of the Breakthrough campaign for their efforts, in particular Benson A. Wilson and Bill Straitton. The major benefactors reached through Breakthrough were the Bank of Montreal, the Birks Family Foundation, and the George Cedric Metcalfe Charitable Foundation. There were, in addition, a gratifying number of individual donors. The response of all has been vital to the project.

Many people at the University of Toronto, including President John Evans, President James Ham, and especially President George Connell, a number of vice-presidential officers, two directors of the Office of Research Administration, members of the comptroller's staff, the dean of Arts and Science, and several chairmen of the Department of Geography, and particularly my administrative assistant, Joanne Wainman, have all been patient, loyal, and strongly supportive of our endeavours, and their efforts have eased our way with friendly advice, guidance, sheer hard work, and, in some instances, financial assistance, as in providing seed money at the outset of the project. The enormous help of the University of Toronto from earliest days to the present, quite apart from affording cartographic work space and a central office, has been a necessary and most gratifying element in the founding, development, and on-going administration of the project.

Finally we acknowledge the magnificent unsolicited grant generously given to the *Atlas* by the Royal Canadian Geographic Society.

These various heart-warming donations and commitments of support have enabled us to compete successfully for further SSHRCC money to help us complete the *Atlas*. Thus, a national, multidisciplinary enterprise, in English and in French, originally funded entirely by an agency of the Government of Canada, has become, in the tradition of so many Canadian enterprises, a combined government and private undertaking. In so doing it nevertheless retains its original purpose and objectives.

The creation of this particular version of a historical atlas of Canada began in 1969. By 1979 funding for the project through the SSHRCC had been obtained and research on the three volumes of the *Atlas* began. We knew then that the task before us was awesomely difficult, cartographically complex, and undoubtedly time-consuming. None of us realized, however, just how time-consuming the reality would be. The creative processes taking place across the whole breadth of Canada and covering historical studies from pre-historic times to 1961 were enormously lengthy. It took over three years, for example, to elaborate our particular historical vision of Canada in order to produce the prospectus for the whole *Atlas*; then those plans were subsequently refined and made more detailed by the editors and editorial boards of each volume. Divergent views were considered by these boards and transformed in a spirit of compromise engendered by mutual trust and respect into the new expressions of Canadian history that are presented in each of these different yet closely related volumes.

The ideals and unique nature of this *Atlas* in themselves became a highly desirable goal. Editors and members of the three editorial boards passed on to scholars across the country their infectious enthusiasm and secured in return an equally enthusiastic response. Many authors unselfishly donated to the *Atlas* much more than normal academic research time; in several cases whole sabbatical leaves were devoted to the project. The enormous financial demands of the project stem largely from remuneration for research assistants, highly labour-intensive cartography, intricate photomechanical processes, publication costs, and the costs of travel and communication across the country. But these equal only a small part of the real monetary value of the time donated by the many participants in the project.

Fundamentally the *Atlas* is an illustration of the feasibility of interpersonal communication and co-operation across the whole of Canada. It is a prime example of Canadian success in overcoming distance and difficulty in order to achieve a common aim. That the process worked as well as it did is a tribute to the unstinting efforts of the editors of the volumes and the members of the editorial boards as well as the many contributors from the academic world and the public and private sectors. The intent of producing a first-class national atlas is now been realized as volumes I and III are published and volume II, depicting the nineteenth century, is under way. One of our other objectives, that of selling these volumes at a relatively low price so that they are widely available to the general public, is also being met. Through its vivid visual presentation of past events in the lives of ordinary Canadians the *Atlas* demonstrates new insights into our past while establishing new thinking in Canadian history as well as an abundance of subjects for further research. Our profound hope is that at the same time the *Atlas* will make a significant contribution to Canadians' understanding of one another and hence to their knowledge about and pride in Canada.

Wm G. Dean
University of Toronto, 1990

II

Charting and mapping the course of Canadian history between 1891 and 1961 have represented a tremendous challenge. During that period the frontiers of settlement expanded towards the West and the North and Canadian society became much more complex. A mostly agrarian society was transformed into an industrial and service-oriented urban society. Distinct regional identities and ethnic diversity persisted as basic features of the Canadian experience. Researchers for volume III of the *Historical Atlas of Canada* had to deal with such diverse phenomena in Canadian history as the peopling of the Prairies, the development of new resources, the expansion of the service sector, the rise of the labour movement, and the appearance of organized sport. Whereas their colleagues working on earlier periods had to struggle with a paucity of sources, the authors of the plates in volume III had to grapple with huge amounts of information.

Thanks to many years of in-depth research the challenge was met and the final product is illuminating. Through its full-colour maps and graphs volume III illustrates the most significant dimensions of the evolution of Canada in the twentieth century and the unique features of the country and its people. It shows the basic trends of its population, its economy, and its society. Most significantly, it also illustrates the complexity of the country and the numerous differences among its regions and in its ethnic and social groups. This volume is thus part of a recent trend in Canadian

historiography: the recognition that diversity is and has been a fundamental component in the shaping of Canadian society.

The editors of volume III were committed to a fair treatment of Québec's distinct characteristics. The various plates show that Québec shared many common features with Ontario, as a component of Central Canada, and also with the rest of the country. Plates dealing with ethnic origins, language, religion, and even politics nevertheless indicate significant differences. Distinct features of Québec such as the *collèges classiques*, the *caisses populaires*, and the *syndicats catholiques* are also portrayed.

The *Atlas* is being published simultaneously in English and French. The translation process was conducted alongside the editing of the original plates, thus permitting a cross-examination of the text and some useful adjustments to the content and wording of many plates. Both the English and the French editions have thus benefited from this close co-operation between the Toronto office and the translation team in Montréal.

My association with this project has been a tremendous experience and I hope that thousands of Canadian and international readers will share my enthusiasm for this magnificent tribute to our history.

Paul-André Linteau
Université du Québec à Montréal, 1990

Preface

In the first six decades of the 20th century Canada's economy and society were transformed, resulting in geographical patterns similar to today's. Agricultural settlement reached its effective limits, links by rail, road, air, and telephone were constructed, and both federal and provincial governments initiated many pivotal social and economic programs. Despite the increased role of international, national, and metropolitan-based enterprises regional identities persisted. At the same time Canada turned from a self-governing British dominion into a nation state, independent but sharing a continent with the dominant United States.

In this volume of the *Historical Atlas of Canada, Addressing the Twentieth Century,* 66 plates depict these complex and diverse patterns of change through a multidisciplinary approach. The *Atlas* does not portray Canada by encyclopaedic single-variable mapping. For that the reader can consult five excellent editions of *The National Atlas of Canada* (1906, 1915, 1957, 1974, and 1985); its maps portray different activities at cross-sections during the 20th century. Instead, this volume examines Canada's past through specific groups and individuals in specific times and places.

If Canada were a homogeneous society, perhaps a broad brush could be used to portray its historical evolution. Our plates make apparent, however, that many generalizations about Canada are simplistic or unconsciously reflect particular regional or class perspectives. Although we can only begin to depict the richness of our history, it is readily apparent that many of the old myths about Canada are unsupported. The stereotype of Canadians as hewers of wood and drawers of water peripheral to an industrial world economy can be discarded. Similarly, it is clear that life did not unilaterally improve for all Canadians in the 20th century. At the turn of the century some Canadians enjoyed prosperity, while others lived in severe deprivation; the birth rate of some groups was high and of others low; some people lived in industrial cities, others on labour-intensive farms; some successfully promoted their own cultural identities, others fought discrimination and cultural repression. In the following decades these differences sometimes faded and sometimes persisted, region by region, place by place. This volume attempts to balance local, regional, and national perspectives in tracking those complex changes.

At the outset the editorial board of this volume agreed on the need to focus on ordinary people, to examine broad issues in social and economic history, and to try to give all regions appropriate attention. What the editorial board thought were the significant topics of 20th-century Canada reflects, of course, the 1980s. This volume is historical in two senses: it tells us about the period under study, and it tells us too about the period in which the study occurred.

Research from a new wave of social historians guided and stimulated *Atlas* endeavours. Class, gender, ethnic diversity, and region are reflected in this volume's perspective on Canada's past. Recent research in economic history has been reinterpreting Canadian development in a more comprehensive and more systematically analytic mould. Such work emphasizes the use of statistical data and has explored numerous new sources. Of particular importance has been a project to provide historical estimates of Canadian national income and its components. Finally, there has been an explosion of research on past urban conditions, and so our portrayal of 20th-century urbanization has been able to take advantage of recent multidisciplinary work that spans social, economic, and regional concerns.

The broader social context of scholarship in the 1980s has affected our choices. Since 1961 a massive restructuring of the world economy has reshaped Canadian corporations, affecting the growth of cities, the composition of the work-force, and regional labour markets; socially debates over multiculturalism, language rights, universal health care, gender equality, and aboriginal rights have come to the fore; politically discussions concerning federal-provincial relations go on, as do debates over free trade with the United States. As these issues have emerged, they have inevitably influenced our choice of research topics.

Our treatment of Canada's development begins in 1891 and ends in 1961. Both dates are census years, and they are convenient markers. The completion of the Canadian Pacific Railway in 1886 had established a vital new cross-country link, and the 1880s were a vibrant economic period. The country grew more slowly in the 1890s; indeed there was a distinct economic lull between 1888 and 1895. The year 1891 thus provides a convenient benchmark to observe 'Canada's Century' from just before its dawn. The choice of a closing date proved controversial. The recent past has received relatively little scholarly consideration; moreover, some distance from the present is required to discern important trends. For some 1958 signalled the beginning of an economic lull after the post-war boom and coincided with a major political change in the country; for others the country's Centennial of 1967 was an important emotional symbol. If one considers the economic boom of the 1960s and 1970s, however, or the tremendous shifts in Québec society then underway, neither year seems appropriate. Instead, 1961, admittedly an arbitrary choice, provides a census-year termination for the first round of post-war growth and change, but leaves the second round of reorganization that followed to future researchers to consider.

The material for the seven decades has been divided into two time periods. The first part, the Great Transformation, covers 1891 to 1929, a period of dramatic structural change in the economy, population, society, and landscape. The second part, Crisis and Response, describes the Depression of the 1930s, the Second World War, and post-war growth to 1961. This division, however, has not been rigid. Many of the changes from the beginning of the century reverberate through the period following the Second World War; similarly, the post-war processes are not always responses to the war itself but are rooted in earlier times. Issues and themes are presented in the section that deals with the most important phases of their development: for example, seven decades of recreational activities are included in the Great Transformation, although there were obvious post-war developments; the plate on university education is located in the section entitled Crisis and Response although significant aspects of university education are relevant to the early 1900s; the evolving railway network is treated in the Great Transformation and the expanding road network is mapped in Crisis and Response, but in both cases critical developments from the other period are included.

The two parts are organized topically. The Great Transformation has been treated in three subsections: patterns of economic change at the national level; regional manifestations of economic growth; and the impact of these changes on society. In Crisis and Response a range of national and regional economic and social issues are examined together, emphasizing the greater integration of the country in this period.

Throughout the volume data have often proved problematic. Rarely has it been possible to assemble systematic and comparable evidence for all places across a long time-period. Some data were available only for one year; others were available only for census years, or only at the scale of the provinces, or only for one industrial sector. Changing census definitions and variable provincial and corporate records make it almost impossible to treat all places equally. Our options therefore were limited by the data, but we have throughout tried to convey key processes at large, as well as in specific places and times.

Geographical regions have been assessed at a variety of scales to portray broad temporal and spatial patterns and processes. The attempt to define intraurban patterns shows that Canadians in the 20th century were participants in an urban and industrial society that shared attributes, whatever their region. Our regional coverage largely ignores the provinces as geographical units, though we recognize that they have become an increasingly important conveyer of economic and social initiatives in a federal system. Often the Maritimes have been grouped together, as have the Prairies, even though each province has a distinctive 'signature' within those regions. Québec has a distinctive cultural and linguistic identity but its economy is linked with Ontario's, and for the purposes of this study southern Québec and southern Ontario are often combined as Central Canada.

Work on volume III proceeded through a series of stages. First themes and topics were identified. After the published material pertaining to them was examined, the research projects required were launched. The response from the scholarly community was overwhelmingly favourable and enthusiastic. Colleagues in a dozen disciplines participated both in discussions on the nature of plates and in the collection of materials. Contributors were enlisted from every region and their research work for the *Atlas* was funded over a number of years.

As the results of research accumulated, a second and overlapping stage began as those results were given shape on the plates themselves. Each plate stands on its own as a piece of research, but it is also interrelated with other plates within the broad scheme of topics and chronology. Preliminary plate designs brought together data from various sources, and the authors of the plates then had to refine their analyses. At this stage, too, the plates were examined from the point of view of cartographic design to ensure that they could in fact be produced as envisaged; as a result many plates went through multiple drafts. In a third overlapping stage of final design and production the editorial, cartographic, and translation teams worked together to check data during the scribing and proofing of plates.

Many individuals have been involved in the production of this work. The editorial board developed the conceptual thrust of the volume, selected the material to be presented on the plates, critically reviewed the draft content of the plates, and helped to shape the linking essays. The first editor of the volume, Thomas F. McIlwraith (1979–80), invited Marvin McInnis (Economics, Queen's University) and James W. Simmons (Geography, University of Toronto) to join the editorial board. Marvin McInnis has worked in population and resource studies and, with his Queen's colleague M.C. Urquhart, is involved in the ongoing monumental task of establishing historical estimates of national income. He wrote important drafts of the essays on national economic patterns and the Great Depression, as well as key elements of the material on demographic change. Jim Simmons is a geographer interested in the long-term workings of the Canadian urban system. After the new administration of the volume took over in 1980, three additional scholars were added to the board. Gregory S. Kealey (History, Memorial University of Newfoundland), a central force in the new field of labour history, offered his critical perspective on the process of industrialization. Chad Gaffield (Histoire, Université d'Ottawa, formerly at University of Victoria) is a social historian sensitive to relations among individuals, groups, and bureaucracies, and he has brought new approaches to looking at Canadian society. L.D. McCann (Geography, Mount Allison University), who has led in a major reinterpretation of Canada's regional geography, lobbied for a non-centralist approach to the study. All the board members contributed research within their own specialties but they also worked productively as a team to review and refine the plates. We have also benefited from the expertise of Paul-André Linteau (Histoire, Université du Québec à Montréal) who undertook the difficult task of supervising the translation of the

volume into French. As a leading Québec social historian he has fine-tuned both perspective and detail on plate texts and essays.

The volume has also drawn on the work of 50 scholars from across Canada who have served as authors or joint authors. They contributed their knowledge, the results of their research, their unremunerated time, and their generosity of spirit. Lynne Marks (doctoral candidate in History, York University), author or coauthor of eight plates, enriched our perspectives on gender and class. Gerald Bloomfield (Geography, University of Guelph) has contributed material generously throughout the work on the volume and his particular contributions are found on nine plates. Although Normand Séguin, René Hardy, and Pierre Lanthier (Sciences humaines, Université du Québec à Trois-Rivières) and Serge Courville (Géographie, Laval) are each named on only one plate, their advice on a range of Québec topics helped shape many others. Fernand Harvey (Institut québécois de recherche sur la culture, Québec) also shared his expertise and material on Québec.

We are grateful to many others for valuable comment, criticism, and suggestions, including Alan F.J. Artibise, Carl Berger, Luc Bureau, Henry W. Castner, Ian M. Drummond, Peter Ennals, Ernest Epp, L.J. Evenden, Kathleen Fraser, Susan W. Friedman, David Gardiner, John B. Garver Jr, Peter G. Goheen, Lawrence Grossman, W.G. Hardwick, Cecil J. Houston, Audrey Kobayashi, Victor A. Konrad, James T. Lemon, Gerald Lenton, Heather MacDougall, Daniel Mackay, Suzanne Mackenzie, Alan G. MacPherson, Aidan McQuillan, Margaret Mattson, Anne E. Mosher, H.V. Nelles, Rosemary E. Ommer, Richard Plant, Steven Plunkett, Mary Powell, Arthur J. Ray, Norbert Robitaille, Abraham Rotstein, Roger Sarty, Joan Schwartz, R.A. Shearer, William J. Smyth, Gilbert A. Stelter, James E. Vance Jr, David Walker, Joan Winearls, and William C. Wonders.

The cumulative research would not have taken the shape it has in this volume without the work of Geoffrey J. Matthews, our cartographic editor. Geoff helped transform tentative and often muddled sketches into clear and imaginative designs that truly convey the essence of the research. His artistry, expressed in nuances of symbol, colour, and layout, capped the phase of intense research and confirmed the board's early hopes for dramatic new portrayals of ideas and material.

In developing 66 plates with the help of over 100 researchers in 30 different institutions we have needed to have experts on specific regions or from different disciplinary perspectives move towards some common ground. Donald Kerr took primary responsibility for developing lines of communications among the board members and with researchers, especially in Central Canada, as well as for budgeting and reporting to both the administration of the project in Toronto and the funding agencies in Ottawa. Deryck W. Holdsworth was primarily responsible for the interaction with researchers in the development of the initial research design, often travelling across the country to visit them in their home institutions; he also supervised the editorial working group on the University of Toronto campus in establishing the final contents of the plates. As assistant editor Susan L. Laskin not only helped to clarify the scholarly thrust of the plates but, above all, functioned as the nerve-centre of the volume in communicating with our many contributors, cartographers, copyeditors, and translators. Research associate Murdo MacPherson was relied on for his careful mapping and graphing of data, persistence in tracking down sources, and meticulous attention to detail. The core group was also fortunate at the later stages of the research process to acquire the skills of Patricia M. Orr, who had previously worked on volume I of the *Historical Atlas of Canada*.

Throughout the long period of producing volume III we have been grateful for the encouragement of R. Cole Harris, whose experience in editing volume I helped us plan a management strategy. At the University of Toronto Press we are indebted to Harald Bohne (director until 1989), Harry van Ierssel (interim director, 1989–90), Ian Montagnes (editor-in-chief), and Peter Scaggs (production manager) for keeping us to schedules, to Joan Bulger (copyeditor) for her meticulous assistance in producing a final manuscript, and to Mary McDougall Maude (freelance editor) for additional editorial help. The French-language edition was undertaken in Montréal by Les Presses de l'Université de Montréal, and we were indeed fortunate that Marcel Paré agreed to act again as translator as he did for volume I. Maurice Saint-Yves has served as toponymic adviser for the plates. Members of the *Atlas* organization – Wm G. Dean (director) and John Warkentin (English co-ordinating editor) – offered valuable comment at the critical early editorial board meetings and on penultimate drafts of the essays.

All those who participated in the creation of this volume would undoubtedly join us in expressing our sincere gratitude to the Social Sciences and Humanities Research Council of Canada for its funding and for its understanding of the complexities of such a mammoth national and multidisciplinary project. We are also appreciative of the efforts of Bill Dean in securing supplementary funds generously made available by the Government of Ontario and, through the University of Toronto's 'Breakthrough' fund-raising campaign, the Bank of Montreal. We wish also to recognize the co-operation of the University of Toronto in providing space and administrative support over the years. Since 1987 we have also had the benefit of the administrative support of the Geography Department at the Pennsylvania State University.

In as much as the archival record of the 20th century is expanding all the time, and particularly as new material becomes available, scholarly interpretations will be added and will change. There are a multitude of research questions to be shaped and then answered in addressing the 20th century. We offer this volume as a contribution to that debate and hope that its arguments provoke scholarship that can build on this portrayal of a still evolving nation.

Donald Kerr, University of Toronto
Deryck W. Holdsworth, Pennsylvania State University
1990

After the euphoria that attended the publication of volume I of the *Historical Atlas of Canada,* and as we moved on to production of the plates on 20th-century Canada, we soon realized that this new volume would be even more technically demanding than the first had been. This challenge we have been able to meet, however, because we have been fortunate to be able to retain almost all the members of the original team of skilled cartographers who worked on volume I. The years of experience that they accumulated during the production of that volume have served us well as we moved on to the cartographic complexities that volume III demanded. The technical specifications had been well established, but within these broad guidelines the cartographers were free to experiment with colour combinations and symbols that would enhance the thematic presentation of the maps.

I wish to thank the cartographic team, the veterans of volume I and also the newcomers, for their invaluable contributions to the success of this volume: Byron Moldofsky, Dorothy Woermke, Vince Corrigan, Diane Ferguson, Ada Cheung, Julienne Patterson, Roddie McNeil, Daniel Poirier, Mariange Beaudry, Fanny Paz, Melita Kosek, and Zhaoyuan Li. Special thanks to production co-ordinator Byron Moldofsky who returned to the project to take on the unenviable task of devising and maintaining a production schedule that would allow us to meet our publication goal. Thanks also to Vince Corrigan who shared with Bryon the task of preparing all the typeset material in English and French for the maps; to Dorothy Woermke for her unfailing reliability; and to Ada Cheung who matured cartographically on this project but never lost her unique blend of humour. Appreciation is extended also to cartographers Chris Grounds, Hedy Later, and Jane Davie of the Department of Geography who aided and contributed to the project with their cartographic expertise.

Thanks to Joanne Wainman who, in addition to her administrative duties, coded and processed all the texts for typesetting, and was always willing to assist the cartographers in times of crisis. Once again John Glover and Louisa Yick of the Faculty of Arts and Science Photographic Laboratory provided almost instant filmwork in response to our never-ending demands for photography. Peter Meyer of Cooper & Beatty was a constant help in alleviating all of our many typesetting problems.

Finally, the photomechanical processes, the science of transforming all our complex cartography into combined negatives and colour proofs, were again entrusted to consultants Leonard Ugarenko, who came out of retirement for this volume, and John Oosterloo at Northway Map Technology Limited who produced reproductions of the finest quality, on schedule, throughout the project.

The production of an atlas requires the interwoven skills of many people in overlapping technologies. Unfortunately they cannot always be acknowledged individually, but to all these people the cartographic staff is forever grateful.

Geoffrey J. Matthews
University of Toronto
1990

Acknowledgments

EXECUTIVE COMMITTEE

Wm G. Dean, Director
Jean-Pierre Wallot,
    Co-Ordinating Editor
John Warkentin,
    Co-Ordinating Editor
Geoffrey J. Matthews,
    Cartographer/Designer
R. Cole Harris, Editor, volume I
R.L. Gentilcore, Editor, volume II
Donald Kerr, Editor,
    volume III
Deryck W. Holdsworth,
    Editor, volume III
Harald Bohne, Director,
    University of Toronto Press,
    1979–89
Harry Van Ierssel, Interim
    Director, University of
    Toronto Press, 1989–90
Ian Montagnes, Editor-in-Chief,
    University of Toronto Press

ADMINISTRATION

Joanne Wainman,
    Administrative Assistant,
    1983–90
James F. Walker,
    Administrative Assistant,
    1979–83

SECRETARIES

Andrew Chatwood
Judy Glucksman
Sandi Koelle
Alison Ward

CORE WORKING GROUP

Susan L. Laskin, 1981–90
Deryck W. Holdsworth, 1982–7
Murdo MacPherson, 1982–9
Patricia M. Orr, 1987–9

**RESEARCH ASSISTANTS
AND ASSOCIATES**

E. Alderdice
Christopher Andreae
Grahame P. Arnould
Lorne Charles Baker
Bradley Bass
Bruce Batchelor
Anne Marie Becker
Stephen Bellinger
Geoffrey Bernardo
David Best
Laura Black
Michael Bloor
Anne Boxall
Karen E. Brown
Curtis Bryan

Carol A. Buckley
Diana Caverhill
Mary Cavett
Ruth Chamberland
Debra Chambers
Kelly Chan
Pauline Chan
Jessie Chisholm
Robert Choinière
Daniel Cichacky
Natalie Crook
Douglas Cruikshank
Peter DeLottinville
Marc Desjardins
Dan Desousa
Kathy Dietrich
Pamela Divinsky
Janet Dixon
Geoffrey Dobilas
Donna Doherty
Joan Ellsworth
Donna Shimamura Everitt
Simon C. Farbrother
John Fitzsimons
Susan W. Friedman
R. Jean Frost
Alain Gelly
Robert Galois
Alain Gamelin
W. Mark Graham
Janine Grant
Lawrence Grossman
David Hanna
Diane Hanna
William Hanziuk
Andrée Héroux
Daniel Hiebert
Norman Hillmer
Margaret Hobbs
Cheryl Hoffman
Diana Hooper
George Horhota
David Hoselton
Carmen Jensen
Dean Jobb
Kyle Jolliffe
Paula Kestleman
John Key
Bruce Kilpatrick
Susan Knox
William Lahey
Shelley M.R. Laskin
Susan L. Laskin
A. Ledoux
Donna Lehto
Robert Lewis
Christina Lloyd
Wolfgang Luftensteiner
Norine McBride
Peter McCaskell
Donna McCririck
Michael J. McGibbon

Mary McInnis
Debra McNabb
Murdo MacPherson
Mary Magwood
Lynne Marks
Steven Maynard
Lourdes Meana
Margaret Meek
Janice Milton
Michael Moir
Marie Constance Morley
Libby Napper
D. Nash
David Neufeld
James A. Nugent
Colin Old
Patricia M. Orr
Charles Parker
S. Passadetti
Christina Mae Paul
Garry Penner
Nova Peters
Robert Pett
M. Portnoff
Pierre Poulin
Marie Puddister
Michael Puddister
Mark Randall
Caroline Rang
Michelle Ryan
Julia Sandquist
Ronald Sawatsky
Kathleen Seaver
Kelly Shaw
Robert M. Shortreed
Henry Sikora
Andrew Skalski
Maria Skoulas
Donna Smith
Mary Jean Smith
Joanne Stewart
Sylvie Taschereau
Richard B. Tillman
Alan Toff
Heather M. Tremble
Sheila Turcon
Peter J. Usher
Michel Vigneault
Ruth Wells
Suzanne Williams
William Williams
Anne Willmot
John P. Wilson
Bruce Wood
Catherine Wood
Douglas Wood
G. Wood
Tom Wyatt
Thomas Robin Wylie

**CARTOGRAPHIC
PRODUCTION**

CARTOGRAPHER/DESIGNER

Geoffrey J. Matthews

**PRODUCTION
CO-ORDINATOR**

Byron Moldofsky

CARTOGRAPHERS

Historical Atlas of Canada

Mariange Beaudry
Ada Cheung
Vincent A. Corrigan
Diane (Paquette) Ferguson
Melita Kosek
Zhaoyuan Li
Roddie McNeil
Byron Moldofsky
Julienne Patterson
Fanny B. Paz
Daniel E. Poirier
Dorothy E. Woermke

*Department of Geography,
University of Toronto*

Jane Davie
Christopher Grounds
Hedy Later

TOPONYMIC ADVISER

Maurice Saint-Yves

**TRANSLATOR FOR THE
FRENCH EDITION**

Marcel Paré,
in consultation with
Paul-André Linteau
and Maurice Saint-Yves
and with the assistance of
Carole Besner
Christian Boisvert
Martine Corbeil
Michèle Dagenais
André Filion
Denis G. Gauvin

HISTORICAL ATLAS OF CANADA

Canada 1891-1961: An Overview

In the seven decades between 1891 and 1961 Canada's economy, society, government structures, and connections to the outside world changed dramatically. Although Canada's historical dependence on the extraction and export of natural resources persisted, the mix of commodities varied over this period, bringing about important changes in the status of its regions. In 1891 Canada's work-force was largely agricultural and male; by 1961 employment in manufacturing, trade, and services had come to predominate and women had established an important role in the paid labour force. Massive waves of immigration, especially before 1914 and after 1945, as well as increasing mobility between regions, changed the composition and distribution of the population. Canada became a predominantly urban society and one increasingly organized through structures of institutions in health, welfare, education, and culture. Globally Canada shifted from being part of the British Empire to being drawn, economically and culturally, into the orbit of the United States.

In 1891, though Canada was at last linked by rail from sea to sea, it was still essentially an archipelago of settlement zones amidst vast areas of undeveloped and even unknown territory (pl 1). Because of the concentration of agricultural and manufacturing wealth in southern Ontario and southwestern Québec, Central Canada stood in marked contrast to the rest of the country. To the east the Maritimes' hopes of becoming the industrial New England of Canada had already been deflated. To the northwest large tracts of rough terrain separated Ontario from the Manitoba lowlands, where the roots of Canada's modern wheat economy had just been established. Even farther west the Canadian Pacific Railway had only just been completed to the Pacific Coast, and in 1891 there were few cities or towns along its route. To the north most of the land mass was still *terra incognita* except to the aboriginal peoples who inhabited it; here missions and fur-trading posts were still the most visible signs of contact between native and European peoples.

Despite its vast undeveloped territory in 1891 Canada was not thought to be especially rich in natural resources. Its situation contrasted sharply with the United States where an abundance of natural resources was already providing a foundation for rapid industrial growth. In Canada all the good farmland in the settled parts of the country had been taken up and the once abundant white-pine forest had been largely cut. Few minerals had been discovered, and, although the Prairie West was believed to contain much valuable land, its potential had yet to be realized. Within a few years, however, perceptions of Canada's resources were to shift dramatically; by the 1920s Canada was considered one of the richest nations of the world in resources.

Technology changed profoundly during the late 19th and early 20th century, and that change led to a re-evaluation of Canada's resources. New techniques of using electricity and generating it from falling water, of making newsprint from spruce wood, and of extracting base metals from complex ores were introduced in quick succession, and rich bodies of ore were discovered. At the same time, strong industrial growth in Europe and the United States after the mid-1890s created a demand for Canada's exports. The rapid exploitation of the forest and mining base to the north and west of the Central Canadian core ensued and the Canadian economy expanded quickly. Of parallel importance was the rapid settlement of the western plains where, through massive capital investments, a new economy was erected upon the production of wheat for export. The resource-based segment of the economy suffered a drastic set-back in the Depression of the 1930s, but it resumed its growth during the Second World War and in the 1950s reached new levels of production.

The other major element in the Canada's economic growth was the development of urban-based manufacturing. Existing industries expanded and new ones came into being, their locations influenced by the growing consumer market, the accessibility of low-cost hydroelectric power, and the decisions of American corporations to establish branch plants in Central Canada. Manufacturing thus became a propellant for the growth of towns and cities in southwestern Ontario and southwestern Québec by the 1920s. Canada's manufacturing production continued its growth after the Second World War in response to a heightened consumerism and an even greater participation by Americans in the economy. Over three-quarters of the value of that production remained solidly entrenched in Central Canada.

In addition to substantial growth in the resource and manufacturing sectors, a considerable service industry developed in response to the structural changes that were occurring in Canada as in all western capitalist countries. Employment in retailing expanded and office work for the management of industrial and financial activities developed especially in the major metropolitan centres. Public-sector employment, including jobs in health and welfare and education as well as in local, provincial, and federal government departments, grew appreciably after the Second World War. In the industrial sector machines replaced skilled workers, and more and more semi- and unskilled workers held routine, assembly-line jobs. Mechanization in mining, forestry, fishing, and agriculture reduced the labour force required within the resource sector from about 50% of the Canadian work-force in 1891 to a mere 14% in 1961 (pl 3). At the same time the number of women in the paid work-force increased from 12% in 1891 to 27% in 1961. At the turn of the century most wage-earning women were in domestic service or held low-paying factory or teaching jobs. Their opportunities improved only slowly. During the Second World War female participation in the work-force increased dramatically, but it was not until the mid-1950s that women, especially married women, became a stable and growing component of the paid work-force.

The great economic expansion of the early 20th century brought a rise in material prosperity. By 1891 Canadians were already well off by world standards. Three generations later, in 1961, they enjoyed a level of income exceeded only in the United States. This greatly increased income, and all that it brought with it in the way of increased consumption, came differentially to Canadians. For the most part workers received limited benefits. Low wages, long hours, dangerous working conditions, and insecure employment prevailed in many sectors. Union attempts to improve wages and working conditions were only partially successful. The labour movement was hindered by schisms and attempts to develop American-based international unions, and in fact only a fraction of the non-agricultural labour force was unionized. The widespread unemployment of the Great Depression further undermined the workers' position. However, strikes during the Second World War finally prompted the federal government in 1944 to give workers the legal right to join a union and to demand that employers recognize and bargain with unions chosen by their employees. In the post-war period unions attained full legal status, but even so less than a third of the non-agricultural labour force was unionized by 1961. For most of this period conservative forces blocked progressive movements, especially in the labour revolt after the First World War.

The population of Canada, from a base of 5 million at the turn of the century, doubled by the late 1920s and almost doubled again to 18 million by 1961, as a result of both natural increase and immigration. A decline in the birth rate paralleled declines in the death rate (with the exception of Québec), and immigration contributed a massive increase in population, not just in the newly opened West but also in Central Canadian cities. To settle the Prairies in the early 20th century the federal government encouraged immigration, and the European backgrounds of these immigrants influenced the social mosaic of the Prairies (pl 4). At least half of all immigrants found employment in cities and mining or lumbering communities. In the late 1940s, and through the 1950s, a second wave of immigrants migrated to Canadian cities.

In 1891 Canada's two dominant cultural and linguistic groups, British and French, together made up almost 90% of the population. By 1961 their proportion remained high at 74%. In 1891 Canada was a strongly British society: 59% of the Canadian population was British in origin. Immigration from the British Isles during the first three decades of the 20th century accounted, in most years, for more than half of all newcomers, but, because of a significant increase in immigration from continental Europe after the Second World War, by 1961 the British component had declined to 44%. French-speaking Canadians comprised 30% of the Canadian population in 1961, and retained their largely Québec base.

At the same time as people were immigrating to Canada, emigration from Canada continued, especially to the United States: Maritimers and French Canadians moved to industrial cities in New England and southern Ontarians moved to the American midwest and west. By the 1950s, however, migration to the United States fell off significantly. More and more Canadians moved within their own country, especially Maritimers to southern Ontario and people from Saskatchewan to coastal British Columbia or southern Ontario.

The indigenous population became even more marginal under the weight of population growth. By 1891 most of the native Indians of southern Canada already lived on reserves where they suffered serious social dislocation. In the 20th century native groups were pushed into economic and social relations compatible with the interests of the dominant European population; there was further erosion of reserve land (pl 2), and throughout the period native attempts to establish legal claims to their traditional lands were unsuccessful. In the North native Indians and Inuit faced social and economic upheaval: contact with the southern economy – first through whaling, the fur trade, and missions, then through mineral exploration and extraction, and in the 1950s through the construction of the American defence system – meant the continual reshaping of their lands.

The proportion of urban dwellers in Canada increased steadily, accounting for about 50% of the population by 1921 and almost 70% by 1961. Rural depopulation, which began in the 1880s in eastern Canada, accelerated during the first third of the 20th century. Industrialization was the basis of urban growth in Central Canada; the urban population also grew with the establishment of service centres on the Prairies and resource-processing towns and cities on the Shield and in British Columbia. The numbers, the increasingly diverse populations, and the range of job opportunities available changed society. Suburbs consumed large areas of land for housing and transportation systems were created to serve them. And the streetcars, buses, and automobiles brought new problems for municipal governments. Those governments were also the front line for the development of educational, welfare, cultural, and recreational facilities for the expanding urban society.

Montréal and Toronto were at the apex of the Canadian urban system, and they rapidly became the metropolitan centres for the national economy. The economy became increasingly concentrated as large corporations superseded small or medium-sized family-owned firms. Symbolic of this transformation was the relocation of management functions away from factory or warehouse and into downtown office buildings in proximity to banks, insurance companies, stockbrokers, lawyers, and accountants. The concentration of financial institutions drew first the Maritimes and then the West under the influence of Montréal and Toronto. In the corporate boardrooms of these cities decisions were made that affected all regions of the country, from the closing of a textile factory in Nova Scotia, to a mortgage foreclosure on a Prairie grain farm, to new investment in British Columbia.

Although Montréal and Toronto exerted great influence on the Canadian economy, they in turn looked to New York and London as centres of the world economy. Even though Canada became an industrial state, it depended on external markets and foreign investment. Consequently traders and entrepreneurs in Montréal and Toronto had to be sensitive to world-wide fluctuations of commodity prices and interest rates. In addition, American businessmen and financiers exerted direct influence on the Canadian economy through branch plants and as a result of money lent to municipalities, provinces, and Canadian enterprises.

In the 1890s Great Britain was Canada's major export market, especially for agricultural products. As the forest and mining industries developed, that dependence shifted in the early decades of the 20th century to the United States where mineral products and newsprint were in demand. By 1961 the United States had become the principal foreign importer of raw materials from Canada and Canada had become the United States' best customer. The source of investment funds followed a similar pattern. In 1900 Britain provided 85% of all foreign capital invested in Canada, but by 1960 its share had dropped to 15%. In the same interval the US share rose from 14% to 75%.

The political link between Britain and Canada remained strong during the early years of this economic reorientation. Canada's role in the First World War marked the beginning of the decline of British influence and the move towards independence, first within the Empire and later within the Commonwealth. After the Second World War Canada began to seek a role as a middle power on the world stage, with an independent voice neither British nor American. From the time of Confederation Canadians have been challenged to build a viable separate nation on a continent shared with the United States. As early as 1879, in its National Policy, the federal government outlined the mechanisms by which Canada could survive and prosper through industrialization. Tariffs protected the nascent Canadian manufacturing industry, although they encouraged direct American investment as well.

Another important strategy in the creation of the Canadian nation was the establishment of strong east-west transportation systems. In the late 19th century the federal government subsidized the construction of railways and, after the First World War, the Canadian National Railways – a crown corporation – amalgamated several previously unsuccessful railways. In 1937 the government created another Crown corporation, Trans-Canada Airlines, to provide domestic air travel from one coast to the other. And in 1947 legislation was introduced to build, in conjunction with the provinces, a trans-Canada highway, completed 20 years later. The federal government was also concerned about the flow of ideas, information, and popular culture from the south, and tried to nourish Canadian cultural development through such agencies as the Canadian Broadcasting Corporation (1936), the National Film Board (1939), and the Canada Council (1957).

The government was slow to involve itself directly in the welfare of its citizens. As late as 1940 most Canadians had little or no protection from illness, injury, or unemployment except that provided by private, voluntarist associations or piecemeal public programs. The devastating effects of the Depression of the 1930s, however, changed political priorities. In 1940 the Unemployment Insurance Act provided modest protection for some unemployed and in 1944 the Family Allowances Act called for Canada-wide payments for children. Although both pieces of legislation could be considered social reforms, they were also intended to sustain purchasing power. By 1961 the federal government had established a universal system of old-age pensions and a cost-sharing agreement with the provinces for universal hospital care.

Big business and big government had become increasingly evident by 1961. National firms emerged in both industrial and service sectors, with branches serving communities across the country. Hierarchies were created and reorganized in religion, education, welfare, and organized labour. In 1961 Canada was urban and industrial. Its economy had grown dramatically and its structure had changed, but it still depended on external markets for the sale of resource products. Economic concentration in Central Canada, especially in Montréal and Toronto, combined with the increased political concentration in Ottawa, aggravated regional tensions. That concentration and the continuing reality of two distinctive linguistic and cultural groups, French and English in origin, made Canada in 1961 still somewhat an archipelago. There were, however, many more areas of settlement than in 1891, along with some remaining undeveloped space and various semi-developed resource peripheries. These areas were interconnected by an increasingly finer mesh of rail, road, air, pipeline, telephone, and telecommunication links, and by increasingly homogeneous tastes, values, and standards.

CANADA IN 1891

Authors: Marvin McInnis, Peter J. Usher (native land use)

In 1891, five years after British Columbia was linked to eastern Canada by rail, the country was still rather fragmented. Vast stretches of territory separated pockets of settled areas where agricultural activity supported most of the people. Southern Ontario and southern Québec, which were better integrated than the rest of the country, had three-quarters of the Canadian population, and their principal cities were founded on a prosperous agricultural economy. A commercially viable farming community had begun in Manitoba. In the Maritime Provinces and in eastern Québec, where the population was much more thinly scattered and the agricultural economy less successful, fishing and forestry still played an important role. The vast Precambrian Shield was only beginning to yield timber and mineral wealth and the abundant resources west of the Rockies were still largely untapped.

Beyond the settled south and its contiguous resource frontier traditional fur trading and fisheries shaped the contact between indigenous and non-indigenous peoples. From a southern Canadian perspective the north was a vast and unknown country. Missions, whaling stations, and fur-trading posts were the only white colonial outposts. From the perspective of the native peoples life still revolved around seasonal limits of resources, although they adapted their traditional way of life to include fur trading.

By 1891, though Canada was heavily dependent on its agricultural base, the country had taken major strides in the direction of becoming a modern, urbanized, industrial nation. Canadians had taken advantage of the industrial technology of the time to establish factories to produce goods for domestic consumption and to equip towns and cities with up-to-date amenities.

The prosperous agricultural economy of Central Canada, especially Ontario, sustained a substantial urban development. In addition to Montréal and Toronto, a network of smaller commercial and manufacturing towns and cities had emerged. Outside this region there were only five cities with any manufacturing presence. The Maritime Provinces, with a much weaker agricultural and resource base, had made a not entirely successful attempt to integrate with the Central Canadian market, and both Saint John and Halifax had some industrial capacity. In British Columbia a resource economy gave rise to resource-processing manufacturing in Vancouver and Victoria. Winnipeg acted as gateway to the developing prairie west.

HISTORICAL ATLAS OF CANADA

THE LAND

 Unexplored by Europeans

Generalized settled area

*Fur seal fleet from Victoria catching in Alaskan waters

NON-NATIVE LAND USE
Value of production

∴: Agriculture
One dot represents $100 000 of net output.

▣ Fishing
● Mining   Each symbol represents
▲ Forestry $500 000 of production.[1]

⬔ Manufacturing value added
One cube represents $1000 000.

1 In most cases symbol locations are approximate and represent general areas of greatest production. Fishing symbols indicate landed value and locations show districts where fish were brought to land rather than caught.

Other economic activity

■ Fur trading post[2]
◊ Whaling station (ca 1891)
· Selected urban place
Place names in bold type indicate a population of more than 10 000.

⟶ Major railway

2 Posts shown are those of the Hudson's Bay Company. Not shown are a small number of independent posts, most of which were in northern Ontario.

Missions
○ Protestant
○ Roman Catho[lic]

PLATE 1

NATIVE LAND USE

Inuit

Virtually self-sufficient hunting and fishing economy; fur trapping for trade exceptional. Some trade in fur and meat established with British and American whaling ships

Indians in non-surrendered areas

Hunting and fishing for subsistence; trapping for trade, mostly with Hudson's Bay Company. As with Inuit, continued extensive use of traditional lands

Indians in surrendered areas

Some hunting and fishing for subsistence, and trapping for trade, in forested areas and along northwestern British Columbia coast; however, use of traditional lands eliminated where taken up for settlement in agricultural areas. Some involvement in wage labour and agriculture

Canada in 1891 was still a thinly populated land. More than one-quarter of the population of almost five million were urban dwellers (places with over 1 000 people), yet only Montréal (219 000) and Toronto (181 000) had populations greater than 70 000. Most of the non-indigenous population lived in cities, towns, and farms within a southern band of agricultural settlement that had almost reached its limits in eastern Canada but which was still expanding rapidly on the central and western Prairies. At the margins of the agricultural frontier in the eastern provinces, and just beginning to expand in British Columbia, were areas of forest exploitation. Much of the population along the Atlantic coast was oriented to the fishing economy. The disparate regions of European settlement in Canada were bound together by a transcontinental railroad and a growing number of branch lines, supplemented sometimes by inland-waterway steamship lines, to outlying agricultural and resource communities.

Some 100 000 indigenous people were spread unevenly across Canada. The northward and westward advance of the resource frontier was accompanied by the formal surrender of Indian lands to the Crown, usually through the signing of treaties. Where this process had already occurred, Indians were confined to small reserves of land and their activities off the reserves were severely constrained, especially where land was taken up for agriculture by the non-indigenous population. To the north, however, Indians and Inuit continued to live as mobile hunting and fishing bands, using large tracts of land and water with few effective restrictions, although non-native activity – fur-trade posts in the sub-Arctic, whaling stations in the Arctic, and missions – reoriented native land use and trade and provided focal points for settlement of the indigenous people.

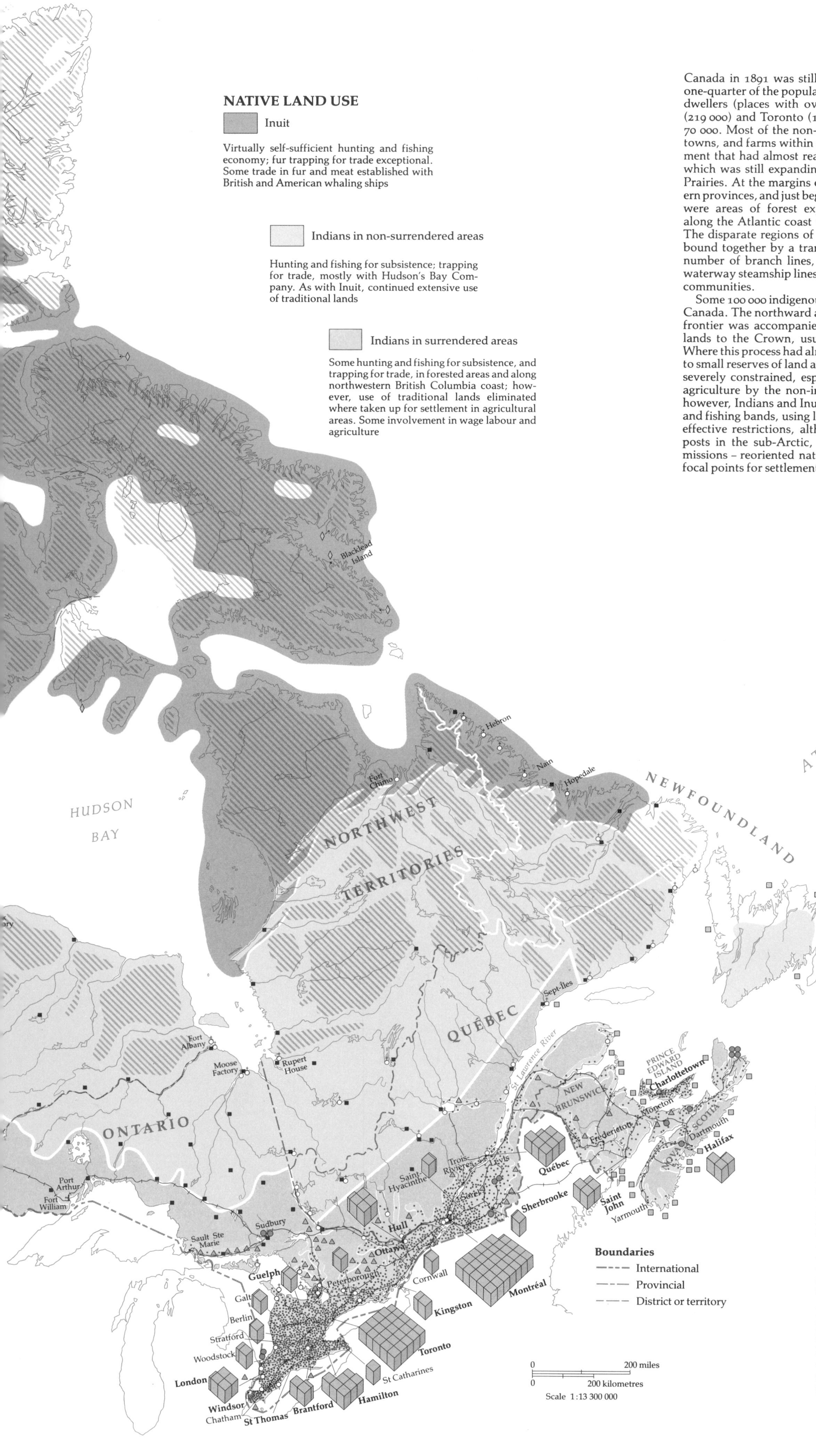

Boundaries

— · — · — International

— — — Provincial

— — — District or territory

0   200 miles
0   200 kilometres
Scale 1:13 300 000

Major urban centres

Manufacturing value added in millions of dollars

Montréal	34.2
Toronto	24.7
Québec	7.4
Hamilton	6.9
Ottawa-Hull	4.3
London	4.3
Saint John	3.5
Halifax	3.1
Vancouver	2.6
Victoria	2.6
Winnipeg	2.5
Brantford	2.4
Kingston	1.7
Woodstock	1.4
Guelph	1.3
Peterborough	1.2
Saint-Hyacinthe	1.2
Berlin (Kitchener)	1.1
Cornwall	1.1
Galt	1.1
Sherbrooke	1.1
St Catharines	1.0

Map labels: HUDSON BAY, NORTHWEST TERRITORIES, QUÉBEC, ONTARIO, NEW BRUNSWICK, PRINCE EDWARD ISLAND, NOVA SCOTIA, NEWFOUNDLAND, ATLANTIC OCEAN, St Lawrence River, Blacklead Island, Hebron, Nain, Hopedale, Fort Chimo, Sept-Îles, Fort Albany, Moose Factory, Rupert House, Port Arthur, Fort William, Sault Ste Marie, Sudbury, Guelph, Peterborough, Cornwall, Berlin, Stratford, Woodstock, London, Windsor, Chatham, St Thomas, Brantford, Hamilton, St Catharines, Toronto, Kingston, Ottawa, Montréal, Hull, Trois-Rivières, Saint-Hyacinthe, Sorel, Lévis, Québec, Sherbrooke, Saint John, Yarmouth, Fredericton, Moncton, Charlottetown, Dartmouth, Halifax, St John's, Galt

TERRITORIAL EVOLUTION

Authors: Norman Nicholson, Robert Galois (BC), Michael Staveley (Nfld)

With the transfer of the arctic islands to Canada in the 1880s Britain completed its withdrawal from the new country. The integration of the vast Northwest Territories (NWT) into a dominion that stretched from the Atlantic to the Pacific proceeded in piecemeal fashion. The Yukon segment of the NWT became a separate territory in 1898 in order to cope better with the Klondike gold rush, but it was the formation of the provinces of Alberta and Saskatchewan in 1905 that brought a significant level of administrative autonomy to the region. In 1912 Ontario, Québec, and Manitoba were also extended northward; thereafter the NWT became an area synonymous with Canada 'north of 60.' On the Labrador coast the historical claims of Newfoundland conflicted with those of an expanded Québec, especially as new timber and mineral resources became accessible. Newfoundland joined the Canadian Confederation in 1949 after an acrimonious internal debate. Across the country, throughout the 20th century, the territorial laws and management systems of native peoples were largely ignored by the demands of resource capital and homesteaders. Amerindians had little success in resolving land claims or in determining their own way of life.

REGIONAL SHARE OF TERRITORY

1891

Maritimes
Québec
Ontario
Manitoba
British Columbia
Rest of Northwest Territories
Keewatin
Assiniboia
Saskatchewan
Alberta   Athabaska

Total land area
3 315 647 sq mi
8 587 194 sq km

1949

Mackenzie
Keewatin
Franklin
Northwest Territories
Yukon Territory
British Columbia
Newfoundland
Maritimes
Québec
Ontario
Manitoba
Saskatchewan
Alberta

Total land area
3 560 238 sq mi
9 220 660 sq km

Compiled under the authority of the hereditary Gitksan and Wet'suwet'en chiefs

GITKSAN AND WET'SUWET'EN TERRITORIES

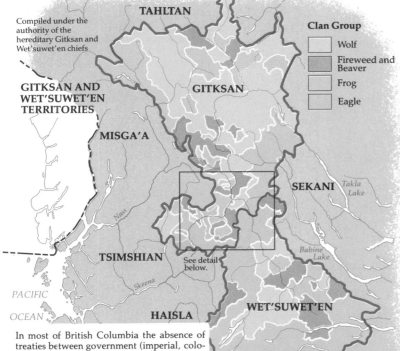

Clan Group
- Wolf
- Fireweed and Beaver
- Frog
- Eagle

TAHLTAN
GITKSAN
MISGA'A
SEKANI
Takla Lake
Babine Lake
TSIMSHIAN
See detail below.
WET'SUWET'EN
HAISLA
CARRIER
PACIFIC OCEAN

Scale 1 : 4 000 000

In most of British Columbia the absence of treaties between government (imperial, colonial, or federal) and indigenous peoples contributed to conflict as settlement advanced. Assertions of ownership by the province and its alienation of land and resources were challenged by Indian claims of an extant aboriginal title to the land. As illustrated in the upper Skeena, the provincial system of land tenure, with Indians confined to reserves, was superimposed on a continuing aboriginal system of territorial ownership and resource allocation. A federal/provincial royal commission (1913-16) endeavoured to resolve this conflict but the ensuing 'settlement' of 1927 between the federal government and British Columbia was never accepted by the Indians.

TWO VIEWS OF LAND IN BRITISH COLUMBIA

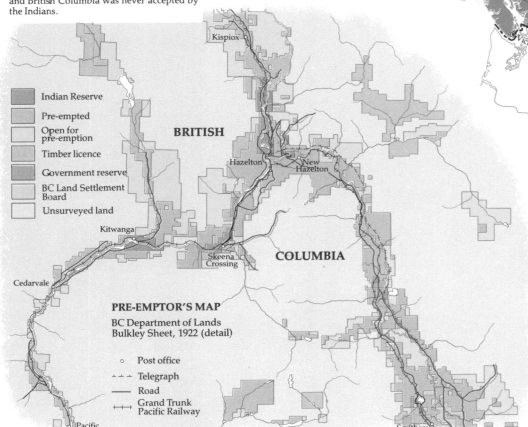

PRE-EMPTOR'S MAP

BC Department of Lands
Bulkley Sheet, 1922 (detail)

- Indian Reserve
- Pre-empted
- Open for pre-emption
- Timber licence
- Government reserve
- BC Land Settlement Board
- Unsurveyed land

BRITISH
COLUMBIA

Kispiox
Hazelton
New Hazelton
Kitwanga
Skeena Crossing
Cedarvale
Smithers
Pacific

- ○ Post office
- ‡‡‡ Telegraph
- —— Road
- ⊢⊣ Grand Trunk Pacific Railway

Scale 1 : 735 000

NORTH POLE

ARCTIC OCEAN
BEAUFORT SEA
DISTRICT OF FRANKLIN 1895
QUEEN ELIZABETH ISLANDS
SVERDRUP IS
DISTRICT OF FRANKLIN 1920
BANKS ISLAND
MELVILLE ISLAND
Viscount Melville Sound
PRINCE OF WALES ISLAND
VICTORIA ISLAND
KING WILLIAM
ARCTIC CIRCLE
CANADA 1925
ALASKA (USA)
YUKON TERRITORY 1898
Whitehorse
DIST. OF YUKON 1895
DIST. OF MACKENZIE 1895
NORTHWEST
DISTRICT OF MACKENZIE
Great Bear Lake
Great Slave Lake
Yellowknife
ARCTIC
DISTRICT OF KEEWATIN
PACIFIC OCEAN
QUEEN CHARLOTTE ISLANDS
Dixon Entrance
Hecate Strait
Queen Charlotte Sound
VANCOUVER ISLAND
Victoria
BRITISH COLUMBIA
DISTRICT OF ATHABASKA 1882
DISTRICT OF ALBERTA 1882, 1895
Edmonton
ALBERTA 1905
Peace
Lake Athabasca
Reindeer Lake
SASKATCHEWAN 1905
DISTRICT OF SASKATCHEWAN 1882
DISTRICT OF SASKATCHEWAN 1882
DISTRICT OF ASSINIBOIA 1882
Regina
Qu'Appelle
UNITED STATES OF AMERICA
MANITOBA 1912
KEEWATIN 1886
Lake Winnipeg
Winnipeg

It is tempting to conjecture what would have been the outcome of later federal/provincial relations had the Prairies been one province, or had any of the other five options that were seriously considered in 1905 been chosen.

PROPOSALS FOR THE PRAIRIE PROVINCES, 1905

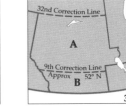

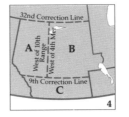

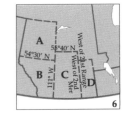

HISTORICAL ATLAS OF CANADA

PLATE 2

The exploration and discovery of the arctic islands, long associated with the search for a northwest passage, extended further north in the late 19th and early 20th centuries. Many of the important voyages were by Scandinavians and Americans. The arctic explorer Stefansson, working for the Canadian government, made the last substantial discovery of new islands in the 1910s. It was not until 1940–4 that an RCMP patrol boat, the *St Roch*, succeeded in traversing the Northwest Passage both ways. While this voyage was a symbolic expression of Canadian sovereignty in the area, NORAD early-warning stations (pll 57, 58) testify to the changing geopolitical position of the Canadian Arctic.

NORTH POLE ★
claimed by Peary
6 Apr 1909

87°06′ Lat
21 Apr 1906

84°17′ Lat
21 Apr 1902

ARCTIC EXPLORATION

GREENLAND
(DENMARK)

POLAR ICE CAP

Norwegian Capt O. Sverdrup
1898–1902 (*Fram*)

American Lieut R.E. Peary, USN
1898–1902 (*Windward*)
1905–1906 (*Roosevelt*)
1908–1909 (*Roosevelt*)

Canadian A.P. Low
1904 (*Neptune*)

Canadian Capt J.E. Bernier
1906–1907 (*Arctic*)
1908–1909 (*Arctic*)
1910–1911 (*Arctic*)

Canadian V. Stefansson
1913–1918 (dog sled)

Canadian Staff-Sgt H.A. Larsen RCMP
1940–1942 (*St Roch*)
1944 (*St Roch*)

1916 WC Winter camp and anchorage of vessel
◀ Movement of exploration

(St Roch)
Depart Vancouver,
23 June 1940
Arrive Vancouver,
16 Oct 1944,
86 days from east to west

Point Barrow

ALASKA (USA)

Martin Point

Herschel Island

Reindeer Depot

Tuktoyaktuk

Cape Kellett

Walker Bay

Holman Island

Pierce Point

Coppermine

Tree River

Cambridge Bay

Pasley Bay
1914 WC

Winter Harbour

Erebus Bay

Dundas Harbour

Arctic Bay 1910 WC

Pond Inlet

C Sheridan
Fort Conger

Cape Columbia

Etah

Godhavn
Egedesminde

To Halifax
To Québec

From Kristiansund, Nor
To Stavanger, Nor

From New York
From Sydney, NS
To Sydney, NS
To New York
From Québec

Low departed Halifax,
Aug 1903; spent a year
in Hudson Bay area.

(St Roch)
Arrive Halifax,
11 Oct 1942
Depart Halifax,
22 July 1944

Scale 1:20 000 000

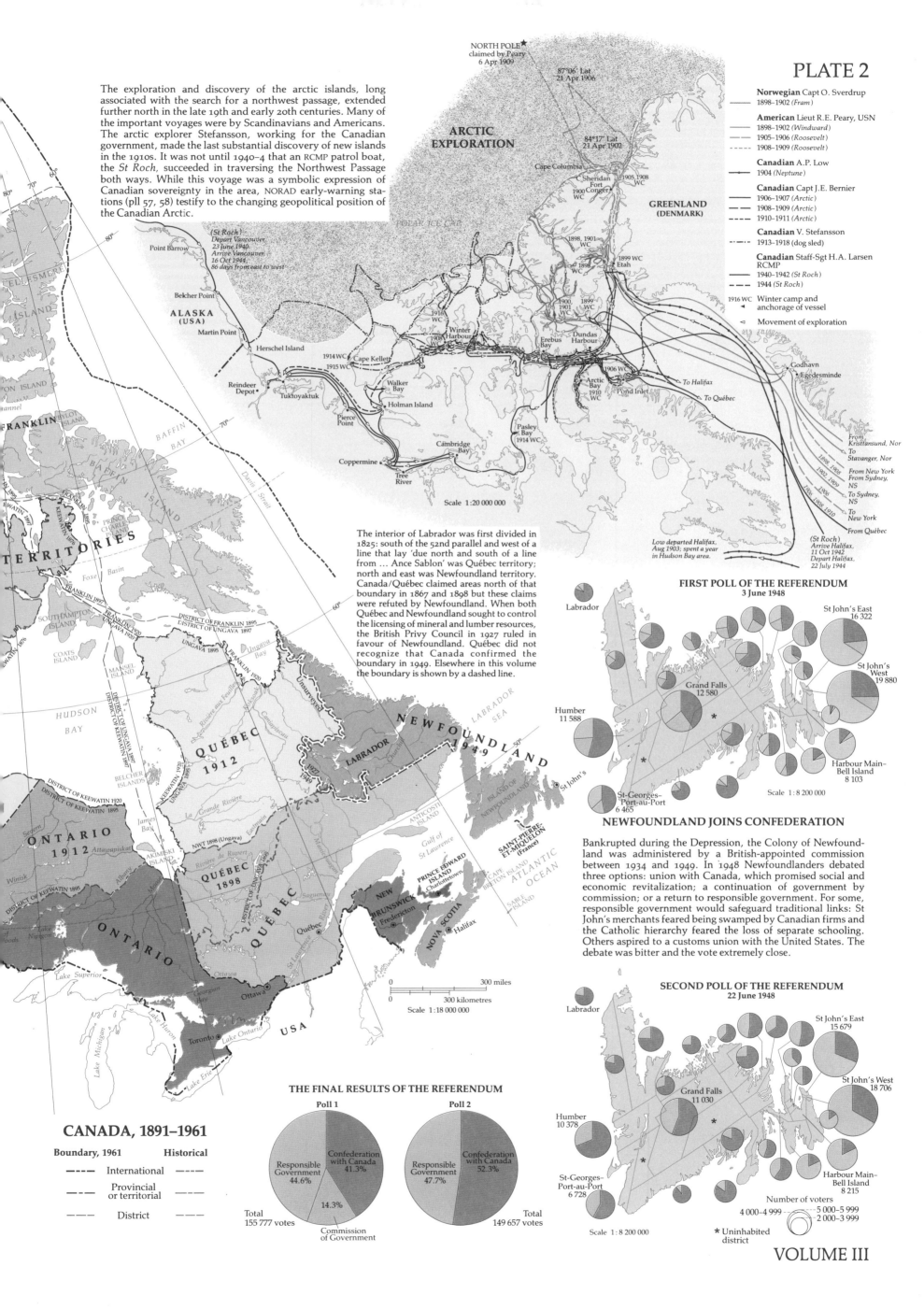

ELLESMERE ISLAND

DEVON ISLAND

FRANKLIN

BYLOT ISLAND

BAFFIN ISLAND

BAFFIN BAY

Davis Strait

PRINCE CHARLES ISLAND

Foxe Basin

DISTRICT OF FRANKLIN 1895

DISTRICT OF UNGAVA 1897

SOUTHAMPTON ISLAND

COATS ISLAND

MANSEL ISLAND

HUDSON BAY

BELCHER ISLANDS

DISTRICT OF KEEWATIN 1920

DISTRICT OF KEEWATIN 1895

QUÉBEC 1912

James Bay

AKIMISKI ISLAND

La Grande Rivière

Rivière de Rupert

QUÉBEC 1898

Eastmain

ONTARIO 1912

Attawapiskat

Winisk

Albany

Severn

ONTARIO

Lake of the Woods

Lake Nipigon

Lake Superior

Lake Michigan

Lake Huron

Georgian Bay

Toronto

Lake Ontario

Lake Erie

USA

Rivière aux Feuilles

Ungava Bay

Unsurveyed

LABRADOR

NEWFOUNDLAND 1949

LABRADOR SEA

Churchill

ISLAND OF NEWFOUNDLAND

St John's

ANTICOSTI ISLAND

Gulf of St Lawrence

SAINT-PIERRE-ET-MIQUELON (France)

PRINCE EDWARD ISLAND Charlottetown

CAPE BRETON ISLAND

NEW BRUNSWICK Fredericton

NOVA SCOTIA Halifax

SABLE ISLAND

ATLANTIC OCEAN

Québec

Saguenay

St Lawrence

Ottawa

Ottawa

The interior of Labrador was first divided in 1825: south of the 52nd parallel and west of a line that lay 'due north and south of a line from … Ance Sablon' was Québec territory; north and east was Newfoundland territory. Canada/Québec claimed areas north of that boundary in 1867 and 1898 but these claims were refuted by Newfoundland. When both Québec and Newfoundland sought to control the licensing of mineral and lumber resources, the British Privy Council in 1927 ruled in favour of Newfoundland. Québec did not recognize that Canada confirmed the boundary in 1949. Elsewhere in this volume the boundary is shown by a dashed line.

FIRST POLL OF THE REFERENDUM
3 June 1948

Labrador

St John's East
16 322

St John's West
19 880

Grand Falls
12 580

Humber
11 588

Harbour Main–Bell Island
8 103

St-Georges–Port-au-Port
6 465

Scale 1:8 200 000

NEWFOUNDLAND JOINS CONFEDERATION

Bankrupted during the Depression, the Colony of Newfoundland was administered by a British-appointed commission between 1934 and 1949. In 1948 Newfoundlanders debated three options: union with Canada, which promised social and economic revitalization; a continuation of government by commission; or a return to responsible government. For some, responsible government would safeguard traditional links: St John's merchants feared being swamped by Canadian firms and the Catholic hierarchy feared the loss of separate schooling. Others aspired to a customs union with the United States. The debate was bitter and the vote extremely close.

CANADA, 1891–1961

Boundary, 1961	Historical
International - - -	— — —
Provincial or territorial — - —	
District — — —	— — —

THE FINAL RESULTS OF THE REFERENDUM

Poll 1
Confederation with Canada 41.3%
Responsible Government 44.6%
Commission of Government 14.3%
Total 155 777 votes

Poll 2
Confederation with Canada 52.3%
Responsible Government 47.7%
Total 149 657 votes

0   300 miles
0   300 kilometres
Scale 1:18 000 000

SECOND POLL OF THE REFERENDUM
22 June 1948

Labrador

St John's East
15 679

St John's West
18 706

Grand Falls
11 030

Humber
10 378

Harbour Main–Bell Island
8 215

St-Georges–Port-au-Port
6 728

Number of voters
4 000–4 999
5 000–5 999
2 000–3 999

* Uninhabited district

Scale 1:8 200 000

ECONOMIC GROWTH

Author: Marvin McInnis

The outstanding characteristic of the Canadian economy between 1891 and 1961 was growth. Canada had one of the fastest-growing economies in the world and it became one of the most prosperous. The growth came from a combination of dramatic urban-industrial development along with a great expansion of the natural resource-based economy. After 1891 the wheat economy of the Prairies was established, and on the Precambrian Shield and in the mountains of British Columbia major mining developments and the world's leading pulp and paper industry grew up.

The change in the structure of the economy (portrayed along with its enormous growth in the three maps on the plate) followed a pattern common to industrial economies generally. An ever-increasing share of production came to be concentrated in cities as first manufacturing then service industries expanded greatly in relative importance. The economy continued to be heavily concentrated in southern Ontario and southern Québec although the western regions made considerable economic gains. Overall, a Canada that in 1891 reflected mainly agricultural and other primary production (pll 1, 5, 10) became by 1961 an industrial economy that reflected essentially the urban system (pll 51, 54, 55).

NATIONAL WORK-FORCE

Other
Government
Service
Finance
Trade
Utilities
Transportation
Construction
Manufacturing
Mining
Fishing
Forestry
Agriculture

Non-agriculture (details not available)

Percentage of work-force

1891 1901 1911 1921 1931 1941 1951 1961

GROSS DOMESTIC PRODUCT PER CAPITA

United States
Sweden
Canada
Australia
*Germany
France
United Kingdom

Hundreds of dollars (1960 US constant)

1890   1913   1926   1960

MANUFACTURING PRODUCTION PER CAPITA

United States
Sweden
United Kingdom
*Germany
Canada
Australia
France

No data for Australia

Hundreds of dollars (1955 US constant)

1899   1913   1929   1957

*See end notes.

FOREIGN INVESTMENT

INVESTMENT IN CANADA

Other countries
United Kingdom
United States

Percentage

Detailed data not available before 1926

1900 1910 1920 1930 1940 1950 1961

TOTAL VALUE

Investment in Canada
Canadian investment abroad
No data

Billions of dollars

1900 1910 1920 1930 1940 1950 1961

CANADIAN INVESTMENT ABROAD

Percentage

1926 1930 1940 1950 1961

Direct capital
Portfolio capital
Government of Canada credits

HISTORICAL ATLAS OF CANADA

GROWTH OF ECONOMIC PRODUCTION

Distribution of GDP

Net value of commodity production (1913 constant dollars)

Manufacturing
Power
Mining
Agriculture
Forestry
Fishing, trapping

Millions of dollars (1913 constant)

One dot represents $10 million of GDP.

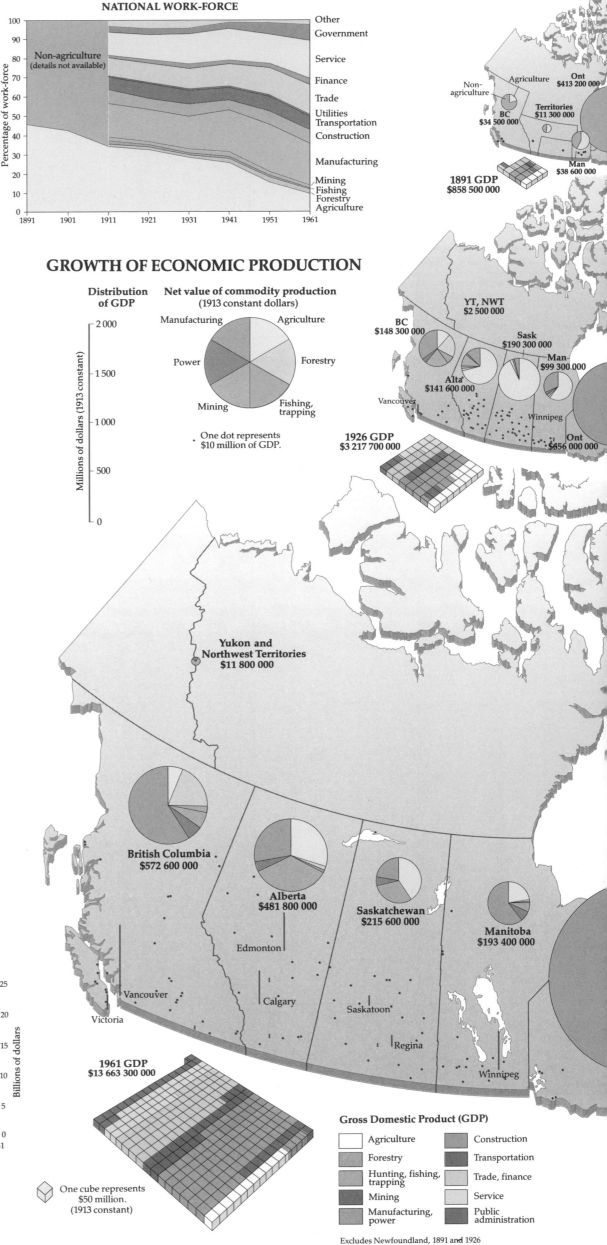

Non-agriculture
Agriculture
Ont $413 200 000
Territories $11 300 000
BC $34 500 000
Man $38 600 000
1891 GDP $858 500 000

YT, NWT $2 500 000
BC $148 300 000
Sask $190 300 000
Alta $141 600 000
Man $99 300 000
Vancouver
Winnipeg
Ont $656 000 000
1926 GDP $3 217 700 000

Yukon and Northwest Territories $11 800 000

British Columbia $572 600 000

Alberta $481 800 000

Saskatchewan $215 600 000

Manitoba $193 400 000

Edmonton
Vancouver
Calgary
Saskatoon
Victoria
Regina
Winnipeg

1961 GDP $13 663 300 000

One cube represents $50 million. (1913 constant)

Gross Domestic Product (GDP)

Agriculture
Forestry
Hunting, fishing, trapping
Mining
Manufacturing, power
Construction
Transportation
Trade, finance
Service
Public administration

Excludes Newfoundland, 1891 and 1926

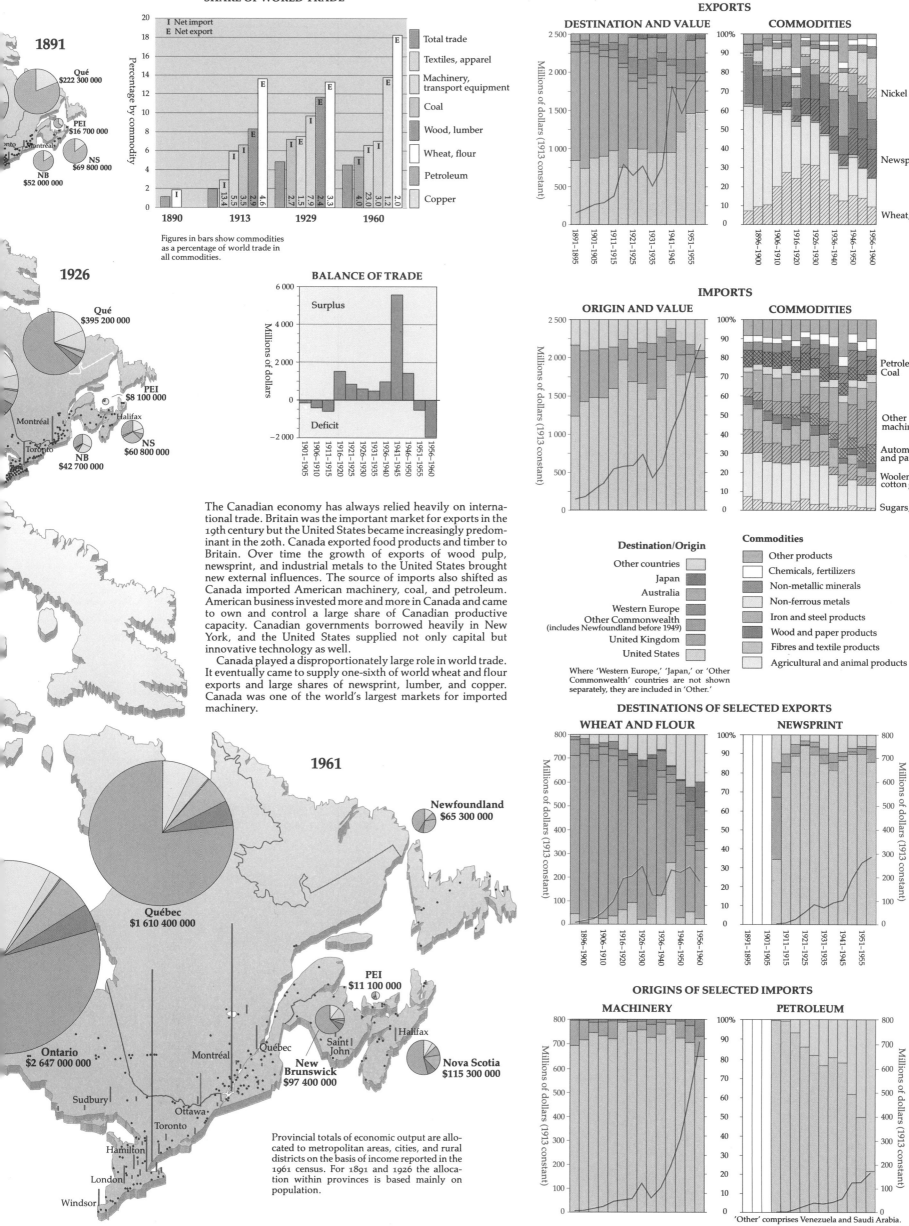

SHARE OF WORLD TRADE

I Net import
E Net export

Total trade
Textiles, apparel
Machinery, transport equipment
Coal
Wood, lumber
Wheat, flour
Petroleum
Copper

Figures in bars show commodities as a percentage of world trade in all commodities.

1891

Qué $222 300 000
PEI $16 700 000
NS $69 800 000
NB $52 000 000

1926

Qué $395 200 000
PEI $8 100 000
Montréal
Halifax
Toronto
NB $42 700 000
NS $60 800 000

BALANCE OF TRADE

Surplus

Deficit

The Canadian economy has always relied heavily on international trade. Britain was the important market for exports in the 19th century but the United States became increasingly predominant in the 20th. Canada exported food products and timber to Britain. Over time the growth of exports of wood pulp, newsprint, and industrial metals to the United States brought new external influences. The source of imports also shifted as Canada imported American machinery, coal, and petroleum. American business invested more and more in Canada and came to own and control a large share of Canadian productive capacity. Canadian governments borrowed heavily in New York, and the United States supplied not only capital but innovative technology as well.

Canada played a disproportionately large role in world trade. It eventually came to supply one-sixth of world wheat and flour exports and large shares of newsprint, lumber, and copper. Canada was one of the world's largest markets for imported machinery.

1961

Newfoundland $65 300 000
Québec $1 610 400 000
PEI $11 100 000
Ontario $2 647 000 000
Montréal
Québec
Saint John
Halifax
New Brunswick $97 400 000
Nova Scotia $115 300 000
Sudbury
Ottawa
Toronto
Hamilton
London
Windsor

Provincial totals of economic output are allocated to metropolitan areas, cities, and rural districts on the basis of income reported in the 1961 census. For 1891 and 1926 the allocation within provinces is based mainly on population.

EXPORTS

DESTINATION AND VALUE

COMMODITIES

Nickel
Newsprint
Wheat, flour

IMPORTS

ORIGIN AND VALUE

COMMODITIES

Petroleum
Coal
Other machinery
Automobiles and parts
Woolen and cotton goods
Sugars, syrups

Destination/Origin

Other countries
Japan
Australia
Western Europe
Other Commonwealth (includes Newfoundland before 1949)
United Kingdom
United States

Commodities

Other products
Chemicals, fertilizers
Non-metallic minerals
Non-ferrous metals
Iron and steel products
Wood and paper products
Fibres and textile products
Agricultural and animal products

Where 'Western Europe,' 'Japan,' or 'Other Commonwealth' countries are not shown separately, they are included in 'Other.'

DESTINATIONS OF SELECTED EXPORTS

WHEAT AND FLOUR

NEWSPRINT

ORIGINS OF SELECTED IMPORTS

MACHINERY

PETROLEUM

'Other' comprises Venezuela and Saudi Arabia.

POPULATION COMPOSITION

Authors: Donald Cartwright, Murdo MacPherson

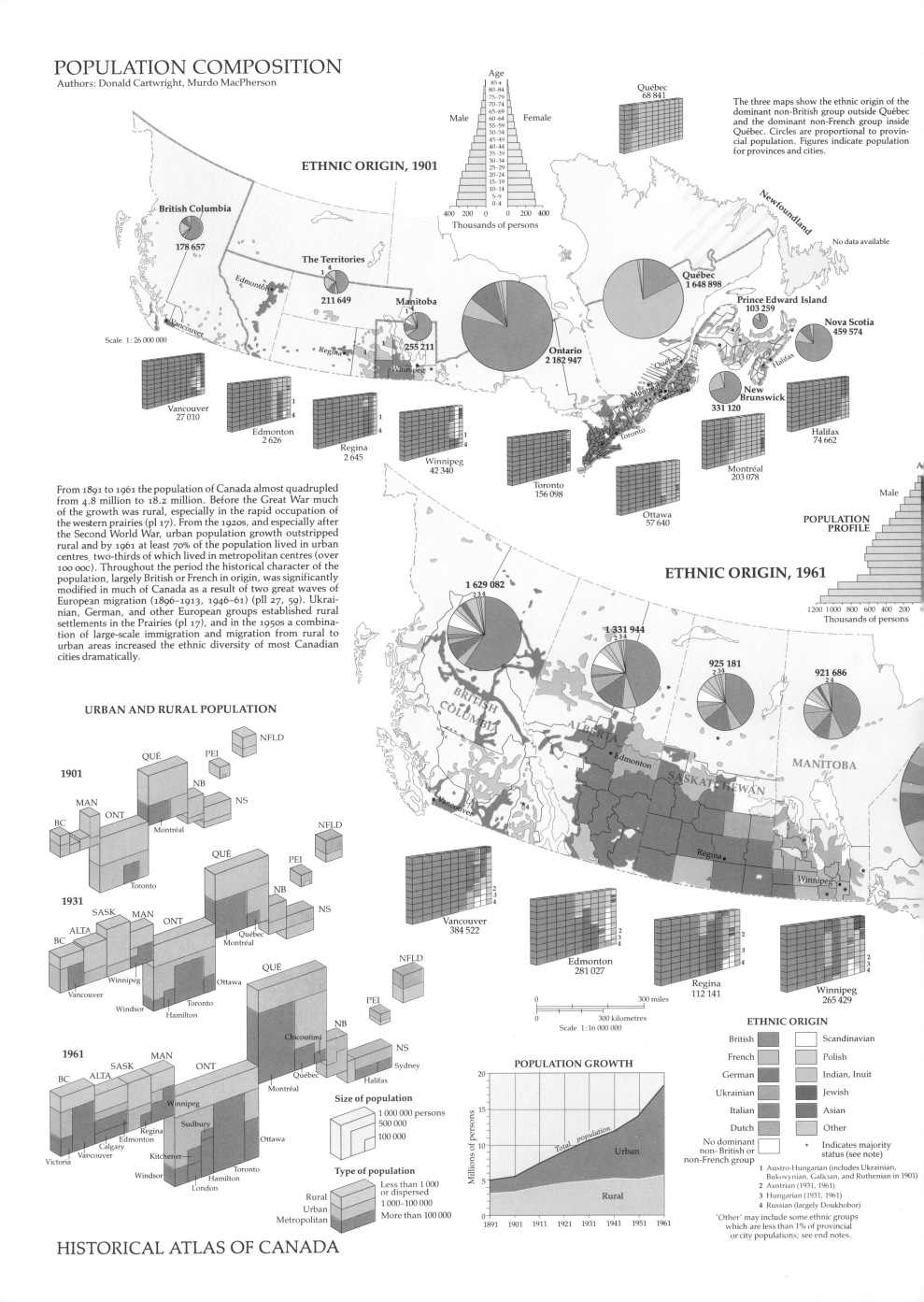

ETHNIC ORIGIN, 1901

Age
85 +
80–84
75–79
70–74
65–69
60–64
55–59
50–54
45–49
40–44
35–39
30–34
25–29
20–24
15–19
10–14
5–9
0–4

Male   Female

400 200 0 200 400
Thousands of persons

The three maps show the ethnic origin of the dominant non-British group outside Québec and the dominant non-French group inside Québec. Circles are proportional to provincial population. Figures indicate population for provinces and cities.

Québec
68 841

Newfoundland

No data available

British Columbia
178 657

The Territories
1 4
211 649

Manitoba
1
255 211

Québec
1 648 898

Prince Edward Island
103 259

Nova Scotia
459 574

New Brunswick
331 120

Ontario
2 182 947

Edmonton

Vancouver

Regina

Winnipeg

Scale 1 : 26 000 000

Vancouver
27 010

Edmonton
2 626

Regina
2 645

Winnipeg
42 340

Toronto
156 098

Ottawa
57 640

Montréal
203 078

Halifax
74 662

From 1891 to 1961 the population of Canada almost quadrupled from 4.8 million to 18.2 million. Before the Great War much of the growth was rural, especially in the rapid occupation of the western prairies (pl 17). From the 1920s, and especially after the Second World War, urban population growth outstripped rural and by 1961 at least 70% of the population lived in urban centres, two-thirds of which lived in metropolitan centres (over 100 000). Throughout the period the historical character of the population, largely British or French in origin, was significantly modified in much of Canada as a result of two great waves of European migration (1896–1913, 1946–61) (pll 27, 59). Ukrainian, German, and other European groups established rural settlements in the Prairies (pl 17), and in the 1950s a combination of large-scale immigration and migration from rural to urban areas increased the ethnic diversity of most Canadian cities dramatically.

POPULATION PROFILE

Male

1200 1000 800 600 400 200
Thousands of persons

ETHNIC ORIGIN, 1961

1 629 082
2 3 4

1 331 944
2 3 4

925 181
2 3 4

921 686
2 4

BRITISH COLUMBIA

ALBERTA

SASKATCHEWAN

MANITOBA

Edmonton

Vancouver

Regina

Winnipeg

URBAN AND RURAL POPULATION

1901

NFLD
QUÉ
PEI
NB
NS
MAN
ONT
BC
Montréal

1931

QUÉ
NFLD
PEI
NB
NS
Toronto
SASK
ALTA
MAN
ONT
BC
Montréal
Québec
Winnipeg
Vancouver
Windsor
Hamilton
Toronto
Ottawa

1961

QUÉ
NFLD
PEI
NB
NS
Sydney
Halifax
Chicoutimi
Québec
Montréal
MAN
SASK
ALTA
BC
ONT
Winnipeg
Sudbury
Regina
Edmonton
Calgary
Vancouver
Victoria
Windsor
Kitchener
Hamilton
London
Toronto
Ottawa

Vancouver
384 522

Edmonton
281 027

Regina
112 141

Winnipeg
265 429

0   300 miles
0   300 kilometres
Scale 1 : 16 000 000

Size of population

1 000 000 persons
500 000
100 000

Type of population

Rural
Urban
Metropolitan

Less than 1 000 or dispersed
1 000–100 000
More than 100 000

ETHNIC ORIGIN

British	Scandinavian
French	Polish
German	Indian, Inuit
Ukrainian	Jewish
Italian	Asian
Dutch	Other
No dominant non-British or non-French group	* Indicates majority status (see note)

1 Austro-Hungarian (includes Ukrainian, Bukovynian, Galician, and Ruthenian in 1901)
2 Austrian (1931, 1961)
3 Hungarian (1931, 1961)
4 Russian (largely Doukhobor)

'Other' may include some ethnic groups which are less than 1% of provincial or city populations; see end notes.

POPULATION GROWTH

20

15

10

5

0

Millions of persons

Total population

Urban

Rural

1891 1901 1911 1921 1931 1941 1951 1961

HISTORICAL ATLAS OF CANADA

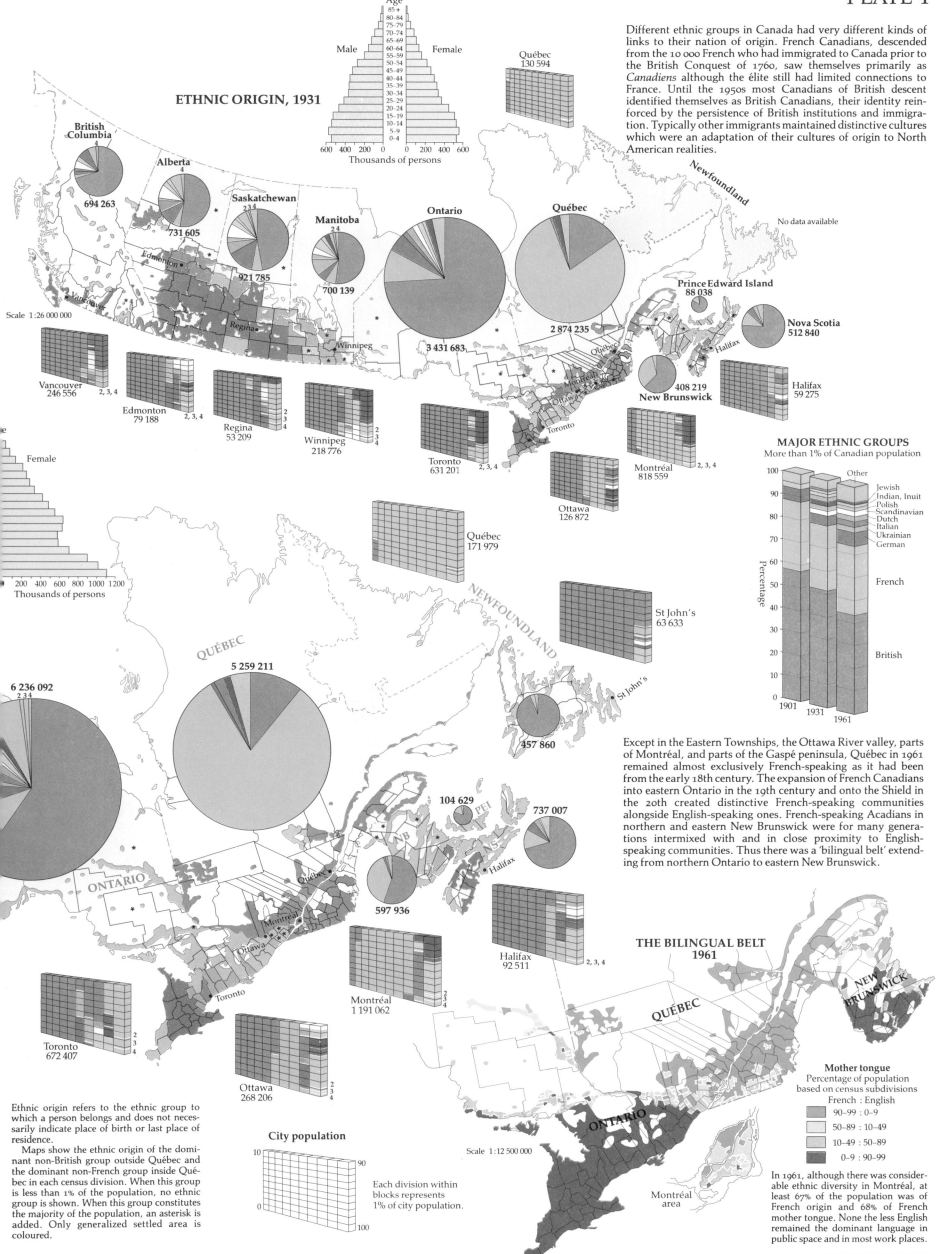

ETHNIC ORIGIN, 1931

Age
85 +
80–84
75–79
70–74
65–69
60–64
55–59
50–54
45–49
40–44
35–39
30–34
25–29
20–24
15–19
10–14
5–9
0–4

Male / Female

600 400 200 0 0 200 400 600
Thousands of persons

Different ethnic groups in Canada had very different kinds of links to their nation of origin. French Canadians, descended from the 10 000 French who had immigrated to Canada prior to the British Conquest of 1760, saw themselves primarily as *Canadiens* although the élite still had limited connections to France. Until the 1950s most Canadians of British descent identified themselves as British Canadians, their identity reinforced by the persistence of British institutions and immigration. Typically other immigrants maintained distinctive cultures which were an adaptation of their cultures of origin to North American realities.

Québec
130 594

Newfoundland

No data available

British Columbia 4
694 263

Alberta 4
731 605

Saskatchewan 234
921 785

Manitoba 24
700 139

Ontario
3 431 683

Québec
2 874 235

Prince Edward Island
88 038

Nova Scotia
512 840

New Brunswick
408 219

Scale 1:26 000 000

Edmonton •
Vancouver •
Regina •
Winnipeg •
Québec
Montréal
Ottawa
Toronto
Halifax

Vancouver
246 556   2, 3, 4

Edmonton
79 188   2, 3, 4

Regina
53 209   234

Winnipeg
218 776   234

Toronto
631 201   2, 3, 4

Montréal
818 559   2, 3, 4

Ottawa
126 872

Québec
171 979

Halifax
59 275

St John's
63 633

MAJOR ETHNIC GROUPS
More than 1% of Canadian population

Percentage

100 — Other
90 — Jewish / Indian, Inuit / Polish / Scandinavian / Dutch / Italian / Ukrainian
80 — German
70
60 — French
50
40
30 — British
20
10
0
1901   1931   1961

Female
200 400 600 800 1000 1200
Thousands of persons

QUÉBEC
5 259 211

6 236 092
234

ONTARIO

104 629
PEI

597 936
NB

737 007
Halifax

457 860

St John's

NEWFOUNDLAND

Québec
Montréal
Ottawa
Toronto
Halifax

Toronto
672 407   234

Ottawa
268 206   234

Montréal
1 191 062   234

Halifax
92 511   2, 3, 4

Except in the Eastern Townships, the Ottawa River valley, parts of Montréal, and parts of the Gaspé peninsula, Québec in 1961 remained almost exclusively French-speaking as it had been from the early 18th century. The expansion of French Canadians into eastern Ontario in the 19th century and onto the Shield in the 20th created distinctive French-speaking communities alongside English-speaking ones. French-speaking Acadians in northern and eastern New Brunswick were for many generations intermixed with and in close proximity to English-speaking communities. Thus there was a 'bilingual belt' extending from northern Ontario to eastern New Brunswick.

THE BILINGUAL BELT 1961

NEW BRUNSWICK

QUÉBEC

ONTARIO

Montréal area

Scale 1:12 500 000

Mother tongue
Percentage of population based on census subdivisions
French : English

90–99 : 0–9
50–89 : 10–49
10–49 : 50–89
0–9 : 90–99

Ethnic origin refers to the ethnic group to which a person belongs and does not necessarily indicate place of birth or last place of residence.

Maps show the ethnic origin of the dominant non-British group outside Québec and the dominant non-French group inside Québec in each census division. When this group is less than 1% of the population, no ethnic group is shown. When this group constitutes the majority of the population, an asterisk is added. Only generalized settled area is coloured.

City population

10
0
90
100

Each division within blocks represents 1% of city population.

In 1961, although there was considerable ethnic diversity in Montréal, at least 67% of the population was of French origin and 68% of French mother tongue. None the less English remained the dominant language in public space and in most work places.

VOLUME III

PART ONE

THE GREAT TRANSFORMATION 1891-1929

National Economic Patterns

The remarkable changes within the Canadian economy in the years between 1891 and 1929 have been called the Great Transformation. The total output of the economy grew dramatically, the population doubled, and there was a great increase in the capital stock of the country. A huge territory, rich in natural resources, was brought into production. At the same time the structure of the economy underwent striking changes. Major new export staples, such as pulp and paper and industrial minerals, were developed. The manufacturing sector grew in stature and complexity as Canada joined the ranks of the leading industrial nations. The electrical, chemical, and metallurgical technology of what has been called the Second Industrial Revolution was brought into play. As the population grew and incomes increased, consumer demand for a wider variety of goods and services enlarged and diversified the activity in trade and services. As the regions of Canada became more closely integrated through investments in transportation and innovations in communication, the economy was centred in and controlled through the main cities.

From 1891 to 1929 the per capita gross national product (GNP) rose by 177%. Only Sweden and the United States had greater growth rates than Canada's annual average of 3.2%. Output per capita grew considerably more rapidly in Canada than it did in such major industrial nations as Great Britain, France, and Germany. Total output grew by more than 5% per annum. Few national economies have expanded so quickly over such an extended period. Canada's population was augmented by a massive influx of immigrants and its capital stock benefited from a substantial inflow of capital from abroad. Canada became one of the world's leading trading nations, with a major industrial economy, and Canadians came to enjoy a level of economic prosperity second only to that of the United States.

The period had not begun auspiciously. The early 1890s marked a low point in the economic fortunes of the Canadian Confederation. The colonies of British North America had come together in 1867 with high hopes of creating a larger and more prosperous national economy, and in the first few decades following Confederation reasonable (if erratic) economic growth had been achieved. The economy was undergoing industrialization and the agricultural sector was prosperous. But high birth rates outpaced the expansion of the labour market and emigration to the United States was high. Extensive railway building had provided links between the regions, especially with the completion of the railway into Manitoba in 1882, but the anticipated agricultural settlement in the West had been confined to a relatively small area. The Maritime Provinces, historically bound up in a maritime and mercantile economy, had received only a modest stimulus from their integration into the larger Canada. More generally the Canadian economy had struggled against a world-wide depression in the 1870s, and another depression in the early 1890s, marked by a long-term slowdown in Britain (Canada's main export market) and steeply protectionist moves in the United States (the other principal market), made prospects look dim indeed.

Circumstances, however, changed dramatically as the 1890s progressed. The economy turned upwards, partly because of the growth in foreign markets for Canadian export staples, and partly because of improvements in Canadian production. The earliest glimmers of optimism originated on the Precambrian Shield. Before 1890 this area had been regarded as an unpromising barrier of granite rock, muskeg, and stunted forest interposed between the older settled parts of Canada and the vast area of exploitable fertile land in the Prairies. Travel to the West was easiest through American territory via Chicago and Minneapolis. But the new techniques of making paper from wood fibre rather than from rags,

which required great amounts of energy, gave new value to the low-grade forest and abundant hydraulic power of the Shield. Nickel and copper ore, discovered in the course of the construction of the Canadian Pacific Railway (CPR), began to be mined for use in the United States. A search for more mineral wealth was on.

Traditional exports also received a boost. The cheese industry, whose products were destined for export to Great Britain, expanded in the 1890s and in that same decade bacon exports came into prominence. The most dramatically revalued commodity, however, was wheat. Canada had ceased to be a net exporter of wheat shortly after Confederation, but in the early 1890s increased production in Manitoba once again provided a surplus for export. Even before 1890 the stage had been set for an export revival by large reductions in trans-Atlantic transport costs and the establishment of rail transport to the Prairies (pl 6). The construction of a network of branch lines thereafter, along with the railways' improved freight-carrying capacity, pushed transport costs down further.

All these circumstances had occurred by the mid-1890s, when world wheat prices began to rise. The pace of agricultural settlement picked up on the Prairies, assisted by the federal government's provision of free homestead land and its active promotion of the glowing economic prospects of the Canadian Prairies. Simultaneously, the exploitation of the resources of the Shield accelerated and in British Columbia the potential of hard-rock mining in the Kootenays and timbering along the coast began to be realized. A protracted investment boom ensued. Between 1898 and 1914 gross investment exceeded 15% of the GNP each year. Much of the investment was directed to the exploitation of the resource frontier – railways, shipping and storage facilities, entire settlements, and financial establishments and managerial offices in the metropolitan centres – but it stimulated growth, with varying intensity, throughout the economy.

Canada's industrial development in this period was, however, not simply a response to the investment boom on the new resource frontiers. The sudden jump in the size of the population, accomplished through the net gain of about a million immigrants by 1914, increased domestic consumer demand and encouraged the expansion of a wide range of manufacturing industries. In addition, significant changes in technology were being implemented as in all the major industrial countries. The principal advance was the generation, transport, and use of electricity. Canada, with an abundance of sites for the generation of hydroelectric power, was in the forefront of this development. Electricity both increased the demand for copper and provided new methods of refining it. Other metallurgical and chemical developments enhanced the value of base metals and led to the manufacture of high-quality machinery and equipment. This was the age of alloy steel, aluminum, and artificial abrasives. The growing popularity and wide circulation of daily newspapers led to a great demand for newsprint, especially in the United States, and a new round of exploitation of Canadian forests for wood pulp. The growing pulp and paper industry in turn demanded acids and other chemicals on a large scale.

Industrialization brought with it a revolution in economic organization. The consolidation of capitalism, particularly the shift from industrial to corporate capitalism, reduced the number and increased the size of economic units. These larger firms were multi-unit organizations, usually with several locations. Their large-scale operations required a high degree of rationalization, the planning of production, and a commitment to research to increase their share of the market. Waves of mergers concentrated more power in the hands of Montréal and Toronto capitalists. The development of scientific management systems redefined labour requirements, often reducing the level of skills needed, but by becoming more efficient stimulating expansion and the growth of employment. In 1890, 2 800 plants produced two-thirds of value-added through manufacturing. By 1922, only 936 plants accounted for the same share. Some consolidations, notably in the textile and agricultural-implements firms, occurred before the turn of the century, but most took place after 1900. Two significant periods of consolidation can be identified during the Great Transformation: from 1909 to 1913, and from 1925 to 1929. The second wave of mergers was marked by the development of large pulp and paper operations and the takeover of many small Canadian automobile companies by large American corporations.

The First World War brought a redirection of the Canadian economy: immigration almost halted; investment declined sharply; and manpower and resources were diverted to the war effort. The growth of the GNP ceased and output per person actually declined. Economic development resumed after 1921, especially between 1925 and 1929, although less vigorously than in the boom between 1896 and 1914. The special dynamic of the earlier boom, the settlement of the Prairie agricultural frontier, had passed. In the 1920s the impetus to growth depended more on pulp and paper, base metals, and the automobile industry (pl 7). An increase in consumerism, triggered by the increased purchasing power of the larger domestic market and the cheaper costs of mass-production items, also fueled growth.

With the end of Prairie settlement railway building also subsided (pl 6). Western settlement had called forth two additional transcontinental main lines – the Canadian Northern and the Grand Trunk Pacific – in the years before 1914. This investment was not justified; the new lines soon faced bankruptcy and they were nationalized in 1917. Although the CPR continued to operate profitably, the government of Canada gathered all of the remaining uneconomic lines into the Canadian National Railways by 1923. This rescue action marked a substantial move by the federal government into economic enterprise, an initiative that was to be extended to other fields. There had been precursors of such government activity in Ontario, in hydroelectricity, and in the western provinces, in telephones. The Great Transformation was largely accomplished by private enterprise, but, as has happened throughout Canadian history, it would not have been possible without large-scale public investment. By the end of the 1920s it was clear that an era of public enterprise had arrived, albeit based on private ideology and run in the same way as capitalist ventures. Government involvement was also a critical component of transport policy: subsidies to keep down freight rates were introduced in order to make east-west trade prosper. The Crow's Nest Pass Agreement of 1897 (which reduced eastbound freight rates for wheat and flour and westbound rates for 'settlers' effects') and the 1927 Maritime Freight Rate Act (which restored low rates between the Maritimes and Central Canada) were two of the most significant interventions for the specific purpose of boosting regional economies. Indeed many aspects of the National Policy, originating in 1879 and redefined for changing times, underpinned the economic development of the Canadian national economy throughout the Great Transformation.

The rapid expansion of the Canadian economy was financed largely by foreign investors, a pattern established well before Confederation. Canada depended on foreign borrowing, mostly in London, to finance large projects but increasingly ventures were financed and directed by entrepreneurs in the United States, some of whom moved to Canada to exercise direct control over their investments, notably in the lumber industry. Many of these Americans became a part of the Canadian business élite and ceased to be regarded as agents of 'foreign' investment.

The emergence of large corporations enabled enterprises to spread themselves across international boundaries without the entrepreneurs themselves having to move. During the Great Transformation there was a large increase in direct American investment in Canada. American firms extended their operations into Canada to take advantage of the rapidly expanding market and they developed much of the new industrial technology and many of the

new products of this period. Canadian patent laws and the high National Policy tariff on finished manufactures encouraged businesses from the United States to establish branch manufacturing activities in Canada (pl 7). In addition, US corporations came increasingly to look to Canada as a source of natural resources, and, as the 20th century proceeded, American ownership reached more and more into the resource sector. Americans invested heavily in pulp mills on the Shield and in British Columbia. The large-scale incursion of American ownership into Canada was closely bound up with the emergence of the corporation as the typical form of business enterprise and the turn-of-the-century merger movement which placed corporate control in relatively few hands.

As the merger movement grew early in the 20th century, bankers and investment dealers formed alliances with industrialists, and the modern corporation took shape. In the 19th century independent merchant wholesalers had been important agents in the economy, controlling the distribution of goods and, through the provision of credit, exerting considerable influence on retailers and manufacturers. Towards the end of the 19th century larger corporations and stock markets provided alternate sources for raising money and the role of independent wholesalers diminished significantly (pl 8). Some manufacturing enterprises could reach customers directly through branch offices which, in addition to looking after distribution, were able to provide instruction on the use of new machines and services for repairs. Wholesalers also faced competition from new forms of retailing. In the 1920s chain stores and department stores expanded dramatically and by 1930 they accounted for 31% of all retail sales. By placing large orders with manufacturers directly or by setting up their own factories, such firms were able to bypass the merchant wholesaler. Many small independent retailers also felt the impact of mass merchandising and disappeared from the scene. The corporate élite, by contrast, became nationally known and nationally influential.

Paralleling the increasingly national significance of the large corporations were the growth and concentration of Canadian financial institutions (pl 9). From 1900 to 1929 the assets of banks rose from $416 million to $2 582 million. Most small banks were absorbed by larger units. By the end of the period ten banks – all with head offices in Toronto and Montréal and with a grand total of 3 970 branches in Canada from coast to coast – controlled the system. Regional banking headquarters disappeared. The relocation of the Halifax-based Royal Bank (to Montréal) and the Bank of Nova Scotia (to Toronto) were the most significant episodes in the closure or absorption of 14 Maritime-based banks. Once established in their new bases, the Royal Bank and the Bank of Nova Scotia grew into national institutions by swallowing up smaller banks. Québec and Winnipeg survived for a time as independent centres, but eventually the banks with headquarters there were also absorbed; by the 1920s both cities had become regional centres for Montréal- and Toronto-based banks. Some grew particularly through their creation of national bank networks, especially the Bank of Montreal and the Toronto-based Canadian Bank of Commerce. Both had close connections with the building of transcontinental railways, and they were therefore able to position themselves as the bankers for many property and resource-development firms in the regions served by those railways.

Insurance head offices were more widely spread. Winnipeg, London, Waterloo, and Ottawa had relatively large operations, though the assets managed in such places were often narrowly based in one firm (even in Montréal Sun Life accounted for 63% of all insurance assets managed in that city). Toronto, by contrast, was the home of a large number of firms, including an increasing number that were American; British companies, traditionally based in Montréal, declined in significance. Trust and loan companies managed to survive in many places across the country, thereby providing a modest amount of local participation in loan and investment decisions, but in that sector, too, mergers and takeovers led to the increasing dominance of Toronto firms.

These structural changes in the Canadian economy had two major effects. First, as in all western countries, urbanization accelerated. Second, the metropolitan centres of Toronto and

Montréal grew ever richer and more powerful. As communication systems improved, first with the postal service and then with telephone connections (pl 10), ideas generated and decisions made in the two metropolitan centres could be quickly disseminated across the country.

The concentration of industrial and financial management in Montréal and Toronto led to widespread regional antagonism towards the two cities. A 1913 survey by western grain growers identified 42 leading plutocrats in Canada, most of whom lived in Toronto and Montréal. Political cartoonists pilloried 'fat-cat' tycoons with their diversified corporate folios. Increasingly, decisions on banking and mortgages were made by managers who were not resident in the locality or the region. On the Prairies, for example, only in grain, where Winnipeg was the focus, was there much sense of regional involvement. In British Columbia Vancouver held some sway over the management of the resource economy, but many critical decisions regarding transport and investment were made in Toronto and Montréal. In the Maritimes the traditional mercantile strengths of Halifax and Saint John diminished. Most middle-sized cities had only limited power to make decisions, whether on interest rates, the size of loans, or the setting of freight rates. On the international scene, however, the same could be said of Montréal and Toronto in relation to New York and London: in the world economic system Canada competed with Australasia, Latin America, and Asia for access to the major industrial markets of Europe and the United States.

PRIMARY PRODUCTION
Author: Marvin McInnis

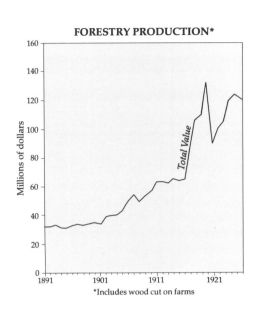

FORESTRY PRODUCTION*

*Includes wood cut on farms

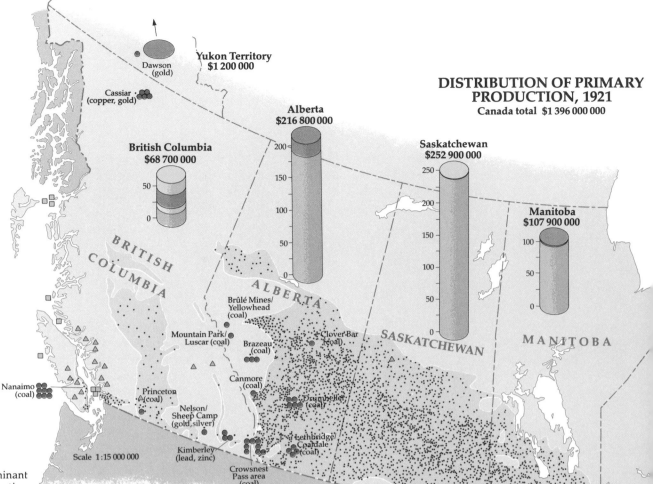

Yukon Territory
$1 200 000

Dawson (gold)

Cassiar (copper, gold)

Alberta
$216 800 000

British Columbia
$68 700 000

Saskatchewan
$252 900 000

Manitoba
$107 900 000

BRITISH COLUMBIA

ALBERTA

SASKATCHEWAN

MANITOBA

Brûlé Mines/ Yellowhead (coal)

Mountain Park/ Luscar (coal)

Brazeau (coal)

Clover Bar (coal)

Canmore (coal)

Drumheller (coal)

Nanaimo (coal)

Princeton (coal)

Nelson/ Sheep Camp (gold, silver)

Lethbridge Coaldale (coal)

Kimberley (lead, zinc)

Crowsnest Pass area (coal)

Scale 1:15 000 000

By the 1920s the primary sector no longer played a dominant role in Canada's economy. Already by 1891 primary production amounted to less than 30% of the national output and by 1926 it had declined to 23%. Agriculture remained most important but its relative position had diminished in spite of the settlement of the western plains in the 1891–1926 period. The value of agricultural production grew on average only 2.6% per annum, more slowly than the economy as a whole with an average annual growth rate of 3.8% between 1891 and 1926. Forestry, which had provided Canada's leading export for most of the 19th century, was on the wane. Although pulpwood production increasingly rose to offset the slower growth of lumber output, and rapid developments in the forest industry in British Columbia to some extent offset decline in eastern Canada, the growth in the forest industry was on average only 3.3% per annum. Fishing was the slowest-growing primary activity with an average annual growth rate of 1.2% in the 35-year period.

Mining with an average annual growth rate of 4.5% gave the most impressive performance of the primary industries. Around the turn of the century the output of gold rose dramatically with the Klondike rush and then during the First World War the mining of both coal and non-ferrous metals increased greatly. The largest increase in the value of mining output occurred in the mid-1920s with new discoveries of complex mineral deposits that included precious metals in combination with base metals.

AGRICULTURAL PRODUCTION

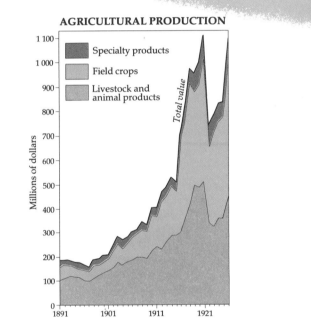

Specialty products
Field crops
Livestock and animal products

Total value

MINING PRODUCTION

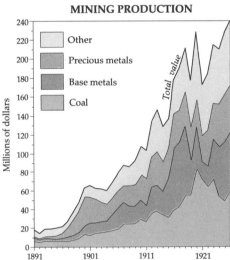

Other
Precious metals
Base metals
Coal

Total value

TOTAL VALUE OF AGRICULTURAL PRODUCTION, 1921*

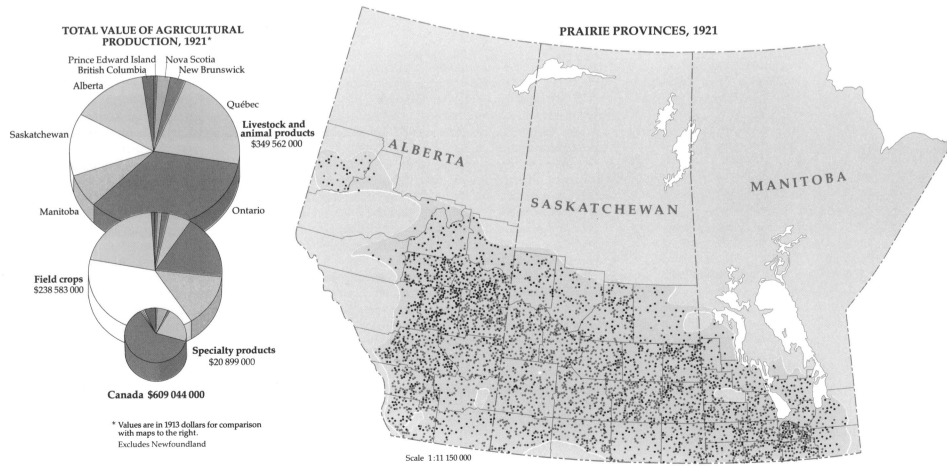

Prince Edward Island
Nova Scotia
British Columbia
New Brunswick
Alberta
Québec
Saskatchewan
Livestock and animal products
$349 562 000
Manitoba
Ontario
Field crops
$238 583 000
Specialty products
$20 899 000

Canada $609 044 000

* Values are in 1913 dollars for comparison with maps to the right.
Excludes Newfoundland

PRAIRIE PROVINCES, 1921

ALBERTA

SASKATCHEWAN

MANITOBA

Scale 1:11 150 000

HISTORICAL ATLAS OF CANADA

PLATE 5

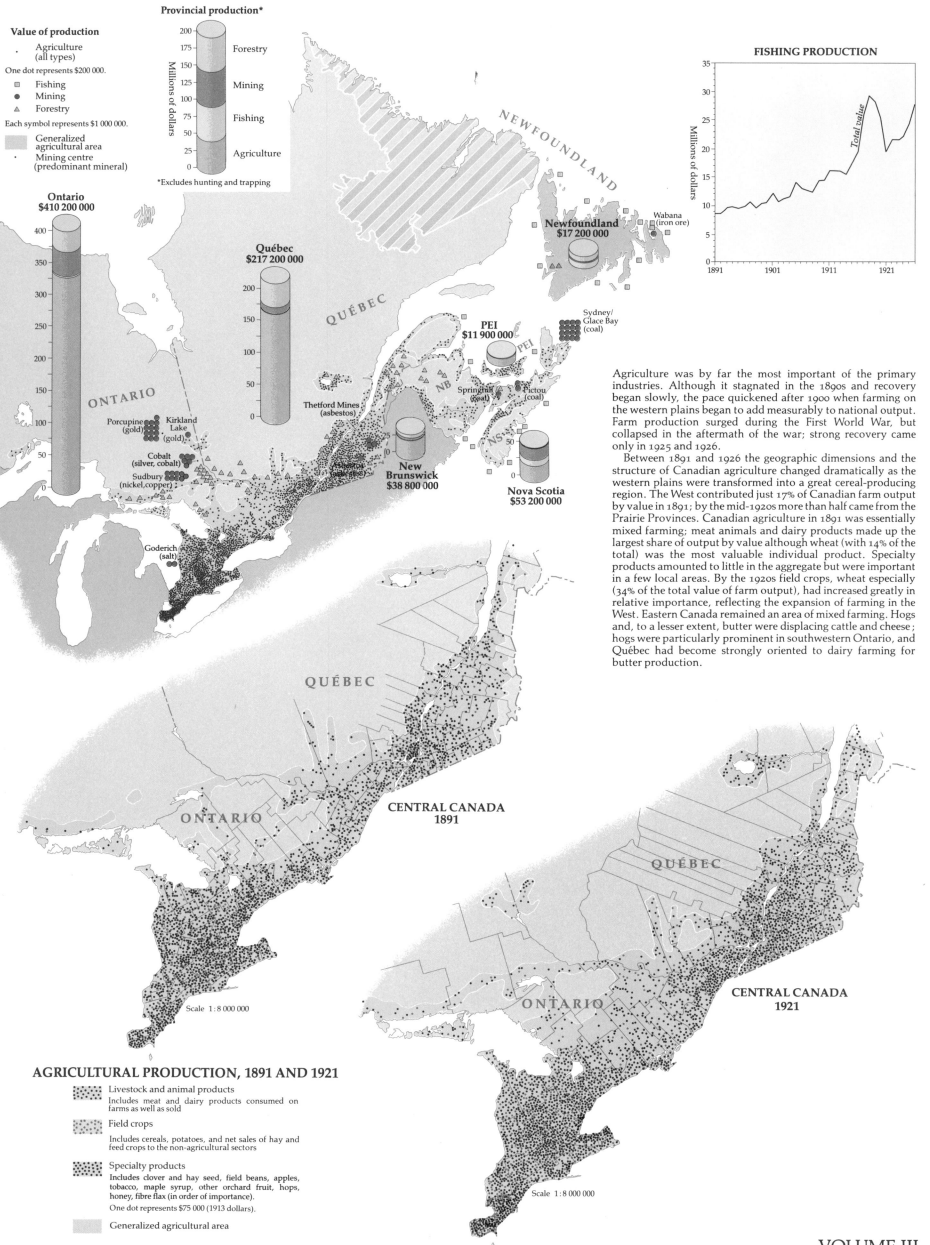

Value of production

. Agriculture (all types)

One dot represents $200 000.

☐ Fishing

● Mining

△ Forestry

Each symbol represents $1 000 000.

Generalized agricultural area

. Mining centre (predominant mineral)

Provincial production*

Millions of dollars

200 — Forestry
175
150
125 — Mining
100
75 — Fishing
50
25 — Agriculture
0

*Excludes hunting and trapping

FISHING PRODUCTION

Millions of dollars

35
30
25
20
15
10
5
0
1891   1901   1911   1921

Total value

Ontario
$410 200 000

400
350
300
250
200
150
100
50
0

ONTARIO

Porcupine (gold)   Kirkland Lake (gold)
Cobalt (silver, cobalt)
Sudbury (nickel, copper)

Goderich (salt)

Québec
$217 200 000

200
150
100
50
0

QUÉBEC

Thetford Mines (asbestos)

Asbestos (asbestos)

New Brunswick
$38 800 000

NB

PEI
$11 900 000

PEI

Springhill (coal)   Pictou (coal)

NS

Sydney/ Glace Bay (coal)

Newfoundland
$17 200 000

NEWFOUNDLAND

Wabana (iron ore)

Nova Scotia
$53 200 000

50
0

Agriculture was by far the most important of the primary industries. Although it stagnated in the 1890s and recovery began slowly, the pace quickened after 1900 when farming on the western plains began to add measurably to national output. Farm production surged during the First World War, but collapsed in the aftermath of the war; strong recovery came only in 1925 and 1926.

Between 1891 and 1926 the geographic dimensions and the structure of Canadian agriculture changed dramatically as the western plains were transformed into a great cereal-producing region. The West contributed just 17% of Canadian farm output by value in 1891; by the mid-1920s more than half came from the Prairie Provinces. Canadian agriculture in 1891 was essentially mixed farming; meat animals and dairy products made up the largest share of output by value although wheat (with 14% of the total) was the most valuable individual product. Specialty products amounted to little in the aggregate but were important in a few local areas. By the 1920s field crops, wheat especially (34% of the total value of farm output), had increased greatly in relative importance, reflecting the expansion of farming in the West. Eastern Canada remained an area of mixed farming. Hogs and, to a lesser extent, butter were displacing cattle and cheese; hogs were particularly prominent in southwestern Ontario, and Québec had become strongly oriented to dairy farming for butter production.

QUÉBEC

ONTARIO

CENTRAL CANADA
1891

Scale 1 : 8 000 000

QUÉBEC

ONTARIO

CENTRAL CANADA
1921

Scale 1 : 8 000 000

AGRICULTURAL PRODUCTION, 1891 AND 1921

Livestock and animal products
Includes meat and dairy products consumed on farms as well as sold

Field crops
Includes cereals, potatoes, and net sales of hay and feed crops to the non-agricultural sectors

Specialty products
Includes clover and hay seed, field beans, apples, tobacco, maple syrup, other orchard fruit, hops, honey, fibre flax (in order of importance).
One dot represents $75 000 (1913 dollars).

Generalized agricultural area

THE EXPANSION AND CONSOLIDATION OF RAILWAYS
Author: Christopher Andreae

CORPORATE STRUCTURE TO 1960

CANADIAN PACIFIC RAILWAY (CPR)
1 Soo Line Railroad (Minneapolis, St Paul and Sault Ste Marie Railway and Wisconsin Central Railway)

NORTHERN ALBERTA RAILWAY (jointly owned by CNR and CPR)

CANADIAN NATIONAL RAILWAY (CNR)
CANADIAN GOVT RAILWAYS
2 Intercolonial Railway
3 National Transcontinental Railway
4 Hudson Bay Railway
GRAND TRUNK RAILWAY
5 Grand Trunk Pacific Railway
CANADIAN NORTHERN RAILWAY
NEWFOUNDLAND RAILWAY
CNR after 1923

WHITE PASS AND YUKON RAILWAY
PACIFIC GREAT EASTERN RAILWAY
ONTARIO NORTHLAND RAILWAY
ALGOMA CENTRAL RAILWAY
CHEMIN DE FER CARTIER
QUEBEC, NORTH SHORE AND LABRADOR RAILWAY
US RAILWAY COMPANIES
6 Great Northern Railway
7 New York Central Railroad
Lines abandoned by 1960 (all colours)

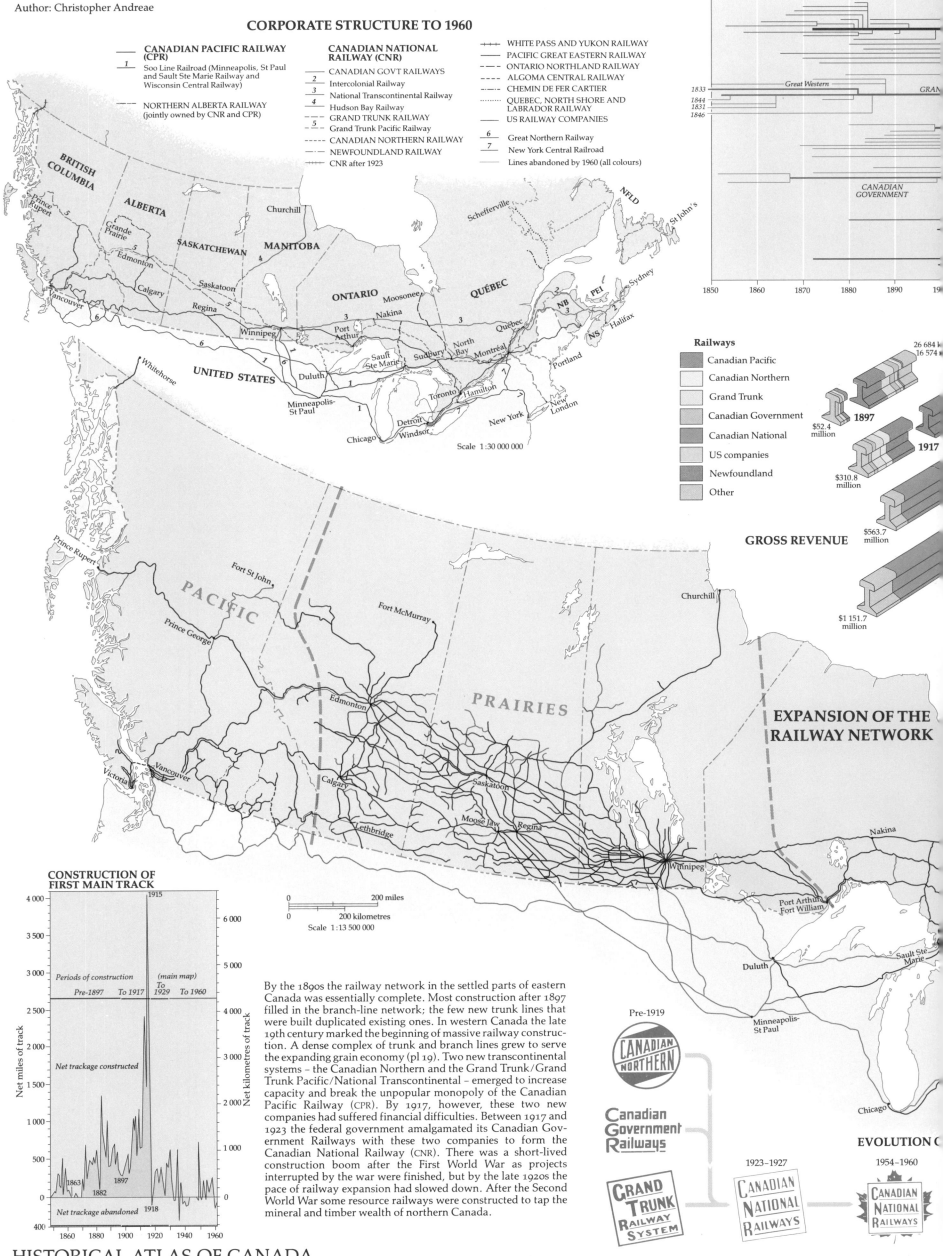

CORPORAT

1833
1844
1831
1846

Great Western

GRA

CANADIAN GOVERNMENT

1850   1860   1870   1880   1890   19

Railways
- Canadian Pacific
- Canadian Northern
- Grand Trunk
- Canadian Government
- Canadian National
- US companies
- Newfoundland
- Other

26 684 k
16 574 k

1897
$52.4 million

1917
$310.8 million

GROSS REVENUE

$563.7 million

$1 151.7 million

EXPANSION OF THE RAILWAY NETWORK

Scale 1:30 000 000

Scale 1:13 500 000

0   200 miles
0   200 kilometres

CONSTRUCTION OF FIRST MAIN TRACK

Periods of construction
Pre-1897   To 1917   (main map) To 1929   To 1960

Net trackage constructed

Net trackage abandoned

1863 1882 1897 1915 1918

Net miles of track: 4 000 / 3 500 / 3 000 / 2 500 / 1 500 / 1 000 / 500 / 0 / 400
Net kilometres of track: 6 000 / 5 000 / 4 000 / 3 000 / 2 000 / 1 000 / 0
1860 1880 1900 1920 1940 1960

By the 1890s the railway network in the settled parts of eastern Canada was essentially complete. Most construction after 1897 filled in the branch-line network; the few new trunk lines that were built duplicated existing ones. In western Canada the late 19th century marked the beginning of massive railway construction. A dense complex of trunk and branch lines grew to serve the expanding grain economy (pl 19). Two new transcontinental systems – the Canadian Northern and the Grand Trunk/Grand Trunk Pacific/National Transcontinental – emerged to increase capacity and break the unpopular monopoly of the Canadian Pacific Railway (CPR). By 1917, however, these two new companies had suffered financial difficulties. Between 1917 and 1923 the federal government amalgamated its Canadian Government Railways with these two companies to form the Canadian National Railway (CNR). There was a short-lived construction boom after the First World War as projects interrupted by the war were finished, but by the late 1920s the pace of railway expansion had slowed down. After the Second World War some resource railways were constructed to tap the mineral and timber wealth of northern Canada.

Pre-1919

CANADIAN NORTHERN

Canadian Government Railways

GRAND TRUNK RAILWAY SYSTEM

1923–1927
CANADIAN NATIONAL RAILWAYS

1954–1960
CANADIAN NATIONAL RAILWAYS

EVOLUTION O

HISTORICAL ATLAS OF CANADA

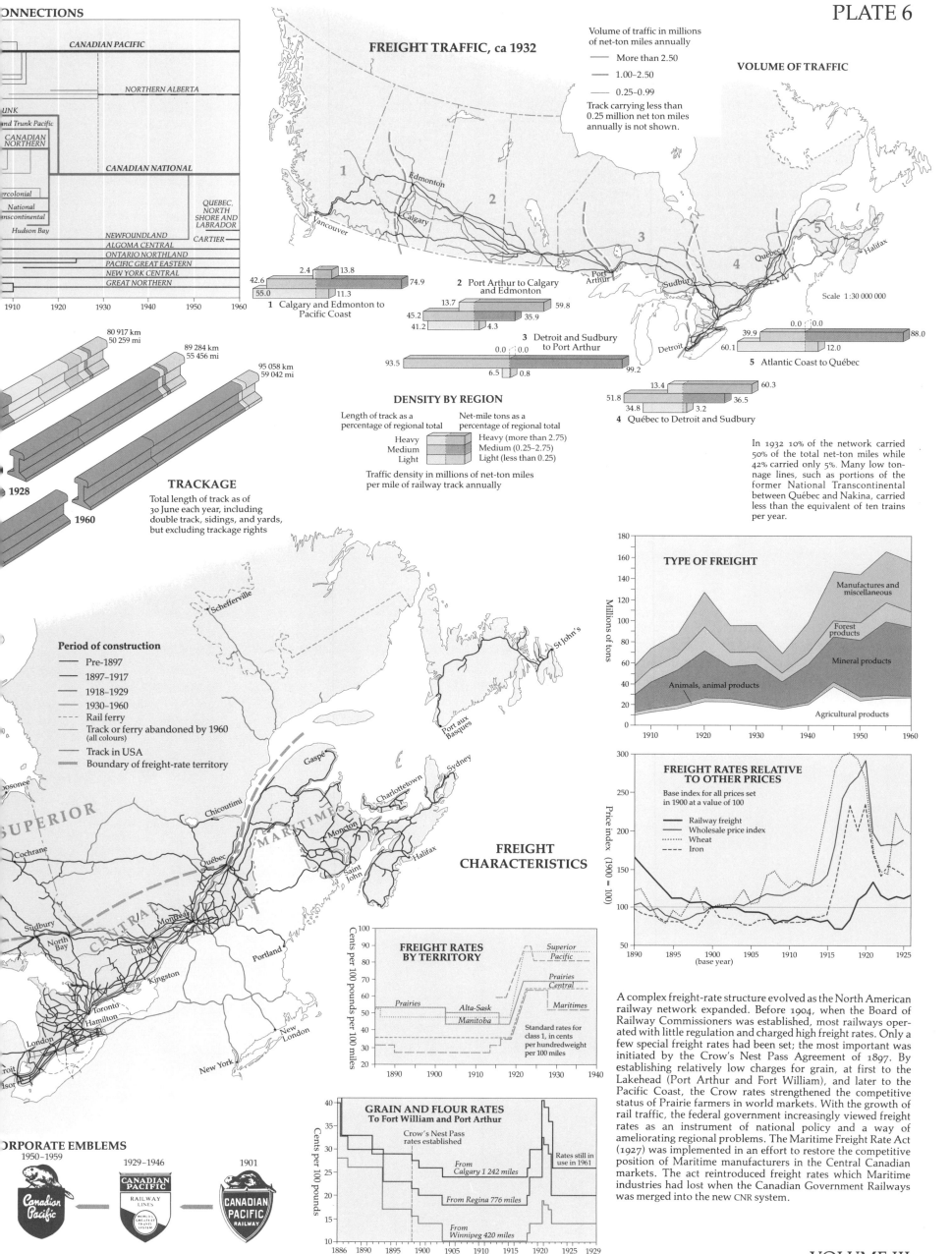

PLATE 6

CONNECTIONS

CANADIAN PACIFIC

NORTHERN ALBERTA

GRAND TRUNK
Grand Trunk Pacific
CANADIAN
NORTHERN

CANADIAN NATIONAL

Intercolonial
National
Transcontinental

Hudson Bay

QUEBEC,
NORTH
SHORE AND
LABRADOR

NEWFOUNDLAND
ALGOMA CENTRAL
ONTARIO NORTHLAND
PACIFIC GREAT EASTERN
NEW YORK CENTRAL
GREAT NORTHERN

CARTIER

1910   1920   1930   1940   1950   1960

FREIGHT TRAFFIC, ca 1932

Volume of traffic in millions
of net-ton miles annually
——— More than 2.50
——— 1.00–2.50
——— 0.25–0.99
Track carrying less than
0.25 million net ton miles
annually is not shown.

VOLUME OF TRAFFIC

Scale 1 : 30 000 000

80 917 km
50 259 mi

89 284 km
55 456 mi

95 058 km
59 042 mi

1928

1960

TRACKAGE

Total length of track as of
30 June each year, including
double track, sidings, and yards,
but excluding trackage rights

2.4   13.8
42.6 ┌──────┐ 74.9
55.0 │ 11.3 │
1 Calgary and Edmonton to
   Pacific Coast

2 Port Arthur to Calgary
   and Edmonton
13.7
45.2   59.8
41.2   35.9
       4.3

3 Detroit and Sudbury
   to Port Arthur
0.0   0.0
93.5   99.2
6.5   0.8

5 Atlantic Coast to Québec
39.9 0.0   0.0   88.0
60.1 12.0

DENSITY BY REGION

Length of track as a
percentage of regional total
Heavy
Medium
Light

Net-mile tons as a
percentage of regional total
Heavy (more than 2.75)
Medium (0.25–2.75)
Light (less than 0.25)

Traffic density in millions of net-ton miles
per mile of railway track annually

4 Québec to Detroit and Sudbury
13.4   60.3
51.8   36.5
34.8   3.2

In 1932 10% of the network carried
50% of the total net-ton miles while
42% carried only 5%. Many low ton-
nage lines, such as portions of the
former National Transcontinental
between Québec and Nakina, carried
less than the equivalent of ten trains
per year.

Period of construction
——— Pre-1897
——— 1897–1917
——— 1918–1929
——— 1930–1960
- - - Rail ferry
——— Track or ferry abandoned by 1960
       (all colours)
——— Track in USA
━━━ Boundary of freight-rate territory

FREIGHT
CHARACTERISTICS

TYPE OF FREIGHT

Manufactures and
miscellaneous

Forest
products

Mineral products

Animals, animal products

Agricultural products

Millions of tons

180
160
140
120
100
80
60
40
20

1910   1920   1930   1940   1950   1960

FREIGHT RATES RELATIVE
TO OTHER PRICES

Base index for all prices set
in 1900 at a value of 100

——— Railway freight
——— Wholesale price index
······ Wheat
- - - Iron

Price index (1900 = 100)

300
250
200
150
100
50

1890 1895 1900 1905 1910 1915 1920 1925
              (base year)

FREIGHT RATES
BY TERRITORY

Superior
Pacific
Prairies
Central
Maritimes

Prairies   Alta-Sask
              Manitoba

Standard rates for
class 1, in cents
per hundredweight
per 100 miles

Cents per 100 pounds per 100 miles

100
90
80
70
60
50
40
30
20

1890   1900   1910   1920   1930   1940

GRAIN AND FLOUR RATES
To Fort William and Port Arthur

Crow's Nest Pass
rates established

From
Calgary 1 242 miles

From Regina 776 miles

From
Winnipeg 420 miles

Rates still in
use in 1961

Cents per 100 pounds

40
35
30
25
20
15
10

1886 1890 1895 1900 1905 1910 1915 1920 1925 1929

A complex freight-rate structure evolved as the North American
railway network expanded. Before 1904, when the Board of
Railway Commissioners was established, most railways operated with little regulation and charged high freight rates. Only a
few special freight rates had been set; the most important was
initiated by the Crow's Nest Pass Agreement of 1897. By
establishing relatively low charges for grain, at first to the
Lakehead (Port Arthur and Fort William), and later to the
Pacific Coast, the Crow rates strengthened the competitive
status of Prairie farmers in world markets. With the growth of
rail traffic, the federal government increasingly viewed freight
rates as an instrument of national policy and a way of
ameliorating regional problems. The Maritime Freight Rate Act
(1927) was implemented in an effort to restore the competitive
position of Maritime manufacturers in the Central Canadian
markets. The act reintroduced freight rates which Maritime
industries had lost when the Canadian Government Railways
was merged into the new CNR system.

CORPORATE EMBLEMS

1950–1959   1929–1946   1901

Canadian Pacific   CANADIAN PACIFIC   CANADIAN
                   RAILWAY LINES   PACIFIC
                   WORLD'S GREATEST   RAILWAY
                   TRAVEL SYSTEM

THE CHANGING STRUCTURE OF MANUFACTURING

Authors: Gerald Bloomfield, Michael Hinton (cotton), Ted Regehr (newsprint), Glen Williams (investment)

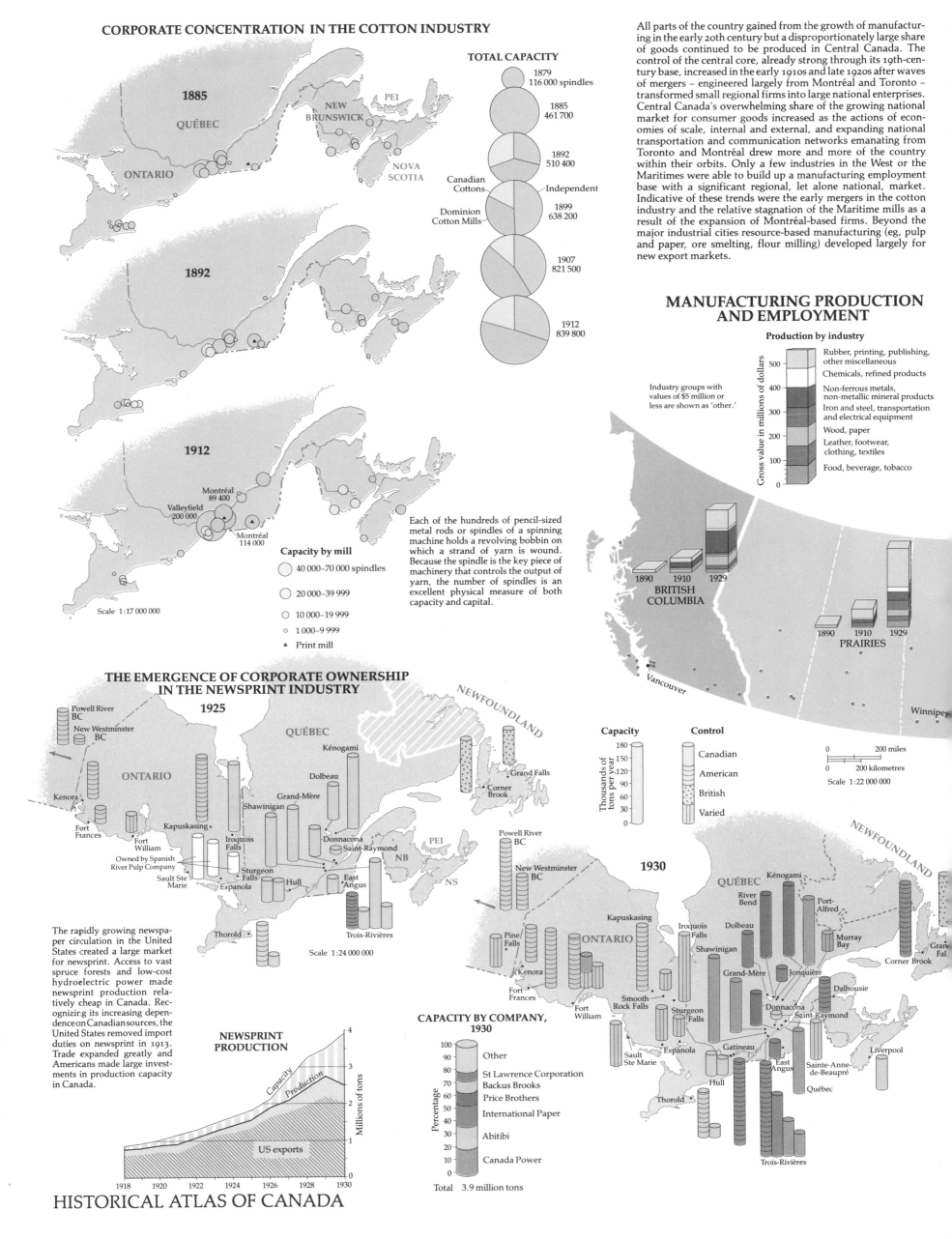

CORPORATE CONCENTRATION IN THE COTTON INDUSTRY

1885

QUÉBEC

NEW BRUNSWICK

PEI

ONTARIO

NOVA SCOTIA

1892

1912

Montréal 89 400

Valleyfield 200 000

Montréal 114 000

TOTAL CAPACITY

1879
116 000 spindles

1885
461 700

1892
510 400

Canadian Cottons — Independent

Dominion Cotton Mills

1899
638 200

1907
821 500

1912
839 800

Capacity by mill

- ◯ 40 000–70 000 spindles
- ◯ 20 000–39 999
- ◯ 10 000–19 999
- ◦ 1 000–9 999
- ▲ Print mill

Scale 1:17 000 000

Each of the hundreds of pencil-sized metal rods or spindles of a spinning machine holds a revolving bobbin on which a strand of yarn is wound. Because the spindle is the key piece of machinery that controls the output of yarn, the number of spindles is an excellent physical measure of both capacity and capital.

All parts of the country gained from the growth of manufacturing in the early 20th century but a disproportionately large share of goods continued to be produced in Central Canada. The control of the central core, already strong through its 19th-century base, increased in the early 1910s and late 1920s after waves of mergers – engineered largely from Montréal and Toronto – transformed small regional firms into large national enterprises. Central Canada's overwhelming share of the growing national market for consumer goods increased as the actions of economies of scale, internal and external, and expanding national transportation and communication networks emanating from Toronto and Montréal drew more and more of the country within their orbits. Only a few industries in the West or the Maritimes were able to build up a manufacturing employment base with a significant regional, let alone national, market. Indicative of these trends were the early mergers in the cotton industry and the relative stagnation of the Maritime mills as a result of the expansion of Montréal-based firms. Beyond the major industrial cities resource-based manufacturing (eg, pulp and paper, ore smelting, flour milling) developed largely for new export markets.

MANUFACTURING PRODUCTION AND EMPLOYMENT

Production by industry

Industry groups with values of $5 million or less are shown as 'other.'

Gross value in millions of dollars

- Rubber, printing, publishing, other miscellaneous
- Chemicals, refined products
- Non-ferrous metals, non-metallic mineral products
- Iron and steel, transportation and electrical equipment
- Wood, paper
- Leather, footwear, clothing, textiles
- Food, beverage, tobacco

BRITISH COLUMBIA
1890 1910 1929

PRAIRIES
1890 1910 1929

Vancouver

Winnipe[g]

0 — 200 miles
0 — 200 kilometres
Scale 1:22 000 000

THE EMERGENCE OF CORPORATE OWNERSHIP IN THE NEWSPRINT INDUSTRY

1925

NEWFOUNDLAND

QUÉBEC

ONTARIO

Powell River BC
New Westminster BC
Kenora
Fort Frances
Fort William
Kapuskasing
Iroquois Falls
Owned by Spanish River Pulp Company
Sault Ste Marie
Espanola
Sturgeon Falls
Hull
Thorold
Shawinigan
Grand-Mère
Dolbeau
Kénogami
Donnacona
Saint-Raymond
East Angus
Trois-Rivières
Grand Falls
Corner Brook
PEI
NB
NS

Scale 1:24 000 000

Capacity

Thousands of tons per year
180
150
120
90
60
30
0

Control

- Canadian
- American
- British
- Varied

The rapidly growing newspaper circulation in the United States created a large market for newsprint. Access to vast spruce forests and low-cost hydroelectric power made newsprint production relatively cheap in Canada. Recognizing its increasing dependence on Canadian sources, the United States removed import duties on newsprint in 1913. Trade expanded greatly and Americans made large investments in production capacity in Canada.

NEWSPRINT PRODUCTION

4
3
2
1
0
Millions of tons

Capacity
Production
US exports

1918 1920 1922 1924 1926 1928 1930

CAPACITY BY COMPANY, 1930

Percentage
100
90
80
70
60
50
40
30
20
10
0

- Other
- St Lawrence Corporation
- Backus Brooks
- Price Brothers
- International Paper
- Abitibi
- Canada Power

Total 3.9 million tons

1930

NEWFOUNDLAND

QUÉBEC

ONTARIO

Powell River BC
New Westminster BC
Pine Falls
Kapuskasing
Iroquois Falls
Kenora
Fort Frances
Fort William
Smooth Rock Falls
Sturgeon Falls
Sault Ste Marie
Espanola
Thorold
Hull
Gatineau
Shawinigan
Grand-Mère
Dolbeau
Kénogami
River Bend
Port-Alfred
Murray Bay
Jonquière
Donnacona
Saint-Raymond
Dalhousie
East Angus
Sainte-Anne-de-Beaupré
Québec
Liverpool
Corner Brook
Gran[d] Fal[ls]
Trois-Rivières

HISTORICAL ATLAS OF CANADA

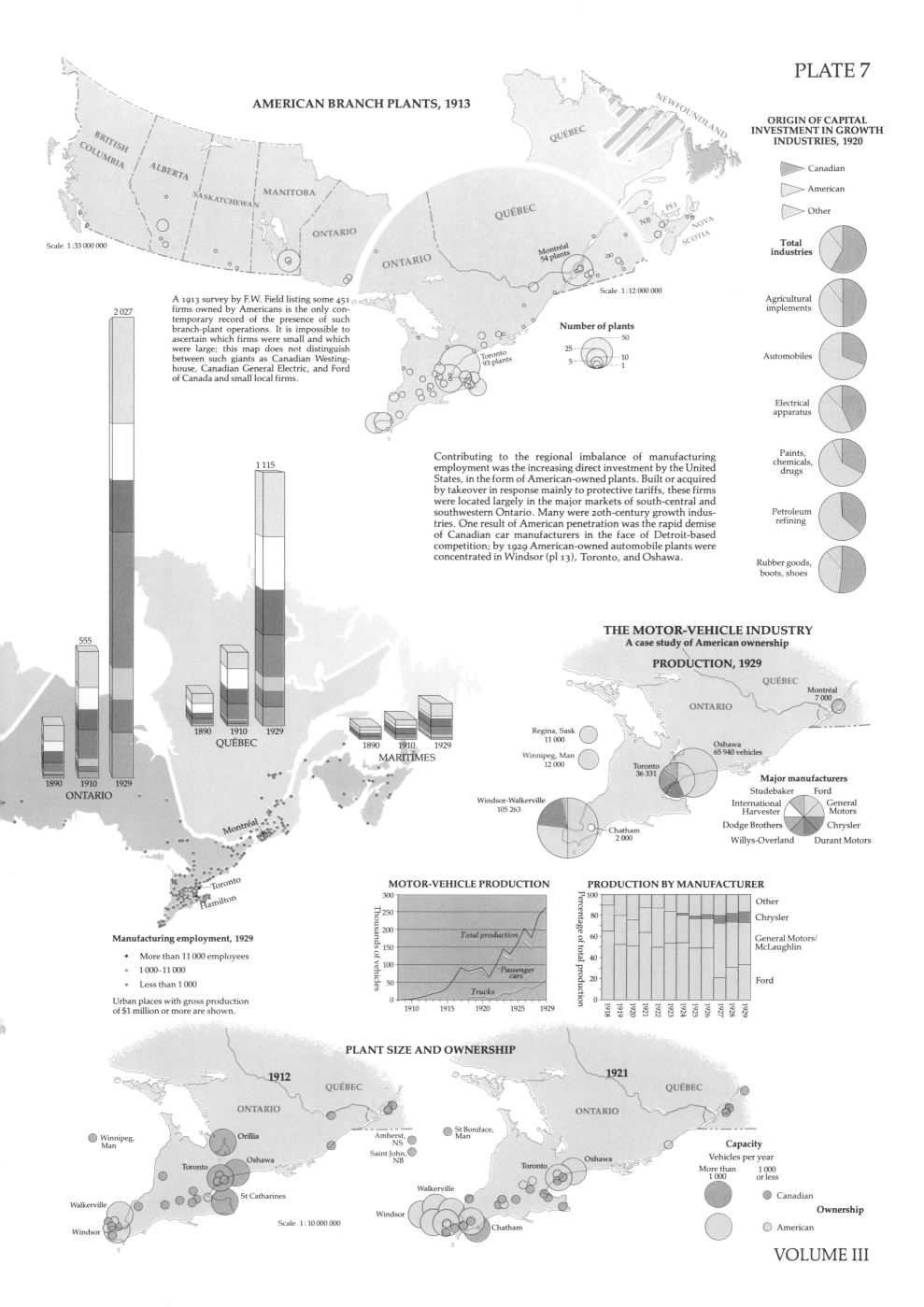

PLATE 7

AMERICAN BRANCH PLANTS, 1913

Scale 1:33 000 000

A 1913 survey by F.W. Field listing some 451 firms owned by Americans is the only contemporary record of the presence of such branch-plant operations. It is impossible to ascertain which firms were small and which were large; this map does not distinguish between such giants as Canadian Westinghouse, Canadian General Electric, and Ford of Canada and small local firms.

Montréal
54 plants

Scale 1:12 000 000

Toronto
93 plants

Number of plants

50
25
10
5
1

ORIGIN OF CAPITAL INVESTMENT IN GROWTH INDUSTRIES, 1920

Canadian
American
Other

Total industries

Agricultural implements

Automobiles

Electrical apparatus

Paints, chemicals, drugs

Petroleum refining

Rubber goods, boots, shoes

Contributing to the regional imbalance of manufacturing employment was the increasing direct investment by the United States, in the form of American-owned plants. Built or acquired by takeover in response mainly to protective tariffs, these firms were located largely in the major markets of south-central and southwestern Ontario. Many were 20th-century growth industries. One result of American penetration was the rapid demise of Canadian car manufacturers in the face of Detroit-based competition; by 1929 American-owned automobile plants were concentrated in Windsor (pl 13), Toronto, and Oshawa.

2 027

1 115

555

1890 1910 1929
ONTARIO

1890 1910 1929
QUÉBEC

1890 1910 1929
MARITIMES

Montréal

Toronto
Hamilton

Manufacturing employment, 1929

- More than 11 000 employees
- 1 000–11 000
- Less than 1 000

Urban places with gross production of $1 million or more are shown.

THE MOTOR-VEHICLE INDUSTRY
A case study of American ownership

PRODUCTION, 1929

QUÉBEC
Montréal
7 000

ONTARIO

Regina, Sask
11 000

Winnipeg, Man
12 000

Oshawa
65 940 vehicles

Toronto
36 331

Windsor-Walkerville
105 263

Chatham
2 000

Major manufacturers

Studebaker   Ford
International   General
Harvester   Motors
Dodge Brothers   Chrysler
Willys-Overland   Durant Motors

MOTOR-VEHICLE PRODUCTION

Thousands of vehicles
300
250
200
150
100
50
0
1910 1915 1920 1925 1929

Total production
Passenger cars
Trucks

PRODUCTION BY MANUFACTURER

Percentage of total production
100
80
60
40
20
0
1918 1919 1920 1921 1922 1923 1924 1925 1926 1927 1928 1929

Other
Chrysler
General Motors/ McLaughlin
Ford

PLANT SIZE AND OWNERSHIP

1912

QUÉBEC
ONTARIO

Winnipeg, Man

Orillia
Oshawa
Toronto
St Catharines
Walkerville
Windsor

Amherst, NS
Saint John, NB

1921

QUÉBEC
ONTARIO

St Boniface, Man

Toronto
Oshawa
Walkerville
Windsor
Chatham

Scale 1:10 000 000

Capacity
Vehicles per year
More than 1 000   1 000 or less

● Canadian
Ownership
○ American

WHOLESALE TRADE

Authors: Donald Kerr, Gerald Bloomfield, G. E. Mills (lumber)

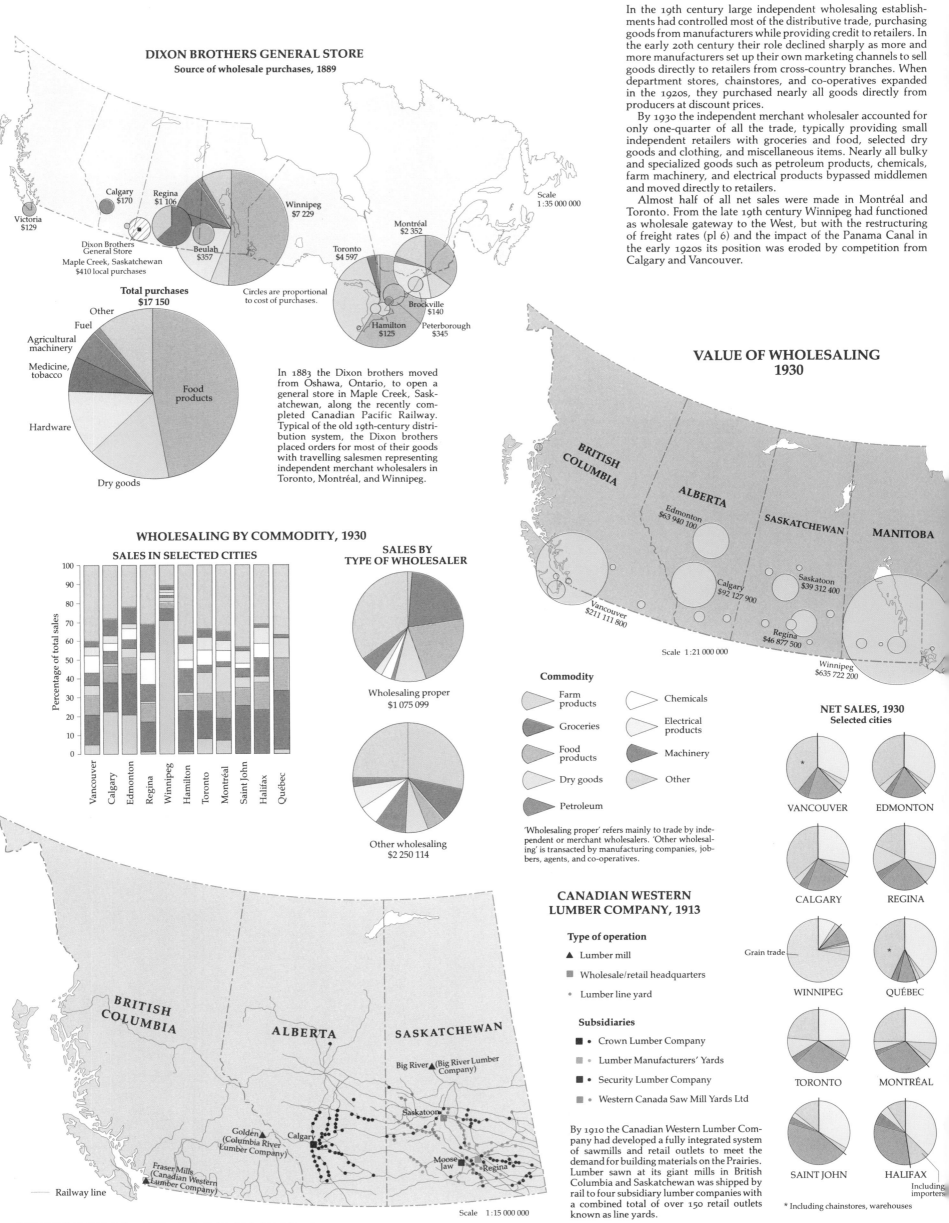

DIXON BROTHERS GENERAL STORE
Source of wholesale purchases, 1889

Victoria $129
Calgary $170
Regina $1 106
Beulah $357
Winnipeg $7 229
Montréal $2 352
Toronto $4 597
Brockville $140
Hamilton $125
Peterborough $345

Dixon Brothers General Store
Maple Creek, Saskatchewan
$410 local purchases

Circles are proportional to cost of purchases.

Scale 1:35 000 000

Total purchases $17 150

Other
Fuel
Agricultural machinery
Medicine, tobacco
Hardware
Food products
Dry goods

In 1883 the Dixon brothers moved from Oshawa, Ontario, to open a general store in Maple Creek, Saskatchewan, along the recently completed Canadian Pacific Railway. Typical of the old 19th-century distribution system, the Dixon brothers placed orders for most of their goods with travelling salesmen representing independent merchant wholesalers in Toronto, Montréal, and Winnipeg.

In the 19th century large independent wholesaling establishments had controlled most of the distributive trade, purchasing goods from manufacturers while providing credit to retailers. In the early 20th century their role declined sharply as more and more manufacturers set up their own marketing channels to sell goods directly to retailers from cross-country branches. When department stores, chainstores, and co-operatives expanded in the 1920s, they purchased nearly all goods directly from producers at discount prices.

By 1930 the independent merchant wholesaler accounted for only one-quarter of all the trade, typically providing small independent retailers with groceries and food, selected dry goods and clothing, and miscellaneous items. Nearly all bulky and specialized goods such as petroleum products, chemicals, farm machinery, and electrical products bypassed middlemen and moved directly to retailers.

Almost half of all net sales were made in Montréal and Toronto. From the late 19th century Winnipeg had functioned as wholesale gateway to the West, but with the restructuring of freight rates (pl 6) and the impact of the Panama Canal in the early 1920s its position was eroded by competition from Calgary and Vancouver.

VALUE OF WHOLESALING 1930

BRITISH COLUMBIA
ALBERTA
SASKATCHEWAN
MANITOBA

Edmonton $63 940 100
Calgary $92 127 900
Saskatoon $39 312 400
Vancouver $211 111 800
Regina $46 877 500
Winnipeg $635 722 200

Scale 1:21 000 000

WHOLESALING BY COMMODITY, 1930
SALES IN SELECTED CITIES

Percentage of total sales

Vancouver, Calgary, Edmonton, Regina, Winnipeg, Hamilton, Toronto, Montréal, Saint John, Halifax, Québec

SALES BY TYPE OF WHOLESALER

Wholesaling proper $1 075 099

Other wholesaling $2 250 114

Commodity

Farm products
Groceries
Food products
Dry goods
Petroleum
Chemicals
Electrical products
Machinery
Other

'Wholesaling proper' refers mainly to trade by independent or merchant wholesalers. 'Other wholesaling' is transacted by manufacturing companies, jobbers, agents, and co-operatives.

NET SALES, 1930
Selected cities

VANCOUVER*
EDMONTON
CALGARY
REGINA
Grain trade
WINNIPEG
QUÉBEC*
TORONTO
MONTRÉAL
SAINT JOHN
HALIFAX
Including importers

* Including chainstores, warehouses

CANADIAN WESTERN LUMBER COMPANY, 1913

Type of operation

▲ Lumber mill
■ Wholesale/retail headquarters
• Lumber line yard

Subsidiaries

■ • Crown Lumber Company
■ • Lumber Manufacturers' Yards
■ • Security Lumber Company
■ • Western Canada Saw Mill Yards Ltd

By 1910 the Canadian Western Lumber Company had developed a fully integrated system of sawmills and retail outlets to meet the demand for building materials on the Prairies. Lumber sawn at its giant mills in British Columbia and Saskatchewan was shipped by rail to four subsidiary lumber companies with a combined total of over 150 retail outlets known as line yards.

BRITISH COLUMBIA
ALBERTA
SASKATCHEWAN

Big River (Big River Lumber Company)
Saskatoon
Golden (Columbia River Lumber Company)
Calgary
Moose Jaw
Regina
Fraser Mills (Canadian Western Lumber Company)

Railway line

Scale 1:15 000 000

HISTORICAL ATLAS OF CANADA

PLATE 8

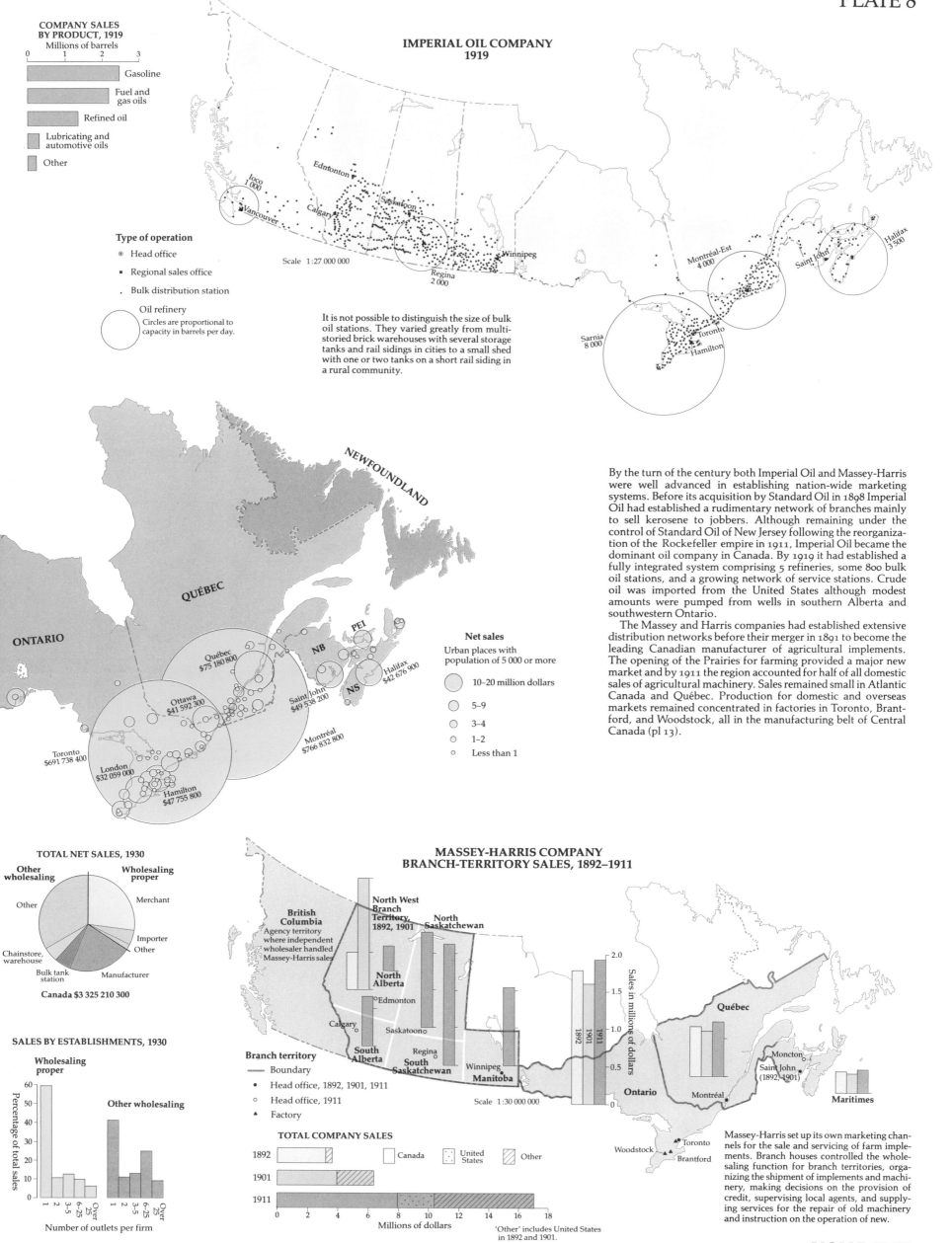

COMPANY SALES BY PRODUCT, 1919
Millions of barrels

Gasoline
Fuel and gas oils
Refined oil
Lubricating and automotive oils
Other

IMPERIAL OIL COMPANY 1919

Type of operation
⊙ Head office
■ Regional sales office
. Bulk distribution station

Oil refinery
Circles are proportional to capacity in barrels per day.

Scale 1:27 000 000

Ioco 1 000
Vancouver
Edmonton
Calgary
Saskatoon
Winnipeg
Regina 2 000
Sarnia 8 000
Toronto
Hamilton
Montréal-Est 4 000
Saint John
Halifax 3 500

It is not possible to distinguish the size of bulk oil stations. They varied greatly from multi-storied brick warehouses with several storage tanks and rail sidings in cities to a small shed with one or two tanks on a short rail siding in a rural community.

NEWFOUNDLAND

QUÉBEC

ONTARIO

PEI
NB
NS

Québec $75 180 800
Ottawa $41 592 300
Toronto $691 738 400
London $32 059 000
Hamilton $47 755 800
Montréal $766 832 800
Saint John $49 538 200
Halifax $42 676 900

Net sales
Urban places with population of 5 000 or more
10–20 million dollars
5–9
3–4
1–2
Less than 1

By the turn of the century both Imperial Oil and Massey-Harris were well advanced in establishing nation-wide marketing systems. Before its acquisition by Standard Oil in 1898 Imperial Oil had established a rudimentary network of branches mainly to sell kerosene to jobbers. Although remaining under the control of Standard Oil of New Jersey following the reorganization of the Rockefeller empire in 1911, Imperial Oil became the dominant oil company in Canada. By 1919 it had established a fully integrated system comprising 5 refineries, some 800 bulk oil stations, and a growing network of service stations. Crude oil was imported from the United States although modest amounts were pumped from wells in southern Alberta and southwestern Ontario.

The Massey and Harris companies had established extensive distribution networks before their merger in 1891 to become the leading Canadian manufacturer of agricultural implements. The opening of the Prairies for farming provided a major new market and by 1911 the region accounted for half of all domestic sales of agricultural machinery. Sales remained small in Atlantic Canada and Québec. Production for domestic and overseas markets remained concentrated in factories in Toronto, Brantford, and Woodstock, all in the manufacturing belt of Central Canada (pl 13).

TOTAL NET SALES, 1930

Other wholesaling
Wholesaling proper
Other
Merchant
Importer
Other
Chainstore, warehouse
Bulk tank station
Manufacturer

Canada $3 325 210 300

SALES BY ESTABLISHMENTS, 1930

Wholesaling proper
Other wholesaling

Percentage of total sales
Number of outlets per firm
1 2 3–5 6–25 Over 25

MASSEY-HARRIS COMPANY BRANCH-TERRITORY SALES, 1892–1911

British Columbia
Agency territory where independent wholesaler handled Massey-Harris sales

North West Branch Territory, 1892, 1901
North Saskatchewan
North Alberta
Edmonton
Calgary
South Alberta
Saskatoon
South Saskatchewan
Regina
Winnipeg
Manitoba

Québec
Ontario
Montréal
Moncton
Saint John (1892, 1901)
Maritimes
Woodstock
Brantford
Toronto

Sales in millions of dollars
2.0
1.5
1.0
0.5
0

1892 1901 1911

Branch territory
— Boundary
● Head office, 1892, 1901, 1911
○ Head office, 1911
▲ Factory

Scale 1:30 000 000

TOTAL COMPANY SALES

1892
1901
1911

Canada
United States
Other

Millions of dollars
0 2 4 6 8 10 12 14 16 18

'Other' includes United States in 1892 and 1901.

Massey-Harris set up its own marketing channels for the sale and servicing of farm implements. Branch houses controlled the wholesaling function for branch territories, organizing the shipment of implements and machinery, making decisions on the provision of credit, supervising local agents, and supplying services for the repair of old machinery and instruction on the operation of new.

FINANCIAL INSTITUTIONS

Authors: Gunter Gad, William Code, Neil Quigley

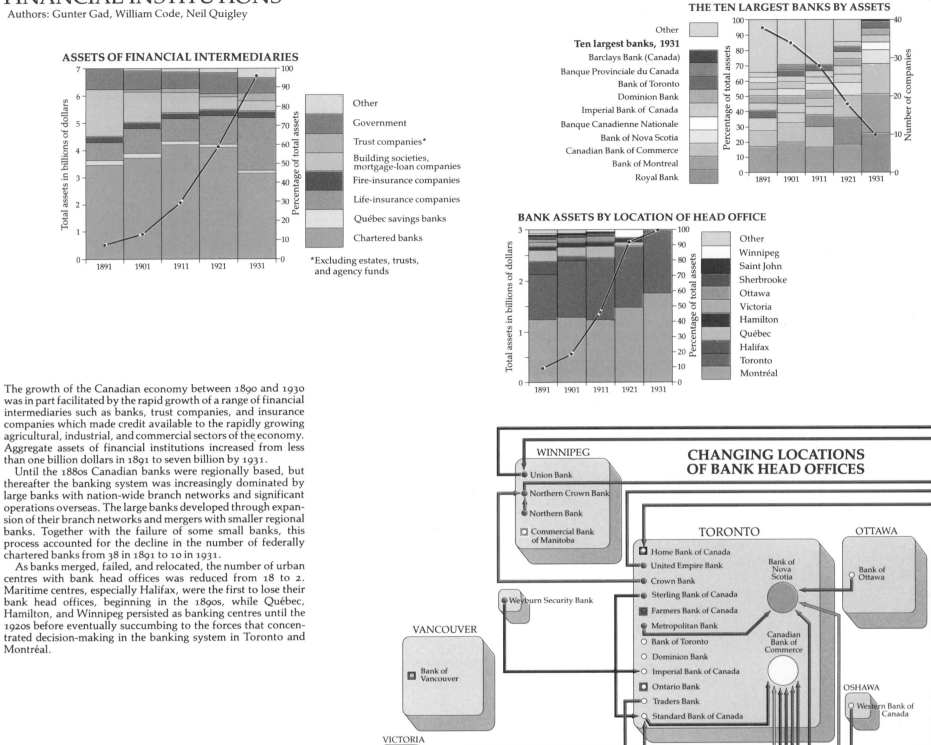

ASSETS OF FINANCIAL INTERMEDIARIES

Total assets in billions of dollars / Percentage of total assets

1891 1901 1911 1921 1931

- Other
- Government
- Trust companies*
- Building societies, mortgage-loan companies
- Fire-insurance companies
- Life-insurance companies
- Québec savings banks
- Chartered banks

*Excluding estates, trusts, and agency funds

THE TEN LARGEST BANKS BY ASSETS

Ten largest banks, 1931

- Other
- Barclays Bank (Canada)
- Banque Provinciale du Canada
- Bank of Toronto
- Dominion Bank
- Imperial Bank of Canada
- Banque Canadienne Nationale
- Bank of Nova Scotia
- Canadian Bank of Commerce
- Bank of Montreal
- Royal Bank

Percentage of total assets / Number of companies

1891 1901 1911 1921 1931

BANK ASSETS BY LOCATION OF HEAD OFFICE

Total assets in billions of dollars / Percentage of total assets

1891 1901 1911 1921 1931

- Other
- Winnipeg
- Saint John
- Sherbrooke
- Ottawa
- Victoria
- Hamilton
- Québec
- Halifax
- Toronto
- Montréal

The growth of the Canadian economy between 1890 and 1930 was in part facilitated by the rapid growth of a range of financial intermediaries such as banks, trust companies, and insurance companies which made credit available to the rapidly growing agricultural, industrial, and commercial sectors of the economy. Aggregate assets of financial institutions increased from less than one billion dollars in 1891 to seven billion by 1931.

Until the 1880s Canadian banks were regionally based, but thereafter the banking system was increasingly dominated by large banks with nation-wide branch networks and significant operations overseas. The large banks developed through expansion of their branch networks and mergers with smaller regional banks. Together with the failure of some small banks, this process accounted for the decline in the number of federally chartered banks from 38 in 1891 to 10 in 1931.

As banks merged, failed, and relocated, the number of urban centres with bank head offices was reduced from 18 to 2. Maritime centres, especially Halifax, were the first to lose their bank head offices, beginning in the 1890s, while Québec, Hamilton, and Winnipeg persisted as banking centres until the 1920s before eventually succumbing to the forces that concentrated decision-making in the banking system in Toronto and Montréal.

CHANGING LOCATIONS OF BANK HEAD OFFICES

WINNIPEG
- Union Bank
- Northern Crown Bank
- Northern Bank
- Commercial Bank of Manitoba

TORONTO
- Home Bank of Canada
- United Empire Bank
- Crown Bank
- Sterling Bank of Canada
- Farmers Bank of Canada
- Metropolitan Bank
- Bank of Toronto
- Dominion Bank
- Imperial Bank of Canada
- Ontario Bank
- Traders Bank
- Standard Bank of Canada

Bank of Nova Scotia

Canadian Bank of Commerce

OTTAWA
- Bank of Ottawa

VANCOUVER
- Bank of Vancouver

- Weyburn Security Bank

OSHAWA
- Western Bank of Canada

VICTORIA
- Bank of British Columbia

HAMILTON
- Bank of Hamilton

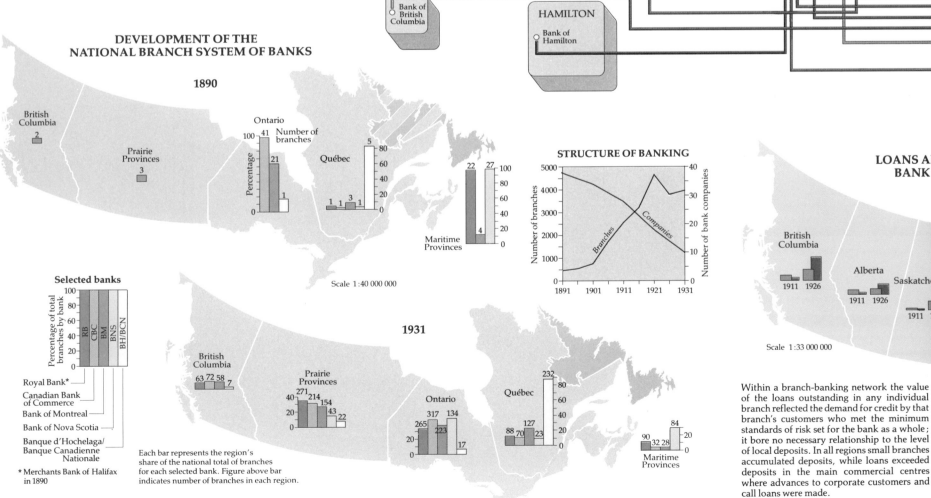

DEVELOPMENT OF THE NATIONAL BRANCH SYSTEM OF BANKS

1890

British Columbia 2

Prairie Provinces 3

Ontario 41 21 1
Number of branches
Percentage

Québec 1 1 3 1 5

Maritime Provinces 22 27 4

Scale 1:40 000 000

Selected banks

Percentage of total branches by bank

RB CBC BM BNS BH/BCN

- Royal Bank*
- Canadian Bank of Commerce
- Bank of Montreal
- Bank of Nova Scotia
- Banque d'Hochelaga / Banque Canadienne Nationale

*Merchants Bank of Halifax in 1890

1931

British Columbia 63 72 58 7

Prairie Provinces 271 214 154 43 22

Ontario 265 317 223 134 17

Québec 88 70 127 23 232

Maritime Provinces 90 32 28 84

Each bar represents the region's share of the national total of branches for each selected bank. Figure above bar indicates number of branches in each region.

STRUCTURE OF BANKING

Number of branches / Number of bank companies

Branches

Companies

1891 1901 1911 1921 1931

LOANS AND BANK ...

British Columbia 1911 1926

Alberta 1911 1926

Saskatche... 1911 19...

Scale 1:33 000 000

Within a branch-banking network the value of the loans outstanding in any individual branch reflected the demand for credit by that branch's customers who met the minimum standards of risk set for the bank as a whole; it bore no necessary relationship to the level of local deposits. In all regions small branches accumulated deposits, while loans exceeded deposits in the main commercial centres where advances to corporate customers and call loans were made.

HISTORICAL ATLAS OF CANADA

PLATE 9

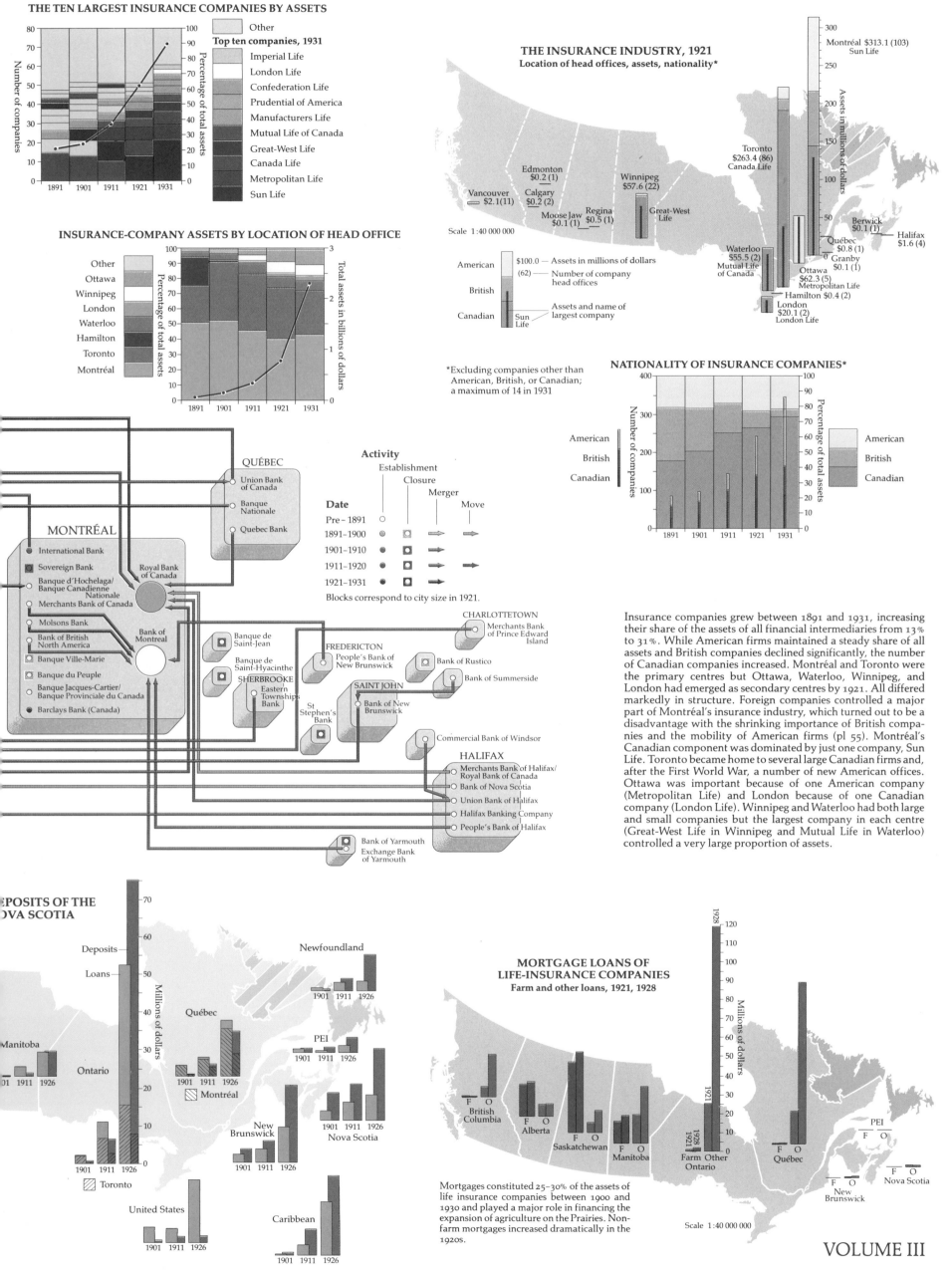

THE TEN LARGEST INSURANCE COMPANIES BY ASSETS

Other

Top ten companies, 1931

Imperial Life
London Life
Confederation Life
Prudential of America
Manufacturers Life
Mutual Life of Canada
Great-West Life
Canada Life
Metropolitan Life
Sun Life

INSURANCE-COMPANY ASSETS BY LOCATION OF HEAD OFFICE

Other
Ottawa
Winnipeg
London
Waterloo
Hamilton
Toronto
Montréal

THE INSURANCE INDUSTRY, 1921
Location of head offices, assets, nationality*

Montréal $313.1 (103)
Sun Life

Toronto
$263.4 (86)
Canada Life

Winnipeg
$57.6 (22)

Edmonton
$0.2 (1)

Vancouver
$2.1 (11)

Calgary
$0.2 (2)

Moose Jaw
$0.1 (1)   Regina
$0.5 (1)

Great-West
Life

Scale 1:40 000 000

Waterloo
$55.5 (2)
Mutual Life
of Canada

Québec
$0.8 (1)

Granby
$0.1 (1)

Berwick
$0.1 (1)

Halifax
$1.6 (4)

Ottawa
$62.3 (5)
Metropolitan Life

Hamilton $0.4 (2)

London
$20.1 (2)
London Life

American
British
Canadian

$100.0 — Assets in millions of dollars

(62) — Number of company
head offices

Sun
Life

Assets and name of
largest company

*Excluding companies other than
American, British, or Canadian;
a maximum of 14 in 1931

NATIONALITY OF INSURANCE COMPANIES*

American
British
Canadian

American
British
Canadian

QUÉBEC

Union Bank
of Canada

Banque
Nationale

Quebec Bank

MONTRÉAL

International Bank
Sovereign Bank
Banque d'Hochelaga/
Banque Canadienne
Nationale
Merchants Bank of Canada
Molsons Bank
Bank of British
North America
Banque Ville-Marie
Banque du Peuple
Banque Jacques-Cartier/
Banque Provinciale
du Canada
Barclays Bank (Canada)

Royal Bank
of Canada

Bank of
Montréal

Activity

	Establishment	Closure	Merger	Move
Date				
Pre – 1891	○			
1891–1900	◐	◻	→	→
1901–1910	◑	◻	→	
1911–1920	●	◻	→	→
1921–1931	●	◼	→	

Blocks correspond to city size in 1921.

CHARLOTTETOWN
Merchants Bank
of Prince Edward
Island

Banque de
Saint-Jean

Banque de
Saint-Hyacinthe

SHERBROOKE
Eastern
Townships
Bank

FREDERICTON
People's Bank of
New Brunswick

Bank of Rustico

St
Stephen's
Bank

SAINT JOHN
Bank of New
Brunswick

Bank of Summerside

Commercial Bank of Windsor

HALIFAX
Merchants Bank of Halifax/
Royal Bank of Canada
Bank of Nova Scotia
Union Bank of Halifax
Halifax Banking Company
People's Bank of Halifax

Bank of Yarmouth
Exchange Bank
of Yarmouth

Insurance companies grew between 1891 and 1931, increasing
their share of the assets of all financial intermediaries from 13%
to 31%. While American firms maintained a steady share of all
assets and British companies declined significantly, the number
of Canadian companies increased. Montréal and Toronto were
the primary centres but Ottawa, Waterloo, Winnipeg, and
London had emerged as secondary centres by 1921. All differed
markedly in structure. Foreign companies controlled a major
part of Montréal's insurance industry, which turned out to be a
disadvantage with the shrinking importance of British companies and the mobility of American firms (pl 55). Montréal's
Canadian component was dominated by just one company, Sun
Life. Toronto became home to several large Canadian firms and,
after the First World War, a number of new American offices.
Ottawa was important because of one American company
(Metropolitan Life) and London because of one Canadian
company (London Life). Winnipeg and Waterloo had both large
and small companies but the largest company in each centre
(Great-West Life in Winnipeg and Mutual Life in Waterloo)
controlled a very large proportion of assets.

...POSITS OF THE
...VA SCOTIA

Deposits
Loans

Newfoundland

1901 1911 1926

Québec

1901 1911 1926
Montréal

PEI

1901 1911 1926

Manitoba

Ontario

...01 1911 1926

New
Brunswick
1901 1911 1926

Nova Scotia
1901 1911 1926

Toronto

United States
1901 1911 1926

Caribbean
1901 1911 1926

MORTGAGE LOANS OF
LIFE-INSURANCE COMPANIES
Farm and other loans, 1921, 1928

1928

1921

British
Columbia

Alberta

F O

Saskatchewan

F O

Manitoba

F O

Farm Other
Ontario

1928

1921

Québec

F O

PEI

F O

New
Brunswick
F O

Nova Scotia
F O

Mortgages constituted 25–30% of the assets of
life insurance companies between 1900 and
1930 and played a major role in financing the
expansion of agriculture on the Prairies. Non-
farm mortgages increased dramatically in the
1920s.

Scale 1:40 000 000

THE EMERGENCE OF THE URBAN SYSTEM

Authors: James W. Simmons, Michael Conzen (railways), Donald Kerr (telephones)

In 1891 30% of the population lived in 297 places of 1 000 people or more, and these urban centres were concentrated in the Maritimes, southern Québec, and southern Ontario. One example of the level of interaction between places is the frequency of passenger-train service. Here it indicates that, although the regions were linked, contacts were generally infrequent and many peripheral locations were still not connected to the rest of the system. Only in southern Ontario were there sufficient branch lines to integrate the region effectively.

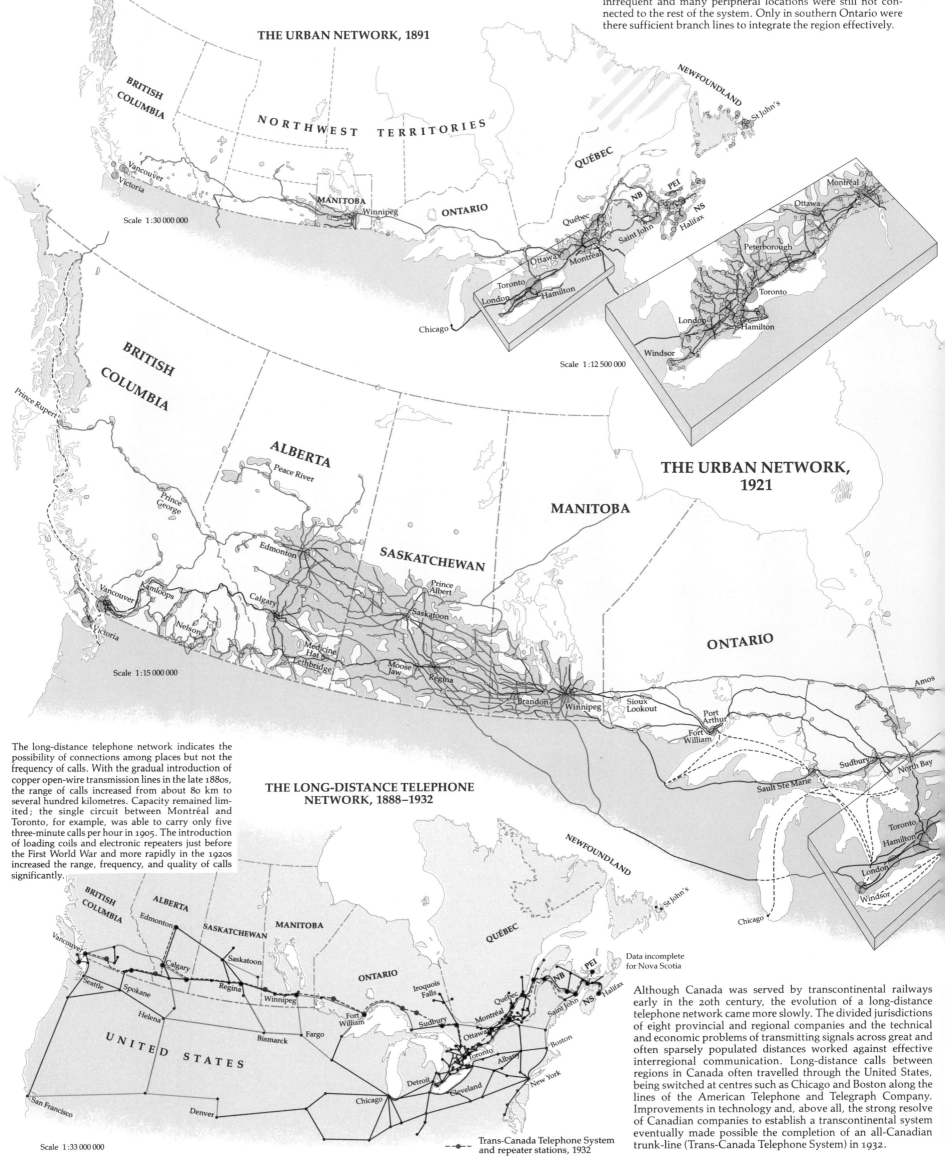

THE URBAN NETWORK, 1891

Scale 1:30 000 000

Scale 1:12 500 000

THE URBAN NETWORK, 1921

Scale 1:15 000 000

The long-distance telephone network indicates the possibility of connections among places but not the frequency of calls. With the gradual introduction of copper open-wire transmission lines in the late 1880s, the range of calls increased from about 80 km to several hundred kilometres. Capacity remained limited; the single circuit between Montréal and Toronto, for example, was able to carry only five three-minute calls per hour in 1905. The introduction of loading coils and electronic repeaters just before the First World War and more rapidly in the 1920s increased the range, frequency, and quality of calls significantly.

THE LONG-DISTANCE TELEPHONE NETWORK, 1888–1932

Data incomplete for Nova Scotia

Scale 1:33 000 000

●—— Trans-Canada Telephone System and repeater stations, 1932

Although Canada was served by transcontinental railways early in the 20th century, the evolution of a long-distance telephone network came more slowly. The divided jurisdictions of eight provincial and regional companies and the technical and economic problems of transmitting signals across great and often sparsely populated distances worked against effective interregional communication. Long-distance calls between regions in Canada often travelled through the United States, being switched at centres such as Chicago and Boston along the lines of the American Telephone and Telegraph Company. Improvements in technology and, above all, the strong resolve of Canadian companies to establish a transcontinental system eventually made possible the completion of an all-Canadian trunk-line (Trans-Canada Telephone System) in 1932.

HISTORICAL ATLAS OF CANADA

PLATE 10

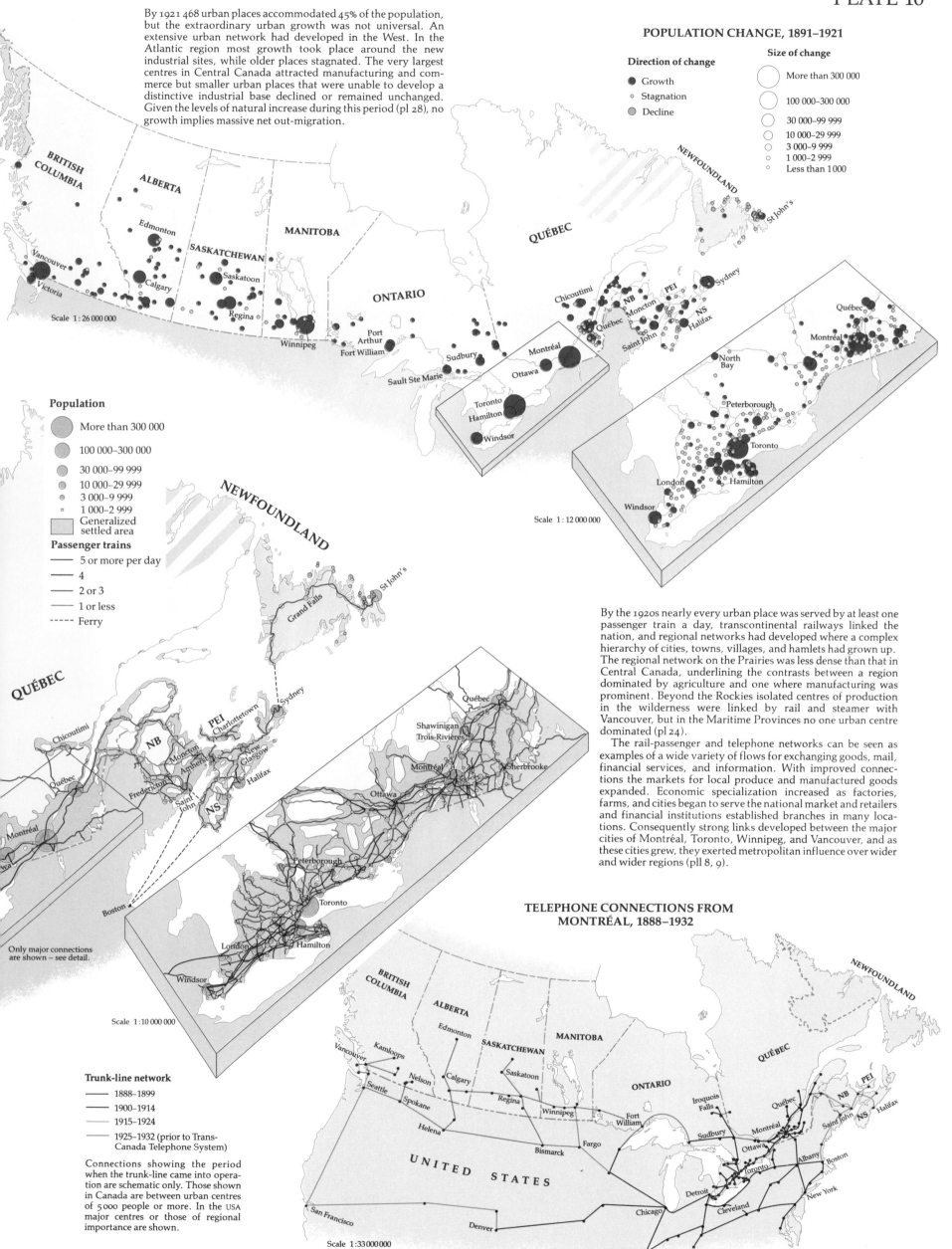

By 1921 468 urban places accommodated 45% of the population, but the extraordinary urban growth was not universal. An extensive urban network had developed in the West. In the Atlantic region most growth took place around the new industrial sites, while older places stagnated. The very largest centres in Central Canada attracted manufacturing and commerce but smaller urban places that were unable to develop a distinctive industrial base declined or remained unchanged. Given the levels of natural increase during this period (pl 28), no growth implies massive net out-migration.

POPULATION CHANGE, 1891–1921

Direction of change
- Growth
- Stagnation
- Decline

Size of change
- More than 300 000
- 100 000–300 000
- 30 000–99 999
- 10 000–29 999
- 3 000–9 999
- 1 000–2 999
- Less than 1 000

Scale 1 : 26 000 000

Scale 1 : 12 000 000

Population
- More than 300 000
- 100 000–300 000
- 30 000–99 999
- 10 000–29 999
- 3 000–9 999
- 1 000–2 999
- Generalized settled area

Passenger trains
- 5 or more per day
- 4
- 2 or 3
- 1 or less
- Ferry

Only major connections are shown – see detail.

Scale 1 : 10 000 000

By the 1920s nearly every urban place was served by at least one passenger train a day, transcontinental railways linked the nation, and regional networks had developed where a complex hierarchy of cities, towns, villages, and hamlets had grown up. The regional network on the Prairies was less dense than that in Central Canada, underlining the contrasts between a region dominated by agriculture and one where manufacturing was prominent. Beyond the Rockies isolated centres of production in the wilderness were linked by rail and steamer with Vancouver, but in the Maritime Provinces no one urban centre dominated (pl 24).

The rail-passenger and telephone networks can be seen as examples of a wide variety of flows for exchanging goods, mail, financial services, and information. With improved connections the markets for local produce and manufactured goods expanded. Economic specialization increased as factories, farms, and cities began to serve the national market and retailers and financial institutions established branches in many locations. Consequently strong links developed between the major cities of Montréal, Toronto, Winnipeg, and Vancouver, and as these cities grew, they exerted metropolitan influence over wider and wider regions (pll 8, 9).

TELEPHONE CONNECTIONS FROM MONTRÉAL, 1888–1932

Trunk-line network
- 1888–1899
- 1900–1914
- 1915–1924
- 1925–1932 (prior to Trans-Canada Telephone System)

Connections showing the period when the trunk-line came into operation are schematic only. Those shown in Canada are between urban centres of 5 000 people or more. In the USA major centres or those of regional importance are shown.

Scale 1 : 33 000 000

Regional Dimensions of the Production System

The extraordinary growth of the Canadian economy and the changes in its structure during the Great Transformation had significant regional consequences. The scale of production, the location of markets, and the degree and pattern of integration in the national economy varied from region to region. The growth in the manufacturing industry occurred at a relatively small number of locations, largely in Central Canada. The Shield and British Columbia attracted highly localized resource development. On the Prairies the wheat economy flourished. The Maritime Provinces struggled to make the difficult adjustment from maritime trade to a continental orientation. During the four decades before 1929 these five broad regions evolved in ways that reflected not only local geography and the demands of the American and British markets but also their connections to an emerging national economic system.

Central Canada

At the heart of the system was Central Canada, whose towns and cities accommodated a growing number of manufacturing industries, distribution facilities, and services. As the economy expanded, manufacturing activity along the corridor between Windsor and Québec increased and enabled Central Canada to strengthen its position as the economic heartland of the nation. The region, which accounted for at least 75% of all industrial output in Canada through the Great Transformation, emerged as the nation's nerve centre, with a distinctive urban core that created innumerable new functions, enterprises, and networks.

From the 1850s the increasing use of steam power had made Central Canada, which had no coal fields of its own, more and more dependent on American coal. Then in the 1890s a rapidly changing technology for the production of hydroelectricity ushered in the modern electrical age (pl 12). Niagara Falls and Shawinigan Falls were exploited first because of their enormous potential. The increasing availability of electrical power, much of it at relatively low cost, was critical to the industrial development of the region, reinforcing earlier growth and greatly reducing dependence on American coal. In 1906 the provincial government of Ontario created the Hydro-Electric Power Commission of Ontario (HEPCO) to ensure wide distribution of Niagara electricity to the industries of southwestern Ontario. By 1910 HEPCO had built transmission lines to London and Toronto and by 1929 it had gained control of most of the production and distribution of electric power. Rates were kept relatively low and the production and sale of a variety of appliances were encouraged, enabling the commission to increase the domestic consumption of electricity, as well as industrial and commercial use. In Québec, by contrast, power production was more closely tied to heavy industry.

As manufacturing grew, the differences in structure between southern Québec and southern Ontario became more pronounced (pl 13). Clothing, textiles, cigarettes, and shoe manufacturing increased in Montréal, Québec, and smaller cities. These labour-intensive industries took advantage of an abundance of labour, reflected in lower wage rates in a province that was weakly unionized (pl 38) and in which a large number of women and children were members of the work-force. At the same time the primary iron and steel, automobile, and electrical-apparatus industries grew in southwestern Ontario, which benefited from proximity to the American manufacturing belt. Many Ontario communities used tax-bonus schemes to attract and keep industrial ventures. Two of Canada's four modern steel plants developed

in southern Ontario around the turn of the century. New large-scale integrated mills, using iron ore from the Upper Great Lakes and coking coal from southwestern Pennsylvania, produced a greater range of items than had been possible in the days of iron smelting. In many ways the emergence of a modern steel industry signalled the coming of age of Canadian industry.

Manufacturing was concentrated in the metropolitan areas of Montréal and Toronto. In 1929 these two cities had a combined manufacturing work-force of 228 000, or one-third of the Canadian total. Two distinctive industrial regions had evolved: one in southern Québec, dominated by metropolitan Montréal, but with important centres from Valleyfield through Saint-Jean, Sherbrooke, and Drummondville to Trois-Rivières and Québec; and the other in southwestern Ontario, focusing on Toronto but extending to the south and west to include Hamilton, St Catharines, Kitchener, London, and Windsor.

Industrialization in Montréal dramatically altered the size and appearance of the city. From early clusterings around the Lachine Canal and near downtown, new factories developed in suburban areas by 1914 (pl 14). There was some heavy industry, primarily iron and steel products related to railways. Dominating the industrial structure, however, were labour-intensive, cheap-wage industries which manufactured garments, textiles, boots and shoes, and tobacco, as well as sugar refineries, breweries, and rubber factories. Although many jobs in the garment industry remained in the central area, the downtown was redeveloped, with an impressive district of warehouses near the docks.

In Toronto a similar transformation took place (pl 15). Firms such as Massey-Harris and the T. Eaton Company reached national markets (pll 8, 52) and the expansion of their factories transformed districts to the west and north of the downtown area. A garment district developed west along King Street near Spadina Avenue, and an extensive zone of railway freight yards and warehouses came into being along the waterfront. Farther along the rail corridors factories for brewing, meat processing, car and bicycle manufacturing, among others, developed in relatively suburban settings.

The financial and managerial functions of Montréal and Toronto intensified and several million square feet of office space were added to each city, along King Street and Bay Street in Toronto and St James Street (rue Saint-Jacques) in Montréal. These offices housed not only banks, but also stockbrokers, lawyers, accountants, insurers, and manufacturers' agents. A very small group of financial and industrial capitalists, split almost evenly between the two cities, emerged as facilitators of new scales of enterprise. Their multiple directorships reflected the interlocking of finance, industry, and transport on an increasingly national level. Largely invisible networks of power and decision-making gradually rationalized the price of capital, of raw materials and consumer products, and of labour – all of which became more alike in more places as the decades passed.

Farming and forestry continued to contribute to the prosperity of Central Canada (pl 11). In the late 19th century Ontario farmers had specialized in dairying, raising hogs and beef cattle, malting barley, and growing apples. In southwestern and eastern Ontario and in southern Québec a profitable dairy industry had developed. Cheese emerged as an important staple in international trade. The expansion of cheese factories and the buoyancy of cheese exports encouraged many farmers to improve the quality of their farming practices by buying and breeding more productive dairy cows, introducing forage crops and ensilage, and improving fields of permanent pasture. Other innovations, such as the cream separator and refrigeration, stimulated the production of butter and fluid milk for urban areas. Although cheese factories remained mostly small and widely scattered (their numbers reached a peak in 1898), other dairy processing – butter, ice cream, milk pasteurization and bottling, and milk condensing and canning – was carried on in much larger factories, mostly in urban centres. As the domestic demand for butter and milk increased, especially after 1905, the cheese export market diminished in importance.

Large-scale flour mills in Central Canada capitalized on, rather than suffered from, the fact that the Prairies had supplanted Ontario as Canada's main wheat-growing area. Leading firms such as Ogilvie and Maple Leaf Mills were quick to establish mills in the West, but they also added substantially to their milling capacity in Central Canada. The new technology of roller-milling, introduced in the late 19th century, made feasible vastly larger plants and flour milling came increasingly to be concentrated in these huge mills, located at important points on the transport system both on the Prairies and especially in Central Canada.

In the United States meat packing had developed as early as the 1840s as a large-scale production-line industry, but in Canada farmers had not succeeded in establishing specialized pig farming on a profitable basis. Cheap feed in the form of by-products from the burgeoning cheese industry and the establishment of markets in Great Britain for Canadian bacon finally brought large-scale meat packing to Canada in the 1890s. The Toronto-based Davis packing empire became the core of the nation-wide Canada Packers business (pl 55).

The Canadian Shield

To the north of Central Canada the Canadian Shield was developed as a new resource hinterland. By the early 20th century technology permitted the exploitation of the Shield's minerals, spruce trees, and fast-flowing rivers. A zone stretching from the Lac-Saint-Jean and Abitibi areas in Québec past Sudbury and on to Michipicoten on the shores of Lake Superior and Pine Falls in Manitoba (pl 16) attracted attention from Toronto, Montréal, British, and American investors who were interested in exploiting the region's potential for hard-rock minerals and pulp and paper.

In mining the initial rush of frenzied development gave way to heavily capitalized hard-rock mining with complex machinery. The discovery of minerals at Cobalt (silver) in 1903, in the Porcupine–Kirkland Lake area (gold) between 1909 and 1912, and at Noranda-Rouyn (gold and copper) in the early 1920s gave rise to single-industry communities. Of long-term importance to northern Ontario was the copper-nickel ore body which had been discovered in the early 1880s when the Canadian Pacific Railway (CPR) was built west of North Bay. The Nickel Belt developed in the first two decades of the 20th century, as nickel came into demand, and Sudbury emerged as the service centre for the many towns which sprang up around mine-shafts. Two other major processing centres on the Shield were the smelting town of Arvida, Québec, where the Pittsburgh-based Alcoa interests exploited the potential for hydroelectric power and deep-water access in order to smelt bauxite, and the steel town of Sault Ste Marie, whose major product was rails for Prairie branch lines. The Shield's mining frontier was more extensive in Ontario than Québec and the financial and management services for this frontier, aided considerably by American interests, developed more in Toronto than in Montréal.

American investment directed much of the development of the pulp and paper industries of the Shield. At the turn of the century these industries were located primarily on the north shore of Lake Huron, in the Ottawa valley, the Lac-Saint-Jean area, and the Saint-Maurice region. There was a boom in the industry on the Shield, however, after provincial legislation limited the export of pulpwood (1900 for Ontario and 1910 for Québec), the US tariff on the import of newsprint was repealed (1913), and the market for

newsprint increased. Forest resources were leased to Canadian and American companies for the production of pulp and paper, but over-investment during the late 1920s caused severe over-capacity and led to many closures in the early years of the Depression (pl 40).

The settlement pattern of the Shield was a mixture of instant camps, company towns, and government-planned communities. Company towns that drew on American and British notions of town planning (Temiskaming, 1919, and Kapuskasing, 1921) replaced boom-towns. Even so, unorganized settlement continued, often on the outskirts of planned communities. Such fringe settlements were generally inhabited by low-skilled labourers and members of distinct ethnic groups. Within the planned communities themselves there was segregation by position within the company and, often, by ethnicity or religion.

The Prairies

The opening of the West was one of the most dramatic elements of the Great Transformation. More than a million settlers from Ontario, the United States, and Europe moved to the Prairies in the early 20th century. Between 1898 and 1914 the population of the Prairies increased from 300 000 to 1.8 million. This enormous increase was not simply a regional event: the creation of a larger domestic market for goods and services had implications for every region. That market made possible the expansion of manufacturing in Central Canada, encouraged the creation of national distribution systems, stimulated the British Columbia forest industry, and made the role of the Maritime Provinces even more marginal in the national economy.

Until the mid-1890s settlement in the Prairies was confined largely to the subhumid lands of southern Manitoba and eastern Assiniboia. The great occupation of a broader zone to the west and northwest (pl 17) followed a spate of branch-line construction by the CPR (and later the Canadian Northern Railway), which was eager to capitalize on its land bonuses, and it was assisted by the federal government which wanted to settle the vast Prairies with immigrants who would help to create wealth and stimulate the domestic market. The Canadian government had established immigrant offices across Europe and the United States (pl 57) to lure both rural and urban workers with visions of land ownership and prosperity in the Last Best West. Government homesteading policies, which followed those used earlier on the American plains, attracted a wide variety of settlers, many of whom came as part of group or block settlements. For some the first Prairie shelter replicated the housing of their former homelands, such as thatched cottages from the European steppes; others resorted to sod houses, dug-outs, log shacks, or tents. The construction of new lumber mills in British Columbia (pl 21) was greatly stimulated by demand in the lumber-scarce prairie and dealers were quick to supply settlers with building materials and house parts (pl 8), even entire houses that could be ordered from catalogues.

Wheat propelled the rapid settlement of the early 1900s (pl 18). 'Dry farming' was essential on the semi-arid lands of the western Canadian plains, where low and erratic rainfall and a short growing season made production difficult. The harvested field was left fallow for a full year, the field kept bare and the surface aerated and free of weeds, so that rain could be stored for growing crops in the following year. Improvements in varieties of wheat, especially the introduction in 1910 of early-ripening Marquis wheat, enabled production to be extended northwards into less arid districts. Canadian farmers were able to grow high-quality grain and high-protein hard wheat for the British market. (Roller-milling had raised the value of hard wheat.) In the early 1890s fewer than 300 000 acres of wheat were planted, almost entirely in Manitoba; by 1901, 2.5 million acres were seeded, which by 1911 had increased to 10 million, and by 1920 to 20 million. By 1928 production exceeded 500 million bushels. Most of the grain was destined for overseas markets, largely British. By the 1920s Canada accounted for almost half of the world's trade in wheat, and wheat contributed between 25% and 30% of Canada's total export trade (pl 3).

Established before the opening of the grain-farming frontier, the cattle-ranching industry in the foothills of the Rockies and on the open ranges of Alberta and southern Saskatchewan persisted even when farming later made necessary the fencing of fields. The success of British and Canadian cattle ranches was based not only upon the generous terms under which extensive leases of land could be obtained from the Canadian government but also upon the growing demand for live cattle in Great Britain. Canadian exports secured a privileged position because the government was able to demonstrate that Canadian cattle were free of pleuropneumonia and that routine inspection and quarantine regulations were of a high standard. Exports of live cattle, already well established at 108 000 head in 1891, rose to 160 000 in 1905. The trade soon declined, however, since the shipment of live cattle was a costly way to deliver meat to a distant market. As refrigeration was perfected and the infrastructure for the distribution of chilled meat established, Canadian live cattle lost their competitive advantage. Cheap, good-quality refrigerated meat from the southern hemisphere undermined the profitability of the Canadian business in Great Britain. Shipments of cattle eastward from Alberta slumped from 85 000 head in 1910 to only 12 000 in 1912. In the years just before the First World War Canadian cattlemen looked to growing domestic demand and the relatively accessible Chicago market rather than to traditional outlets in Great Britain.

The Prairies had been slow to develop as a wheat-growing region not only because of adverse growing conditions but also because of distance from the markets. Great Britain was the predominant market and the world price of wheat was set at Liverpool. The United States, Russia, India, Argentina, and Australia had all responded to the growing British market and the outpouring of wheat from those countries kept prices so low that Canada could not compete effectively. To transport the wheat more than a railway was needed. A complete transportation system had to be developed with storage and transshipment at the Lakehead, transport on the Great Lakes in large, special-purpose vessels (which after 1899 could benefit from deeper canals that bypassed Niagara Falls and the rapids of the upper St Lawrence), and efficient storage and transshipment again at the port of Montréal. Grain elevators were built at Georgian Bay ports and some grain was taken by rail over a short-cut to Montréal. Buffalo, NY, at the eastern end of Lake Erie, took increasing amounts of Canadian grain, which was milled there 'in transit' or shipped to New York City in bond. Freight rates to Liverpool had long been higher from Montréal than from New York (where wheat was shipped as ballast in trans-Atlantic liners). Yet with efficient port facilities Montréal succeeded in garnering a good portion of the Canadian wheat trade.

Western farmers could not influence the price of wheat, but they blamed the high cost of shipping and distribution on the monopolies at home which controlled those operations. At the local grain elevator farmers met the system head on (pl 19). As early as 1900 two-thirds of all elevators were controlled by five large grain companies. As the branch-line rail system was extended in the first three decades of the 20th century, elevator companies, some of them American and controlled by firms based in Minneapolis and others controlled by Winnipeg merchants, enjoyed special relationships with railway companies. Farmers faced high storage charges and improper grading procedures. To make matters worse, the banks demanded repayments on loans at the time of threshing, forcing farmers to sell their product in a glutted market. Discontent drove the farmers to challenge the cartels in the courts and to demand political action. They also began to build their own grain elevators and establish their own distribution systems. After a number of false starts they successfully organized co-operative wheat pools for the storing and marketing of grain. By 1929 farmer-owned concerns handled half of the grain that moved through

the 'country elevators,' and the three provincially based wheat pools also operated terminal elevators at the Lakehead and on the west coast.

Farmers were able to modify the shipping system, but the railway determined the location of hamlet, town, and city. Grain delivery centres were located about 11 km apart (the effective distance for haulage by wagon), a spacing which imposed a uniform pattern of settlement. Smaller towns had a lumber yard, a general store, perhaps an implements dealer and a hardware store, a post office, a bank, and two or more elevators. Larger towns, usually located at railway divisional points, had several banks, and perhaps four or more elevators. The major cities enjoyed much more than a superior trading status. They were also provincial capitals, seats of universities, regional railway centres, or places in which specialized manufacturing was undertaken. Winnipeg functioned as a gateway city for the entire West into the 1920s, when it lost some of its importance through the rise of Vancouver as an alternative shipping point (after the opening of the Panama Canal) and the centralization of financial management in Central Canada (pl 9). Calgary was able to replace its early dependence on cattle by becoming the organizing centre for the Alberta oil industry in the 1920s.

Real-estate speculation also helped to determine the shape and structure of Prairie cities. In Edmonton (pl 20) the land-holdings of the Hudson's Bay Company influenced the direction of residential growth, while in Calgary and Winnipeg the CPR was the major landowner around which others positioned speculative subdivisions. Suburban land was treated as a commodity, just like the crops of the field, and 'booster' rhetoric stimulated rounds of real-estate booms and absentee ownership. The drying up of overseas investment by 1913 and the decline in immigration during the First World War ended this speculative boom and in many western cities vast tracts of suburban land were left for several decades with an irregular scattering of houses set amidst second-growth scrub, making the provision of services such as sewers, water, and public transport inefficient and expensive.

British Columbia

The settlement of British Columbia was determined by the natural resources on which its economy was built. Although a few thousand non-native people had established permanent residence in the area by 1871, when British Columbia entered Confederation, substantial population growth dated from the completion of the CPR in 1886. During the Great Transformation the population of British Columbia increased sevenfold to reach 700 000 by 1929, three-quarters of it concentrated in the southwestern corner of the province, especially in Vancouver, which served as a transshipment and processing centre for the lumber, fishing, and mining industries.

From its historical base on the Burrard Inlet near Vancouver the lumber industry expanded up the coast (pl 21), where many fjords along Georgia Strait gave access to mammoth stands of red cedar and Douglas fir. The exploitation of inland valleys required heavy capitalization, and technology and entrepreneurial talents came west to build the lumber industry. Steam engines to haul cut logs to marshalling areas and robust Shea engines to pull trains of logs had been developed in Michigan and Minnesota in the 1880s. Both American capital and eastern Canadian lumbermen were attracted to this resource-rich region, where a generous provincial government placed few restrictions on timber leases or the volume of the cut.

External capital also developed the salmon-canning industry in British Columbia, after its early beginnings in the days of the Cariboo gold rush. British interests acquired existing American-owned concerns and developed production geared almost entirely to British markets. Most of the early canneries were in Steveston, at the mouth of the Fraser River, but the Nass, Skeena, and other northern inlets also developed as important centres. The brevity of the fishing season and the subsequent urgency to can the catch demanded high levels of seasonal labour. Conflict ensued, not only between capital and labour over piece-rates, but between European, Japanese, and native workers who all received different rates of pay. Ethnic segregation of the work-force was prevalent in Vancouver Island coal-mining towns as well as in the coastal cannery camps (pl 22).

Most of the settlement in the BC interior was also tied to resource extraction. The discovery and development of a variety of mineral resources in the Kootenays, especially in the late 1890s, opened up a remote, somewhat inaccessible area. Railways, including spur lines from American systems, were built into mountain valleys. Indeed, the Kootenays could be seen as an extension of the American mining frontier then active in Idaho, Colorado, and Montana. Settlements rose and fell. Towns like Phoenix and Sandon largely disappeared when ore veins were exhausted or the costs of extraction and smelting priced the ore out of the market; but other towns like Nelson persisted as service centres. By 1906 the mining industry was more solidly established when the three large mines at Rossland were linked to the smelter at Trail by the CPR-controlled conglomerate, Consolidated Mining and Smelting (COMINCO). Three years later it added the immense Sullivan mine at Kimberley to its holdings. Through COMINCO the CPR widened its sphere of influence and inserted a Canadian presence in this largely American-dominated region.

Vancouver developed as the terminus of the CPR, the point of transshipment to Pacific markets, and the focal point of the corporate organization of the province's resource industries. The opening of the Panama Canal increased Vancouver's global accessibility in the 1920s. The province's lumber could be shipped to the eastern United States and Canada, and some grain shipments from the Prairies could be diverted from the Lakehead to the Pacific. Vancouver's False Creek and Burrard Inlet waterfronts were the sites of a dozen sawmills that processed the logs boomed in from camps up the coast; and communities in the lower Fraser valley that were based on salmon canning, sawmilling, and farming were linked to the city by an extensive interurban rail network. Vancouver, even more than Halifax and Winnipeg, lived in the shadow of Montréal and Toronto.

The Maritime Provinces and Newfoundland

While most of the West and parts of the Canadian Shield were experiencing rapid growth and integration into the national, market, the Maritime Provinces and Newfoundland were entering a difficult period of transition. Their industrial base was much smaller than that of Central Canada at Confederation, and their industrial growth was hampered by the small size and dispersion of local markets and the distance from Central and western Canadian markets. By and large the Maritimes missed out on the Great Transformation.

The relatively slow pace of development is evident in the fishing industry, though it remained important in both Newfoundland and the Maritimes (pl 23). In Newfoundland, especially, the inshore fishery, which was controlled by the merchants, showed remarkable stability. Modest technological improvements, such as the introduction of gasoline motors and cod traps, increased productivity and enabled the small-boat fishery to survive. This change, however, discouraged investment in the offshore bank fishery conducted from schooners, and in Newfoundland the banks fishery declined between the 1890s and the 1920s. In the more diversified Nova Scotian fishery many of the sail-powered schooners acquired motors in the 1920s. Several steam trawlers were operating from Nova Scotia by the 1920s, but many fishermen and politicians, fearful that the trawlers would put fishermen out of work, opposed their use. New technology was indeed gradually displacing labour and protective associations and unions of fishermen began to develop in this period.

Although the Maritimes and Newfoundland remained major fish-producing regions, their share of world markets was diminishing.

The value of their output decreased and employment declined. The geographical advantages enjoyed by Norway and other fishing nations competing for the European market took their toll, as did the failure of fishermen to weaken merchant control and implement a more efficient system of production and marketing. For many people fishing was merely one of several occupations. The seasonal round of labour also involved some farming, some work in the woods in winter, boat building or shipbuilding, and sometimes mining. Agriculture was chiefly for local markets; only highly specialized products, such as apples or seed potatoes as well as fox furs, were sold to markets beyond the region. Newfoundland attempted to develop an industrial base by building railways and encouraging mining and forestry (there were pulp mills at Corner Brook and Grand Falls), but the effort was undermined by the island's distance from major markets.

In the Maritimes textile manufacturing, sugar refining, glass making, and metal working, industries that had been established after Confederation, had faced strong competition from Central Canadian producers. Enterprises had either closed down or fallen victim to acquisitions and mergers by the 1880s, and control had passed outside the region. In the mid-1890s a limited second phase of industrialization in the Maritimes occurred (pl 24). Coal fields in Cape Breton and Pictou and iron-ore deposits at Wabana, Nfld, provided the raw materials for the region's iron and steel industries. The embryonic Nova Scotia Steel and Coal Corporation built a fully integrated works at Sydney Mines on the coal fields of Cape Breton between 1901 and 1905. In 1905 the Dominion Coal Company built a primary iron and steel mill across the harbour at Sydney. By building on the remnants of the earlier industrialization, chiefly iron and steel metal working, and by establishing new industries, such as the manufacture of furniture, farm machinery, and confectionery, the region participated in a small way in national economic growth. Of particular importance was the policy of the Intercolonial Railway in providing cheap freight rates that allowed Maritime manufacturers to compete in the Central Canadian market. By 1917, however, the Intercolonial Railway was drawn into the plans for the reorganization of the bankrupt Canadian Northern and Grand Trunk Pacific, thereby losing its regional identity and its ability to set rates. The once-competitive rate structure from Halifax to Toronto disappeared (pl 6).

By the early 1920s the Maritime region had lost control of most of its industries through mergers with either Central Canadian or foreign corporations and most of its financial institutions had moved to headquarters in Central Canada (pl 9). Urban development was weak: less than 50% of the population was living in urban areas by 1931. Its physical, political, and historical fragmentation meant that the region lacked a single metropolitan centre in which manufacturing industries could achieve economies of scale. Although well located for processing imports, such as refining sugar, neither Saint John nor Halifax was a viable location for major manufacturing industries to serve the domestic market. The two cities, moreover, had similar functions and were therefore more competitive than complementary. As ocean-shipping cities, both faced increasing competition from Montréal and the Atlantic seaboard ports of the United States. Saint John had declined as a shipbuilding centre with the ascendancy of iron ships. Halifax retained its function as a centre for Nova Scotia's fishing trade, but had only limited success in developing its infrastructure to capture Canada's winter-port rail trade (pl 25). Grandiose plans for extending docks and piers to the south of the 19th-century harbour were only minimally executed. Despite its magnificent natural harbour Halifax was not well sited to become a major port. Even though it was icebound for four months of the year, Montréal retained its primacy as the nation's main port, mainly because of its proximity to Central Canadian industrial and consumer markets. Only in the two world wars did Halifax take on great importance, as a convoy departure point and as a military base. In peacetime the port took second place to Montréal, and after the 1920s it dropped to third place behind Vancouver.

The Great War

The Great War of 1914–18 (pl 26) had a number of important regional economic effects across Canada: an increased demand for Prairie wheat and a rise in prices (followed by post-war decline and hardship for overextended farmers); a growth in the demand for non-ferrous metals on the Shield and in British Columbia and hence the expansion of smelters and refineries; and an expansion of manufacturing, especially in Central Canada. Some important aspects of government involvement with everyday life began to develop during the war. Food and fuel prices were controlled in 1916 and 1917 respectively, and a wheat board operated between 1917 and 1920. War bonds issued between the fall of 1915 and the fall of 1919 brought in $2 billion; Toronto's control of this financing initiated a shift in the competitive positions of Montréal and Toronto. In 1917 personal income tax was introduced, plus taxes on profits in trade and on the gross revenues of insurance companies. These taxes came too late to pay for the war, but they were retained as an important source of revenue to reduce the heavy national debt.

The political aspects of the war had severe repercussions for future generations. Although voluntary enlistment was initially high, especially among British-born immigrants in the West, it dropped off by 1917, and the increasing demands for soldiers for the trenches led to calls for conscription. In the federal referendum on the issue in 1917 Canadian civilians of German and Austrian background who had arrived since 1905 were stripped of their franchise (earlier there had been internment of enemy aliens, including Ukrainians); women who had husbands or sons in military service were given the vote for the first time. Francophones, who, by and large, saw the war as a British affair, voted overwhelmingly against conscription and later ignored call-up orders. Many farmers also resisted conscription, and labour groups voiced their opposition. In the end only about 83 000 recruits were gained by conscription, yet it significantly hardened divisions within the country.

Four decades of economic transformation profoundly altered the relative economic positions of Canada's regions. The development of the Prairies as a wheat-exporting region and the Shield and British Columbia as forest and mining regions, barely begun in 1891, contributed enormously to the national economy. By comparison, the Maritimes and Newfoundland grew much more slowly. The leading cities of all regions had their metropolitan ambitions thwarted by the tightening grip of Toronto and Montréal in a wide array of manufacturing, financial, and service endeavours. In southwestern and south-central Ontario the growth of urban-based industrial activities overwhelmed the transformations in agriculture while in southern Québec economic growth did not extend far outside Montréal and a few other centres. A series of regions had been connected to form an emerging national system during the Great Transformation but development was uneven and integration was variable.

RESOURCE-BASED INDUSTRIES IN CENTRAL CANADA

Author: Marvin McInnis

The first-stage processing of natural resources was a significant component of Canadian manufacturing. The forest supported the sawmilling and pulp and paper industries and agriculture provided the essential raw materials for a number of industries – flour milling, meat packing, butter and cheese manufacturing. These industries did not, however, always process nearby resources.

Sawmilling had been the leading manufacturing industry of Canada during most of the 19th century. By 1926 the sawmill industry in Central Canada was still substantial but western Canadian mills had come to produce a far greater share of output (pll 8, 22). The utilization of the forests in Ontario and Québec had been largely redirected to the pulp and paper industries. In 1891 these industries were essentially market-oriented, located at good power sites especially in the Niagara Peninsula and in the Eastern Townships. After 1900 the American market became more important but pulp-mill sites gravitated northward to the abundant forest resources on the Shield and to major power sources on the Saint-Maurice River north of Trois-Rivières (pll 12, 16); the most dramatic growth of the pulp and paper industries came between 1911 and 1926.

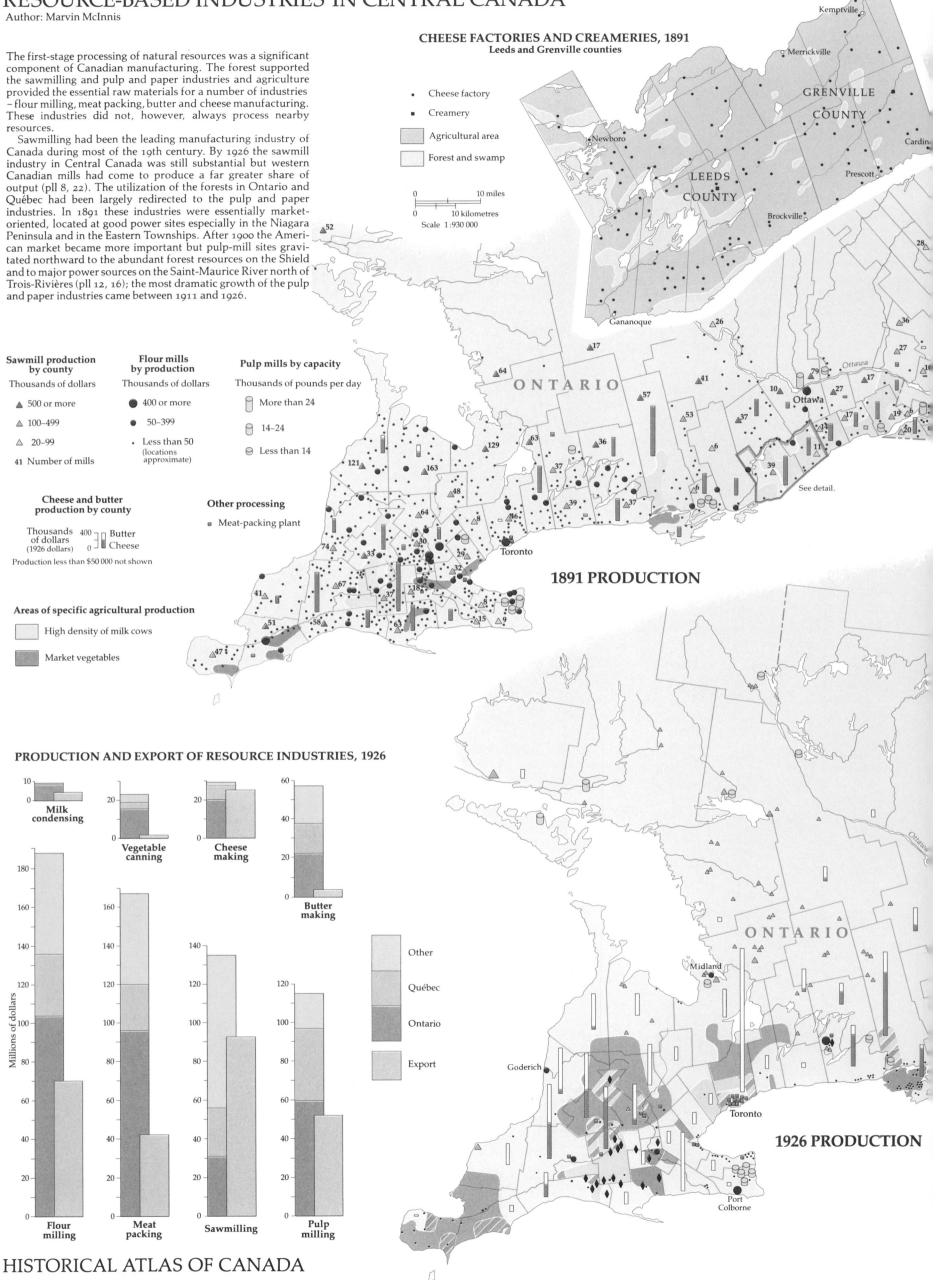

CHEESE FACTORIES AND CREAMERIES, 1891
Leeds and Grenville counties

- • Cheese factory
- ▪ Creamery

Agricultural area

Forest and swamp

Scale 1:930 000
0   10 miles
0   10 kilometres

Sawmill production by county
Thousands of dollars
- ▲ 500 or more
- △ 100–499
- △ 20–99
- 41 Number of mills

Flour mills by production
Thousands of dollars
- ● 400 or more
- ● 50–399
- · Less than 50 (locations approximate)

Pulp mills by capacity
Thousands of pounds per day
- More than 24
- 14–24
- Less than 14

Cheese and butter production by county
Thousands of dollars (1926 dollars) 400 / 0 — Butter / Cheese
Production less than $50 000 not shown

Other processing
- ▪ Meat-packing plant

Areas of specific agricultural production
- High density of milk cows
- Market vegetables

1891 PRODUCTION

1926 PRODUCTION

PRODUCTION AND EXPORT OF RESOURCE INDUSTRIES, 1926

Milk condensing
Vegetable canning
Cheese making
Butter making

Other
Québec
Ontario
Export

Millions of dollars

Flour milling
Meat packing
Sawmilling
Pulp milling

HISTORICAL ATLAS OF CANADA

PLATE 11

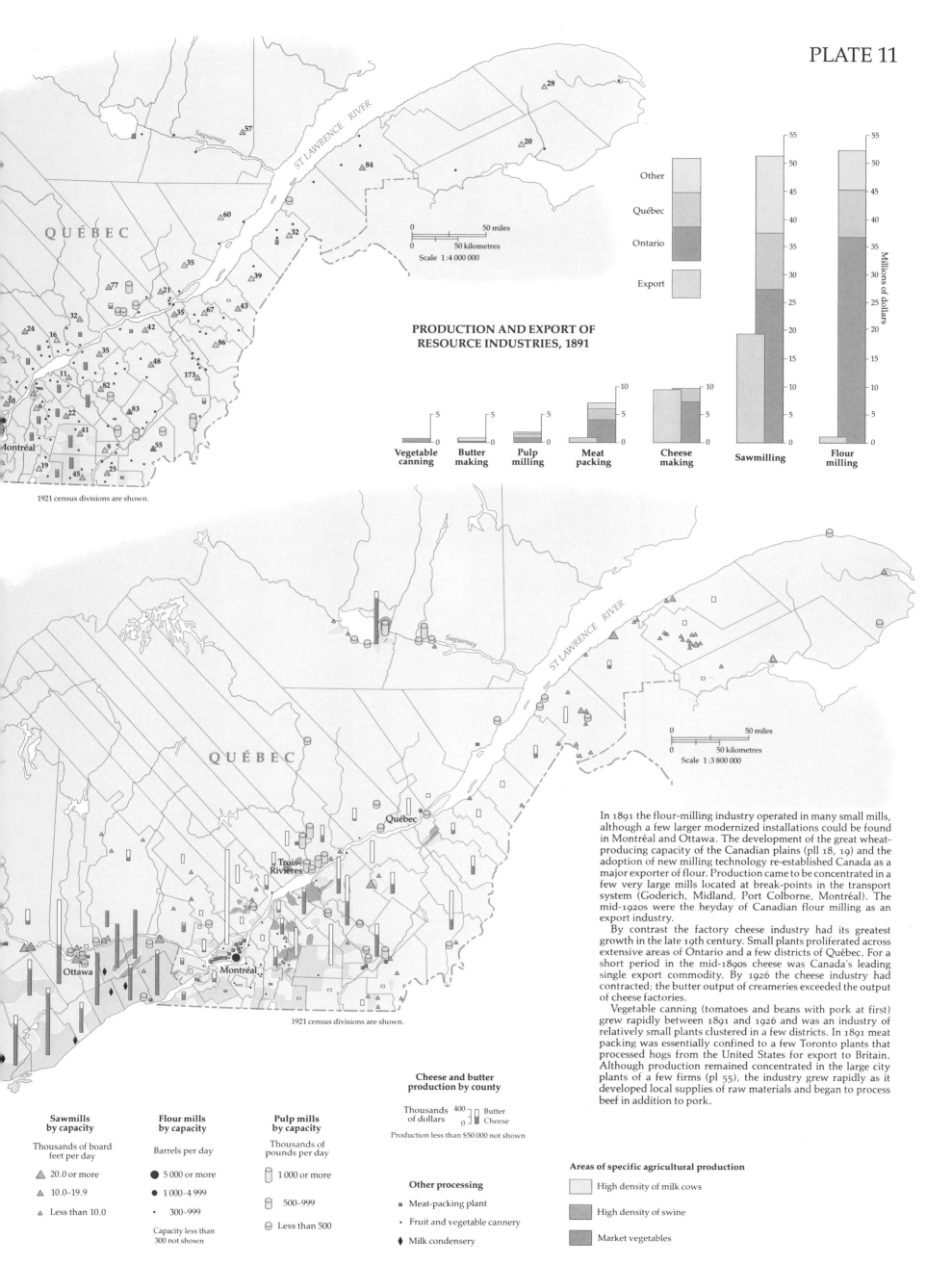

**PRODUCTION AND EXPORT OF
RESOURCE INDUSTRIES, 1891**

Other
Québec
Ontario
Export

Millions of dollars

Vegetable
canning

Butter
making

Pulp
milling

Meat
packing

Cheese
making

Sawmilling

Flour
milling

QUÉBEC

57

28

20

84

60

32

35

77

21

39

35

67

43

24

16

32

35

86

42

48

173

11

82

83

7

6

22

10

41

9

55

19

45

25

Montréal

1921 census divisions are shown.

ST LAWRENCE RIVER

Saguenay

0   50 miles
0   50 kilometres
Scale 1:4 000 000

QUÉBEC

Québec

Trois-
Rivières

Ottawa

Montréal

ST LAWRENCE RIVER

Saguenay

0   50 miles
0   50 kilometres
Scale 1:3 800 000

1921 census divisions are shown.

In 1891 the flour-milling industry operated in many small mills, although a few larger modernized installations could be found in Montréal and Ottawa. The development of the great wheat-producing capacity of the Canadian plains (pll 18, 19) and the adoption of new milling technology re-established Canada as a major exporter of flour. Production came to be concentrated in a few very large mills located at break-points in the transport system (Goderich, Midland, Port Colborne, Montréal). The mid-1920s were the heyday of Canadian flour milling as an export industry.

By contrast the factory cheese industry had its greatest growth in the late 19th century. Small plants proliferated across extensive areas of Ontario and a few districts of Québec. For a short period in the mid-1890s cheese was Canada's leading single export commodity. By 1926 the cheese industry had contracted; the butter output of creameries exceeded the output of cheese factories.

Vegetable canning (tomatoes and beans with pork at first) grew rapidly between 1891 and 1926 and was an industry of relatively small plants clustered in a few districts. In 1891 meat packing was essentially confined to a few Toronto plants that processed hogs from the United States for export to Britain. Although production remained concentrated in the large city plants of a few firms (pl 55), the industry grew rapidly as it developed local supplies of raw materials and began to process beef in addition to pork.

**Sawmills
by capacity**

Thousands of board
feet per day

△ 20.0 or more

△ 10.0–19.9

△ Less than 10.0

**Flour mills
by capacity**

Barrels per day

● 5 000 or more

● 1 000–4 999

· 300–999

Capacity less than
300 not shown

**Pulp mills
by capacity**

Thousands of
pounds per day

▯ 1 000 or more

▯ 500–999

▯ Less than 500

**Cheese and butter
production by county**

Thousands
of dollars

400

0

Butter
Cheese

Production less than $50 000 not shown

Other processing

▪ Meat-packing plant

· Fruit and vegetable cannery

◆ Milk condensery

Areas of specific agricultural production

☐ High density of milk cows

☐ High density of swine

☐ Market vegetables

ELECTRICITY AND INDUSTRIAL DEVELOPMENT IN CENTRAL CANADA

Authors: Gerald Bloomfield, René Hardy, Pierre Lanthier, Normand Séguin

The harnessing of water for the generation of low-cost electric power was an important factor in consolidating the industrial position of southern Québec and Ontario. In Québec large quantities of power were used by a few industrial consumers for the production of chemicals, pulp and paper, and metals. In Ontario the effect was more indirect through the substitution of electrical power for imported coal in a wide range of existing industries and locations.

With a multiplicity of power sites and a limited market outside Montréal, the hydroelectric power industry in Québec remained under private control. While individual companies developed regional markets, the system was connected by transmission lines and interlocking directorships. In Ontario, by contrast, the anxieties of industrialists in southwestern Ontario that they would be denied power from the province's dominant site at Niagara (then controlled by Toronto and Buffalo interests) led to political action. In 1906 the government created the publicly owned Hydro-Electric Power Commission of Ontario (HEPCO) to administer the transmission, sale, and, later, production of power. HEPCO deliberately set low rates for domestic consumption while the private companies in Québec maintained significantly higher domestic rates and consumption per capita was less.

INDUSTRIAL GENERATING CAPACITY

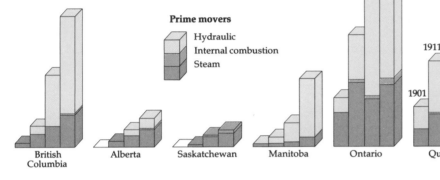

Prime movers
- Hydraulic
- Internal combustion
- Steam

Thousands of horsepower

British Columbia · Alberta · Saskatchewan · Manitoba · Ontario · Québec · New Brunswick · Nova Scotia

PEI figures too small to show

1928 · 1921 · 1911 · 1901

Electric light systems
- △ Private
- ▲ Private (signed first contract with HEPCO, May 1908)
- △ Municipal
- ▲ Municipal (signed first contract with HEPCO, May 1908)
- ○─ Generating station and transmission line

HEPCO DOMESTIC-SERVICE RATES, SOUTHERN ONTARIO
Net cost per kilowatt

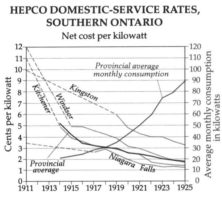

Cents per kilowatt · Average monthly consumption in kilowatts

Provincial average monthly consumption

Kitchener · Windsor · Kingston · Niagara Falls · *Provincial average*

1911 1913 1915 1917 1919 1921 1923 1925

Development of hydroelectric power and electrochemical industries at Niagara Falls, first in the United States and then in Canada, triggered much economic growth. Canadian power companies served local manufacturing plants on both sides of the border but, as power came increasingly under the control of HEPCO, it was widely distributed to municipalities for resale to industries and households in southern Ontario.

NIAGARA FALLS, ONTARIO: POWER GENERATION AND EXPORTS
Figures in millions of kilowatts

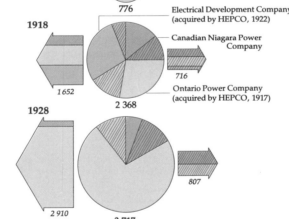

To Ontario · *Exports to New York State*

1911 — 254 · 522 · 776

1918 — 1652 · 716 · 2 368

Electrical Development Company (acquired by HEPCO, 1922)
Canadian Niagara Power Company
Ontario Power Company (acquired by HEPCO, 1917)

1928 — 2 910 · 807 · 3 717

THE NIAGARA REGION

GROWTH OF MANUFACTURING

LAKE ONTARIO

St Catharines · Merriton · Thorold · Niagara Falls · *Welland Canal* · Welland · Port Colborne · Bridgeburg, Fort Erie · Buffalo

NEW YORK · ONTARIO · LAKE ERIE

1929 · 1914 · 1904 · Niagara Falls

Millions of dollars (100 75 50 25 0)

POWER PRODUCTION AND INDUSTRIAL CONSUMPTION, 1929

LAKE ONTARIO

Queenston · De Cew Falls · Niagara Falls · Niagara electro-chemical complex · *Welland Canal* · Chippawa · Welland · Port Colborne · Fort Erie · Bridgeburg Buffalo

NEW YORK · ONTARIO · LAKE ERIE

Scale 1:670 000

- ● Hydroelectric generating station
- ■ Major electrochemical and metallurgical plant
- — Major transmission line
- -- Power canal

GENERATING STATIONS AT NIAGARA FALLS

Ontario Power Company · Niagara Falls Power Company · *American Falls* · Canadian Niagara Power Company · *Horseshoe Falls* · Toronto Power Company

LAKE ONTARIO

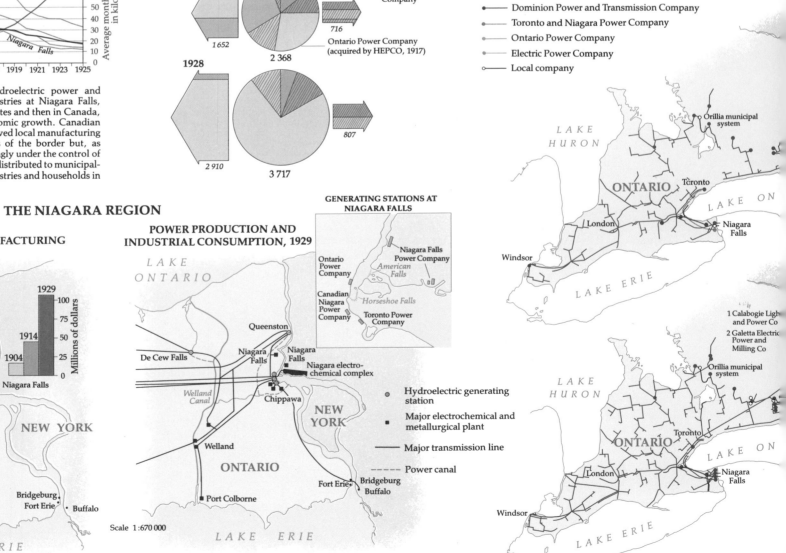

ONTARIO

Orillia municipal system
Lindsay Light, He[at] and Power Co
LAKE HURON
Toronto
LAKE ONT[ARIO]
Niagara Falls
Windsor
LAKE ERIE

Bracebridge and Gravenhurst municipal system
Orillia municipal system
Simcoe Railway and Power Co
Lindsay Light, Heat and Power Co
LAKE HURON
ONTARIO
Toronto
London
LAKE ONT[ARIO]
Niagara Falls
LAKE ERIE

0 ——— 100 miles
0 ——— 100 kilometres
Scale 1:6 800 000

Ontario transmission systems
- ●─ Hydro-Electric Power Commission of Ontario (HEPCO)
- ●─ Dominion Power and Transmission Company
- ●─ Toronto and Niagara Power Company
- ●─ Ontario Power Company
- ●─ Electric Power Company
- ○─ Local company

LAKE HURON
ONTARIO
Orillia municipal system
Toronto
London
LAKE ONT[ARIO]
Niagara Falls
Windsor
LAKE ERIE

1 Calabogie Light and Power Co
2 Galetta Electric Power and Milling Co
Orillia municipal system
LAKE HURON
ONTARIO
Toronto
London
LAKE ON[TARIO]
Niagara Falls
Windsor
LAKE ERIE

HISTORICAL ATLAS OF CANADA

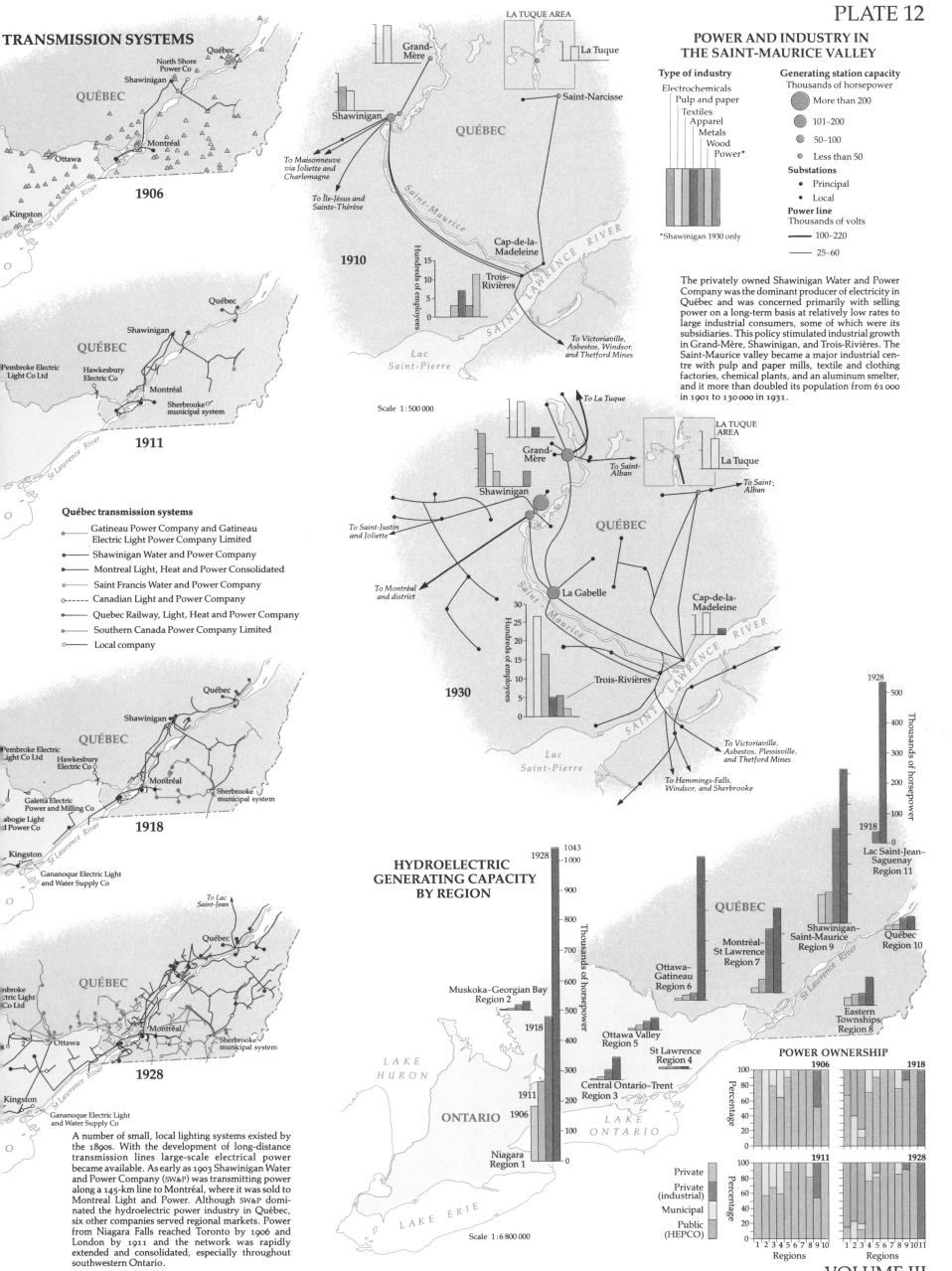

PLATE 12

TRANSMISSION SYSTEMS

POWER AND INDUSTRY IN THE SAINT-MAURICE VALLEY

Type of industry
- Electrochemicals
- Pulp and paper
- Textiles
- Apparel
- Metals
- Wood
- Power*

*Shawinigan 1930 only

Generating station capacity
Thousands of horsepower
- More than 200
- 101–200
- 50–100
- Less than 50

Substations
- Principal
- Local

Power line
Thousands of volts
- 100–220
- 25–60

The privately owned Shawinigan Water and Power Company was the dominant producer of electricity in Québec and was concerned primarily with selling power on a long-term basis at relatively low rates to large industrial consumers, some of which were its subsidiaries. This policy stimulated industrial growth in Grand-Mère, Shawinigan, and Trois-Rivières. The Saint-Maurice valley became a major industrial centre with pulp and paper mills, textile and clothing factories, chemical plants, and an aluminum smelter, and it more than doubled its population from 61 000 in 1901 to 130 000 in 1931.

QUÉBEC

1906

QUÉBEC
1911

Scale 1:500 000

LA TUQUE AREA
La Tuque
Grand-Mère
Shawinigan
QUÉBEC
1910
Saint-Narcisse
Cap-de-la-Madeleine
Trois-Rivières
Lac Saint-Pierre
To Maisonneuve via Joliette and Charlemagne
To Île-Jésus and Sainte-Thérèse
To Victoriaville, Asbestos, Windsor, and Thetford Mines

Québec transmission systems
- Gatineau Power Company and Gatineau Electric Light Power Company Limited
- Shawinigan Water and Power Company
- Montreal Light, Heat and Power Consolidated
- Saint Francis Water and Power Company
- Canadian Light and Power Company
- Quebec Railway, Light, Heat and Power Company
- Southern Canada Power Company Limited
- Local company

1918

1928

LA TUQUE AREA
La Tuque
Grand-Mère
Shawinigan
La Gabelle
QUÉBEC
Cap-de-la-Madeleine
Trois-Rivières
Lac Saint-Pierre
1930
To La Tuque
To Saint-Alban
To Saint-Justin and Joliette
To Montréal and district
To Victoriaville, Asbestos, Plessisville, and Thetford Mines
To Hemmings-Falls, Windsor, and Sherbrooke

HYDROELECTRIC GENERATING CAPACITY BY REGION

LAKE HURON
ONTARIO
LAKE ONTARIO
LAKE ERIE

Niagara Region 1
Muskoka–Georgian Bay Region 2
Central Ontario–Trent Region 3
St Lawrence Region 4
Ottawa Valley Region 5
Ottawa–Gatineau Region 6
Montréal–St Lawrence Region 7
Eastern Townships Region 8
Shawinigan–Saint-Maurice Region 9
Québec Region 10
Lac Saint-Jean–Saguenay Region 11

QUÉBEC

Scale 1:6 800 000

POWER OWNERSHIP

1906   1918
1911   1928

- Private
- Private (industrial)
- Municipal
- Public (HEPCO)

Regions

A number of small, local lighting systems existed by the 1890s. With the development of long-distance transmission lines large-scale electrical power became available. As early as 1903 Shawinigan Water and Power Company (SW&P) was transmitting power along a 145-km line to Montréal, where it was sold to Montreal Light and Power. Although SW&P dominated the hydroelectric power industry in Québec, six other companies served regional markets. Power from Niagara Falls reached Toronto by 1906 and London by 1911 and the network was rapidly extended and consolidated, especially throughout southwestern Ontario.

URBAN INDUSTRIAL DEVELOPMENT IN CENTRAL CANADA

Authors: Elizabeth Bloomfield, Gerald Bloomfield, Marc Vallières (Québec)

REGIONAL SHARE OF MANUFACTURING

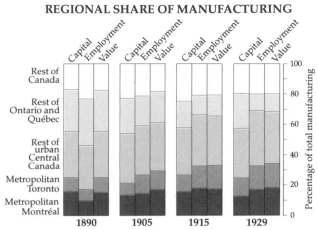

MANUFACTURING STRUCTURE, 1911
15 largest centres

Total employment in manufacturing

Manufacturing employment as a percentage of total labour force

Women employed in manufacturing as a percentage of total manufacturing employment

Centre		Total employment	% labour force	% women
Montréal		61 018	33	27
Toronto		59 283	35	26
Hamilton		18 978	51	20
Québec		8 856	32	33
London		8 292	42	26
Ottawa		6 861	20	24
Brantford		5 512	54	13
Berlin[1]		3 816	60	30
Hull		3 643	55	21
Peterborough		3 501	48	22
Maisonneuve[2]		3 184	49	23
Guelph		2 514	42	18
Windsor		2 437	33	22
Kingston		2 227	31	27
Sherbrooke		2 050	33	25

Percentage of manufacturing

Type of industry

Food, beverages, tobacco
Leather and products
Clothing
Furniture
Printing
Metal fabricating
Transportation equipment
Non-metallic mineral products
Miscellaneous manufactures

Rubber and products
Textiles, knitting mills
Wood products
Pulp and paper
Primary metal processing
Machinery
Electrical goods
Chemicals and products
Other[3]

1 Berlin became Kitchener in 1916.

2 Maisonneuve became part of Montréal in 1918.

3 Electricity and gas works as well as other factory occupations, office employees, and manufacturing labourers.

Urban centres in Central Canada, especially Montréal (pl 14) and Toronto (pl 15), developed as the nation's leading producers of manufactured goods, largely as a result of the protection of National Policy tariffs and the proximity of a large domestic market. The pace of change varied according to location, industrial base, and local entrepreneurial energy which often resulted in municipal tax incentives to attract or retain enterprises. The rise of iron and steel in Hamilton and of rubber products, furniture, and food processing in Kitchener and other towns of the Grand River valley kept these areas in the vanguard of industrial growth. New developments in motor-vehicle industries brought rapid growth to the Windsor area and to Oshawa. Along the Niagara frontier metal refining and the production of electrical goods accounted for much industrial development. In the Saint-Maurice valley smelting, pulp and paper mills, chemicals, and textiles were at the heart of rapid industrialization, particularly in Trois-Rivières and Shawinigan (pl 12). Textiles were responsible for a great deal of the development in Sherbrooke, Drummondville, and other towns of the Eastern Townships.

Most urban centres in southwestern Ontario expanded their industrial base throughout the Great Transformation, while in Québec it was not until the late 1910s that there was any comparable non-metropolitan growth. Southwestern Ontario received much American investment (pl 7) and had a high proportion of skilled workers, especially in metal industries. In contrast, Québec's traditional labour-intensive industries, such as shoes and textiles, suffered a relative decline in the early 1900s as they adjusted to modern technology. The rise of new resource-oriented manufacturing such as pulp and paper and aluminum smelting contributed to Québec's industrial development in the 1920s.

INDUSTRIALIZATION 1905

Type of industry

Canadian control		American control
○	Chemicals, drugs	⊖
●	Motor vehicles and parts	●
◐	Other	⊖

Size of firm
○ 50 or more employees
○ 1–49

Railways
Street
Interurban
Regional or national

WORKPLACE AND RESIDENCE:
The Ford Motor Company, 1926–1927

Type of worker
· Blue-collar
· White-collar

Ford Motor Company
Built-up area

Scale 1:80 000

Ford City became East Windsor in 1929.

THE WINDSOR AREA

INDUSTRIALIZATION 1926–1927

Scale 1:110 000

The border cities of Windsor, Walkerville, and Ford City were the gateway to Canada for many American enterprises. An early industrial base of salt, liquor, pharmaceuticals, and metal fabrication was overshadowed when Ford (1904), General Motors (1919), and Chrysler (1924) established automobile plants. In 1927 over 50% of the area's manufacturing employees worked at Ford.

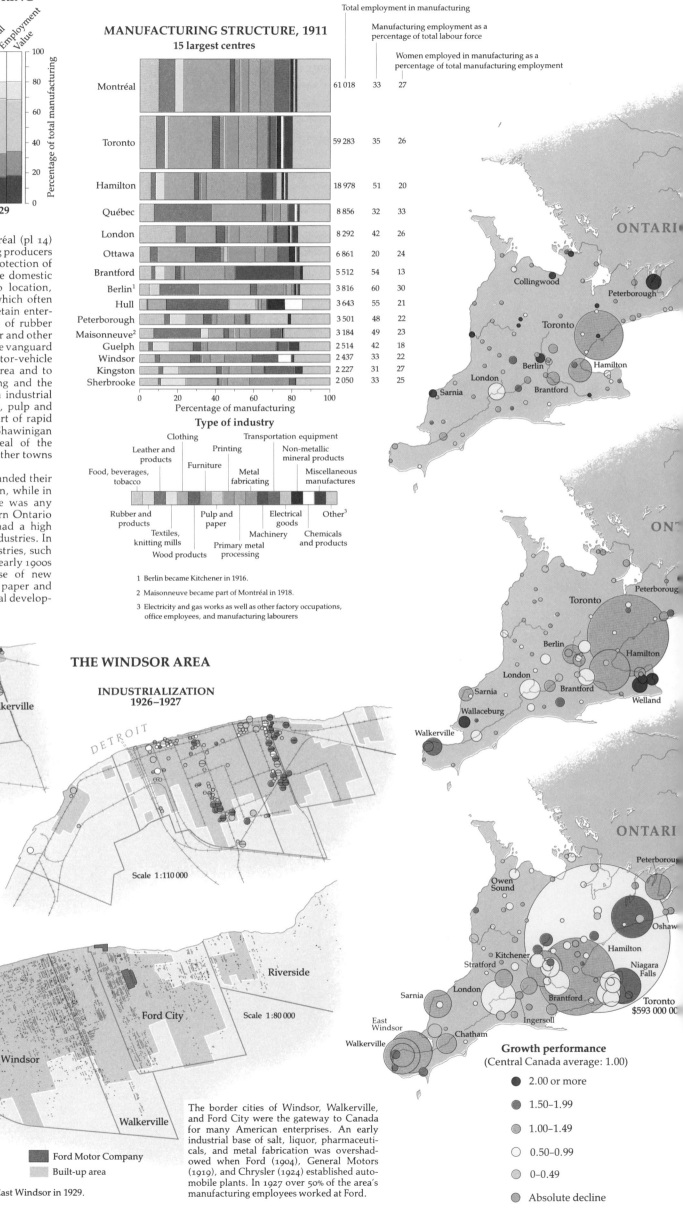

Growth performance
(Central Canada average: 1.00)
● 2.00 or more
● 1.50–1.99
◐ 1.00–1.49
○ 0.50–0.99
◑ 0–0.49
● Absolute decline

HISTORICAL ATLAS OF CANADA

PLATE 13

MANUFACTURING: DISTRIBUTION AND CHANGE

Value of manufacturing production for
urban places with population over 1 500

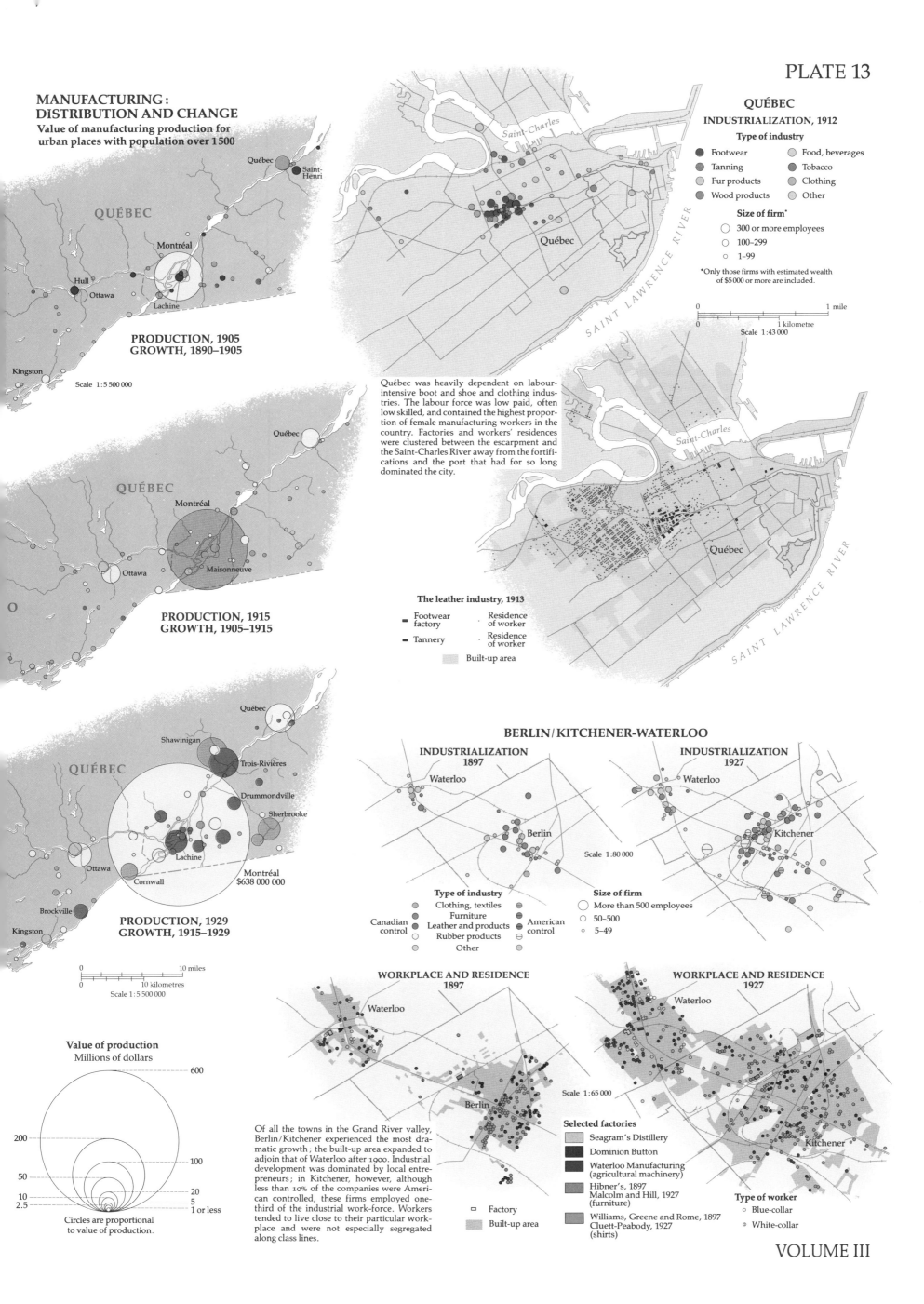

PRODUCTION, 1905
GROWTH, 1890–1905

Scale 1:5 500 000

PRODUCTION, 1915
GROWTH, 1905–1915

PRODUCTION, 1929
GROWTH, 1915–1929

Montréal
$638 000 000

0   10 miles
0   10 kilometres
Scale 1:5 500 000

Value of production
Millions of dollars

600
200
100
50
20
10
5
2.5
1 or less

Circles are proportional
to value of production.

QUÉBEC
INDUSTRIALIZATION, 1912
Type of industry

- Footwear
- Tanning
- Fur products
- Wood products
- Food, beverages
- Tobacco
- Clothing
- Other

Size of firm*

- ○ 300 or more employees
- ○ 100–299
- ∘ 1–99

*Only those firms with estimated wealth
of $5 000 or more are included.

0   1 mile
0   1 kilometre
Scale 1:43 000

Québec was heavily dependent on labour-
intensive boot and shoe and clothing industries. The labour force was low paid, often
low skilled, and contained the highest proportion of female manufacturing workers in the
country. Factories and workers' residences
were clustered between the escarpment and
the Saint-Charles River away from the fortifi-
cations and the port that had for so long
dominated the city.

The leather industry, 1913

- ▬ Footwear factory
- ▬ Tannery
- · Residence of worker
- · Residence of worker
- Built-up area

BERLIN/KITCHENER-WATERLOO

INDUSTRIALIZATION 1897

INDUSTRIALIZATION 1927

Scale 1:80 000

Type of industry

Canadian control
- Clothing, textiles
- Furniture
- Leather and products
- Rubber products
- Other

- American control

Size of firm

- ○ More than 500 employees
- ○ 50–500
- ∘ 5–49

WORKPLACE AND RESIDENCE 1897

WORKPLACE AND RESIDENCE 1927

Scale 1:65 000

Selected factories

- Seagram's Distillery
- Dominion Button
- Waterloo Manufacturing (agricultural machinery)
- Hibner's, 1897 Malcolm and Hill, 1927 (furniture)
- Williams, Greene and Rome, 1897 Cluett-Peabody, 1927 (shirts)

- □ Factory
- Built-up area

Type of worker

- ∘ Blue-collar
- ⊕ White-collar

Of all the towns in the Grand River valley,
Berlin/Kitchener experienced the most dramatic growth; the built-up area expanded to
adjoin that of Waterloo after 1900. Industrial
development was dominated by local entrepreneurs; in Kitchener, however, although
less than 10% of the companies were American controlled, these firms employed one-
third of the industrial work-force. Workers
tended to live close to their particular workplace and were not especially segregated
along class lines.

THE INDUSTRIAL DEVELOPMENT OF MONTRÉAL

Authors: Paul-André Linteau, Sylvie Taschereau

THE PROCESS OF ANNEXATION

- By 1879
- 1880–1899
- 1900–1909
- 1910
- 1911–1918

Streetcar lines extending beyond the area shown on the 1915 map

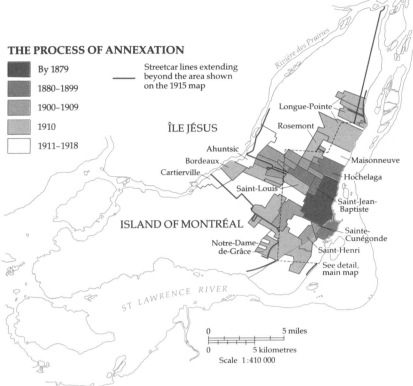

ÎLE JÉSUS

Rivière des Prairies

Longue-Pointe
Rosemont
Ahuntsic
Bordeaux
Cartierville
Maisonneuve
Saint-Louis
Hochelaga
Saint-Jean-Baptiste
ISLAND OF MONTRÉAL
Notre-Dame-de-Grâce
Sainte-Cunégonde
Saint-Henri
See detail, main map

ST LAWRENCE RIVER

0   5 miles
0   5 kilometres
Scale 1:410 000

POPULATION AND THE BUILDING CYCLE

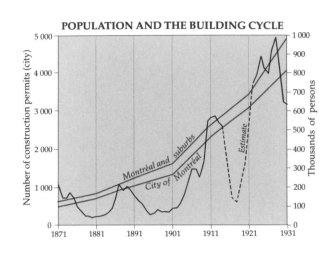

Number of construction permits (city)

Montréal and suburbs
City of Montréal
Estimate

Thousands of persons

1871 1881 1891 1901 1911 1921 1931

The population of Montréal grew steadily throughout the late 19th and early 20th centuries, particularly after 1901. The built-up area expanded considerably during several cycles of construction activity. Growth was concentrated along the two axes which had characterized the city's development since the 18th century: the St Lawrence River and Saint-Laurent Boulevard.

An extensive streetcar system, electrified in 1892, facilitated urban expansion, which from the 1880s increasingly took place in the suburban towns around the city. Montréal gradually annexed most of these municipalities, beginning with Hochelaga in 1883 and ending with Maisonneuve in 1918; only affluent Westmount and Outremont maintained their independence. During this process, which reached a peak in 1910, Montréal absorbed 23 municipalities, some of which, especially along the Rivière des Prairies, were still quite rural with only small clusters of population until after the Second World War.

GROWTH OF MANUFACTURING

Thousands of employees

Employees
Value of goods produced
Capital

Millions of dollars

1880 1890 1900 1910 1920

MAJOR INDUSTRIAL SITES AND BUILT-UP AREA, 1879

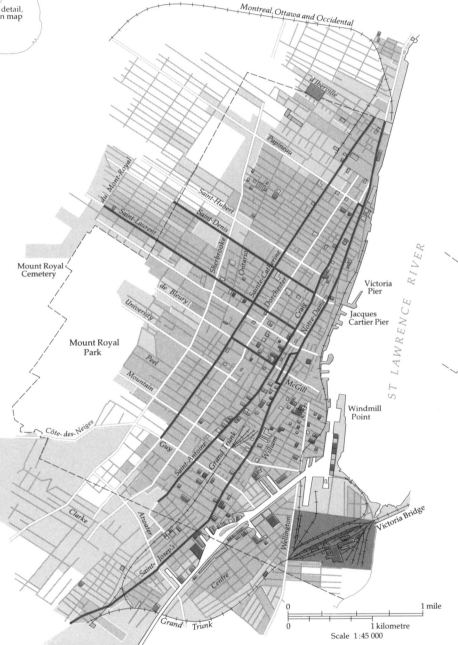

Montreal, Ottawa and Occidental
d'Iberville
Papineau
du Mont-Royal
Saint-Hubert
Saint-Denis
Saint-Laurent
Saint-Catherine
Sherbrooke
Ontario
Dorchester
Craig
Notre-Dame
de Bleury
University
Mount Royal Cemetery
Mount Royal Park
Peel
Mountain
McGill
Guy
Saint-Antoine
Grand Trunk
William
Clarke
Atwater
Wellington
Saint-Joseph
Centre
Grand Trunk
Côte-des-Neiges

Victoria Pier
Jacques Cartier Pier
Windmill Point
ST LAWRENCE RIVER
Victoria Bridge

OUTREMONT
Côte-Sainte-Cathe
Notre-Da-des-Nei Cemete (Cathol
Victoria
Canadian Pacific
Grand Trunk

0   1 mile
0   1 kilometre
Scale 1:45 000

Manufacturing

- Iron, steel, non-ferrous metals
- Transportation equipment
- Leather
- Clothing
- Textiles
- Wood products

Built-up area

- 50% or more
- Less than 50%
- Streetcar line
- Municipal boundary

Montréal, 1889

HISTORICAL ATLAS OF CANADA

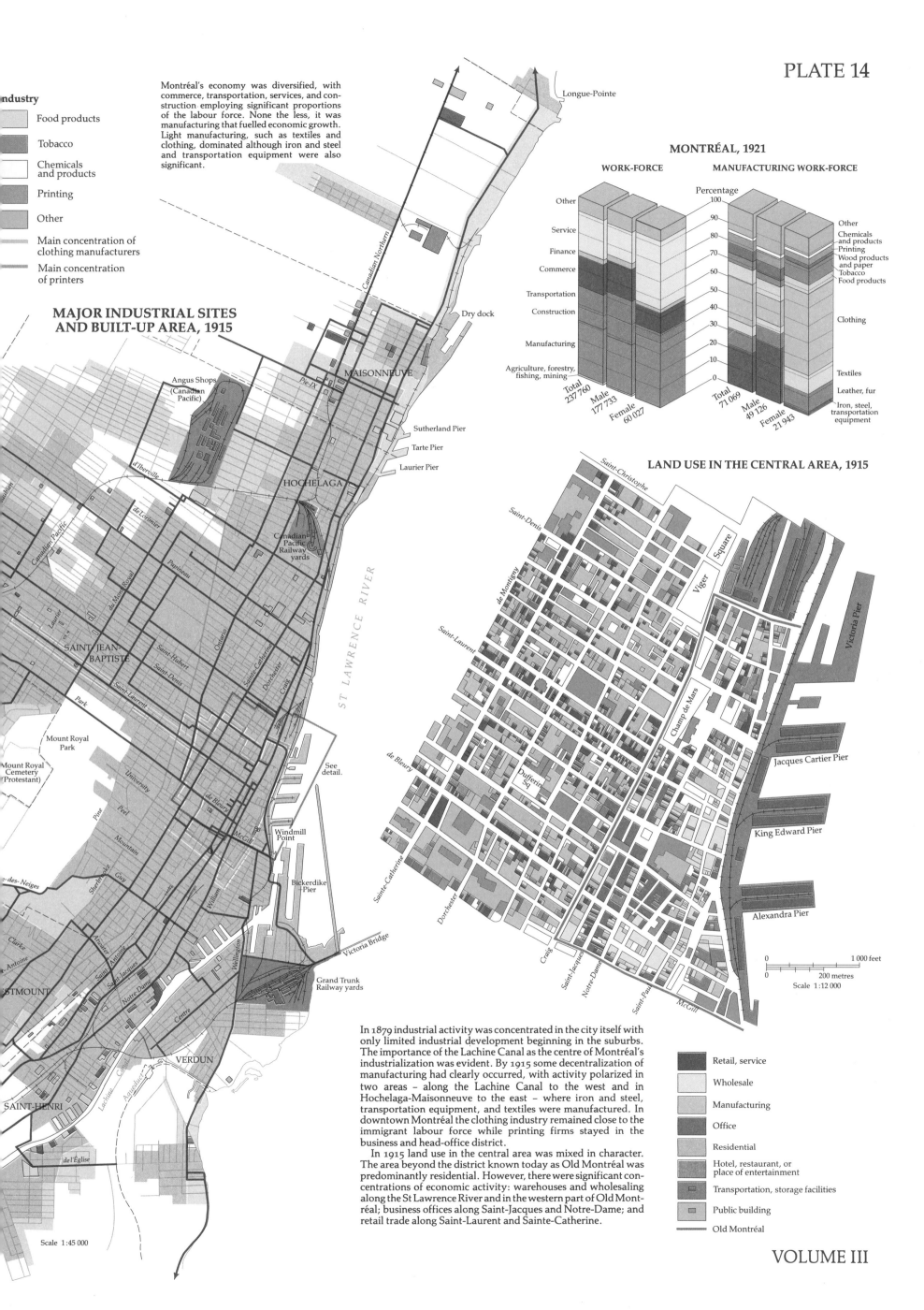

PLATE 14

Industry

Food products

Tobacco

Chemicals and products

Printing

Other

Main concentration of clothing manufacturers

Main concentration of printers

Montréal's economy was diversified, with commerce, transportation, services, and construction employing significant proportions of the labour force. None the less, it was manufacturing that fuelled economic growth. Light manufacturing, such as textiles and clothing, dominated although iron and steel and transportation equipment were also significant.

MAJOR INDUSTRIAL SITES AND BUILT-UP AREA, 1915

Longue-Pointe

Dry dock

Canadian Northern

MAISONNEUVE

Pie-IX

Angus Shops (Canadian Pacific)

d'Iberville

de Lorimier

Sutherland Pier

Tarte Pier

Laurier Pier

HOCHELAGA

Canadian Pacific

Canadian Pacific Railway yards

Papineau

Saint-Hubert

Saint-Denis

Ontario

Sainte-Catherine

Dorchester

Craig

ST LAWRENCE RIVER

SAINT-JEAN-BAPTISTE

Laurier

du Mont-Royal

Saint-Laurent

Park

Mount Royal Park

Mount Royal Cemetery (Protestant)

University

de Bleury

McGill

See detail.

Pine

Peel

Mountain

Sherbrooke

Guy

-des-Neiges

William

Windmill Point

Bickerdike Pier

Clarke

Atwater

Saint-Antoine

Saint-Jacques

Notre-Dame

Wellington

Victoria Bridge

STMOUNT

Centre

Grand Trunk Railway yards

VERDUN

SAINT-HENRI

Lachine Canal

Aqueduct

de l'Église

Scale 1:45 000

MONTRÉAL, 1921

WORK-FORCE

MANUFACTURING WORK-FORCE

Percentage

Other
Service
Finance
Commerce
Transportation
Construction
Manufacturing
Agriculture, forestry, fishing, mining

Total 237 760
Male 177 733
Female 60 027

Other
Chemicals and products
Printing
Wood products and paper
Tobacco
Food products

Clothing

Textiles

Leather, fur

Iron, steel, transportation equipment

Total 71 069
Male 49 126
Female 21 943

LAND USE IN THE CENTRAL AREA, 1915

Saint-Christophe

Saint-Denis

de Montigny

Viger Square

Saint-Laurent

Victoria Pier

Champ de Mars

de Bleury

Jacques Cartier Pier

Dufferin Sq.

King Edward Pier

Sainte-Catherine

Dorchester

Alexandra Pier

Craig

Saint-Jacques

Notre-Dame

Saint-Paul

McGill

0   1 000 feet

0   200 metres

Scale 1:12 000

In 1879 industrial activity was concentrated in the city itself with only limited industrial development beginning in the suburbs. The importance of the Lachine Canal as the centre of Montréal's industrialization was evident. By 1915 some decentralization of manufacturing had clearly occurred, with activity polarized in two areas – along the Lachine Canal to the west and in Hochelaga-Maisonneuve to the east – where iron and steel, transportation equipment, and textiles were manufactured. In downtown Montréal the clothing industry remained close to the immigrant labour force while printing firms stayed in the business and head-office district.

In 1915 land use in the central area was mixed in character. The area beyond the district known today as Old Montréal was predominantly residential. However, there were significant concentrations of economic activity: warehouses and wholesaling along the St Lawrence River and in the western part of Old Montréal; business offices along Saint-Jacques and Notre-Dame; and retail trade along Saint-Laurent and Sainte-Catherine.

Retail, service

Wholesale

Manufacturing

Office

Residential

Hotel, restaurant, or place of entertainment

Transportation, storage facilities

Public building

Old Montréal

THE EMERGENCE OF CORPORATE TORONTO

Authors: Gunter Gad, Deryck W. Holdsworth

By 1914 Toronto had consolidated its position as the leading industrial centre for Ontario (pl 13). Industrial growth occurred close to the city centre, along the railroad corridors, and at the outer edge of the city. The printing and later the garment industry moved west from the King/Bay area to Spadina Avenue; engineering and transportation-equipment firms expanded along the railroad belts; and meat-packing and other food-processing industries dominated the city's northwest corner. Significant expansion occurred at the edges of the central business district. Substantial blocks of land in public use for most of the 19th century became sites for railroad freight yards, factories, and warehouses. As King Street was transformed from the city's specialty retail street into a canyon of Edwardian office towers, Yonge and Queen, where the rapidly expanding Eaton's and Simpson's department stores were located, became the new focus for retailing. Increasingly serving national markets (pl 52) and relying to some extent on their own manufacturing, Eaton's and Simpson's developed large mail-order operations and factories which, in the case of Eaton's, were adjacent to the retail store.

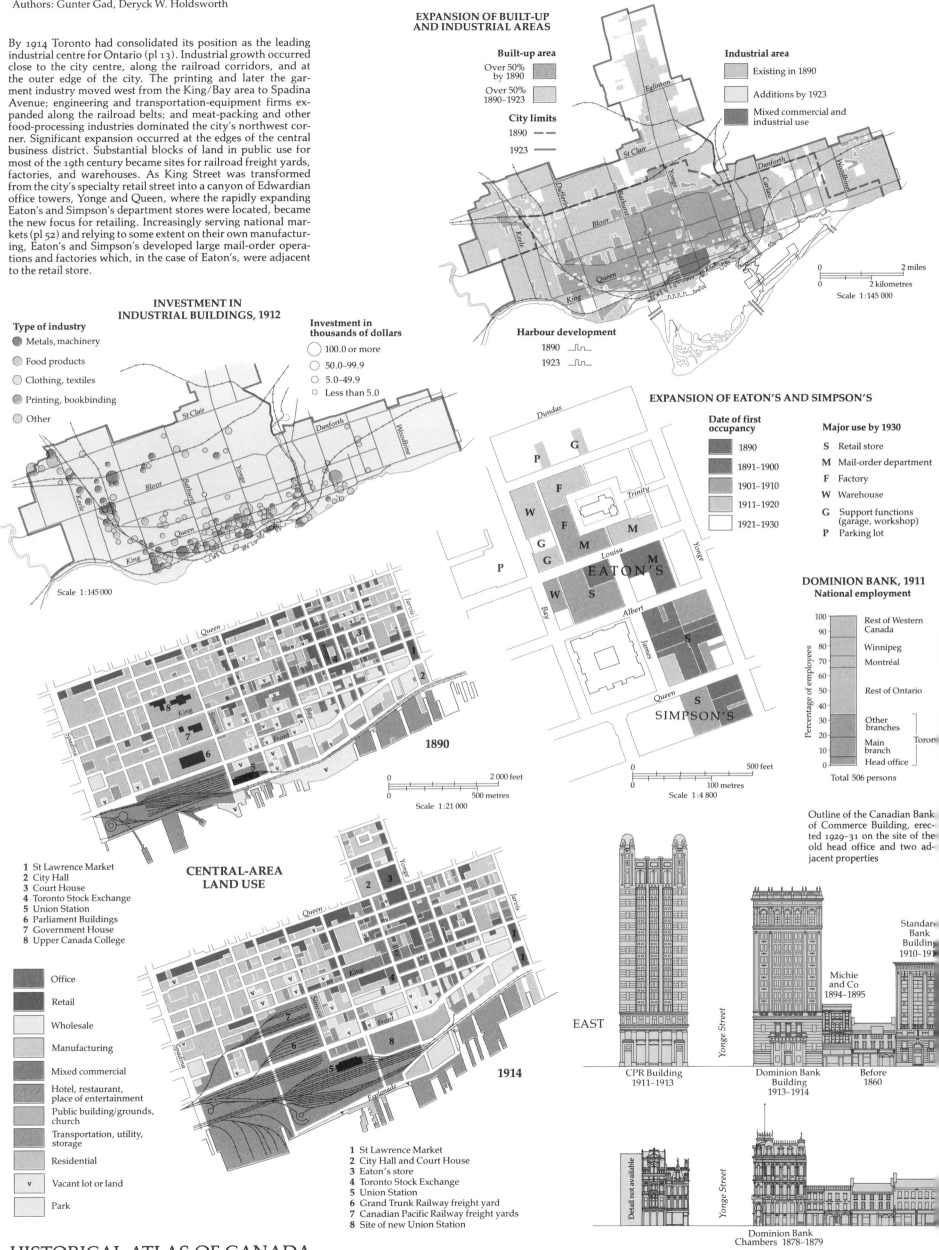

EXPANSION OF BUILT-UP AND INDUSTRIAL AREAS

Built-up area
- Over 50% by 1890
- Over 50% 1890–1923

City limits
- 1890 – – –
- 1923 ——

Industrial area
- Existing in 1890
- Additions by 1923
- Mixed commercial and industrial use

0   2 miles
0   2 kilometres
Scale 1:145 000

Harbour development
- 1890
- 1923

INVESTMENT IN INDUSTRIAL BUILDINGS, 1912

Type of industry
- Metals, machinery
- Food products
- Clothing, textiles
- Printing, bookbinding
- Other

Investment in thousands of dollars
- 100.0 or more
- 50.0–99.9
- 5.0–49.9
- Less than 5.0

Scale 1:145 000

EXPANSION OF EATON'S AND SIMPSON'S

Date of first occupancy
- 1890
- 1891–1900
- 1901–1910
- 1911–1920
- 1921–1930

Major use by 1930
- S   Retail store
- M   Mail-order department
- F   Factory
- W   Warehouse
- G   Support functions (garage, workshop)
- P   Parking lot

EATON'S

SIMPSON'S

0   500 feet
0   100 metres
Scale 1:4 800

DOMINION BANK, 1911
National employment

Percentage of employees
- Rest of Western Canada
- Winnipeg
- Montréal
- Rest of Ontario
- Other branches
- Main branch — Toronto
- Head office

Total 506 persons

Outline of the Canadian Bank of Commerce Building, erected 1929–31 on the site of the old head office and two adjacent properties

1890

0   2 000 feet
0   500 metres
Scale 1:21 000

1 St Lawrence Market
2 City Hall
3 Court House
4 Toronto Stock Exchange
5 Union Station
6 Parliament Buildings
7 Government House
8 Upper Canada College

CENTRAL-AREA LAND USE

- Office
- Retail
- Wholesale
- Manufacturing
- Mixed commercial
- Hotel, restaurant, place of entertainment
- Public building/grounds, church
- Transportation, utility, storage
- Residential
- v   Vacant lot or land
- Park

1914

1 St Lawrence Market
2 City Hall and Court House
3 Eaton's store
4 Toronto Stock Exchange
5 Union Station
6 Grand Trunk Railway freight yard
7 Canadian Pacific Railway freight yards
8 Site of new Union Station

EAST

CPR Building 1911–1913

Dominion Bank Building 1913–1914

Michie and Co 1894–1895

Before 1860

Standard Bank Building 1910–19

Detail not available

Dominion Bank Chambers 1878–1879

Yonge Street

HISTORICAL ATLAS OF CANADA

PLATE 15

PRESIDENCIES AND DIRECTORSHIPS OF TORONTO'S PLUTOCRATS

Leading companies by sector	Head-office location	Assets in $millions*	Cox	Hanna	Wood	Pellatt	Lash	Mackenzie	Matthews	Nicholls	Osler	Jaffray	Morrow	Moore	Plummer	Jones	Walker	Flavelle	Mann	Mulock	Wilkie
MANUFACTURING																					
Dominion Steel	Sydney, NS/Montréal	76.6																			
Canada Cement	Montréal	31.9																			
Massey-Harris	Toronto	(30.0)																			
Steel Co of Canada	Hamilton	28.9																			
Nova Scotia Steel and Coal	New Glasgow, NS	16.8																			
Canadian General Electric	Toronto	15.5																			
Maple Leaf Milling	Toronto	6.5																			
Standard Chemical, Iron & Lumber	Toronto	6.5																			
TRANSPORTATION, UTILITIES (CANADIAN)																					
Canadian Pacific Railway	Montréal	1000.0																			
Canadian Northern Railway	Toronto	234.6																			
Grand Trunk Pacific Railway	Montréal	100.0																			
Shawinigan Water and Power	Montréal	21.1																			
Toronto Railway	Toronto	19.9																			
Winnipeg Electric Railway	Winnipeg	17.1																			
Electrical Development Co of Ontario	Toronto	(12.0)																			
Consumers' Gas Co of Toronto	Toronto	8.7																			
TRANSPORTATION, UTILITIES (FOREIGN)																					
Rio de Janeiro Tramway, Light & Power	Toronto	98.2																			
Mexico Light & Power	Toronto	48.3																			
Mexico North-Western Railway	Toronto/New York	47.9																			
Twin City Rapid Transit	Minneapolis	47.6																			
Mississippi River Power	Boston	(41.6)																			
Mexico Tramways	Toronto	37.4																			
Sao Paulo Tramway, Light & Power	Toronto	23.3																			
Mexican Northern Power	Montréal	(22.6)																			
FINANCE																					
Canadian Bank of Commerce	Toronto	233.2																			
Bank of Nova Scotia	Halifax/Toronto	80.1																			
Dominion Bank	Toronto	79.9																			
Imperial Bank	Toronto	78.0																			
Toronto General Trusts	Toronto	45.1																			
Canada Life Assurance	Toronto	44.2																			
Canada Permanent Mortgage	Toronto	30.0																			
National Trust	Toronto	28.2																			
MISCELLANEOUS																					
Bell Telephone	Montréal	27.1																			
Hudson's Bay	London, UK/Winnipeg	10.4																			
Robert Simpson	Toronto	8.2																			
Consolidated Mining & Smelting	Toronto	7.4																			

Number of positions in leading companies . . . 11 3 12 6 11 8 8 6 5 2 5 5 1 3 2 3 2 2 2
Number of positions in other companies . . . 18 24 13 17 9 11 10 12 9 9 5 5 6 4 5 3 4 3 3
Total number of positions in leading and other companies . . . **29 27 25 23 20 19 18 18 14 11 10 10 7 7 7 6 6 5 5**

Parentheses indicate estimated assets.

■ President
▨ Vice-President
□ Director

TORONTO 'PLUTOCRATS'
Identified by the *Grain Growers' Guide*, 1913
(see end notes)

INTERLOCKING DIRECTORSHIPS
Companies with Toronto plutocrats as president

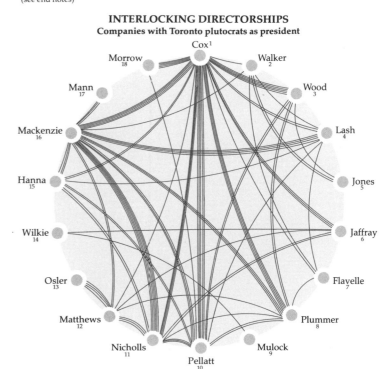

Red connecting lines indicate number of interlocking directorships. Red numbers refer to locations of offices of plutocrats on the map below left. Messrs Jones, Flavelle, and Nichols were located outside this core area. Moore (whose office was located at #19) is not shown in the diagram, INTERLOCKING DIRECTORSHIPS; see end notes.

Toronto-based enterprises became increasingly important nationally during the first decades of the 20th century. Toronto banks and insurance companies grew in stature, sometimes through acquisitions and mergers, sometimes by relocation from other cities to Toronto, to profit from new economic activity in Central Canada, the West, and the United States (pl 9). A small group of Toronto entrepreneurs created new companies to develop utilities, streetcar systems, railroad lines, real estate, and mines across the nation and beyond (pl 8). Many of these 'plutocrats' sat as directors on each others' boards.

New forms of enterprises and the concentration of business in Toronto created the need for stockbrokers, lawyers, accountants, and other services ancillary to corporate capitalism. Demand for office space led to new, taller buildings. The first structures over six storeys were built in the 1890s, and by 1928 there were more than 40 buildings over six storeys high. The core of the office district moved westward along King Street to Yonge Street and its western limit reached Bay Street. A new city hall and court house at Bay and Queen added to the westward shift of the office district. The new office towers housed more than their names suggest: the Canadian Pacific Railway (CPR) and Dominion Bank buildings contained many legal, financial, and manufacturing firms as well as their primary occupants. The Canadian Bank of Commerce outgrew its 1890 head-office building by the 1920s and its new 32-storey tower, the tallest in the British Empire, anticipated further expansion of the company; most of the tower was rented out, and the bank's main branch and head office occupied only the first seven floors.

OFFICES OF COMPANY PRESIDENTS, 1913

Scale 1:18 000

1 Court House
2 Toronto Stock Exchange

Scale 1:15 400

1890

Scale 1:15 400

1914

1 City Hall and Court House
2 Toronto Stock Exchange

OFFICES OF BANKS AND LAW FIRMS

Banks
■ Toronto head office
▲ Head office elsewhere (see pl 9)

Law firms
◎ 3 or more
◉ 2
○ 1

KING STREET, SOUTH SIDE, 1890 AND 1914

Building name and date of construction indicated where possible

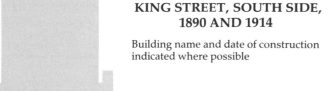

Bank of Nova Scotia 1902–1904
Colonial Building 1880

Bay Street
WEST
1914

Bank of Commerce Building 1889–1890
1880 1872
Quebec Bank 1911–1912
Trusts and Guarantee Building remodelled 1908
Union Bank Chambers 1910–1911
Bank of Toronto 1911–1913

0 ——— 100 feet

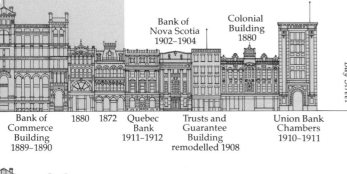

Bank of Commerce Building 1889–1890
Bay Street
Evening Telegram 1879
1890

BUILDING OCCUPANCY
King Street, south side

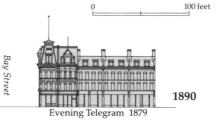

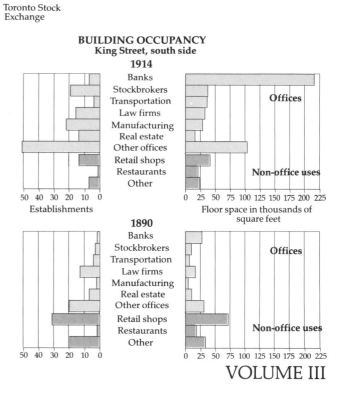

1914

Banks
Stockbrokers
Transportation
Law firms
Manufacturing
Real estate
Other offices
Retail shops
Restaurants
Other

50 40 30 20 10 0
Establishments

Offices
Non-office uses

0 25 50 75 100 125 150 175 200 225
Floor space in thousands of square feet

1890

Banks
Stockbrokers
Transportation
Law firms
Manufacturing
Real estate
Other offices
Retail shops
Restaurants
Other

50 40 30 20 10 0

Offices
Non-office uses

0 25 50 75 100 125 150 175 200 225

RESOURCE DEVELOPMENT ON THE SHIELD
Author: Susan L. Laskin

At the end of the 19th and the beginning of the 20th century the Shield was transformed from a largely undeveloped territory into a resource hinterland for Central Canada (and to some extent the United States). The changing technology in the production of pulp from wood, the new techniques of producing hydroelectric power from running water, American demand for newsprint, provincial legislation prohibiting the export of pulpwood (1900 in Ontario, 1910 in Québec), and American legislation allowing the import of duty-free newsprint (1913) gave rise to large-scale pulp and paper mills based on the Shield's spruce forests and power from its fast-flowing rivers.

New processes to refine complex ores (both separating copper and nickel and separating out gold), new techniques of producing hydroelectric power, demand for minerals in the growing industrial economies of Central Canada and the United States, and the discovery of silver- and gold-bearing veins of rock produced a mining boom in northern Ontario.

By the late 1920s the heavy investment in the pulp and paper industry of the late 1910s and early 1920s was beginning to create overcapacity (pl 40). The enormous power potential of the Shield was confirmed in the establishment of an American-controlled aluminum smelter at Arvida based on imported bauxite and a planned hydroelectric capacity of 800 000 hp. The number of head offices of mining companies located in Toronto confirmed Toronto's pre-eminent position in developing the Shield's mining frontier.

SILVER SHIPMENTS

Value in millions of dollars / Total number of producing mines

Other / Cobalt area

A Northern Silver Mine, Franklin Carmichael, 1930

Courtesy of McMichael Canadian Art Collection, gift of Mrs. A. J. Latner, 1971.9.

RESOURCE DEVELOPMENT, 1928

Edge of the Precambrian Shield
Railway
Proposed railway
Road
Generalized agricultural area

Scale 1:5 015 000

0   100 miles
0   100 kilometres

CENTRAL MANITOBA MINES AREA

Lake Winnipeg
Pine Falls
Au
Red Lake
Au
Cu Ni Li
MANITOBA
Winnipeg
Kenora
Dryden
Au
Lac Seul
Cu
Au
Fe
CNR
ONTARIO
Au
Fe
Au
Lake Nipigon
Au
Fe
Au
CPR
CANADA / UNITED STATES
Lake of the Woods
Au
CPR
Hearst
Albany
Nipigon
Port Arthur
Ag
Pb
Zn
Fort William
Au
Atikokan
CNR
Fe
Fort Frances
Fe
Ag
Fe
Algoma Central Railway
Fe
Au
Michipicoten
SUDBURY AREA
Sault Ste Marie
Pb
Zn Cu
Bruce Mines

PLAN OF A MODEL TOWNSITE KAPUSKASING, August 1922

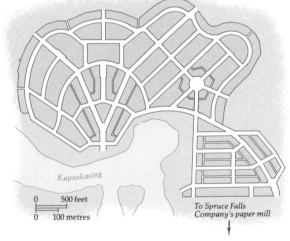

Kapuskasing

0   500 feet
0   100 metres

To Spruce Falls Company's paper mill

In the late 19th century settlement around small-scale mining operations was unplanned and growth was haphazard. When later resource developments required large-scale capital investment, companies increasingly built their own towns. The layout of these townsites created spatial segregation based on job status at the workplace. In Kapuskasing, the first community on the Shield where a provincial government became involved in planning, curvilinear streets, attention to topography, and other aspects of contemporary British garden-city planning were adopted.

Resource communities on the Shield, like Copper Cliff, depended on a single industry and attracted immigrant labour. Sudbury initially developed as a service centre for the surrounding mining communities and its work-force and ethnic composition were more diversified.

THE SUDBURY AREA

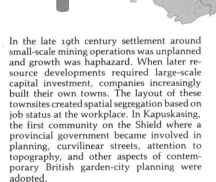

Levack
Zn
Pb
Ni
Cu
Frood
Garson
SUDBURY
Coniston
Creighton
Pt
Copper Cliff

Scale 1:1 200 000

ETHNIC ORIGIN OF POPULATION, 1931

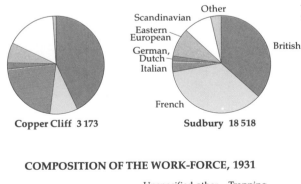

Other
Scandinavian
Eastern European
German, Dutch
Italian
British
French

Copper Cliff 3 173   **Sudbury 18 518**

COMPOSITION OF THE WORK-FORCE, 1931

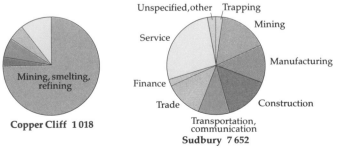

Unspecified, other   Trapping
Mining
Service
Manufacturing
Finance
Trade
Construction
Transportation, communication

Mining, smelting, refining

Copper Cliff 1 018   **Sudbury 7 652**

SMELTING IN THE SUDBURY AREA

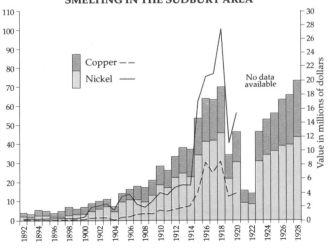

Thousands of tons / Value in millions of dollars

Copper ---
Nickel

No data available

Mineral production

△ Major mine
◇ Smelter
♠ Smelter and refinery

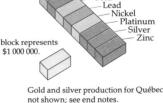

Cobalt
Copper
Gold
Lead
Nickel
Platinum
Silver
Zinc

One block represents $1 000 000.

Gold and silver production for Québec not shown; see end notes.

HISTORICAL ATLAS OF CANADA

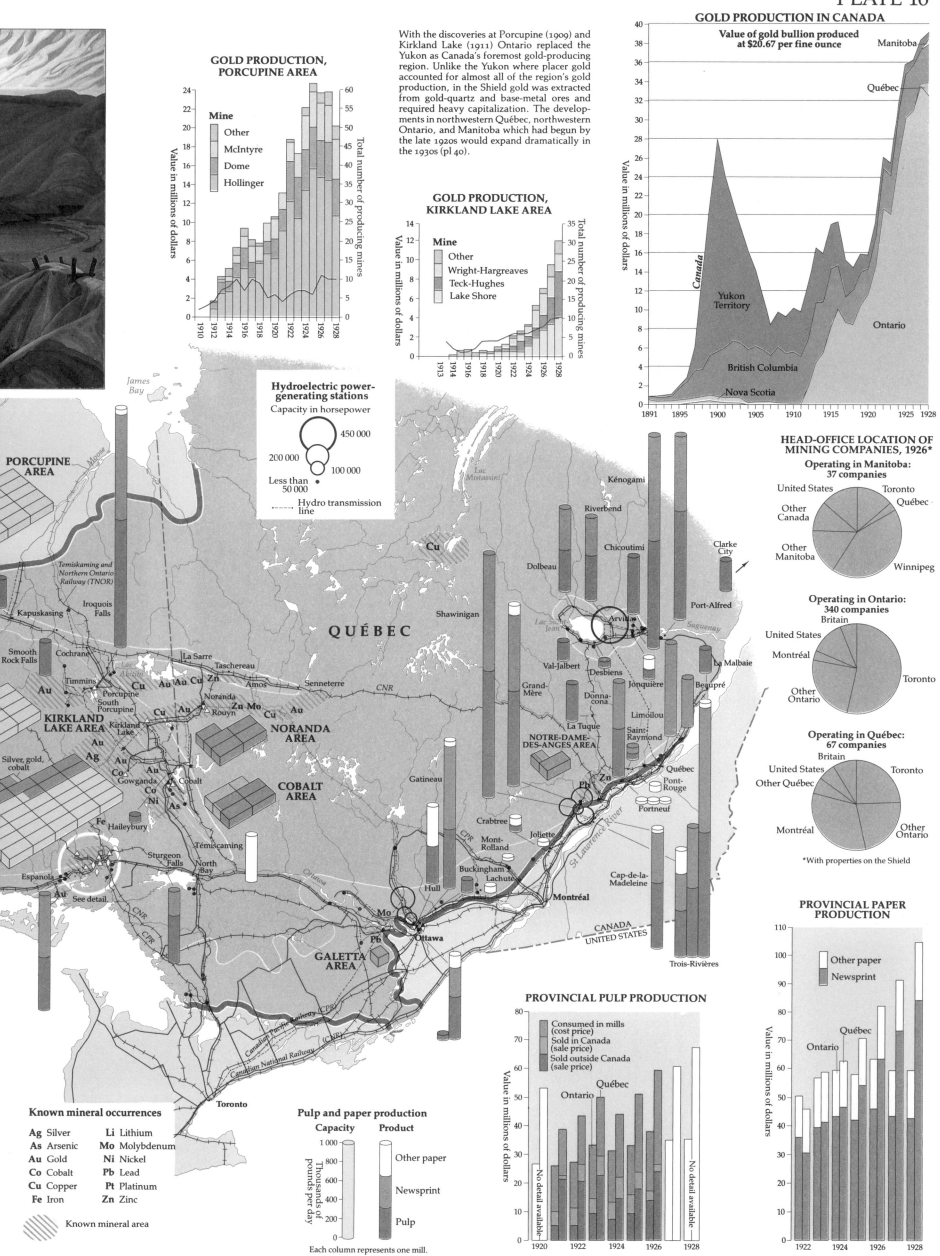

PLATE 16

GOLD PRODUCTION IN CANADA

Value of gold bullion produced at $20.67 per fine ounce

Manitoba
Québec
Canada
Yukon Territory
Ontario
British Columbia
Nova Scotia

GOLD PRODUCTION, PORCUPINE AREA

Mine
- Other
- McIntyre
- Dome
- Hollinger

Value in millions of dollars
Total number of producing mines

With the discoveries at Porcupine (1909) and Kirkland Lake (1911) Ontario replaced the Yukon as Canada's foremost gold-producing region. Unlike the Yukon where placer gold accounted for almost all of the region's gold production, in the Shield gold was extracted from gold-quartz and base-metal ores and required heavy capitalization. The developments in northwestern Québec, northwestern Ontario, and Manitoba which had begun by the late 1920s would expand dramatically in the 1930s (pl 40).

GOLD PRODUCTION, KIRKLAND LAKE AREA

Mine
- Other
- Wright-Hargreaves
- Teck-Hughes
- Lake Shore

Value in millions of dollars
Total number of producing mines

Hydroelectric power-generating stations
Capacity in horsepower
450 000
200 000
100 000
Less than 50 000
- - - Hydro transmission line

HEAD-OFFICE LOCATION OF MINING COMPANIES, 1926*

Operating in Manitoba: 37 companies
United States, Toronto, Québec, Other Canada, Other Manitoba, Winnipeg

Operating in Ontario: 340 companies
Britain, United States, Montréal, Other Ontario, Toronto

Operating in Québec: 67 companies
Britain, United States, Toronto, Other Québec, Montréal, Other Ontario

*With properties on the Shield

PROVINCIAL PAPER PRODUCTION

- Other paper
- Newsprint

Value in millions of dollars

Ontario
Québec

PROVINCIAL PULP PRODUCTION

- Consumed in mills (cost price)
- Sold in Canada (sale price)
- Sold outside Canada (sale price)

Ontario
Québec
No detail available

Value in millions of dollars

Known mineral occurrences

Ag Silver		**Li** Lithium	
As Arsenic		**Mo** Molybdenum	
Au Gold		**Ni** Nickel	
Co Cobalt		**Pb** Lead	
Cu Copper		**Pt** Platinum	
Fe Iron		**Zn** Zinc	

Known mineral area

Pulp and paper production
Capacity — Thousands of pounds per day
Product
- Other paper
- Newsprint
- Pulp

Each column represents one mill.

Map labels: James Bay, PORCUPINE AREA, Moose, Temiskaming and Northern Ontario Railway (TNOR), Kapuskasing, Iroquois Falls, Cochrane, Smooth Rock Falls, Timmins, Porcupine, South Porcupine, KIRKLAND LAKE AREA, Kirkland Lake, Lac Abitibi, La Sarre, Taschereau, Amos, Senneterre, Noranda, Rouyn, NORANDA AREA, Silver, gold, cobalt, Gowganda, Cobalt, COBALT AREA, Haileybury, Témiscaming, Sturgeon Falls, North Bay, Espanola, See detail, QUÉBEC, Kénogami, Riverbend, Chicoutimi, Dolbeau, Clarke City, Port-Alfred, Shawinigan, Lac Saint-Jean, Arvida, Saguenay, La Malbaie, Val-Jalbert, Desbiens, Jonquière, Beaupré, Grand-Mère, Donnacona, Limoilou, Saint-Raymond, La Tuque, NOTRE-DAME-DES-ANGES AREA, Québec, Pont-Rouge, Portneuf, Gatineau, Crabtree, Mont-Rolland, Joliette, Buckingham, Lachute, Hull, Cap-de-la-Madeleine, Montréal, GALETTA AREA, Ottawa, Trois-Rivières, CANADA, UNITED STATES, St Lawrence River, Ottawa, CPR, CNR, Canadian Pacific Railway (CPR), Canadian National Railway (CNR), Toronto, Lac Mistassini

VOLUME III

PEOPLING THE PRAIRIES
Authors: William J. Carlyle, John C. Lehr, G.E. Mills (homesteaders' shelter)

The Canadian Prairies were seen as the Last Best West: their settlement marked the end of an era of agricultural settlement that had brought millions of homesteaders to the North American plains since the 1860s. At the margins of agriculture, in terms of both climate and soils, the Prairies could be settled only after effective seed types and transportation systems had been developed. Settlement followed the parkland belt northwest from Winnipeg towards Edmonton, and between Edmonton and Calgary, filling in the margins to the south and north in the 1920s. Land was surveyed into 160-acre parcels by the Dominion Lands Survey. The government and other agencies, including railroad companies, the Hudson's Bay Company, and land colonization companies, disposed of the land to settlers. Not all the land was appropriate for farming, and in many townships outmigration began during the 1920s.

URBAN AND RURAL POPULATION

Millions of persons

2.4, 2.2, 2.0, 1.8, 1.6, 1.4, 1.2, 1.0, 0.8, 0.6, 0.4, 0.2, 0

Rural

Urban

1891 1901 1911 1921 1931

POPULATION OF THE 'NORTH WEST,' 1904
Ethnic origin by township

- Canadian of British origin
- French Canadian and French
- Recent colonies of British origin
- American (including Canadians repatriated from the United States)
- German
- Scandinavian
- Icelandic
- Ukrainian (Galician and Bukovynian)

ETHNIC ORIGIN, 1931

Native Indian Other

Other European

French

Scandinavian

Ukrainian

German

British

Railway
Proposed railway

Scale 1:5 000 000

Townships predominantly settled by Mormons from Utah and Idaho

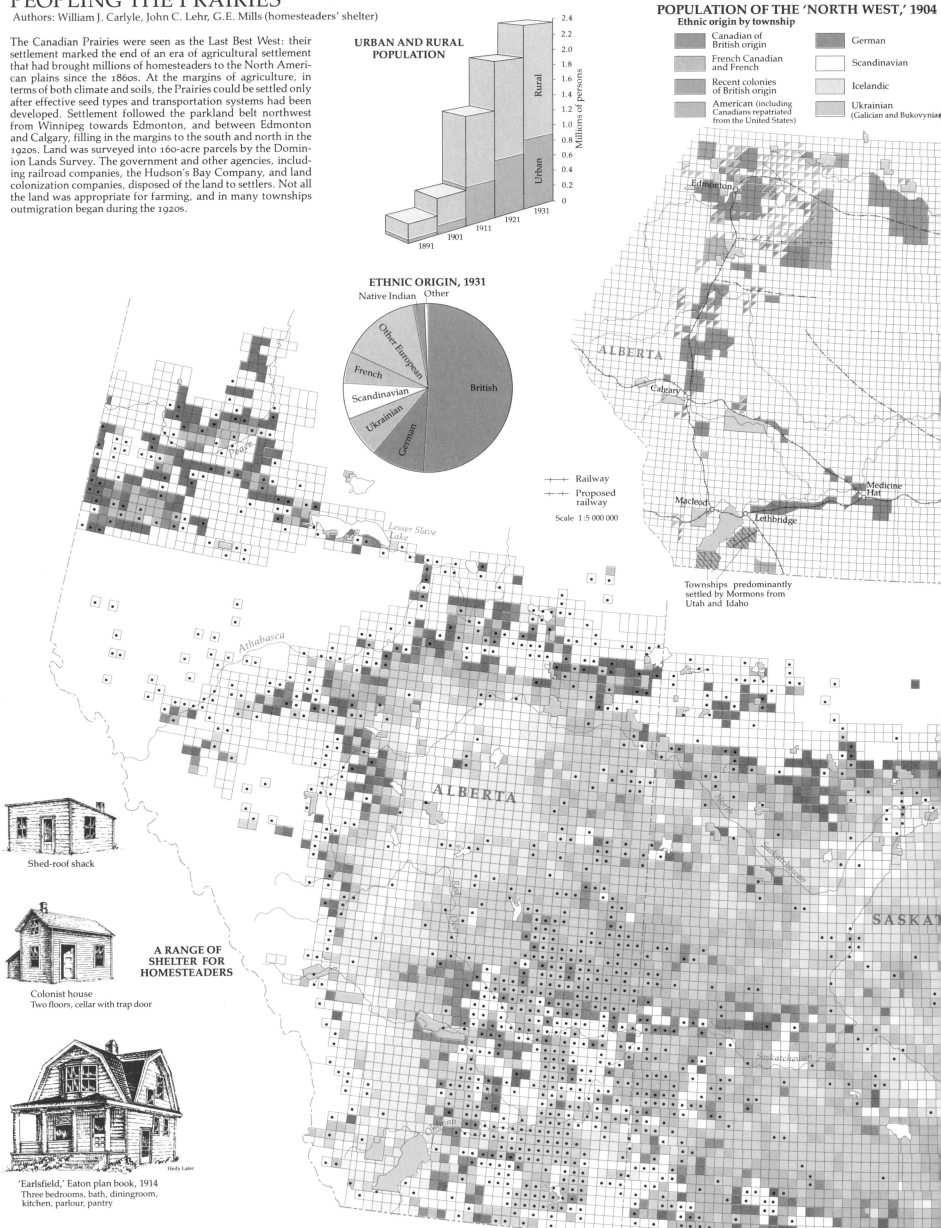

Edmonton

ALBERTA

Calgary

Medicine Hat

Macleod

Lethbridge

Peace

Lesser Slave Lake

Athabasca

ALBERTA

Red Deer

North Saskatchewan

Saskatchewan

SASKAT

Bow

Shed-roof shack

A RANGE OF SHELTER FOR HOMESTEADERS

Colonist house
Two floors, cellar with trap door

Hedy Later

'Earlsfield,' Eaton plan book, 1914
Three bedrooms, bath, diningroom, kitchen, parlour, pantry

HISTORICAL ATLAS OF CANADA

PLATE 17

Doukhobor

Other European

Indian Reserve

Métis (mixed French or
Scottish and native Indian)

Townships are coloured according to approximate proportion of land taken up for homesteading. Based on federal Department of
Interior map: see end notes.

Settlers of British origin from Ontario were among the first to
move into the Manitoba lowlands, and subsequently into the
other two provinces (pl 27). By 1904 distinctive groups of other
migrants had created ethnic enclaves. Group settlement
schemes were more prevalent than had been the case in the
American experience, in part because of strong government
and railroad recruitment practices. Chain migration also
strengthened the tendency of settlers to seek out familiar social,
cultural, and religious milieux, thereby reinforcing the development of ethnically homogeneous blocs.

Distinctive clusters of European, American, and American-
born European groups were to be found. Language, folk
customs, and ethnic landscapes persisted despite the geometry
of the homestead land system and the necessity for individual
farmsteads that went against European nucleated farm-village
settlement practices. In the case of Ukrainian settlement, Gali-
cians and Bukovynians usually settled separately in the same
general areas. Thus old-world distinctions between them were
perpetuated in the landscape of the Canadian West. Although
adjustment, expansion, and infilling took place after 1904, the
early distribution of ethnic groups in rural areas persisted.

UKRAINIAN SETTLEMENT IN SOUTHERN MANITOBA, 1901

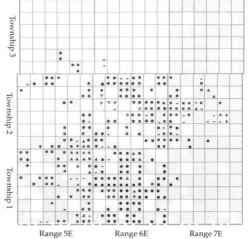

Place of origin

Bukovyna
• Chernivci District
▪ Zastavna District

Galicia
✶ Borshchiv District
▲ Husiatyn District
▽ Zalishchyky District
▿ Kolomya District

- Ukrainian, province of
origin not determined

Not open for homestead
settlement, 1895–1901

Range 5E   Range 6E   Range 7E

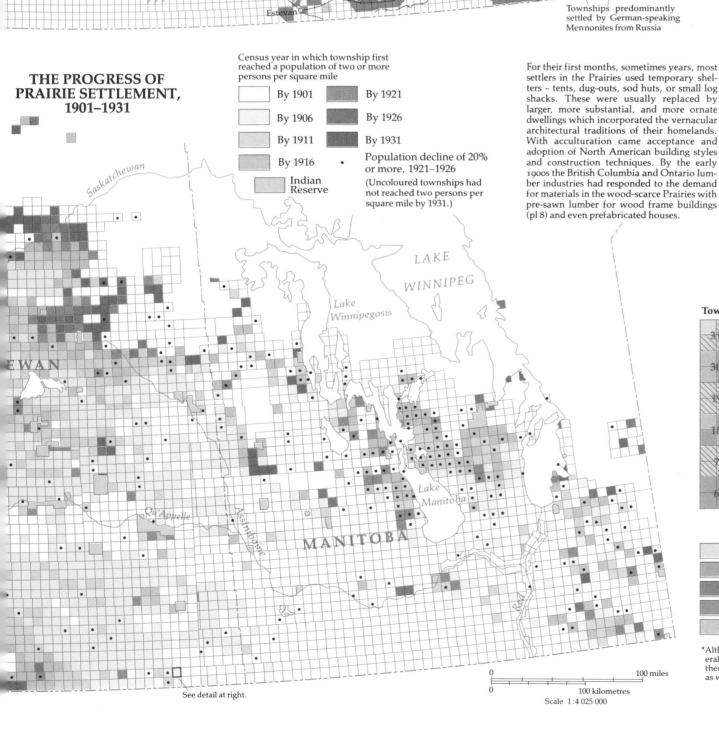

See detail
above.

Townships predominantly
settled by German-speaking
Mennonites from Russia

House built by
Bukovynian settler

**UKRAINIAN
SETTLERS' HOUSES**

**THE PROGRESS OF
PRAIRIE SETTLEMENT,
1901–1931**

Census year in which township first
reached a population of two or more
persons per square mile

By 1901   By 1921

By 1906   By 1926

By 1911   By 1931

By 1916   • Population decline of 20%
            or more, 1921–1926

Indian   (Uncoloured townships had
Reserve   not reached two persons per
           square mile by 1931.)

For their first months, sometimes years, most
settlers in the Prairies used temporary shel-
ters – tents, dug-outs, sod huts, or small log
shacks. These were usually replaced by
larger, more substantial, and more ornate
dwellings which incorporated the vernacular
architectural traditions of their homelands.
With acculturation came acceptance and
adoption of North American building styles
and construction techniques. By the early
1900s the British Columbia and Ontario lumber industries had responded to the demand
for materials in the wood-scarce Prairies with
pre-sawn lumber for wood frame buildings
(pl 8) and even prefabricated houses.

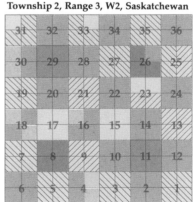

Hedy Later

House built by
Galician settler

**DISPOSITION OF LAND
Township 2, Range 3, W2, Saskatchewan**

31	32	33	34	35	36
30	29	28	27	26	25
19	20	21	22	23	24
18	17	16	15	14	13
7	8	9	10	11	12
6	5	4	3	2	1

Original disposition of land

Railway   Sold by Crown
                   to individuals*

Homestead   **Railway lands sold
                   (where known) to:**

Hudson's Bay   American land
Company   companies

School land   Individual
                   Americans

Special grant to   Individual
Canadian Land Co   Canadians

*Although no pre-emptions are shown here, sev-
eral quarter-sections were pre-empted by settlers,
then later cancelled and disposed of otherwise,
as with NE4.

See detail at right.

0   100 miles

0   100 kilometres
                     Scale 1:4 025 000

PRAIRIE AGRICULTURE

Authors: Philip D. Keddie, Simon Evans (ranching)

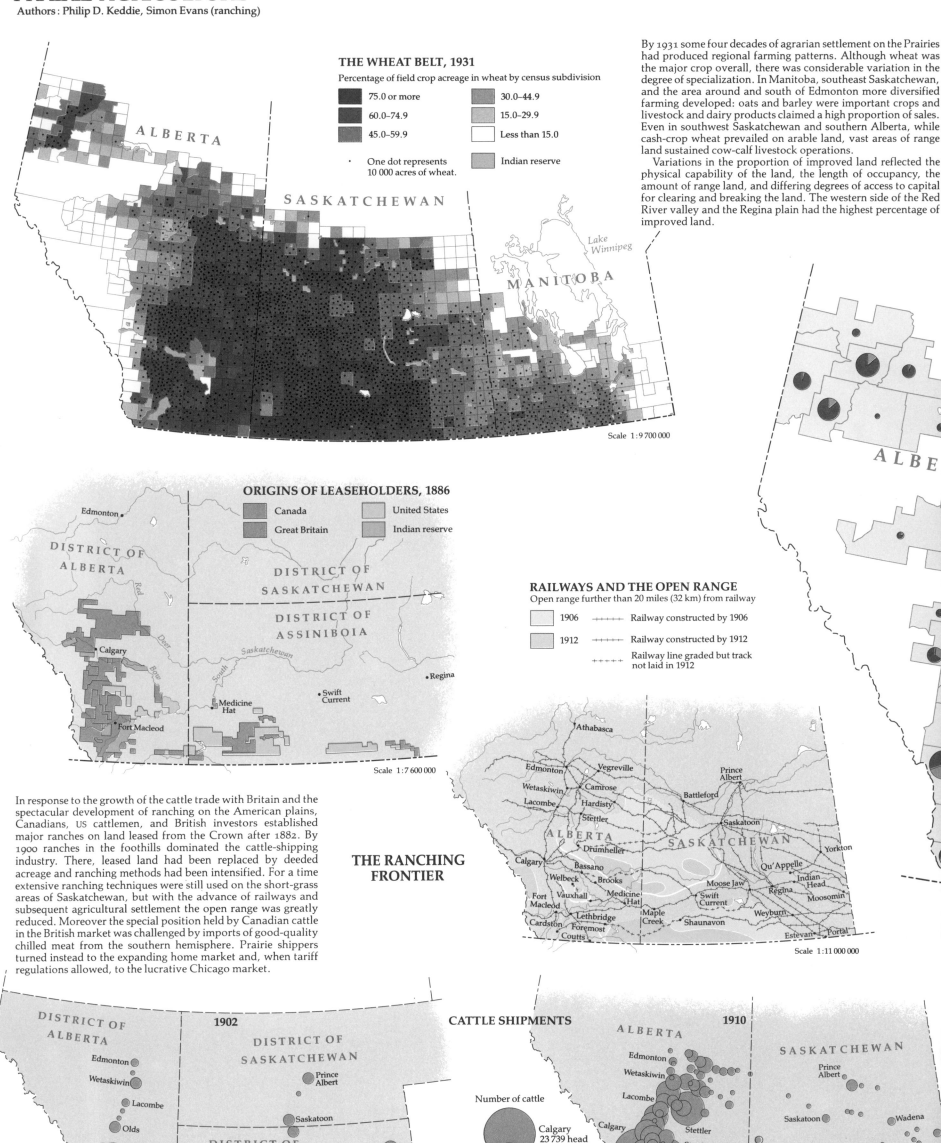

THE WHEAT BELT, 1931

Percentage of field crop acreage in wheat by census subdivision

- 75.0 or more
- 60.0–74.9
- 45.0–59.9
- 30.0–44.9
- 15.0–29.9
- Less than 15.0
- Indian reserve

· One dot represents 10 000 acres of wheat.

ALBERTA

SASKATCHEWAN

Lake Winnipeg

MANITOBA

Scale 1:9 700 000

By 1931 some four decades of agrarian settlement on the Prairies had produced regional farming patterns. Although wheat was the major crop overall, there was considerable variation in the degree of specialization. In Manitoba, southeast Saskatchewan, and the area around and south of Edmonton more diversified farming developed: oats and barley were important crops and livestock and dairy products claimed a high proportion of sales. Even in southwest Saskatchewan and southern Alberta, while cash-crop wheat prevailed on arable land, vast areas of range land sustained cow-calf livestock operations.

Variations in the proportion of improved land reflected the physical capability of the land, the length of occupancy, the amount of range land, and differing degrees of access to capital for clearing and breaking the land. The western side of the Red River valley and the Regina plain had the highest percentage of improved land.

ORIGINS OF LEASEHOLDERS, 1886

- Canada
- Great Britain
- United States
- Indian reserve

Edmonton

DISTRICT OF ALBERTA

DISTRICT OF SASKATCHEWAN

DISTRICT OF ASSINIBOIA

Red Deer

Bow

Saskatchewan

Calgary

Medicine Hat

Swift Current

Regina

Fort Macleod

Scale 1:7 600 000

RAILWAYS AND THE OPEN RANGE

Open range further than 20 miles (32 km) from railway

- 1906
- 1912
- +++++ Railway constructed by 1906
- +++++ Railway constructed by 1912
- +++++ Railway line graded but track not laid in 1912

ALBE

THE RANCHING FRONTIER

Athabasca

Edmonton   Vegreville   Prince Albert

Wetaskiwin   Camrose   Battleford

Lacombe   Hardisty   Saskatoon

Stettler

ALBERTA   Drumheller   SASKATCHEWAN   Yorkton

Calgary   Bassano   Moose Jaw   Qu'Appelle   Indian Head

Welbeck   Brooks   Swift Current   Regina   Moosomin

Fort Macleod   Vauxhall   Medicine Hat   Maple Creek   Shaunavon   Weyburn

Lethbridge   Cardston   Foremost   Estevan   Portal

Coutts

Scale 1:11 000 000

In response to the growth of the cattle trade with Britain and the spectacular development of ranching on the American plains, Canadians, US cattlemen, and British investors established major ranches on land leased from the Crown after 1882. By 1900 ranches in the foothills dominated the cattle-shipping industry. There, leased land had been replaced by deeded acreage and ranching methods had been intensified. For a time extensive ranching techniques were still used on the short-grass areas of Saskatchewan, but with the advance of railways and subsequent agricultural settlement the open range was greatly reduced. Moreover the special position held by Canadian cattle in the British market was challenged by imports of good-quality chilled meat from the southern hemisphere. Prairie shippers turned instead to the expanding home market and, when tariff regulations allowed, to the lucrative Chicago market.

CATTLE SHIPMENTS

1902

DISTRICT OF ALBERTA   DISTRICT OF SASKATCHEWAN

Edmonton   Prince Albert

Wetaskiwin

Lacombe   Saskatoon

Olds   Yorkton

Calgary   DISTRICT OF ASSINIBOIA   Qu'Appelle

Gleichen   Regina

High River   Medicine Hat   Swift Current

Fort Macleod   Maple Creek

Lethbridge

Scale 1:11 000 000

Number of cattle

Calgary 23 739 head

- 8 000–12 000
- 4 000–7 999
- 2 000–3 999
- 1 000–1 999
- 500–999
- 100–499

1910

ALBERTA   SASKATCHEWAN

Edmonton   Prince Albert

Wetaskiwin

Lacombe   Saskatoon

Calgary   Wadena

Stettler

Strathmore

Gleichen   Brooks   Qu'Appelle

High River

Fort Macleod   Crane Lake

Medicine Hat   Maple Creek

Coutts

Scale 1:11 000 000

HISTORICAL ATLAS OF CANADA

PLATE 18

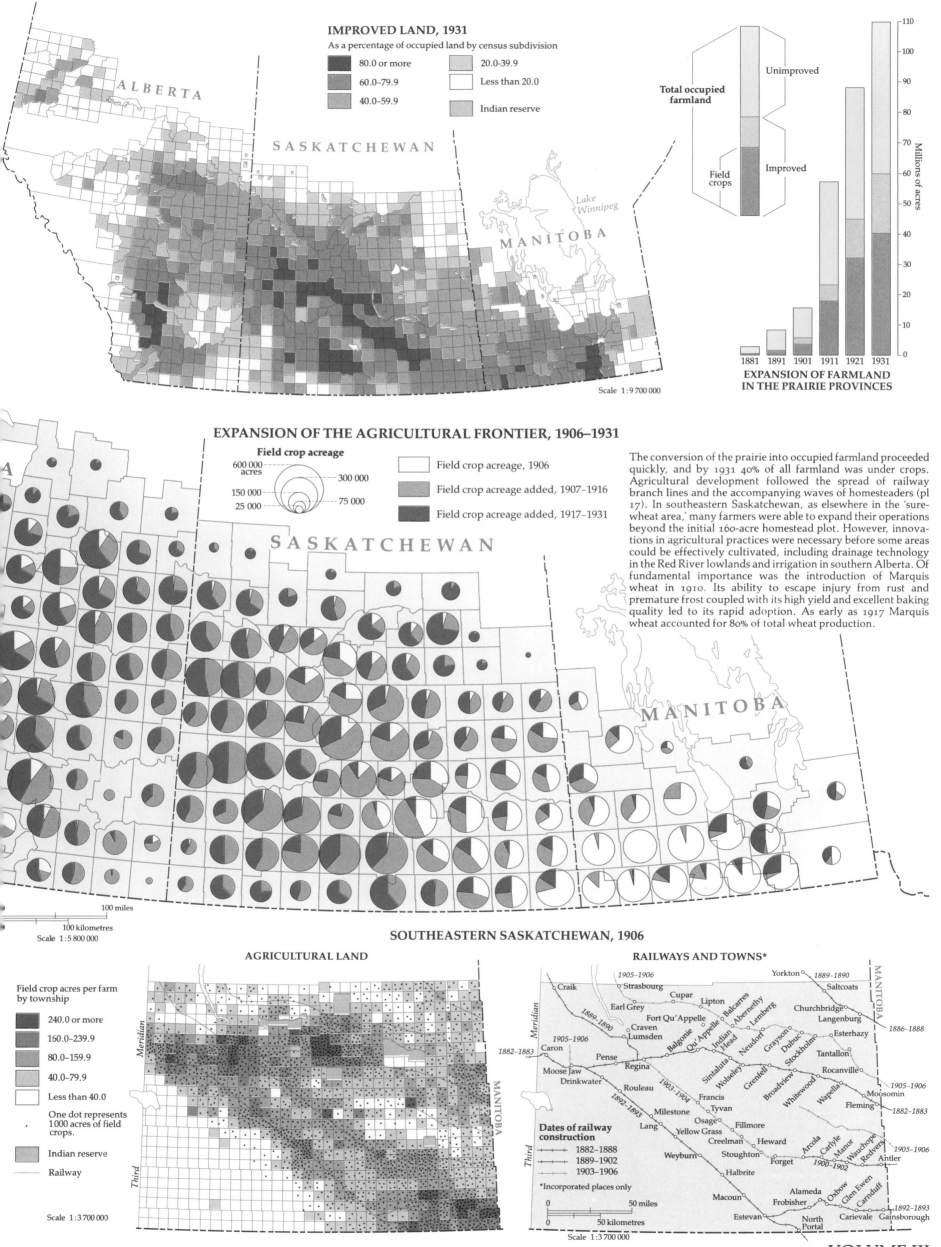

IMPROVED LAND, 1931

As a percentage of occupied land by census subdivision

- 80.0 or more
- 60.0–79.9
- 40.0–59.9
- 20.0–39.9
- Less than 20.0
- Indian reserve

ALBERTA

SASKATCHEWAN

MANITOBA

Lake Winnipeg

Scale 1:9 700 000

Total occupied farmland

Field crops

Unimproved

Improved

Millions of acres

1881 1891 1901 1911 1921 1931

EXPANSION OF FARMLAND IN THE PRAIRIE PROVINCES

EXPANSION OF THE AGRICULTURAL FRONTIER, 1906–1931

Field crop acreage

600 000 acres
300 000
150 000
75 000
25 000

- Field crop acreage, 1906
- Field crop acreage added, 1907–1916
- Field crop acreage added, 1917–1931

SASKATCHEWAN

MANITOBA

The conversion of the prairie into occupied farmland proceeded quickly, and by 1931 40% of all farmland was under crops. Agricultural development followed the spread of railway branch lines and the accompanying waves of homesteaders (pl 17). In southeastern Saskatchewan, as elsewhere in the 'sure-wheat area,' many farmers were able to expand their operations beyond the initial 160-acre homestead plot. However, innovations in agricultural practices were necessary before some areas could be effectively cultivated, including drainage technology in the Red River lowlands and irrigation in southern Alberta. Of fundamental importance was the introduction of Marquis wheat in 1910. Its ability to escape injury from rust and premature frost coupled with its high yield and excellent baking quality led to its rapid adoption. As early as 1917 Marquis wheat accounted for 80% of total wheat production.

100 miles

100 kilometres

Scale 1:5 800 000

SOUTHEASTERN SASKATCHEWAN, 1906

AGRICULTURAL LAND

Field crop acres per farm by township

- 240.0 or more
- 160.0–239.9
- 80.0–159.9
- 40.0–79.9
- Less than 40.0

· One dot represents 1 000 acres of field crops.

- Indian reserve
- Railway

Scale 1:3 700 000

Meridian

Third

MANITOBA

RAILWAYS AND TOWNS*

1905–1906
Craik
Strasbourg
Cupar
Lipton
Earl Grey
Fort Qu'Appelle
Balcarres
Abernethy
Lemberg
Craven
Balgonie
Indian Head
Neudorf
Grayson
Dubuc
Lumsden
Qu'Appelle
Wolseley
Sintaluta
Grenfell
Stockholm
Caron
Pense
Broadview
Whitewood
Moose Jaw
Regina
Drinkwater
Rouleau
Francis
Milestone
Osage
Tyvan
Fillmore
Lang
Yellow Grass
Heward
Creelman
Weyburn
Stoughton
Forget
Arcola
Carlyle
Manor
Halbrite
Wauchope
Redvers
Antler
Macoun
Alameda
Frobisher
Oxbow
Glen Ewen
Carnduff
North Portal
Estevan
Carievale
Gainsborough

Yorkton
1889–1890
Saltcoats
Churchbridge
Langenburg
Esterhazy
Tantallon
Rocanville
Moosomin
Wapella
Fleming

MANITOBA

1889–1890
1886–1888
1905–1906
1882–1883
1905–1906
1882–1883
1900–1902
1905–1906
1892–1893

1905–1906
1889–1902
1882–1883
1903–1904
1892–1893

Meridian

Third

Dates of railway construction
- 1882–1888
- 1889–1902
- 1903–1906

*Incorporated places only

0   50 miles
0   50 kilometres

Scale 1:3 700 000

THE GRAIN-HANDLING SYSTEM

Authors: John C. Everitt, Donna Shimamura Everitt, Susan L. Laskin (the Lakehead)

Prairie farmers encountered the world market at the grain elevators in their nearest hamlet. These elevators, combined with and dependent upon the rapidly developing railway system, enabled the vast amounts of grain that were grown in the Prairies to be marketed in a relatively cheap and efficient manner. Within a short period of time, and partly as a result of amalgamations, these elevators became increasingly controlled by groups of Winnipeg-based individuals who owned 'line-elevator' companies, the first being organized in 1893. Many more elevators were owned by the major milling companies which used lines of elevators to obtain choice grain for flour production.

The major elevator syndicates, many American owned and/or operated, soon joined together as an openly run cartel, or a 'syndicate of syndicates.' Farmers believed the cartel was 'fleecing' them, and their protests eventually led to government action and farmer-owned elevator companies. After several unsuccessful attempts by farmers to organize the handling of grain, the Grain Growers Grain Company (the United Grain Growers after 1916) was begun in 1906, to be followed by the provincially organized wheat pools in the 1920s. The pools were soon responsible for marketing over half of the crop.

Elevator hamlets, spaced some 11 km (7 miles) apart on myriad railroad branch lines and thus within one day's wagon distance for farmers, were at the heart of the Prairie settlement system. Waskada, Manitoba, exhibits many of the typical characteristics of such a settlement. From this town the grain would have been routed through the grain trade-centre of Winnipeg, and then shipped to the Lakehead for eventual export.

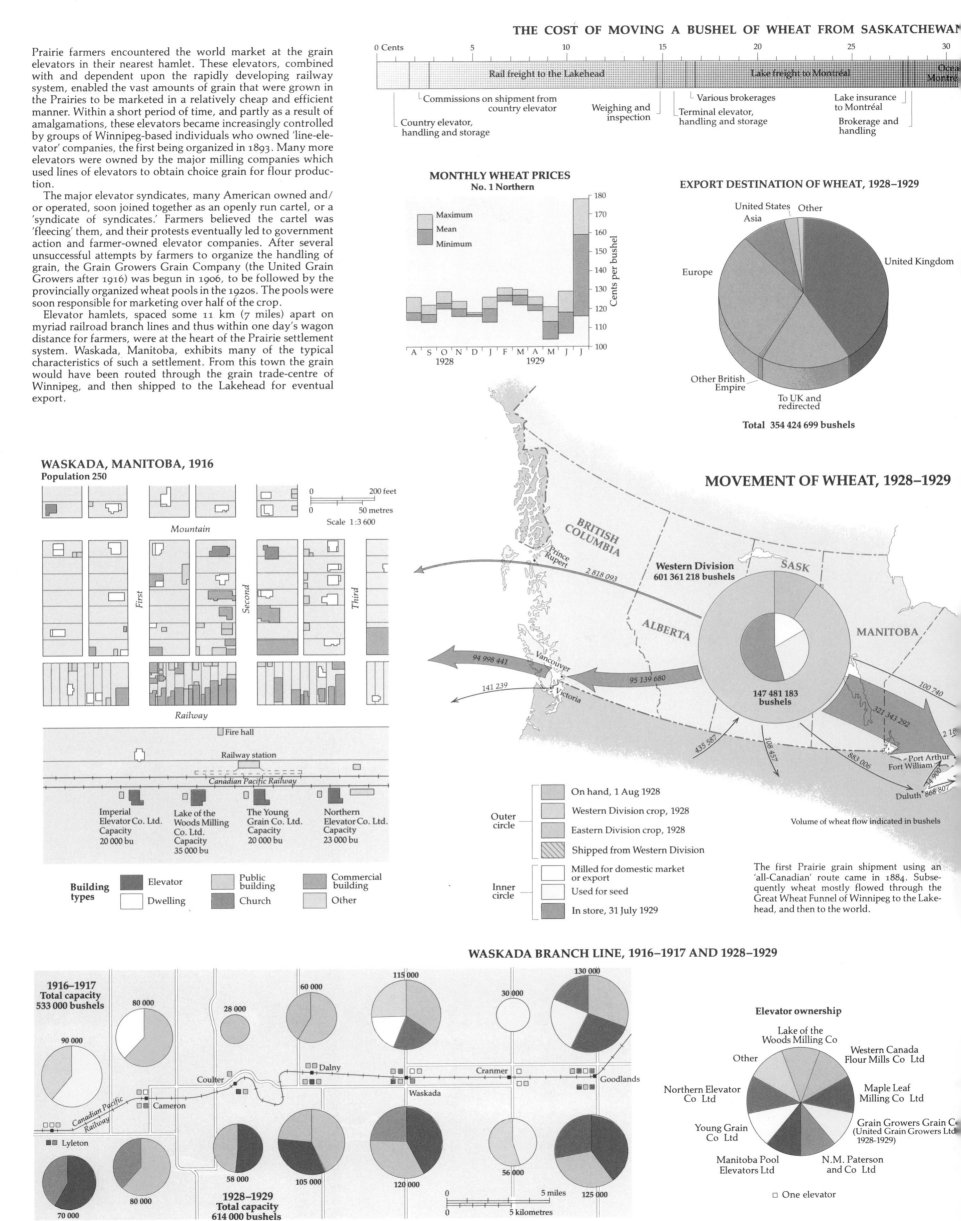

THE COST OF MOVING A BUSHEL OF WHEAT FROM SASKATCHEWAN

MONTHLY WHEAT PRICES
No. 1 Northern

Maximum
Mean
Minimum

EXPORT DESTINATION OF WHEAT, 1928–1929

United States
Asia
Other
Europe
United Kingdom
Other British Empire
To UK and redirected

Total 354 424 699 bushels

WASKADA, MANITOBA, 1916
Population 250

Mountain

First
Second
Third

Railway

Fire hall
Railway station
Canadian Pacific Railway

Imperial Elevator Co. Ltd. Capacity 20 000 bu
Lake of the Woods Milling Co. Ltd. Capacity 35 000 bu
The Young Grain Co. Ltd. Capacity 20 000 bu
Northern Elevator Co. Ltd. Capacity 23 000 bu

Building types
Elevator
Dwelling
Public building
Church
Commercial building
Other

MOVEMENT OF WHEAT, 1928–1929

BRITISH COLUMBIA
Prince Rupert
2 818 093
Western Division 601 361 218 bushels
SASK
94 998 441
95 139 680
Vancouver
141 239
Victoria
ALBERTA
MANITOBA
147 481 183 bushels
100 740
321 343 292
435 587
108 457
883 006
Port Arthur Fort William
Duluth 868 807

Volume of wheat flow indicated in bushels

Outer circle
On hand, 1 Aug 1928
Western Division crop, 1928
Eastern Division crop, 1928
Shipped from Western Division

Inner circle
Milled for domestic market or export
Used for seed
In store, 31 July 1929

The first Prairie grain shipment using an 'all-Canadian' route came in 1884. Subsequently wheat mostly flowed through the Great Wheat Funnel of Winnipeg to the Lakehead, and then to the world.

WASKADA BRANCH LINE, 1916–1917 AND 1928–1929

1916–1917 Total capacity 533 000 bushels
90 000
80 000
28 000
60 000
115 000
30 000
130 000
Canadian Pacific Railway
Coulter
Cameron
Lyleton
Dalny
Cranmer
Waskada
Goodlands
58 000
105 000
120 000
56 000
125 000
70 000
80 000
1928–1929 Total capacity 614 000 bushels

0   5 miles
0   5 kilometres
Scale 1:245 000

Elevator ownership
Lake of the Woods Milling Co
Other
Western Canada Flour Mills Co Ltd
Northern Elevator Co Ltd
Maple Leaf Milling Co Ltd
Young Grain Co Ltd
Grain Growers Grain Co (United Grain Growers Ltd 1928–1929)
Manitoba Pool Elevators Ltd
N.M. Paterson and Co Ltd

□ One elevator

HISTORICAL ATLAS OF CANADA

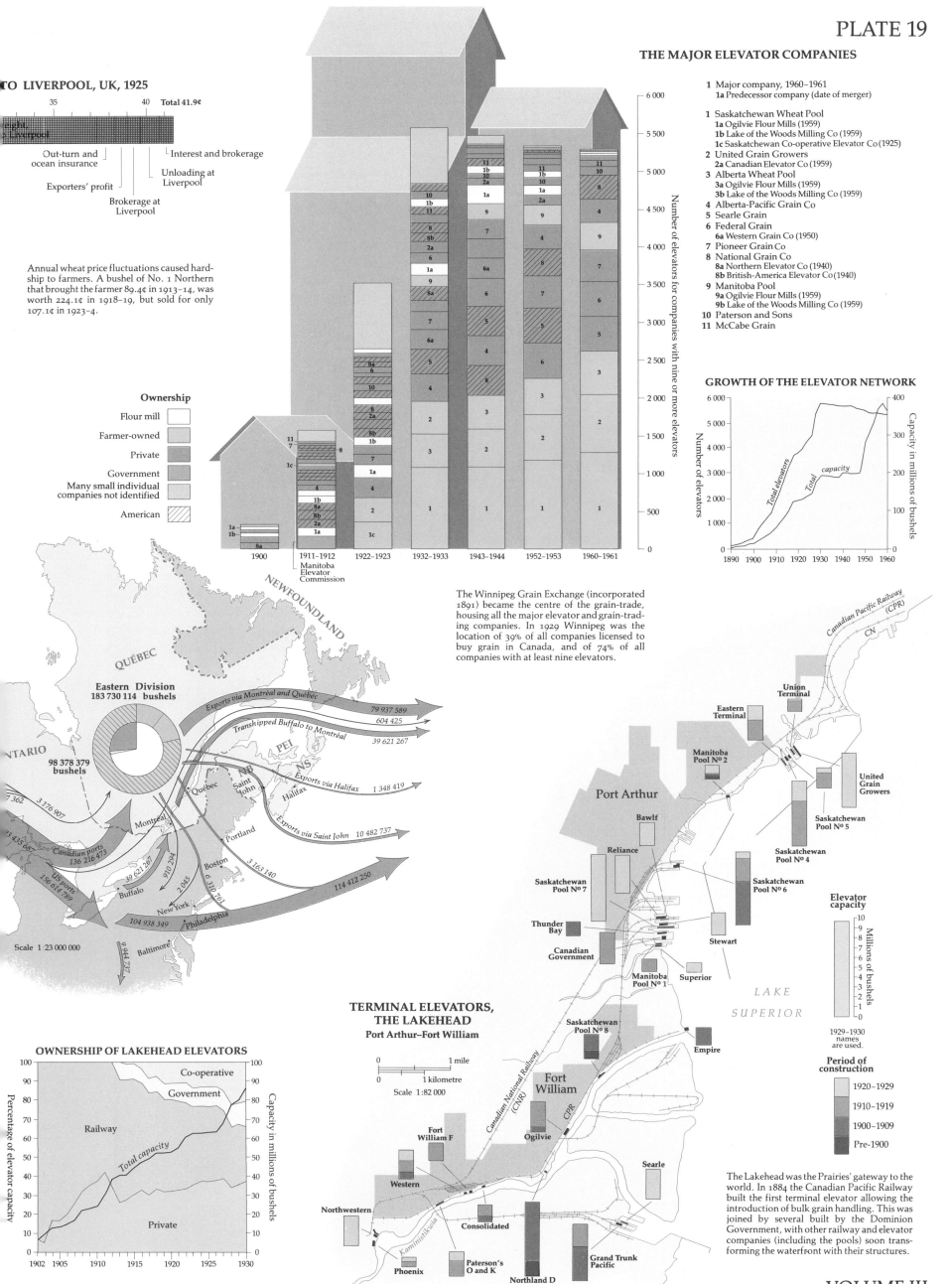

PLATE 19

TO LIVERPOOL, UK, 1925

35   40   Total 41.9¢

Freight,
Liverpool

Out-turn and
ocean insurance

Interest and brokerage

Unloading at
Liverpool

Exporters' profit

Brokerage at
Liverpool

Annual wheat price fluctuations caused hardship to farmers. A bushel of No. 1 Northern
that brought the farmer 89.4¢ in 1913–14, was
worth 224.1¢ in 1918–19, but sold for only
107.1¢ in 1923–4.

Ownership

Flour mill
Farmer-owned
Private
Government
Many small individual
companies not identified
American

THE MAJOR ELEVATOR COMPANIES

1   Major company, 1960–1961
   1a   Predecessor company (date of merger)

1   Saskatchewan Wheat Pool
   1a   Ogilvie Flour Mills (1959)
   1b   Lake of the Woods Milling Co (1959)
   1c   Saskatchewan Co-operative Elevator Co (1925)
2   United Grain Growers
   2a   Canadian Elevator Co (1959)
3   Alberta Wheat Pool
   3a   Ogilvie Flour Mills (1959)
   3b   Lake of the Woods Milling Co (1959)
4   Alberta-Pacific Grain Co
5   Searle Grain
6   Federal Grain
   6a   Western Grain Co (1950)
7   Pioneer Grain Co
8   National Grain Co
   8a   Northern Elevator Co (1940)
   8b   British-America Elevator Co (1940)
9   Manitoba Pool
   9a   Ogilvie Flour Mills (1959)
   9b   Lake of the Woods Milling Co (1959)
10   Paterson and Sons
11   McCabe Grain

Number of elevators for companies with nine or more elevators

6 000
5 500
5 000
4 500
4 000
3 500
3 000
2 500
2 000
1 500
1 000
500
0

1900   1911–1912   1922–1923   1932–1933   1943–1944   1952–1953   1960–1961

Manitoba
Elevator
Commission

GROWTH OF THE ELEVATOR NETWORK

Number of elevators

6 000
5 000
4 000
3 000
2 000
1 000

Capacity in millions of bushels

400
300
200
100

1890   1900   1910   1920   1930   1940   1950   1960

Total elevators
Total capacity

The Winnipeg Grain Exchange (incorporated
1891) became the centre of the grain-trade,
housing all the major elevator and grain-trad-
ing companies. In 1929 Winnipeg was the
location of 39% of all companies licensed to
buy grain in Canada, and of 74% of all
companies with at least nine elevators.

NEWFOUNDLAND

QUÉBEC

Eastern Division
183 730 114 bushels

Exports via Montréal and Québec   79 937 589

Transshipped Buffalo to Montréal   604 425

39 621 267

98 378 379
bushels

ONTARIO

PEI

NB

NS

Québec

Saint
John

Halifax

Exports via Halifax   1 348 419

7 362   3 176 907

Montréal

Portland

Exports via Saint John   10 482 737

3 435 687

Canadian ports
136 216 473

39 621 267
910 294
2 045

Boston

3 163 140

US ports
156 614 789

Buffalo

New York

114 412 250

104 938 349

Philadelphia

Scale 1:23 000 000

Baltimore

9 944 737

OWNERSHIP OF LAKEHEAD ELEVATORS

Percentage of elevator capacity

100
90
80
70
60
50
40
30
20
10

Co-operative
Government
Railway
Total capacity
Private

Capacity in millions of bushels

100
90
80
70
60
50
40
30
20
10

1902   1905   1910   1915   1920   1925   1930

TERMINAL ELEVATORS, THE LAKEHEAD
Port Arthur–Fort William

0   1 mile
0   1 kilometre
Scale 1:82 000

Canadian Pacific Railway (CPR)

CN (CPR)

Union
Terminal

Eastern
Terminal

Manitoba
Pool No 2

Port Arthur

Bawlf

Reliance

United
Grain
Growers

Saskatchewan
Pool No 5

Saskatchewan
Pool No 4

Saskatchewan
Pool No 7

Saskatchewan
Pool No 6

Thunder
Bay

Canadian
Government

Stewart

Manitoba
Pool No 1

Superior

LAKE
SUPERIOR

**Elevator
capacity**

10
9
8
7
6
5
4
3
2
1
0

Millions of bushels

1929–1930
names
are used.

Saskatchewan
Pool No 8

Empire

Canadian National Railway (CNR)

Fort
William

CPR

**Period of
construction**

1920–1929
1910–1919
1900–1909
Pre-1900

Ogilvie

Searle

Fort
William F

Western

Kaministikaia

Northwestern

Consolidated

Paterson's
O and K

Phoenix

Northland D

Grand Trunk
Pacific

The Lakehead was the Prairies' gateway to the
world. In 1884 the Canadian Pacific Railway
built the first terminal elevator allowing the
introduction of bulk grain handling. This was
joined by several built by the Dominion
Government, with other railway and elevator
companies (including the pools) soon transforming the waterfront with their structures.

LAND DEVELOPMENT IN EDMONTON

Author: P.J. Smith

SUBDIVIDED AND DEVELOPED LAND, 1914

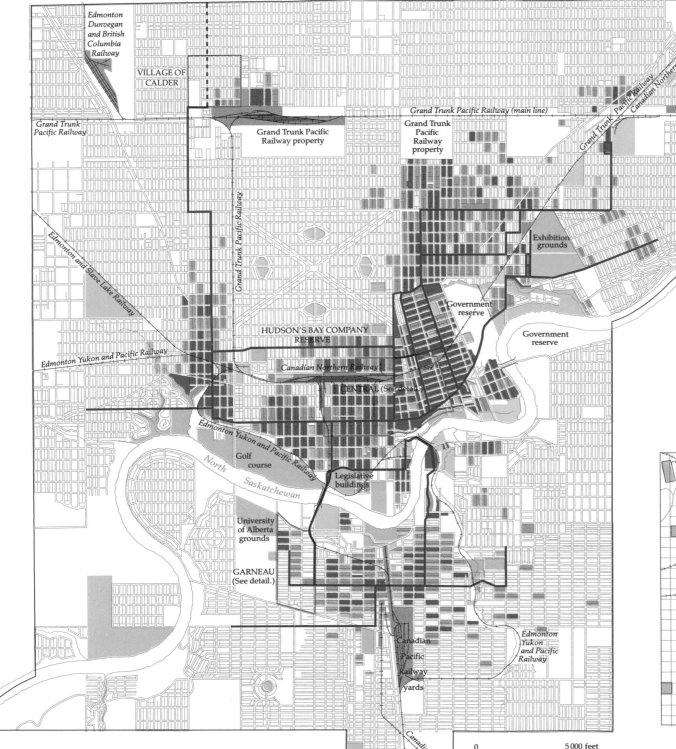

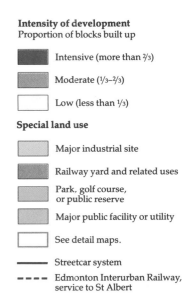

Intensity of development
Proportion of blocks built up

- Intensive (more than 2/3)
- Moderate (1/3–2/3)
- Low (less than 1/3)

Special land use

- Major industrial site
- Railway yard and related uses
- Park, golf course, or public reserve
- Major public facility or utility
- See detail maps.
- ——— Streetcar system
- - - - Edmonton Interurban Railway, service to St Albert

Before zoning regulations came into force in 1933, the need for water and sewer services gave the City of Edmonton its only effective control over the location of residential development. After 1914 most houses were built on serviced land, allowing partially built neighbourhoods, such as Garneau in River Lot 7, to be gradually filled in.

SUBDIVISIONS IN THE GREATER EDMONTON AREA, 1914

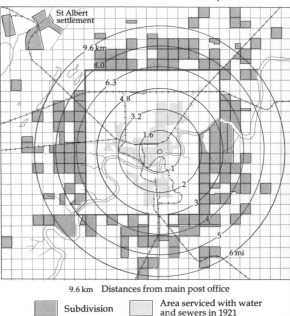

9.6 km Distances from main post office

- Subdivision
- Area serviced with water and sewers in 1921

In 1914 Edmonton was at the end of its pioneer development phase, securely established as the trading centre for a vast hinterland that had been opened in central and northern Alberta. Yet the short, intense boom that had resulted from agricultural settlement was already over. The speculative land market had collapsed in 1913, and although Edmonton's population reached a record 72 500 in 1914, it fell by 20 000 over the next two years. The construction boom also ended in 1914, leaving Edmonton with a physical fabric that largely persisted until the 1950s.

The initial elements of Edmonton's layout were determined after Rupert's Land was transferred to the Crown in 1870. Private land claims could then be staked, on the traditional river-lot system. A village developed in the 1880s, following the edge of the valley in the river lots east of the Hudson's Bay Company reserve. For the next 25 years development was concentrated there, but by 1914 it had spilled through the southern half of the reserve and northward along its eastern and western margins. A secondary centre had also formed across the river in Strathcona, around the terminus of the Edmonton and Calgary Railway.

From 1905 to 1914 Edmonton matured rapidly as a city. It became the provincial capital in 1905 and the seat of the university in 1907. Civic beautification was a popular issue, and numerous parks and park reserves were established. A full range of urban services was installed – water and sewers, streetcars, electricity, telephones – all operated as municipal utilities. Schools and public buildings were constructed, often in handsome and substantial style. Yet the optimism of the period ran easily to excess, and that too became imprinted on Edmonton's form. Repeated and unnecessary extensions to the city's boundaries, over-ambitious railway schemes, streetcar lines on unbuilt streets, a broad fringe zone of scattered development, and a still broader fringe of empty speculative subdivisions were the negative legacy of Edmonton's years as a frontier city.

DEVELOPMENT IN GARNEAU NEIGHBOURHOOD

Dates on which subdivision plans were registered

By 1919

Scale 1:16 500

PLATE 20

CENTRAL AREA DEVELOPMENT, 1914

Retail

Commercial and service

Lumber yard

Warehouse and wholesale

Industrial

Public building or municipal utility

Transportation

Single-family dwelling or apartment

Hotel or rooming house

Building vacant or under construction, August 1914

Ancillary buildings (stable, garage, shed, etc)

In 1914 the commercial core of Edmonton was concentrated on the original village site, but it had begun to shift westward, drawn by the railways to new axes on Jasper Avenue West and 101 Street. A central wholesale district emerged as well, framed by the railway yards and the two main business streets.

Scale 1:12 300

FIRST SURVEY, EDMONTON SETTLEMENT, 1882

Scale 1:140 000

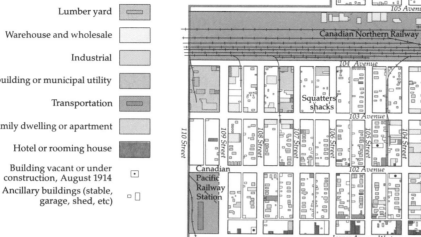

EDMONTON BUILDING PERMITS, 1905–1951

Residential

Non-residential

Total value of construction

MUNICIPAL BOUNDARY CHANGES

Cities of Edmonton and Strathcona at incorporation

Boundary of Edmonton after amalgamation with Strathcona in 1912

Boundary of Edmonton in 1914

THE STREETCAR NETWORK

Dates of construction

— 1908–1909
- - - 1909
— 1910–1911
- - - 1911–1912
— 1913
- - - 1915–1920

······ Edmonton Interurban Railway (EIR) service to St Albert, 1913–1914

▪▪▪▪ Link track to EIR

* Lines discontinued in 1913

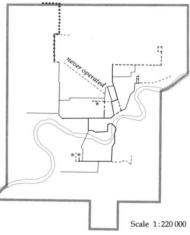

Scale 1:220 000

By 1929

By 1939

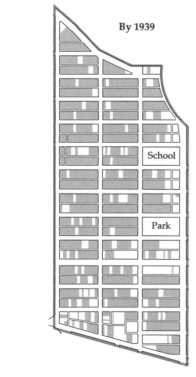

School

Park

LAND FORFEITED TO THE MUNICIPALITY, 1920–1929

After 1914 most owners of undeveloped land defaulted on property taxes. Their land was often forfeited to the City of Edmonton, which then tried to sell it, usually without success. The municipality thus accumulated a huge land bank during the 1920s, unwelcome at the time but invaluable 30 years later.

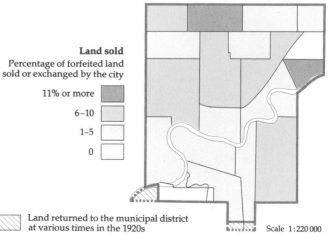

Land sold
Percentage of forfeited land sold or exchanged by the city

11% or more

6–10

1–5

0

Land forfeited
Percentage of developable land forfeited for tax delinquency

80% or more

60–79

40–59

20–39

0–19

Land returned to the municipal district at various times in the 1920s

Scale 1:220 000

BRITISH COLUMBIA RESOURCES
Author: Robert Galois

Prior to the opening of the Canadian Pacific Railway (CPR) to Vancouver in 1887, the economy of British Columbia was dependent on maritime linkages, via the south coast, for the export of staple commodities (coal, gold, fish, fur, and lumber). On the mainland the Cariboo road served as the axis of economic activity for placer mining and ranching.

In 1891 the geographic pattern of staples extraction had changed relatively little but coal, lumber, and fish had assumed greater importance. Overseas markets still predominated. The railway constituted a new axis of development on the mainland but, as yet, the effective transportation corridor remained narrow; the lack of branch lines left much of the southern interior poorly integrated, hampering resource development, especially lode mining. Victoria, the provincial capital, remained the largest city but the emergence of Vancouver at the intersection of the rail and ocean transport systems signalled a new importance for the Lower Mainland as a processing and transportation centre.

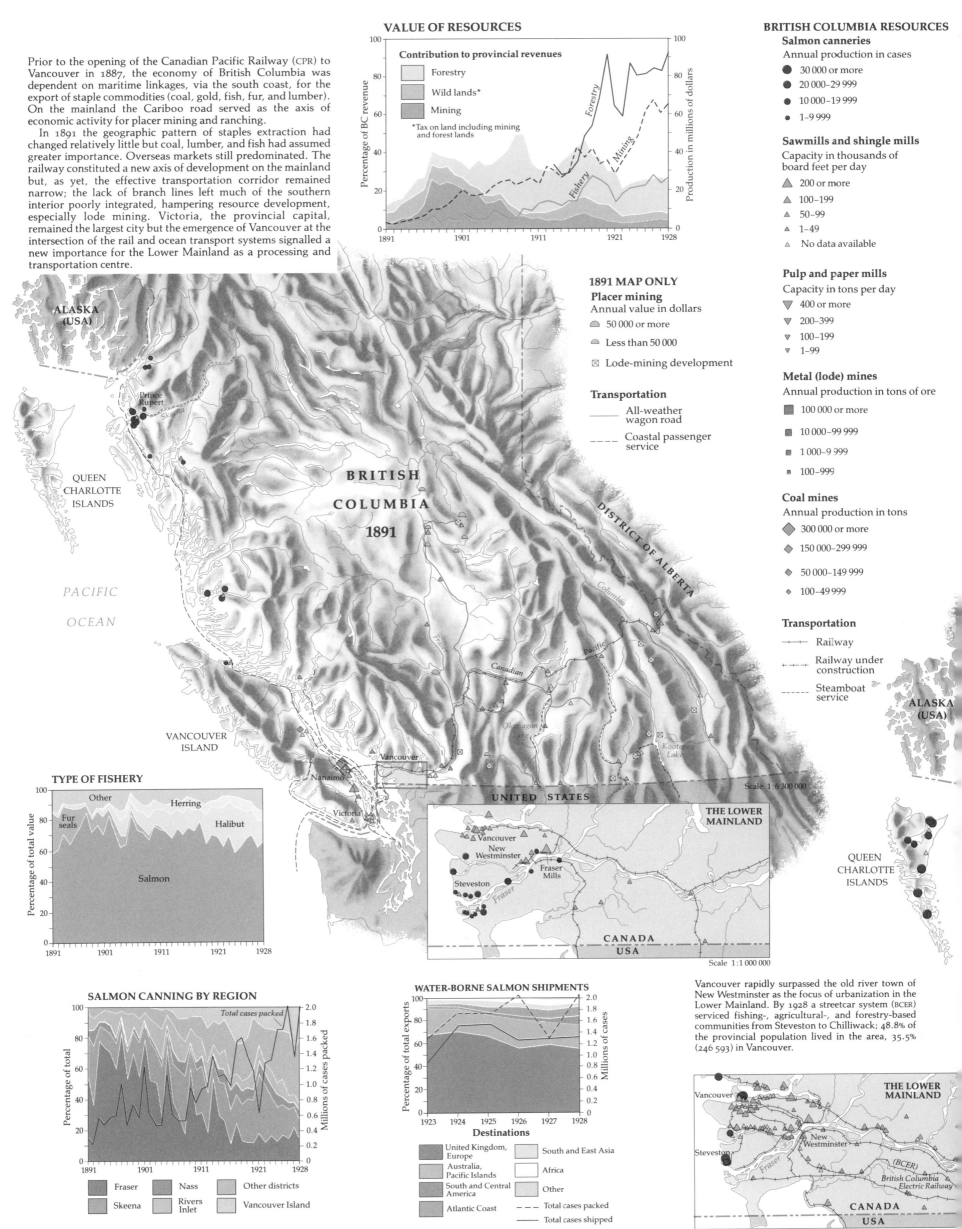

VALUE OF RESOURCES

Contribution to provincial revenues
- Forestry
- Wild lands*
- Mining

*Tax on land including mining and forest lands

Percentage of BC revenue / Production in millions of dollars

Forestry
Mining
Fishery

1891 1901 1911 1921 1928

BRITISH COLUMBIA RESOURCES

Salmon canneries
Annual production in cases
- 30 000 or more
- 20 000–29 999
- 10 000–19 999
- 1–9 999

Sawmills and shingle mills
Capacity in thousands of board feet per day
- 200 or more
- 100–199
- 50–99
- 1–49
- No data available

Pulp and paper mills
Capacity in tons per day
- 400 or more
- 200–399
- 100–199
- 1–99

Metal (lode) mines
Annual production in tons of ore
- 100 000 or more
- 10 000–99 999
- 1 000–9 999
- 100–999

Coal mines
Annual production in tons
- 300 000 or more
- 150 000–299 999
- 50 000–149 999
- 100–49 999

Transportation
- Railway
- Railway under construction
- Steamboat service

1891 MAP ONLY

Placer mining
Annual value in dollars
- 50 000 or more
- Less than 50 000
- ⊠ Lode-mining development

Transportation
- All-weather wagon road
- Coastal passenger service

ALASKA (USA)

Prince Rupert
Skeena

QUEEN CHARLOTTE ISLANDS

PACIFIC OCEAN

BRITISH COLUMBIA 1891

DISTRICT OF ALBERTA

Columbia
Fraser
Canadian
Pacific
Okanagan Lake
Kootenay Lake

VANCOUVER ISLAND

Vancouver

Nanaimo

Victoria

Scale 1:6 300 000

ALASKA (USA)

QUEEN CHARLOTTE ISLANDS

TYPE OF FISHERY

Percentage of total value

Other
Herring
Fur seals
Halibut
Salmon

1891 1901 1911 1921 1928

THE LOWER MAINLAND

UNITED STATES

Vancouver
New Westminster
Fraser Mills
Steveston
Fraser

CANADA
USA

Scale 1:1 000 000

SALMON CANNING BY REGION

Percentage of total / Millions of cases packed

Total cases packed

1891 1901 1911 1921 1928

- Fraser
- Skeena
- Nass
- Rivers Inlet
- Other districts
- Vancouver Island

WATER-BORNE SALMON SHIPMENTS

Percentage of total exports / Millions of cases

1923 1924 1925 1926 1927 1928

Destinations
- United Kingdom, Europe
- Australia, Pacific Islands
- South and Central America
- Atlantic Coast
- South and East Asia
- Africa
- Other
- Total cases packed
- Total cases shipped

Vancouver rapidly surpassed the old river town of New Westminster as the focus of urbanization in the Lower Mainland. By 1928 a streetcar system (BCER) serviced fishing-, agricultural-, and forestry-based communities from Steveston to Chilliwack; 48.8% of the provincial population lived in the area, 35.5% (246 593) in Vancouver.

THE LOWER MAINLAND

Vancouver
New Westminster
Steveston
Fraser
(BCER)
British Columbia Electric Railway

CANADA
USA

HISTORICAL ATLAS OF CANADA

PLATE 21

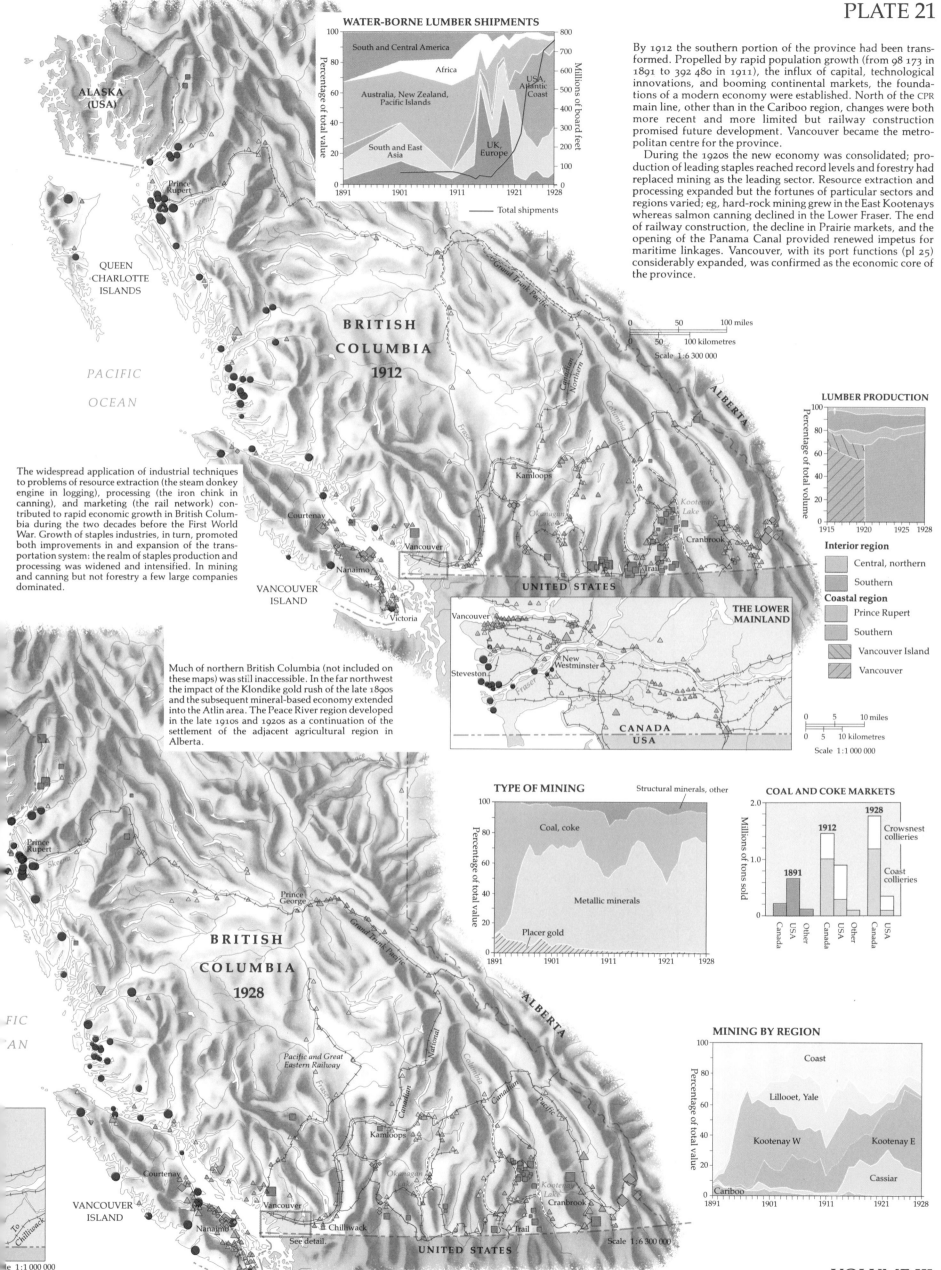

WATER-BORNE LUMBER SHIPMENTS

South and Central America
Africa
Australia, New Zealand, Pacific Islands
South and East Asia
USA, Atlantic Coast
UK, Europe

Percentage of total value
Millions of board feet

Total shipments

By 1912 the southern portion of the province had been transformed. Propelled by rapid population growth (from 98 173 in 1891 to 392 480 in 1911), the influx of capital, technological innovations, and booming continental markets, the foundations of a modern economy were established. North of the CPR main line, other than in the Cariboo region, changes were both more recent and more limited but railway construction promised future development. Vancouver became the metropolitan centre for the province.

During the 1920s the new economy was consolidated; production of leading staples reached record levels and forestry had replaced mining as the leading sector. Resource extraction and processing expanded but the fortunes of particular sectors and regions varied; eg, hard-rock mining grew in the East Kootenays whereas salmon canning declined in the Lower Fraser. The end of railway construction, the decline in Prairie markets, and the opening of the Panama Canal provided renewed impetus for maritime linkages. Vancouver, with its port functions (pl 25) considerably expanded, was confirmed as the economic core of the province.

ALASKA (USA)

Prince Rupert

QUEEN CHARLOTTE ISLANDS

PACIFIC OCEAN

BRITISH COLUMBIA 1912

Kamloops

Okanagan Lake

Kootenay Lake

Cranbrook

ALBERTA

Courtenay

Vancouver

Nanaimo

VANCOUVER ISLAND

Victoria

UNITED STATES

Trail

0 50 100 miles
0 50 100 kilometres
Scale 1:6 300 000

LUMBER PRODUCTION

Percentage of total volume
1915 1920 1925 1928

Interior region
Central, northern
Southern

Coastal region
Prince Rupert
Southern
Vancouver Island
Vancouver

The widespread application of industrial techniques to problems of resource extraction (the steam donkey engine in logging), processing (the iron chink in canning), and marketing (the rail network) contributed to rapid economic growth in British Columbia during the two decades before the First World War. Growth of staples industries, in turn, promoted both improvements in and expansion of the transportation system: the realm of staples production and processing was widened and intensified. In mining and canning but not forestry a few large companies dominated.

Much of northern British Columbia (not included on these maps) was still inaccessible. In the far northwest the impact of the Klondike gold rush of the late 1890s and the subsequent mineral-based economy extended into the Atlin area. The Peace River region developed in the late 1910s and 1920s as a continuation of the settlement of the adjacent agricultural region in Alberta.

THE LOWER MAINLAND

Vancouver
Steveston
New Westminster
Fraser

CANADA
USA

0 5 10 miles
0 5 10 kilometres
Scale 1:1 000 000

Prince Rupert

Skeena

Prince George

BRITISH COLUMBIA 1928

Pacific and Great Eastern Railway

Grand Trunk Pacific

Canadian National

Columbia

Canadian Pacific

ALBERTA

Kamloops

Okanagan Lake

Kootenay Lake

Cranbrook

Courtenay

Vancouver

Chilliwack

See detail.

Nanaimo

VANCOUVER ISLAND

Victoria

Trail

UNITED STATES

To Chilliwack

1:1 000 000

Scale 1:6 300 000

TYPE OF MINING

Structural minerals, other
Coal, coke
Metallic minerals
Placer gold

Percentage of total value
1891 1901 1911 1921 1928

COAL AND COKE MARKETS

Millions of tons sold

2.0

1.0

1891 1912 1928
Canada USA Other

Crowsnest collieries
Coast collieries

MINING BY REGION

Percentage of total value

Coast
Lillooet, Yale
Kootenay W
Kootenay E
Cassiar
Cariboo

1891 1901 1911 1921 1928

RESOURCE COMMUNITIES IN BRITISH COLUMBIA
Author: Robert Galois

FISH PROCESSING, NASS RIVER, 1891–1928

Pacific Northern (1903–1904)
Observatory Inlet
Greenville
Mill Bay (1891–1928) See detail.
Douglas (Pre-1891)
Croasdailes (Pre-1891)
Kincolith
Nass
Arrandale (1905–1928)
Port Nelson (1905–1910)
Nass Bay
Cascade (1891–1893)
Nass Harbour (1892–1927)
Portland Inlet

Scale 1:510 000
0   5 miles
0   5 kilometres

○ Village in 1913
■ Salmon cannery (Dates of operation may have been intermittent.)

Indian Reserve
Pre-1891 | 1913–1928

MILL BAY, 1913

Wooden flume
Mess house
Office
Shed
Gas tank
Cold storage
Warehouse
Plank walk
Warehouse
Cannery
Boat building
NASS
Boat house
Smoke house

The encounter between an evolving aboriginal world and the new industrial system was apparent in the lower Nass valley: salmon canneries were built amid two mission villages, a number of reserves, and a major eulachon fishing site. The canneries provided seasonal employment for native people (men as fisherman, women as cannery workers) as well as for Chinese, Japanese, and Caucasians. Ethnic divisions were clearly visible on the landscape.

Occupants of dwellings
Caucasian | Japanese
Native | Chinese

Non-residential building

Salmon catch by ethnic group
Japanese	293 699
Native	44 325
Caucasian	16 626
Total	**354 650**

0   200 feet
0   50 metres
Scale 1:2 700

SEASONAL ACTIVITY
Mill Bay cannery

Preparation | Fishing

Processing | Shipping

PROVINCIAL SALMON CANNING
Three largest companies by year

Millions of cases packed / Percentage of total production
Total production
1902 1905 1910 1915 1920 1925 1928

Ownership
BC Packers
Anglo-BC Packing Company
John Todd and Sons
Northern BC Canning Company
Canadian Fishing Company
Gosse Packing Company
Wallace Fisheries

THE NANAIMO COAL FIELDS, 1891–1928

Two corporate groupings, the Dunsmuirs and Western Fuel Company (WFC), dominated coal mining on Vancouver Island. In 1910 Dunsmuir sold to Central Canadian interests who, in 1928, purchased WFC. The landscape of mining settlements, collieries, and railways focused on Nanaimo. A poor safety record, absentee ownership, and the employment of Chinese and Japanese labourers contributed to bitter confrontations.

The economic and social landscapes of British Columbia were transformed in the half-century following the construction of the Canadian Pacific Railway. A corporate and industrial system of resource extraction (minerals, forest products, and fish) spread across much of the province (pl 21). Terrain and climate conspired to minimize agriculture and the family farm.

Industrial production of staples entailed an influx of labour and capital and a heavy reliance upon external markets. Economic and spatial instability was inherent in this structure: communities that blossomed as part of the rapidly expanding resource frontier could fade and disappear equally rapidly. The Lower Mainland and southern Vancouver Island were important exceptions to this pattern. These areas were more diverse, containing both older resource communities and cities that linked the fragments of the resource periphery with the world beyond.

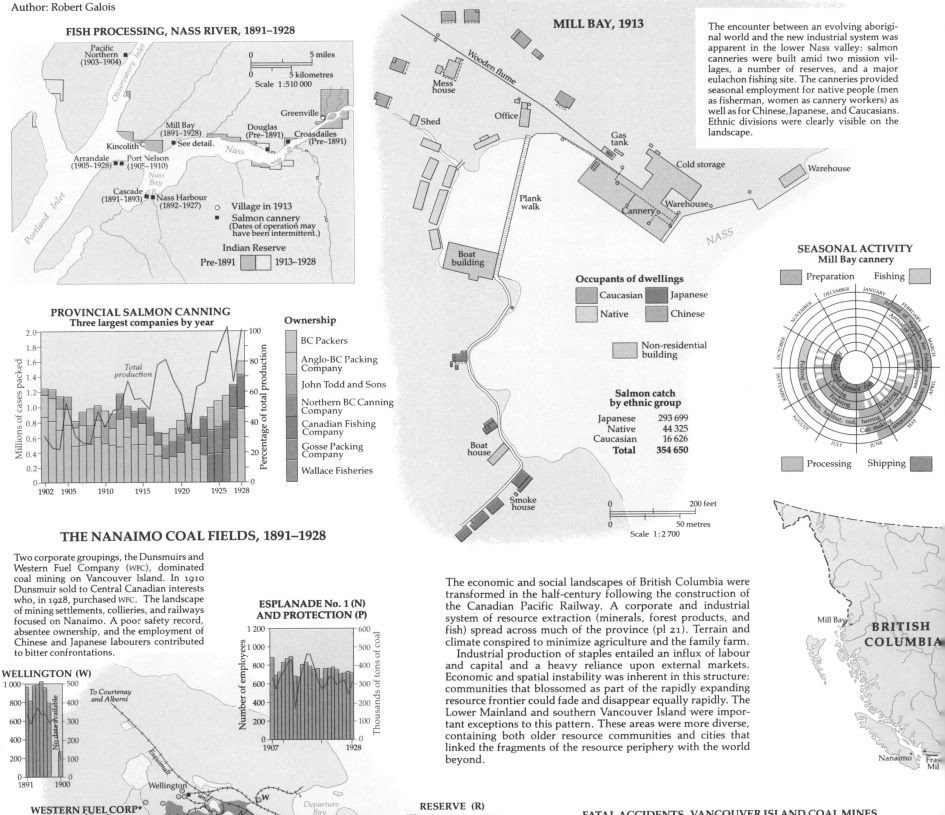

ESPLANADE No. 1 (N) AND PROTECTION (P)
Number of employees / Thousands of tons of coal
1907   1928

WELLINGTON (W)
No data available
1891   1900

WESTERN FUEL CORP* (combined)
No data available
1891   1906
*Includes Esplanade No. 1 and Protection prior to 1907; see end notes.

To Courtenay and Alberni
Wellington
Esquimalt
Nanaimo
Departure Bay
Newcastle Island
Railway
NANAIMO
Protection Island
RESERVE (R)
1913   1928
FIDDICK (F)
1908   1917

Mine ownership
Western Fuel Corporation
Grandby Consolidated Mining and Smelting Company
○ Mine
■ Townsite
Nanaimo built-up area
Coal seam
Indian Reserve
Canadian Collieries
Other companies

Railway
+–+–+ Public
+–+–+ Private
+–+–+ Private (narrow gauge)

EXTENSION (E)
No data available | No data available
1897 1900 1910 1920 1928
E
Extension
South Wellington
To Boat Harbour
R
F

CASSIDY (C)
1918   1928
C
To Victoria

0   2 miles
0   2 kilometres
Scale 1:150 000

FATAL ACCIDENTS, VANCOUVER ISLAND COAL MINES

Employment
Chinese, Japanese
Caucasian

Fatalities
Chinese, Japanese (—)
Caucasian (- - -)

Number of employees / Fatalities per 1 000 employees
87
Rate not available
1891 1895 1900 1905 1910 1915 1920 1925 1928

PROVINCIAL COAL PRODUCTION
Three largest companies by year

Thousands of tons / Percentage of total production
Total production
1891 1895 1900 1905 1910 1915 1920 1925 1928

Ownership
Crow's Nest Pass Coal Company
Canadian Collieries (Dunsmuir)
Western Fuel Corporation
Grandby Consolidated Mining and Smelting Company

BRITISH COLUMBIA
Mill Bay
Nanaimo
Fras Mill

HISTORICAL ATLAS OF CANADA

PLATE 22

CANADIAN WESTERN LUMBER COMPANY, FRASER MILLS, 1931

ETHNIC COMPOSITION OF THE WORK-FORCE

Canadian Western Lumber Company, part of the Mackenzie and Mann empire (pll 8, 15), became the largest lumber producer in the province, its mill processing logs drawn largely from Vancouver Island. By 1931 the work-force was ethnically diverse but English Canadians and Americans dominated managerial and supervisory positions. French Canadian labourers, recruited in Québec, established the nearby settlement of Maillardville.

THE TOWN

Other
East Indian
Japanese
Chinese
American
British
Scandinavian
French Canadian
English Canadian

Percentage

Total 653

THE COMPANY

Number of employees

0 10 20 30 40 50 60

Shingle mill
Planing mill
Sawmill
Veneer plant
Machine shop
Chain
Dry kilns
Grading shed
Tram
Yard
Shipping
Door factory
Power plant

By department
433 employees

Percentage of caucasian work-force

0 20 40 60 80 100

Managerial, supervisory 16
Skilled 68
Semi-, unskilled 404
Clerical 7

By occupational group
495 employees

THE COMPANY'S CAUCASIAN WORK-FORCE

Residential location

Fraser Mills — 150
Maillardville — 173
New Westminster — 141
Other — 26

SELECTED LAND USE, FRASER MILLS

Land use
General residential
Industrial
Other

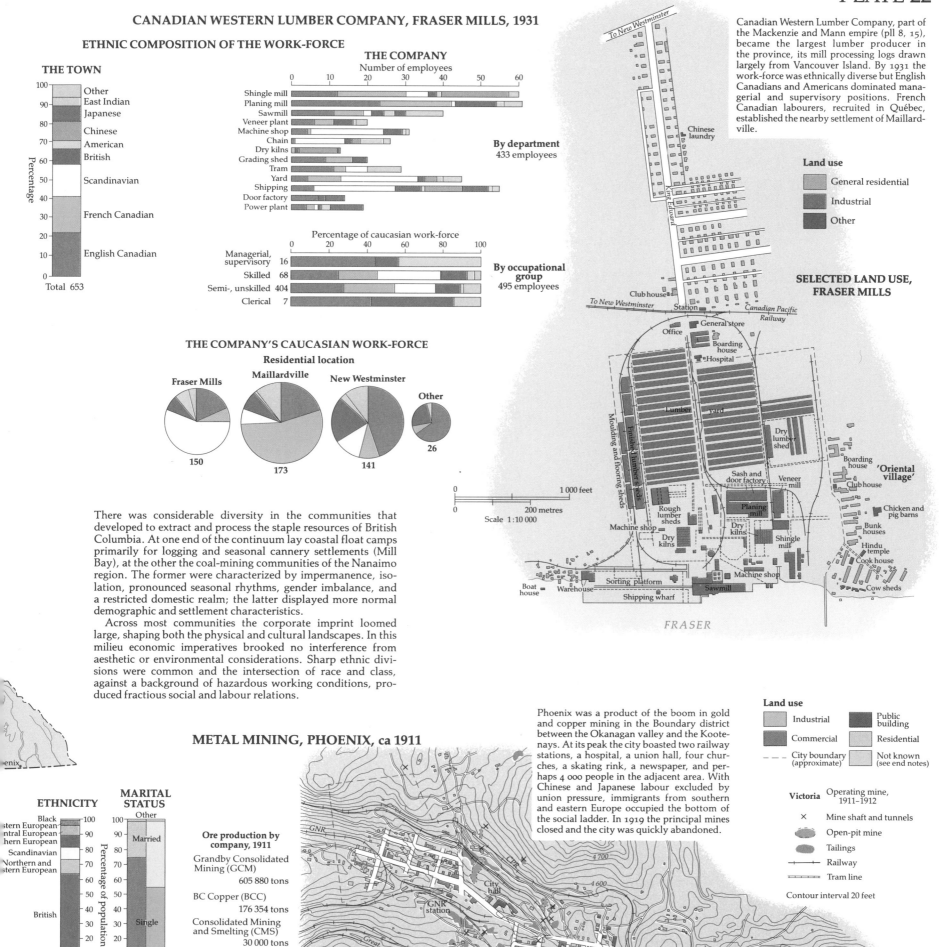

To New Westminster
Chinese laundry
Club house
To New Westminster
Station
Canadian Pacific Railway
General store
Office
Boarding house
Hospital
Lumber yard
Moulding and flooring sheds
Fraser lumber sheds
Dry lumber shed
Boarding house
'Oriental village'
Club house
Chicken and pig barns
Sash and door factory
Veneer mill
Bunk houses
Rough lumber sheds
Planing mill
Hindu temple
Machine shop
Dry kilns
Dry kilns
Shingle mill
Cook house
Boat house
Warehouse
Sorting platform
Machine shop
Cow sheds
Shipping wharf
Sawmill

0 1 000 feet
0 200 metres
Scale 1:10 000

FRASER

There was considerable diversity in the communities that developed to extract and process the staple resources of British Columbia. At one end of the continuum lay coastal float camps primarily for logging and seasonal cannery settlements (Mill Bay), at the other the coal-mining communities of the Nanaimo region. The former were characterized by impermanence, isolation, pronounced seasonal rhythms, gender imbalance, and a restricted domestic realm; the latter displayed more normal demographic and settlement characteristics.

Across most communities the corporate imprint loomed large, shaping both the physical and cultural landscapes. In this milieu economic imperatives brooked no interference from aesthetic or environmental considerations. Sharp ethnic divisions were common and the intersection of race and class, against a background of hazardous working conditions, produced fractious social and labour relations.

METAL MINING, PHOENIX, ca 1911

Phoenix was a product of the boom in gold and copper mining in the Boundary district between the Okanagan valley and the Kootenays. At its peak the city boasted two railway stations, a hospital, a union hall, four churches, a skating rink, a newspaper, and perhaps 4 000 people in the adjacent area. With Chinese and Japanese labour excluded by union pressure, immigrants from southern and eastern Europe occupied the bottom of the social ladder. In 1919 the principal mines closed and the city was quickly abandoned.

Land use
Industrial
Commercial
– – – City boundary (approximate)
Public building
Residential
Not known (see end notes)

Victoria Operating mine, 1911–1912
× Mine shaft and tunnels
Open-pit mine
Tailings
Railway
Tram line

Contour interval 20 feet

ETHNICITY

Black
Eastern European
Central European
Southern European
Scandinavian
Northern and Western European
British

Percentage of population

656

MARITAL STATUS

Other
Married
Single

464 Male
198 Female

Ore production by company, 1911

Grandby Consolidated Mining (GCM)
605 880 tons

BC Copper (BCC)
176 354 tons

Consolidated Mining and Smelting (CMS)
30 000 tons

Total 812 234 tons

Rawhide, Gold Drop, and Snowshoe mines, Phoenix, 1909

Courtesy of British Columbia Archives and Record Service, HP 18382.

GNR
CPR
City hall
GNR station
Great Northern (GNR) Railway
PHOENIX
CPR station
Canadian Pacific Railway
Victoria (GCM)
Old Ironsides (GCM)
Snowshoe (CMS)
Gold Drop (GCM)
Knob Hill (GCM)
Monarch (GCM)
Rawhide (BCC)
Curlew (GCM)

0 1000 feet
0 200 metres
Scale 1:14 500

SEA AND LIVELIHOOD IN ATLANTIC CANADA

Authors: Eric W. Sager, John J. Mannion (Point Lance)

The sea provided a livelihood for many people in Newfoundland and the Maritimes well into the 20th century. In 1900 Newfoundland was still the world's largest producer of salt cod. Half of the cod catch came from the Grand Banks and Labrador fisheries, but these fisheries declined after the 1890s and the inshore fishery increased in relative importance. The total number of those employed in this labour-intensive fishery remained fairly stable between 1884 and 1921, but the percentage of the labour force engaged in fishing declined. After the 1920s absolute decline occurred: the number of those engaged in fishing fell by 25% between 1921 and 1945. In the more diversified economy of the Maritimes, fishing was less important than in Newfoundland, a greater variety of species was caught, and technological change was more rapid. Labour was displaced even more quickly than in Newfoundland and employment in fishing declined by 30% between the 1890s and 1920s.

FISHERMEN

Percentage of total work-force

| 0 | 10 | 20 | 30 | 40 | 50 |

1891 — Maritimes / Newfoundland
1901
1911
1921
1931 — Nfld 1935

In 1900 Nova Scotians had almost 700 000 lobster traps; Newfoundlanders had 240 000. Official figures suggest 2.9 nets or seines per fisherman in Nova Scotia compared to 0.8 per fisherman in Newfoundland. In 1900 Nova Scotians had about 7 000 trawls; Newfoundlanders had over 4 000 cod traps.

Scale 1:9 800 000

NETS AND LOBSTER TRAPS, 1900

Number of nets*

- 10 000 or more
- 6 000–9 999
- 3 000–5 999
- 1 000–2 999
- Less than 1 000
- 10 000 lobster traps

*Includes gills, seines, trawls, cod traps (Nfld)

All vessels are drawn to scale.

A Lunenburg dory-fishing power schooner, ca 1930s, with diesel engine and trawl dories

Nova Scotian steam trawler, ca 1920s

Trawl dory-rigged for sailing

In the early 1900s technological changes occurred in the fishing industry. In Newfoundland the cod trap and the motorized dory increased output per person and improved inshore catch relative to the offshore Bank catch. Mechanization reduced the number of small boats and vessels after 1911 but the fleet was still only partially motorized by the 1930s. In the Maritimes the number of vessels and boats also declined. By the 1920s most boats were gasoline-powered, more trawls were used, and motorized schooners grew in importance; in 1925 there were 10 steam trawlers in Nova Scotia.

A Lunenburg deep-sea fishing schooner, ca 1900, carrying full canvas and hand-line dories

HISTORICAL ATLAS OF CANADA

FISHERMEN AND THEIR CATCH, 1890 AND 1900*

Percentage of adult male population

- 80.0 or more
- 60.0–79.9
- 40.0–59.9
- 20.0–39.9
- 10.0–19.9
- Less than 10.0

Only generalized settled area is coloured.

Pie graphs indicate the composition of the catch.

Value of landings by county

1 500 000
1 000 000
500 000
250 000
100 000

Dollars

*Data are based on the average of these two years.

GULF DIVISION, QUÉBEC*

Other / Fish oil / Seal, seal oil / Bait / Herring / Mackerel / Salmon / Lobster / Cod

$1 412 790

*Counties of Gaspé, Bonaventure, and Saguenay

PRINCE EDWARD ISLAND

Haddock / Smelt / Hake / Oyster / Cod / Mackerel / Other / Lobster / Herring

$1 050 673

NEW BRUNSWICK

Pollock / Oyster / Haddock / Alewife / Mackerel / Hake / Sardine / Salmon / Smelt / Other / Herring / Lobster / Cod

$3 234 401

NOVA SCOTIA

Salmon / Halibut / Pollock / Hake / Herring / Haddock / Mackerel / Other / Cod / Lobster

$7 208 176

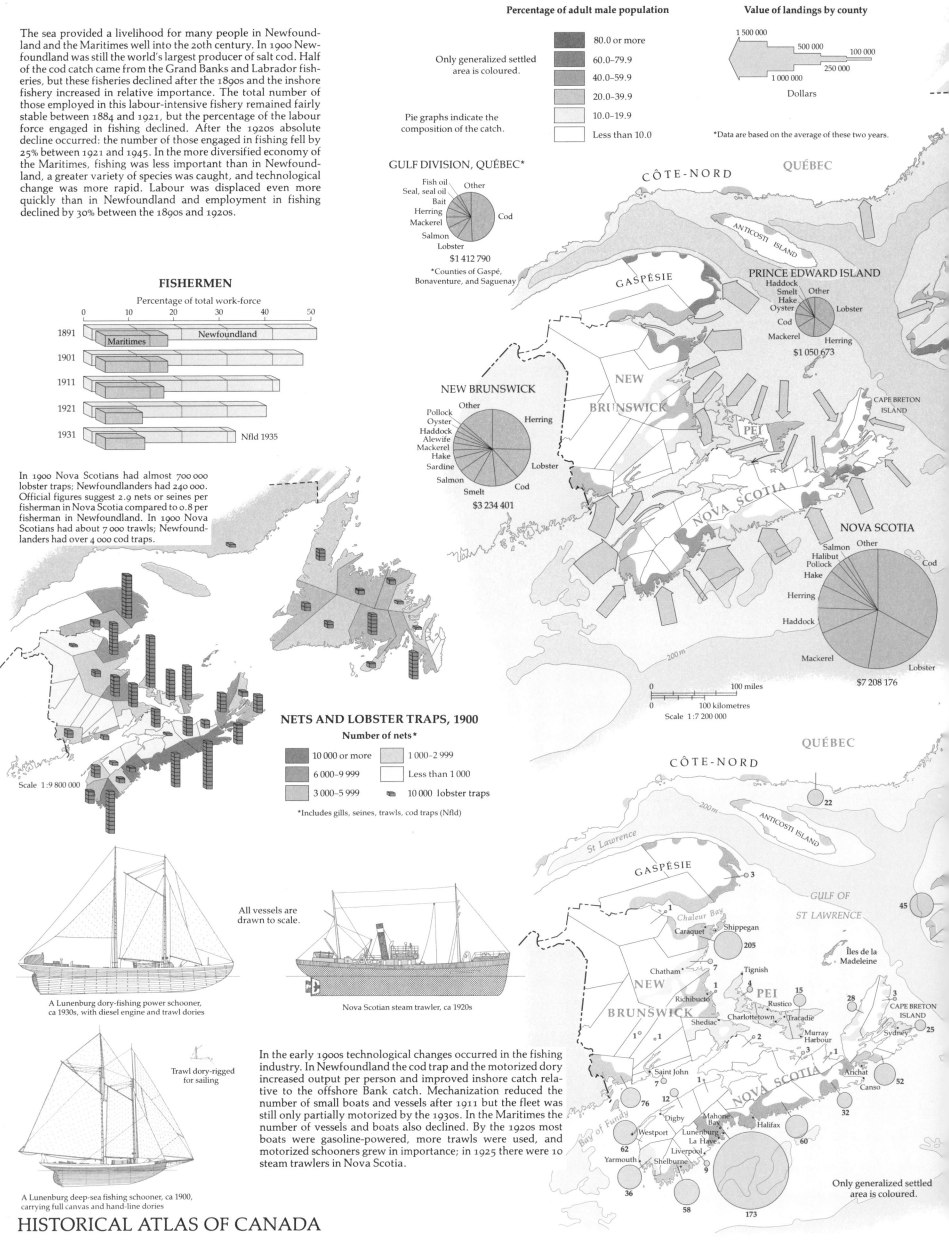

0   100 miles
0   100 kilometres
Scale 1:7 200 000

PLATE 23

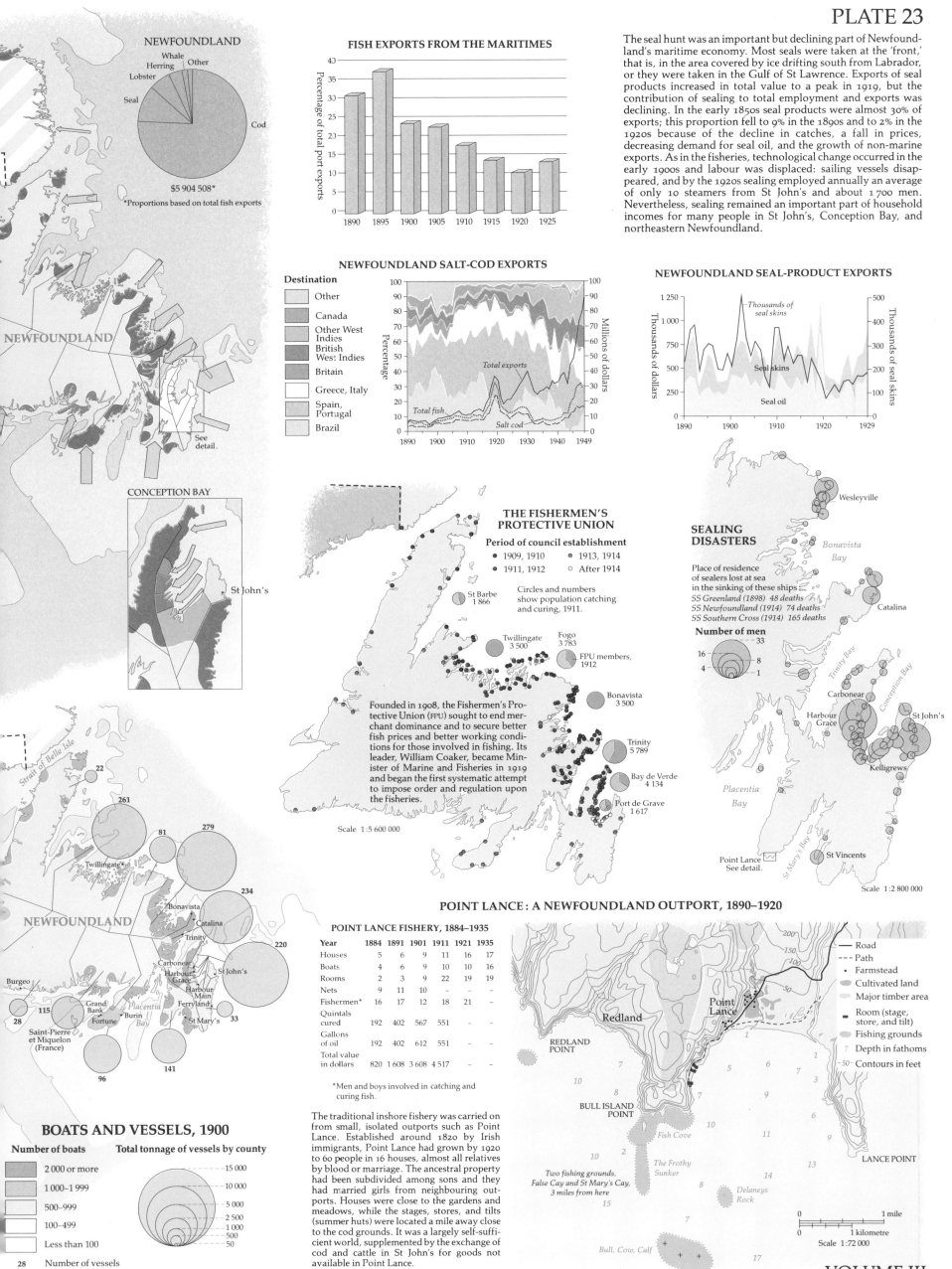

NEWFOUNDLAND

Whale
Herring
Lobster
Other

Seal

Cod

$5 904 508*

*Proportions based on total fish exports

FISH EXPORTS FROM THE MARITIMES

Percentage of total port exports

1890 1895 1900 1905 1910 1915 1920 1925

The seal hunt was an important but declining part of Newfoundland's maritime economy. Most seals were taken at the 'front,' that is, in the area covered by ice drifting south from Labrador, or they were taken in the Gulf of St Lawrence. Exports of seal products increased in total value to a peak in 1919, but the contribution of sealing to total employment and exports was declining. In the early 1850s seal products were almost 30% of exports; this proportion fell to 9% in the 1890s and to 2% in the 1920s because of the decline in catches, a fall in prices, decreasing demand for seal oil, and the growth of non-marine exports. As in the fisheries, technological change occurred in the early 1900s and labour was displaced: sailing vessels disappeared, and by the 1920s sealing employed annually an average of only 10 steamers from St John's and about 1 700 men. Nevertheless, sealing remained an important part of household incomes for many people in St John's, Conception Bay, and northeastern Newfoundland.

NEWFOUNDLAND SALT-COD EXPORTS

Destination

- Other
- Canada
- Other West Indies
- British West Indies
- Britain
- Greece, Italy
- Spain, Portugal
- Brazil

Total exports
Total fish
Salt cod

1890 1900 1910 1920 1930 1940 1949

NEWFOUNDLAND SEAL-PRODUCT EXPORTS

Thousands of seal skins
Seal skins
Seal oil

1890 1900 1910 1920 1929

CONCEPTION BAY

St John's

See detail.

THE FISHERMEN'S PROTECTIVE UNION

Period of council establishment

- 1909, 1910
- 1913, 1914
- 1911, 1912
- After 1914

Circles and numbers show population catching and curing, 1911.

St Barbe 1 866

Twillingate 3 500

Fogo 3 783

FPU members, 1912

Bonavista 3 500

Trinity 5 789

Bay de Verde 4 134

Port de Grave 1 617

Founded in 1908, the Fishermen's Protective Union (FPU) sought to end merchant dominance and to secure better fish prices and better working conditions for those involved in fishing. Its leader, William Coaker, became Minister of Marine and Fisheries in 1919 and began the first systematic attempt to impose order and regulation upon the fisheries.

Scale 1:5 600 000

SEALING DISASTERS

Place of residence of sealers lost at sea in the sinking of these ships:
SS Greenland (1898) 48 deaths
SS Newfoundland (1914) 74 deaths
SS Southern Cross (1914) 165 deaths

Number of men

16
4
33
8
1

Wesleyville

Bonavista Bay

Catalina

Trinity Bay

Carbonear

Conception Bay

Harbour Grace

St John's

Kelligrews

Placentia Bay

St Mary's Bay

St Vincents

Point Lance
See detail.

Scale 1:2 800 000

BOATS AND VESSELS, 1900

Number of boats

- 2 000 or more
- 1 000–1 999
- 500–999
- 100–499
- Less than 100

Total tonnage of vessels by county

15 000
10 000
5 000
2 500
1 000
500
50

28 Number of vessels

22
261
81
279
234
220
141
96
33
115
28

Twillingate
Bonavista
Catalina
Trinity
Carbonear
Harbour Grace
Harbour Main
Ferryland
St John's
St Mary's
Burgeo
Grand Bank
Fortune
Burin
Placentia Bay
Saint-Pierre et Miquelon (France)

NEWFOUNDLAND

POINT LANCE: A NEWFOUNDLAND OUTPORT, 1890–1920

POINT LANCE FISHERY, 1884–1935

Year	1884	1891	1901	1911	1921	1935
Houses	5	6	9	11	16	17
Boats	4	6	9	10	10	16
Rooms	2	3	9	22	19	19
Nets	9	11	10	–	–	–
Fishermen*	16	17	12	18	21	–
Quintals cured	192	402	567	551	–	–
Gallons of oil	192	402	612	551	–	–
Total value in dollars	820	1 608	3 608	4 517	–	–

*Men and boys involved in catching and curing fish.

The traditional inshore fishery was carried on from small, isolated outports such as Point Lance. Established around 1820 by Irish immigrants, Point Lance had grown by 1920 to 60 people in 16 houses, almost all relatives by blood or marriage. The ancestral property had been subdivided among sons and they had married girls from neighbouring outports. Houses were close to the gardens and meadows, while the stages, stores, and tilts (summer huts) were located a mile away close to the cod grounds. It was a largely self-sufficient world, supplemented by the exchange of cod and cattle in St John's for goods not available in Point Lance.

- Road
- Path
- Farmstead
- Cultivated land
- Major timber area
- Room (stage, store, and tilt)
- Fishing grounds
- Depth in fathoms
- Contours in feet

Redland

Point Lance

REDLAND POINT

BULL ISLAND POINT

Fish Cove

The Frothy Sunker

LANCE POINT

Two fishing grounds, False Cay and St Mary's Cay, 3 miles from here

Delaneys Rock

Bull, Cow, Calf

0 1 mile
0 1 kilometre
Scale 1:72 000

INDUSTRIALIZATION AND THE MARITIMES

Author: L.D. McCann

During the Great Transformation a strong, industrial economy did not materialize in the Maritimes despite the fact that at Confederation the region held Canada's only proven reserves of coal and iron ore. Entrepreneurs with capital gained from the staples trade and shipbuilding invested locally in textile and woollen mills, glass and machinery works, and railway-car plants in scattered, often isolated communities. Investment never became concentrated and an integrated network of industrial places failed to develop (pl 10). Even towns along the Intercolonial Railroad functioned largely independently of each other.

The coal and iron and steel industries of Pictou County and Cape Breton Island were an exception to this pattern and accounted, both directly and indirectly, for about 20% of Nova Scotia's industrial labour force in 1910. In particular, the Nova Scotia Steel and Coal Company, which employed over 6 000 workers, operated a fully integrated iron and steel works at Sydney Mines. Iron ore from Wabana, Newfoundland, and local coal were assembled to produce primary steel which was delivered by rail to the company's Pictou County rolling mills, forging division, axle works, and railway-car plant in Trenton. Other companies in nearby New Glasgow produced a variety of metal products, including farm implements and mining equipment.

MAJOR CORPORATE CHANGES IN THE IRON AND STEEL INDUSTRY

GENERAL MINING ASSOCIATION, 1827

HOPE IRON WORKS, 1872

NOVA SCOTIA FORGE CO, 1874

NOVA SCOTIA STEEL AND FORGE CO, 1889

NOVA SCOTIA STEEL CO, 1895

NOVA SCOTIA STEEL AND COAL CO, 1900

ACADIA COAL CO, 1919

NOVA SCOTIA STEEL CO, 1882

NEW GLASGOW COAL, IRON AND RAILWAY CO, 1889

HALIFAX SHIPYARDS LTD, 1918

BRITISH EMPIRE STEEL CORP, 1921

DOMINION STEEL AND COAL CORP, 1926

THE LABOUR FORCE

Finance
Utilities
Domestic trade

Service, government

Transportation

Construction

Manufacturing

Mining

Forestry, fishing, trapping

Agriculture

1891 · 1929

Thousands of persons

Prince Edward Island · New Brunswick · Nova Scotia

Nova Scotia Steel and Coal Company, 1910
Divisions

- Coal
- Coke
- Iron ore
- Limestone
- Pig iron
- Primary steel products
- Fabricating steel, axles, forging

Production (circles) and shipment (arrows) totals are shown in tons.

Employment in manufacturing, 1911

- More than 1 000
- 751–1 000
- 376–750
- 126–375
- 1–125

To St Lawrence port
To Ontario 18 148
To Québec 5 041
To other Maritimes
To other North America

Pictou 20 165
Trenton 86 21
Westville
New Glasg

Scale 1 : 4 900 000
0 — 50 miles
0 — 50 kilometres

NEW BRUNSWICK FOREST INDUSTRY

1891

1911

1931

Assets of sawmills in dollars
- · More than 75 000
- · 5 000–75 000
- · Less than 5 000
- ∘ No data

Control of pulp and paper mills
- ▲ Within province
- △ External

In the early decades of the 20th century lumbering was replaced by the pulp and paper industry as New Brunswick's leading generator of manufacturing employment and profit. Sawmilling remained important in some localities; new technology increased sawmill capacity and concentrated the industry near major export centres.

PRODUCTION AND EMPLOYMENT

Production in millions of dollars

Thousands of employees

Production
Employees

1891 1901 1911 1921 1931

— Sawmilling   — Pulp and paper

METAL MANUFACTURERS IN PICTOU COUNTY

Figures and circles represent assets in thousands of dollars.

1911–1912

SCOTIA STEEL 2000

TRENTON

BROWN MACHINE CO 42.5

BAILEY UNDERWOOD (agricultural implements) 27.5

NEW GLASGOW

MARITIME BRIDGE 42.5

CANADA TOOL 4

I. MATHESON & CO (founders) 42.5

MUNRO WIRE WORKS 42.5

FRASER MACHINE & MOTOR 27.5

STEEL FURNISHING 42.5

J.W. CUMMING (tools, mining equipment) 27.5

1931

SCOTIA STEEL 750

EASTERN CAR (rolling stock) 1000

TRENTON

NEW GLASGOW

I. MATHESON & CO (founders) 42.5

NEW GLASGOW FOUNDRY 2.5

J.W. CUMMING (tools, mining equipment) 250

Scale 1 : 63 360
0 — 2 500 feet
0 — 300 metres

HISTORICAL ATLAS OF CANADA

PLATE 24

The Maritimes were heavily dependent on the federal government for tariff protection, subsidies, and bounties as well as for freight-rate concessions on the Intercolonial Railway. This peripheral region suffered from a limited local market and was far from the growing central and western Canadian markets. As manufacturing firms in Ontario and Québec reduced production costs by adopting new technologies and achieving economies of scale, they competed successfully against their Maritime counterparts. Maritime industrialists could not borrow capital to introduce new technologies because of their weakening position, and their firms became increasingly vulnerable to take-over bids.

As recession set in after the First World War, the federal government bowed to western and central Canadian demands and dismantled the region's preferential freight-rate structure. Rates jumped as much as 240% (pl 6) despite arguments from Maritime politicians, businessmen, and community leaders that the previous structure was a condition of Confederation. Some rate concessions occurred in 1926, but by the early 1920s most manufacturing – even the once successful coal and iron and steel industries – was in decline. Particularly hard hit were the industrial towns of Cape Breton and Pictou County, and those along the major rail lines.

CHANGE IN MANUFACTURING EMPLOYMENT, 1920–1929

Urban places with 200 or more employees
Percentage change
- Increase
- Decrease
  - 0–24.9
  - 25.0–49.9
  - 50.0–74.9
  - 75.0–99.9

Scale 1 : 6 300 000

Railways
- Canadian National (Canadian Government before 1920)
- Canadian Pacific
- Other

Source of control
- Local
- Regional
- National
- International

DOMINION COAL CO, 1893

DOMINION IRON AND STEEL CO, 1899

DOMINION STEEL CORP, 1909

NOVA SCOTIA STEEL AND THE STRUCTURE OF MANUFACTURING, 1910–1911

The coal produced at Sydney Mines that was not exported was used in Nova Scotia Steel's operations.

METROPOLITAN OUTREACH

After Confederation neither Halifax nor Saint John was able to fend off the metropolitan outreach of Montréal. Gradually Toronto-based enterprises competed against those based in Montréal, and during the 1920s they began to dominate the expanding service economy of retailing, wholesale distribution (pl 8), and banking (pl 9).

BRANCH OUTLETS IN THE MARITIMES

41% | 4% | 1% | 2% | 66%
3.7% of total establishments (8 120)

26% | 6% | 13% | 2% | 79%
4.1% of total establishments (14 660)

6.4% of total establishments (15 030)
19% | 11% | 23% | 3% | 99%

Resources | Manufacturing | Wholesaling | Retailing | Finance

19% Branch outlets as a percentage of total establishments per sector

- Internal (region-based)
- External

DECLINE IN INDUSTRIAL CAPE BRETON

1911
9 109 517
Glace Bay
Sydney Mines
North Sydney
Sydney 5 447 000
NOVA SCOTIA

Type of industry
- Primary metal
- Chemical
- Metal fabricating
- Machinery
- Other
- Coal
- Coal mine

Value in dollars*
1 000 000–2 000 000
500 000–999 999
150 000–499 999
50 000–149 999
Less than 50 000

*Circles are proportional to the assets of industries and the value of coal production in dollars.

1931
Glace Bay
North Sydney
Sydney 3 006 500

0   5 miles
0   5 kilometres
Scale 1 : 550 000

1881
QUÉBEC
ONTARIO
Montréal 13
Saint John 22
Halifax 65
NB
PEI
NS

1911
Montréal 147
Toronto 83
Saint John 49
Halifax 35

1931
Montréal 229
Toronto 228
Saint John 58
Halifax 60

Scale 1 : 20 000 000

60 Number of metropolitan branches

Number of business linkages
10 25 50 75 100 125

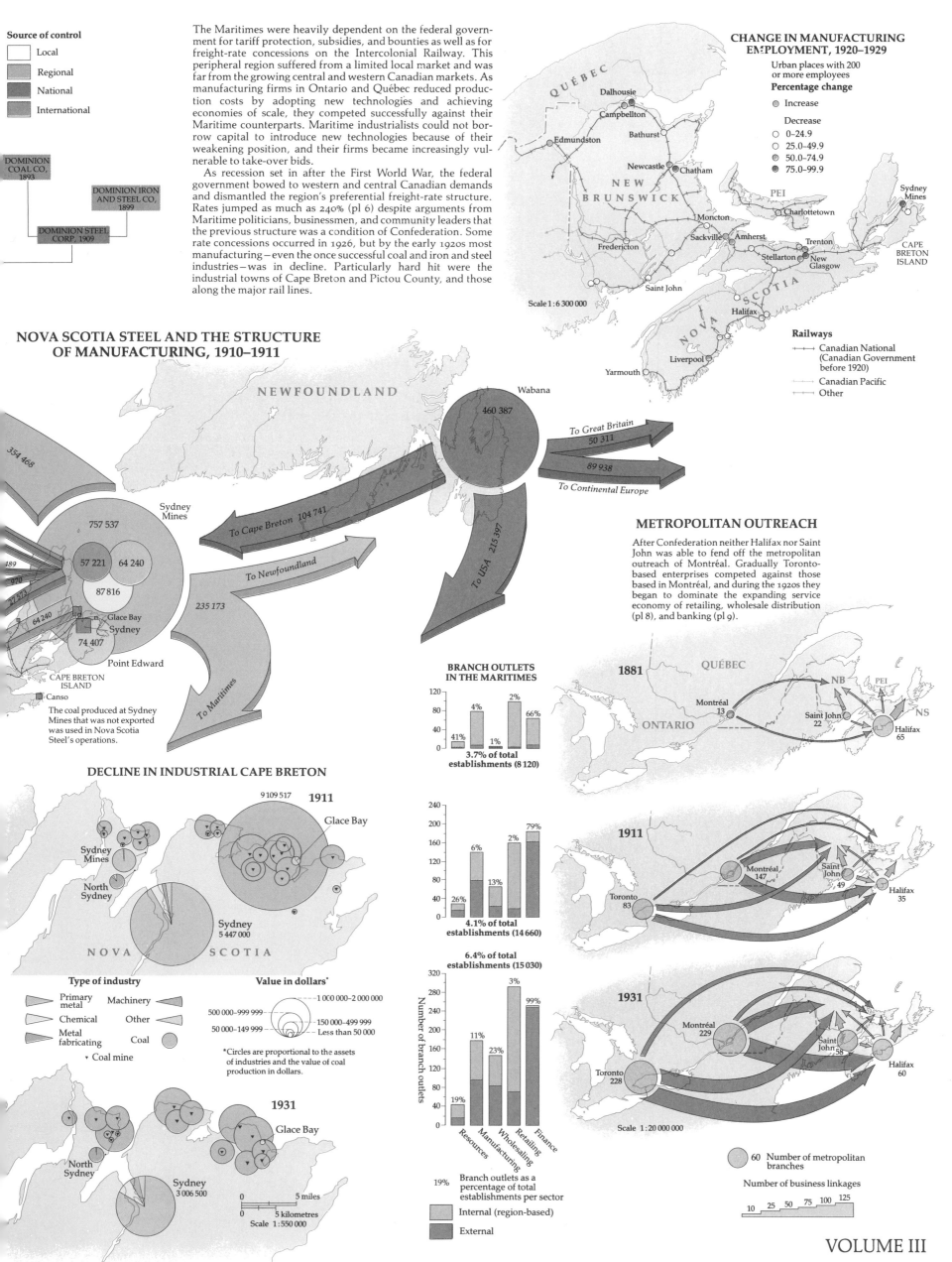

PORT DEVELOPMENT IN HALIFAX

Author: L.D. McCann

HALIFAX, 1896

Rockhead Prison

Richmond Depot, Intercolonial Railway (ICR)

Dry dock

Windsor

Young

Bayers

NORTH END

Gottingen

HM Naval Yard

ICR Deepwater Terminal

S. Cunard & Co

Chebucto

Common

Furness Withy & Co

Pickford & Black

City ferry dock

Quinpool

Citadel

Robie

Oxford

Jubilee

Coburg

South Park

South

Dominion Coal Co

Halifax Electrical Tram Co

Pleasant

Scale 1:37 000

North West Arm

Marlborough Woods

Inglis

SOUTH END

Royal Nova Scotia Yacht Squadron

Point Pleasant Park

In an attempt to become a major Canadian port Halifax envisaged an extensive harbour redevelopment that would transform much of the Halifax waterfront. Four alternatives were considered and scheme D, the Ocean Terminals in the South End, was chosen.

LABOUR FORCE, 1881

Total 12 959

Percentage

Other
Labourers — L
Commercial clerks — C — Industry unspecified
Government (including defence)
Service
Finance, insurance, real estate
Trade
Transportation
Construction
Manufacturing
Primary

HALIFAX AREA

To Truro

To Sheet Harbour (Sherbrooke)

CNR (Intercolonial before 1923)

NOVA SCOTIA

Bedford Basin

Dartmouth

Halifax

Halifax Harbour

Halifax & South Western

To Lunenburg, Yarmouth

CNR (Intercolonial before 1923)

Scale 1:400 000

ATLANTIC OCEAN

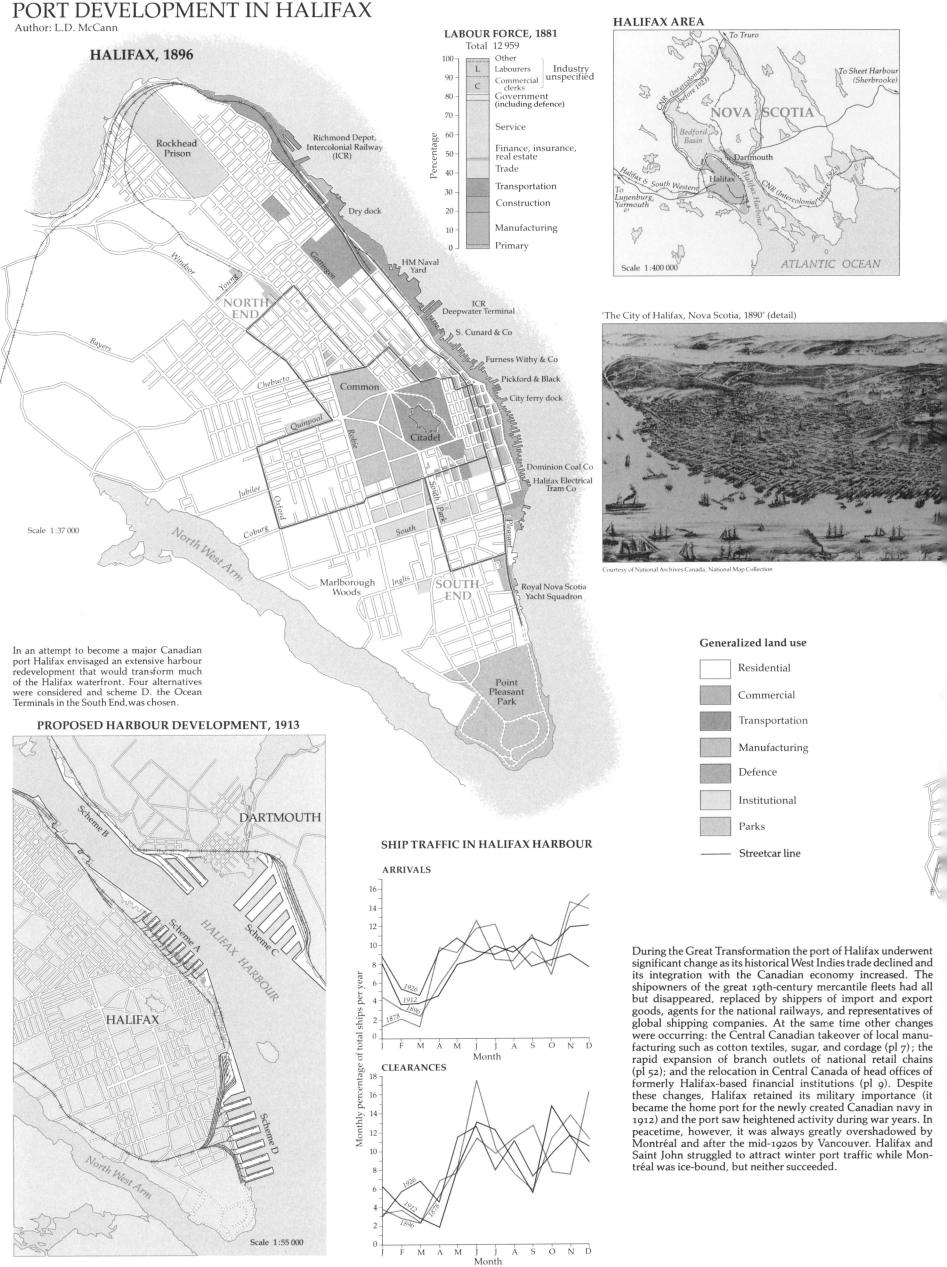

'The City of Halifax, Nova Scotia, 1890' (detail)

Courtesy of National Archives Canada, National Map Collection

Generalized land use

Residential
Commercial
Transportation
Manufacturing
Defence
Institutional
Parks
— Streetcar line

PROPOSED HARBOUR DEVELOPMENT, 1913

Scheme B

DARTMOUTH

Scheme C

Scheme A

HALIFAX HARBOUR

HALIFAX

Scheme D

North West Arm

Scale 1:55 000

SHIP TRAFFIC IN HALIFAX HARBOUR

ARRIVALS

Monthly percentage of total ships per year

1926
1912
1878
1896

J F M A M J J A S O N D
Month

CLEARANCES

1926
1912
1878
1896

J F M A M J J A S O N D
Month

During the Great Transformation the port of Halifax underwent significant change as its historical West Indies trade declined and its integration with the Canadian economy increased. The shipowners of the great 19th-century mercantile fleets had all but disappeared, replaced by shippers of import and export goods, agents for the national railways, and representatives of global shipping companies. At the same time other changes were occurring: the Central Canadian takeover of local manufacturing such as cotton textiles, sugar, and cordage (pl 7); the rapid expansion of branch outlets of national retail chains (pl 52); and the relocation in Central Canada of head offices of formerly Halifax-based financial institutions (pl 9). Despite these changes, Halifax retained its military importance (it became the home port for the newly created Canadian navy in 1912) and the port saw heightened activity during war years. In peacetime, however, it was always greatly overshadowed by Montréal and after the mid-1920s by Vancouver. Halifax and Saint John struggled to attract winter port traffic while Montréal was ice-bound, but neither succeeded.

HISTORICAL ATLAS OF CANADA

PLATE 25

HALIFAX, 1912

LABOUR FORCE, 1911
Total 17 909

- Industry unspecified
- Government (including defence)
- Service
- Finance, insurance, real estate
- Trade
- Transportation
- Construction
- Manufacturing
- Primary

Percentage (0–100)

Map labels: Rockhead Prison, Robie, Railway wharves, Halifax Graving Dock, HM Dockyard, NORTH END, Bayers, Windsor, Gottingen, Chebucto, Common, Quinpool, Robie, Citadel, ICR Deepwater Terminal, S. Cunard & Co, Furness Withy & Co, Pickford & Black, City ferry dock, Robin, Jones, Whitman, Halifax Electrical Tram Co, Jubilee, Coburg, South, South Park, Marlborough Woods, Inglis, SOUTH END, North West Arm, Point Pleasant Park

Scale 1:37 000

HALIFAX, 1926

Map labels: Robie, Hydrastone, Railway wharves, Halifax Graving Dock, HM Dockyard, Windsor, Barrington, Gottingen, NORTH END, Bayers, Federal government wharves, Deepwater Terminals, S. Cunard & Co, Furness Withy & Co, Federal government wharves, Pickford & Black, City ferry dock, Chebucto, Common, Quinpool, Citadel, Robie, Robin, Jones, Whitman, Nova Scotia Light & Power Co, Jubilee, Coburg, South, South Park, Marlborough Woods, Inglis, SOUTH END, Ocean Terminals, Federal government wharves, North West Arm, Point Pleasant Park

LABOUR FORCE, 1931
Total 23 011

- Industry unspecified
- Defence
- Government
- Service
- Finance, insurance, real estate
- Trade
- Transportation
- Construction
- Manufacturing
- Primary

Percentage (0–100)

0 1 mile
0 1 kilometre
Scale 1:37 000

THE HALIFAX EXPLOSION, 1917

Early on the morning of 6 December 1917 the munitions carrier *Mont Blanc* and the Belgian Relief steamer *Imo* collided in the Narrows of Halifax Harbour. The subsequent explosion, fires, and flying glass killed some 1 600 people, injured thousands more, and caused millions of dollars in damage.

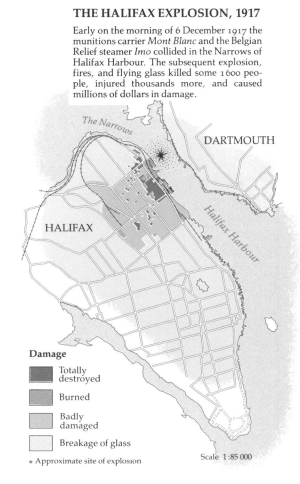

Map labels: The Narrows, DARTMOUTH, HALIFAX, Halifax Harbour

Damage
- Totally destroyed
- Burned
- Badly damaged
- Breakage of glass
- * Approximate site of explosion

Scale 1:85 000

Halifax's economic transformation brought major changes to its physical form. The most dramatic of these, and a direct function of port development, was the construction, beginning in 1913, of the Intercolonial Railway through the western suburbs and the South End and the building of the huge Ocean Terminals. The finger wharves, home to the sailing ships of the old colonial city, were upgraded to facilitate the growing number of steamships that now docked in Halifax. Manufacturing gained little ground. Except for a small area in the North End, factories generally avoided Halifax, preferring the better serviced industrial sites of neighbouring Dartmouth.

As the city's population grew from 38 437 in 1891 to 59 275 in 1931, residential areas expanded. To the west newly developed suburbs housed white-collar workers employed in trade, government, and other expanding service sectors. With the Ocean Terminals in place, working-class port and railway workers moved into the South End adjacent to the longstanding élite area near Point Pleasant Park. The North End underwent widespread rebuilding after the explosion of 1917; the new Hydrastone neighbourhood, built according to the planning principles behind English garden cities, contained a mixture of working-class occupants.

CARGO MOVEMENT THROUGH MAJOR PORTS

Major Canadian ports
- Montréal
- Vancouver
- **Halifax**
- Saint John
- Québec

Sea-borne cargo in millions of tons (0–13)

1890 1900 1910 1920 1930 1940 1950 1960

THE GREAT WAR

Author: Christopher A. Sharpe

ENLISTMENT AND MILITARY INSTALLATIONS

Yukon Territory and

British Columbia 158 272

Alberta 122 915

Saskatchewan 158 907

Manitoba 122 762

Québec 390 897

Ontario 582 246

New Brunswick 68 710

Nova Scotia and PEI 115 361

Newfoundland 33 708

Scale 1:40 000 000

Scale 1:20 000 000

- Canadian Expeditionary Force training camp
- Royal Flying Corps aerodrome
- Royal Canadian Navy signal station
- ▲ 'Alien' internment camp

Canadian Expeditionary Force (CEF) (excluding Newfoundland)

CEF Canada 189 588

CEF Overseas 417 486

Untapped manpower 1 112 996

Total eligible male population (18–45 years) 1 720 070

CASUALTY RATES OF SELECTED BATTALIONS

Percentage of men

Battalion		Total number of men
Royal Newfoundland Regiment		6 241
2nd (Eastern Ontario)		5 326
24th (Victoria Rifles)		4 827
46th (South Saskatchewan)		5 374
49th (Loyal Edmonton)		4 050
72nd (Seaforth Highlanders)		3 791
77th (Ottawa)		1 368

■ Killed □ Wounded ▨ Not injured

ST JOHN'S

0   1 500 feet
0   400 metres
Scale 1:18 000

VICTORY LOAN CAMPAIGNS, 1917, 1918

BC
Alta
Sask
Man
Ont
Qué
NB
NS
PEI
Canada
Nfld (1918 only)

0   40   80   120   160   200
Per capita contributions in dollars

The strain of financing the war effort led to war taxes on business profits, personal income, and luxuries. There were also three Victory Loan campaigns aimed at the patriotism of small-scale savers. In 1917 the campaign raised $546 million, far in excess of the $150 million target. A further $678 million and $587 million were realized in the next two years.

CANADIAN PATRIOTIC FUND, 1914–1919

BC
Alta
Sask
Man
Ont
Qué
NB
NS
PEI
Canada
Nfld

Contributions □ Deficit spending ▨ Surplus

Canada total $ 46 348 931

0   4   8   12   16   20   24   38   46
Millions of dollars

The Canadian Patriotic Fund was a voluntary organization which co-ordinated fundraising and provided monthly grants to wives and dependents of soldiers. Widows and dependents received pensions from the fund until the federal government assumed that responsibility in 1916. While most contributions were voluntary, Alberta and New Brunswick used taxes to levy funds.

IMPERIAL MUNITIONS BOARD CONTRACTS, 1915–1919

The British government established the Imperial Munitions Board in Canada to bring order to the country's fledgling munitions industry. In addition to co-ordinating contracts for ships, aircraft, chemicals, explosives, weapons, and ammunition at existing factories, the board also established seven new 'national factories' to produce war matériel.

Scale 1:40 000 000

BRITISH COLUMBIA
ALBERTA
SASKATCHEWAN
MANITOBA
ONTARIO
QUÉBEC
NEWFOUNDLAND
NB
PEI
NS

UK BC Alta Sask Man
USA
NS
NB
Qué
Ont

Value of contracts
Millions of dollars
- ● More than 100.0
- ● 15.1–100.0
- · 1.0–15.0
- · Less than 1.0

Total contracts $1 104 155 604

Scale 1:20 000 000

PROVINCIAL SHARE OF MANUFACTURING AND WAR TRADE, 1915

50
40
30
20
10
0

War trade   Manufacturing trade

BC Alta Sask Man Ont Qué NB NS
Percentage of trade

MILITARY SERVICE ACT, 1917

150
140
130
120
110
100
90
80
70
60
50
40
30
20
10
0
Thousands of men

□ Conscripted or volunteered
▨ Defaulted

BC Alta Sask Man Ont Qué NB NS and PEI **Canada**

British Columbia 18 169

Alberta 28 076

Saskatchewan 45 536

Manitoba 24 512

Québec 115 602

Ontario 122 968

Newfoundland
3 629 called up
1 573 medically acceptable

New Brunswick 16 902

Nova Scotia and Prince Edward Island 30 117

Canada

Class 1 registration 401 882

Taken on strength 124 588

Occupational exemptions

Discharged

Exemption refused

Signed reports for service

On strength as of Armistice Day

Medical exemptions

Agricultural exemptions

PLATE 26

THE ROYAL NEWFOUNDLAND REGIMENT
Final tally, St John's enlistment

▲ Enlisted and returned without medical discharge 1460

▲ Killed in action or died of wounds 365

▲ Discharged as medically unfit 352

Not shown are 33 men who were called up but did not serve overseas.

☐ Generalized residential areas

In most areas of Canada more than one regiment recruited men, but in St John's in Newfoundland only the Royal Newfoundland Regiment (RNR) was active. As in other places the impact of service was devastating on the local community. Of the 24% of the RNR that came from St John's almost half sustained casualties, many at Beaumont Hamel on 1 July 1916, the first day of the Battle of the Somme. The war killed or injured 15% of the city's men between 18 and 32 years of age.

ST JOHN'S HARBOUR

REVENUE AND PUBLIC DEBT

Millions of dollars (3 200 to 0)

Net public debt

Total war-tax revenue

1900 1910 1920 1930 1939

TAXES

Millions of dollars (300 to 0)

Business-profits war tax (to 1920); war tax on financial institutions

Income war tax

Custom and excise taxes

Total revenue

1915 1920 1925 1930 1935 1939

In 1914 Canada, as part of the British Empire, went to war against Germany and the Austro-Hungarian Empire. By 1918 the Canadian army had become an independent fighting unit, and in 1919 Canada insisted on signing the Versailles peace treaty on its own behalf. A growing sense of independent nationhood, fostered by battlefield victories and enormous casualties, was one critical consequence of the Great War. War memorials in almost every city, town, and hamlet recorded the devastating local impact of this overseas conflict. Other lasting effects of the war included a larger federal bureaucracy resulting from new social responsibility for veterans and war widows, precedent-setting revenue generation through income and other taxes, and a growing public debt. Female participation in the home-front war effort contributed to federal legislation on women's suffrage during the war.

All regions contributed manpower to the Canadian Expeditionary Force (CEF), which received basic training at some sixty centres across Canada before going overseas. The needs of modern machine warfare created a wartime manufacturing effort, which used the existing expertise and infrastructure in Central Canada and thus reinforced the favoured position of this area. Varying regional contributions to the war effort were also evident in the Victory Loan and Canadian Patriotic Fund campaigns. In 1917 the conscription issue revealed deep divisions within Canada: many French Canadians regarded the struggle in Europe as a British and imperial war rather than a defence of Canada; western Canadian farmers objected to conscription taking away necessary farm labourers; and union leaders argued that 'equality' of sacrifice should involve the conscription of wealth as well as manpower. The War Measures Act, which was enacted during the early enthusiasm for the war, allowed for the disenfranchisement, denial of civil rights, and often internment of 'enemy aliens' and radicals.

Number of beds

More than 1000 / 501–1000 / 1–500

Type of hospital

♦ Canadian General Hospital

■ Convalescent

▲ Special

Final resting place by campaign

—9000 men
—5000
—1000

• Canadian military cemetery

CANADIAN MILITARY HOSPITALS AND CEMETERIES IN EUROPE

Most fighting occurred along a 160-km front in France and Belgium. Conflict in eight regions that now have hauntingly familiar names led to a final resting place in this area for some 39 000 of the 61 000 Canadians who died.

Non-combatant Canadian troops also contributed through forestry projects in Scotland and railway building behind the front.

ENGLAND

LONDON — Thames

Dover — STRAIT OF DOVER

Brighton

Calais — Dunkirk

NETHERLANDS

Antwerp

BELGIUM — Scheldt

PASSCHENDAELE, 26 Oct–10 Nov 1917

Ypres — Passchendaele — Courtrai

THE YPRES SALIENT, 1915

THE DEFENCE OF YPRES, Jan–Sep 1916

Brussels

Lille

Boulogne

Béthune — Lens — Vimy — Douai

HILL 70 AND LENS, 15–25 Aug 1917

VIMY RIDGE, 1917

Mons

Valenciennes

THE FINAL ADVANCE, 12 Oct–11 Nov 1918

Arras

Cambrai

Saint-Quentin

THE BATTLES OF ARRAS, THE CANAL DU NORD, AND CAMBRAI, 26 Aug–9 Oct 1918

Abbeville — Somme

THE SOMME, 1916 — Albert

AMIENS, Winter 1917–1918 — Amiens

FRANCE

Compiègne

Reims

Le Havre

Rouen — Seine

Marne

PARIS

50 miles
0   50 kilometres
Scale 1:2 500 000

CASUALTIES AND MEDICAL-CARE FACILITIES

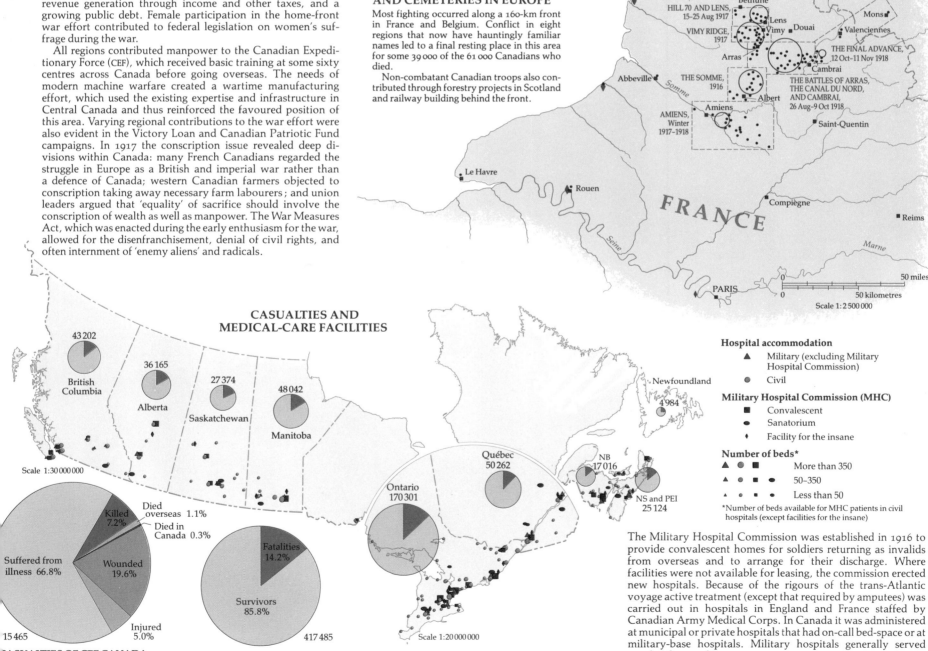

British Columbia 43 202

Alberta 36 165

Saskatchewan 27 374

Manitoba 48 042

Scale 1:30 000 000

Québec 50 262

Newfoundland 4 984

Ontario 170 301

NB 17 016

NS and PEI 25 124

Hospital accommodation

▲ Military (excluding Military Hospital Commission)

● Civil

Military Hospital Commission (MHC)

■ Convalescent

◆ Sanatorium

♦ Facility for the insane

Number of beds*

▲ ● ■ More than 350

▲ ● ■ 50–350

▲ ● ■ Less than 50

*Number of beds available for MHC patients in civil hospitals (except facilities for the insane)

The Military Hospital Commission was established in 1916 to provide convalescent homes for soldiers returning as invalids from overseas and to arrange for their discharge. Where facilities were not available for leasing, the commission erected new hospitals. Because of the rigours of the trans-Atlantic voyage active treatment (except that required by amputees) was carried out in hospitals in England and France staffed by Canadian Army Medical Corps. In Canada it was administered at municipal or private hospitals that had on-call bed-space or at military-base hospitals. Military hospitals generally served non-battle casualties.

Killed 7.2%
Died overseas 1.1%
Died in Canada 0.3%
Wounded 19.6%
Suffered from illness 66.8%
Injured 5.0%
15 465

CASUALTIES OF CEF CANADA AND CEF OVERSEAS (repetitions included)

Fatalities 14.2%
Survivors 85.8%
417 485

FATALITIES OF CEF OVERSEAS

Scale 1:20 000 000

Canadian Society during the Great Transformation

At the close of the 19th century Canada was a predominantly rural society, although a number of small towns and a handful of larger urban centres served regional economies based on agriculture, resource extraction, and a few industries. By 1921, however, more Canadians lived in cities than in the countryside and the nation's economy had been reorganized on industrial, corporate, and metropolitan lines. These changes reflected the social and economic forces characteristic of most western capitalist nations, but also the imprint of various individuals, groups, and classes who sought to direct, extend, or challenge these forces. Not all Canadians were successful in their attempts to shape their own world; ethnic, class, gender, and regional disparities remained.

Many of the profound changes which occurred in Canadian society derived from substantial declines in fertility and mortality rates, massive immigration, and significant redistributions of settlement (pll 27, 28, 29). In Canada, as in most western industrializing countries, there was a shift from high to low fertility. In the first half of the 19th century the birth rate in Canada was about as high as has ever occurred in human history. After 1851 the rate gradually decreased, as young men and women tended to delay marriage; later, marital fertility was itself in decline, until, by the early 1930s, the transition to modern fertility patterns was essentially complete. The chief cause of this latter drop in the fertility rate was the increased use of various methods of birth control within marriage.

Regional economic and cultural differences produced variations in the rate of decline in fertility. In rural Ontario families in long-settled communities with restricted amounts of land for sons to inherit were more likely to limit the number of children they had than families in more recently and less densely settled areas. Cultural factors also played their part: fertility remained high in long-settled areas in rural Québec decades after it had declined in rural Ontario. Infant-mortality rates in Québec were also much higher. Cities experienced a greater decline in marital fertility than rural areas. Indeed, the reduction of fertility rates in Montréal, a primarily French Canadian city, was almost as great as the decline in Toronto, Hamilton, and Vancouver. One result of declining fertility in cities was greater concern for the quality of childhood experience. Programs to improve sanitation and to provide pure milk for children contributed to significant decreases in infant and child mortality (pl 32). The impact of these and other developments was uneven, however, and infant and child death rates remained at high levels in those urban neighbourhoods where working-class poverty was prevalent (pl 31).

Complementing these changes was a movement of population to the newly settled West and from rural to urban areas (pl 27). In the eastern half of the country the limits of available agricultural land had been reached by the end of the 19th century and the lack of land nearby for the children of farmers encouraged rural out-migration. From rural Ontario people moved to farmland in the Prairies, to the American midwest, and to Ontario's own towns and cities. The Maritimes lost both rural and urban population, especially in the 1920s, when already limited economic opportunities worsened. After 1921 the Prairies, too, experienced rural out-migration, foreshadowing adjustments that would intensify during the Depression (pl 43). People from Québec were more likely to move to the New England states than to participate in the general westward movement within Canada.

During the Great Transformation massive immigration fueled population growth and a buoyant Canadian economy discour-

aged emigration to the United States. The encouragement of large-scale immigration had been one of the original cornerstones of the Conservatives' National Policy in the late 1870s; immigration was quite high in the 1880s, though not sufficient to offset high emigration. By the 1890s knowledge of 'dry farming' and lower rail and water freight rates to Montréal made the Prairies a viable agricultural region and led to dramatic increases in Canadian immigration rates. With a total population of less than five million in 1891, Canada attracted three million more people between 1896 and 1914. Although the majority of immigrants in this period were British, or Americans of European background, they were joined by many continental Europeans and a smaller number of Chinese and Japanese. Together they established an ethnocultural diversity in Canadian society (pl 4).

Although the official aim of the government immigration policy was to encourage the agricultural settlement of the Prairies, less than half of all immigrants became farmers. Many found employment in cities, mines, or railway construction. For some immigrants wage-labour provided the money needed to equip themselves for Prairie farming. Others saw themselves only as temporary sojourners in Canada and sought to save as much money as possible before they returned to their homelands. Large employers, such as the Canadian Pacific Railway (CPR), preferred to hire immigrant labourers, whom they perceived as docile and cheap. Businessmen helped to keep the doors open for immigrants who were willing to do mining, factory, and construction work, despite the professed government preference for farmers and a growing Canadian hostility to Asians and eastern and southern Europeans.

Racial tensions were especially severe in British Columbia, where ghettos of Chinese, Japanese, and East Indians developed (pl 22). Asians were the targets of riots on several occasions, as well as of exclusionary employment practices advocated by white Canadians, who argued that their standard of living was threatened by Asian workers. Governments were exhorted to prohibit immigration from Asia; such actions reflected the fear and mistrust that were to find dramatic expression in 1941 in the forced internment of Japanese Canadians (pl 48).

Canada's expanding cities were divided by both class and ethnicity. In Winnipeg, for example, the main immigrant working-class section, composed of a number of cohesive ethnic communities, was north of the CPR yards (pl 31); the area was characterized by dilapidated and overpriced housing, overcrowding, poor sanitation, and high rates of mortality. South of the Assiniboine River the city's élite, almost entirely Anglo-Saxon, occupied large houses on extensive lots along tree-lined, curving streets. Clearly defined immigrant working-class sections also existed in other Canadian cities.

In many urban areas non-immigrants were also divided by class. In Montréal's working-class districts, for example, French Canadians shared common problems of poor housing, overcrowding, and impure milk and water with British and European immigrants. Workers had only to look up the lower slopes of the Mountain to the large houses of business and professional people, primarily of British Canadian background, to be reminded of the inequality in their society (pl 30).

Such inequalities were underscored in the workplace, where low wages, long hours, dangerous working conditions, and insecurity of employment were the norm for working-class Canadians. They increasingly found themselves in larger workplaces, with complex machinery and detailed divisions of labour. Earlier labour units based on artisanal skills, in which workers participated in several if not all phases of the manufacturing process, gave way to new technological and managerial methods which lowered costs and gave employers more control over the pace and nature of the labour process. The assembly line, so critical to 20th-century mass-production industries like the automobile industry, epitomized the lack of worker control in large-scale workplaces. The 'de-skilling' of work proceeded at different paces from industry to industry. For example, the traditional skills of coopers were re-placed by new technology in the late 1870s while machinists' skills were retained into the 20th century. In certain industries, such as steel, the introduction of new technology resulted in the development of specialized semiskilled positions related to the handling of new machines.

In the retail and clerical fields urbanization, larger workplaces, and the consequent subdivision and de-skilling of work altered the composition of the work-force. Clerical and retail jobs began to absorb female labour, providing new occupational options for women, although employment for women continued in domestic service, teaching, nursing, and work in textile factories (pl 37). The low wages paid to women (half the wages paid to men) en-couraged employers to hire them. Between 1891 and 1931 the employment of children continued to decline as a result both of child-labour legislation and of the changing demands of indus-try, but many working-class and immigrant families continued to require the income of older children (and rent from boarders) to get by.

Some traditional patterns of work persisted. Most agricultural work continued to be performed by family labour, supplemented by seasonal paid help at harvest time. Until threshing machines were replaced by combines, the Prairie grain harvest relied on migratory workers brought in each year on special trains from the east. Logging also used seasonal labour and, despite technological advances, the work remained hard and dangerous. The fishing industry, especially in Newfoundland, continued to be dominat-ed by the merchants who controlled the outport economy. The nature of all these industries meant that many Canadians, par-ticularly on the east coast, continued to shift occupations with the seasons. Fishermen often became loggers at the end of the fish-ing season, while longshoremen worked in the sawmills when the ports closed down. Companies in the new resource industries attracted workers to isolated areas by providing housing, stores, and other necessities. Although some firms employed transient male labour, accommodated in bunkhouses in primitive camps, others sought to create family settings through company towns (pll 16, 21, 37).

The Canadian working class was seriously divided by skill, reli-gion, and ethnicity. Only a minority of Canadian workers were unionized in this period, and the union movement itself was divided by different approaches to the nature and purpose of unions (pl 38). Many union members were organized by occupa-tion in craft unions which were affiliated with the Trades and Labor Congress (TLC), and, frequently, part of larger international (or American) unions. As a result the TLC was closely linked to the conservative leadership of the American Federation of Labor (AFL), which viewed the primary purpose of unions to be the provision of increased material benefits to its members. The AFL shunned independent political action and instead pursued a policy of rewarding its friends and punishing its enemies in the mainstream political parties. The AFL leadership also promoted a narrow craft unionism and discouraged organization by industry, although there was always a vocal radical minority in favour of syndicalism and socialism. Not all international unions fit into this mould, however. Some, like the Western Federation of Miners (WFM) and the United Mine Workers of America (UMWA), were industrial rather than craft unions and organized all workers in a particular industry regardless of occupation. These associations tended to have a more radical political vision than craft unions. Many members of the WFM and the UMWA were socialists who saw the bitter struggles waged in the mines of Alberta, British

Columbia, and Nova Scotia as part of a broader pattern of class war between the producers of wealth and their exploiters. Other unions saw unionization and strikes as weapons in a more limited struggle to humanize capitalism. Revolutionary industrial unions, such as the Industrial Workers of the World and the One Big Union (OBU), looked forward to the day when a general strike would overthrow capitalism. During the Canadian labour revolt of 1917–20 this view became widespread among Canadian workers (pl 39).

Other labour organizations reflected particular Canadian reali-ties. In 1927 a number of Canadian unions joined together to form the All-Canadian Congress of Labour (ACCL), an organization which opposed the American dominance of the TLC. As well as being a nationalist organization, the ACCL also supported industrial unionism; although it contained some very conservative elements, it was somewhat to the left of the TLC. Another Canadian labour organization was the Confédération des travailleurs catholiques du Canada (CTCC). Founded in 1921 by Catholic labour leaders and churchmen, the CTCC was intended to counter, among Catholic workers in Québec, what the Roman Catholic Church perceived to be the godless, materialistic influence of American unions. Al-though the priests who were the chaplains of the unions argued against industrial conflict and preached a message of co-operation between labour and capital, the unions themselves became in-creasingly willing to defend their members' interests by traditional union tactics, and the intransigence of employers led CTCC unions into a number of strikes.

Some working-class leaders argued that action in the workplace alone would not solve the problems facing Canadian workers. As a result labour and socialist candidates came forward in an effort to provide a voice within government for the concerns of working people (pl 38). Although these candidates sometimes en-joyed success in local municipal governments, they made only limited gains at the provincial and federal levels. Many working-class Canadians voted for Liberal or Conservative candidates, and many others either lacked the vote or dissociated themselves from the electoral process. Those labour or socialist candidates who were elected were sometimes able to press governments into passing legislation that improved the situation of working-class Canadians, but labour electoral success did not lead to major social and economic change in this period.

During the First World War radical labour leaders focused on the general strike as an instrument of social change (pl 39). Their hopes of radical social transformation were raised by the Russian Revolution of 1917. By the end of the war social and economic conditions were ripe for significant working-class action: hopes which had been raised by the war had not been fulfilled, unem-ployment was a significant problem, and inflation had drastically reduced the already limited purchasing power of working-class Canadians. In the spring of 1919 western Canadian labour leaders met to begin planning the development of the OBU, whose primary object was the organization of all workers. Before the formal creation of the OBU, Canadians across the country witnessed the potential force of the general strike. The most significant strike was the Winnipeg General Strike of 1919, in which the vast majority of both organized and unorganized workers took part. The strike was called in support of collective bargaining rights for the city's metal- and building-trades workers, but government officials and many of the Winnipeg labour leaders recognized the broader potential of a general strike, as did certain leaders of general strikes across Canada that were called either in support of the Winnipeg strike or in response to local issues. The opponents of these strikes saw them as the first stages of a Bolshevik revolution in Canada. In Winnipeg the Anglo-Saxon middle-class inhabi-tants of the South End formed themselves into a Citizens' Commit-tee of One Thousand to oppose the strike, which they argued was fomented by 'foreign agitators' (even though most of the strike leaders were also Anglo-Saxon). This group was able to call on the state to defend its interests. The authorities moved in to protect property, arresting strike leaders and firing on strikers on 'Bloody

Saturday,' and effectively breaking the strike. The crushing of the Winnipeg General Strike was a serious setback for labour and the 1920s brought major anti-union offensives by employers.

Struggles in the workplace were linked in part to the desire for a better material life at home, and campaigns by social reformers throughout Canada also focused on home and community. In Winnipeg church missions were established in the immigrant North End, and in Montréal a major social survey chronicled the poverty and poor housing conditions of residents in the 'city below the hill.' Some middle-class individuals put forward their own vision of a revitalized Canada, one which incorporated a humanitarian concern for the position of immigrant and working-class Canadians with a desire to reassert control by middle-class Anglo-Saxons of a society which appeared to be becoming alarmingly heterogeneous and disorderly. The social-gospel movement reflected a practical, active Christianity, concerned with improving society here on earth. Temperance was a major concern, since reformers viewed liquor as the primary cause of poverty and working-class disorder. Women played an active role in many of the reform campaigns, especially those whose objects were to provide parks, pure milk and water, education, and other services for all children.

Among the major targets of social reformers throughout Canada were health and welfare issues (pl 32). The belief that the easing of economic hardship was an individual responsibility (support was typically provided by religious charities) continued to make the government reluctant to involve itself in such matters. But as the limitations of voluntary initiatives in the urbanized and industrialized society of the 20th century became more evident, reformers increasingly lobbied governments. Children, who could not be blamed for their own misfortune, were the main concern of social reformers, who viewed youth as an important national resource, the future guardians of Canadian society. Efforts were made to keep children off the streets and in 'proper' environments through the development of foster homes, the introduction of mothers' allowances, and the creation of juvenile courts. Some reformers, doctors, and members of the newly emerging profession of social work also sought to shape the future by advocating the sterilization of the 'feeble-minded.' Legislation to that end was passed in Alberta and British Columbia.

Infectious disease also attracted attention. The control of tuberculosis and the provision of sanatoriums were the focus of a variety of private and public initiatives in the areas of public health. The extent of such efforts differed significantly among the provinces, as did provincial death rates from the disease, though overall the death rate from tuberculosis dropped during this period. Venereal disease, a significant problem during the First World War, was the subject of federal legislation in 1919 which provided a measure of consistency in treatment. This intervention, however, like the passage of federal legislation for old-age pensions in 1927, was an exception to the continuing reluctance of federal and provincial governments to involve themselves in matters of health and social welfare. Their policy led to a strong dependence on local welfare initiatives. Although achievements varied from locality to locality as a result, there were widespread initiatives to improve the quality of water, sanitary services, and other aspects of public hygiene.

Except in Québec, where the Catholic Church continued to dominate, education had been fully accepted as the responsibility of the provinces. Standardized compulsory schooling had already become the norm for most children in the primary grades and the structure of secondary schooling was expanded to include a diverse range of programs appropriate for different types of students (pl 33). By the 1920s educators promoted what are now regarded as culturally biased IQ tests as they sought 'scientific' bases for allocating children to different schools. New schools, geared to technical and commercial training rather than the pursuit of more academic skills, adjusted educational curricula to meet the labour requirements of an increasingly technological economy.

Parents in turn became more willing to send their children to school for longer periods, since secondary education was seen as necessary to equip children for employment. Some families, however, continued to have a pressing need for their children's income or labour at home and on the farm. These children attended school irregularly and left as soon as they legally could, if not before. Such realities, especially rural/urban differences, explain the divergent patterns of secondary-school attendance across the country more than the differing nature of local and provincial school systems.

Cultural and religious conflicts also affected education. The most politically explosive issue concerned schooling for francophones outside Québec. By the late 19th century francophone minorities had established themselves in the Maritimes, Ontario, and the West (pl 4). Efforts by Protestant English Canadians in these regions to enforce religious and linguistic conformity through the school systems led to disputes in New Brunswick, Alberta, Saskatchewan, Ontario, and, most famous of all, Manitoba, where the dispute over French-language schooling was of major significance in the federal election of 1896.

The use of schools to impose the dominant culture on reluctant minorities was also evident in the education of native children. The attempt by church and state officials to enforce a western, Christian, and individualistic attitude of mind was not only unsuccessful but destructive. Children who were removed from their communities and placed in poorly equipped missionary schools to be trained as industrious, disciplined mechanics, farm labourers, domestic servants, and housewives often learned little save hostility towards white Canadian society.

Although religion could be a potent source of conflict, it could also enhance order and stability in a rapidly changing world. In many parts of the country, especially the newly settled West, there was an overwhelming desire to build churches. Houses, converted stores, and other non-religious structures served as places of worship until sufficient resources became available to build formal structures. Geography sometimes encouraged a blurring of divisions within Protestantism. In many areas of the West sparse settlement made it impossible for each denomination to build its own church and the solution was to establish 'union' churches whose ministers and congregations dispensed with denominational distinctions. New intellectual forces in Protestantism were undermining the basis of many theological distinctions, thereby reducing the significance of denominational differences. Congregationalists, Presbyterians, and Methodists formed the United Church of Canada in 1925, which answered the need for a strong and broadly based, self-consciously Canadian church (pl 34). Revealingly, it was chiefly in long established communities, especially in the Maritimes and Ontario, that Presbyterian congregations voted against joining this new national organization.

As well as providing the basis for religious fellowship, churches were the centre of many of the leisure activities available to Canadians, especially in small villages and isolated areas. Church-sponsored concerts, socials, and Ladies' Aid meetings provided many women with the best opportunities for social activity outside the home. Men had more leisure options, including fraternal societies and service clubs. Taverns remained largely the preserve of working-class men and their importance persisted despite attempts to impose prohibition during the 1920s.

Sports gained importance as the gradual shortening of the working day allowed for more regular enjoyment of activities which had previously been confined to informal challenge matches on holidays (pl 35). The growth of amateur sports organizations dominated by the middle class and the promotion of sport by churches and schools ensured the propagation of the amateur ideal. However, in rural areas the popularity of tournaments, exhibitions, and challenge matches reflected different influences, creating a form of sport that incorporated elements of amateurism and professionalism.

The development of professional and commercial (spectator) sport was strongly associated with urbanization. League networks expanded rapidly in this period and professional sport, financed by entrepreneurs, filled leisure hours and provided a focus for community identity. Spectator sport was increasingly Americanized. Symptomatic was the transformation of ice hockey: initially teams from across Canada competed for the Stanley Cup, but by 1927 that competition involved only the teams of the National Hockey League; by the late 1930s the league had diminished to six teams, only two of which were based in Canada (although most were staffed with Canadian general managers, coaches, and players). The vastness of Canada meant that sports leagues were very often organized on a regional or local basis, since teams had little money to pay for travel expenses. Few national organizations existed. Competition for football's Grey Cup (which began in 1909) was confined to eastern Canada until 1921, when the Edmonton Eskimos journeyed east to meet the Toronto Argonauts. Interest in the contest grew after 1935, when the Winnipeg Blue Bombers became the first western team to win the cup, and even more so after 1948, when supporters of the Calgary Stampeders arrived in Toronto to transform the event into a national festival. The game's popularity was associated with increased participation by American players and coaches and with changes in the rules that made the Canadian game more like American football.

Leisure activity at all levels of society helped to alter urban and rural land use (pl 36). Urban parks, once areas for contemplative strolls in floral or botanical gardens, more often came to be flat, grassed playing fields for amateur sports. Schools, social clubs, and church- and work-related groups all sought to use this recreational space. In addition, the desire of reformers to provide fresh-air activities for inner-city youths (and to get them off the streets) led to the development of school playgrounds, rural day-camps, and church-organized day-trips to the beach or the countryside. In larger cities giant amusement parks offered activities at the end of a streetcar ride.

The boom in railway construction, which had facilitated mining and logging activities, also opened people's eyes to the aesthetic value of untouched vistas of rock and forest and encouraged attempts to preserve areas of wilderness. The creation of Algonquin Park by the province of Ontario in 1893 was, in part, a response to the pace of logging that was occurring on the Shield. The construction of elegant railway hotels by the CPR and the development of the federal government's first National Park in the Rockies were also a means of promoting Canada as a tourist destination to Europeans and Americans. Other federal parks developed in the first decades of the 20th century, often as a way of managing scarce natural resources as well as protecting scenic beauty.

For most Canadians access to recreational land was precluded by a lack of money or transport. In addition, some areas of lakes, forests, and fishing streams were bought up by the business and professional classes for their private enjoyment. From the 1880s, and especially in the early 1900s, commercial steamer and railway companies also developed recreational areas in different parts of the country, where they built hotels and cottages for wealthy city-dwellers. The Muskokas and the lower St Lawrence were opened up for Americans as well as Torontonians, the Laurentians for vacationers from Montréal. For the non-élite, steamships took day-trippers from Vancouver up the British Columbia coast and railway companies developed Lake Winnipeg beaches. Although the Grand Trunk Railway to Portland opened up the Maine beaches as a summer holiday area for a few tourists from Montréal, significant tourism began only in the late 1920s with the building of highways and the increased use of the automobile. Only when automobile ownership became more general and the road network expanded did a more egalitarian recreational landscape, with cottages, tourist cabins, and campgrounds, begin to develop.

It was in this period that many Canadians began consciously to realize what was distinctively Canadian about their landscape. The development of a Canadian tradition in painting, associated with Tom Thomson and the painters of the Toronto-based Group of Seven, came at a time when the wilderness of the Shield and the West was being made accessible to industry and tourism (pll 16, 21). These paintings of autumnal woods, northern lakes and spruce forests, west-coast rain forests, and the snow-capped peaks in the Rockies captured some of the eternal qualities of Canadian space beyond its farms, towns, and cities. In architecture a Canadian 'signature' emerged. Undoubtedly inspired in part by the design of the major railway hotels across the country, the Confederation Building in Ottawa in the 1920s established the motif of a château style that was used for subsequent public buildings in Ottawa (pl 56). The distinctive château roof was copied in smaller post offices, museums, and national park buildings across the country.

The impulse for nationalism was most strongly kindled by the sense of identity that emerged from Canada's involvement in the First World War (pl 26). None the less, in this period British immigrants composed more than half of the immigrant stream, British institutions and the British monarchy continued to have widespread value among British Canadians, and both francophone and new ethnocultural groups for the most part had to adjust to the British Canadian vision of Canada. This template for society faded only slowly during the course of the 20th century.

MIGRATION
Author: Marvin McInnis

As the 19th century drew to a close the influx of immigrants to Canada accelerated greatly, reaching a peak in the years 1909–13. There were many immigrants from eastern Europe, especially Poland, Austria, and Russia. Scandinavians also came in large numbers, often having first emigrated to the United States. A significant number of Americans came, mostly to the areas of agricultural settlement in the West. Britain, the traditional source of immigrants to Canada, continued to provide the greatest number. Canada was not, however, equally open to all immigrants: Asians were required to pay restrictive head taxes.

The outstanding attraction of Canada was farming on the plains, where 160-acre farms were offered free under homestead policy. Almost as many immigrants came to non-agricultural jobs, however, especially in railway construction, mining, and logging in the West and manufacturing and other jobs in the cities of Central Canada. Canadians continued to emigrate to the United States in large numbers, particularly to industrial cities near the border such as Detroit and Buffalo.

THE MOVE TO THE WEST, 1891–1914

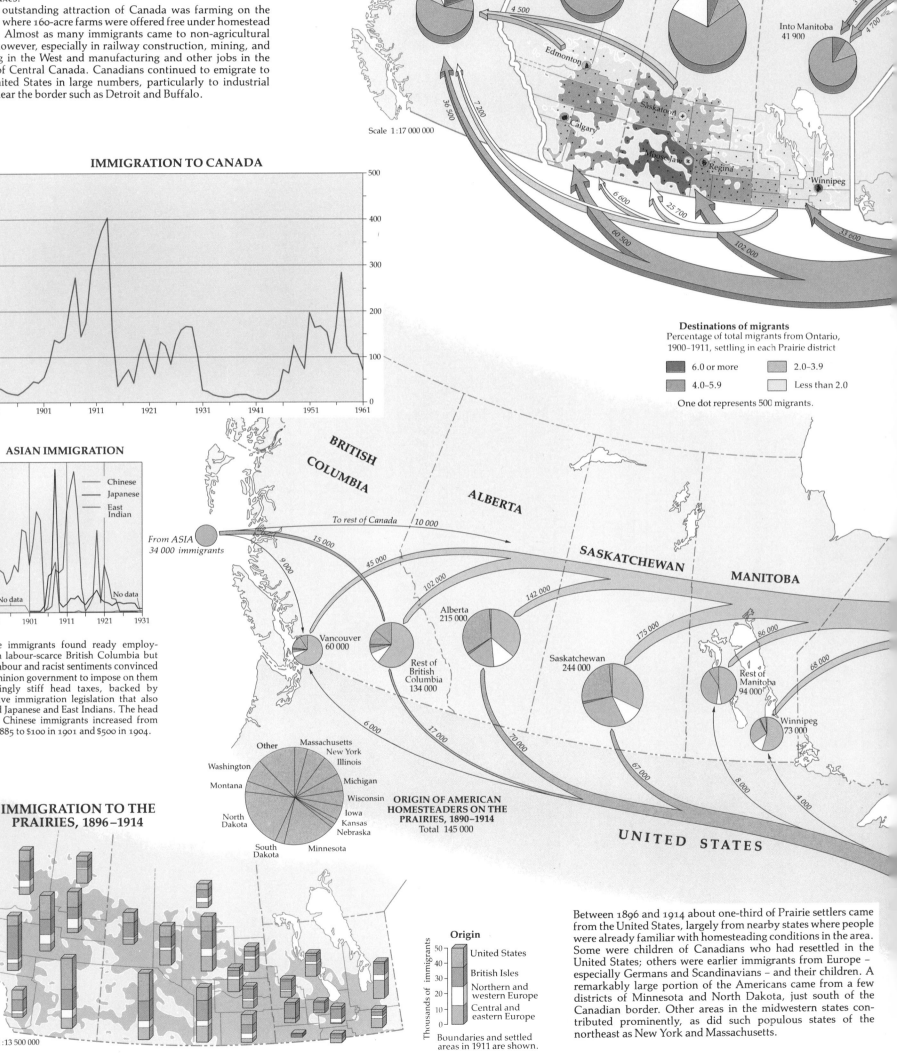

Scale 1:17 000 000

Total migration into British Columbia 66 700 migrants

Into Alberta 90 100

Into Saskatchewan 150 000

Into Manitoba 41 900

Edmonton · Saskatoon · Calgary · Moose Jaw · Regina · Winnipeg

Destinations of migrants
Percentage of total migrants from Ontario, 1900–1911, settling in each Prairie district

- 6.0 or more
- 4.0–5.9
- 2.0–3.9
- Less than 2.0

One dot represents 500 migrants.

IMMIGRATION TO CANADA

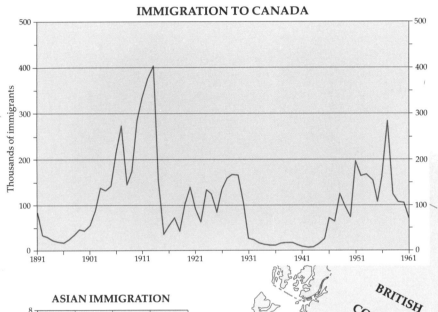

Thousands of immigrants
500 / 400 / 300 / 200 / 100 / 0
1891 1901 1911 1921 1931 1941 1951 1961

ASIAN IMMIGRATION

Thousands of immigrants
8 / 7 / 6 / 5 / 4 / 3 / 2 / 1 / 0

— Chinese
— Japanese
— East Indian

No data / No data
1891 1901 1911 1921 1931

Chinese immigrants found ready employment in labour-scarce British Columbia but white labour and racist sentiments convinced the dominion government to impose on them increasingly stiff head taxes, backed by restrictive immigration legislation that also affected Japanese and East Indians. The head tax for Chinese immigrants increased from $50 in 1885 to $100 in 1901 and $500 in 1904.

BRITISH COLUMBIA · ALBERTA · SASKATCHEWAN · MANITOBA

To rest of Canada 10 000

From ASIA 34 000 immigrants

15 000 / 9 000 / 45 000 / 102 000 / 142 000 / 175 000 / 86 000 / 68 000

Vancouver 60 000
Rest of British Columbia 134 000
Alberta 215 000
Saskatchewan 244 000
Rest of Manitoba 94 000
Winnipeg 73 000

6 000 / 17 000 / 70 000 / 67 000 / 8 000 / 4 000

ORIGIN OF AMERICAN HOMESTEADERS ON THE PRAIRIES, 1890–1914
Total 145 000

Other · Massachusetts · New York · Illinois · Washington · Michigan · Montana · Wisconsin · Iowa · Kansas · Nebraska · North Dakota · Minnesota · South Dakota

UNITED STATES

Between 1896 and 1914 about one-third of Prairie settlers came from the United States, largely from nearby states where people were already familiar with homesteading conditions in the area. Some were children of Canadians who had resettled in the United States; others were earlier immigrants from Europe – especially Germans and Scandinavians – and their children. A remarkably large portion of the Americans came from a few districts of Minnesota and North Dakota, just south of the Canadian border. Other areas in the midwestern states contributed prominently, as did such populous states of the northeast as New York and Massachusetts.

IMMIGRATION TO THE PRAIRIES, 1896–1914

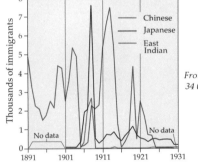

Scale 1:13 500 000

Origin

Thousands of immigrants
50 / 40 / 30 / 20 / 10 / 0

- United States
- British Isles
- Northern and western Europe
- Central and eastern Europe

Boundaries and settled areas in 1911 are shown.

HISTORICAL ATLAS OF CANADA

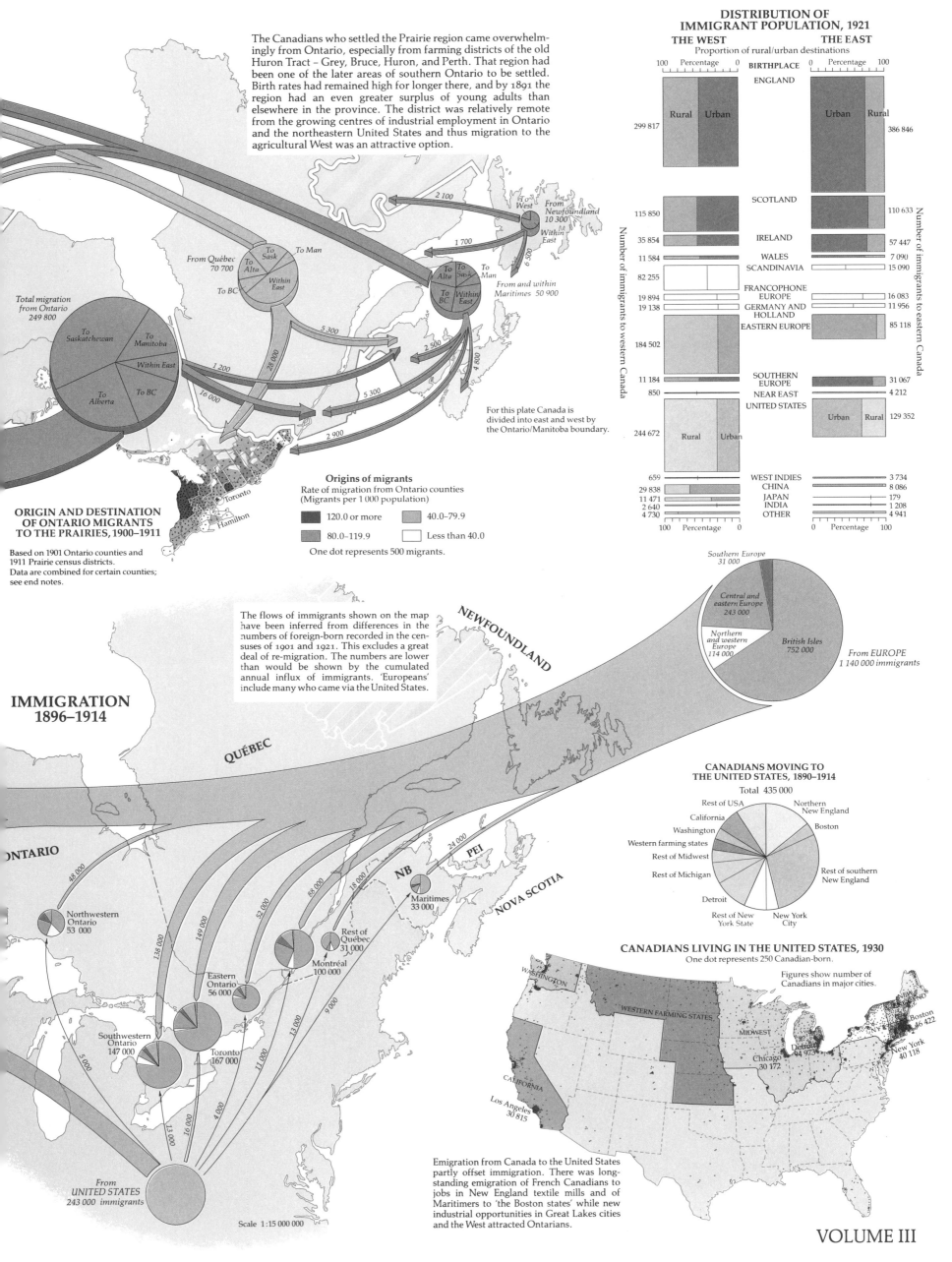

PLATE 27

DISTRIBUTION OF
IMMIGRANT POPULATION, 1921

The Canadians who settled the Prairie region came overwhelmingly from Ontario, especially from farming districts of the old Huron Tract – Grey, Bruce, Huron, and Perth. That region had been one of the later areas of southern Ontario to be settled. Birth rates had remained high for longer there, and by 1891 the region had an even greater surplus of young adults than elsewhere in the province. The district was relatively remote from the growing centres of industrial employment in Ontario and the northeastern United States and thus migration to the agricultural West was an attractive option.

THE WEST   THE EAST
Proportion of rural/urban destinations

ORIGIN AND DESTINATION OF ONTARIO MIGRANTS TO THE PRAIRIES, 1900–1911

Based on 1901 Ontario counties and 1911 Prairie census districts. Data are combined for certain counties; see end notes.

Origins of migrants
Rate of migration from Ontario counties (Migrants per 1 000 population)

- 120.0 or more
- 80.0–119.9
- 40.0–79.9
- Less than 40.0

One dot represents 500 migrants.

For this plate Canada is divided into east and west by the Ontario/Manitoba boundary.

The flows of immigrants shown on the map have been inferred from differences in the numbers of foreign-born recorded in the censuses of 1901 and 1921. This excludes a great deal of re-migration. The numbers are lower than would be shown by the cumulated annual influx of immigrants. 'Europeans' include many who came via the United States.

IMMIGRATION
1896–1914

From EUROPE 1 140 000 immigrants

CANADIANS MOVING TO THE UNITED STATES, 1890–1914
Total 435 000

CANADIANS LIVING IN THE UNITED STATES, 1930
One dot represents 250 Canadian-born.
Figures show number of Canadians in major cities.

Emigration from Canada to the United States partly offset immigration. There was long-standing emigration of French Canadians to jobs in New England textile mills and of Maritimers to 'the Boston states' while new industrial opportunities in Great Lakes cities and the West attracted Ontarians.

Scale 1:15 000 000

ELEMENTS OF POPULATION CHANGE
Author: Marvin McInnis

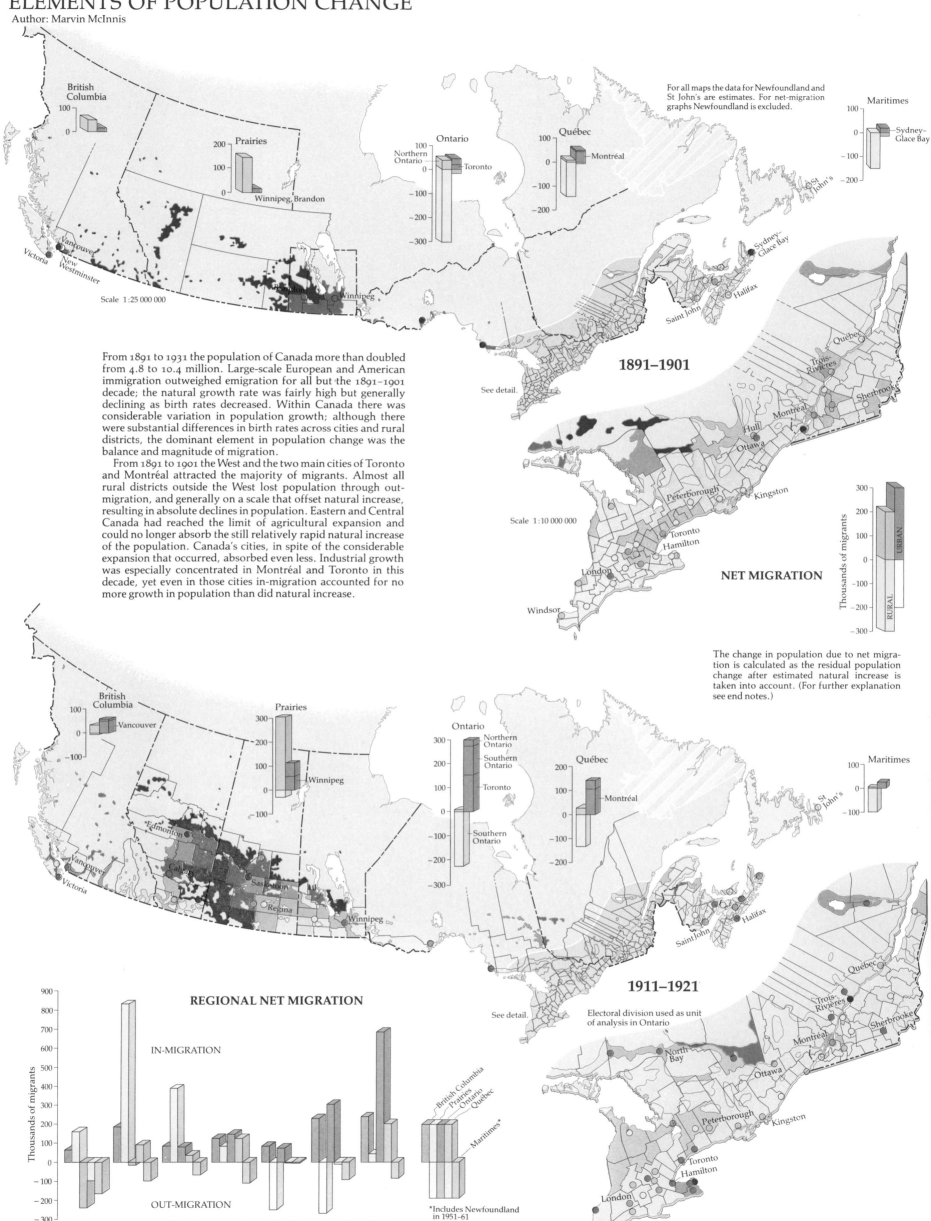

For all maps the data for Newfoundland and St John's are estimates. For net-migration graphs Newfoundland is excluded.

From 1891 to 1931 the population of Canada more than doubled from 4.8 to 10.4 million. Large-scale European and American immigration outweighed emigration for all but the 1891–1901 decade; the natural growth rate was fairly high but generally declining as birth rates decreased. Within Canada there was considerable variation in population growth; although there were substantial differences in birth rates across cities and rural districts, the dominant element in population change was the balance and magnitude of migration.

From 1891 to 1901 the West and the two main cities of Toronto and Montréal attracted the majority of migrants. Almost all rural districts outside the West lost population through out-migration, and generally on a scale that offset natural increase, resulting in absolute declines in population. Eastern and Central Canada had reached the limit of agricultural expansion and could no longer absorb the still relatively rapid natural increase of the population. Canada's cities, in spite of the considerable expansion that occurred, absorbed even less. Industrial growth was especially concentrated in Montréal and Toronto in this decade, yet even in those cities in-migration accounted for no more growth in population than did natural increase.

1891–1901

Scale 1:10 000 000

NET MIGRATION

The change in population due to net migration is calculated as the residual population change after estimated natural increase is taken into account. (For further explanation see end notes.)

1911–1921

Electoral division used as unit of analysis in Ontario

REGIONAL NET MIGRATION

IN-MIGRATION

OUT-MIGRATION

*Includes Newfoundland in 1951–61

1891–1901 1901–1911 1911–1921 1921–1931 1931–1941 1941–1951 1951–1961

HISTORICAL ATLAS OF CANADA

PLATE 28

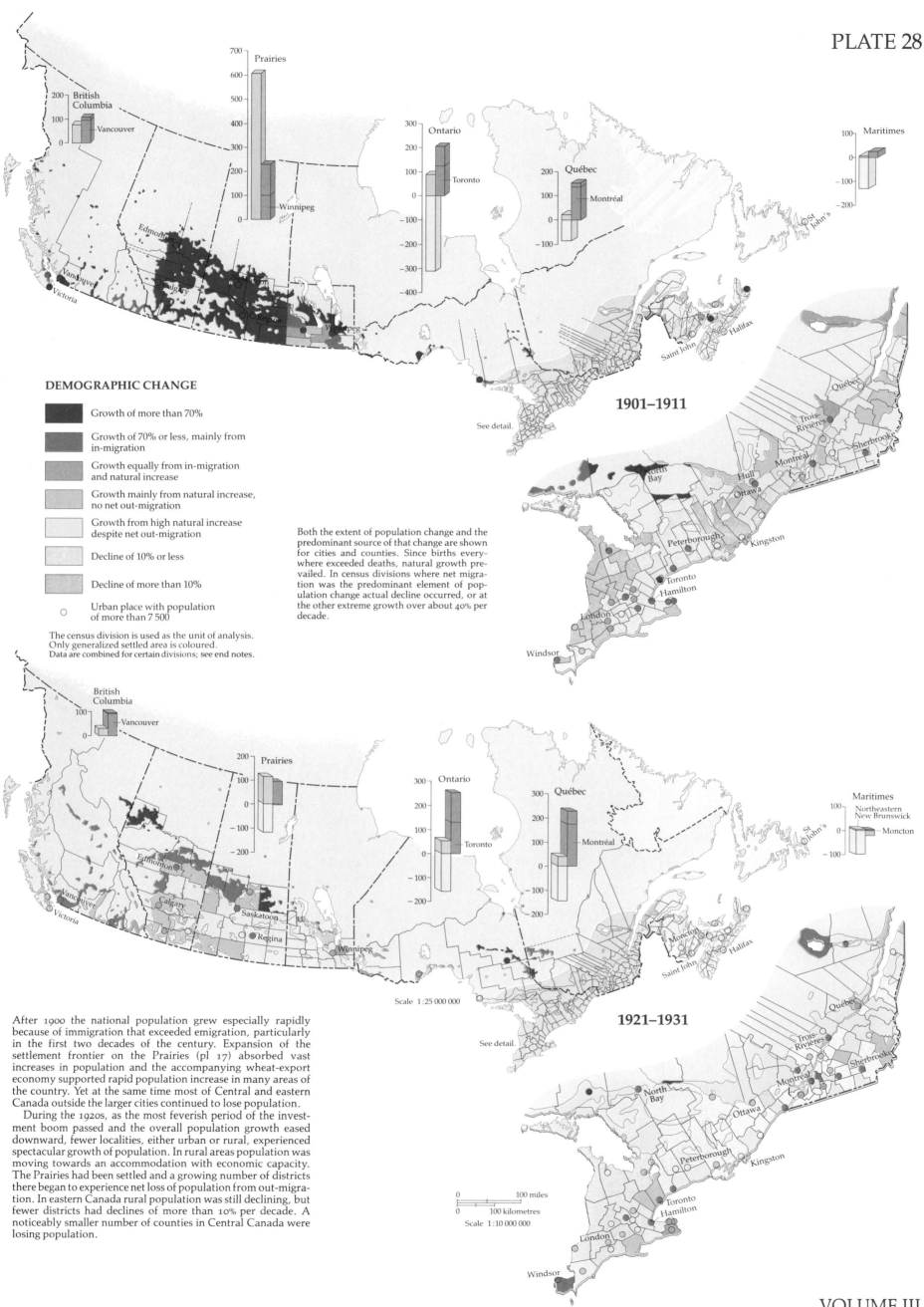

DEMOGRAPHIC CHANGE

Growth of more than 70%

Growth of 70% or less, mainly from in-migration

Growth equally from in-migration and natural increase

Growth mainly from natural increase, no net out-migration

Growth from high natural increase despite net out-migration

Decline of 10% or less

Decline of more than 10%

○ Urban place with population of more than 7 500

The census division is used as the unit of analysis.
Only generalized settled area is coloured.
Data are combined for certain divisions; see end notes.

Both the extent of population change and the predominant source of that change are shown for cities and counties. Since births everywhere exceeded deaths, natural growth prevailed. In census divisions where net migration was the predominant element of population change actual decline occurred, or at the other extreme growth over about 40% per decade.

1901–1911

1921–1931

After 1900 the national population grew especially rapidly because of immigration that exceeded emigration, particularly in the first two decades of the century. Expansion of the settlement frontier on the Prairies (pl 17) absorbed vast increases in population and the accompanying wheat-export economy supported rapid population increase in many areas of the country. Yet at the same time most of Central and eastern Canada outside the larger cities continued to lose population.

During the 1920s, as the most feverish period of the investment boom passed and the overall population growth eased downward, fewer localities, either urban or rural, experienced spectacular growth of population. In rural areas population was moving towards an accommodation with economic capacity. The Prairies had been settled and a growing number of districts there began to experience net loss of population from out-migration. In eastern Canada rural population was still declining, but fewer districts had declines of more than 10% per decade. A noticeably smaller number of counties in Central Canada were losing population.

Scale 1:25 000 000

0   100 miles
0   100 kilometres

Scale 1:10 000 000

THE DEMOGRAPHIC TRANSITION
Author: Marvin McInnis

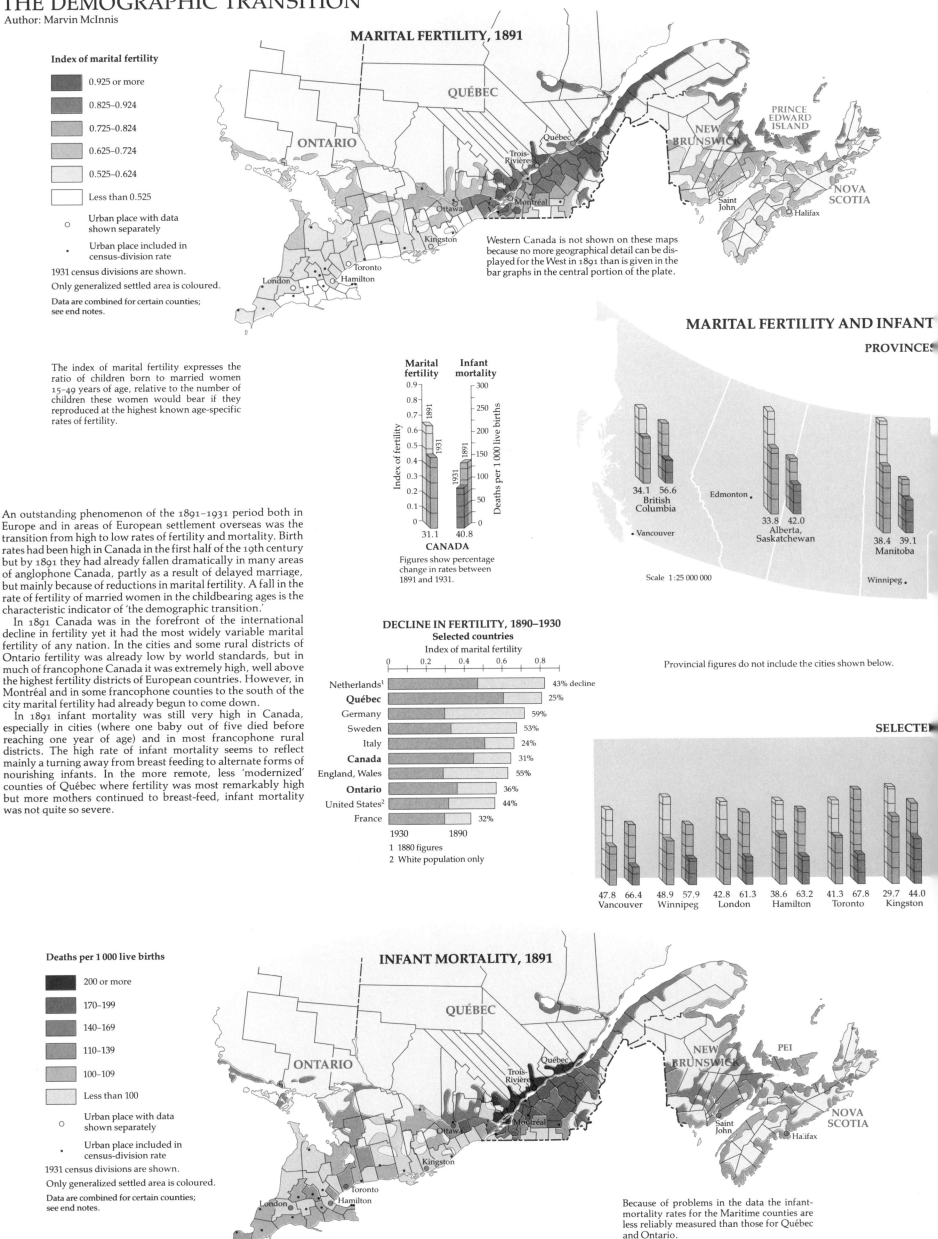

MARITAL FERTILITY, 1891

Index of marital fertility

- 0.925 or more
- 0.825–0.924
- 0.725–0.824
- 0.625–0.724
- 0.525–0.624
- Less than 0.525

○ Urban place with data shown separately

• Urban place included in census-division rate

1931 census divisions are shown.

Only generalized settled area is coloured.

Data are combined for certain counties; see end notes.

Western Canada is not shown on these maps because no more geographical detail can be displayed for the West in 1891 than is given in the bar graphs in the central portion of the plate.

The index of marital fertility expresses the ratio of children born to married women 15–49 years of age, relative to the number of children these women would bear if they reproduced at the highest known age-specific rates of fertility.

An outstanding phenomenon of the 1891–1931 period both in Europe and in areas of European settlement overseas was the transition from high to low rates of fertility and mortality. Birth rates had been high in Canada in the first half of the 19th century but by 1891 they had already fallen dramatically in many areas of anglophone Canada, partly as a result of delayed marriage, but mainly because of reductions in marital fertility. A fall in the rate of fertility of married women in the childbearing ages is the characteristic indicator of 'the demographic transition.'

In 1891 Canada was in the forefront of the international decline in fertility yet it had the most widely variable marital fertility of any nation. In the cities and some rural districts of Ontario fertility was already low by world standards, but in much of francophone Canada it was extremely high, well above the highest fertility districts of European countries. However, in Montréal and in some francophone counties to the south of the city marital fertility had already begun to come down.

In 1891 infant mortality was still very high in Canada, especially in cities (where one baby out of five died before reaching one year of age) and in most francophone rural districts. The high rate of infant mortality seems to reflect mainly a turning away from breast feeding to alternate forms of nourishing infants. In the more remote, less 'modernized' counties of Québec where fertility was most remarkably high but more mothers continued to breast-feed, infant mortality was not quite so severe.

Marital fertility / Infant mortality

Index of fertility / Deaths per 1 000 live births

1891 / 1931

CANADA
31.1 / 40.8

Figures show percentage change in rates between 1891 and 1931.

MARITAL FERTILITY AND INFANT

PROVINCES

- British Columbia: 34.1 / 56.6
- Alberta, Saskatchewan: 33.8 / 42.0
- Manitoba: 38.4 / 39.1

Edmonton
• Vancouver
Winnipeg •

Scale 1:25 000 000

Provincial figures do not include the cities shown below.

SELECTED

- Vancouver: 47.8 / 66.4
- Winnipeg: 48.9 / 57.9
- London: 42.8 / 61.3
- Hamilton: 38.6 / 63.2
- Toronto: 41.3 / 67.8
- Kingston: 29.7 / 44.0

DECLINE IN FERTILITY, 1890–1930
Selected countries

Index of marital fertility

- Netherlands[1] — 43% decline
- Québec — 25%
- Germany — 59%
- Sweden — 53%
- Italy — 24%
- Canada — 31%
- England, Wales — 55%
- Ontario — 36%
- United States[2] — 44%
- France — 32%

1930 / 1890

1 1880 figures
2 White population only

INFANT MORTALITY, 1891

Deaths per 1 000 live births

- 200 or more
- 170–199
- 140–169
- 110–139
- 100–109
- Less than 100

○ Urban place with data shown separately

• Urban place included in census-division rate

1931 census divisions are shown.

Only generalized settled area is coloured.

Data are combined for certain counties; see end notes.

Because of problems in the data the infant-mortality rates for the Maritime counties are less reliably measured than those for Québec and Ontario.

HISTORICAL ATLAS OF CANADA

PLATE 29

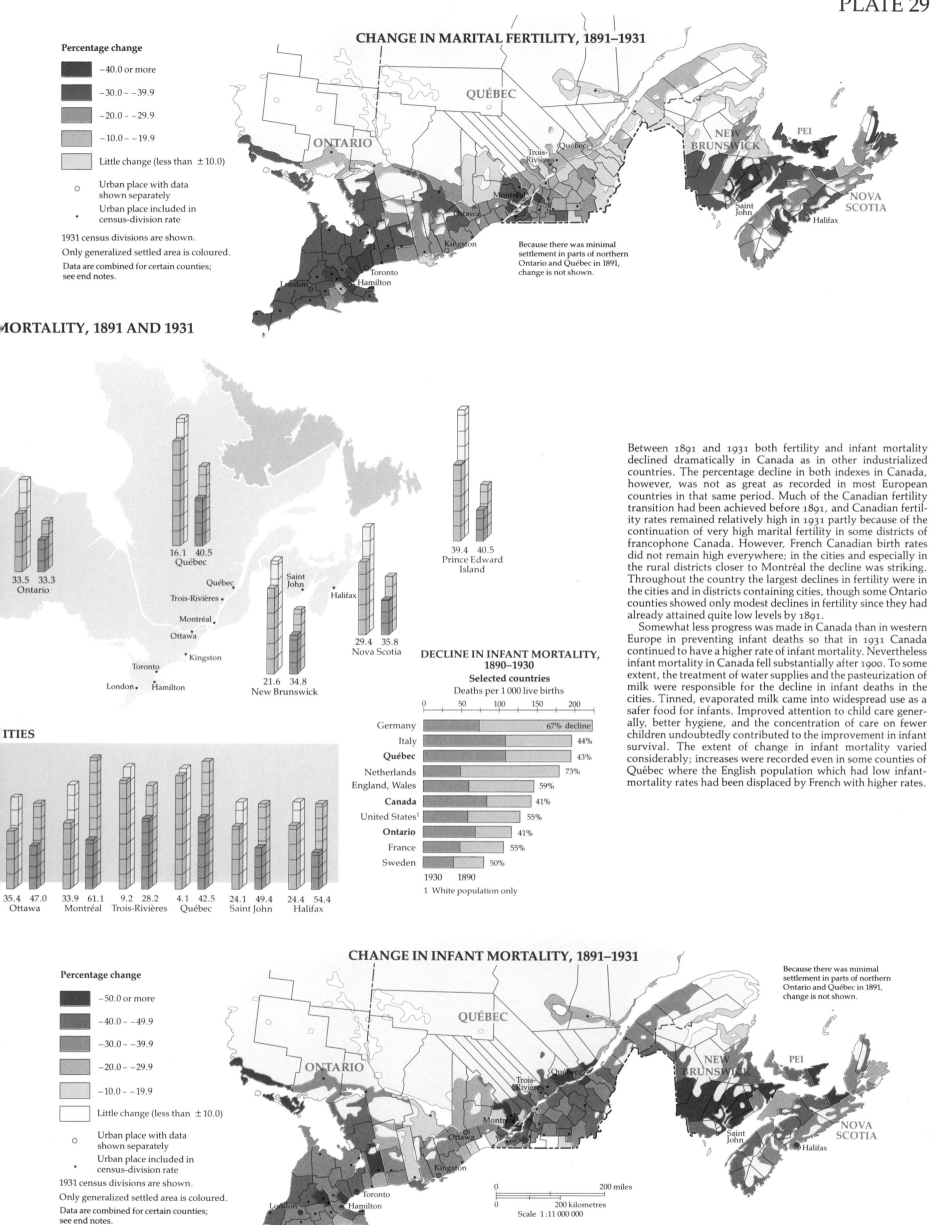

Percentage change

- −40.0 or more
- −30.0 – −39.9
- −20.0 – −29.9
- −10.0 – −19.9
- Little change (less than ±10.0)

○ Urban place with data shown separately

• Urban place included in census-division rate

1931 census divisions are shown.

Only generalized settled area is coloured.

Data are combined for certain counties; see end notes.

CHANGE IN MARITAL FERTILITY, 1891–1931

QUÉBEC

ONTARIO

NEW BRUNSWICK

PEI

NOVA SCOTIA

Trois-Rivières
Québec
Montréal
Ottawa
Kingston
Toronto
Hamilton
London
Saint John
Halifax

Because there was minimal settlement in parts of northern Ontario and Québec in 1891, change is not shown.

MORTALITY, 1891 AND 1931

33.5 33.3
Ontario

16.1 40.5
Québec

Québec
Trois-Rivières
Montréal
Ottawa
Toronto
Kingston
London Hamilton

Saint John

Halifax

39.4 40.5
Prince Edward Island

29.4 35.8
Nova Scotia

21.6 34.8
New Brunswick

ITIES

35.4 47.0
Ottawa

33.9 61.1
Montréal

9.2 28.2
Trois-Rivières

4.1 42.5
Québec

24.1 49.4
Saint John

24.4 54.4
Halifax

DECLINE IN INFANT MORTALITY, 1890–1930
Selected countries
Deaths per 1 000 live births

	0	50	100	150	200
Germany				67% decline	
Italy			44%		
Québec			43%		
Netherlands		73%			
England, Wales			59%		
Canada			41%		
United States[1]			55%		
Ontario			41%		
France		55%			
Sweden		50%			

1930 1890

1 White population only

Between 1891 and 1931 both fertility and infant mortality declined dramatically in Canada as in other industrialized countries. The percentage decline in both indexes in Canada, however, was not as great as recorded in most European countries in that same period. Much of the Canadian fertility transition had been achieved before 1891, and Canadian fertility rates remained relatively high in 1931 partly because of the continuation of very high marital fertility in some districts of francophone Canada. However, French Canadian birth rates did not remain high everywhere; in the cities and especially in the rural districts closer to Montréal the decline was striking. Throughout the country the largest declines in fertility were in the cities and in districts containing cities, though some Ontario counties showed only modest declines in fertility since they had already attained quite low levels by 1891.

Somewhat less progress was made in Canada than in western Europe in preventing infant deaths so that in 1931 Canada continued to have a higher rate of infant mortality. Nevertheless infant mortality in Canada fell substantially after 1900. To some extent, the treatment of water supplies and the pasteurization of milk were responsible for the decline in infant deaths in the cities. Tinned, evaporated milk came into widespread use as a safer food for infants. Improved attention to child care generally, better hygiene, and the concentration of care on fewer children undoubtedly contributed to the improvement in infant survival. The extent of change in infant mortality varied considerably; increases were recorded even in some counties of Québec where the English population which had low infant-mortality rates had been displaced by French with higher rates.

CHANGE IN INFANT MORTALITY, 1891–1931

Because there was minimal settlement in parts of northern Ontario and Québec in 1891, change is not shown.

QUÉBEC

ONTARIO

NEW BRUNSWICK

PEI

NOVA SCOTIA

Trois-Rivières
Québec
Montréal
Ottawa
Kingston
Toronto
Hamilton
London
Saint John
Halifax

Percentage change

- −50.0 or more
- −40.0 – −49.9
- −30.0 – −39.9
- −20.0 – −29.9
- −10.0 – −19.9
- Little change (less than ±10.0)

○ Urban place with data shown separately

• Urban place included in census-division rate

1931 census divisions are shown.

Only generalized settled area is coloured.

Data are combined for certain counties; see end notes.

0 200 miles
0 200 kilometres
Scale 1:11 000 000

THE SOCIAL LANDSCAPE OF MONTRÉAL, 1901

Authors: Sherry Olson, David Hanna

The rapid industrialization of Montréal in the late 19th century attracted migrants from rural Québec, as well as immigrants from the British Isles and elsewhere. The population of Montréal, Canada's largest city, doubled in thirty years to nearly a third of a million people, including suburbs, by 1901. Within broadly segregated areas a complex mosaic of social and economic groups existed. French and English, rich and poor, doctors and shoemakers were separated by more and more distance.

The blue-collar city was differentiated into specialized industrial districts, in response to the pull of port, canal, and railways. Most workers still lived within walking distance of their jobs. White-collar workers and professionals were more likely to live at a distance from their work-place as an expanding network of tramways opened up suburbs.

The economic patterns were made more complex by ethnic divisions. The city south of Mount Royal to the Canadian Pacific Railway (CPR) was heavily Protestant and English-speaking. Although the area northeast of Saint-Laurent Boulevard was considered French, it contained sizeable islands of English-speaking Protestants and Irish Catholics. Around the Lachine Canal lay the largest Irish neighbourhoods. Other groups, including Jewish immigrants, German speakers, and French Protestants, gravitated to the new garment district centred on Saint-Laurent Boulevard and de Lagauchetière. This district was the root of the 'immigrant corridor' which in the following decades would extend along Saint-Laurent Boulevard.

The contrasts between the 'city above the hill' and the city below the hill' can be seen in the range of housing and rental levels. As densities increased, conditions below the hill deteriorated. Epidemics led in 1897 to the first investigation of urban social problems in a Canadian city and spawned initiatives to improve management of the urban community.

CONCENTRATIONS OF SKILLED WORKERS

MONTRÉAL

Occupation

| Carter |
| Glass blower |
| Machinist |
| Nail maker |
| Printer |
| Shoemaker |
| Stone cutter |
| Tailor |
| Weaver |

Scale 1:60 000

RENTAL AND OCCUPATIONAL PROFILE ALONG MOUNTAIN STREET

Occupation
- Merchant
- Agent
- Clerk
- Joiner
- Labourer

Elevation played a pivotal role in Montréal's social geography. On Mountain Street the poor occupied the low ground (15 m) close to the Lachine Canal and the Grand Trunk Railway. The wealthy lived on the terrace (35 m) upon which the CPR embankment rested, reinforcing the separation.

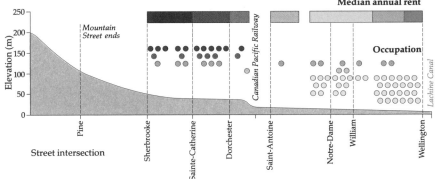

Median annual rent

Occupation

Street intersection

MONTRÉAL RENT DISTRIBUTION
CENTRED ON SAINT-LAURENT BOULEVARD

The relationship between rent and topography is evident in districts southwest of Saint-Laurent Boulevard, but to the northeast people living on the terrace had rents no higher than those below. Here poverty and wealth were found at all elevations.

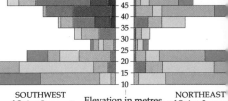

Bars are proportional to number of street segments, colour-coded according to rent class.

SOUTHWEST of Saint-Laurent Boulevard — Elevation in metres — NORTHEAST of Saint-Laurent Boulevard

A SCALE OF LIVING SPACE
A typology of new housing

No street in Montréal ever featured quite the array of housing illustrated below. Most offered a range of two or three classes of dwelling. The overwhelming majority of Montrealers lived in houses like the two models at the poor end of the scale. About 40% of all households occupied cramped dwellings in high-density streets, shown in dark green, while the élite (4%) occupied larger houses on more spacious streets, shown in maroon and brown.

Carmen Jensen

$1200 $850 $500 $275 / $225 $140 / $130 / $130 $140 / $130 / $130 $100 / $100 $120 / $90

HISTORICAL ATLAS OF CANADA

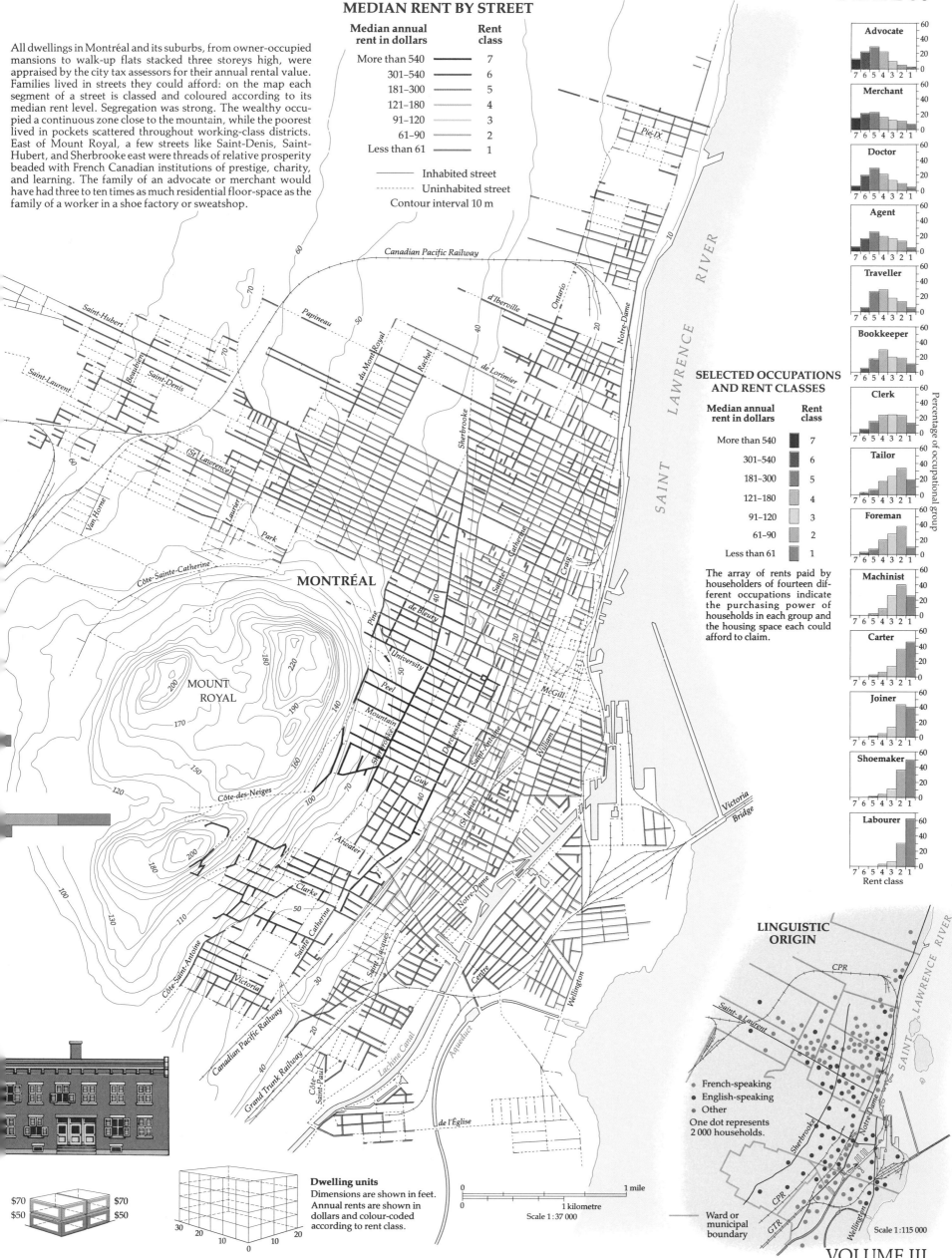

PLATE 30

MEDIAN RENT BY STREET

Median annual rent in dollars	Rent class
More than 540	7
301–540	6
181–300	5
121–180	4
91–120	3
61–90	2
Less than 61	1

—— Inhabited street
- - - Uninhabited street
Contour interval 10 m

All dwellings in Montréal and its suburbs, from owner-occupied mansions to walk-up flats stacked three storeys high, were appraised by the city tax assessors for their annual rental value. Families lived in streets they could afford: on the map each segment of a street is classed and coloured according to its median rent level. Segregation was strong. The wealthy occupied a continuous zone close to the mountain, while the poorest lived in pockets scattered throughout working-class districts. East of Mount Royal, a few streets like Saint-Denis, Saint-Hubert, and Sherbrooke east were threads of relative prosperity beaded with French Canadian institutions of prestige, charity, and learning. The family of an advocate or merchant would have had three to ten times as much residential floor-space as the family of a worker in a shoe factory or sweatshop.

MONTRÉAL

MOUNT ROYAL

SAINT LAWRENCE RIVER

SELECTED OCCUPATIONS AND RENT CLASSES

Median annual rent in dollars	Rent class
More than 540	7
301–540	6
181–300	5
121–180	4
91–120	3
61–90	2
Less than 61	1

The array of rents paid by householders of fourteen different occupations indicate the purchasing power of households in each group and the housing space each could afford to claim.

Advocate
Merchant
Doctor
Agent
Traveller
Bookkeeper
Clerk
Tailor
Foreman
Machinist
Carter
Joiner
Shoemaker
Labourer

Percentage of occupational group

Rent class

Dwelling units
Dimensions are shown in feet. Annual rents are shown in dollars and colour-coded according to rent class.

$70 $70
$50 $50

0 — 1 mile
0 — 1 kilometre
Scale 1:37 000

LINGUISTIC ORIGIN

SAINT LAWRENCE RIVER

• French-speaking
• English-speaking
• Other

One dot represents 2 000 households.

—— Ward or municipal boundary

Scale 1:115 000

WINNIPEG: A DIVIDED CITY
Author: Daniel J. Hiebert

POPULATION BY ETHNIC ORIGIN
AND PLACE OF RESIDENCE, 1891–1921

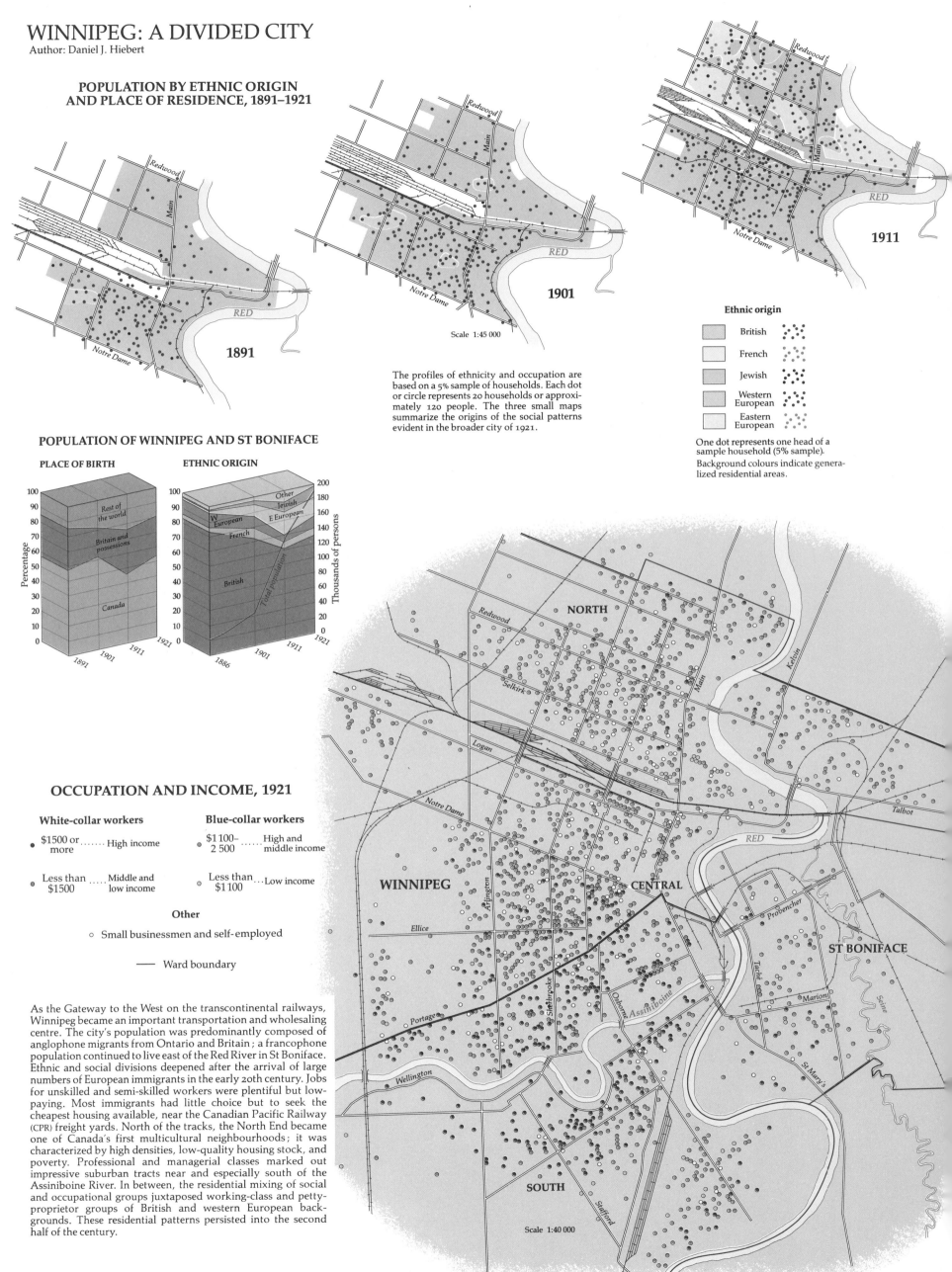

1891

1901

Scale 1:45 000

1911

The profiles of ethnicity and occupation are based on a 5% sample of households. Each dot or circle represents 20 households or approximately 120 people. The three small maps summarize the origins of the social patterns evident in the broader city of 1921.

Ethnic origin

- British
- French
- Jewish
- Western European
- Eastern European

One dot represents one head of a sample household (5% sample). Background colours indicate generalized residential areas.

POPULATION OF WINNIPEG AND ST BONIFACE

PLACE OF BIRTH

Rest of the world
Britain and possessions
Canada

Percentage

100 90 80 70 60 50 40 30 20 10 0

1891 1901 1911 1921

ETHNIC ORIGIN

Other
Jewish
E European
W European
French
British
Total population

100 90 80 70 60 50 40 30 20 10 0

Thousands of persons
200 180 160 140 120 100 80 60 40 20 0

1886 1901 1911 1921

OCCUPATION AND INCOME, 1921

White-collar workers

- $1500 or more .... High income
- Less than $1500 ..... Middle and low income

Blue-collar workers

- $1 100– 2 500 ..... High and middle income
- Less than $1 100 ...Low income

Other

- Small businessmen and self-employed

— Ward boundary

As the Gateway to the West on the transcontinental railways, Winnipeg became an important transportation and wholesaling centre. The city's population was predominantly composed of anglophone migrants from Ontario and Britain; a francophone population continued to live east of the Red River in St Boniface. Ethnic and social divisions deepened after the arrival of large numbers of European immigrants in the early 20th century. Jobs for unskilled and semi-skilled workers were plentiful but low-paying. Most immigrants had little choice but to seek the cheapest housing available, near the Canadian Pacific Railway (CPR) freight yards. North of the tracks, the North End became one of Canada's first multicultural neighbourhoods; it was characterized by high densities, low-quality housing stock, and poverty. Professional and managerial classes marked out impressive suburban tracts near and especially south of the Assiniboine River. In between, the residential mixing of social and occupational groups juxtaposed working-class and petty-proprietor groups of British and western European backgrounds. These residential patterns persisted into the second half of the century.

HISTORICAL ATLAS OF CANADA

PLATE 31

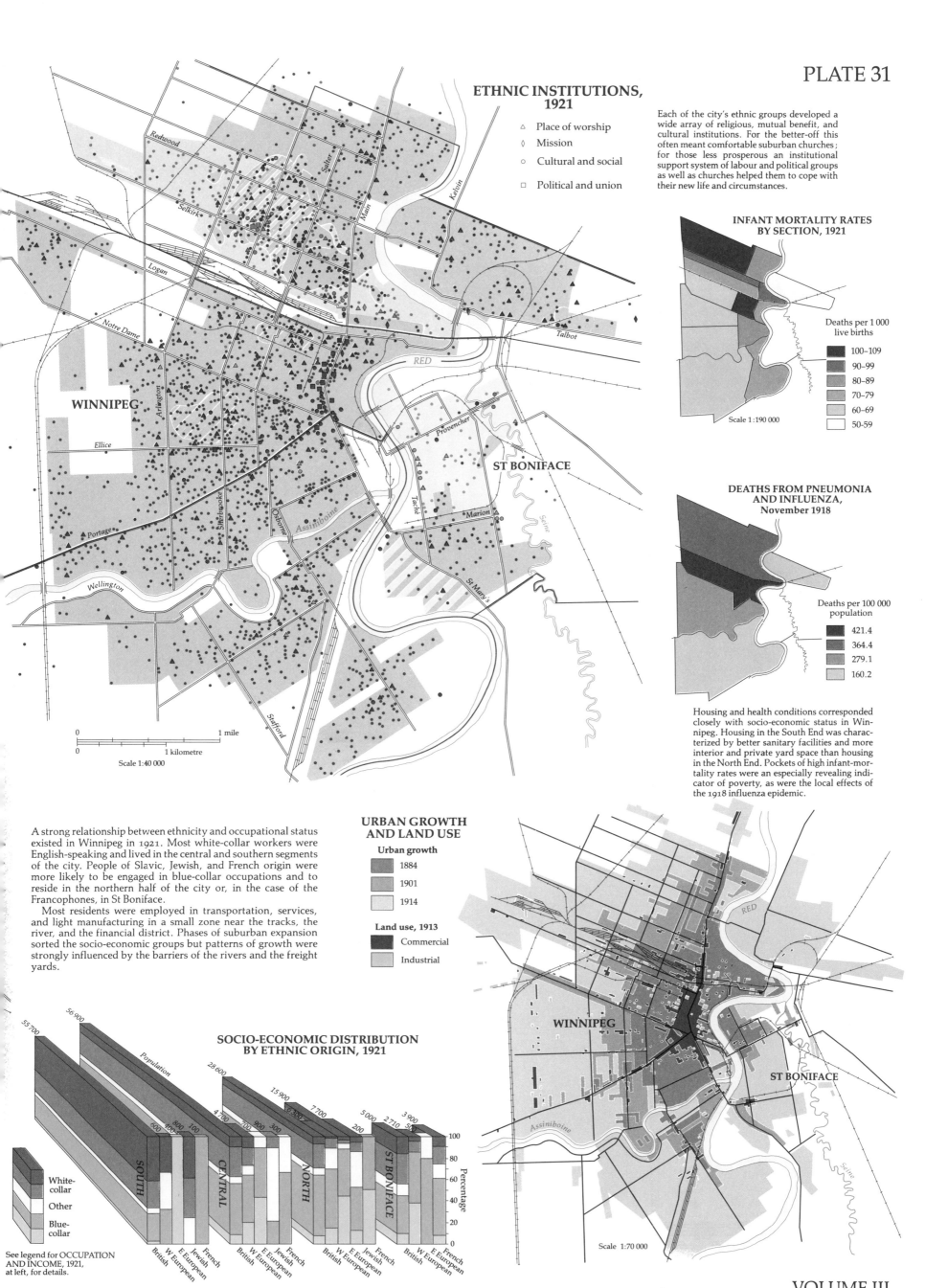

ETHNIC INSTITUTIONS, 1921

△ Place of worship

◊ Mission

○ Cultural and social

□ Political and union

Each of the city's ethnic groups developed a wide array of religious, mutual benefit, and cultural institutions. For the better-off this often meant comfortable suburban churches; for those less prosperous an institutional support system of labour and political groups as well as churches helped them to cope with their new life and circumstances.

Redwood

Selkirk

Salter

Main

Kelvin

Logan

Notre Dame

Talbot

RED

WINNIPEG

Ellice

Arlington

Sherbrooke

Osborne

Assiniboine

Tache

Provencher

ST BONIFACE

Marion

Seine

Portage

Wellington

St Mary's

Stafford

0   1 mile

0   1 kilometre

Scale 1:40 000

INFANT MORTALITY RATES BY SECTION, 1921

Scale 1:190 000

Deaths per 1 000 live births

■ 100–109
■ 90–99
■ 80–89
■ 70–79
■ 60–69
□ 50–59

DEATHS FROM PNEUMONIA AND INFLUENZA, November 1918

Deaths per 100 000 population

■ 421.4
■ 364.4
■ 279.1
□ 160.2

Housing and health conditions corresponded closely with socio-economic status in Winnipeg. Housing in the South End was characterized by better sanitary facilities and more interior and private yard space than housing in the North End. Pockets of high infant-mortality rates were an especially revealing indicator of poverty, as were the local effects of the 1918 influenza epidemic.

A strong relationship between ethnicity and occupational status existed in Winnipeg in 1921. Most white-collar workers were English-speaking and lived in the central and southern segments of the city. People of Slavic, Jewish, and French origin were more likely to be engaged in blue-collar occupations and to reside in the northern half of the city or, in the case of the Francophones, in St Boniface.

Most residents were employed in transportation, services, and light manufacturing in a small zone near the tracks, the river, and the financial district. Phases of suburban expansion sorted the socio-economic groups but patterns of growth were strongly influenced by the barriers of the rivers and the freight yards.

URBAN GROWTH AND LAND USE

Urban growth

■ 1884
■ 1901
□ 1914

Land use, 1913

■ Commercial
■ Industrial

WINNIPEG

RED

Assiniboine

ST BONIFACE

Seine

Scale 1:70 000

SOCIO-ECONOMIC DISTRIBUTION BY ETHNIC ORIGIN, 1921

Population

55 700
56 900
28 600
15 900
7 700
5 000
3 900

■ White-collar
□ Other
■ Blue-collar

SOUTH
CENTRAL
NORTH
ST BONIFACE

British
W European
E European
Jewish
French

Percentage
100
80
60
40
20
0

See legend for OCCUPATION AND INCOME, 1921, at left, for details.

NEW APPROACHES TO DISEASE AND PUBLIC DEPENDENCY

Author: Lynne Marks

INFANT MORTALITY

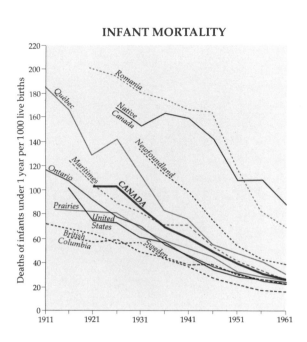

IMPACT OF SANITATION AND PASTEURIZATION IN TORONTO

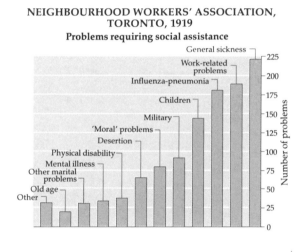

Chlorination began
Chlorination completed
Filtration completed
Pasteurization compulsory

Victorian beliefs in the demoralizing effects of welfare persisted in early 20th-century Canada and fostered a reluctance to assist individuals considered capable of providing for themselves, such as the able-bodied unemployed. This attitude, in combination with the desire to create a 'strong and healthy Canada,' led to a focus on children by those concerned with improving social and health conditions.

A major issue for child-centred reformers was Canada's infant mortality rate, which was high by international standards, especially in the newly crowded cities. Reformers pressured governments to launch programs such as well-baby clinics and health inspection of school children. Interest in the health and strength of future Canadians also had a darker side. Members of the mental hygiene movement agitated against the rights to reproduce of those judged mentally 'unfit', resulting in sterilization programs in Alberta and British Columbia.

Concern for child health often prompted broader public-health initiatives such as milk pasteurization, water filtration, and public-health nursing. To deal with tuberculosis, the largest single cause of death by disease among younger adults, clinics to test for the disease were set up in both rural and urban areas and sanatoriums were established in most provinces, generally away from large cities. Most health and welfare programs, however, were founded in major urban areas, where a complex array of institutions was supported by religious and lay efforts often with government assistance. Early social-work organizations such as Toronto's Neighbourhood Workers' Association attempted to centralize, organize, and prevent 'duplication and waste' among disparate private relief agencies.

STERILIZATION OF THE MENTALLY 'UNFIT'
Alberta's Sexual Sterilization Act

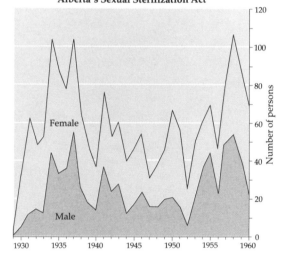

NEIGHBOURHOOD WORKERS' ASSOCIATION, TORONTO, 1919
Problems requiring social assistance

General sickness
Work-related problems
Influenza-pneumonia
Children
Military
'Moral' problems
Desertion
Physical disability
Mental illness
Other marital problems
Old age
Other

ESTABLISHED INSTITUTIONS AND NEW

Old
Hospital
Mental hospital
Home for incurables
Poor house
Home for the aged
Orphanage
Day nursery
Reformatory
Multifunctional institutions

THE MANDATE OF THE JUVENILE COURT, HALIFAX, 1912–1913
Supervision and control

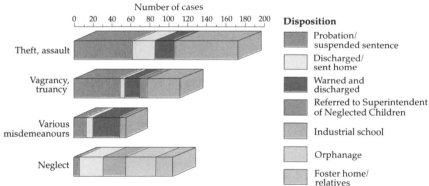

Number of cases

Theft, assault
Vagrancy, truancy
Various misdemeanours
Neglect

Disposition
- Probation/ suspended sentence
- Discharged/ sent home
- Warned and discharged
- Referred to Superintendent of Neglected Children
- Industrial school
- Orphanage
- Foster home/ relatives

TORONTO

LAKE ONTARIO

CHILDREN UNDER PUBLIC CARE, 1941

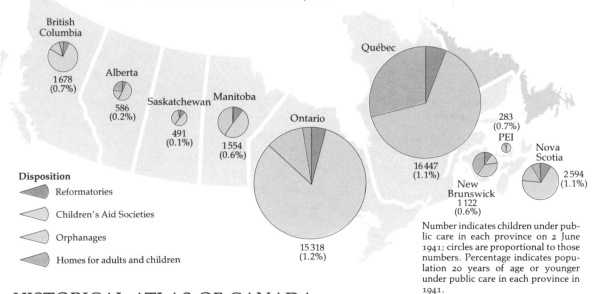

British Columbia
1 678 (0.7%)

Alberta
586 (0.2%)

Saskatchewan
491 (0.1%)

Manitoba
1 554 (0.6%)

Ontario
15 318 (1.2%)

Québec
16 447 (1.1%)

PEI
283 (0.7%)

New Brunswick
1 122 (0.6%)

Nova Scotia
2 594 (1.1%)

Disposition
- Reformatories
- Children's Aid Societies
- Orphanages
- Homes for adults and children

Number indicates children under public care in each province on 2 June 1941; circles are proportional to those numbers. Percentage indicates population 20 years of age or younger under public care in each province in 1941.

Orphaned, neglected, and delinquent children were perceived as a threat to public order, and it was feared that they would grow up to be criminals. In English Canada reformers argued that a 'proper' home environment was essential for these children, and, as a result, many were placed in foster homes under the auspices of Children's Aid Societies. The creation of juvenile courts meant that the specific problems of children could be dealt with away from the contaminating influences of adult criminals. By broadening the definition of behaviour that could result in judicial intervention these courts increased the public control exercised over children.

Idealization of the home as an environment for children was also instrumental in securing passage of provincial mothers' allowance legislation. In effect widowed mothers who were judged suitable were paid to raise their children.

HISTORICAL ATLAS OF CANADA

PLATE 32

PUBLIC HEALTH PROGRAMS, NEW BRUNSWICK, 1928

By the 1920s the health problems facing overcrowded cities had begun to be addressed through preventive public-health measures, but the situation in rural areas and smaller towns remained serious because of a lack of financial resources. As a result most provincial governments became involved in public health. Funding was extremely limited, however, and costs were still shared with local organizations and municipalities where possible, making the provision of services very uneven.

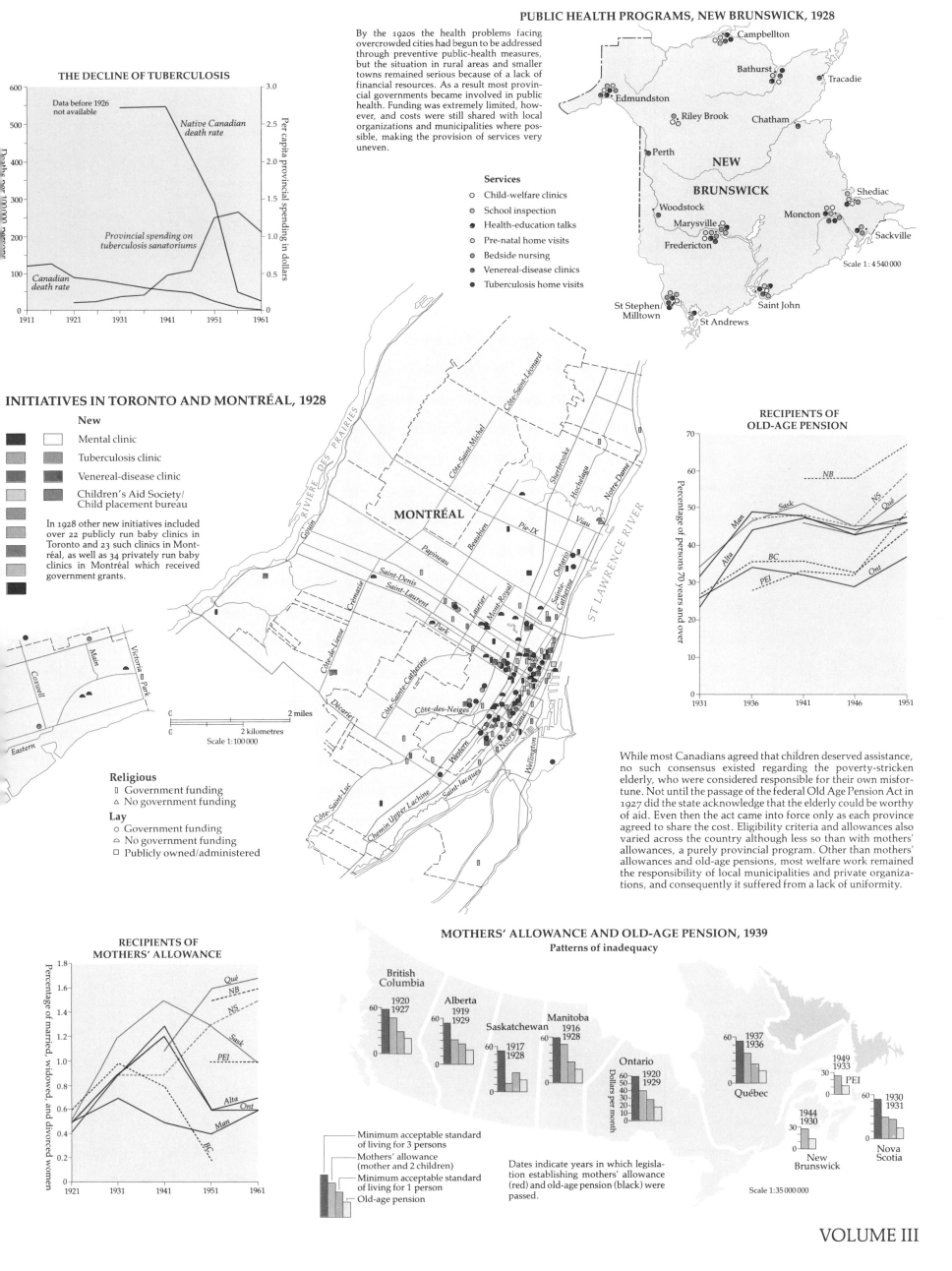

Services
- ○ Child-welfare clinics
- ◑ School inspection
- ● Health-education talks
- ○ Pre-natal home visits
- ◔ Bedside nursing
- ◕ Venereal-disease clinics
- ● Tuberculosis home visits

Campbellton
Bathurst
Tracadie
Edmundston
Riley Brook
Chatham
Perth
NEW
BRUNSWICK
Shediac
Woodstock
Moncton
Marysville
Sackville
Fredericton
Scale 1 : 4 540 000
St Stephen/
Milltown
St Andrews
Saint John

THE DECLINE OF TUBERCULOSIS

Deaths per 100000 persons

600
500
400
300
200
100
0

Per capita provincial spending in dollars

3.0
2.5
2.0
1.5
1.0
0.5
0

Data before 1926 not available

Native Canadian death rate

Provincial spending on tuberculosis sanatoriums

Canadian death rate

1911 1921 1931 1941 1951 1961

INITIATIVES IN TORONTO AND MONTRÉAL, 1928

New

- Mental clinic
- Tuberculosis clinic
- Venereal-disease clinic
- Children's Aid Society/ Child placement bureau

In 1928 other new initiatives included over 22 publicly run baby clinics in Toronto and 23 such clinics in Montréal, as well as 34 privately run baby clinics in Montréal which received government grants.

Coxwell
Main
Victoria Park
Eastern

2 miles
2 kilometres
Scale 1:100 000

Religious
- ▫ Government funding
- △ No government funding

Lay
- ○ Government funding
- ⬠ No government funding
- ▢ Publicly owned/administered

MONTRÉAL

RIVIÈRE DES PRAIRIES
Côte-Saint-Léonard
Côte-Saint-Michel
Sherbrooke
Hochelaga
Notre-Dame
Gouin
Côte-de-Liesse
Pie-IX
Viau
Beaubien
Papineau
Saint-Denis
Saint-Laurent
Crémazie
Laurier
Mont-Royal
Ontario
Sainte-Catherine
ST LAWRENCE RIVER
Park
Côte-Sainte-Catherine
Décarie
Côte-des-Neiges
Western
Notre-Dame
Wellington
Côte-Saint-Luc
Chemin Upper Lachine
Saint-Jacques

RECIPIENTS OF OLD-AGE PENSION

Percentage of persons 70 years and over

70
60
50
40
30
20
10
0

NB
NS
Qué
Man
Sask
Alta
BC
Ont
PEI

1931 1936 1941 1946 1951

While most Canadians agreed that children deserved assistance, no such consensus existed regarding the poverty-stricken elderly, who were considered responsible for their own misfortune. Not until the passage of the federal Old Age Pension Act in 1927 did the state acknowledge that the elderly could be worthy of aid. Even then the act came into force only as each province agreed to share the cost. Eligibility criteria and allowances also varied across the country although less so than with mothers' allowances, a purely provincial program. Other than mothers' allowances and old-age pensions, most welfare work remained the responsibility of local municipalities and private organizations, and consequently it suffered from a lack of uniformity.

RECIPIENTS OF MOTHERS' ALLOWANCE

Percentage of married, widowed, and divorced women

1.8
1.6
1.4
1.2
1.0
0.8
0.6
0.4
0.2

Qué
NB
NS
Sask
PEI
Alta
Ont
Man
BC

1921 1931 1941 1951 1961

MOTHERS' ALLOWANCE AND OLD-AGE PENSION, 1939
Patterns of inadequacy

British Columbia
1920
1927
60

Alberta
1919
1929
60

Saskatchewan
1917
1928
60

Manitoba
1916
1928
60

Ontario
1920
1929
Dollars per month
60
40
30
20
10
0

Québec
1937
1936
60

PEI
1949
1933
30

New Brunswick
1944
1930
30

Nova Scotia
1930
1931
60

- Minimum acceptable standard of living for 3 persons
- Mothers' allowance (mother and 2 children)
- Minimum acceptable standard of living for 1 person
- Old-age pension

Dates indicate years in which legislation establishing mothers' allowance (red) and old-age pension (black) were passed.

Scale 1:35 000 000

SCHOOLING AND SOCIAL STRUCTURE

Authors: Chad Gaffield, Lynne Marks

THE 'RURAL SCHOOL PROBLEM'

SECONDARY-SCHOOL ATTENDANCE, 1921 AND 1951

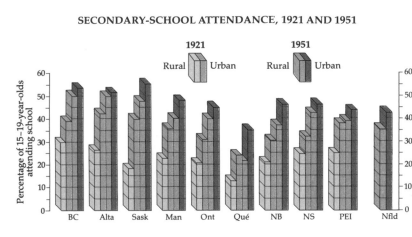

1921 — Rural Urban 1951 — Rural Urban

Percentage of 15–19-year-olds attending school

BC Alta Sask Man Ont Qué NB NS PEI Nfld

ENROLMENT IN SECONDARY GRADES, SASKATCHEWAN, 1930

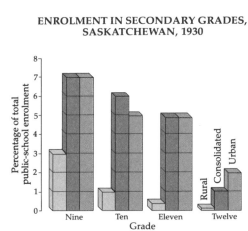

Percentage of total public-school enrolment

Nine Ten Eleven Twelve

Rural Consolidated Urban

Grade

SECONDARY SCHOOLING

ENROLMENT BY REGION

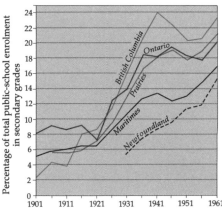

Percentage of total public-school enrolment in secondary grades

British Columbia · Ontario · Prairies · Maritimes · Newfoundland

1901 1911 1921 1931 1941 1951 1961

SCHOOL ENROLMENT

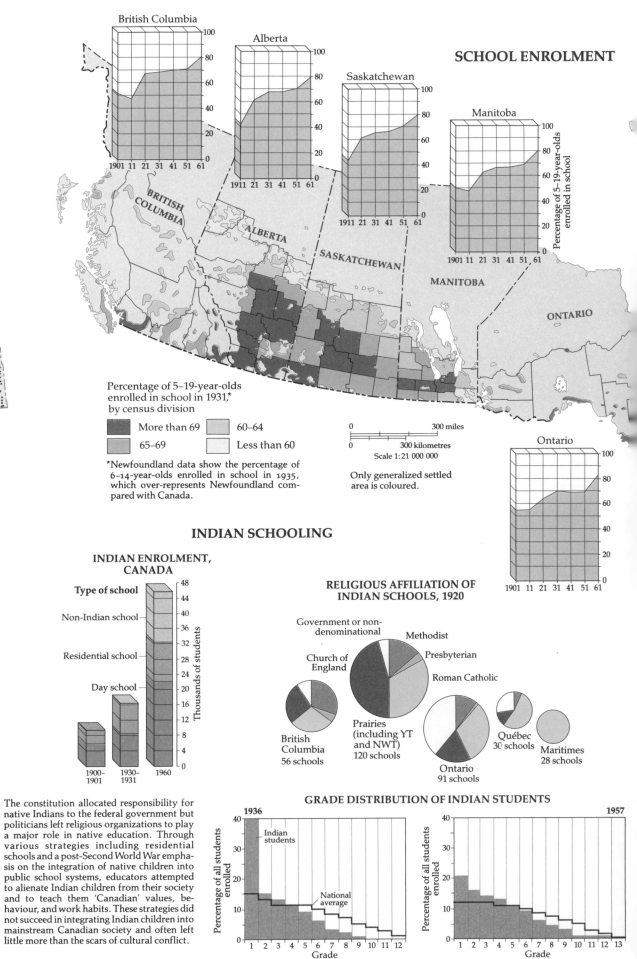

British Columbia · Alberta · Saskatchewan · Manitoba · Ontario

Percentage of 5–19-year-olds enrolled in school

Percentage of 5–19-year-olds enrolled in school in 1931,* by census division

- More than 69
- 65–69
- 60–64
- Less than 60

*Newfoundland data show the percentage of 6–14-year-olds enrolled in school in 1935, which over-represents Newfoundland compared with Canada.

Only generalized settled area is coloured.

0 — 300 miles
0 — 300 kilometres
Scale 1:21 000 000

SASKATCHEWAN SCHOOLS, 1931

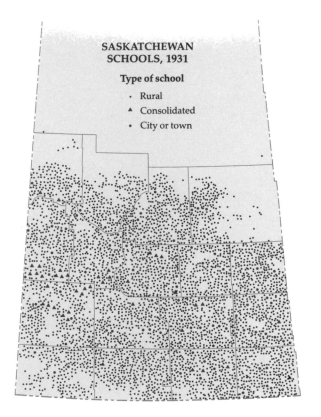

Type of school

- · Rural
- ▲ Consolidated
- ● City or town

INDIAN ENROLMENT, ALBERTA, 1911

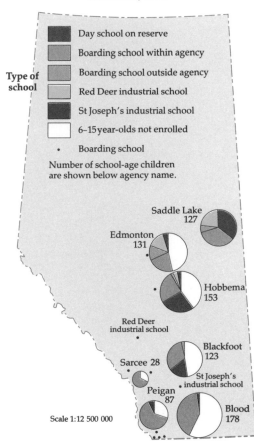

Type of school

- Day school on reserve
- Boarding school within agency
- Boarding school outside agency
- Red Deer industrial school
- St Joseph's industrial school
- 6–15 year-olds not enrolled
- ● Boarding school

Number of school-age children are shown below agency name.

Saddle Lake 127
Edmonton 131
Hobbema 153
Red Deer industrial school
Blackfoot 123
Sarcee 28
St Joseph's industrial school
Peigan 87
Blood 178

Scale 1:12 500 000

INDIAN SCHOOLING

INDIAN ENROLMENT, CANADA

Type of school

Non-Indian school
Residential school
Day school

Thousands of students

1900–1901 1930–1931 1960

RELIGIOUS AFFILIATION OF INDIAN SCHOOLS, 1920

Government or non-denominational
Methodist
Church of England
Presbyterian
Roman Catholic

British Columbia 56 schools
Prairies (including YT and NWT) 120 schools
Ontario 91 schools
Québec 30 schools
Maritimes 28 schools

The constitution allocated responsibility for native Indians to the federal government but politicians left religious organizations to play a major role in native education. Through various strategies including residential schools and a post-Second World War emphasis on the integration of native children into public school systems, educators attempted to alienate Indian children from their society and to teach them 'Canadian' values, behaviour, and work habits. These strategies did not succeed in integrating Indian children into mainstream Canadian society and often left little more than the scars of cultural conflict.

GRADE DISTRIBUTION OF INDIAN STUDENTS

1936
Percentage of all students enrolled
Indian students
National average
Grade 1 2 3 4 5 6 7 8 9 10 11 12

1957
Percentage of all students enrolled
Grade 1 2 3 4 5 6 7 8 9 10 11 12 13

HISTORICAL ATLAS OF CANADA

PLATE 33

NEW AGENDAS IN EDUCATION

ENROLMENT BY GENDER

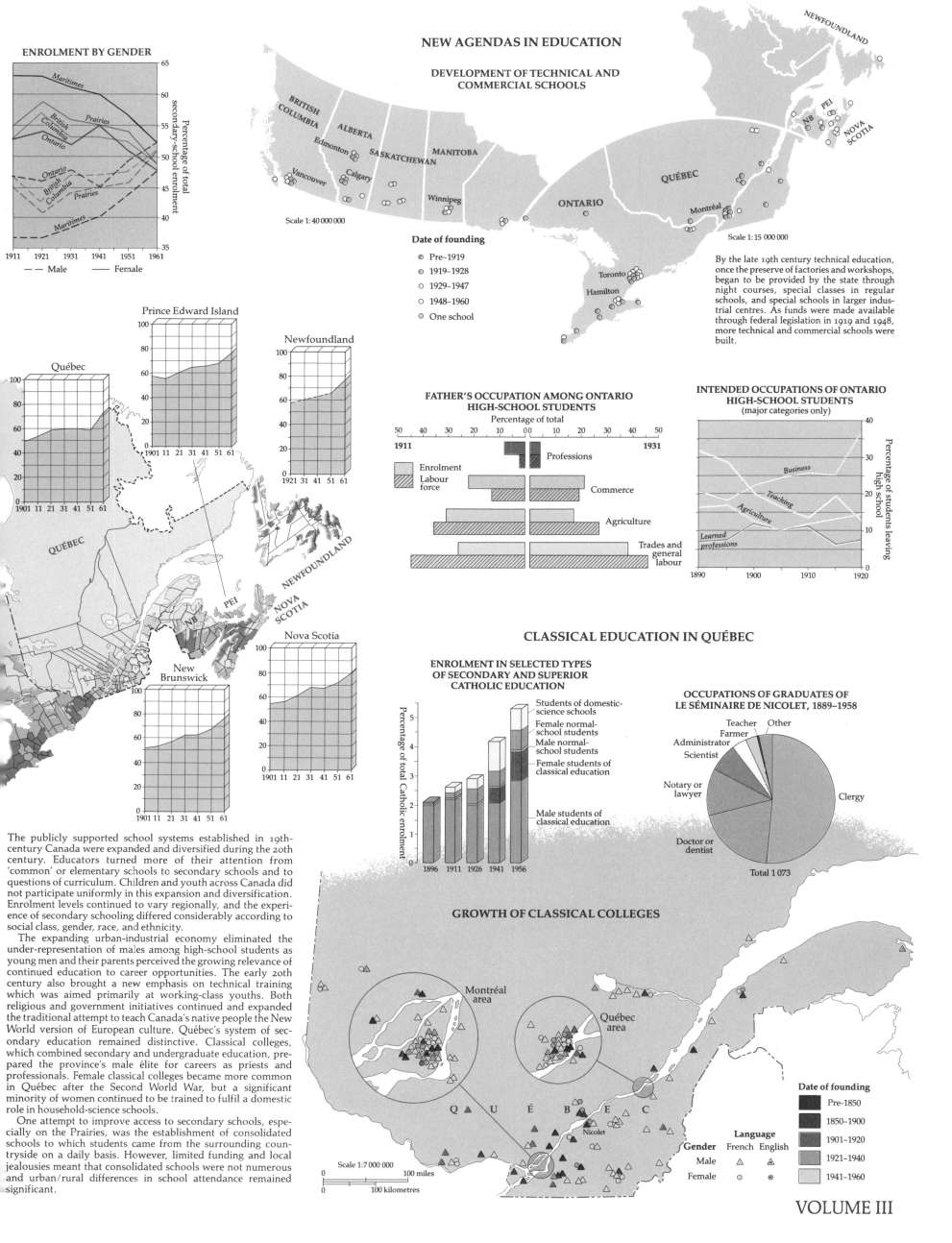

Percentage of total secondary-school enrolment

Maritimes
British Columbia
Prairies
Ontario
Ontario
British Columbia
Prairies
Maritimes

1911 1921 1931 1941 1951 1961

— Male   — Female

DEVELOPMENT OF TECHNICAL AND COMMERCIAL SCHOOLS

NEWFOUNDLAND

BRITISH COLUMBIA
ALBERTA
SASKATCHEWAN
MANITOBA
Edmonton
Calgary
Vancouver
Winnipeg
ONTARIO
QUÉBEC
Montréal
NB
PEI
NOVA SCOTIA
Toronto
Hamilton

Scale 1:40 000 000

Scale 1:15 000 000

Date of founding

- ◉ Pre–1919
- ◎ 1919–1928
- ○ 1929–1947
- ○ 1948–1960
- ○ One school

By the late 19th century technical education, once the preserve of factories and workshops, began to be provided by the state through night courses, special classes in regular schools, and special schools in larger industrial centres. As funds were made available through federal legislation in 1919 and 1948, more technical and commercial schools were built.

Provincial enrolment charts

Prince Edward Island
100 80 60 40 20
1901 11 21 31 41 51 61

Newfoundland
100 80 60 40 20
1921 31 41 51 61

Québec
100 80 60 40 20
1901 11 21 31 41 51 61

QUÉBEC
NEWFOUNDLAND
PEI
NOVA SCOTIA
NB

New Brunswick
100 80 60 40 20
1901 11 21 31 41 51 61

Nova Scotia
100 80 60 40 20
1901 11 21 31 41 51 61

FATHER'S OCCUPATION AMONG ONTARIO HIGH-SCHOOL STUDENTS

Percentage of total

50 40 30 20 10 0 10 20 30 40 50

1911   **1931**

Professions
Commerce
Agriculture
Trades and general labour

Enrolment
Labour force

INTENDED OCCUPATIONS OF ONTARIO HIGH-SCHOOL STUDENTS
(major categories only)

Percentage of students leaving high school

40 30 20 10 0

Business
Teaching
Agriculture
Learned professions

1890 1900 1910 1920

CLASSICAL EDUCATION IN QUÉBEC

ENROLMENT IN SELECTED TYPES OF SECONDARY AND SUPERIOR CATHOLIC EDUCATION

Percentage of total Catholic enrolment

5 4 3 2 1

Students of domestic-science schools
Female normal-school students
Male normal-school students
Female students of classical education
Male students of classical education

1896 1911 1926 1941 1956

OCCUPATIONS OF GRADUATES OF LE SÉMINAIRE DE NICOLET, 1889–1958

Teacher
Farmer
Other
Administrator
Scientist
Notary or lawyer
Clergy
Doctor or dentist

Total 1 073

GROWTH OF CLASSICAL COLLEGES

Montréal area
Québec area
Q U É B E C
Nicolet

Scale 1:7 000 000
0   100 miles
0   100 kilometres

Date of founding
- ■ Pre–1850
- ■ 1850–1900
- ■ 1901–1920
- ■ 1921–1940
- ■ 1941–1960

Language   French English
Gender
Male   △   ▲
Female ○   ◉

The publicly supported school systems established in 19th-century Canada were expanded and diversified during the 20th century. Educators turned more of their attention from 'common' or elementary schools to secondary schools and to questions of curriculum. Children and youth across Canada did not participate uniformly in this expansion and diversification. Enrolment levels continued to vary regionally, and the experience of secondary schooling differed considerably according to social class, gender, race, and ethnicity.

The expanding urban-industrial economy eliminated the under-representation of males among high-school students as young men and their parents perceived the growing relevance of continued education to career opportunities. The early 20th century also brought a new emphasis on technical training which was aimed primarily at working-class youths. Both religious and government initiatives continued and expanded the traditional attempt to teach Canada's native people the New World version of European culture. Québec's system of secondary education remained distinctive. Classical colleges, which combined secondary and undergraduate education, prepared the province's male élite for careers as priests and professionals. Female classical colleges became more common in Québec after the Second World War, but a significant minority of women continued to be trained to fulfil a domestic role in household-science schools.

One attempt to improve access to secondary schools, especially on the Prairies, was the establishment of consolidated schools to which students came from the surrounding countryside on a daily basis. However, limited funding and local jealousies meant that consolidated schools were not numerous and urban/rural differences in school attendance remained significant.

RELIGIOUS ADHERENCE

Authors: Murdo MacPherson, Douglas Campbell (Votes of congregations, NS)

Except for the formation of the United Church of Canada in 1925, the modern patterns of religious adherence across Canada had largely emerged by 1921. In eastern Canada these patterns reflected traditions brought by migrants from Europe and the United States over three centuries. The varied origins of late 19th- and early 20th-century immigrants were apparent in the patchwork pattern of adherence on the Prairies. The diversity was even more dramatic at the local level. In Saskatchewan, for example, the band of Presbyterians and Methodists mirrored the earliest line of settlement by migrants from Ontario, the United States, and Britain, while the scattering of Lutherans on either side corresponded with settlement by Germans and Scandinavians. The presence of adherents of Greek churches* indicated Ukrainian group settlement on the prairie fringes. In British Columbia the predominance of Anglicans was a consequence of the largely British background of the population; however, the Confucian and Buddhist elements of Vancouver's population showed the significant presence of Chinese and Japanese migrants. Similarly, it is clear that Winnipeg, Toronto, and Montréal were the preferred destinations of most Jewish immigrants.

RELIGIOUS DIVERSITY IN SASKATCHEWAN, 1921

Census subdivisions

Colour shows major group only, not percentage of adherence. See central legend.

FIRST RANK

Saskatoon

Regina •

Mormons 17.6%

SECOND RANK

Saskatoon

Regina •

Scale 1:11 300 000

Congregationalists 11.6%

Percentage of population

Roman Catholic		Anglican		Baptist	
50.0 or more		50.0 or more		50.0 or more	
25.0–49.9		25.0–49.9		25.0–49.9	
10.0–24.9		10.0–24.9		10.0–24.9	

Presbyterian		Methodist		Lutheran	
50.0 or more		50.0 or more		25.0–49.9	
25.0–49.9		25.0–49.9		10.0–24.9	
10.0–24.9		10.0–24.9			

First statistical rank refers to the single religious group with the greatest number of adherents per census unit and second statistical rank is the group with the next highest percentage of adherents. Religious populations are most diverse in census units where under 25% of adherents belong to the first rank.

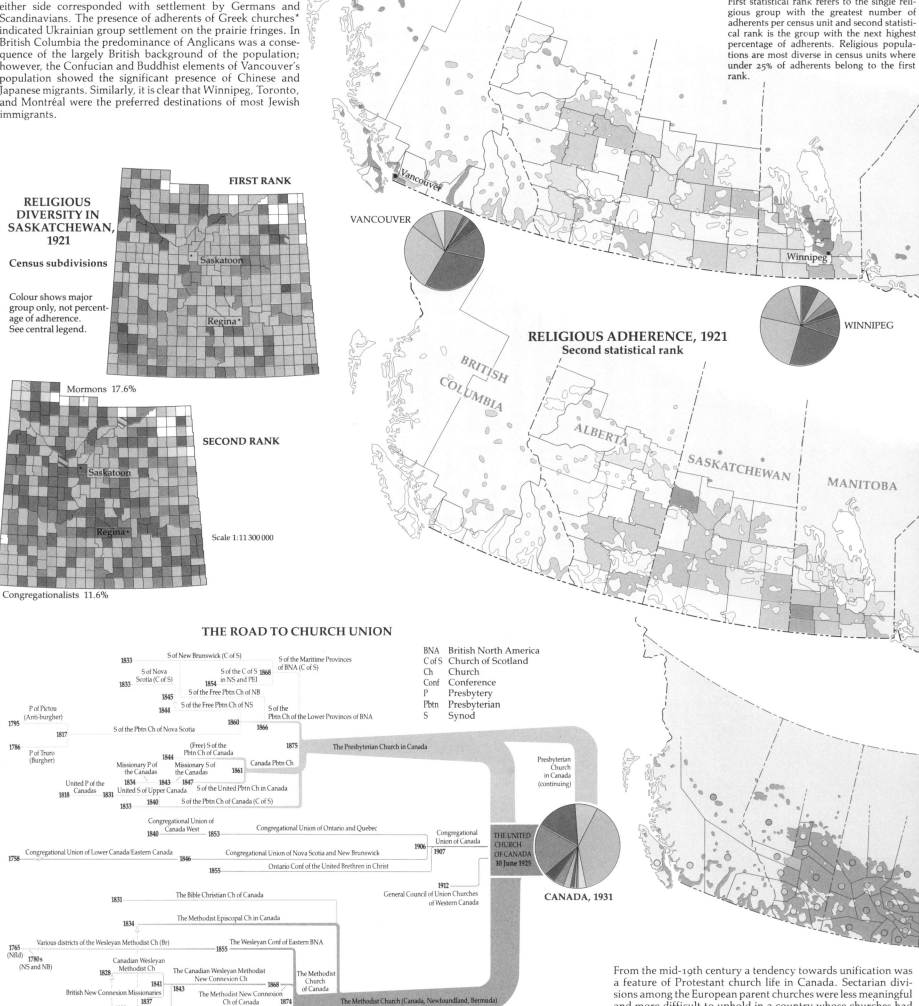

RELIGIOUS ADHERENCE, 1921
First statistical rank

VANCOUVER

Winnipeg

Vancouver

RELIGIOUS ADHERENCE, 1921
Second statistical rank

WINNIPEG

BRITISH COLUMBIA

ALBERTA

SASKATCHEWAN

MANITOBA

THE ROAD TO CHURCH UNION

BNA	British North America
C of S	Church of Scotland
Ch	Church
Conf	Conference
P	Presbytery
Pbtn	Presbyterian
S	Synod

1833 — S of New Brunswick (C of S)
1833 — S of Nova Scotia (C of S)
1868 — S of the C of S in NS and PEI
S of the Maritime Provinces of BNA (C of S)
1854 — S of the Free Pbtn Ch of NB
1845 — S of the Free Pbtn Ch of NS
1844
S of the Pbtn Ch of the Lower Provinces of BNA
1795 — P of Pictou (Anti-burgher)
1817
1786 — P of Truro (Burgher)
1860
1866
S of the Pbtn Ch of Nova Scotia
(Free) S of the Pbtn Ch of Canada — 1875
Missionary P of the Canadas — 1844
Missionary S of the Canadas
1834 1843 1847 — S of the United Pbtn Ch in Canada
United P of the Canadas — 1818 — 1831 — United S of Upper Canada
1861 — Canada Pbtn Ch
1840
1833 — S of the Pbtn Ch of Canada (C of S)
The Presbyterian Church in Canada
Presbyterian Church in Canada (continuing)

Congregational Union of Canada West — 1840 — 1853
Congregational Union of Ontario and Quebec
1758 — Congregational Union of Lower Canada/Eastern Canada — 1846
Congregational Union of Nova Scotia and New Brunswick
1855 — Ontario Conf of the United Brethren in Christ
1906 — Congregational Union of Canada
1907

THE UNITED CHURCH OF CANADA 10 June 1925

CANADA, 1931

1831 — The Bible Christian Ch of Canada
1834 — The Methodist Episcopal Ch in Canada
1765 (Nfld) — Various districts of the Wesleyan Methodist Ch (Br)
1780s (NS and NB)
1855 — The Wesleyan Conf of Eastern BNA
1828 — Canadian Wesleyan Methodist Ch
1841 — The Canadian Wesleyan Methodist New Connexion Ch — 1868
British New Connexion Missionaries — 1843
1837 — The Methodist New Connexion Ch of Canada — 1874
1780s — Methodist Episcopal Ch (USA)
1832 — Protestant Methodists
1814 — British Wesleyan (Ont)
1833 — 1840 — 1847 — Wesleyan Methodist Ch in Canada
1854
1790s — District of the British Wesleyan Methodist Conf (Qué)
1829 — The Primitive Methodist Ch in Canada
The Methodist Church of Canada
The Methodist Church (Canada, Newfoundland, Bermuda) — 1884
1912 — General Council of Union Churches of Western Canada

Approximate number of adherents

Thousands: 10 100 500 1000 2000

From the mid-19th century a tendency towards unification was a feature of Protestant church life in Canada. Sectarian divisions among the European parent churches were less meaningful and more difficult to uphold in a country whose churches had limited resources to serve a population that in the West was widely scattered. The series of unions within the Methodist, Presbyterian, and Congregational Churches culminated in the formation of the United Church of Canada. The Presbyterian vote on union across Canada revealed anti-union feeling in the long-established eastern areas, while the more recently settled west was heavily pro-union.

HISTORICAL ATLAS OF CANADA

PLATE 34

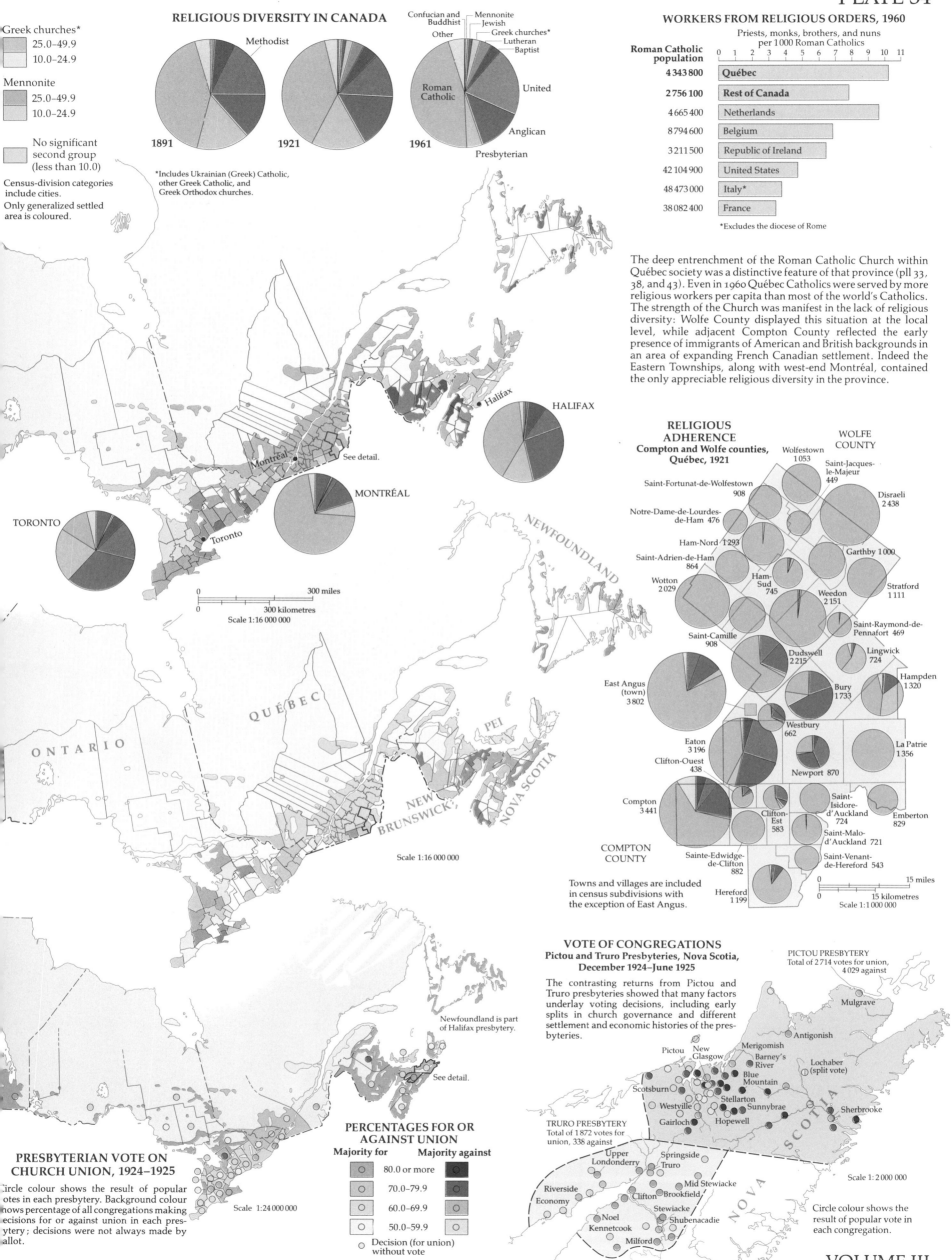

RELIGIOUS DIVERSITY IN CANADA

Greek churches*
- 25.0–49.9
- 10.0–24.9

Mennonite
- 25.0–49.9
- 10.0–24.9

No significant second group (less than 10.0)

Census-division categories include cities.
Only generalized settled area is coloured.

*Includes Ukrainian (Greek) Catholic, other Greek Catholic, and Greek Orthodox churches.

Confucian and Buddhist
Other
Mennonite
Jewish
Greek churches*
Lutheran
Baptist

Methodist

1891   **1921**   **1961**

Roman Catholic
United
Anglican
Presbyterian

WORKERS FROM RELIGIOUS ORDERS, 1960

Priests, monks, brothers, and nuns per 1 000 Roman Catholics
0 1 2 3 4 5 6 7 8 9 10 11

Roman Catholic population	
4 343 800	Québec
2 756 100	Rest of Canada
4 665 400	Netherlands
8 794 600	Belgium
3 211 500	Republic of Ireland
42 104 900	United States
48 473 000	Italy*
38 082 400	France

*Excludes the diocese of Rome

The deep entrenchment of the Roman Catholic Church within Québec society was a distinctive feature of that province (pll 33, 38, and 43). Even in 1960 Québec Catholics were served by more religious workers per capita than most of the world's Catholics. The strength of the Church was manifest in the lack of religious diversity: Wolfe County displayed this situation at the local level, while adjacent Compton County reflected the early presence of immigrants of American and British backgrounds in an area of expanding French Canadian settlement. Indeed the Eastern Townships, along with west-end Montréal, contained the only appreciable religious diversity in the province.

HALIFAX

MONTRÉAL

See detail.

TORONTO

Toronto

Montréal

Halifax

0 _____ 300 miles
0 _____ 300 kilometres
Scale 1:16 000 000

ONTARIO

QUÉBEC

NEWFOUNDLAND

NEW BRUNSWICK

PEI

NOVA SCOTIA

Scale 1:16 000 000

RELIGIOUS ADHERENCE
Compton and Wolfe counties, Québec, 1921

WOLFE COUNTY

Wolfestown 1 053
Saint-Jacques-le-Majeur 449
Saint-Fortunat-de-Wolfestown 908
Disraeli 2 438
Notre-Dame-de-Lourdes-de-Ham 476
Ham-Nord 1 293
Garthby 1 000
Saint-Adrien-de-Ham 864
Ham-Sud 745
Wotton 2 029
Weedon 2 151
Stratford 1 111
Saint-Raymond-de-Pennafort 469
Saint-Camille 908
Dudswell 2 215
Lingwick 724
East Angus (town) 3 802
Bury 1 733
Hampden 1 320
Eaton 3 196
Westbury 662
La Patrie 1 356
Clifton-Ouest 438
Newport 870
Compton 3 441
Clifton-Est 583
Saint-Isidore-d'Auckland 724
Emberton 829
Saint-Malo-d'Auckland 721
Sainte-Edwidge-de-Clifton 882
Saint-Venant-de-Hereford 543
Hereford 1 199

COMPTON COUNTY

Towns and villages are included in census subdivisions with the exception of East Angus.

0 _____ 15 miles
0 _____ 15 kilometres
Scale 1:1 000 000

VOTE OF CONGREGATIONS
Pictou and Truro Presbyteries, Nova Scotia, December 1924–June 1925

The contrasting returns from Pictou and Truro presbyteries showed that many factors underlay voting decisions, including early splits in church governance and different settlement and economic histories of the presbyteries.

PICTOU PRESBYTERY
Total of 2 714 votes for union, 4 029 against

Mulgrave
Antigonish
Merigomish
Pictou   New Glasgow
Barney's River
Lochaber (split vote)
Scotsburn   Blue Mountain
Westville   Stellarton
Gairloch   Hopewell   Sunnybrae
Sherbrooke

TRURO PRESBYTERY
Total of 1 872 votes for union, 338 against

Upper Londonderry
Springside
Riverside
Truro
Economy
Clifton   Mid Stewiacke
Brookfield
Noel   Stewiacke
Kennetcook   Shubenacadie
Milford

NOVA SCOTIA

Scale 1:2 000 000

Circle colour shows the result of popular vote in each congregation.

Newfoundland is part of Halifax presbytery.

See detail.

PRESBYTERIAN VOTE ON CHURCH UNION, 1924–1925

Circle colour shows the result of popular votes in each presbytery. Background colour shows percentage of all congregations making decisions for or against union in each presbytery; decisions were not always made by ballot.

Scale 1:24 000 000

PERCENTAGES FOR OR AGAINST UNION

Majority for   Majority against

- 80.0 or more
- 70.0–79.9
- 60.0–69.9
- 50.0–59.9
- Decision (for union) without vote

ORGANIZED SPORT

Authors: Alan Metcalfe, William Humber, Lynne Marks (Peterborough, 1890s)

By the turn of the century some form of organized sport was found in every town and city in Canada. Challenges, tournaments, and league play were local or sometimes regional, there being very few national competitions. Middle- and upper-class Canadian men joined clubs which provided facilities for sporting activities and formed associations to promote and control amateur sport. In spite of efforts by amateur associations to advance the playing of lacrosse, cricket, and soccer, baseball grew in popularity as a summer sport, reflecting the pervasive influence of the United States. Ice hockey was played during the long Canadian winter, and with the introduction of artificial ice on the west coast in the early 1910s hockey became a truly national sport. Because of the widespread popularity of ice hockey there were even some women's teams. However, female participation in organized sport generally was limited because of contemporary views on the role of women.

In the early 20th century increasing leisure time encouraged local participation in organized sport. Local teams were sponsored by a widening range of organizations including schools and churches. Sport was also becoming a marketable commodity, and professionalism in sport increased dramatically. There were more urban places that could support sports facilities and provide large crowds with the money and leisure time to attend sporting events. Entrepreneurs seized upon the financial potential of sport as spectacle. As the commercialization and professionalization of sport grew, ties to the United States, with its large market, strengthened.

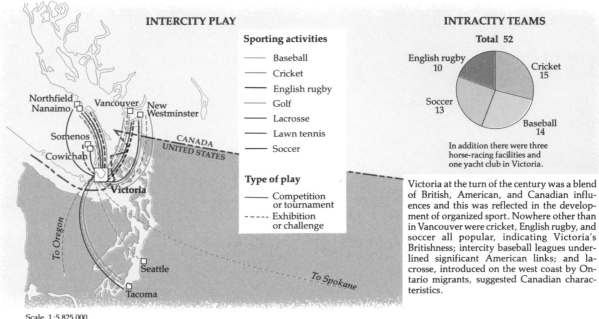

ORGANIZED SPORT, VICTORIA, BRITISH COLUMBIA, 1895

INTERCITY PLAY

Sporting activities
- Baseball
- Cricket
- English rugby
- Golf
- Lacrosse
- Lawn tennis
- Soccer

Type of play
- Competition or tournament
- Exhibition or challenge

Scale 1:5 825 000

INTRACITY TEAMS

Total 52
- English rugby 10
- Cricket 15
- Soccer 13
- Baseball 14

In addition there were three horse-racing facilities and one yacht club in Victoria.

Victoria at the turn of the century was a blend of British, American, and Canadian influences and this was reflected in the development of organized sport. Nowhere other than in Vancouver were cricket, English rugby, and soccer all popular, indicating Victoria's Britishness; intercity baseball leagues underlined significant American links; and lacrosse, introduced on the west coast by Ontario migrants, suggested Canadian characteristics.

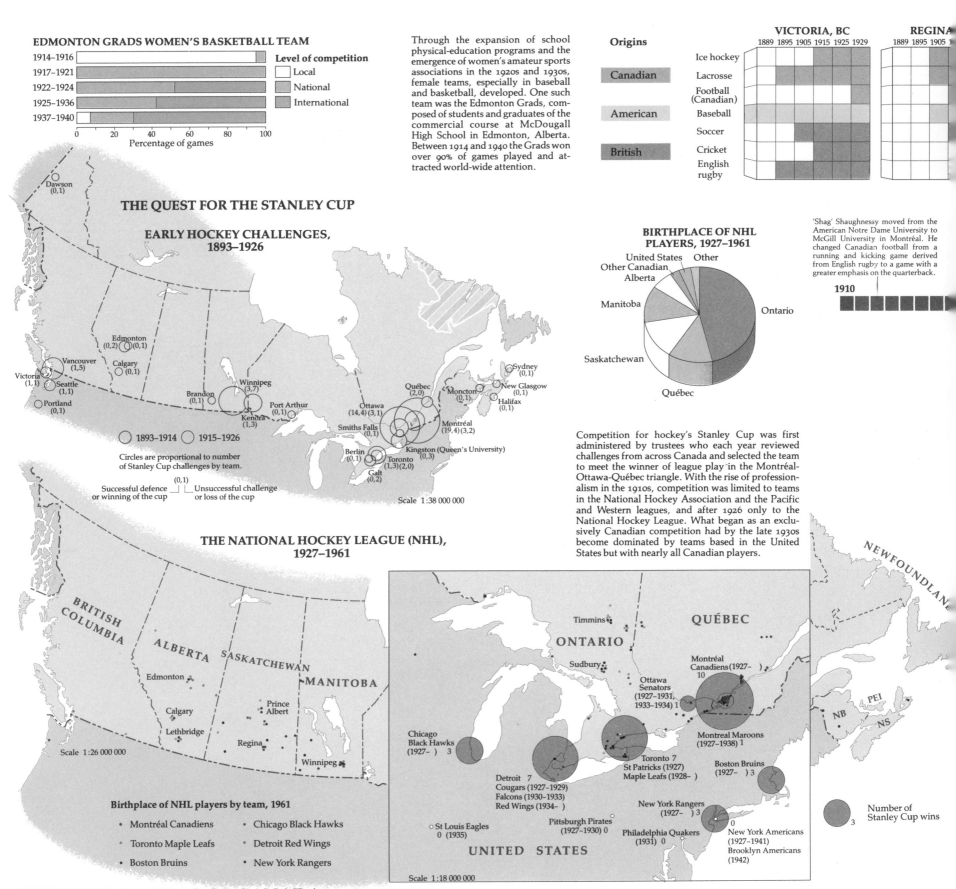

EDMONTON GRADS WOMEN'S BASKETBALL TEAM

1914–1916
1917–1921
1922–1924
1925–1936
1937–1940

Level of competition
- Local
- National
- International

Percentage of games

Through the expansion of school physical-education programs and the emergence of women's amateur sports associations in the 1920s and 1930s, female teams, especially in baseball and basketball, developed. One such team was the Edmonton Grads, composed of students and graduates of the commercial course at McDougall High School in Edmonton, Alberta. Between 1914 and 1940 the Grads won over 90% of games played and attracted world-wide attention.

Origins
- Canadian
- American
- British

VICTORIA, BC / REGINA

1889 1895 1905 1915 1925 1929

- Ice hockey
- Lacrosse
- Football (Canadian)
- Baseball
- Soccer
- Cricket
- English rugby

THE QUEST FOR THE STANLEY CUP

EARLY HOCKEY CHALLENGES, 1893–1926

Dawson (0,1)
Victoria (1,1)
Seattle (1,1)
Portland (0,1)
Vancouver (1,5)
Calgary (0,1)
Edmonton (0,2) (0,1)
Brandon (0,1)
Kenora (1,3)
Winnipeg (3,7)
Port Arthur (0,1)
Smiths Falls (0,1)
Berlin (0,1)
Toronto (1,3)(2,0)
Galt (0,2)
Ottawa (14,4)(3,1)
Kingston (Queen's University) (0,3)
Québec (2,0)
Montréal (19,4)(3,2)
Moncton (0,1)
Halifax (0,1)
New Glasgow (0,1)
Sydney (0,1)

1893–1914   1915–1926
Circles are proportional to number of Stanley Cup challenges by team.

(0,1) Successful defence or winning of the cup | Unsuccessful challenge or loss of the cup

Scale 1:38 000 000

BIRTHPLACE OF NHL PLAYERS, 1927–1961

- United States
- Other
- Other Canadian
- Alberta
- Manitoba
- Saskatchewan
- Québec
- Ontario

'Shag' Shaughnessy moved from the American Notre Dame University to McGill University in Montréal. He changed Canadian football from a running and kicking game derived from English rugby to a game with a greater emphasis on the quarterback.

1910

Competition for hockey's Stanley Cup was first administered by trustees who each year reviewed challenges from across Canada and selected the team to meet the winner of league play in the Montréal-Ottawa-Québec triangle. With the rise of professionalism in the 1910s, competition was limited to teams in the National Hockey Association and the Pacific and Western leagues, and after 1926 only to the National Hockey League. What began as an exclusively Canadian competition had by the late 1930s become dominated by teams based in the United States but with nearly all Canadian players.

THE NATIONAL HOCKEY LEAGUE (NHL), 1927–1961

BRITISH COLUMBIA
ALBERTA
SASKATCHEWAN
MANITOBA
Edmonton
Calgary
Lethbridge
Prince Albert
Regina
Winnipeg

Scale 1:26 000 000

Birthplace of NHL players by team, 1961
- Montréal Canadiens
- Toronto Maple Leafs
- Boston Bruins
- Chicago Black Hawks
- Detroit Red Wings
- New York Rangers

Timmins
ONTARIO
QUÉBEC
Sudbury
Ottawa Senators (1927–1931, 1933–1934) 1
Montréal Canadiens (1927–) 10
Montréal Maroons (1927–1938) 1
NEWFOUNDLAND
Chicago Black Hawks (1927–) 3
Detroit Cougars (1927–1929) Falcons (1930–1933) Red Wings (1934–) 7
Toronto 7 St Patricks (1927) Maple Leafs (1928–)
Boston Bruins (1927–) 3
NB
PEI
NS
St Louis Eagles 0 (1935)
Pittsburgh Pirates (1927–1930) 0
Philadelphia Quakers (1931) 0
New York Rangers (1927–) 3
New York Americans (1927–1941) Brooklyn Americans (1942) 0
UNITED STATES

Number of Stanley Cup wins

Scale 1:18 000 000

HISTORICAL ATLAS OF CANADA

PLATE 35

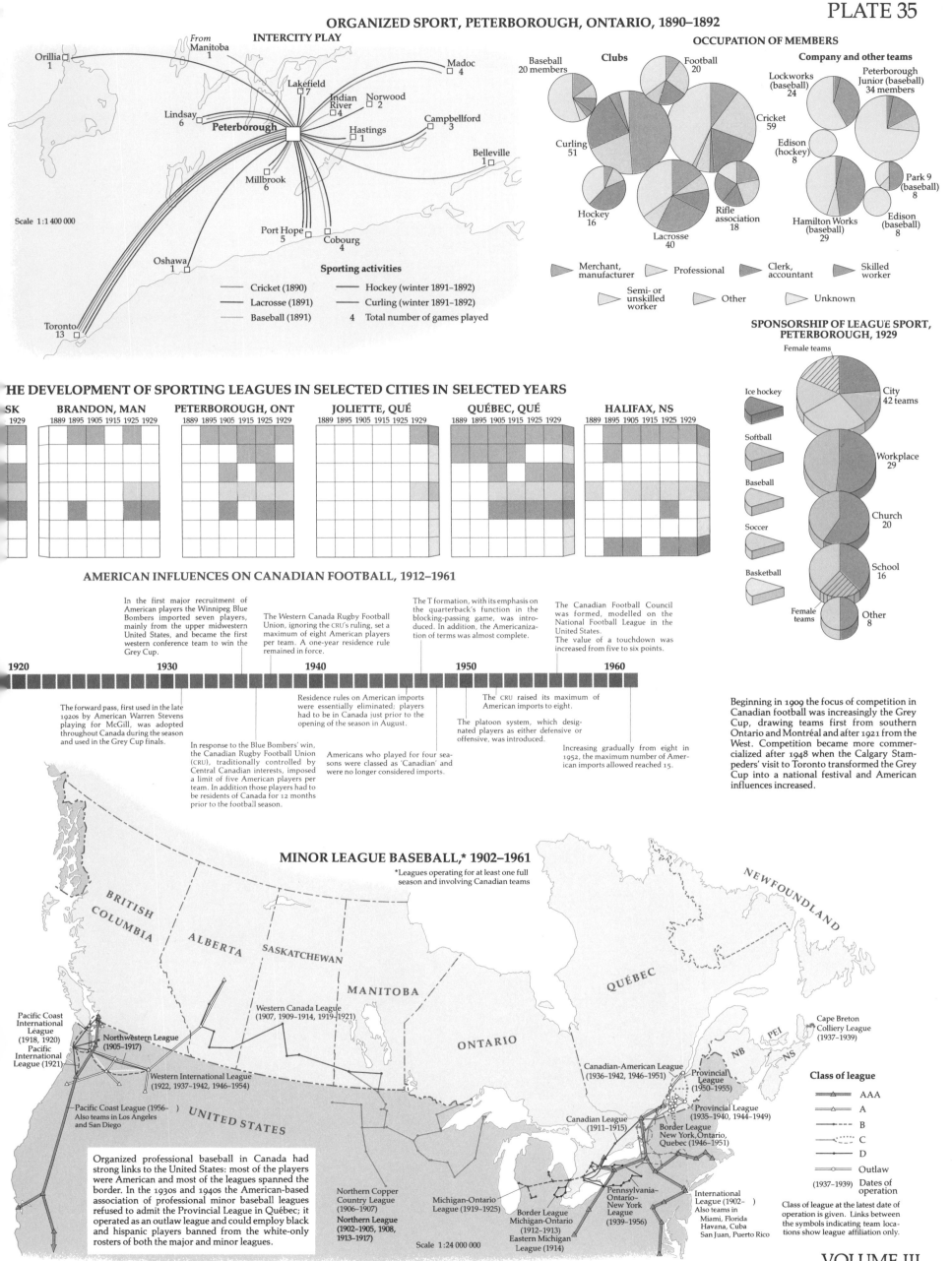

ORGANIZED SPORT, PETERBOROUGH, ONTARIO, 1890–1892

INTERCITY PLAY

From Manitoba 1
Orillia 1
Madoc 4
Lakefield 7
Indian River 4
Norwood 2
Lindsay 6
Peterborough
Campbellford 3
Hastings 1
Belleville 1
Millbrook 6
Port Hope 5
Cobourg 4
Oshawa 1
Toronto 13

Scale 1:1 400 000

Sporting activities
— Cricket (1890)
— Lacrosse (1891)
— Baseball (1891)
— Hockey (winter 1891–1892)
— Curling (winter 1891–1892)
4 Total number of games played

OCCUPATION OF MEMBERS

Clubs
Baseball 20 members
Football 20
Curling 51
Cricket 59
Hockey 16
Rifle association 18
Lacrosse 40

Company and other teams
Lockworks (baseball) 24
Peterborough Junior (baseball) 34 members
Edison (hockey) 8
Park 9 (baseball) 8
Hamilton Works (baseball) 29
Edison (baseball) 8

Merchant, manufacturer
Professional
Clerk, accountant
Skilled worker
Semi- or unskilled worker
Other
Unknown

SPONSORSHIP OF LEAGUE SPORT, PETERBOROUGH, 1929

Female teams
Ice hockey
Softball
Baseball
Soccer
Basketball
City 42 teams
Workplace 29
Church 20
School 16
Other 8
Female teams

HE DEVELOPMENT OF SPORTING LEAGUES IN SELECTED CITIES IN SELECTED YEARS

SK	BRANDON, MAN	PETERBOROUGH, ONT	JOLIETTE, QUÉ	QUÉBEC, QUÉ	HALIFAX, NS
1929	1889 1895 1905 1915 1925 1929	1889 1895 1905 1915 1925 1929	1889 1895 1905 1915 1925 1929	1889 1895 1905 1915 1925 1929	1889 1895 1905 1915 1925 1929

AMERICAN INFLUENCES ON CANADIAN FOOTBALL, 1912–1961

In the first major recruitment of American players the Winnipeg Blue Bombers imported seven players, mainly from the upper midwestern United States, and became the first western conference team to win the Grey Cup.

The Western Canada Rugby Football Union, ignoring the CRU's ruling, set a maximum of eight American players per team. A one-year residence rule remained in force.

The T formation, with its emphasis on the quarterback's function in the blocking-passing game, was introduced. In addition, the Americanization of terms was almost complete.

The Canadian Football Council was formed, modelled on the National Football League in the United States.
The value of a touchdown was increased from five to six points.

1920 1930 1940 1950 1960

The forward pass, first used in the late 1920s by American Warren Stevens playing for McGill, was adopted throughout Canada during the season and used in the Grey Cup finals.

In response to the Blue Bombers' win, the Canadian Rugby Football Union (CRU), traditionally controlled by Central Canadian interests, imposed a limit of five American players per team. In addition those players had to be residents of Canada for 12 months prior to the football season.

Residence rules on American imports were essentially eliminated; players had to be in Canada just prior to the opening of the season in August.

Americans who played for four seasons were classed as 'Canadian' and were no longer considered imports.

The CRU raised its maximum of American imports to eight.

The platoon system, which designated players as either defensive or offensive, was introduced.

Increasing gradually from eight in 1952, the maximum number of American imports allowed reached 15.

Beginning in 1909 the focus of competition in Canadian football was increasingly the Grey Cup, drawing teams first from southern Ontario and Montréal and after 1921 from the West. Competition became more commercialized after 1948 when the Calgary Stampeders' visit to Toronto transformed the Grey Cup into a national festival and American influences increased.

MINOR LEAGUE BASEBALL,* 1902–1961

*Leagues operating for at least one full season and involving Canadian teams

BRITISH COLUMBIA
ALBERTA
SASKATCHEWAN
MANITOBA
ONTARIO
QUÉBEC
NEWFOUNDLAND
NB
PEI
NS
UNITED STATES

Pacific Coast International League (1918, 1920)
Pacific International League (1921)
Northwestern League (1905–1917)
Western International League (1922, 1937–1942, 1946–1954)
Pacific Coast League (1956–) Also teams in Los Angeles and San Diego
Western Canada League (1907, 1909–1914, 1919–1921)

Cape Breton Colliery League (1937–1939)

Canadian-American League (1936–1942, 1946–1951)
Provincial League (1950–1955)
Provincial League (1935–1940, 1944–1949)
Canadian League (1911–1915)
Border League New York, Ontario, Quebec (1946–1951)
International League (1902–) Also teams in Miami, Florida Havana, Cuba San Juan, Puerto Rico
Pennsylvania-Ontario-New York League (1939–1956)

Northern Copper Country League (1906–1907)
Northern League (1902–1905, 1908, 1913–1917)
Michigan-Ontario League (1919–1925)
Border League Michigan-Ontario (1912–1913)
Eastern Michigan League (1914)

Scale 1:24 000 000

Organized professional baseball in Canada had strong links to the United States: most of the players were American and most of the leagues spanned the border. In the 1930s and 1940s the American-based association of professional minor baseball leagues refused to admit the Provincial League in Québec; it operated as an outlaw league and could employ black and hispanic players banned from the white-only rosters of both the major and minor leagues.

Class of league
———△——— AAA
———△——— A
——————— B
·········○········· C
——————— D
———○——— Outlaw
(1937–1939) Dates of operation
Class of league at the latest date of operation is given. Links between the symbols indicating team locations show league affiliation only.

RECREATIONAL LANDS

Author: Geoffrey Wall

In the midst of the assault on vast areas of Canada's resource regions (pll 5, 16, 21) there were concerns about the depletion of natural resources and the destruction of scenic places as well as pressures from an urban population seeking recreational space in natural settings. Beginning in the Canadian Rockies in the 1880s, efforts were made to set aside land for parks. Both the federal government and the Canadian Pacific Railway (CPR) began to develop visitor facilities; indeed the CPR hotels, an amalgam of Scottish castle and French château styles, became synonymous with the marketing of the Rockies, and Canada, for many American and European tourists. The first provincial park was established in Ontario in 1893 in the face of an advancing lumbering frontier (pl 16). Major provincial parks developed in British Columbia, Ontario, and Québec in the 1910s. Most provincial parks, however, were established during and after the Depression.

As surpluses of time and money became available to an urban, industrial society, the demand for rural or wilderness settings for day-trips and vacations mounted. Railroad and steamboat facilities serviced grand hotels, private cottages, and lakeside beaches, as in the Muskoka lakes region in Ontario and the Laurentians in Québec. As automobile ownership increased, motels and camp sites developed in more accessible places. A considerable portion of recreational land was alienated for private use to wealthy clients, many of whom were American.

Within towns and cities demands for recreational and leisure space prompted the establishment of park systems. Here too there was competition from private, commercial interests that ran amusement parks or private clubs (pl 35), but with the development of neighbourhood parks and the use of school playgrounds most neighbourhoods had access to open space.

ROCKY MOUNTAINS NATIONAL PARK,* ALBERTA

*Became Banff National Park in 1911

Modifications in park boundaries reflected different meanings of conservation and the changing balance of power among proponents of resource extraction, the development of tourism, and the preservation of Canada's natural heritage.

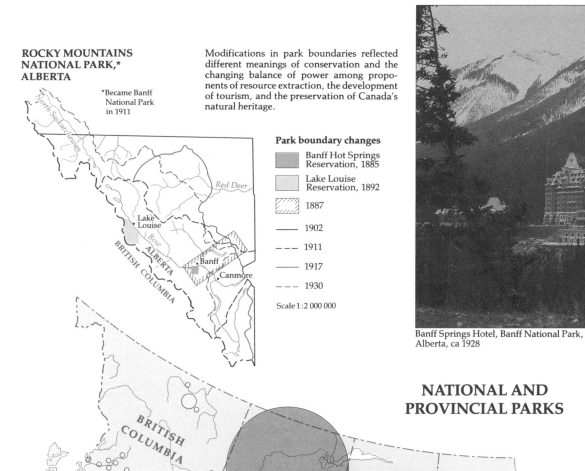

Park boundary changes

- Banff Hot Springs Reservation, 1885
- Lake Louise Reservation, 1892
- 1887
- 1902
- 1911
- 1917
- 1930

Scale 1:2 000 000

Banff Springs Hotel, Banff National Park, Alberta, ca 1928

NATIONAL AND PROVINCIAL PARKS

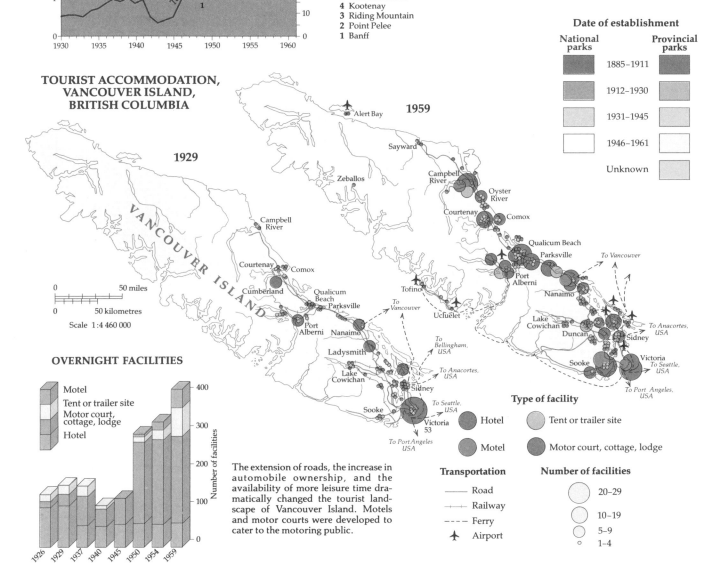

A Glacier
B Mount Revelstoke
C Yoho
D Kootenay

Scale 1:19 000 000

NATIONAL-PARK ATTENDANCE

11 Other
10 Fundy
9 Cape Breton Highlands
8 Prince Edward Island
7 Elk Island
6 Jasper
5 Waterton Lakes
4 Kootenay
3 Riding Mountain
2 Point Pelee
1 Banff

Date of establishment

National parks	Provincial parks
1885–1911	1885–1911
1912–1930	1912–1930
1931–1945	1931–1945
1946–1961	1946–1961
Unknown	

The early national parks were developed on western mountain land already under federal control. Special places of awesome beauty and wilderness areas were protected by provincial governments as well. In the Prairie Provinces the development of parks largely awaited the transfer of control over natural resources from federal powers in 1930. In Ontario and Québec the major catalyst was a demand for recreational settings for urbanites. A similar impetus in the Maritimes was not realized until the 1950s.

TOURIST ACCOMMODATION, VANCOUVER ISLAND, BRITISH COLUMBIA

1929

1959

0 — 50 miles
0 — 50 kilometres
Scale 1:4 460 000

Type of facility

- Hotel
- Motel
- Tent or trailer site
- Motor court, cottage, lodge

Transportation
- Road
- Railway
- Ferry
- Airport

Number of facilities
- 20–29
- 10–19
- 5–9
- 1–4

OVERNIGHT FACILITIES

- Motel
- Tent or trailer site
- Motor court, cottage, lodge
- Hotel

1926 1929 1937 1940 1945 1950 1954 1959

The extension of roads, the increase in automobile ownership, and the availability of more leisure time dramatically changed the tourist landscape of Vancouver Island. Motels and motor courts were developed to cater to the motoring public.

PUBLIC RECREATIONAL FACILITIES, TORONTO, 1955

- ○ Municipal park
- ● School (used by City Parks Department)
- ▲ Recreation centre operated by private agency
- ▲ Recreation or community centre operated by city
- ■ Amusement park

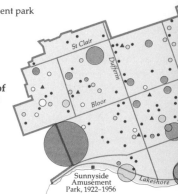

Date of establishment of municipal park
- By 1891
- By 1921
- By 1946
- By 1955

Sunnyside Amusement Park, 1922-1956

HISTORICAL ATLAS OF CANADA

PLATE 36

COTTAGES AND HOTELS, MUSKOKA DISTRICT, ONTARIO

Origin of cottage owner, 1915

Toronto	⊙	▲ Hotel
Other Ontario	◉	● Urban place
United States	○	┼┼ Railway
Other	◐	---- Lake steamer

The Muskoka region of the Canadian Shield developed as a summer resort and cottage area in those parts accessible by rail and steamboat. As the prime vacation sites were occupied, mainly by Torontonians and by Americans from the industrial cities of the bordering states, public access to the larger lakes became limited. The recreational value of the region intensified during the automobile era but the origins of cottage owners remained essentially unchanged.

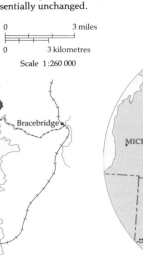

Port Cockburn
Rosseau
Lake Joseph
Cleveland's
Lake Rosseau
Windermere
Port Sandfield
Port Carling
MUSKOKA
Bala
Lake Muskoka
Bracebridge
Gravenhurst

0 ___ 3 miles
0 ___ 3 kilometres
Scale 1:260 000

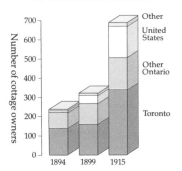

Courtesy of National Archives of Canada, Ottawa. PA-804067

PRIMARY RESIDENCE OF COTTAGE OWNERS

Number of cottage owners
700 / 600 / 500 / 400 / 300 / 200 / 100 / 0
1894 1899 1915

Other
United States
Other Ontario
Toronto

PLACE OF PRIMARY RESIDENCE OF COTTAGE OWNERS, 1915

ONTARIO / QUÉBEC
Muskoka District 44
Toronto 343
Hamilton 30
Buffalo 15
MICHIGAN
NEW YORK
OHIO
PENNSYLVANIA
Pittsburgh 48
WEST VIRGINIA
MARYLAND
NJ
VIRGINIA

Scale 1:16 000 000

One dot represents one cottage owner.

Other
11 From western Canada
1 From Nova Scotia
28 From other USA
3 From England

HUNTING AND SPORT FISHING, NEW BRUNSWICK

Type of licence

Hunter
Non-resident ----
Resident ——

Game
Deer ——
Big game ——
Special deer ——
Moose and deer ——
Deer and game bird ——

Hunting and fishing, once primarily sources of food, became popular sporting activities for local residents, important tourist attractions, and sources of government revenue. Maintenance of stocks required regulation of users and management of resources. Many waterways became the preserve of wealthy foreigners.

HUNTING LICENCES

Non-resident licences: 5 000 / 4 000 / 3 000 / 2 000 / 1 000 / 0
Resident licences: 50 000 / 40 000 / 30 000 / 20 000 / 10 000 / 0
1902 1910 1920 1930 1940 1950 1961

Start of deer licence
Ban on caribou hunting begins
Reintroduction of deer licence
Change to moose and deer licence
Special deer licence
Ban on moose hunting
Change to deer and game-bird licence

NEWFOUNDLAND
QUÉBEC
Mistassini
Chics-Chocs
Chibougamau
Prince Edward Island PEI
Terra Nova
Cape Breton Highlands
La Vérendrye
NB
Laurentides
Fundy
NS
Mont-Tremblant
Lake Superior
Algonquin
Georgian Bay Islands
St Lawrence Islands
Point Pelee

Park area, 1961
Thousands of hectares

4 500 Wood Buffalo
3 000 Mistassini
1 000–1 999
500–999
100–499
50–99
Less than 50

Large parcels of land from 19th-century estate owners provided the foundation of a park system in Toronto; it was complemented by the city's ravine network and developed in response to its citizens' concern for outdoor recreational space. Beginning in the early 1900s, waterfront amusement parks drew wide audiences.

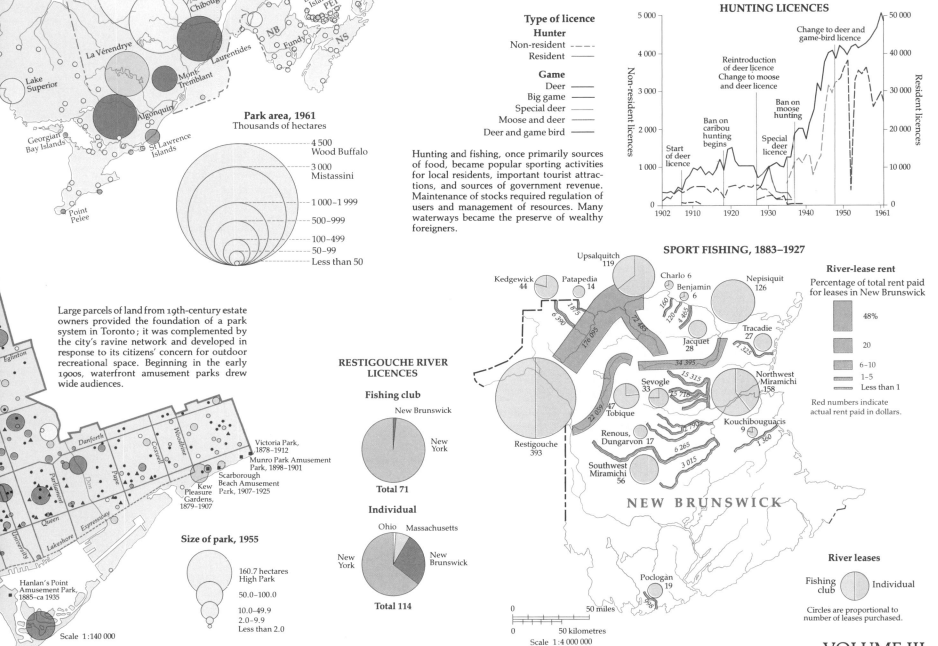

Eglinton
Danforth
Woodbine
Coxwell
Pape
Don
Parliament
University
Lakeshore
Queen
Expressway

Victoria Park, 1878–1912
Munro Park Amusement Park, 1898–1901
Scarborough Beach Amusement Park, 1907–1925
Kew Pleasure Gardens, 1879–1907
Hanlan's Point Amusement Park, 1885–ca 1935

Size of park, 1955

160.7 hectares High Park
50.0–100.0
10.0–49.9
2.0–9.9
Less than 2.0

Scale 1:140 000

RESTIGOUCHE RIVER LICENCES

Fishing club
New Brunswick
New York
Total 71

Individual
Ohio / Massachusetts
New York
New Brunswick
Total 114

SPORT FISHING, 1883–1927

Upsalquitch 119
Kedgewick 44
Patapedia 14
Charlo 6
Benjamin 6
Nepisiquit 126
Restigouche 393
Jacquet 28
Tracadie 27
Sevogle 33
Northwest Miramichi 158
Tobique
Renous, Dungarvon 17
Kouchibouguacis 9
Southwest Miramichi 56
Poclogan 19

NEW BRUNSWICK

River-lease rent
Percentage of total rent paid for leases in New Brunswick

48%
20
6–10
1–5
Less than 1

Red numbers indicate actual rent paid in dollars.

River leases

Fishing club | Individual

Circles are proportional to number of leases purchased.

0 ___ 50 miles
0 ___ 50 kilometres
Scale 1:4 000 000

WORKING WORLDS

Authors: Lynne Marks, Debra McNabb (Glace Bay)

By the end of the 19th century, although many Canadians remained on farms, people were becoming increasingly reliant on wage labour, often within the country's growing factories. The low wages and frequent periods of unemployment that characterized an economy undergoing industrialization meant that many male workers could not earn enough to support a family. As a result the wages of unmarried children were often essential to a family's survival. Depending on a family's circumstances, some children might begin earning wages at age 13, although 15 or 16 was more common. In certain industries, such as the textile industry, informal family networks often led to the hiring of several members of the same family by one factory.

While both sons and daughters contributed to the family economy, sons were more likely to be employed, at least partly because they could bring home more money. Women earned approximately half of what men earned for the same job, and could obtain employment only in low-wage industries such as textiles or new female-dominated occupations like clerical work. In most of the heavy industries of the early 20th century, like steel and pulp and paper, and in the resource-extracting activities that fueled these industries, only men were employed. This meant that in many single-industry towns, such as Glace Bay, families were completely dependent on the wages of fathers and sons. These families, like other working-class families, depended on the skills of married women who performed the arduous domestic labour necessary for the family's survival and who used a variety of strategies, including taking in boarders, to help stretch meagre family incomes.

AGRICULTURAL-IMPLEMENT WORKERS

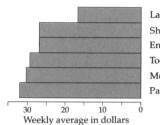

Labourer
Sheet-metal worker
Engineer
Tool maker
Moulder
Pattern maker

Weekly average in dollars

PULP AND PAPER WORKERS

Beaterman
Finisher*
Grinderman
Millwright
Backtender

Weekly average in dollars
*(mai

FARM-HELP WAGES, 1921
National average wage including board

Monthly in summer season	
Male $67 ($22 board)	Female $42 ($18 board)
Annual	
Male $669	Female $449

PROVINCIAL MINIMUM

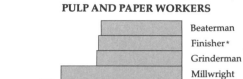

	British Columbia All wage-earning women except domestic and farm labourers, fruit pickers	Québec Women in industrial establishments
Year of enactment	**1918**	**1919**
	Manitoba Women in shops, offices, factories, places of amusement (cities)	Saskatchewan Women in shops, factories, hotels, restaurants (cities)

THE WORK-FORCE, 1921

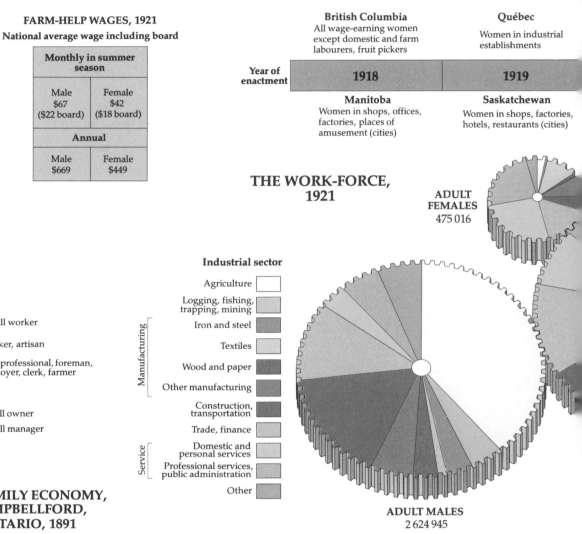

Industrial sector

Agriculture
Logging, fishing, trapping, mining
Iron and steel — Manufacturing
Textiles
Wood and paper
Other manufacturing
Construction, transportation
Trade, finance — Service
Domestic and personal services
Professional services, public administration
Other

ADULT FEMALES
475 016

ADULT MALES
2 624 945

WOOLEN-MILL WORKERS BY HOUSEHOLD

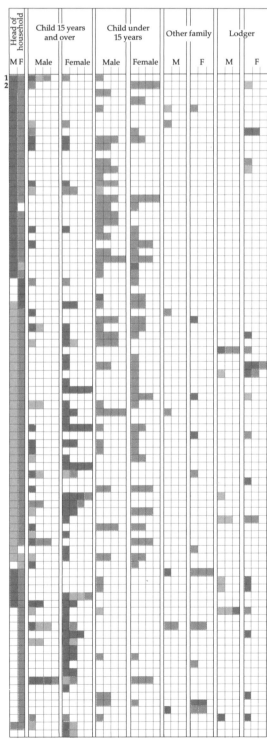

Employment

- Woolen-mill worker
- Other worker, artisan
- Merchant, professional, foreman, small employer, clerk, farmer
- At home
1 Woolen-mill owner
2 Woolen-mill manager

THE FAMILY ECONOMY, CAMPBELLFORD, ONTARIO, 1891

Many wage-earning children were in their twenties and thirties. Even as adults they contributed their wages to the family until they married and left home. Wages were generally given to the mother, who managed the family budget. Contemporary views on the role of women and the heavy demands of domestic work meant that few married women worked outside the home.

WAGE-EARNING CHILDREN
By father's occupation*

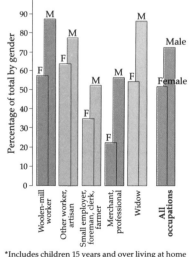

*Includes children 15 years and over living at home
Mother's occupation is used if father was deceased.

WORK, BIRTHPLACE, AND GENDER, 1921

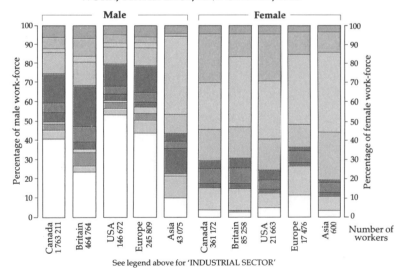

Male | Female

Percentage of male work-force

Canada 1 763 211
Britain 464 764
USA 146 672
Europe 245 809
Asia 43 075

Canada 361 172
Britain 85 258
USA 21 663
Europe 17 476
Asia 600

Percentage of female work-force
Number of workers

See legend above for 'INDUSTRIAL SECTOR'

Millions of immigrants entered Canada in the early 20th century (pl 27), both encouraged by government to settle the western Prairies and sought by businessmen who wanted cheap and docile labour to build railways, fell timber, and work in the growing factories. Some came to Canada only to earn money to help their families back in Europe. These 'sojourners' worked for a season or two in a variety of jobs and then left Canada, often returning later as family needs required.

Racial and sexual inequality limited the options available to many immigrants. Central and eastern Europeans had little choice but to accept low-paying, semi- or unskilled jobs, while Asians, both male and female, were concentrated in the personal-service sector. Many British and European women also worked as servants, but the low status and poor working conditions meant that most moved on to other work when possible.

PLATE 37

OCCUPATIONS, 1921

TELEPHONE-COMPANY WORKERS

*Operator
Installer
Lineman
Repairman
Cableman

(ale)

Weekly average in dollars
0   10   20   30   40

GARMENT WORKERS

Female
Machine operator
General handsewer
Buttonhole maker

Male
Cutter
Presser
Machine operator
Pocket maker

Weekly average in dollars
0   10   20   30   40

WAGE LEGISLATION

Ontario	Alberta
All wage-earning women except domestic and farm labourers	All wage-earning women except domestic labourers (cities and towns over 1 500)
1920	**1922**
Nova Scotia	New Brunswick
Women in shops and factories (cities and towns)	Fixed-wage scales for male and female teachers

CHILDREN
under 15 years
73 208

Total work-force comprises men, women, and children, both union and non-union workers. Union members as shown are a subset of total work-force, classified separately according to type of union.

Union membership

- Mining and quarrying
- Building trades
- Metal trades
- Printing trades
- Clothing, boot, and shoe trades
- Railway employees
- Other transportation trades
- Personal service, amusement trades
- Other trades, general labour

TOTAL
3 173 169

UNION MEMBERS
313 320

THE FACTORY SYSTEM, EATON'S, TORONTO, 1915

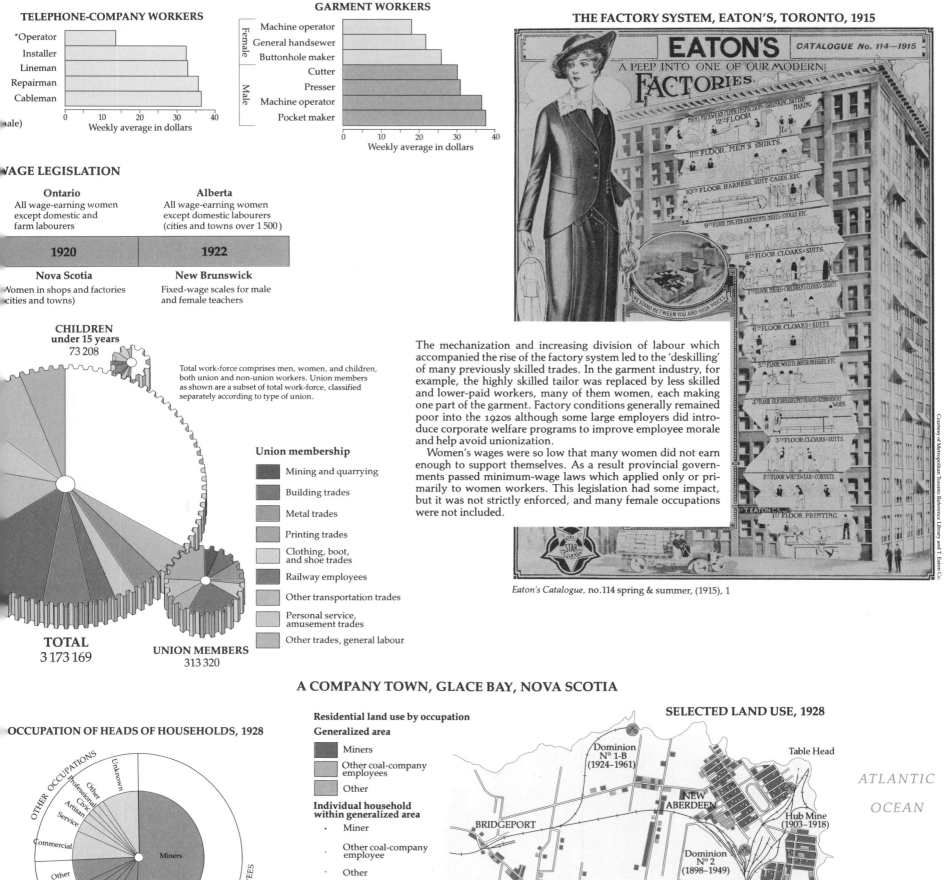

EATON'S CATALOGUE No. 114—1915
A PEEP INTO ONE OF OUR MODERN FACTORIES.

Courtesy of Metropolitan Toronto Reference Library and T. Eaton Co.

The mechanization and increasing division of labour which accompanied the rise of the factory system led to the 'deskilling' of many previously skilled trades. In the garment industry, for example, the highly skilled tailor was replaced by less skilled and lower-paid workers, many of them women, each making one part of the garment. Factory conditions generally remained poor into the 1920s although some large employers did introduce corporate welfare programs to improve employee morale and help avoid unionization.

Women's wages were so low that many women did not earn enough to support themselves. As a result provincial governments passed minimum-wage laws which applied only or primarily to women workers. This legislation had some impact, but it was not strictly enforced, and many female occupations were not included.

Eaton's Catalogue, no.114 spring & summer, (1915), 1

A COMPANY TOWN, GLACE BAY, NOVA SCOTIA

OCCUPATION OF HEADS OF HOUSEHOLDS, 1928

OTHER OCCUPATIONS
Unknown
Other
Professional
Civic
Artisan
Service
Commercial
Other
Other underground
Supervisory
Tradesman
Surface
Miners
COAL-COMPANY EMPLOYEES

A FAMILY BUDGET, CAPE BRETON, 1917

OTHER
COMPANY
Other
Rent
Coal
Flour
Children's
CLOTHING
Women's
Men's other
Men's work clothes
Other
Tea
Sugar
Milk
Fish
Meat
Potatoes
Butter
FOOD AND HOUSEHOLD

An average based on a Cape Breton Island family of one miner, his wife, and five children with a daily income of $3.50 and a yearly income of $1 071

Residential land use by occupation

Generalized area
- Miners
- Other coal-company employees
- Other

Individual household within generalized area
- · Miner
- · Other coal-company employee
- · Other

Other land use
- Commercial
- Mine (Dates of operation)

SELECTED LAND USE, 1928

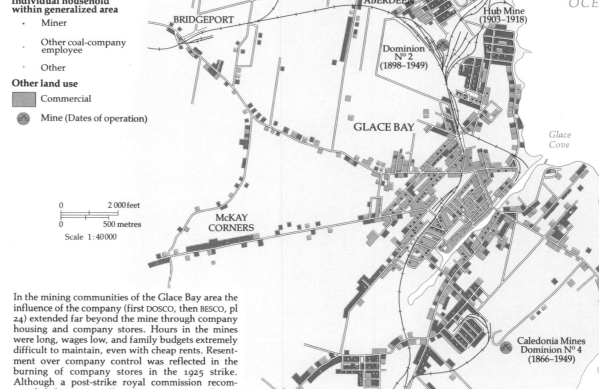

ATLANTIC OCEAN

Dominion Nº 1-B (1924–1961)
Table Head
NEW ABERDEEN
BRIDGEPORT
Hub Mine (1903–1918)
Dominion Nº 2 (1898–1949)
GLACE BAY
Glace Cove
McKAY CORNERS
Caledonia Mines Dominion Nº 4 (1866–1949)
Dominion Nº 11 (1913–1949)

0   2 000 feet
0   500 metres
Scale 1:40 000

In the mining communities of the Glace Bay area the influence of the company (first DOSCO, then BESCO, pl 24) extended far beyond the mine through company housing and company stores. Hours in the mines were long, wages low, and family budgets extremely difficult to maintain, even with cheap rents. Resentment over company control was reflected in the burning of company stores in the 1925 strike. Although a post-strike royal commission recommended that BESCO sell its houses, its control over shelter persisted for another two decades.

ORGANIZED LABOUR

Authors: Gregory S. Kealey, Douglas Cruikshank

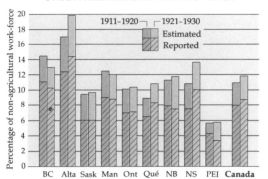

UNION MEMBERSHIP BY PROVINCE

1911–1920 ☐ 1921–1930 ⬛
Estimated
Reported

Percentage of non-agricultural work-force

BC Alta Sask Man Ont Qué NB NS PEI **Canada**

UNION MEMBERSHIP BY INDUSTRY

Percentage of total membership / Thousands of members

- Other
- Service
- Transportation
- Building trades
- Metal trades
- Clothing, footwear
- Mining
- —— Total membership

UNION MEMBERSHIP BY AFFILIATION

Percentage of total membership

National
- Other or unaffiliated
- National and Catholic
- Trades and Labor Congress (TLC) only
- One Big Union (OBU)
- Canadian Federation of Labour (CFL)
- All-Canadian Congress of Labour (ACCL)

International
- Other or unaffiliated
- American Federation of Labor (AFL) only
- TLC/AFL

Data on union membership, while often unreliable for these early years, suggest periods of particularly rapid growth at the beginning of the 20th century and towards the end of and immediately after the First World War. The movement enjoyed its greatest successes in British Columbia, Alberta, and Nova Scotia, and in the nation's transportation and construction industries. Labour in the new mass-production industries proved far more difficult to organize. Despite the efforts of a new industrial unionism, which peaked in 1919, Canada's manufacturers battled to maintain or to create union-free environments. Although the Trades and Labor Congress maintained its position as the dominant trade-union centre, its close ties to the American Federation of Labor proved controversial. A series of significant challenges to its hegemony were mounted by alternative bodies representing dissenting ideologies, sometimes syndicalist and socialist or later, in the case of Québec, Catholic and corporatist.

RAILWAY UNIONS*

*Canadian Brotherhood of Railway Employees (CBRE founded 1908), Brotherhood of Railway and Steamship Clerks, Freight Handlers, Express and Station Employees (BRSC)

- CBRE joins TLC; BRSC begins in Canada
- CBRE expelled from TLC after failing to merge with BRSC
- BRSC suspended from AFL in jurisdictional dispute with teamsters; reinstated 1927
- CBRE helps found ACCL

Thousands of members

Affiliation
- Independent
- AFL/TLC
- TLC only
- ACCL

Union
- CBRE
- BRSC

See legend on affiliation graph above for acronyms.

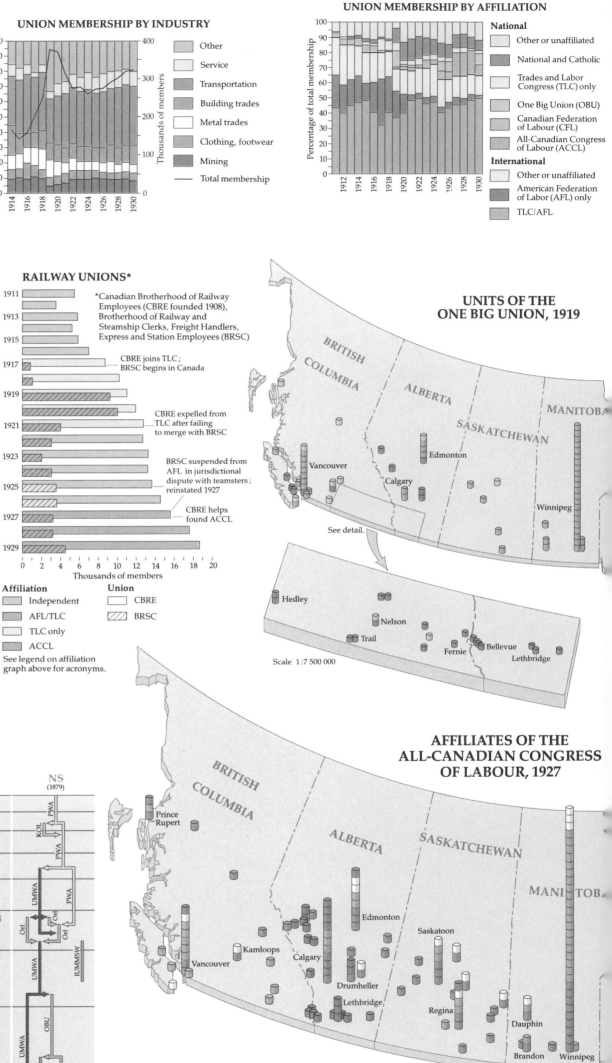

UNITS OF THE ONE BIG UNION, 1919

BRITISH COLUMBIA ALBERTA SASKATCHEWAN MANITOBA

Vancouver Edmonton Calgary Winnipeg

See detail.

Hedley Nelson Trail Fernie Bellevue Lethbridge

Scale 1:7 500 000

AFFILIATES OF THE ALL-CANADIAN CONGRESS OF LABOUR, 1927

BRITISH COLUMBIA ALBERTA SASKATCHEWAN MANITOBA

Prince Rupert Vancouver Kamloops Calgary Edmonton Saskatoon Drumheller Lethbridge Regina Dauphin Brandon Winnipeg

BRICKLAYERS AND MASONS INTERNATIONAL UNION OF AMERICA

50
- Percentage of employees unionized
- Non-members employed in union localities
- Union members employed

Hundreds employed

87 88 74 69 70 67 65 70 72 73 72 83 86 87 85 87 84

1890 1892 1894 1896 1898 1900 1902 1904 1906

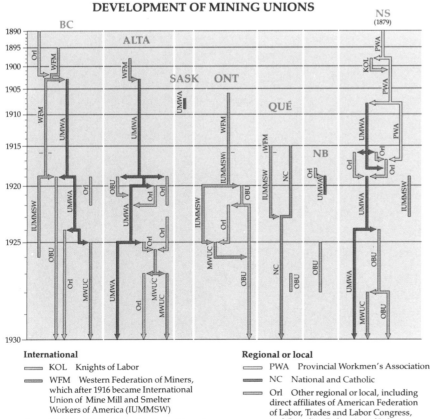

DEVELOPMENT OF MINING UNIONS

BC ALTA SASK ONT QUÉ NB NS (1879)

KOL WFM UMWA OBU Orl IUMMSW NC MWUC PWA

Development of Mining Unions legend:

International
- KOL Knights of Labor
- WFM Western Federation of Miners, which after 1916 became International Union of Mine Mill and Smelter Workers of America (IUMMSW)
- UMWA United Mine Workers of America

National
- OBU One Big Union
- MWUC Mine Workers' Union of Canada

Regional or local
- PWA Provincial Workmen's Association
- NC National and Catholic
- Orl Other regional or local, including direct affiliates of American Federation of Labor, Trades and Labor Congress, and Canadian Federation of Labour

By international standards the Canadian labour movement was highly fragmented: witness the brief insurgency of the One Big Union, a revolutionary industrial union, in 1919, the rise of Catholic unionism in Québec in the 1920s, and the rise of an independent Canadian unionism in the All-Canadian Congress of Labour. In part this was a consequence of the sheer geographical scale of the nation; the extraordinarily diverse history of miners' unionism, for example, derived as much from regional and provincial settings as from ideological disputes.

- Direct charter
- Other
- Mine Workers' Union of Canada
- Lumber Workers' Industrial Union
- Former Canadian Federation of Labour affiliate
- One Big Union
- Canadian Brotherhood of Railway Employees

PLATE 38

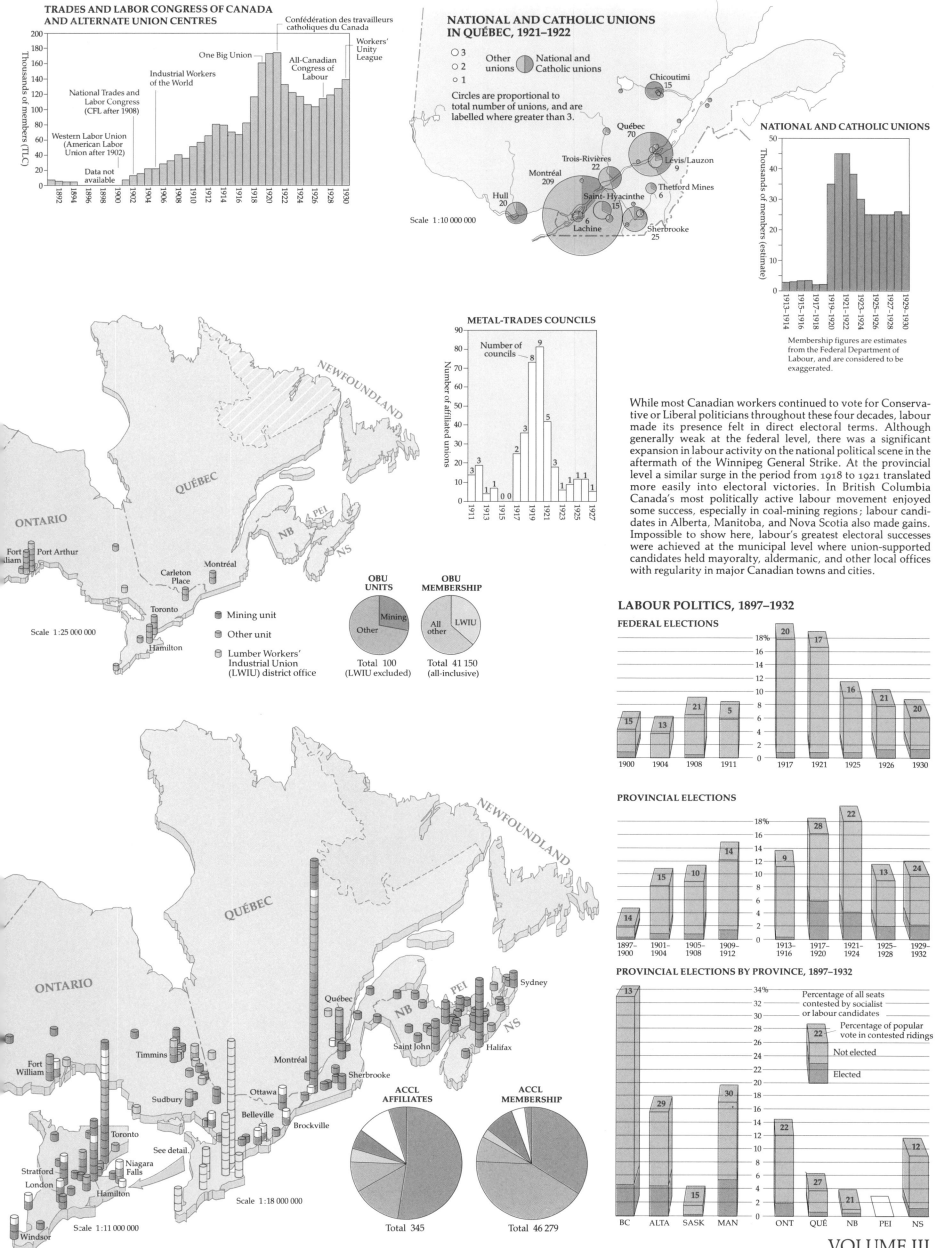

TRADES AND LABOR CONGRESS OF CANADA
AND ALTERNATE UNION CENTRES

NATIONAL AND CATHOLIC UNIONS
IN QUÉBEC, 1921–1922

○ 3 Other unions ◑ National and Catholic unions
○ 2
○ 1

Circles are proportional to total number of unions, and are labelled where greater than 3.

Scale 1:10 000 000

NATIONAL AND CATHOLIC UNIONS

Membership figures are estimates from the Federal Department of Labour, and are considered to be exaggerated.

METAL-TRADES COUNCILS

OBU UNITS

OBU MEMBERSHIP

● Mining unit
◐ Other unit
◑ Lumber Workers' Industrial Union (LWIU) district office

Total 100 (LWIU excluded)

Total 41 150 (all-inclusive)

Scale 1:25 000 000

Scale 1:18 000 000

Scale 1:11 000 000

ACCL AFFILIATES

ACCL MEMBERSHIP

Total 345

Total 46 279

While most Canadian workers continued to vote for Conservative or Liberal politicians throughout these four decades, labour made its presence felt in direct electoral terms. Although generally weak at the federal level, there was a significant expansion in labour activity on the national political scene in the aftermath of the Winnipeg General Strike. At the provincial level a similar surge in the period from 1918 to 1921 translated more easily into electoral victories. In British Columbia Canada's most politically active labour movement enjoyed some success, especially in coal-mining regions; labour candidates in Alberta, Manitoba, and Nova Scotia also made gains. Impossible to show here, labour's greatest electoral successes were achieved at the municipal level where union-supported candidates held mayoralty, aldermanic, and other local offices with regularity in major Canadian towns and cities.

LABOUR POLITICS, 1897–1932

FEDERAL ELECTIONS

PROVINCIAL ELECTIONS

PROVINCIAL ELECTIONS BY PROVINCE, 1897–1932

Percentage of all seats contested by socialist or labour candidates

Percentage of popular vote in contested ridings

Not elected

Elected

STRIKES
Authors: Gregory S. Kealey, Douglas Cruikshank

STRIKE ISSUES

Against change in rate of earnings
For change in rate of earnings

(y-axis: Percentage of total strikes, 0–100; x-axis: years 1891–1929)

STRIKE SETTLEMENT METHODS

(left y-axis: Percentage of total strikes, 0–100; right y-axis: Total number of strikes, 0–500; x-axis: years 1891–1929)

- Indefinite or unterminated
- Replacement of workers
- Return of workers
- Third-party involvement
- Negotiations between parties
- Total strikes

STRIKE RESULTS

(y-axis: Percentage of total strikes, 0–100; x-axis: years 1891–1929)

- Indefinite or unterminated
- Compromise or partially successful
- In favour of employers
- In favour of workers

The strike – a collective and complete cessation of work – represents the most accessible measure of overt conflict between workers and employers. The pattern of strike activity in the years 1891 to 1930 varied dramatically. Nationally the size of strikes grew over the years, as did their frequency, until the aftermath of the labour revolt of 1919. The mean duration of strikes, however, remained remarkably constant. Contrasts existed across industries and provinces. In Nova Scotia the dominance of the coal and steel industries, especially the former, meant that strikes were both frequent and large and, unlike the national pattern, peaked in the 1920s rather than in the First World War period. Strikes in the mining industry were by far the largest and most frequent, although shorter in duration than strikes in manufacturing.

The issues over which strikes were fought, the settlements reached, and the final outcomes varied greatly. In periods of economic downturn workers tended to engage in defensive strikes, that is, strikes aimed at preserving what the workers already had. These were generally not solved through negotiation and they were often defeated. In periods of economic upturn, the reverse held.

FREQUENCY, SIZE, AND DURATION OF STRIKES, 1891–1930

Type of industry	Time period
Service	1891–1900
Transportation	1901–1910
Construction	1911–1920
Manufacturing	1921–1930
Mining	

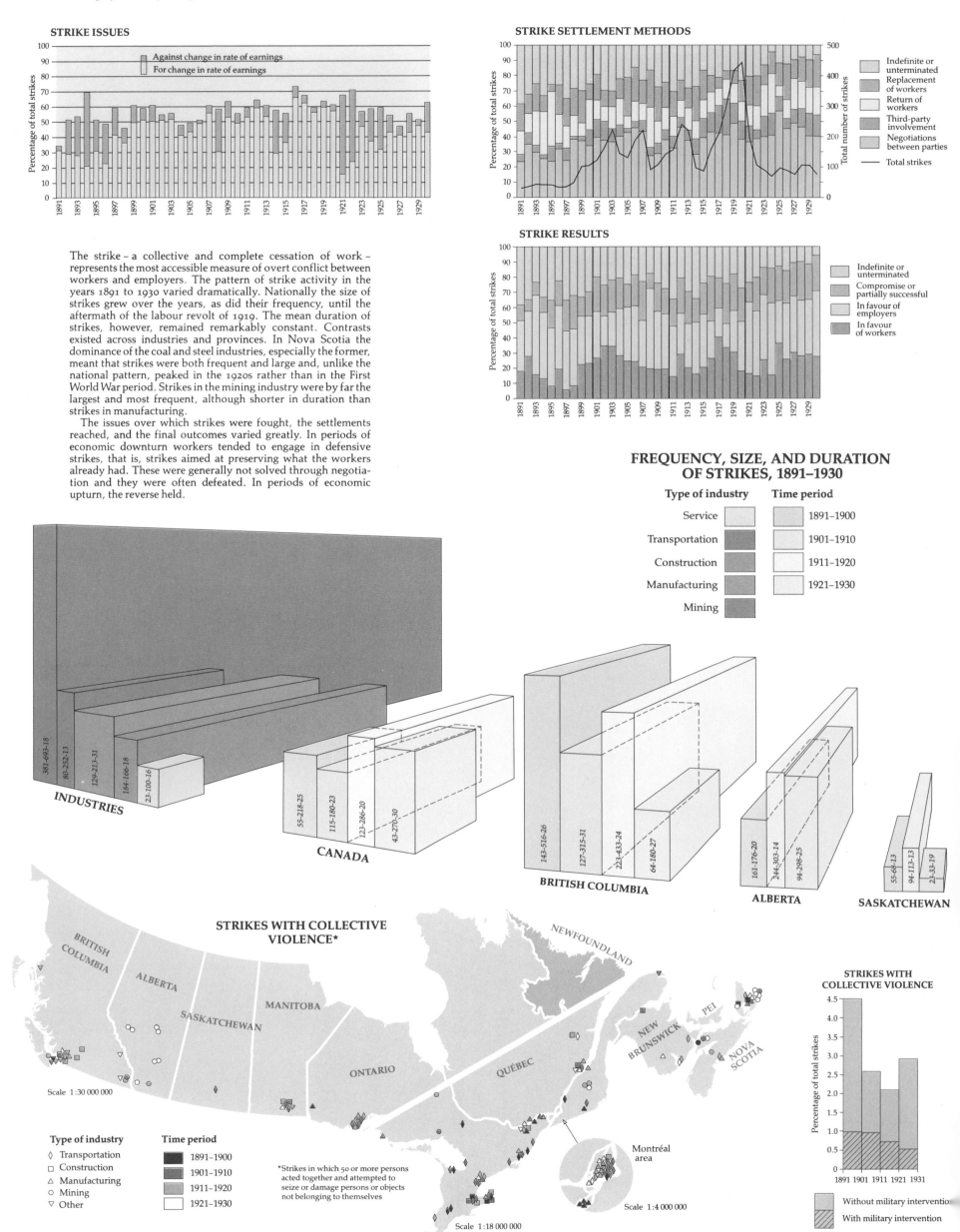

INDUSTRIES
381-693-18 80-252-13 129-213-31 184-166-18 23-100-16

CANADA
55-218-25 115-180-23 123-286-20 43-270-30

BRITISH COLUMBIA
143-516-26 127-315-31 223-433-24 64-180-27

ALBERTA
161-176-20 244-303-14 94-208-25

SASKATCHEWAN
55-68-13 94-113-13 23-33-19

STRIKES WITH COLLECTIVE VIOLENCE*

Scale 1:30 000 000

BRITISH COLUMBIA, ALBERTA, SASKATCHEWAN, MANITOBA, ONTARIO, QUÉBEC, NEW BRUNSWICK, PEI, NOVA SCOTIA, NEWFOUNDLAND

Montréal area
Scale 1:4 000 000

Scale 1:18 000 000

Type of industry	Time period
◇ Transportation	■ 1891–1900
□ Construction	■ 1901–1910
△ Manufacturing	▨ 1911–1920
○ Mining	□ 1921–1930
▽ Other	

*Strikes in which 50 or more persons acted together and attempted to seize or damage persons or objects not belonging to themselves

STRIKES WITH COLLECTIVE VIOLENCE

(y-axis: Percentage of total strikes, 0–4.5; x-axis: 1891, 1901, 1911, 1921, 1931)

Without military intervention
With military intervention

PLATE 39

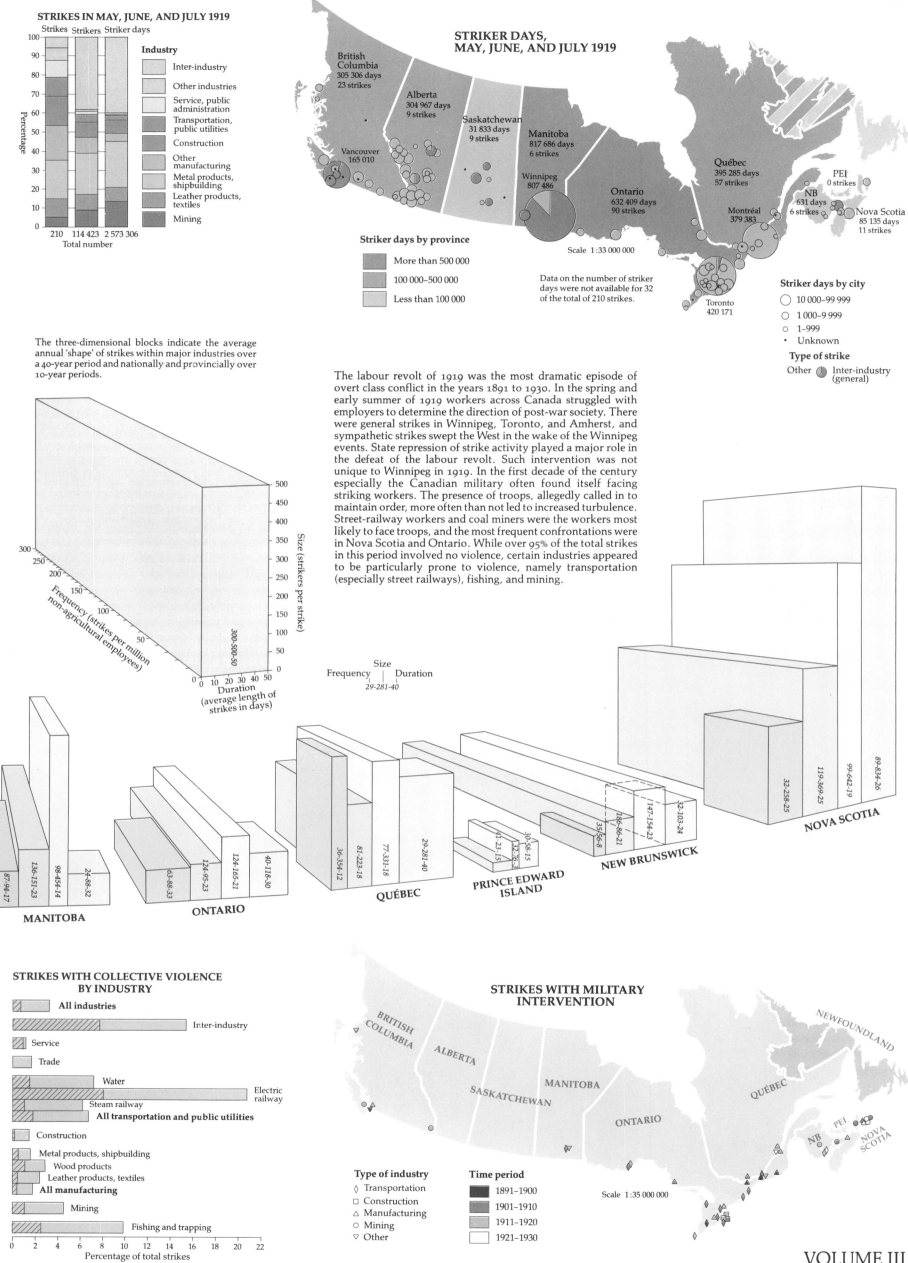

STRIKES IN MAY, JUNE, AND JULY 1919

Strikes   Strikers   Striker days

Industry

- Inter-industry
- Other industries
- Service, public administration
- Transportation, public utilities
- Construction
- Other manufacturing
- Metal products, shipbuilding
- Leather products, textiles
- Mining

Percentage

210   114 423   2 573 306

Total number

STRIKER DAYS, MAY, JUNE, AND JULY 1919

British Columbia
305 306 days
23 strikes

Vancouver
165 010

Alberta
304 967 days
9 strikes

Saskatchewan
31 833 days
9 strikes

Manitoba
817 686 days
6 strikes

Winnipeg
807 486

Ontario
632 409 days
90 strikes

Québec
395 285 days
57 strikes

Montréal
379 383

NB
631 days
6 strikes

PEI
0 strikes

Nova Scotia
85 135 days
11 strikes

Toronto
420 171

Scale 1:33 000 000

Striker days by province

- More than 500 000
- 100 000–500 000
- Less than 100 000

Data on the number of striker days were not available for 32 of the total of 210 strikes.

Striker days by city

- ○ 10 000–99 999
- ○ 1 000–9 999
- ○ 1–999
- · Unknown

Type of strike

Other ◐ Inter-industry (general)

The three-dimensional blocks indicate the average annual 'shape' of strikes within major industries over a 40-year period and nationally and provincially over 10-year periods.

The labour revolt of 1919 was the most dramatic episode of overt class conflict in the years 1891 to 1930. In the spring and early summer of 1919 workers across Canada struggled with employers to determine the direction of post-war society. There were general strikes in Winnipeg, Toronto, and Amherst, and sympathetic strikes swept the West in the wake of the Winnipeg events. State repression of strike activity played a major role in the defeat of the labour revolt. Such intervention was not unique to Winnipeg in 1919. In the first decade of the century especially the Canadian military often found itself facing striking workers. The presence of troops, allegedly called in to maintain order, more often than not led to increased turbulence. Street-railway workers and coal miners were the workers most likely to face troops, and the most frequent confrontations were in Nova Scotia and Ontario. While over 95% of the total strikes in this period involved no violence, certain industries appeared to be particularly prone to violence, namely transportation (especially street railways), fishing, and mining.

Frequency (strikes per million non-agricultural employees)

Duration (average length of strikes in days)

Size (strikers per strike)

Size
Frequency │ Duration
29–281–40

MANITOBA

87-94-17
136-151-23
98-454-14
24-88-32

ONTARIO

63-88-33
124-95-23
124-165-21
40-118-30

QUÉBEC

36-354-12
81-223-18
77-331-18
29-281-40

PRINCE EDWARD ISLAND

41-23-15
32-26-3
30-58-15

NEW BRUNSWICK

35-56-8
186-86-21
147-154-23
32-103-24

NOVA SCOTIA

32-258-25
119-369-25
99-642-19
89-834-26

STRIKES WITH COLLECTIVE VIOLENCE BY INDUSTRY

- All industries
- Inter-industry
- Service
- Trade
- Water
- Electric railway
- Steam railway
- All transportation and public utilities
- Construction
- Metal products, shipbuilding
- Wood products
- Leather products, textiles
- All manufacturing
- Mining
- Fishing and trapping

0 2 4 6 8 10 12 14 16 18 20 22
Percentage of total strikes

STRIKES WITH MILITARY INTERVENTION

BRITISH COLUMBIA
ALBERTA
SASKATCHEWAN
MANITOBA
ONTARIO
QUÉBEC
NEWFOUNDLAND
NB
PEI
NOVA SCOTIA

Scale 1:35 000 000

Type of industry

- ◇ Transportation
- □ Construction
- △ Manufacturing
- ○ Mining
- ▽ Other

Time period

- 1891–1900
- 1901–1910
- 1911–1920
- 1921–1930

PART TWO

CRISIS AND RESPONSE
1929 - 1961

The Great Depression

The world came crashing down on many Canadians in the Great Depression of the 1930s. The severe economic decline which Canada suffered after 1929 was part of an international crisis that had its origins in world overproduction of primary commodities. The downturn in the economy in Canada began as early as April 1929, while that in the United States came in August; both started before the crash of the stock market in October 1929. The crisis of the 1930s is notable as much for its duration as for its severity. In 1931 the Depression in North America deepened as the world financial system collapsed (precipitated by a series of currency depreciations and the abandonment of the gold standard). The bottom was finally reached for both Canada and the United States in March 1933, but recovery was weak and hesitant. The economy was still far from sustaining full employment when there was a severe setback in 1937.

In the years after the First World War the Canadian economy had become closely linked to that of the United States. The newsprint industry had become dependent on the American market; the automobile-assembly industry was completely under American control; and the radio and movie industries contributed to making Canada part of a single North American market. Great Britain, by contrast, became a secondary trading partner because of the decline of its economy after the war. A depression in the United States was, therefore, certain to exacerbate any economic downturn in Canada.

The stock-market crash caught Canadian businessmen off guard, but the collapse of wheat prices on the Winnipeg Grain Exchange had a more profound effect, since wheat was so important to the Canadian economy. During the early part of 1929 wheat prices on the world market declined; but throughout the summer prices at Winnipeg were pushed up by speculation, only to collapse dramatically in the fall and winter. The wheat pool, which had made cash advances on the basis of summer prices, was financially crippled. Canada had contributed significantly to the world oversupply of wheat in 1929 with a bumper crop and all-time high exports, and the price of wheat dropped 20% in that year. In 1930 Canada had a very small wheat crop, the first of several poor crops during the Depression years, and although prices recovered to their former levels in that year, in 1931 the bottom fell out of the world price of wheat. The Canadian wheat price for the year fell by 53% and for the rest of the decade oversupply and competition among wheat-exporting nations kept the price depressed.

Overcapacity in other sectors also contributed to Canada's economic predicament. Although the initial downturn seemed to be part of a familiar business cycle, the collapse was unusually severe, following as it did upon the feverish upswing of the late 1920s. That investment boom had resulted in severe overcapacity in some major industries, notably flour milling, pulp and paper, and automobile manufacturing (where by 1930 capacity was one-third greater than production). The housing market was saturated and large cities had a great excess of commercial office space. Since similar circumstances had driven the US economy into depression, its demand for Canada's exports fell off, especially for newsprint and lumber. Canada's close trading ties with the United States ensured that the recession would be deep; reinforcing this effect were American trade practices, such as the Smoot-Hawley tariff of 1930, which restricted all agricultural imports, and the imposition of import duties in 1932 on such products as lumber and copper. Canada also suffered from the protectionist measures undertaken by other western economies. Although many countries came out of the Depression by the mid-1930s, in Canada the intimate relationship between industrial and agricultural distress perpetuated the misery almost to the end of the decade.

The grave international situation was not solely responsible for Canada's woes. Accumulated investment debt contributed to the depth of the crisis and the slowness of recovery. The costs of servicing the debt that had accumulated from borrowing in the pre-1914 and post-war investment booms placed a severe burden on businesses and farmers when incomes plummeted after 1929. Canadian banks cut back severely on lending in the early years of the Depression. This policy kept Canadian banking solvent (unlike what happened in the United States and Europe), but it denied credit to firms that had previously been financially stable. As a result, their inability to meet interest payments on accumulated debts provoked commercial failures. Mortgage foreclosures on farms also became commonplace.

The prevailing government view at the onset of the Depression was that it was a short-term recession brought on by external factors. Some belt-tightening and fiscal responsibility were considered the appropriate response. As the recession deepened, government revenues were reduced and the cost of maintaining unemployment relief and heavy fixed-debt charges led to deficits in the federal budget. Between 1930 and 1937 the national debt increased by more than $1 billion, and provincial and municipal debt by more than $700 million. Balanced budgets became difficult if not impossible for all levels of government.

Initially the only significant government initiative was to place high tariffs on the import of manufactured goods in 1930 and 1931. These gave some shelter to Canadian manufacturers and their employees, but they also had the less desirable effect of making the manufacturing industry resistant to price changes. The tariffs did nothing to help hard-pressed export industries, whose problems were not addressed until the 1932 Ottawa agreement on British Empire trade preferences and the 1935 reciprocity treaty with the United States. In any event the gradual re-expansion of world trade had the most important effect on Canadian recovery.

Government efforts to respond to the crisis were limited by orthodox laissez-faire notions and by lack of funds. Even so the federal government expanded its financial commitment to deal with the problem of massive public unemployment. Depleted revenues and the threat of financial collapse at the provincial level forced the federal government to disburse grants-in-aid to the Prairies to pay for mounting relief costs. Eleven successive relief acts were passed between 1930 and 1940. The decision to bail out the provinces, which had already come to the rescue of the municipalities (the traditional source of relief), forced a re-evaluation of the roles and responsibilities of the three levels of government. Federal responsibility for unemployment relief was finally acknowledged in 1940, when a national unemployment insurance scheme was set in place.

Other significant instances of expanded federal responsibility, both dating from 1935, were the formation of the Canadian Wheat Board (the main purchaser and supplier of wheat), and the founding of the Bank of Canada (it was believed that the lack of a central bank to manage foreign exchange and the money supply may have contributed to Canada's difficulties in dealing with the Depression). The Prairie Farm Rehabilitation Act (PFRA) of the same year represented an intrusion of the federal government into provincial jurisdictions through its establishment of community pastures. Because this involved the unprecedented step of transferring control of land to federal authority, Alberta refused to implement the strategy of community pastures until 1960.

The Depression hit Canada's primary producers first, but the impact was quickly felt by other sectors of the economy (pl 40). The severe blow dealt to Prairie agriculture, from slackening demand compounded by drought, was transmitted to transport companies through a reduction of wheat movements. Capital-goods manufacturers were subsequently affected, with both farm-machinery and rolling-stock manufacturers losing sales; this in turn hurt the iron and steel industry and consequently coal mining. The unemployment which resulted reduced consumer demand and so damaged the retail and service industries. In addition, reduced American demand for pulp and paper and a slump in the construction industry in Canada and the United States hit the forestry sector. Economic recovery began in 1933 but, like the United States, Canada was slow to recover compared to Europe. A second recession set in again after 1937, and it was only the economic stimulus provided by the Second World War that allowed complete recovery to take place.

Canada essentially closed the door on immigration during the Depression. The number of immigrants dropped by some 93% between 1929 and 1935 (the denial of entry to European Jews fleeing Nazism is a particularly shameful aspect of Canada's record) and relief rolls were reduced by deporting some 17 000 foreign 'public dependents' before the newly elected Liberal government stopped the practice in 1935.

At the nadir of the Depression in 1933 almost one-third of workers were out of work (pl 41) and at the outbreak of war in 1939 the unemployment rate was still 10%. For the two-thirds of Canadians who were fortunate enough to remain employed the experience of the Depression sharply contrasted with that of their neighbours on relief. A 23% drop in average living costs between 1929 and 1933 meant that many employees, especially those in the manufacturing and service sectors, gained greater purchasing power and enjoyed a higher standard of living despite reduced wage levels. Lack of job security, however, was a constant worry and inhibited many from enjoying a better life. The prospects for unemployed workers and their families in the Depression years were grim. Unemployment insurance did not exist and individuals were not expected to turn to the government for help until they had exhausted other means of support. Public relief, based on the 19th-century English poor law, was designed to be as unattractive as possible in order to discourage individuals from claiming it 'too readily' or remaining dependent on it. By providing less remuneration than the lowest paid work relief was intended to be only a last resort for the destitute and those incapable of work. Even so, some 15% of Canadians (1.5 million) were dependent on direct relief in April 1933.

Relief was given either directly in the form of cash payments and vouchers for specific items, or indirectly through the provision of some form of paid work. Paid work was seen as less demoralizing for the individual, but make-work projects normally required only unskilled labour. Organized in the first instance by municipal governments, make-work projects were later supervised by provincial and federal authorities. It should be noted that Canada did not have an abundance of major public works, such as the construction of big dams or bridges, or the writers' projects that were used to create employment in the United States.

Many single Canadians became transients in search of work (pl 41). Riding the rails became an acquired skill, as the young and not so young crisscrossed the country on top of, in, and even under boxcars. They picked up odd jobs on farms, washed restaurant dishes for a meal, and received occasional relief money from municipalities either sympathetic to their plight or eager to see them on their way. Many sought food at individual houses in return for doing a chore, while others found a few weeks of employment in logging or mining.

Collections of makeshift shacks and tents – 'hobo jungles' –

were to be found on waste land in most major urban areas. Their inhabitants, like those who filled the hostels for single men, were perceived as a growing threat by citizens and governments alike. The federal government, through the Department of National Defence, established relief work camps (pl 42) and the single, homeless unemployed had little choice but to go to them after municipalities cut them off relief. These camps brought together unemployed single men in remote locations and kept them occupied with menial tasks connected with the building of airports and highways and the improvement of national parks. But camp life quickly produced dissatisfaction and the inmates formed a ready audience for the organizers of the Communist-led Relief Camp Workers Union (RCWU). The RCWU organized relief-camp strikes in 1934 and 1935 in British Columbia, Ontario, and Québec, and it also organized the On-to-Ottawa Trek of 1935 (pl 45). The Liberal government closed the camps in 1936, leaving the problems of the single transients unsolved.

The Prairies were the region most severely affected by the Depression (pl 43). A collapse in the wheat market for Prairie produce was aggravated by prolonged periods of drought. In almost every year Saskatchewan had more people per capita on relief than any other province. When the dust clouds enveloped the land and farmers could no longer earn enough to meet the costs of production, many Prairie families abandoned their land to the dust bowls or the mortgage company. Some left the Prairies forever. Others, assisted by government schemes, moved to districts on the northern fringe of settlement that were less affected by drought. There they faced new hardships – forest clearing, heavy soils, swamp fever that infected livestock animals, and, in 1937, even drought. That same drought stifled recovery in the more established areas. Under the provisions of the PFRA a water-development program was introduced to construct small dugout reservoirs on individual farms to catch rainwater and runoff for watering stock (large irrigation projects were not the agency's focus until after the Second World War). Badly eroded land was taken out of production and turned into community pastures.

To alleviate the burden of urban relief schemes of rural colonization were implemented, especially in Québec. There land settlement as a counterbalance to the problems of urban/industrial life and the migration of francophones to non-French, non-Catholic areas had been fostered by the Catholic Church as early as the mid-19th century. The Depression brought the state more fully into this movement (pl 44). While colonization was encouraged throughout the province, attention was directed to establishing settlers in the Clay Belt of northwestern Québec, especially the Abitibi district. Under three settlement plans which operated during the Depression some 12 000 settler households were established, 5 500 of these in the Abitibi district alone.

The Maritimes were economically depressed throughout the 1920s and the region therefore had less distance to fall after 1929. Heavy out-migration during the 1920s had helped to reduce local pressure and, by taking several jobs, many people kept themselves off the relief rolls. None the less, the hardships of the Depression were real enough and efforts were made to ameliorate suffering. At the heart of these efforts was the Antigonish Movement, established in 1928 as an extension program of St Francis Xavier University and directed by Father Moses Coady. The movement sought to use co-operative methods to improve social and economic conditions. Its objective, to find a middle road between the excesses of individualistic capitalism on the one hand and state communism on the other, had been formulated in the years between 1918 and 1928 when there had been vigorous debate on rural decline, migration, and the industrial class system and on the responses to them by the Catholic Church and educational institutions. In the fishing villages and farms along the Northumberland Strait and Gulf of St Lawrence shore, especially in Acadian and Scottish Catholic communities, study clubs, credit unions, co-operative stores, and fishing co-operatives were developed in the early 1930s. The program spread into the mining communities of Cape Breton. As with the PFRA, the success of this movement ensured its continued development after the Depression (although it became increasingly international in focus).

In British Columbia the relief rolls swelled, not only from unemployment in fishing, forestry, and mining, but also from an influx of transients in search of mild winters as much as work. While the provincial government's 'work and wages' programs were perhaps the most innovative in extending government's role during the Depression, progress was hampered by the province's diminished financial resources. Some of the discontent bred in the relief camps and soup lines of British Columbia found dramatic expression. The On-to-Ottawa Trek began in the BC camps, the participants congregating in Vancouver and heading east on trains in April 1935, gathering strength as others joined in along the route (pl 45). To prevent the trekkers from meeting up with a contingent in Winnipeg, the authorities decided to stop them in Regina. Mounted troops charged the trekkers, a riot ensued, one person died, and the trek ended. Machine-gun fire left nicks that are still visible on buildings.

More broadly, there was a climate of confrontation between capital and labour throughout the 1930s. Virulent anti-union forces, especially in Québec, but also in Ontario mining towns such as Sudbury, sought to exclude union organizers from the workplace and both the Ontario and Québec governments supported them. In general, union membership declined during the decade, though efforts (especially by Communists) to organize new unions such as the Workers' Unity League and the Relief Camp Workers Union led to a spate of strikes and outbreaks of collective violence (pl 45).

Throughout these years of turmoil Canada's two main political parties were hard pressed to come up with solutions. The Liberal government suffered defeat early, in 1930, and its Conservative successor, despite publicized intentions of creating new markets for Canadian exports and providing 'work instead of dole,' had no answers to the slump. Constitutional difficulties delayed its attempts to enact legislation for a New Deal program which was to include labour standards, marketing boards and price codes, the encouragement of competition, and unemployment insurance. Most of the reforms were implemented too late to prevent a disgruntled public from giving the Liberals a landslide victory in the election of 1935 (pl 46).

The most depressed areas of the country turned to politically radical solutions. The two most successful 'third parties,' the Social Credit Party and the Co-operative Commonwealth Federation (CCF), appealed essentially to Prairie farmers, although the CCF also gained support from western urban workers. Social Credit, a political movement founded in Alberta in 1932, sought to limit the power of the banks and to control the supply and distribution of money. Its populist policies were regionally focused and in Alberta the party enjoyed landslide success from its initial victories in 1935 down to the 1960s. The CCF, also founded in 1932, adopted a program of public ownership and the establishment of a welfare state, drawn up by the League for Social Reconstruction. It attracted national support, but its strength derived principally from the western electorate. Although it was the most successful of the third parties in the 1935 federal election, the CCF had to await the coming of the Second World War to achieve its greatest success, by which time its growth had inspired the federal Liberals to adjust their policies to head off defeat.

There were other third parties. The Communist Party of Canada, effectively illegal between 1931 and 1936, played an important national role in organizing the unemployed. It also organized the clandestine sending of volunteers to fight in the Spanish Civil War, once the Foreign Enlistment Act of April 1937 made it illegal to enlist and fight in a foreign war. The growth of the Union nationale in Québec owed part of its success to the belief among many French Canadians that the province's economic woes were brought on by English Canadian and American owners of business and industry. Although the origins of the party lay among the reformist and nationalist ex-Liberals of the Action libérale nationale, the conservative half of the union, led by Maurice Duplessis, seized full control in 1936. Duplessis swung the party well to the right. The Union nationale remained in power to the end of the 1950s, except for the period 1939–44.

Perversely, it was the misery of another world war that brought an end to the economic and social distress of the Great Depression. But the meaning of the Depression persisted well into the period of prosperity which followed the Second World War and the experience of it lodged itself in the collective memory of the nation.

ECONOMIC CRISIS

Authors: Elizabeth Bloomfield, Gerald Bloomfield, Deryck W. Holdsworth, Murdo MacPherson

The Canadian economy, heavily dependent on the export of raw and semi-processed goods, was profoundly affected by the collapse of world trade in 1929. Among the western economies the United States was most deeply hurt, and since the United States was Canada's main trading partner, a severe decline in the Canadian economy was inevitable. Between 1929 and 1933 total Canadian export prices declined by some 60% and earnings from the top export commodities, wheat and flour, fell by over 70%. Economic activity was sharply reduced and by 1933 national income was half that of 1929. A contraction in the money supply over this period followed and helped to reinforce the price and production slump.

After 1933 the Canadian economy was slow to recover. Although total export volume exceeded its 1929 level by 1937, export prices were still 16% below. In addition, heavy domestic overinvestment in the 1920s had exhausted the opportunity for new investment during the early 1930s. After 1933 investment, as a stimulus to recovery, was slow to return and reflected a climate of pessimism and caution among Canadian investors.

Agriculture was the economic sector that was most affected because it was export-oriented, and in 1939 it still lagged behind its 1929 contribution to the national income. The Prairie economy was devastated (pl 43). Manufacturing, aided by some tariff protection, slowly returned to its 1929 level by 1939. Because of expansion in the production of metals, the mining industry was the only sector of the economy to show a strong recovery.

INDEX OF INTERNATIONAL INCOMES

For the graphs showing indices relative change is measured in relation to 1929 values which are considered to be equal to 100. All other values are adjusted accordingly; actual value is not shown.

SELECTED EXPORTS

MONEY SUPPLY

GROSS DOMESTIC INVESTMENT*

*Excluding change in inventories

NATIONAL INCOME, SELECTED SECTORS

EMPLOYMENT INDEX, SELECTED SECTORS

For actual employment figures in 1931 see pl 3.

EMPLOYMENT INDEX
By regions and selected cities

MINERAL PRODUCTION

THE GOLD-MINING BOOM

Gold played the strongest role in the exceptional recovery of the mining industry. The price of gold was stable in the downswing and increased between 1933 and 1934; a ready market in the United States resulted in a steep rise in output and new mining developments on the Shield. Nickel and copper, used in producer goods, suffered in the downswing but recovered strongly with the revitalization of industrial activity in the United Kingdom and the United States.

Scale 1:17 000 000

Number of major mines, 1939
- 6–10
- 2–5
- 1

HISTORICAL ATLAS OF CANADA

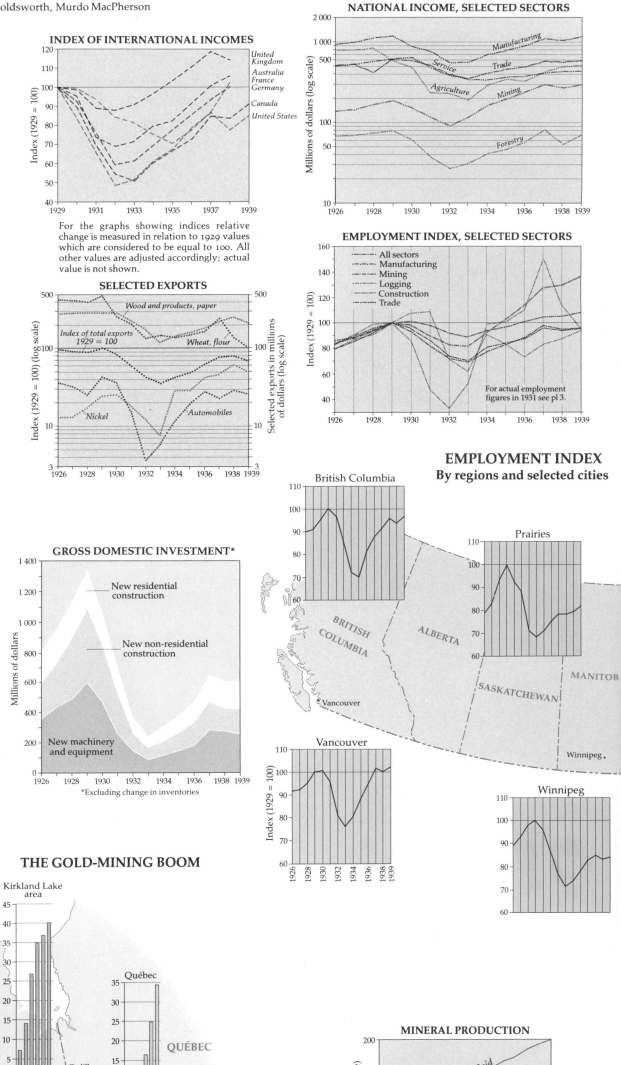

PLATE 40

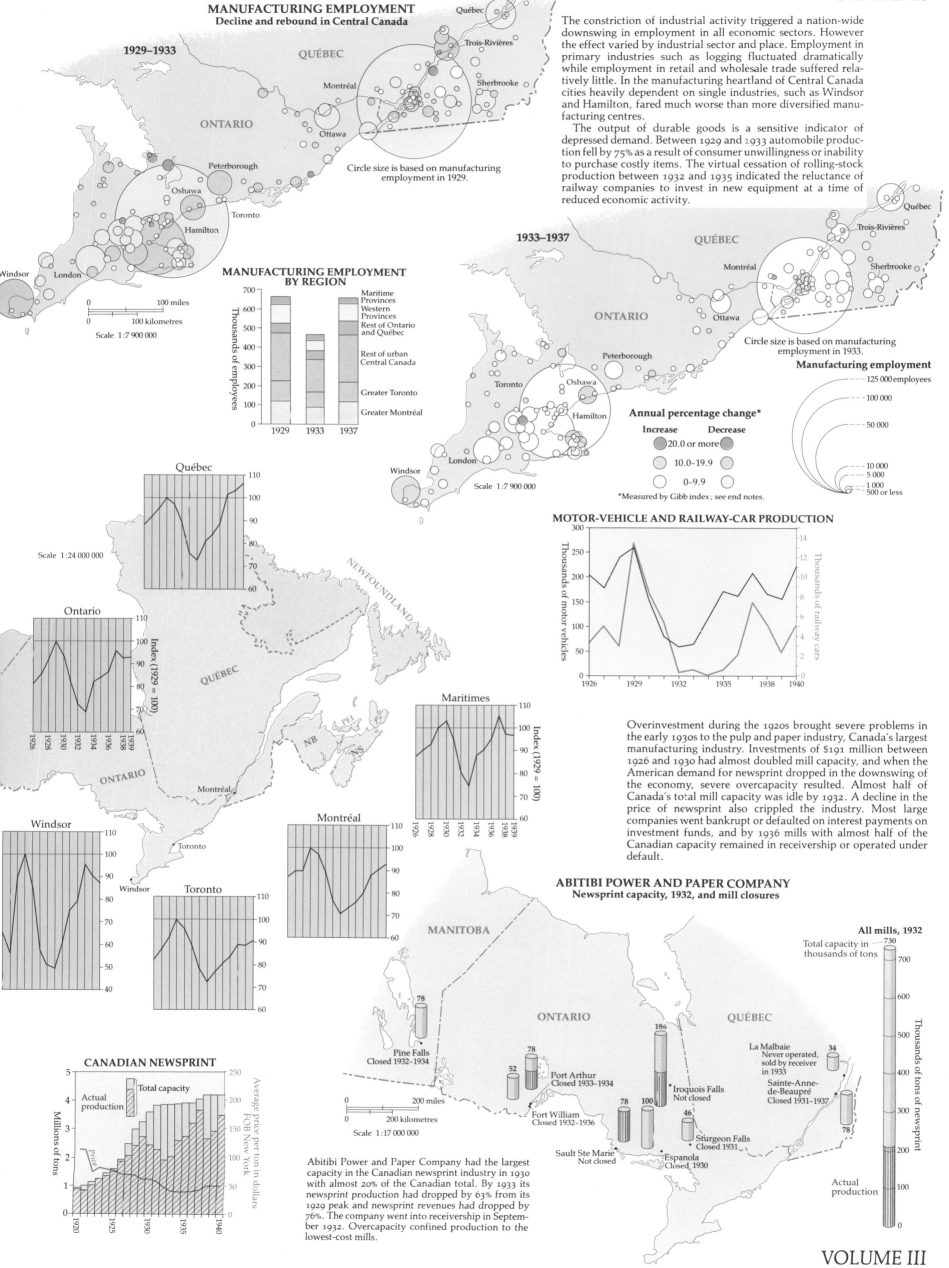

MANUFACTURING EMPLOYMENT
Decline and rebound in Central Canada

1929–1933

QUÉBEC

Québec

Trois-Rivières

Montréal

Sherbrooke

ONTARIO

Ottawa

Peterborough

Oshawa

Toronto

Hamilton

Windsor   London

0   100 miles
0   100 kilometres
Scale 1:7 900 000

Circle size is based on manufacturing employment in 1929.

The constriction of industrial activity triggered a nation-wide downswing in employment in all economic sectors. However the effect varied by industrial sector and place. Employment in primary industries such as logging fluctuated dramatically while employment in retail and wholesale trade suffered relatively little. In the manufacturing heartland of Central Canada cities heavily dependent on single industries, such as Windsor and Hamilton, fared much worse than more diversified manufacturing centres.

The output of durable goods is a sensitive indicator of depressed demand. Between 1929 and 1933 automobile production fell by 75% as a result of consumer unwillingness or inability to purchase costly items. The virtual cessation of rolling-stock production between 1932 and 1935 indicated the reluctance of railway companies to invest in new equipment at a time of reduced economic activity.

MANUFACTURING EMPLOYMENT BY REGION

Thousands of employees

Maritime Provinces
Western Provinces
Rest of Ontario and Québec
Rest of urban Central Canada
Greater Toronto
Greater Montréal

1929 1933 1937

1933–1937

QUÉBEC

Québec

Trois-Rivières

Montréal

Sherbrooke

ONTARIO

Ottawa

Peterborough

Toronto

Oshawa

Hamilton

Windsor   London

Scale 1:7 900 000

Circle size is based on manufacturing employment in 1933.

Manufacturing employment

125 000 employees
100 000
50 000
10 000
5 000
1 000
500 or less

Annual percentage change*

Increase   Decrease
20.0 or more
10.0–19.9
0–9.9

*Measured by Gibb index; see end notes.

Québec

Scale 1:24 000 000

NEWFOUNDLAND

Ontario

Index (1929 = 100)

1926 1928 1930 1932 1934 1936 1938 1939

QUÉBEC

ONTARIO

PEI

NB   NS

Montréal

Maritimes

Index (1929 = 100)

1926 1928 1930 1932 1934 1936 1938 1939

Windsor

Toronto

Toronto

Windsor

Montréal

MOTOR-VEHICLE AND RAILWAY-CAR PRODUCTION

Thousands of motor vehicles

Thousands of railway cars

1926 1929 1932 1935 1938 1940

Overinvestment during the 1920s brought severe problems in the early 1930s to the pulp and paper industry, Canada's largest manufacturing industry. Investments of $191 million between 1926 and 1930 had almost doubled mill capacity, and when the American demand for newsprint dropped in the downswing of the economy, severe overcapacity resulted. Almost half of Canada's total mill capacity was idle by 1932. A decline in the price of newsprint also crippled the industry. Most large companies went bankrupt or defaulted on interest payments on investment funds, and by 1936 mills with almost half of the Canadian capacity remained in receivership or operated under default.

ABITIBI POWER AND PAPER COMPANY
Newsprint capacity, 1932, and mill closures

MANITOBA

ONTARIO

QUÉBEC

78
Pine Falls
Closed 1932–1934

78
52   Port Arthur
Closed 1933–1934

186

78
Fort William
Closed 1932–1936

78 100   46
Sault Ste Marie
Not closed

Espanola
Closed 1930

Iroquois Falls
Not closed

Sturgeon Falls
Closed 1931

La Malbaie
Never operated, sold by receiver in 1933

34

Sainte-Anne-de-Beaupré
Closed 1931–1937

78

0   200 miles
0   200 kilometres
Scale 1:17 000 000

All mills, 1932

730
Total capacity in thousands of tons

700

600

500

400

300

Thousands of tons of newsprint

200

Actual production

100

0

CANADIAN NEWSPRINT

Millions of tons

Average price per ton in dollars FOB New York

Actual production

Total capacity

Price

1920 1925 1930 1935 1940

Abitibi Power and Paper Company had the largest capacity in the Canadian newsprint industry in 1930 with almost 20% of the Canadian total. By 1933 its newsprint production had dropped by 63% from its 1929 peak and newsprint revenues had dropped by 76%. The company went into receivership in September 1932. Overcapacity confined production to the lowest-cost mills.

THE IMPACT OF THE DEPRESSION ON PEOPLE
Authors: Murdo MacPherson, Deryck W. Holdsworth (trekking)

By the winter of 1933 some 32% of the Canadian work-force was jobless and by April over 1.5 million Canadians, 15% of the population, depended on direct relief for survival. Even by 1939 a million people were still on relief. Direct relief, formerly a public charity granted to the chronically poor, was extended in the Depression to those whose destitution was caused solely by unemployment or by loss of the means of livelihood, as in the case of drought-stricken farmers. The distribution of relief reflected the pattern of hardship across the country. Saskatchewan, with its devastated farming economy (pl 43), had the highest proportion of relief recipients in its population. In contrast, Maritimers were less likely to go on relief because of their traditional access to basic sustenance.

The relief rolls of urban areas were disproportionately large, reflecting not only the main concentrations of unemployment but also the in-migration of those seeking help. Many municipalities experienced great difficulties coping with this influx (pl 42). Soup kitchens, queues for job openings, and 'hobo jungles' became the habitual world for many unemployed. Some travelled from place to place – usually 'riding the rails' on freight cars – seeking 'work and wages' instead of 'the pogey' or instead of work in a relief camp (pl 42). This could bring a stint of work on a farm, in a logging camp, or in a gold mine, sometimes interspersed with an excursion to the milder BC coast in winter.

THE UNEMPLOYED AND RELIEF

Legend:
- Unemployed wage-earners not on relief
- Farm placement
- Youth training
- Schemes for single men
- Works projects
- Individuals / Head of families } Direct relief

Farm relief, other than direct relief, is not shown. Relief for resettlement is too small to be shown.

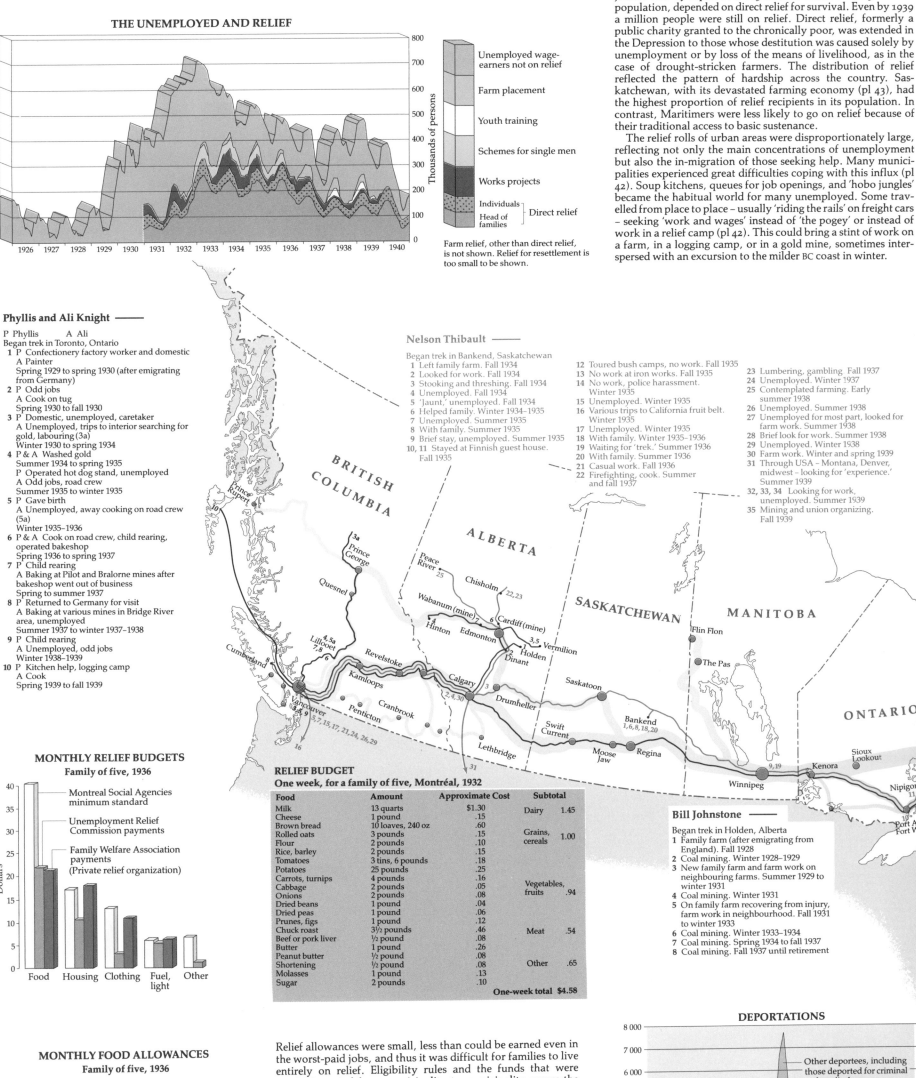

Phyllis and Ali Knight

P Phyllis A Ali
Began trek in Toronto, Ontario
1 P Confectionery factory worker and domestic
  A Painter
  Spring 1929 to spring 1930 (after emigrating from Germany)
2 P Odd jobs
  A Cook on tug
  Spring 1930 to fall 1930
3 P Domestic, unemployed, caretaker
  A Unemployed, trips to interior searching for gold, labouring (3a)
  Winter 1930 to spring 1934
4 P & A Washed gold
  Summer 1934 to spring 1935
  P Operated hot dog stand, unemployed
  A Odd jobs, road crew
  Summer 1935 to winter 1935
5 P Gave birth
  A Unemployed, away cooking on road crew (5a)
  Winter 1935–1936
6 P & A Cook on road crew, child rearing, operated bakeshop
  Spring 1936 to spring 1937
7 P Child rearing
  A Baking at Pilot and Bralorne mines after bakeshop went out of business
  Spring to summer 1937
8 P Returned to Germany for visit
  A Baking at various mines in Bridge River area, unemployed
  Summer 1937 to winter 1937–1938
9 P Child rearing
  A Unemployed, odd jobs
  Winter 1938–1939
10 P Kitchen help, logging camp
  A Cook
  Spring 1939 to fall 1939

Nelson Thibault

Began trek in Bankend, Saskatchewan
1 Left family farm. Fall 1934
2 Looked for work. Fall 1934
3 Stooking and threshing. Fall 1934
4 Unemployed. Fall 1934
5 'Jaunt,' unemployed. Fall 1934
6 Helped family. Winter 1934–1935
7 Unemployed. Summer 1935
8 With family. Summer 1935
9 Brief stay, unemployed. Summer 1935
10, 11 Stayed at Finnish guest house. Fall 1935
12 Toured bush camps, no work. Fall 1935
13 No work at iron works. Fall 1935
14 No work, police harassment. Winter 1935
15 Unemployed. Winter 1935
16 Various trips to California fruit belt. Winter 1935
17 Unemployed. Winter 1935
18 With family. Winter 1935–1936
19 Waiting for 'trek.' Summer 1936
20 With family. Summer 1936
21 Casual work. Fall 1936
22 Firefighting, cook. Summer and fall 1937
23 Lumbering, gambling. Fall 1937
24 Unemployed. Winter 1937
25 Contemplated farming. Early summer 1938
26 Unemployed. Summer 1938
27 Unemployed for most part, looked for farm work. Summer 1938
28 Brief look for work. Summer 1938
29 Unemployed. Winter 1938
30 Farm work. Winter and spring 1939
31 Through USA – Montana, Denver, midwest – looking for 'experience.' Summer 1939
32, 33, 34 Looking for work, unemployed. Summer 1939
35 Mining and union organizing. Fall 1939

Bill Johnstone

Began trek in Holden, Alberta
1 Family farm (after emigrating from England). Fall 1928
2 Coal mining. Winter 1928–1929
3 New family farm and farm work on neighbouring farms. Summer 1929 to winter 1931
4 Coal mining. Winter 1931
5 On family farm recovering from injury, farm work in neighbourhood. Fall 1931 to winter 1933
6 Coal mining. Winter 1933–1934
7 Coal mining. Spring 1934 to fall 1937
8 Coal mining. Fall 1937 until retirement

MONTHLY RELIEF BUDGETS
Family of five, 1936

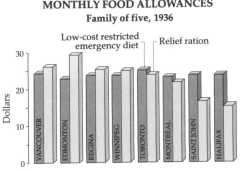

- Montreal Social Agencies minimum standard
- Unemployment Relief Commission payments
- Family Welfare Association payments (Private relief organization)

Categories: Food, Housing, Clothing, Fuel, light, Other

RELIEF BUDGET
One week, for a family of five, Montréal, 1932

Food	Amount	Approximate Cost	Subtotal	
Milk	13 quarts	$1.30	Dairy	1.45
Cheese	1 pound	.15		
Brown bread	10 loaves, 240 oz	.60	Grains, cereals	1.00
Rolled oats	3 pounds	.15		
Flour	2 pounds	.10		
Rice, barley	2 pounds	.15		
Tomatoes	3 tins, 6 pounds	.18	Vegetables, fruits	.94
Potatoes	25 pounds	.25		
Carrots, turnips	4 pounds	.16		
Cabbage	2 pounds	.05		
Onions	2 pounds	.08		
Dried beans	1 pound	.04		
Dried peas	1 pound	.06		
Prunes, figs	1 pound	.12		
Chuck roast	3½ pounds	.46	Meat	.54
Beef or pork liver	½ pound	.08		
Butter	1 pound	.26	Other	.65
Peanut butter	½ pound	.08		
Shortening	½ pound	.08		
Molasses	1 pound	.13		
Sugar	2 pounds	.10		
			One-week total	$4.58

MONTHLY FOOD ALLOWANCES
Family of five, 1936

- Low-cost restricted emergency diet
- Relief ration

Cities: VANCOUVER, EDMONTON, REGINA, WINNIPEG, TORONTO, MONTREAL, SAINT JOHN, HALIFAX

Relief allowances were small, less than could be earned even in the worst-paid jobs, and thus it was difficult for families to live entirely on relief. Eligibility rules and the funds that were available varied from municipality to municipality across the country. Rarely were the necessities of life – food, housing, fuel, and clothing – adequately covered by relief. Only in western cities did the relief ration permit the maintenance of a 'restricted emergency diet' (a minimum standard, regarded by health agencies as nutritionally inadequate for prolonged periods). Most Canadians on relief suffered from poor health and cases of scurvy and rickets attested to malnutrition.

In an attempt to deal with the enormity of the relief burden a 'Canadians first' policy surfaced and over 17 000 foreign 'public charges' were deported between 1929 and 1935. The policy was stopped after the 1935 election.

DEPORTATIONS

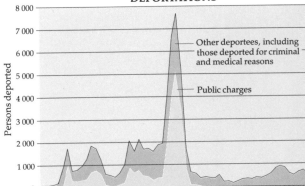

- Other deportees, including those deported for criminal and medical reasons
- Public charges

PLATE 41

RELIEF RECIPIENTS BY PROVINCE

Direct relief by province

Type of relief

Indirect
Direct

Average number on relief per month

Proportion of direct relief in selected urban areas, 1935

Rest of province

Specified urban area

Costs of relief
Relief recipients
Population

British Columbia

Alberta

Saskatchewan

Manitoba

Ontario

Percentage of provincial population

Thousands of recipients

Québec

Newfoundland

St John's

PEI

New Brunswick

Nova Scotia

Scale 1:27 000 000

Vancouver

Calgary and Edmonton

Regina

Winnipeg

Toronto

Montréal

Halifax and cities in Cape Breton

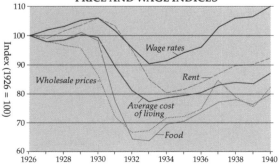

Courtesy of the Glenbow Archives, Calgary, NC6-12955(b)

'Riding the rails'

This map illustrates both the general movement of people seeking employment and the actual journeys of some people engaged in the search. Shown here are the experiences of Nelson Thibault, a Prairie farmer's son who was in his teens when the Depression began; Bill Johnstone, in his early twenties and the son of an immigrant ex-miner from northern England; and Phyllis and Ali Knight, a married couple in their late twenties from Germany.

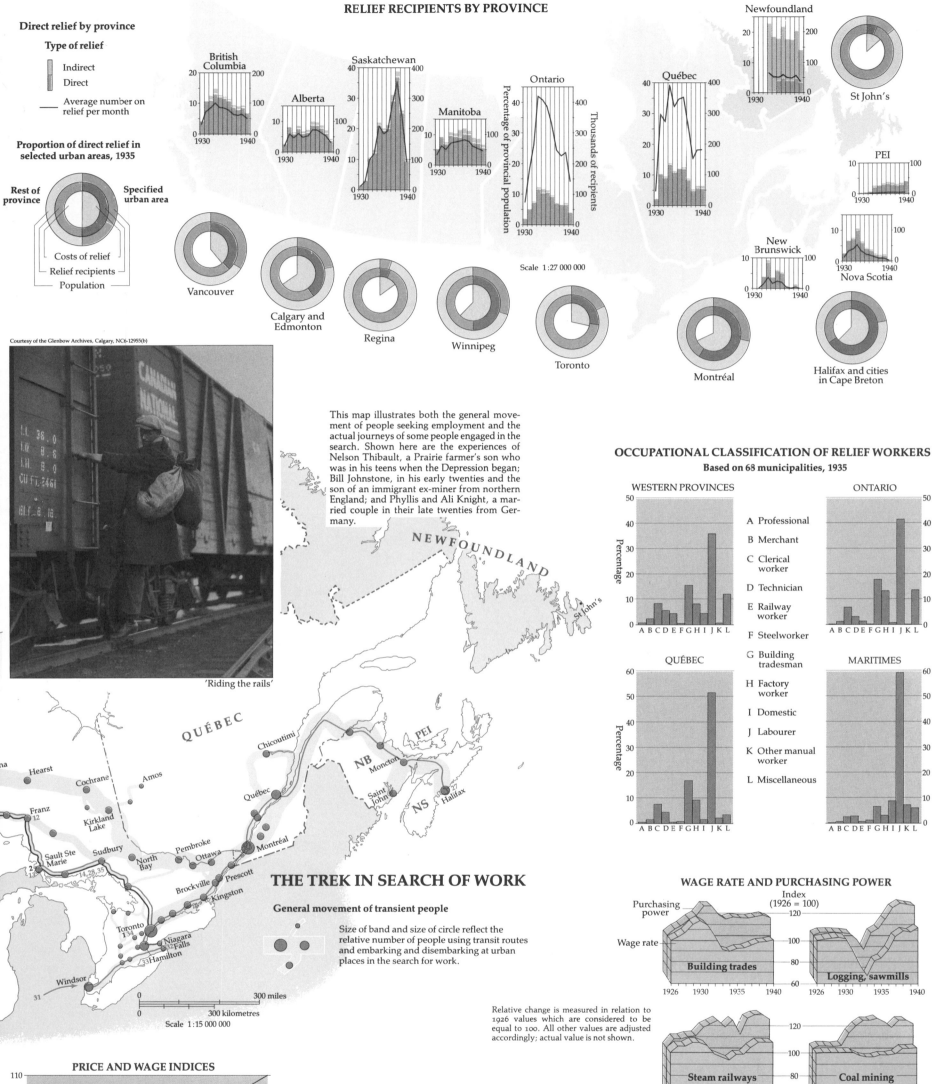

NEWFOUNDLAND

St John's

QUÉBEC

Hearst
Cochrane
Amos
Chicoutimi
PEI
NB
Moncton
Québec
Saint John
NS
Halifax
Franz
Kirkland Lake
Sault Ste Marie
Sudbury
North Bay
Pembroke
Ottawa
Montréal
Brockville
Prescott
Kingston
Toronto
Niagara Falls
Hamilton
Windsor

THE TREK IN SEARCH OF WORK

General movement of transient people

Size of band and size of circle reflect the relative number of people using transit routes and embarking and disembarking at urban places in the search for work.

0   300 miles
0   300 kilometres
Scale 1:15 000 000

OCCUPATIONAL CLASSIFICATION OF RELIEF WORKERS
Based on 68 municipalities, 1935

WESTERN PROVINCES

ONTARIO

QUÉBEC

MARITIMES

Percentage

A Professional
B Merchant
C Clerical worker
D Technician
E Railway worker
F Steelworker
G Building tradesman
H Factory worker
I Domestic
J Labourer
K Other manual worker
L Miscellaneous

WAGE RATE AND PURCHASING POWER

Purchasing power

Index (1926 = 100)

Wage rate

Building trades

Logging, sawmills

Steam railways

Coal mining

Factory trades

Factory labour

Relative change is measured in relation to 1926 values which are considered to be equal to 100. All other values are adjusted accordingly; actual value is not shown.

PRICE AND WAGE INDICES

Index (1926 = 100)

Wage rates
Wholesale prices
Rent
Average cost of living
Food

Labourers and blue-collar workers were most seriously affected by unemployment, particularly by the collapse of the construction industry and the widespread loss of manufacturing jobs. Civil servants and professional and managerial groups were least touched. Those fortunate to remain employed faced job insecurity and suffered cuts in wages, although this was less of a problem for salaried or unionized workers. The decline in prices reduced the cost of living, however, and some workers even benefited from an enhanced purchasing power and could enjoy a higher standard of living than in the pre-Depression years.

MANAGING THE RELIEF BURDEN

Author: Murdo MacPherson

GOVERNMENT RELIEF

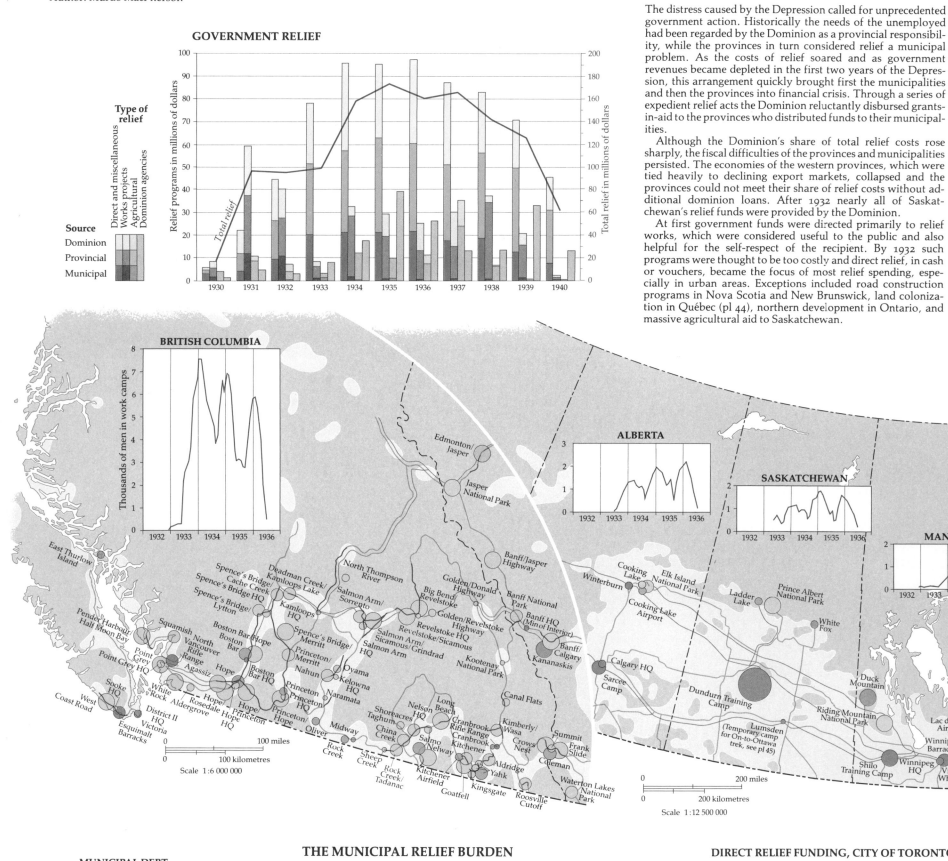

Type of relief

- Direct and miscellaneous
- Works projects
- Agricultural
- Dominion agencies

Source

- Dominion
- Provincial
- Municipal

Relief programs in millions of dollars (left axis)

Total relief in millions of dollars (right axis)

Total relief

Years: 1930 1931 1932 1933 1934 1935 1936 1937 1938 1939 1940

BRITISH COLUMBIA

Thousands of men in work camps
1932 1933 1934 1935 1936

ALBERTA
1932 1933 1934 1935 1936

SASKATCHEWAN
1932 1933 1934 1935 1936

MANITOBA
1932 1933 1934

The distress caused by the Depression called for unprecedented government action. Historically the needs of the unemployed had been regarded by the Dominion as a provincial responsibility, while the provinces in turn considered relief a municipal problem. As the costs of relief soared and as government revenues became depleted in the first two years of the Depression, this arrangement quickly brought first the municipalities and then the provinces into financial crisis. Through a series of expedient relief acts the Dominion reluctantly disbursed grants-in-aid to the provinces who distributed funds to their municipalities.

Although the Dominion's share of total relief costs rose sharply, the fiscal difficulties of the provinces and municipalities persisted. The economies of the western provinces, which were tied heavily to declining export markets, collapsed and the provinces could not meet their share of relief costs without additional dominion loans. After 1932 nearly all of Saskatchewan's relief funds were provided by the Dominion.

At first government funds were directed primarily to relief works, which were considered useful to the public and also helpful for the self-respect of the recipient. By 1932 such programs were thought to be too costly and direct relief, in cash or vouchers, became the focus of most relief spending, especially in urban areas. Exceptions included road construction programs in Nova Scotia and New Brunswick, land colonization in Québec (pl 44), northern development in Ontario, and massive agricultural aid to Saskatchewan.

Scale 1:6 000 000
0   100 miles
0   100 kilometres

Scale 1:12 500 000
0   200 miles
0   200 kilometres

THE MUNICIPAL RELIEF BURDEN

MUNICIPAL DEBT 1931–1934

Millions of dollars

- British Columbia
- Alberta
- Saskatchewan
- Manitoba
- Ontario
- Québec
- Maritimes

Total debt / Amount in default

BANKRUPT ONTARIO MUNICIPALITIES 1931–1934

ONTARIO

Sturgeon Falls 1933
Sudbury 1933
Pembroke 1934
Hawkesbury 1932
Rockland 1933
Eastview Date not available
Dysart Township 1932
Trenton 1934
York 1933 $15 000 000
North York 1933
Scarborough 1932
Weston 1934
East York 1933
Etobicoke 1933
Leaside 1933
New Toronto 1933
Mimico 1933
Brantford RC School District Date not available
Thorold 1934
Niagara Falls 1933
Fort Erie 1934
Walkerville 1934
Riverside 1931
Windsor 1932
Tecumseh 1932
East Windsor 1931
$13 000 000
West Sandwich 1931
East Sandwich 1931
Leamington 1934
La Salle 1932
Kingsville 1934
Sandwich 1932
Essex 1933
Pelee Township Date not available

Public debentures

- ● More than 6 000 000 dollars
- ● 4 000 000–6 000 000
- ● 2 000 000–3 999 999
- ○ 1 000 000–1 999 999
- ○ Less than 1 000 000

1934 Date of bankruptcy

Scale 1:6 250 000
0   100 miles
0   100 kilometres

DIRECT RELIEF FUNDING, CITY OF TORONTO

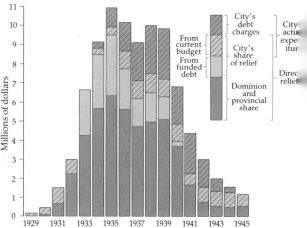

Millions of dollars

- From current budget
- From funded debt
- City's debt charges
- City's share of relief
- Dominion and provincial share
- City's actual expenditure
- Direct relief

Years: 1929 1931 1933 1935 1937 1939 1941 1943 1945

Many industrial municipalities experienced financial crisis when unemployment mounted, real-estate values shrank, and property taxes became increasingly difficult to collect. Relief was funded on credit, and when this could no longer be extended, bankruptcy followed. Despite high relief costs the City of Toronto's superior credit rating made it possible for it to borrow the bulk of its share of relief between 1933 and 1939 and defer its relief burden. This resulted in debt charges forming the majority of the city's expenditures after 1934 and repayment was not completed until 1944.

HISTORICAL ATLAS OF CANADA

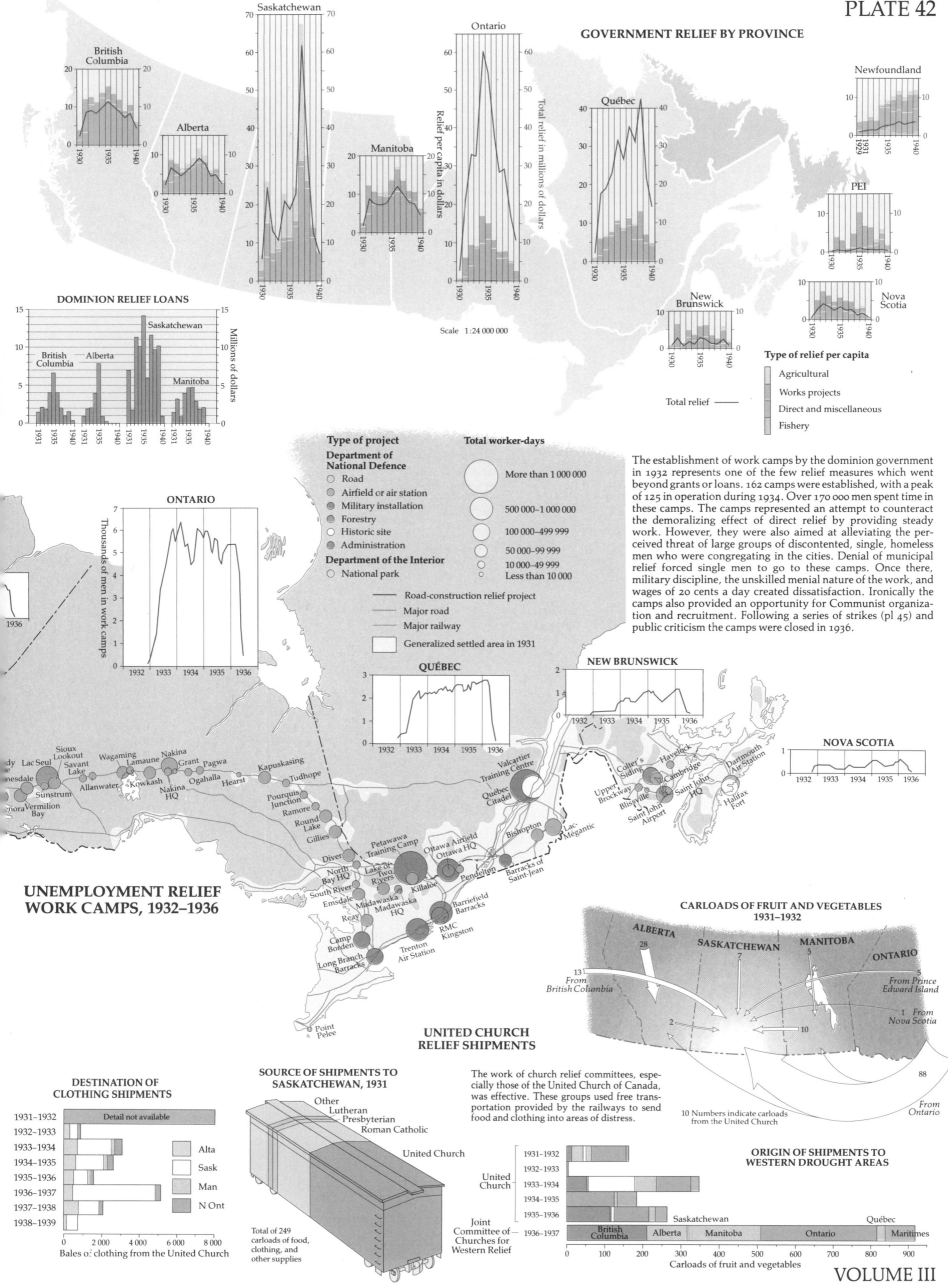

GOVERNMENT RELIEF BY PROVINCE

British Columbia

Saskatchewan

Alberta

Manitoba

Ontario

Québec

Newfoundland

PEI

Nova Scotia

New Brunswick

Relief per capita in dollars

Total relief in millions of dollars

Scale 1:24 000 000

DOMINION RELIEF LOANS

British Columbia

Alberta

Saskatchewan

Manitoba

Millions of dollars

Type of relief per capita

Agricultural

Works projects

Direct and miscellaneous

Fishery

Total relief ———

Type of project

Department of National Defence
○ Road
◔ Airfield or air station
◑ Military installation
◕ Forestry
○ Historic site
● Administration

Department of the Interior
○ National park

Total worker-days

More than 1 000 000

500 000–1 000 000

100 000–499 999

50 000–99 999

10 000–49 999

Less than 10 000

——— Road-construction relief project
——— Major road
——— Major railway
▭ Generalized settled area in 1931

The establishment of work camps by the dominion government in 1932 represents one of the few relief measures which went beyond grants or loans. 162 camps were established, with a peak of 125 in operation during 1934. Over 170 000 men spent time in these camps. The camps represented an attempt to counteract the demoralizing effect of direct relief by providing steady work. However, they were also aimed at alleviating the perceived threat of large groups of discontented, single, homeless men who were congregating in the cities. Denial of municipal relief forced single men to go to these camps. Once there, military discipline, the unskilled menial nature of the work, and wages of 20 cents a day created dissatisfaction. Ironically the camps also provided an opportunity for Communist organization and recruitment. Following a series of strikes (pl 45) and public criticism the camps were closed in 1936.

ONTARIO

Thousands of men in work camps

QUÉBEC

NEW BRUNSWICK

NOVA SCOTIA

UNEMPLOYMENT RELIEF WORK CAMPS, 1932–1936

CARLOADS OF FRUIT AND VEGETABLES 1931–1932

ALBERTA 28

SASKATCHEWAN 7

MANITOBA 5

ONTARIO 5

13 *From British Columbia*

5 *From Prince Edward Island*

1 *From Nova Scotia*

2

10

88

From Ontario

10 Numbers indicate carloads from the United Church

UNITED CHURCH RELIEF SHIPMENTS

DESTINATION OF CLOTHING SHIPMENTS

1931–1932 Detail not available
1932–1933
1933–1934
1934–1935
1935–1936
1936–1937
1937–1938
1938–1939

Bales of clothing from the United Church

Alta
Sask
Man
N Ont

SOURCE OF SHIPMENTS TO SASKATCHEWAN, 1931

Other
Lutheran
Presbyterian
Roman Catholic

United Church

Total of 249 carloads of food, clothing, and other supplies

The work of church relief committees, especially those of the United Church of Canada, was effective. These groups used free transportation provided by the railways to send food and clothing into areas of distress.

United Church

Joint Committee of Churches for Western Relief

1931–1932
1932–1933
1933–1934
1934–1935
1935–1936
1936–1937

ORIGIN OF SHIPMENTS TO WESTERN DROUGHT AREAS

British Columbia
Alberta
Manitoba
Saskatchewan
Ontario
Québec
Maritimes

Carloads of fruit and vegetables

DROUGHT AND DEPRESSION ON THE PRAIRIES

Author : Murdo MacPherson

WHEAT RETURNS BY AREA, 1921–1929 AND 1930–1938

Scale 1:20 000 000

Generalized drought areas are based on crop districts.

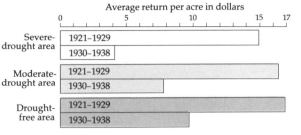

Average return per acre in dollars

	0	5	10	15	17
Severe-drought area	1921–1929				
	1930–1938				
Moderate-drought area	1921–1929				
	1930–1938				
Drought-free area	1921–1929				
	1930–1938				

The effect of economic depression alone is seen in the reduced returns for the drought-free area. The addition of severe drought rendered economic wheat production impossible. Little more than subsistence was possible in the moderate-drought area.

MARKET VALUE OF WHEAT

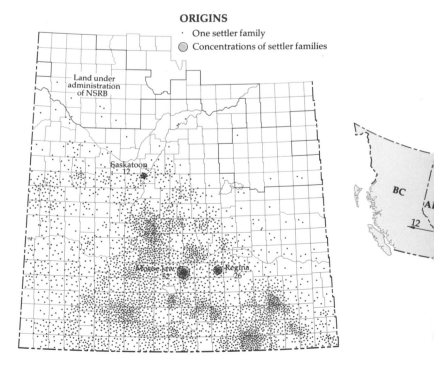

— Wholesale price of No. 1 Northern wheat at Fort William

--- Wheat price at local elevator in Saskatchewan

— Estimated value of wheat sold from Saskatchewan farms

INDEX OF NET FARM INCOME

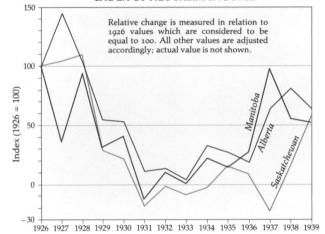

Relative change is measured in relation to 1926 values which are considered to be equal to 100. All other values are adjusted accordingly; actual value is not shown.

The combined effects of economic collapse and prolonged drought meant that the Depression was felt more severely in the Prairies than in any other part of Canada. Restriction of the world export grain market, as a result of newly erected tariff barriers and increased foreign production, reduced the value of Prairie wheat by almost one-third between 1929 and 1932. At the same time a series of droughts between 1930 and 1937 brought about complete or partial crop failures over extensive areas.

Although there was yearly variation in the effects of the drought across the Prairies, there was little respite for south-central Saskatchewan and the wheat crop there was severely and consistently devastated. Low wheat prices and low yields resulted in a steep drop in net farm income. In Saskatchewan per capita income plunged by 72% between 1928 and 1933 and returns from farming could not cover costs from 1931 to 1934 and again during the severe drought of 1937, when farmers in Manitoba and Alberta were well on the way to recovery. It was impossible for most Prairie farmers, and especially those in Saskatchewan, to survive without some form of government relief (pl 42). Saskatchewan's relief payments reflected the severity of the drought in that province, and in the worst-hit areas entire municipalities were at times supported by relief.

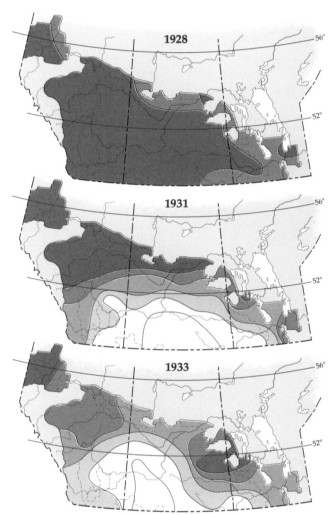

1928

1931

1933

Scale 1:22 000 000

WHEAT YIELDS

Bushels per acre

	20
	16
	12
	8
	4
	0
	Non-agricultural land

--- Primary wheat-growing area

(Wheat is grown outside this area but as a secondary crop.)

Wheat yields reflect the cumulative effect of various natural forces. Although deficiency of rainfall was undoubtedly the single most important factor, other problems such as a grasshopper plague in 1933 and rust disease in 1935 contributed to crop devastation. Destruction of crop and vegetation cover also left the land susceptible to soil erosion under the high prairie winds, and dust bowls further reduced productive capacity.

GOVERNMENT-ASSISTED SETTLERS

FARM RELIEF, SASKATCHEWAN, 1929–1938

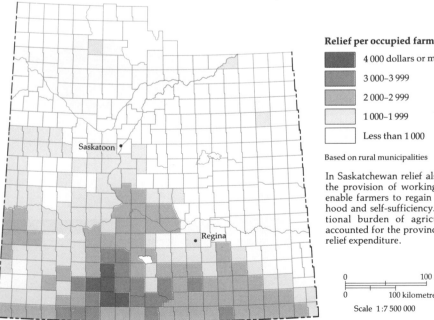

Relief per occupied farm

	4 000 dollars or more
	3 000–3 999
	2 000–2 999
	1 000–1 999
	Less than 1 000

Based on rural municipalities

In Saskatchewan relief also involved the provision of working capital to enable farmers to regain their livelihood and self-sufficiency. This additional burden of agricultural aid accounted for the province's massive relief expenditure.

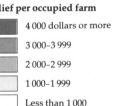

0 ————— 100 miles
0 ————— 100 kilometres
Scale 1:7 500 000

ORIGINS

· One settler family
⊙ Concentrations of settler families

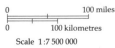

HISTORICAL ATLAS OF CANADA

PLATE 43

THE WORK OF THE PRAIRIE FARM REHABILITATION ADMINISTRATION

SMALL WATER PROJECTS CONSTRUCTED BY 1938

Number of projects per rural municipality

- 30 or more
- 20–29
- 10–19
- 1–9

Scale 1:8 200 000

By the mid-1930s it appeared that large areas of the prairie would be lost to agriculture. In April 1935 the dominion government responded with the Prairie Farm Rehabilitation Act (PFRA) which established remedial programs. New agricultural practices, such as strip farming, cover cropping, and shelter belts were introduced. Submarginal crop land was fenced, re-grassed, and permanently converted into community pastures which counteracted the worst of the soil drifting. The limited water resources of the Prairies were more effectively utilized through development of water-holding and irrigation projects. The smaller of these water projects were most immediately beneficial to farmers while the larger and more expensive ones attempted to provide long-term solutions. In combination, water and pasture development enabled a diversification in Prairie agriculture through expanded livestock production.

Small water projects consisted of dugouts, ponds for watering stock, and small irrigation works constructed relatively cheaply on individual farms. Dugouts, on average 60 ft by 160 ft and 10 ft deep (18 m by 49 m and 3 m deep), were the most numerous and effective of these projects.

Large water projects were mainly concerned with irrigation and aided the resettlement of farmers. The management of community pastures was under federal jurisdiction but such an arrangement was resisted by Alberta until 1962.

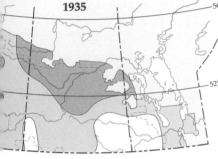

1935

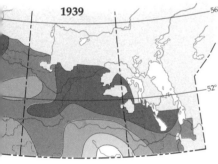

1937

1939

LARGE WATER PROJECTS AND COMMUNITY PASTURES COMPLETED BY 1940

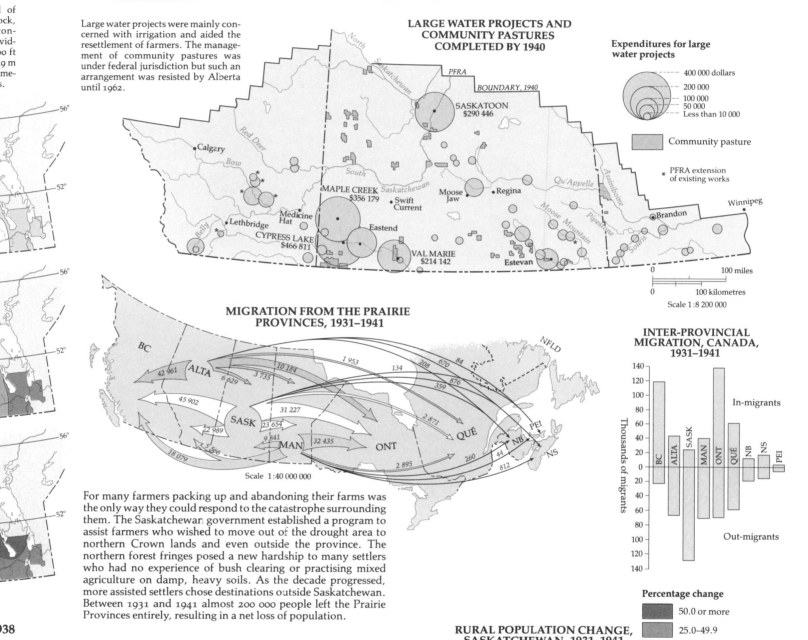

Expenditures for large water projects

- 400 000 dollars
- 200 000
- 100 000
- 50 000
- Less than 10 000

- Community pasture
- * PFRA extension of existing works

SASKATOON $290 446
MAPLE CREEK $356 179
CYPRESS LAKE $466 811
VAL MARIE $214 142

Scale 1:8 200 000

MIGRATION FROM THE PRAIRIE PROVINCES, 1931–1941

Scale 1:40 000 000

INTER-PROVINCIAL MIGRATION, CANADA, 1931–1941

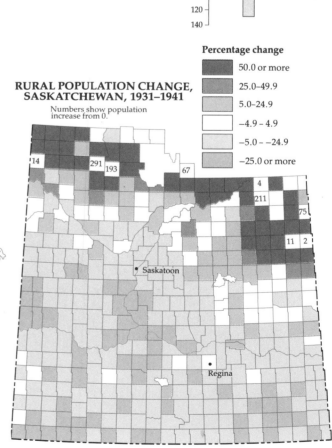

In-migrants

Out-migrants

Thousands of migrants

For many farmers packing up and abandoning their farms was the only way they could respond to the catastrophe surrounding them. The Saskatchewan government established a program to assist farmers who wished to move out of the drought area to northern Crown lands and even outside the province. The northern forest fringes posed a new hardship to many settlers who had no experience of bush clearing or practising mixed agriculture on damp, heavy soils. As the decade progressed, more assisted settlers chose destinations outside Saskatchewan. Between 1931 and 1941 almost 200 000 people left the Prairie Provinces entirely, resulting in a net loss of population.

SASKATCHEWAN, 1930–1938

DESTINATIONS

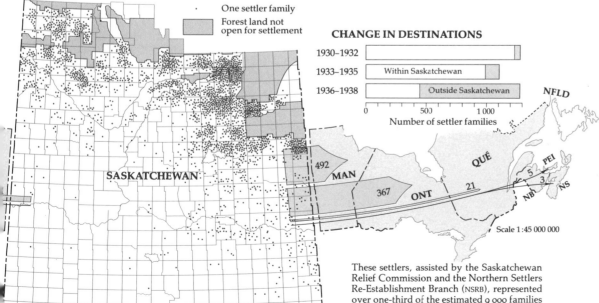

- One settler family
- Forest land not open for settlement

CHANGE IN DESTINATIONS

1930–1932	
1933–1935	Within Saskatchewan
1936–1938	Outside Saskatchewan

0   500   1 000
Number of settler families

Scale 1:45 000 000

These settlers, assisted by the Saskatchewan Relief Commission and the Northern Settlers Re-Establishment Branch (NSRB), represented over one-third of the estimated 9 000 families who moved into the northern Crown lands during the Depression.

Scale 1:7 500 000

RURAL POPULATION CHANGE, SASKATCHEWAN, 1931–1941

Numbers show population increase from 0.

Percentage change

- 50.0 or more
- 25.0–49.9
- 5.0–24.9
- −4.9 – 4.9
- −5.0 – −24.9
- −25.0 or more

COLONIZATION AND CO-OPERATION

Authors: Murdo MacPherson, Serge Courville (new parishes), Daniel MacInnes (Antigonish movement)

In eastern Canada relief schemes based on self-help or co-operation emerged as significant responses to the hardships of the Depression. In Québec the colonization of new agricultural land in marginal areas was seen as a viable alternative to unemployment and dependency on direct relief. Since the mid-19th century the Roman Catholic Church and the Québec government had combined to encourage colonization and provide an economic and social infrastructure in the new settlements. While the parish and the local priest remained important during the Depression, the state greatly expanded its role in land settlement by implementing major colonization schemes. 12 000 new farms were opened under three settlement plans: the federal-provincial Gordon Plan (1932-5); the provincial Vautrin Plan (1935-7); and the federal-provincial Rogers-Auger Plan (1937-46). Grants for transportation and construction, premiums for land clearing and ploughing, and technical advice were offered to former urban dwellers and farmers from across the province. The Abitibi region was the main destination for migrants while the Gaspé and southern Gulf shore were also important areas for new settlers. More than half of the settlers were sponsored under the Vautrin Plan.

Relief settlement plans were established in other provinces, but by 1940 much of the newly settled land had been abandoned. Although there was also considerable land abandonment in Québec, the impact was less; the move to the land was much greater, and new settlers were encouraged to move onto previously abandoned land.

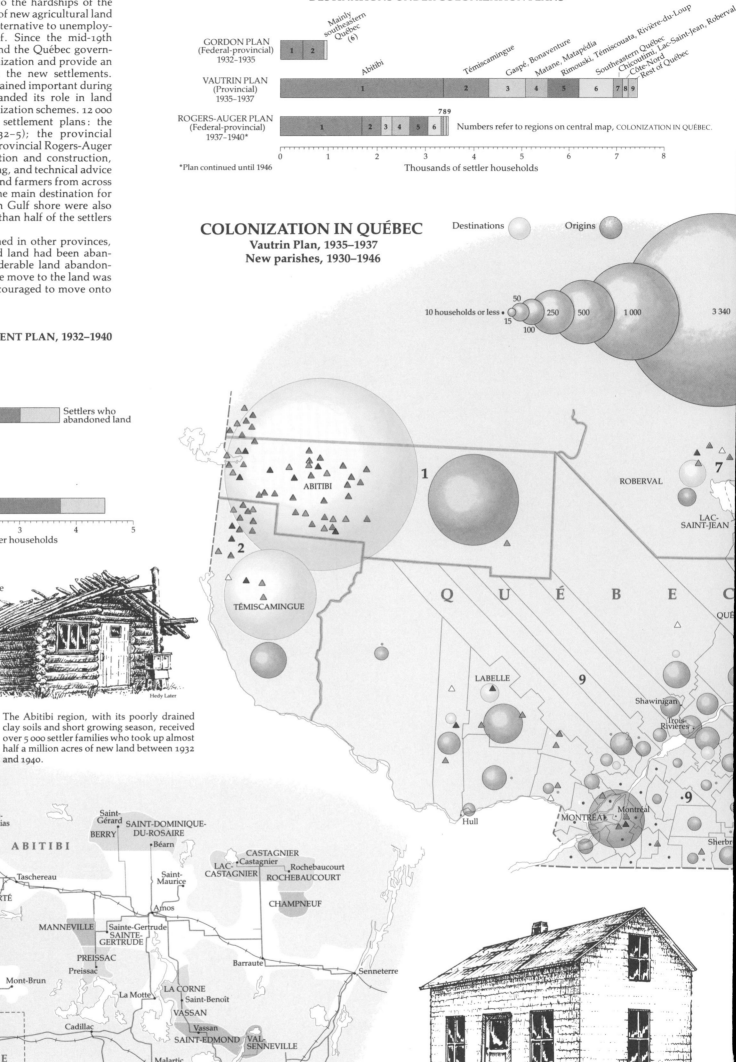

DESTINATIONS UNDER COLONIZATION PLANS

*Plan continued until 1946

Numbers refer to regions on central map, COLONIZATION IN QUÉBEC.

COLONIZATION IN QUÉBEC
Vautrin Plan, 1935–1937
New parishes, 1930–1946

Destinations   Origins

10 households or less •

DOMINION RELIEF SETTLEMENT PLAN, 1932–1940

Settlers who remained   Settlers who abandoned land

Thousands of settler households

Settler's initial dwelling, Roquemaure

Hedy Later

The Abitibi region, with its poorly drained clay soils and short growing season, received over 5 000 settler families who took up almost half a million acres of new land between 1932 and 1940.

COLONIZATION IN ABITIBI REGION, QUÉBEC

Areas of settlement

Settled area, 1932

Gordon Plan, 1932–1935

Vautrin Plan, 1935–1937

Rogers-Auger Plan, 1937–1946

ROQUEMAURE New parishes formed under colonization plans

Roads, 1946
Paved
Gravel
Earth

Scale 1:1 250 000

0   20 miles
0   20 kilometres

Typical settler's house, Roquemaure

Hedy Later

Although a colonist's initial shelter may have been quite primitive, there were guidelines and grants for house building established by the Québec Department of Colonization; typical houses were one and a half or two storeys, shingle-sided, and with a square plan.

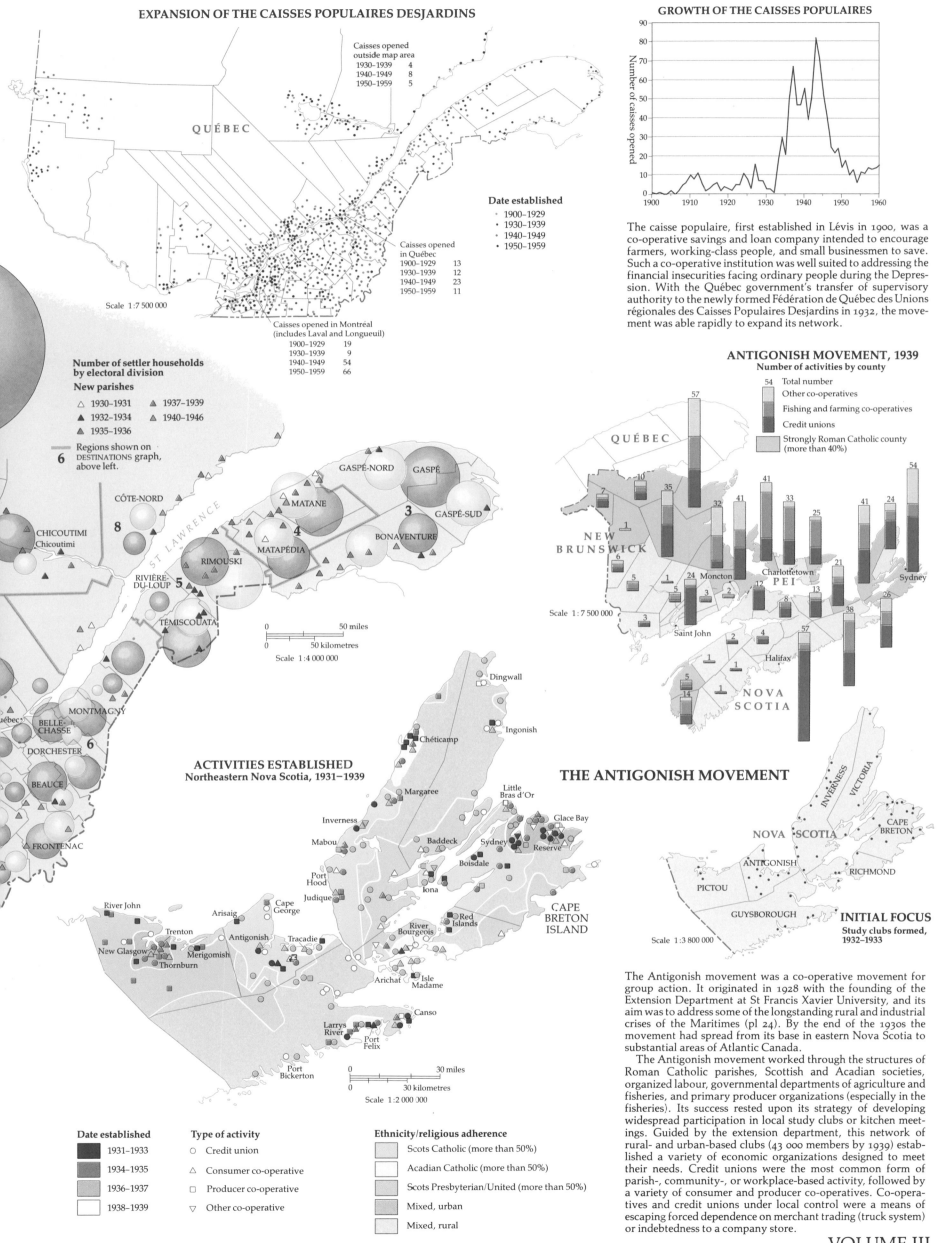

PLATE 44

EXPANSION OF THE CAISSES POPULAIRES DESJARDINS

Caisses opened outside map area
1930–1939 4
1940–1949 8
1950–1959 5

QUÉBEC

Date established
· 1900–1929
· 1930–1939
· 1940–1949
· 1950–1959

Caisses opened in Québec
1900–1929 13
1930–1939 12
1940–1949 23
1950–1959 11

Caisses opened in Montréal (includes Laval and Longueuil)
1900–1929 19
1930–1939 9
1940–1949 54
1950–1959 66

Scale 1:7 500 000

Number of settler households by electoral division
New parishes
△ 1930–1931 ▲ 1937–1939
▲ 1932–1934 ▲ 1940–1946
▲ 1935–1936

6 Regions shown on DESTINATIONS graph, above left.

GASPÉ-NORD GASPÉ
CÔTE-NORD 8
MATANE
CHICOUTIMI Chicoutimi 4 GASPÉ-SUD 3
MATAPÉDIA BONAVENTURE
RIMOUSKI
RIVIÈRE-DU-LOUP 5
ST LAWRENCE
TÉMISCOUATA

0   50 miles
0   50 kilometres
Scale 1:4 000 000

MONTMAGNY
BELLE-CHASSE
DORCHESTER 6
BEAUCE
FRONTENAC

GROWTH OF THE CAISSES POPULAIRES

The caisse populaire, first established in Lévis in 1900, was a co-operative savings and loan company intended to encourage farmers, working-class people, and small businessmen to save. Such a co-operative institution was well suited to addressing the financial insecurities facing ordinary people during the Depression. With the Québec government's transfer of supervisory authority to the newly formed Fédération de Québec des Unions régionales des Caisses Populaires Desjardins in 1932, the movement was able rapidly to expand its network.

ANTIGONISH MOVEMENT, 1939
Number of activities by county

54 Total number
Other co-operatives
Fishing and farming co-operatives
Credit unions
Strongly Roman Catholic county (more than 40%)

QUÉBEC
NEW BRUNSWICK
Moncton Charlottetown PEI Sydney
Scale 1:7 500 000
Saint John Halifax NOVA SCOTIA

ACTIVITIES ESTABLISHED
Northeastern Nova Scotia, 1931–1939

Dingwall
Ingonish
Chéticamp
Margaree Little Bras d'Or Glace Bay
Inverness Baddeck Sydney Reserve
Mabou Boisdale
Port Hood Iona
Judique
River John Cape George Red Islands
Arisaig
Trenton Antigonish Tracadie River Bourgeois
New Glasgow Merigomish
Thornburn CAPE BRETON ISLAND
Arichat Isle Madame
Canso
Larrys River Port Felix
Port Bickerton

0   30 miles
0   30 kilometres
Scale 1:2 000 000

THE ANTIGONISH MOVEMENT

INVERNESS VICTORIA
NOVA SCOTIA CAPE BRETON
ANTIGONISH RICHMOND
PICTOU
GUYSBOROUGH **INITIAL FOCUS**
Scale 1:3 800 000 Study clubs formed, 1932–1933

The Antigonish movement was a co-operative movement for group action. It originated in 1928 with the founding of the Extension Department at St Francis Xavier University, and its aim was to address some of the longstanding rural and industrial crises of the Maritimes (pl 24). By the end of the 1930s the movement had spread from its base in eastern Nova Scotia to substantial areas of Atlantic Canada.

The Antigonish movement worked through the structures of Roman Catholic parishes, Scottish and Acadian societies, organized labour, governmental departments of agriculture and fisheries, and primary producer organizations (especially in the fisheries). Its success rested upon its strategy of developing widespread participation in local study clubs or kitchen meetings. Guided by the extension department, this network of rural- and urban-based clubs (43 000 members by 1939) established a variety of economic organizations designed to meet their needs. Credit unions were the most common form of parish-, community-, or workplace-based activity, followed by a variety of consumer and producer co-operatives. Co-operatives and credit unions under local control were a means of escaping forced dependence on merchant trading (truck system) or indebtedness to a company store.

Date established
■ 1931–1933
■ 1934–1935
■ 1936–1937
□ 1938–1939

Type of activity
○ Credit union
△ Consumer co-operative
□ Producer co-operative
▽ Other co-operative

Ethnicity/religious adherence
Scots Catholic (more than 50%)
Acadian Catholic (more than 50%)
Scots Presbyterian/United (more than 50%)
Mixed, urban
Mixed, rural

WORKERS' RESPONSES

Authors: Gregory S. Kealey, Douglas Cruikshank

UNION MEMBERSHIP BY PROVINCE, 1931–1940

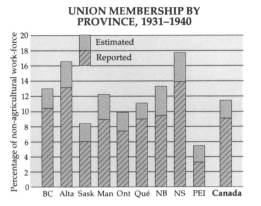

UNION MEMBERSHIP BY INDUSTRY

Other
Service
Transportation
Building trades
Metal trades
Clothing, footwear
Mining
— Total membership

UNION MEMBERSHIP BY AFFILIATION

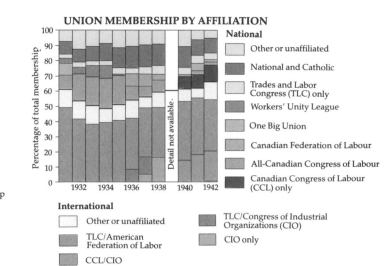

National
- Other or unaffiliated
- National and Catholic
- Trades and Labor Congress (TLC) only
- Workers' Unity League
- One Big Union
- Canadian Federation of Labour
- All-Canadian Congress of Labour
- Canadian Congress of Labour (CCL) only

International
- Other or unaffiliated
- TLC/American Federation of Labor
- CCL/CIO
- TLC/Congress of Industrial Organizations (CIO)
- CIO only

Detail not available.

The experience of the Great Depression provided new impetus for organizing within the Canadian working class, whether employed or unemployed. Trade unions had in previous depressions suffered severe erosions in membership but in the 1930s membership did not fall. Fragmentation of the labour movement, however, increased with the rise of the Congress of Industrial Organizations (CIO) and its Canadian affiliate the Canadian Congress of Labour. In 1934 Canadian national unions represented a small majority of unionized workers but the rise of the CIO restored the dominance of international unions.

Early in the Depression most strikes were defensive and in opposition to wage decreases, but over the decade workers increasingly took the offensive and struggles to force employers to bargain with the union became more important. Strikes were more frequent than in the 1920s but less than from 1901 to 1920. They also involved fewer workers and were shorter because of Depression conditions. Nova Scotia again led the nation in both the frequency and size of strikes, and mining again led all industries in frequency.

FREQUENCY, SIZE, AND DURATION

Type of industry
- Service
- Transportation
- Construction
- Manufacturing
- Mining

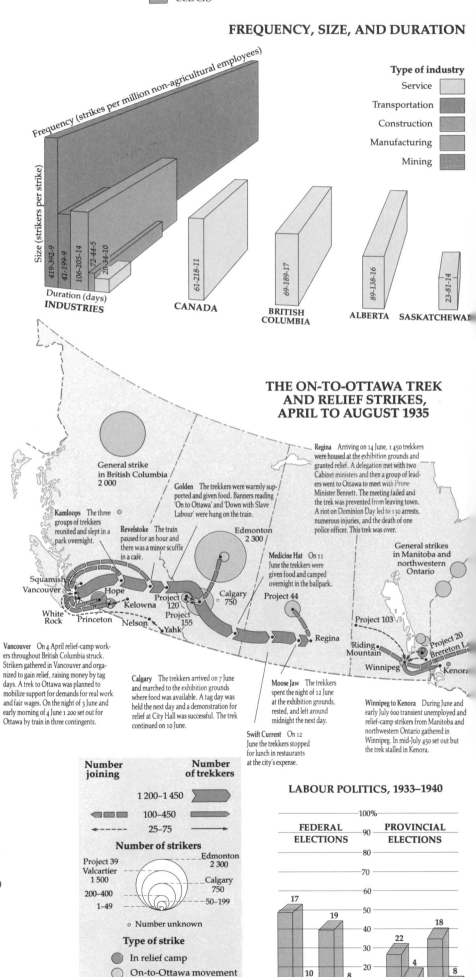

WORKERS' UNITY LEAGUE AND CONGRESS OF INDUSTRIAL ORGANIZATIONS UNIONS

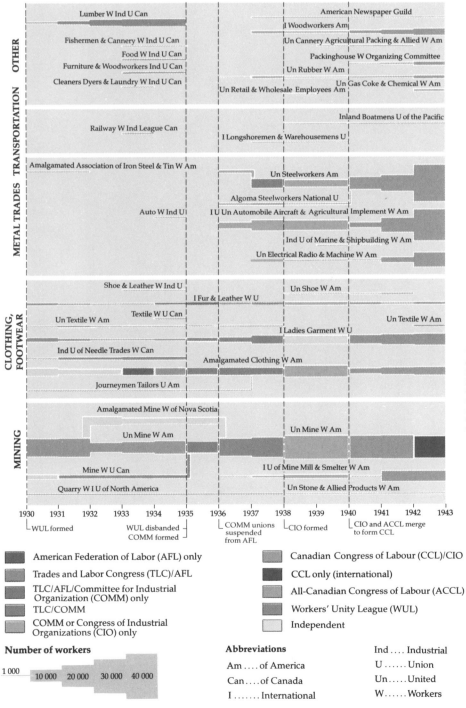

1930 1931 1932 1933 1934 1935 1936 1937 1938 1939 1940 1941 1942 1943

└ WUL formed
WUL disbanded / COMM formed
COMM unions suspended from AFL
CIO formed
CIO and ACCL merge to form CCL

- American Federation of Labor (AFL) only
- Trades and Labor Congress (TLC)/AFL
- TLC/AFL/Committee for Industrial Organization (COMM) only
- TLC/COMM
- COMM or Congress of Industrial Organizations (CIO) only
- Canadian Congress of Labour (CCL)/CIO
- CCL only (international)
- All-Canadian Congress of Labour (ACCL)
- Workers' Unity League (WUL)
- Independent

Number of workers
1 000   10 000   20 000   30 000   40 000

Abbreviations
Am ....of America
Can ....of Canada
I .... International
Ind .... Industrial
U ...... Union
Un ..... United
W ...... Workers

THE ON-TO-OTTAWA TREK AND RELIEF STRIKES, APRIL TO AUGUST 1935

General strike in British Columbia 2 000

Golden The trekkers were warmly supported and given food. Banners reading 'On to Ottawa' and 'Down with Slave Labour' were hung on the train.

Kamloops The three groups of trekkers reunited and slept in a park overnight.

Revelstoke The train paused for an hour and there was a minor scuffle in a café.

Edmonton 2 300

Medicine Hat On 11 June the trekkers were given food and camped overnight in the ballpark.

Regina Arriving on 14 June, 1 450 trekkers were housed at the exhibition grounds and granted relief. A delegation met with two Cabinet ministers and then a group of leaders went to Ottawa to meet with Prime Minister Bennett. The meeting failed and the trek was prevented from leaving town. A riot on Dominion Day led to 130 arrests, numerous injuries, and the death of one police officer. This trek was over.

General strikes in Manitoba and northwestern Ontario

Squamish
Vancouver
White Rock   Hope   Kelowna   Project 120
Princeton   Nelson   Project 155
Yahk   Calgary 750   Project 44
Regina
Project 103
Riding Mountain
Winnipeg   Project 20
Brereton L.
Kenora

Vancouver On 4 April relief-camp workers throughout British Columbia struck. Strikers gathered in Vancouver and organized to gain relief, raising money by tag days. A trek to Ottawa was planned to mobilize support for demands for real work and fair wages. On the night of 3 June and early morning of 4 June 1 200 set out for Ottawa by train in three contingents.

Calgary The trekkers arrived on 7 June and marched to the exhibition grounds where food was available. A tag day was held the next day and a demonstration for relief at City Hall was successful. The trek continued on 10 June.

Moose Jaw The trekkers spent the night of 12 June at the exhibition grounds, rested, and left around midnight the next day.

Swift Current On 12 June the trekkers stopped for lunch in restaurants at the city's expense.

Winnipeg to Kenora During June and early July 600 transient unemployed and relief-camp strikers from Manitoba and northwestern Ontario gathered in Winnipeg. In mid-July 450 set out but the trek stalled in Kenora.

Number joining   **Number of trekkers**
1 200–1 450
100–450
25–75

Number of strikers
Project 39
Valcartier 1 500
Edmonton 2 300
Calgary 750
200–400
1–49
50–199
○ Number unknown

Type of strike
● In relief camp
○ On-to-Ottawa movement
○ Other

For identification of projects see pl 42.

LABOUR POLITICS, 1933–1940

FEDERAL ELECTIONS
17   19   10

PROVINCIAL ELECTIONS
22   4   18   8

1935   1940   1933–1936   1937–1940

HISTORICAL ATLAS OF CANADA

PLATE 45

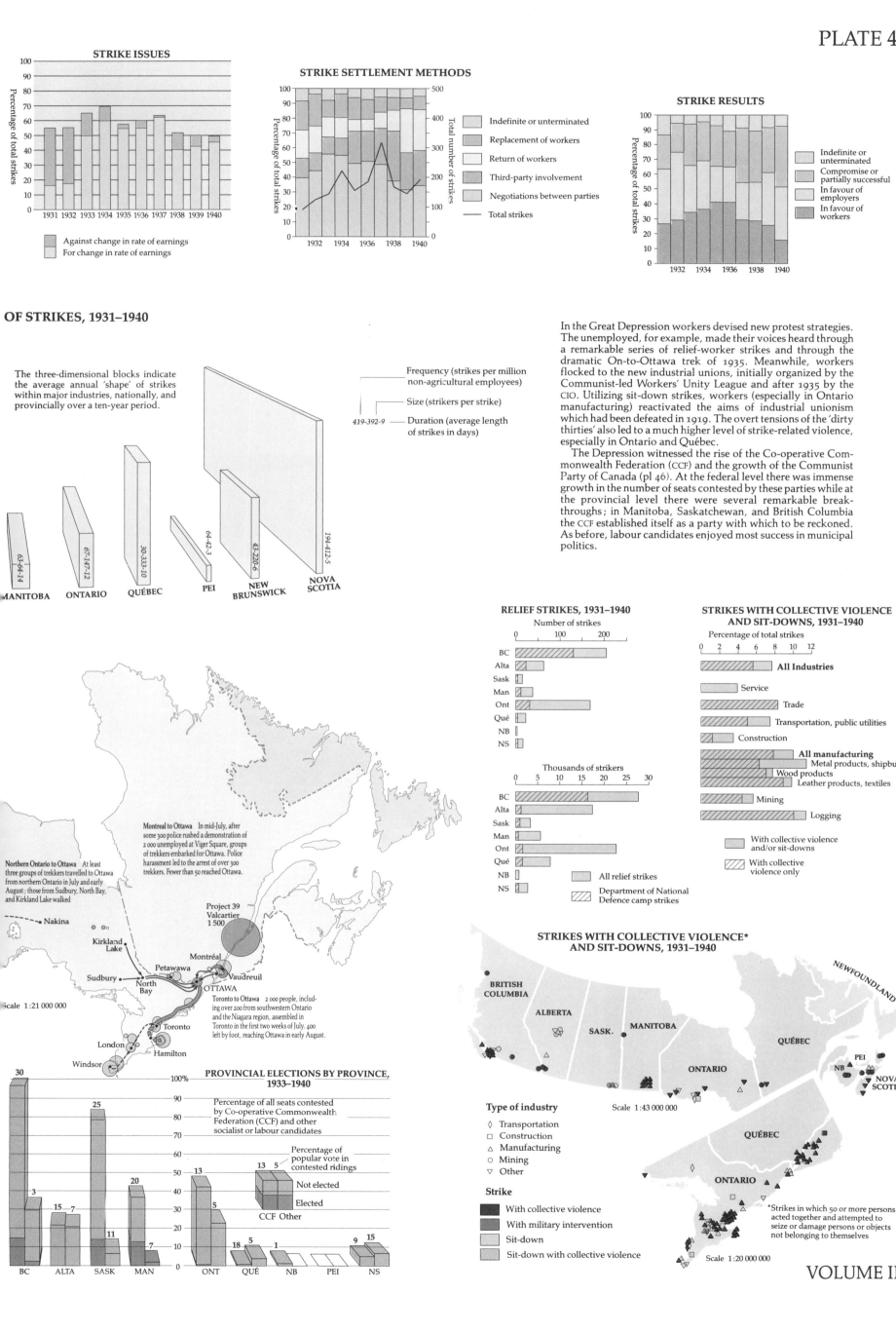

STRIKE ISSUES

Percentage of total strikes

1931 1932 1933 1934 1935 1936 1937 1938 1939 1940

Against change in rate of earnings
For change in rate of earnings

STRIKE SETTLEMENT METHODS

Percentage of total strikes / Total number of strikes

1932 1934 1936 1938 1940

Indefinite or unterminated
Replacement of workers
Return of workers
Third-party involvement
Negotiations between parties
Total strikes

STRIKE RESULTS

Percentage of total strikes

1932 1934 1936 1938 1940

Indefinite or unterminated
Compromise or partially successful
In favour of employers
In favour of workers

OF STRIKES, 1931–1940

The three-dimensional blocks indicate the average annual 'shape' of strikes within major industries, nationally, and provincially over a ten-year period.

Frequency (strikes per million non-agricultural employees)
Size (strikers per strike)
419-392-9
Duration (average length of strikes in days)

63-64-14 MANITOBA
67-147-12 ONTARIO
30-333-10 QUÉBEC
64-42-3 PEI
43-220-6 NEW BRUNSWICK
194-412-5 NOVA SCOTIA

In the Great Depression workers devised new protest strategies. The unemployed, for example, made their voices heard through a remarkable series of relief-worker strikes and through the dramatic On-to-Ottawa trek of 1935. Meanwhile, workers flocked to the new industrial unions, initially organized by the Communist-led Workers' Unity League and after 1935 by the CIO. Utilizing sit-down strikes, workers (especially in Ontario manufacturing) reactivated the aims of industrial unionism which had been defeated in 1919. The overt tensions of the 'dirty thirties' also led to a much higher level of strike-related violence, especially in Ontario and Québec.

The Depression witnessed the rise of the Co-operative Commonwealth Federation (CCF) and the growth of the Communist Party of Canada (pl 46). At the federal level there was immense growth in the number of seats contested by these parties while at the provincial level there were several remarkable breakthroughs; in Manitoba, Saskatchewan, and British Columbia the CCF established itself as a party with which to be reckoned. As before, labour candidates enjoyed most success in municipal politics.

RELIEF STRIKES, 1931–1940

Number of strikes
0 100 200

BC
Alta
Sask
Man
Ont
Qué
NB
NS

Thousands of strikers
0 5 10 15 20 25 30

BC
Alta
Sask
Man
Ont
Qué
NB
NS

All relief strikes
Department of National Defence camp strikes

STRIKES WITH COLLECTIVE VIOLENCE AND SIT-DOWNS, 1931–1940

Percentage of total strikes
0 2 4 6 8 10 12

All Industries
Service
Trade
Transportation, public utilities
Construction
All manufacturing
Metal products, shipbuilding
Wood products
Leather products, textiles
Mining
Logging

With collective violence and/or sit-downs
With collective violence only

Montreal to Ottawa
In mid-July, after some 300 police rushed a demonstration of 2 000 unemployed at Viger Square, groups of trekkers embarked for Ottawa. Police harassment led to the arrest of over 300 trekkers. Fewer than 50 reached Ottawa.

Northern Ontario to Ottawa
At least three groups of trekkers travelled to Ottawa from northern Ontario in July and early August; those from Sudbury, North Bay, and Kirkland Lake walked

Nakina
Kirkland Lake
Sudbury
North Bay
Petawawa
Montréal
Vaudreuil
OTTAWA
Toronto
London
Hamilton
Windsor

Project 39
Valcartier
1 500

Scale 1:21 000 000

Toronto to Ottawa
2 000 people, including over 200 from southwestern Ontario and the Niagara region, assembled in Toronto in the first two weeks of July. 400 left by foot, reaching Ottawa in early August.

STRIKES WITH COLLECTIVE VIOLENCE* AND SIT-DOWNS, 1931–1940

NEWFOUNDLAND
BRITISH COLUMBIA
ALBERTA
SASK.
MANITOBA
QUÉBEC
ONTARIO
PEI
NB
NOVA SCOTIA
QUÉBEC
ONTARIO

Scale 1:43 000 000

Type of industry
◇ Transportation
□ Construction
△ Manufacturing
○ Mining
▽ Other

Strike
With collective violence
With military intervention
Sit-down
Sit-down with collective violence

*Strikes in which 50 or more persons acted together and attempted to seize or damage persons or objects not belonging to themselves

Scale 1:20 000 000

PROVINCIAL ELECTIONS BY PROVINCE, 1933–1940

Percentage of all seats contested by Co-operative Commonwealth Federation (CCF) and other socialist or labour candidates

Percentage of popular vote in contested ridings

Not elected
Elected

CCF   Other

30
3
25
7
15
11
20
13
5
13 5
18 5
1
9 15
7

BC ALTA SASK MAN ONT QUÉ NB PEI NS

NEW POLITICAL DIRECTIONS
Author: Murdo MacPherson, Mary Magwood (1935 results)

R.B. Bennett's Conservatives proved incapable of dealing with the severity of the Depression and were swept out of office in 1935. Mackenzie King and the Liberals returned to power with a landslide. The Liberal victory, with only 45% of the national vote, was made possible by the emergence of new third parties and independent members who captured 26% of the vote.

In 1932 social democrats, small labour parties, and radical farmers had come together to form the Co-operative Common-wealth Federation (CCF). Although not running candidates in the Maritimes and Québec, the party gained 9% of the national vote; its success was concentrated in western Canada. The short-lived Reconstruction Party proposed a regulated and reformed capitalism; it too gained 9% of the vote, but its support was widely scattered and only its founder, H.H. Stevens, was elected. The Social Credit Party, which emphasized control of banks and the money supply ran federal candidates in the Prairies and in British Columbia and dominated Alberta poli-tics, at both the provincial and federal levels, until the 1960s.

A new political departure in Québec drew upon dissatisfac-tion with the provincial Liberal government that was seen to be selling out the province and its cultural heritage to external economic interests. The 1935 provincial election showed that a union of the Conservatives and reformist ex-Liberals of the Action libérale nationale (ALN) could defeat the Liberals and bring about a nationalist program. In 1936 the newly formed Union nationale ended 40 years of Liberal rule. The Conserva-tive leader, Duplessis, quickly gained control of the party, replaced the reformism of the ALN with economic conserva-tism, and headed a particularly right-wing government until 1959 (except for the period 1939–44).

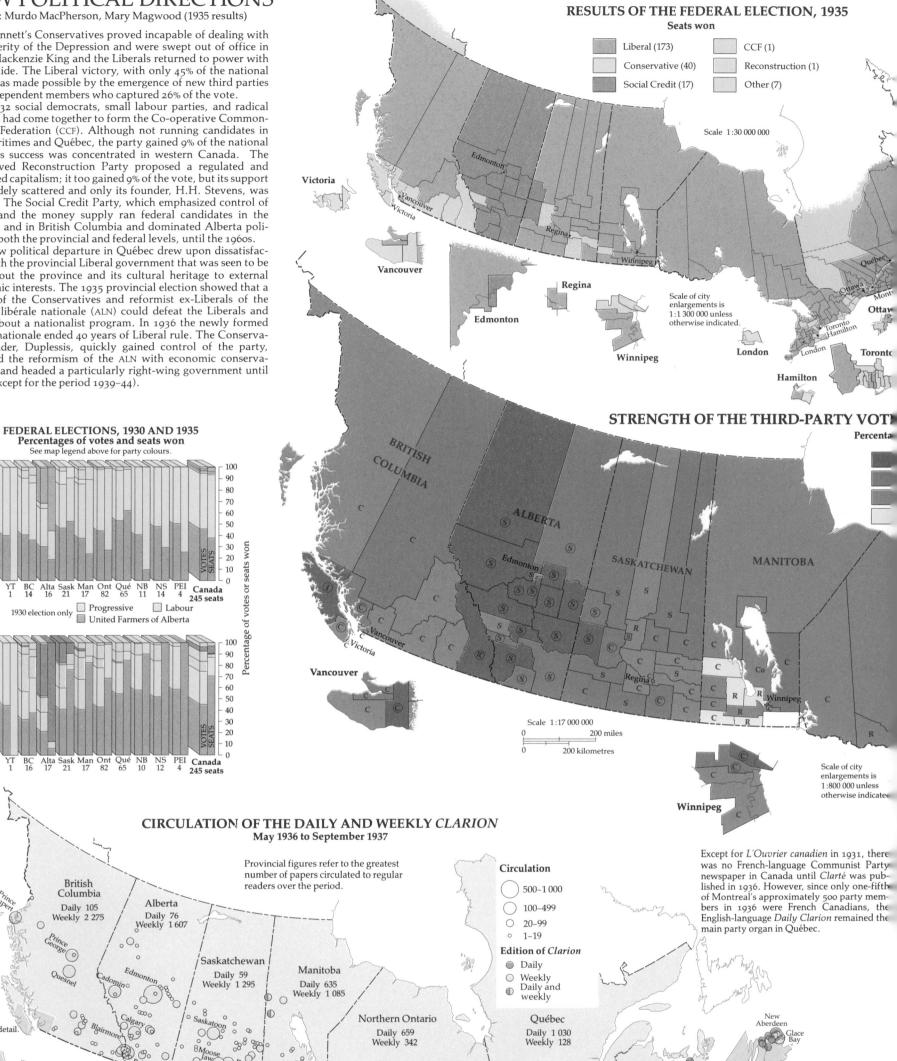

RESULTS OF THE FEDERAL ELECTION, 1935
Seats won

- Liberal (173)
- Conservative (40)
- Social Credit (17)
- CCF (1)
- Reconstruction (1)
- Other (7)

Scale 1:30 000 000

Scale of city enlargements is 1:1 300 000 unless otherwise indicated.

FEDERAL ELECTIONS, 1930 AND 1935
Percentages of votes and seats won
See map legend above for party colours.

1930

1930 election only:
- Progressive
- Labour
- United Farmers of Alberta

1935

STRENGTH OF THE THIRD-PARTY VOTE

Percentage

Scale 1:17 000 000

0 — 200 miles
0 — 200 kilometres

Scale of city enlargements is 1:800 000 unless otherwise indicated

CIRCULATION OF THE DAILY AND WEEKLY *CLARION*
May 1936 to September 1937

Provincial figures refer to the greatest number of papers circulated to regular readers over the period.

Circulation
- 500–1 000
- 100–499
- 20–99
- 1–19

Edition of *Clarion*
- Daily
- Weekly
- Daily and weekly

British Columbia
Daily 105
Weekly 2 275

Alberta
Daily 76
Weekly 1 607

Saskatchewan
Daily 59
Weekly 1 295

Manitoba
Daily 635
Weekly 1 085

Northern Ontario
Daily 659
Weekly 342

Québec
Daily 1 030
Weekly 128

New Brunswick and PEI, no circulation

Nova Scotia
Daily 0
Weekly 745

Southern Ontario
Daily 5 077
Weekly 0

Daily 200
Weekly 850

Scale 1:26 000 000
Scale 1:6 000 000
Scale 1:6 000 000
Scale 1:10 000 000

Except for *L'Ouvrier canadien* in 1931, there was no French-language Communist Party newspaper in Canada until *Clarté* was pub-lished in 1936. However, since only one-fifth of Montréal's approximately 500 party mem-bers in 1936 were French Canadians, the English-language *Daily Clarion* remained the main party organ in Québec.

Tripling its membership between 1934 and 1937, the Communist Party of Canada grew in popularity during the Depression. Although its membership remained small (16 000 by 1939), the party effectively campaigned on behalf of the unemployed and trade unions (pl 45). The circulation of the party newspaper, the *Clarion*, showed the party's strength in resource communities and industrial centres. Fervent anti-communism in Québec and the party's refusal to recognize the special status of a French Canadian nation confined the party to Montréal's immigrant population.

HISTORICAL ATLAS OF CANADA

PLATE 46

THE RISE TO POWER OF THE UNION NATIONALE
Québec provincial elections, 1935 and 1936

1935

QUÉBEC

Îles-de-la-Madeleine
Scale 1:7 500 000

Québec
Scale 1:1 200 000

Montréal
Scale 1:1 400 000

Scale 1:11 000 000

Québec
Scale 1:625 000

Montréal
Scale 1:1 400 000

Seats won, 1935	Seats won, 1936
Liberal (48)	Liberal (14)
Conservative (16)	Union nationale (76)
Action libérale nationale (26)	

▲ Liberal by acclamation

* A winning majority of 60% or more of the vote

1936

QUÉBEC

Îles-de-la-Madeleine
Scale 1:7 500 000

Scale 1:11 000 000

Québec
Scale 1:625 000

Montréal
Scale 1:1 400 000

Support for the Union nationale was widespread. The party's strength in rural ridings was based on its promotion of farmers' interests. In urban areas (except English-speaking west Montréal) its popularity related to the party's policy on nationalism.

N THE FEDERAL ELECTION, 1935

vote

.0 or more

.0–59.9

.0–39.9

ss than 20.0

Largest third-party vote

C CCF
S Social Credit
R Reconstruction
L Independent Liberal
I Independent
U United Farmers of Ontario
La Labour
Co Communist
A Anti-Communist

◯ Candidate elected

Where there was no third-party candidate the electoral division is uncoloured.

NEWFOUNDLAND

Québec
Scale 1:625 000

ONTARIO

QUÉBEC

NEW BRUNSWICK

PEI

NOVA SCOTIA

Toronto
Hamilton

Montréal

Southwestern Ontario

London

Scale 1:10 000 000

Ottawa

See detail for party.

Toronto

Scale 1:625 000

Hamilton

MAJOR PARTIES IN FEDERAL ELECTIONS

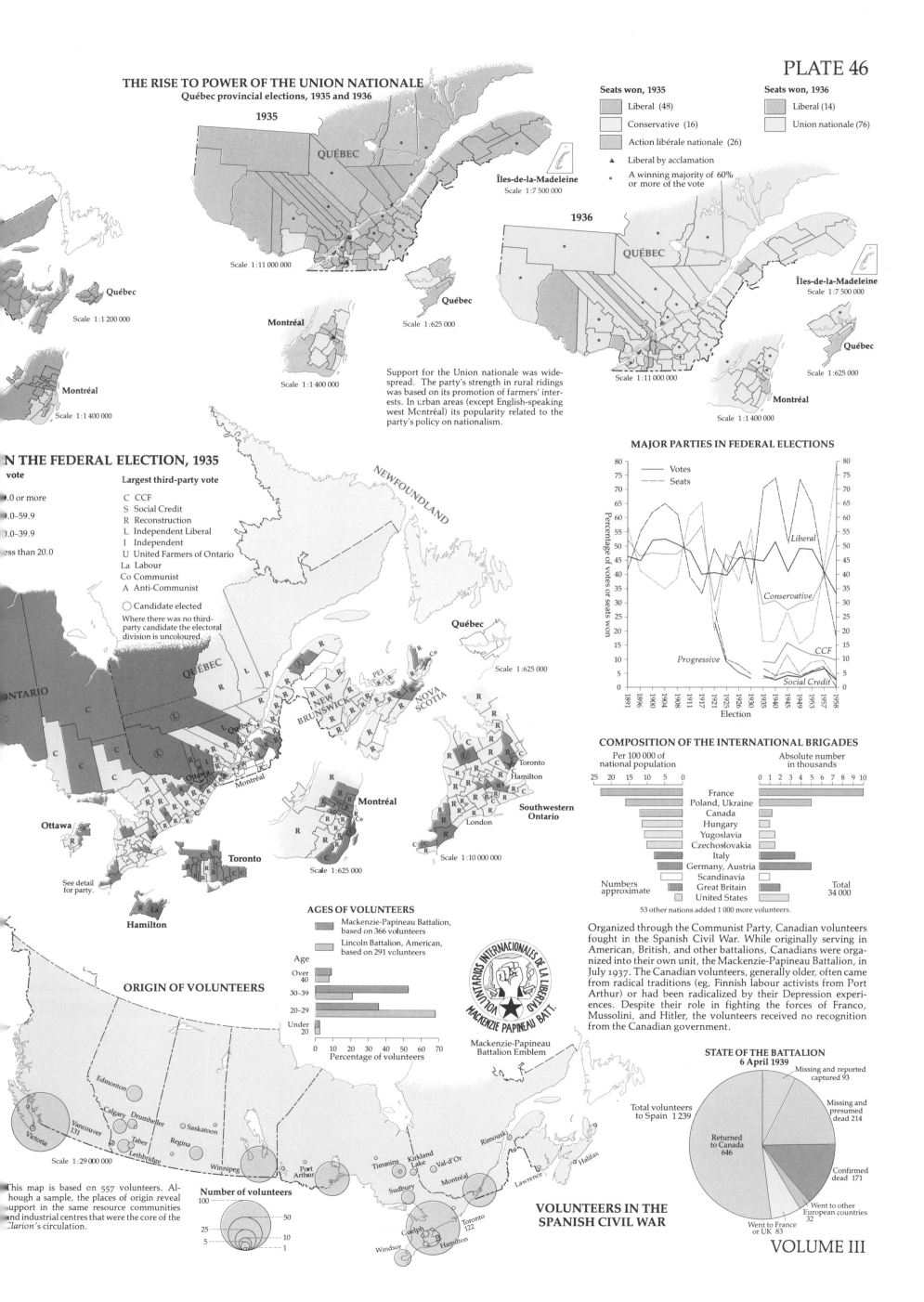

Liberal

Conservative

Progressive

CCF

Social Credit

Percentage of votes or seats won

Votes
Seats

Election: 1891 1896 1900 1904 1908 1911 1917 1921 1925 1926 1930 1935 1940 1945 1949 1953 1957 1958

COMPOSITION OF THE INTERNATIONAL BRIGADES

Per 100 000 of national population
25 20 15 10 5 0

Absolute number in thousands
0 1 2 3 4 5 6 7 8 9 10

France
Poland, Ukraine
Canada
Hungary
Yugoslavia
Czechoslovakia
Italy
Germany, Austria
Scandinavia
Great Britain
United States

Numbers approximate

Total 34 000

53 other nations added 1 000 more volunteers.

Organized through the Communist Party, Canadian volunteers fought in the Spanish Civil War. While originally serving in American, British, and other battalions, Canadians were organized into their own unit, the Mackenzie-Papineau Battalion, in July 1937. The Canadian volunteers, generally older, often came from radical traditions (eg, Finnish labour activists from Port Arthur) or had been radicalized by their Depression experiences. Despite their role in fighting the forces of Franco, Mussolini, and Hitler, the volunteers received no recognition from the Canadian government.

AGES OF VOLUNTEERS

Mackenzie-Papineau Battalion, based on 366 volunteers

Lincoln Battalion, American, based on 291 volunteers

Age
Over 40
30–39
20–29
Under 20

0 10 20 30 40 50 60 70
Percentage of volunteers

VOLUNTARIOS INTERNACIONALES DE LA LIBERTAD
MACKENZIE PAPINEAU BATT.

Mackenzie-Papineau Battalion Emblem

ORIGIN OF VOLUNTEERS

Edmonton
Calgary Drumheller
Vancouver 131
Victoria
Taber
Lethbridge
Saskatoon
Regina
Winnipeg
Port Arthur
Timmins
Kirkland Lake
Val-d'Or
Sudbury
Rimouski
Montréal
Lawrence
Halifax

Scale 1:29 000 000

his map is based on 557 volunteers. Although a sample, the places of origin reveal upport in the same resource communities nd industrial centres that were the core of the Clarion's circulation.

Number of volunteers
100
50
25
10
5
1

Toronto 122
Guelph
Windsor
Hamilton

VOLUNTEERS IN THE SPANISH CIVIL WAR

STATE OF THE BATTALION
6 April 1939

Missing and reported captured 93

Missing and presumed dead 214

Confirmed dead 171

Went to other European countries 32

Went to France or UK 83

Returned to Canada 646

Total volunteers to Spain 1 239

The Second World War and the Post-War Period

The Second World War was a major turning-point for Canada. Changes occurred in Canada's relationship with the outside world, in the role of government, in the nature of the economy and society, and in Canadians' sense of themselves. Dynamic economic growth was associated with post-war prosperity, and waves of immigration, population growth, and suburbanization changed the composition and distribution of the population. None the less, differences based on class, language, ethnicity, and region remained embedded in the very different society that emerged during the 1940s and 1950s.

The Second World War transformed Canada's relationship with the rest of the world. With the fall of France in the spring of 1940 Canada was called upon to play an important role, providing food and military equipment for the war effort, as well as direct military service. During the war more than a million Canadians served overseas (pl 47). Although casualty rates were lower than in the Great War, more than 40 000 Canadians died in the conflict. High casualty rates in the First World War had contributed to post-war isolationism, but the sacrifices of the Second World War prompted Canada in the post-war period to take on the role of a middle power in world affairs. Ironically, however, though Canada's achievements in the war effort generated a growing sense of pride and nationhood, the demands of the war increased political ties with the United States, ties which would eventually limit Canada's geopolitical independence.

Before 1940 Canada's primary political links had always been with Britain, but, with the fall of France, Britain's weakness became apparent. The Ogdensburg Agreement of 1940 provided for the creation of a Permanent Joint Board of Defence with the United States to handle issues of shared concern in the defence of North America. The Hyde Park Agreement of 1941 reflected an equally important initiative in the economic sphere. This agreement dealt with the strain on Canada's balance of payments that arose from the effort to supply Britain with war matériel. It enabled imported American components used in goods for Britain to be charged to the British account under the lend-lease agreement between the United States and Britain. The Americans also agreed to purchase more Canadian goods, thereby reducing Canada's shortage of American dollars. The agreement solved Canadian problems for the time, but it also represented a shift towards that integration of the Canadian and American economies which was to become so marked after the war.

The war years were a period of rapid growth for the Canadian economy. The gross national product (GNP) more than doubled between 1939 and 1945 as production for the war effort caused employment in manufacturing to soar. By the end of the war Canada had produced 16 000 aircraft, 6 500 tanks, almost a million rifles, a quarter of a million machine guns, thousands of cargo and escort vessels, and almost a million motor vehicles. Although that economic expansion was caused by the demands of the war, it was possible because the federal government was willing to become actively involved in the economy. The scope of government involvement can be seen in the phenomenal growth of federal government expenditure – from $680 million in 1939 to $5 136 million in 1945.

The federal civil service, which more than doubled during the war years, gained experience as a directly influential force in regulating the economy. There had been economic planners in government in the 1930s, particularly in the Department of Finance, but it was only during the war that government planning came into its own. Federal control of the war industry was based in the Department of Munitions and Supply, headed by C.D. Howe. Howe created Crown companies to run various aspects of the war effort, from building bombers to refining fuel (pl 48). His department used the powers of the War Measures Act to regulate the use of a wide range of materials by private industry and control the kind of goods produced; many plants that were producing 'non-essential' goods were required to convert to war production. The federal government strictly regulated wages and prices, and rationed scarce commodities, through the Wartime Prices and Trade Board. By 1941 the economy had returned to virtually full employment, and by 1942 there was such a labour shortage that Canadians had to get permission from the government's National Selective Service before changing jobs.

Increased government control took place almost exclusively at the federal level. The move to centralization had begun before the war in response to the Depression. In 1937 the Royal Commission on Dominion-Provincial Relations had recommended that the federal government exercise exclusive jurisdiction over income tax, corporation tax, and succession duty. And in 1942 the provincial governments signed tax-rental agreements with the federal government, giving up the power to collect taxes in return for federal payments equal to previous revenues. Control over provincial taxation gave the federal government better financial resources for the war economy.

Government intervention in the economy, according to the orthodox Keynesian theories of the day, was intended to pave the way to recovery by massive doses of public spending to increase purchasing power. Built-in stabilizers included social-welfare programs (pl 63) to sustain purchasing power. Unemployment insurance, introduced in 1940, also injected money into the economy in periods of depression. The Unemployment Insurance Act provided only a limited safety-net however. Benefits were restricted to 50% of wages for single men, and 65% for married men. More than a quarter of the Canadian labour force, including government, agricultural, and domestic workers, was left outside the scheme.

As the war continued, pressure mounted for further social-welfare legislation. A symptom of this pressure was the rise in the fortunes of the socialist Co-operative Commonwealth Federation (CCF): in 1943 the CCF narrowly led the two mainstream federal parties in national opinion polls, and in the Ontario election of that year it gained enough seats to form the official opposition; in 1944 it formed the government in Saskatchewan.

The federal government had been presented with its own blueprint for social welfare in the Marsh Report, submitted in 1943 to the Committee on Reconstruction and Rehabilitation. The report's recommendations, based on assumed full employment, included social insurance to cover both employment risks and the economic problems of old age, a system of health insurance, and a system of family allowances to all Canadian children. The government was not prepared to put into practice all the recommendations of the report, but, alarmed by the successes of the CCF, it introduced the Family Allowance Act in 1944. The act, which provided for payments for all children up to age sixteen, gave many married women an income of their own for the first time while reinforcing their responsibility for child rearing.

The federal government's White Paper on Employment and Income, issued in April 1945, announced a more active future role for government in everyday life. It proclaimed the 'maintenance of a high and stable level of employment and income' to be a 'major aim of government policy.' To this end the government pledged its willingness to run budgetary deficits to 'prime the pump' in periods of recession, while cutting back expenditures in good times. Unemployment insurance and family allowances were identified as essential elements of economic policy. Some efforts were made to address regional inequalities. The Royal Commission on Dominion-Provincial Relations had recommended payment to the poorer provinces of national adjustment grants which would enable them to maintain social and educational services at a Canadian average, but efforts to move strongly towards equalization of provincial revenues were blocked by opposition from Ontario, Alberta, and British Columbia, provinces that would not have been eligible for such grants.

Full wartime employment did increase the prosperity of the Canadian worker and consumption levels rose, but stringent wage controls also led to a massive wave of strikes during the war years (pl 62). The chief objective of many strikes was union recognition. Workers feared the return of pre-war conditions and used their new bargaining power, in a full-employment economy, to gain recognition for unions that would protect their rights. As in the past, federal and provincial governments were sometimes willing to help suppress strikes with police and troops. But in 1944 the federal parliament passed PC 1003, which guaranteed the right to organize and bargain collectively and provided a system of regulations which required employers to recognize unions that were supported by a majority of the workers.

The war opened up employment opportunities for women in such traditionally male jobs as welding, machine-shop work, shipbuilding, and aircraft assembly (pl 48), though the Campaign for Women Workers reflected the traditional attitude that a woman's primary responsibility was the home. Campaigns to recruit women war-workers focused initially only on single women. The Day Nurseries Agreement, which provided for federal-provincial cost-sharing in the development of day-care services, was implemented only in Ontario and Québec and was cancelled after the war.

During the war almost 10 000 people of German and Italian origin were interned. In British Columbia long-standing racist attitudes towards Japanese Canadians were exacerbated by fear of a Japanese invasion. Although the federal government had been informed by its own security forces that the Japanese Canadians posed no threat, political pressures led them to round up all Japanese Canadians on the coast, including those born in Canada, confiscate their property, and send them to camps in the interior of British Columbia or farther east (pl 48).

To the wonderment of many Canadians, wartime prosperity continued and grew stronger well into the post-war period. Trends established during the war continued. Consumerism helped define a larger home market. Canada as a nation gained a clearer identity; it was a destination for displaced Europeans, a middle power internationally, and a source for American industrial and strategic resource needs.

For the first few years after the war the strength of the Canadian economy, in comparison to the devastated economies of Europe, allowed Canada to play an enhanced role in international affairs. Canada provided generous credits to Britain and to other countries in western Europe to help them restore their shattered economies. Canada's willingness to aid the Europeans reflected its traditional concern with external trade, and through credits to European countries Canada sought both to increase its volume of trade and to diversify its trading links, thus reducing its reliance on trade with the British and the Americans. Economic considerations also help to explain the role played by Canadian diplomats in the development of the North Atlantic Treaty Organization (NATO). Although NATO was essentially a military alliance, Canadian efforts led to the insertion of Article II in the agreement, which encouraged the reduction of trade barriers and the development of economic co-operation between member nations. At the same time Canada explicitly rejected more thorough economic integration with the United States by breaking off in 1948 secret free-trade negotiations that had started in 1947.

During this 'golden age' of Canadian diplomacy the country was a significant player on the world stage, acting as peace keeper in places such as the Middle East, Kashmir, and the Belgian Congo (pl 57). During the Suez crisis of 1956 Canada played a key role in the negotiations which led to the sending of a United Nations peace-keeping force to the region to separate Egyptian from French, English, and Israeli combatants. Canada's role in the crisis reflect-ed a shifting of Canadian political ties, with Canada being willing to act against British interests in support of the American position.

While Canadian ties with Britain weakened in the post-war world, efforts to develop multilateral trading links did little to reduce the ever-increasing influence of the United States in Canadian political, economic, and cultural life. Although Canadians were proof against the worst extremes of Cold War hysteria current in the United States in the late 1940s and early 1950s, they largely shared the American world-view concerning communism. This was reflected in Canada's involvement both in NATO and in the Korean war. In the nuclear age Canada was of strategic importance to the United States, which meant a continued strengthening of the alliance forged at Ogdensburg. In the mid-1950s the Americans built the Distant Early Warning (DEW) line, which consisted of a series of radar stations intended to detect any Soviet attack in the Canadian north (pll 57, 58). Canadians further strengthened their military ties with the Americans through Defence Production Sharing agreements and through the North American Air Defence Command (NORAD), established in 1957 as a joint air-defence force which came ultimately under American command.

Canada was also increasingly tied to the United States by direct American investment in the Canadian economy in the post-war period. Fears about the depletion of their own natural resources in the face of the military needs of the Cold War and the requirements of an increasingly technological society led Americans to invest heavily in the Canadian resource sector. Those sectors in which the United States was already involved, such as pulp and paper and metallic mineral mining, grew rapidly. The discovery and development of oil and gas fields and the significance of Canadian uranium in a nuclear age added new energy staples to the traditional export mix (pl 50). These new fuel sources within Canada also lowered the costs of manufacturing and the cost of living for Canadian consumers.

American investment in manufacturing in Canada increased significantly in this period. By 1961 a number of important industries, such as chemicals, electrical apparatus, and rubber, were largely controlled by Americans (pl 51). Although this investment contributed to economic prosperity, the expansion in the number of American branch plants in Canada increased dependence on American technology and decision making. Decisions on production runs, export markets, and other critical issues came more and more to be made in the United States. The closing down and relocation of plants brought distress to more than a few Canadian communities. National control of the economy became a political issue, leading to a series of government studies, the best known of which, the Gordon Report of 1957, tried to forecast Canada's economic prospects in the light of the fact that the United States produced 50% of the non-Communist world's industrial output, earned 40% of the world's money income, and participated in 16% of international trade.

Research and development (R&D) was generally conducted in the United States and by 1961 Canada had one of the lowest ratios of R&D expenditure to GNP in the industrialized world. Canadian plants in large multinational enterprises – firms increasingly working in a global rather than merely a national market – became assembly-plant operations for which most or all of the components came from abroad. Proximity to the United States, the technical and economic leadership of the United States at the time, and the disparity in size of the two countries meant that in the 1950s there appeared to be burgeoning American ownership of Canada's industry.

In contrast to many other sectors, most of the Canadian steel industry was able to equal its American competitors in the development and use of new technology and the production of high-quality steel. During the 1950s DOFASCO in Hamilton was one of the few North American companies to introduce the efficient oxygen furnace from Europe, and the firm became very competitive. Indeed the steel industry in Ontario expanded significantly. STELCO and DOFASCO in Hamilton fed a growing number of consumer-products industries in Central Canada, and Algoma in Sault Ste Marie produced structural steel for the construction industry and pipe for the western oil and gas industries. In the

Maritimes DOSCO's production at Sydney, NS, continued to stagnate with old technology and bad management, and the future of the industry in this increasingly peripheral region was as bleak as it had been in the 1920s.

For those Canadians returning from the war, and especially those seeking to start families, the need for housing was crucial. The federal government created the Central Mortgage and Housing Corporation in 1946, which made it easier for Canadians to obtain mortgages by lengthening periods of amortization and lowering down payments. The massive suburban boom in the 1950s contributed substantially to the health of both the retail sector and the construction industry through the building of houses, schools, roads, and the first shopping plazas (pll 52, 60). This suburban explosion changed the lives of millions of people across the country. The 1950s were an era of unprecedented prosperity: the purchase of a house was just one item on an incredible shopping list that included a radio, an automobile, kitchen appliances, a vacation, and perhaps even a cottage. Many Canadians began to think of themselves as middle-class.

The economy was also fueled by the increased domestic demand which was the inevitable consequence of a rapid growth in population (pl 59). From 12 million in 1946 the population grew to more than 18 million by 1961, including 2 million immigrants (most of whom were European). More than 280 000 immigrants arrived in 1957 alone. Couples who had delayed starting families because of the Depression and the war began to have children. There was a striking fall in the average age at marriage and a shift in attitude towards childbearing. The resulting 'baby boom' was responsible for a significant proportion of the overall growth in population. Most of this growth occurred in urban areas, the prime destinations for immigrants and those leaving rural areas and small towns within Canada. The most dramatic increases in population were in the rapidly expanding suburban tracts on the periphery of Canada's metropolitan areas (pl 60).

The federal government left much of the economy to operate unfettered in the free market and a wave of mergers led to the emergence of a small number of nationally prominent firms in finance, media, retailing, and manufacturing. Many regional breweries, for example, came under national, corporate ownership. The T. Eaton Company, which had expanded from its Toronto base (pl 15) to operate a quasinational business through its mail-order catalogues, branch stores, groceteria, and warehouses in the 1920s, had, with a series of mail-order outlets and more branch stores, become a truly national company in the early 1950s (pl 52). Chain stores, which had also risen to prominence in the 1920s, accounted for over 50% of all retail trade by 1961. F.W. Woolworth's and other 'five and dime' stores challenged the traditional merchant's world, and these were imitated by Canada's own Metropolitan stores. 'Voluntary' chains of wholesalers and retailers, such as Independent Grocers' Association and Red & White, came together to meet the competition of supermarket food chains. And the main streets of major urban centres were beginning to face growing competition from the new, suburban, automobile-oriented shopping plazas on the edges of towns.

National transportation and communication networks provided the infrastructure necessary for the emergence of a growing number of national firms. Railways, the early mainstay in the consolidation of Canada, shared the growing market with motor vehicles, aircraft, and pipelines (pll 50, 53). As motor-vehicle registration increased dramatically in the 1920s, the demand grew for paved streets in cities and for intercity roads (pl 53). Roads and highways consumed an increasing share of municipal and provincial government budgets. Until the 1950s road networks were generally locally oriented and the highways were more closely linked to the United States than to neighbouring provinces. In 1950 construction began on the Trans-Canada Highway to provide an east-west highway link across the entire country. Costs were shared by the federal and provincial governments.

The early years of airline services reflected a north-south regional pattern within Canada. In the 1920s and 1930s local lines operated by bush pilots had developed all across Canada to serve isolated communities in the north. Several lines grew by acquisitions and

mergers, and by the 1950s distinctive regional carriers, such as Pacific Western and Québecair, were in operation. The only east-west transcontinental service in the 1940s and 1950s was that run by Trans-Canada Airlines (TCA), a federal Crown corporation created in 1937 to provide airline services from coast to coast. Little significant growth occurred until after the war, and travel by air for both business and pleasure was really a development of the 1950s. In 1960, after 30 years of public development, the federal government allowed the private Canadian Pacific Airlines to compete with TCA in the east-west service.

The increasing demand for energy, not only to drive the industrial machine and serve the transport network, but also to satisfy consumer needs, led the federal government in 1956 to develop a pipeline which gave Central Canada ready access to Alberta's natural gas (pl 50). The simplest and cheapest route would have been through the United States, but, as with railroads and telephones earlier, nationalist concerns forced the pipeline to run only through Canadian territory. The government did not itself build the pipeline, but instead backed Trans-Canada Pipelines, a largely American-controlled company. Major oil pipelines were also constructed, primarily to serve the Canadian market from Vancouver to Toronto. Approximately 30% of the oil produced in Canada was exported to the United States. Another major transportation project of the 1950s was the St Lawrence Seaway, which involved the deepening of the St Lawrence River channel and the construction of larger canals to allow the passage of bulk carriers and some ocean-going ships between the Great Lakes and the Atlantic. After some initial American reluctance, a treaty was signed between the two countries in 1954 to provide for joint construction and ownership of the Seaway, which opened in 1959. The pipeline and the Seaway helped to develop the transport network that laid the basis for an increasingly integrated national economy.

At the 1945 Dominion-Provincial Conference on Reconstruction the federal government proposed the development of national health insurance, old-age pensions, and unemployment-assistance programs. The financing of such programs required the continuation of the wartime tax-rental agreements with the provinces, by which the federal government collected corporate and income taxes in return for grants to the provinces. Control of those revenues and of major new social programs would have increased Ottawa's ability to manage the economy. Ontario and Québec both refused to continue the tax-rental agreement, however, since they also opposed Ottawa's centralizing efforts in both economic and social policy.

While the opposition of Ontario and Québec delayed the introduction of certain national social programs, it did not prevent progress at the provincial level. In 1946 Saskatchewan's CCF government introduced a provincial hospital-insurance plan; British Columbia did the same in 1948. However, most other provinces did nothing until 1957, when the federal government enacted a national hospital-insurance arrangement (pl 63). Even so, the late 1940s and early 1950s ushered in a new era of health care in Canada. Hospitalization for treatment became nearly universal; pharmaceuticals that could control disease came into widespread use for the first time; there were dramatic advances in surgery; and there were some important advances in the understanding of mental health. Another significant development was the passage in 1951 of old-age-pension legislation, which provided pensions for all Canadians over 70; this replaced a means test, which was left to cover only those aged 65 to 69.

Although the provinces generally followed the federal lead in the provision of welfare services, they were more ready to innovate in the field of education, which was a provincial responsibility. The high birth rate and immigration after the war meant that enrolment in primary and secondary schools grew rapidly in the 1950s (pl 33) and increased enrolment, combined with the growth of the suburbs, meant the building of new schools and the expansion and renovation of old ones. Parents were increasingly aware of the importance of education, and their improved material circumstances enabled them to encourage children to remain in school and, in many cases, to attend university. The buoyant labour market of the 1950s made it possible for many students to finance post-secondary education themselves from summer earnings. Others, who had never expected to be able to afford university, did so through the federal government's veterans' grants schemes.

As regional universities expanded and more and more professional schools came into existence, more students were able to receive university education in their own region. For postgraduate degrees, however, most Canadians still went outside the country. Postgraduate programs remained limited, chiefly from lack of funds. The Royal Commission on National Development in the Arts, Letters and Sciences (1949–51) recommended the establishment of a Canada Council to support university research and the council was founded in 1957, when inheritance taxes on the estate of wealthy Montréal financier Isaak Killam enabled the government to set up an endowment.

In the popular arts American influence threatened to overwhelm a distinctive Canadian culture. Attempts to develop Canadian drama, music, and dance included the Dominion Drama Festival, the Stratford Festival, and Montréal's Théâtre du Nouveau Monde, but these were small voices in a louder and more assertive popular trend. Canadians near the border tuned in to American radio and television stations (pl 65), and at night Canadians all across the country could listen to powerful, clear-channel American radio stations. American television programming was also readily available to those living away from the border, since Canadian stations bought much American material.

The Canadian Broadcasting Corporation (CBC), founded in 1936, had become a veritable Canadian institution during the war, when CBC reporters assigned to the European theatre of war transmitted up-to-the-minute accounts of the Canadian forces. The CBC worked conscientiously to provide Canadian content, and though its schedules contained a large number of American programs in the late 1950s, it also fostered a cultural identity in English-speaking Canada with such programs as the 'Happy Gang' and discussion programs like 'Citizen's Forum.' 'Wednesday Night,' a three-hour program that mixed original drama, symphony concerts, opera, and documentaries, gave employment to Canadian writers and artists. These programs, and others such as 'Hockey Night in Canada' and 'Wayne and Shuster,' had a profound effect on the development of English Canadian culture. In Québec the presentation of distinctive programs on French-language radio, both on the CBC and the independent CKAC, reduced direct American influence. By the mid-1930s daytime serials and evening drama had gained immense popularity. In the 1950s writers, actors, musicians, and comedians produced innovative TV programs that set the stage for a later cultural movement in Québec.

The expansion of activity in almost every aspect of the federal government greatly increased the size of the civil service across the country and in Ottawa. From the beginning of the century planners had sought to transform the nation's capital, a lumber town on the edge of the Shield, into a modern, sophisticated city full of symbolic buildings. Successive generations of public buildings, consciously aligned to the picturesque Gothic-revival style used for the original Parliament Buildings, had gradually transformed downtown Ottawa (pl 56). During the Second World War inelegant 'temporaries' were built on and around Parliament Hill but their use for office work continued after the war. During the 1950s the government moved some of its departments to suburban fringes of the city, thereby dramatically expanding the government's visibility in the Ottawa region, already heightened by the National Capital Commission's accumulation of property in the Gatineau hills.

In the post-war period historic French-English tensions remained powerful, and Québec's grievances were articulated by the province's premier, Maurice Duplessis. Duplessis's frequent confrontations with Ottawa arose from his concern to retain Québec's autonomy against what he viewed as the efforts of the federal government to usurp provincial rights. Québec rejected the federal proposals of the post-war conference on reconstruction and refused to accept federal grants to Québec universities, viewing them as an infringement upon provincial responsibility for education. The Québec government also claimed the right to institute a provincial income tax, and through successful negotiations with the federal government it was able to avoid the imposition of double taxation on the people of Québec. It was, none the less, happy to receive cash equalization payments.

Duplessis's battles for Québec autonomy were based on a Québec nationalism rooted in traditional rural and Catholic values. Education and social services took distinctive forms in Québec. Social services were largely run by the Catholic Church, and, though the government assisted it with grants, welfare was chronically underfunded. Nor was there a ministry of education in Québec; the educational system was managed by separate Catholic and Protestant committees. Most secondary and early post-secondary education in the Catholic system was still provided by the classical colleges, educational institutions largely run by religious orders (pl 33). These colleges tended to focus primarily on the humanities (although mathematics and sciences were introduced in the 1950s) and the student bodies of the majority of them remained exclusively male. An increasing number of women's classical colleges were founded in the post-war years, but young Québec women were as likely to attend domestic-science schools as classical colleges.

There were hints of social change in the province. The prolonged and violent Asbestos Strike of 1949 revealed an unwillingness among Québec workers to tolerate conditions endured in the past. And support for the strike by individuals within the hierarchy of the Catholic Church testified to the stirrings of a new, less conservative spirit among the Québec clergy, stirrings that were somewhat in keeping with the appearance of two new groups within the Québec intelligentsia. One group, associated with the publication Cité libre, devoted itself to the principles of liberal democracy and argued for the separation of church and state and a reduction in the power of the Catholic Church in Québec society. The other group, known as neonationalists and attached to the newspaper Le Devoir, also wished to increase the power of the state at the expense of the church and was critical of Duplessis's brand of nationalism, which it perceived as granting English Canadian and American businessmen a free hand in controlling the Québec economy. Unlike the cité librists, the neonationalists still saw themselves as nationalists, but they argued for a more modern nationalism, one suited to an urban, industrial society. The neonationalists were ultimately to triumph in the Quiet Revolution which followed the Liberal election victory of 1960. With the onset of the Quiet Revolution the church was rapidly replaced by the state as the provider of education and social services. The state also became the primary defender of a new, more active, Québec nationalism, which attempted to gain for the people of Québec increasing control over their own province.

Toronto and Montréal dominated the national urban system (pl 54). Long-distance air travel and improved long-distance telephone communications consolidated the centralization of financial and industrial management in the two cities, whose domination of corporate decision making, financial transactions, and the money market deepened (pl 55). Toronto grew more rapidly than Montréal because of the strong and varied economy of southwestern Ontario and the American preference for Toronto as the location for the head offices of their Canadian businesses. Both immigration and internal migration contributed to Toronto's rapid growth; the population of the metropolitan area increased by two-thirds between 1946 and 1961 (pl 60). Its prosperity was visibly attested by new office buildings, the construction of Canada's first subway line beneath Yonge Street, and imaginative schemes for suburbs with mixed land use, as in Don Mills. The rapidity of suburban growth caused a crisis in services and infrastructure and was a major factor in the formation of a metropolitan government in 1953.

Some efforts were made in the post-war years to boost the economic performance of regions that did not share in the prosperity of Toronto, southwestern Ontario, and Montréal. Federal grants that had first been awarded to the poorer provinces under the tax-rental agreements during the war were increased, and in 1957 they were given more systematic and permanent form as equalization payments – payments which brought the proportion of the provincial tax revenues under federal control up to the average of the two wealthiest provinces, Ontario and British Columbia (the latter, along with Alberta, was enjoying a boom based on the demand for its natural resources). Those payments did not eliminate regional economic disparities (pll 3, 66). The great bulk of secondary industry continued to be located in Central Canada (pl 51). The major form of manufacturing found in other regions involved the processing of raw materials – pulp and paper mills, fish-processing plants, or metal refineries. Regions dependent on traditional exports such as grain and fish also underwent change in this period. Some Prairie railway lines were abandoned and the 'elevator landscape' was rationalized through mergers. The sizeable inshore fishery of the Atlantic Provinces remained profitable, but its continued success acted as a disincentive to heavy capital investment in an offshore Atlantic fleet, and the day was to come when Canada would not be able to meet the challenge of the heavily capitalized factory-fishing fleets of other nations (pl 49). Similarly, the mechanization of farming reduced the labour requirements of the agricultural sector, and most rural areas of eastern and Central Canada as well as the Prairies suffered a fall in population (pl 59).

In the North the fur-trading frontier expanded (pl 58). Competition from non-native trappers led to the establishment of substantial native game reserves in which traditional hunting and trapping could continue. An improved health-care system for native Canadians somewhat reduced the exceedingly high native mortality rates. Increased activity in the defence and resource-extraction sectors of the North, combined with improved transport and communications, linked the region more closely to the rest of Canada, but provided little employment for native peoples.

The late 1940s and 1950s witnessed a variety of struggles by working people to retain the gains of the war years and to improve their situation (pl 62). The early struggles were often concerned with union security. One of the most important of these was the strike at the Ford works in Windsor, Ontario, which gained for the union the right to have union dues collected from all workers, even those who did not belong to the union. Other strikes, notably those in the steel and rubber industries, were called to increase wages. Labour strife was a factor in getting the wartime legislation PC 1003 (which required employers to recognize a union if a majority of the labour force were members of it) permanently on the statute books as part of the Industrial Relations and Disputes Investigation Act of 1948. The provinces passed similar legislation and, in general, the period saw a growth in the state's role in labour relations, especially in the establishment of systematic conciliation procedures.

A major battle to prevent Communists from gaining control of the Canadian union movement was waged in the late 1940s, and by the early 1950s Communist members had been expelled from their unions and Communist-led unions from the Canadian Congress of Labour (CCL). That internal battle may have weakened the labour movement in the immediate post-war years, but the merger of the CCL and the Trades and Labor Congress into the Canadian Labour Congress (CLC) in 1956 brought a new unity to the movement, one of the fruits of which was the decision of the CLC to join with the CCF in the late 1950s in an effort to develop a new party dedicated to improving the quality of life of working-class Canadians. The founding of the New Democratic Party in 1961 reflected the willingness of Canadian union leaders to participate directly in politics, unlike their American counterparts, who tended to restrict their activities to industrial actions.

The vulnerability of workers in a cyclical capitalist economy was brought home to many Canadians when, even in a society with greatly improved welfare services, unemployment began to climb in the late 1950s. Other workers were made insecure by technological change. The wage differential between unskilled and skilled workers had narrowed significantly in the 1940s, and although the demand for clerical workers continued to soar, the introduction of new business machines meant that clerical work was made increasingly more routine (pl 61). Most Canadian women in the work-force remained outside the union movement. Women were increasingly employed in the growing service sector of the economy, a sector that was particularly difficult to organize, as the failure by the Retail, Wholesale and Department Store Union to organize the workers employed by Eaton's in the late 1940s and early 1950s had demonstrated.

The lack of union representation was only one of the difficulties facing women workers. For the most part in the immediate post-war period they were forced out of the relatively highly paid non-traditional jobs which they had been encouraged to enter during the war and compelled to return to traditional low-paid jobs; in addition, younger women were less likely to enter the paid work-force, choosing instead to marry and have children. However, as the 1950s progressed, more and more married women, a high proportion of them immigrants, entered the work-force, especially in the service sector (pl 61). By taking on paid work married immigrant women helped to establish their families in a new land.

Canada changed fundamentally during the Second World War and in the years from 1945 to 1961. Trends which first emerged during the war continued and many areas of Canadian life were transformed by 1961. The state came to influence culture and social welfare to an extent previously unknown in the nation's history. Government economic efforts, such as the National Policy in the late 19th century, had long attempted to build a more integrated nation, but the array of interventions and support systems introduced immediately after the Second World War made available federal social programs as well as assistance for business and economic development. Those programs provided Canadians across the country with a common safety-net. Country-wide transportation and communication links also nurtured the growth of a national Canadian economy and society, though government reports of the late 1950s described a nation still beset by regional inequalities and disfigured by pockets of poverty and deprivation (pl 66).

Canada's population in 1961 stood at 18.2 million; 14.0 million people lived in urban places and 8.4 million in cities with populations greater than 100 000. Places such as Sudbury and Chicoutimi-Jonquière joined the group of large cities. Calgary, Edmonton, and Vancouver were riding waves of prosperity based on their provinces' revitalized mining sectors. Many of these cities were also the home of significant numbers of European immigrants – Germans in Vancouver, Italians in Toronto and Montréal, to name but two important groups – and ethnic retail outlets invigorated many neighbourhoods.

Rural Canada, by contrast, was in decline. Canada's agricultural sector, especially wheat-growing, was still important, but the agricultural labour force was almost halved between 1921 and 1961. Technological improvements meant that tractors replaced horses, and combines replaced harvest labour; pesticides and fertilizers improved yields and increased productivity. In some parts of the Maritimes and Québec the rural landscape and rural society were not much altered. And in outports along the Atlantic Coast and the shores of the Gulf of St Lawrence, an occupational pluralism of fishing, lumbering, and farming persisted. Agriculture in Central Canada, especially in the most fertile southwestern counties of Ontario and the plains around Montréal, continued to undergo adjustments as these areas specialized in products for the urban market. On the Prairies wheat farmers still faced periodic drought and worried about the number of frost-free days. Anxieties persisted, too, about the highly variable overseas market; a glut of wheat on the Prairies in the late 1950s led to the introduction of delivery quotas.

The late 1950s brought a pause economically, and with it came a political adjustment. The post-war Liberal ascendancy was broken by the overwhelming Conservative victory in the federal election of 1958. In the 1960s an economic upswing was to bring more prosperity and more national integration, but many of the regional divides, as well as those divides based on ethnicity, language, gender, and class, would survive and become the issues that the next generation would face.

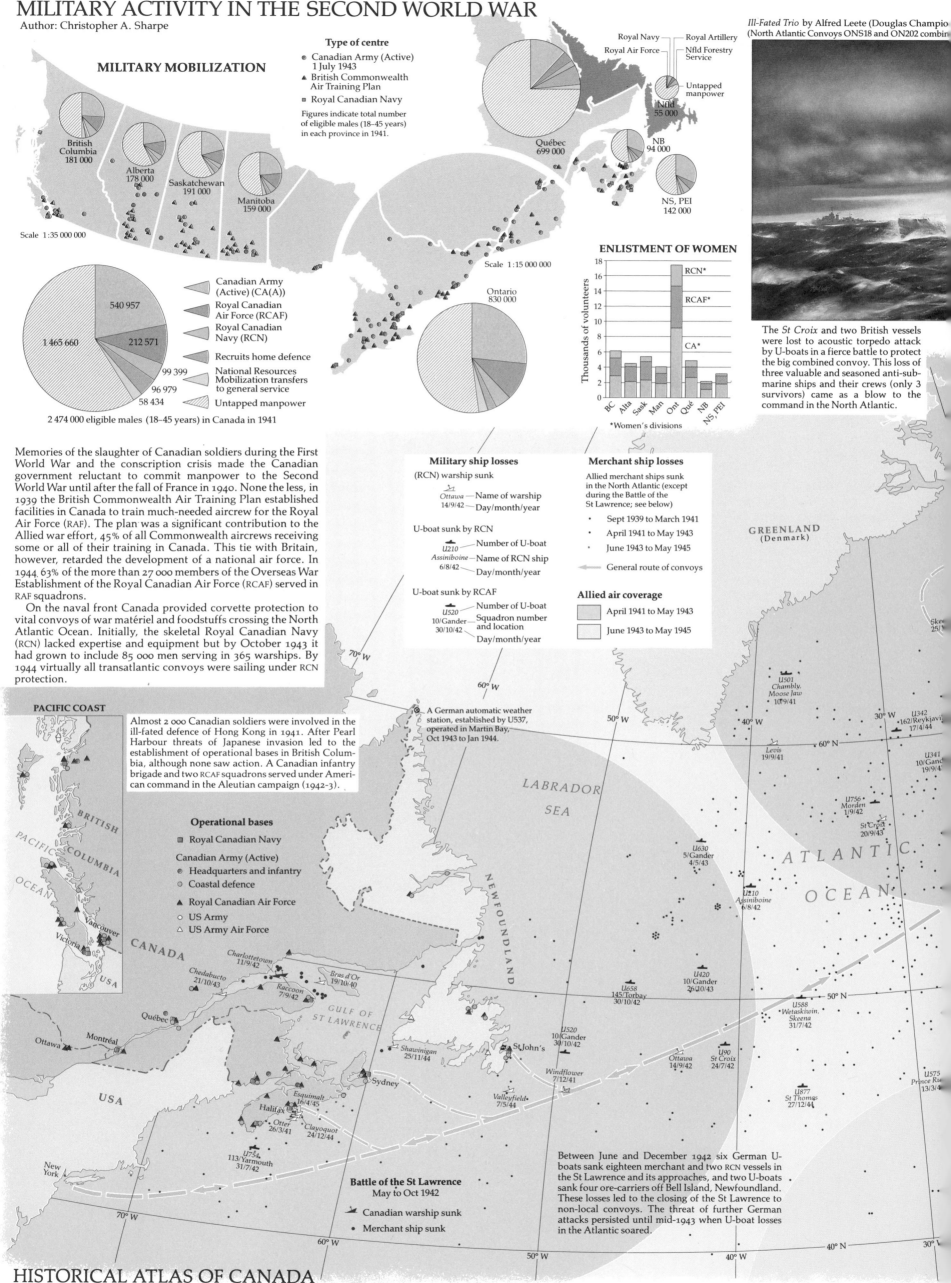

MILITARY ACTIVITY IN THE SECOND WORLD WAR

Author: Christopher A. Sharpe

MILITARY MOBILIZATION

Type of centre

- Canadian Army (Active) 1 July 1943
- ▲ British Commonwealth Air Training Plan
- ■ Royal Canadian Navy

Figures indicate total number of eligible males (18–45 years) in each province in 1941.

British Columbia 181 000
Alberta 178 000
Saskatchewan 191 000
Manitoba 159 000

Scale 1:35 000 000

Royal Navy — Royal Artillery
Royal Air Force — Nfld Forestry Service
Untapped manpower

Nfld 55 000
Québec 699 000
NB 94 000
NS, PEI 142 000
Ontario 830 000

Scale 1:15 000 000

1 465 660
540 957
212 571
99 399
96 979
58 434

- Canadian Army (Active) (CA(A))
- Royal Canadian Air Force (RCAF)
- Royal Canadian Navy (RCN)
- Recruits home defence
- National Resources Mobilization transfers to general service
- Untapped manpower

2 474 000 eligible males (18–45 years) in Canada in 1941

ENLISTMENT OF WOMEN

Thousands of volunteers

RCN*
RCAF*
CA*

BC Alta Sask Man Ont Qué NB NS,PEI

*Women's divisions

Ill-Fated Trio by Alfred Leete (Douglas Champio (North Atlantic Convoys ONS18 and ON202 combin

The *St Croix* and two British vessels were lost to acoustic torpedo attack by U-boats in a fierce battle to protect the big combined convoy. This loss of three valuable and seasoned anti-submarine ships and their crews (only 3 survivors) came as a blow to the command in the North Atlantic.

Memories of the slaughter of Canadian soldiers during the First World War and the conscription crisis made the Canadian government reluctant to commit manpower to the Second World War until after the fall of France in 1940. None the less, in 1939 the British Commonwealth Air Training Plan established facilities in Canada to train much-needed aircrew for the Royal Air Force (RAF). The plan was a significant contribution to the Allied war effort, 45% of all Commonwealth aircrews receiving some or all of their training in Canada. This tie with Britain, however, retarded the development of a national air force. In 1944 63% of the more than 27 000 members of the Overseas War Establishment of the Royal Canadian Air Force (RCAF) served in RAF squadrons.

On the naval front Canada provided corvette protection to vital convoys of war matériel and foodstuffs crossing the North Atlantic Ocean. Initially, the skeletal Royal Canadian Navy (RCN) lacked expertise and equipment but by October 1943 it had grown to include 85 000 men serving in 365 warships. By 1944 virtually all transatlantic convoys were sailing under RCN protection.

Military ship losses

(RCN) warship sunk
Ottawa — Name of warship
14/9/42 — Day/month/year

U-boat sunk by RCN
U210 — Number of U-boat
Assiniboine — Name of RCN ship
6/8/42 — Day/month/year

U-boat sunk by RCAF
U520 — Number of U-boat
10/Gander — Squadron number and location
30/10/42 — Day/month/year

Merchant ship losses

Allied merchant ships sunk in the North Atlantic (except during the Battle of the St Lawrence; see below)

- Sept 1939 to March 1941
- April 1941 to May 1943
- June 1943 to May 1945

← General route of convoys

Allied air coverage
April 1941 to May 1943
June 1943 to May 1945

PACIFIC COAST

Almost 2 000 Canadian soldiers were involved in the ill-fated defence of Hong Kong in 1941. After Pearl Harbour threats of Japanese invasion led to the establishment of operational bases in British Columbia, although none saw action. A Canadian infantry brigade and two RCAF squadrons served under American command in the Aleutian campaign (1942-3).

Operational bases
- ■ Royal Canadian Navy

Canadian Army (Active)
- ● Headquarters and infantry
- ○ Coastal defence

- ▲ Royal Canadian Air Force
- □ US Army
- △ US Army Air Force

A German automatic weather station, established by U537, operated in Martin Bay, Oct 1943 to Jan 1944.

GREENLAND (Denmark)

LABRADOR SEA

ATLANTIC OCEAN

NEWFOUNDLAND

GULF OF ST LAWRENCE

BRITISH COLUMBIA
PACIFIC OCEAN
CANADA
USA

Vancouver
Victoria

Charlottetown 11/9/42
Chedabucto 21/10/43
Raccoon 7/9/42
Bras d'Or 19/10/40

Québec
Ottawa
Montréal

Shawinigan 25/11/44
St John's
Windflower 7/12/41

Sydney
Valleyfield 7/5/44

Esquimalt 16/4/45
Halifax
Otter 26/3/41
Clayoquot 24/12/44

New York
U754 113/Yarmouth 31/7/42

Battle of the St Lawrence
May to Oct 1942

- ▲ Canadian warship sunk
- ● Merchant ship sunk

U501 Chambly, Moose Jaw 10/9/41
U342 162/Reykjavi 17/4/44
Levis 19/9/41
U341 10/Gand 19/9/41
U756 Morden 1/9/42
St Croix 20/9/43
U630 5/Gander 4/5/43
U210 Assiniboine 6/8/42
U420 10/Gander 26/10/43
U588 Wetaskiwin, Skeena 31/7/42
U658 145/Torbay 30/10/42
U520 10/Gander 30/10/42
Ottawa 14/9/42
U90 St Croix 24/7/42
U575 Prince Ru 13/3/4
U877 St Thomas 27/12/44

Between June and December 1942 six German U-boats sank eighteen merchant and two RCN vessels in the St Lawrence and its approaches, and two U-boats sank four ore-carriers off Bell Island, Newfoundland. These losses led to the closing of the St Lawrence to non-local convoys. The threat of further German attacks persisted until mid-1943 when U-boat losses in the Atlantic soared.

HISTORICAL ATLAS OF CANADA

PLATE 47

(ptember 1943)

CANADIAN FATALITIES IN TWO WORLD WARS

| 1914–1918 | CEF* | | RCN, RAF |
| 1939–1945 | CA(A) | RCAF | RCN |

Thousands of men
0 5 10 15 20 25 30 35 40 45 50 55 60 65
*Candian Expeditionary Force

Courtesy of the Canadian War Museum, Ottawa

Canadian fatalities were fewer than in the Great War, but nevertheless substantial. Almost 43 000 Canadian and Newfoundland service personnel were killed; 63% were buried in the graves shown here.

PACIFIC THEATRE

Yokohama
Hong Kong
Rangoon
Singapore

MILITARY FATALITIES IN THE SECOND WORLD WAR
Selected countries

Soviet Union
7 500 000 fatalities

Germany
2 850 000

Japan
1 506 000

United Kingdom
397 800

Canada
42 042

France
210 700

United States
292 100

Italy
77 500

Percentage of fatalities in the armed forces
0 5 10 15 20 25 30 35 40

CANADIAN WAR GRAVES

Bremen
Hamburg
Berlin
Leeds
London
Antwerp
Arnhem
Hanover
Brussels
Boulogne
Dieppe
Caen
Munich

Bologna
Florence
Ancona
Ortona
Rome
Cassino
Bari
Naples
Agira
Malta

Type of cemetery
- Canadian Army (Active)
- Royal Canadian Air Force
- Royal Canadian Navy

Number of graves
- More than 2 000
- 1 000–2 000
- 500–999
- 100–499
- Less than 100

Scale 1:19 300 000

CANADIAN FORCES IN EUROPE AND THE NORTH ATLANTIC

NORWEGIAN SEA

To Murmansk USSR
To Murmansk USSR

ICELAND
Reykjavik

NORWAY
SWEDEN

NORTH SEA

DENMARK

UNITED KINGDOM

IRELAND

Kiel
Hamburg
Münster
Wilhelmshaven
Cologne
Frankfurt
Stuttgart
Berlin

NETHERLANDS
The Scheldt 10/11/44
Dunkirk 6–17/11/44
Calais 1/10/44
Boulogne 27/9/44
BELGIUM
Zeebrugge 27/9/44
The Rhineland 2–3/45
The Rhineland 9/11/44
Mons
LUX.

FRANCE
D-Day 6/6/44
Falaise Gap
Lorient
L'Isle-Adam

SWITZERLAND

Biennais

BAY OF BISCAY

SPAIN
PORTUGAL

CORSICA (France)

SARDINIA (Italy)

ITALY
YUGOSLAVIA
ALBANIA
ADRIATIC SEA
Adriatic Sector 8/44–2/45
Advance to the Arno 6–8/44
Liri Valley 5/44
Cassino 3/44
The Sangro 11/43

TYRRHENIAN SEA
SICILY (Italy)
MEDITERRANEAN SEA

GIBRALTAR (UK)
ALGERIA
TUNISIA
MALTA

Royal Canadian Air Force

Type of base
- ▲ Coastal command
- △ Bomber
- ▲ Fighter

Targets bombed
- More than 1 000 sorties per target
- 500–1 000
- 250–499
- 100–249
- Mining sorties

Canadian Army (Active)

Troop movements
1st Canadian Corps
- ← 1st Canadian Division
- ← 5th Canadian Armoured Division
- ← 1st Canadian Armoured Brigade

2nd Canadian Corps
- ← 2nd Canadian Division
- ← 3rd Canadian Division
- ← 4th Canadian Armoured Division

Newfoundland
- ← 59th Regiment
- ← 166th Regiment
- ☼ 166th gun position

1939 international boundaries are shown.

By the end of 1939 the first 23 000 men of the 1st Division of the Canadian Active Service Force (CASF) were in the United Kingdom. Although naval and air force personnel had been engaged since early in the war in Europe, it was not until 19 August 1942 that the CASF saw action in the disastrous raid on Dieppe; 18% of the 5 000-man force died in the raid and only 2 210 returned. The Canadian army made significant contributions to eventual Allied victory in the Sicilian and Italian campaigns in 1943–5 and in the North West European theatre in 1944–5.

0   300 miles
0   300 kilometres
Scale at 50° N approximately 1:15 760 000

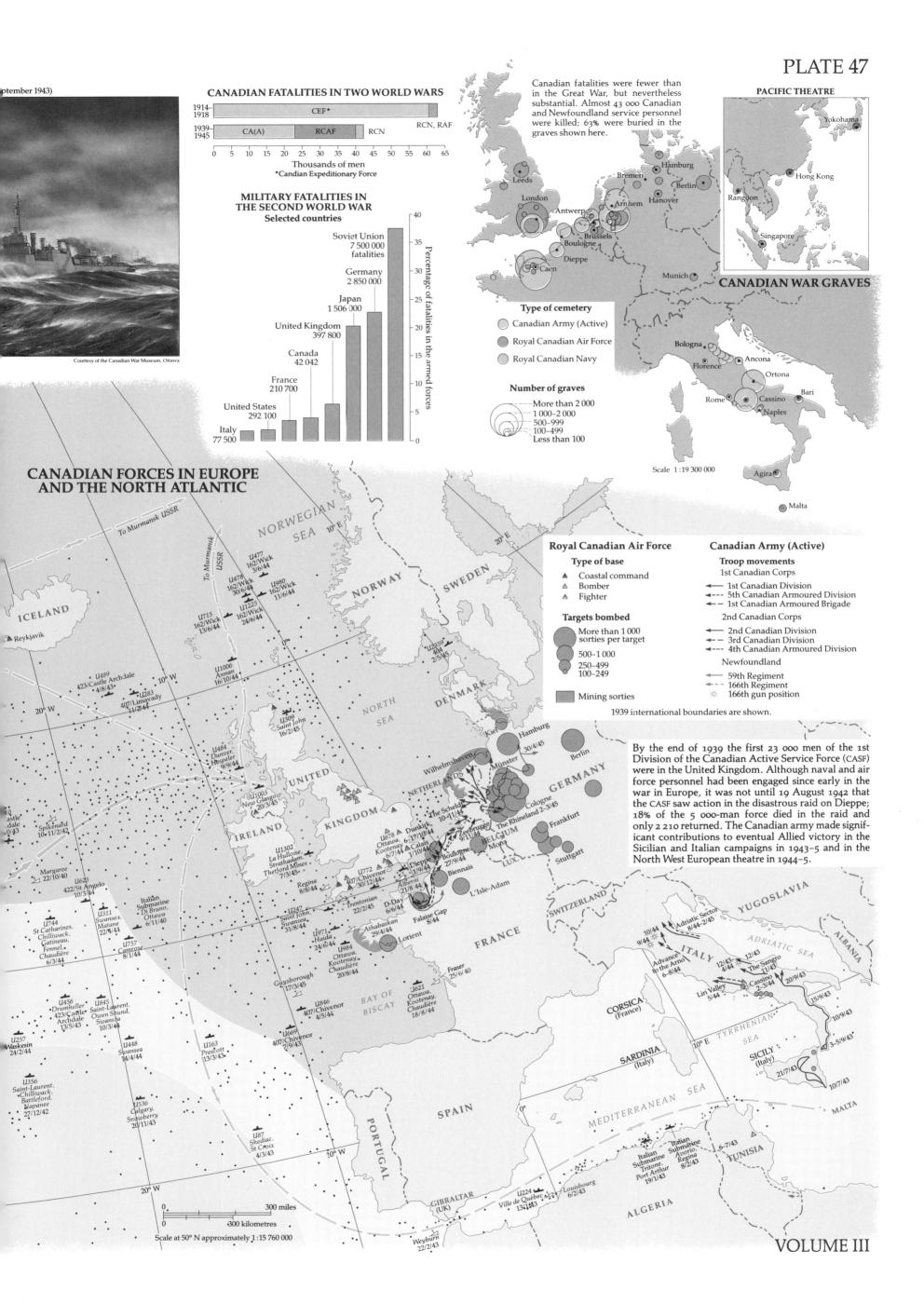

THE HOME FRONT IN THE SECOND WORLD WAR

Authors: Christopher A. Sharpe, Lynne Marks

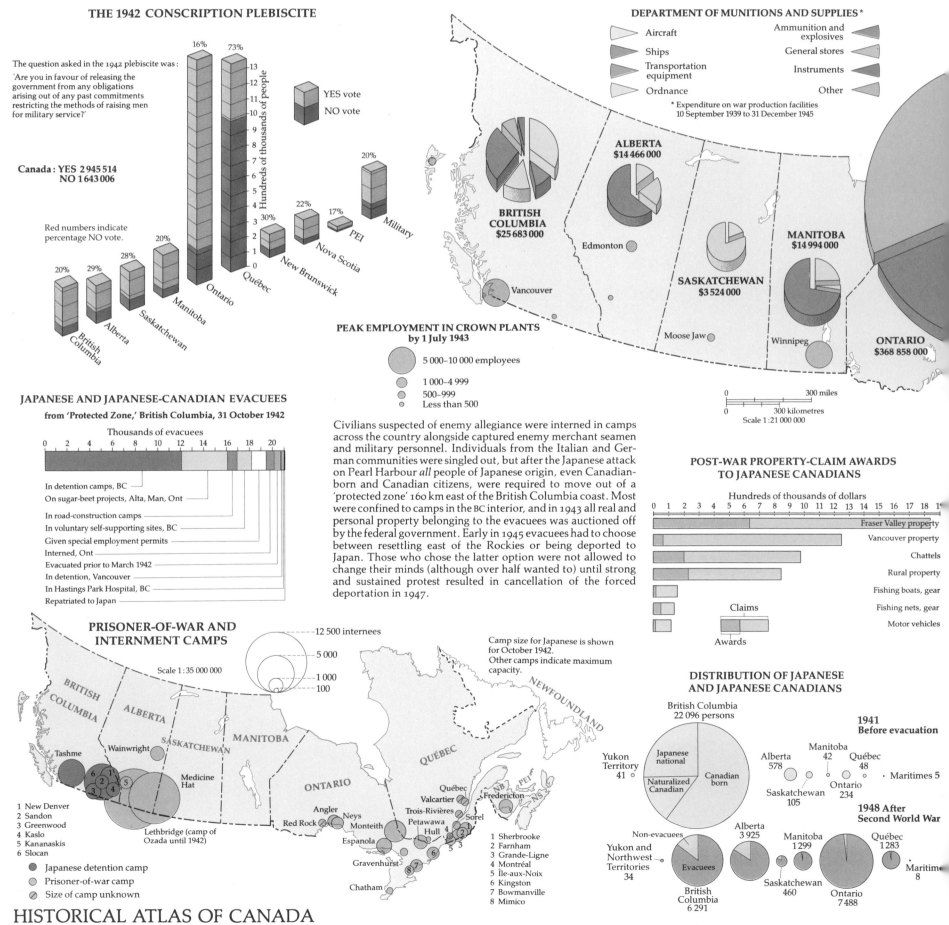

COST OF THE WAR

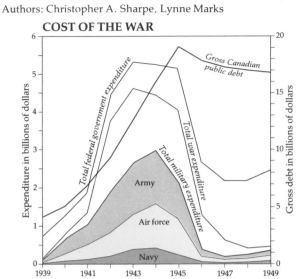

VICTORY LOAN CAMPAIGNS, 1940–1945

The Second World War had significant effects on Canada's domestic scene. Under the federal Department of Munitions and Supplies the government established over a hundred Crown plants for the production of war *matériel*. Old factories were adapted and new ones built, providing employment for nearly a quarter of a million people. Most of the investment was concentrated in Central Canada, using existing plants and skilled labour. Canada provided critical war machinery and foodstuffs for Europe and exports increased, albeit through risky convoy methods.

Britain's dependence on Canadian goods caused a financial crisis when Britain was unable to meet the costs of its Canadian imports; in turn Canada could not pay for industrial components imported from the United States, and its debt increased. Under a 1941 American Lend-Lease agreement American *matériel* for British war needs was supplied on a deferred payment basis, and this allowed Canada to sustain its war production. Victory loans raised domestic funds for the war effort.

As in the Great War, conscription was a controversial issue. A 1942 plebiscite released the government from an earlier pledge not to conscript for overseas service, and in 1944 about 13 000 conscripts were sent overseas, although only 2 500 were posted to battlefield units.

THE 1942 CONSCRIPTION PLEBISCITE

The question asked in the 1942 plebiscite was:
'Are you in favour of releasing the government from any obligations arising out of any past commitments restricting the methods of raising men for military service?'

Canada: YES 2 945 514
NO 1 643 006

Red numbers indicate percentage NO vote.

FEDERAL GOVERNMENT INVOLVEMENT IN WAR INDUSTRY

DEPARTMENT OF MUNITIONS AND SUPPLIES *

* Expenditure on war production facilities
10 September 1939 to 31 December 1945

PEAK EMPLOYMENT IN CROWN PLANTS
by 1 July 1943

5 000–10 000 employees
1 000–4 999
500–999
Less than 500

JAPANESE AND JAPANESE-CANADIAN EVACUEES
from 'Protected Zone,' British Columbia, 31 October 1942

Civilians suspected of enemy allegiance were interned in camps across the country alongside captured enemy merchant seamen and military personnel. Individuals from the Italian and German communities were singled out, but after the Japanese attack on Pearl Harbour *all* people of Japanese origin, even Canadian-born and Canadian citizens, were required to move out of a 'protected zone' 160 km east of the British Columbia coast. Most were confined to camps in the BC interior, and in 1943 all real and personal property belonging to the evacuees was auctioned off by the federal government. Early in 1945 evacuees had to choose between resettling east of the Rockies or being deported to Japan. Those who chose the latter option were not allowed to change their minds (although over half wanted to) until strong and sustained protest resulted in cancellation of the forced deportation in 1947.

POST-WAR PROPERTY-CLAIM AWARDS TO JAPANESE CANADIANS

PRISONER-OF-WAR AND INTERNMENT CAMPS

Camp size for Japanese is shown for October 1942.
Other camps indicate maximum capacity.

DISTRIBUTION OF JAPANESE AND JAPANESE CANADIANS

HISTORICAL ATLAS OF CANADA

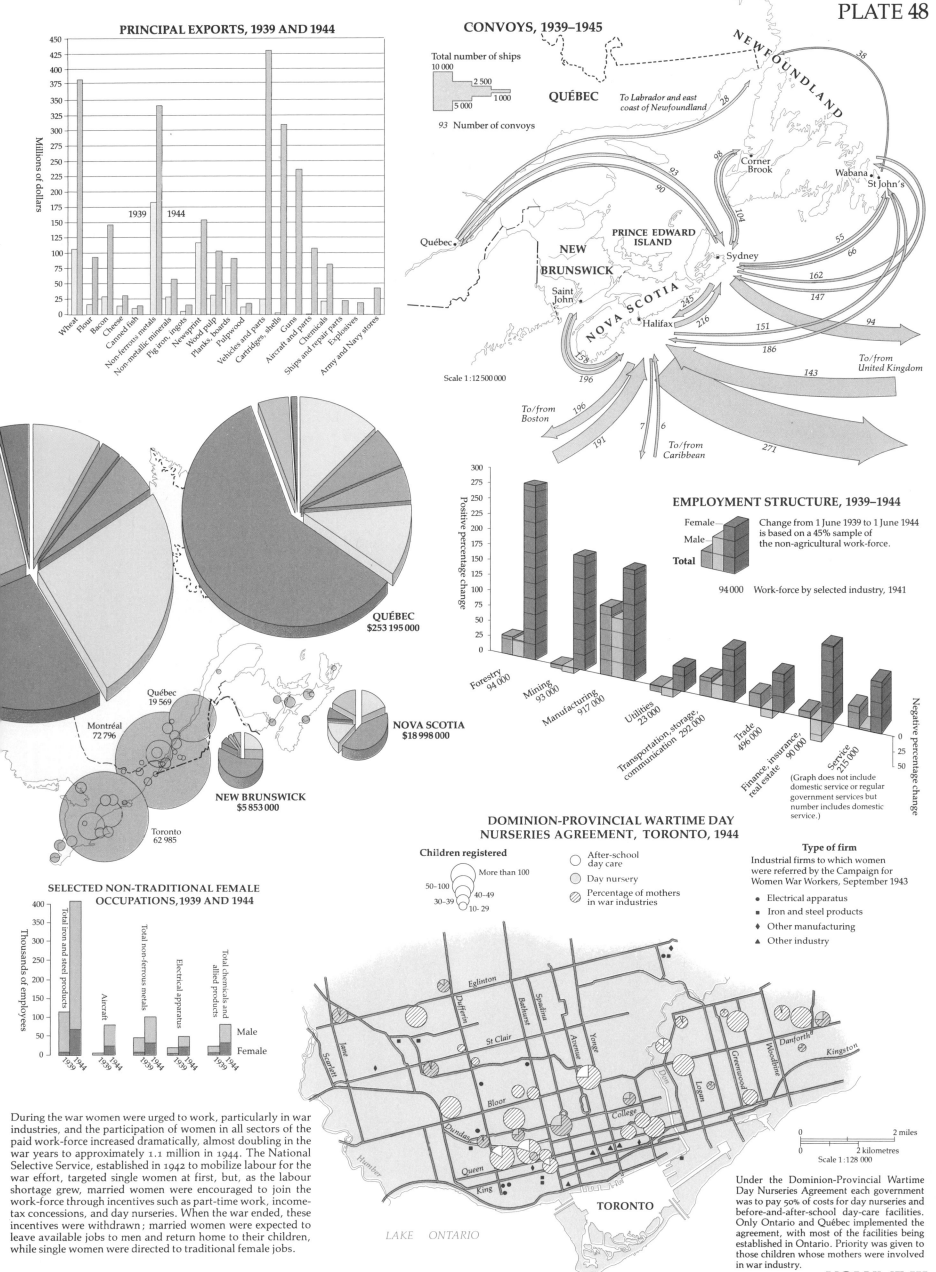

PLATE 48

PRINCIPAL EXPORTS, 1939 AND 1944

Millions of dollars

1939 1944

Wheat
Flour
Bacon
Cheese
Canned fish
Non-ferrous metals
Non-metallic minerals
Pig iron, ingots
Newsprint
Wood pulp
Planks, boards
Pulpwood
Vehicles and parts
Cartridges, shells
Guns
Aircraft and parts
Chemicals
Ships and repair parts
Explosives
Army and Navy stores

CONVOYS, 1939–1945

Total number of ships
10 000
2 500
5 000
1 000

93 Number of convoys

To Labrador and east
coast of Newfoundland

QUÉBEC

NEWFOUNDLAND

Corner
Brook

Wabana
St John's

PRINCE EDWARD
ISLAND

NEW
BRUNSWICK

Québec

Saint
John

NOVA SCOTIA

Sydney

Halifax

To/from
United Kingdom

To/from
Boston

To/from
Caribbean

Scale 1:12 500 000

EMPLOYMENT STRUCTURE, 1939–1944

Positive percentage change

Female
Male
Total

Change from 1 June 1939 to 1 June 1944
is based on a 45% sample of
the non-agricultural work-force.

94 000 Work-force by selected industry, 1941

Forestry
94 000

Mining
93 000

Manufacturing
917 000

Utilities
23 000

Transportation, storage,
communication 292 000

Trade
496 000

Finance, insurance,
real estate 90 000

Service
215 000

Negative percentage change

(Graph does not include
domestic service or regular
government services but
number includes domestic
service.)

QUÉBEC
$253 195 000

Québec
19 569

Montréal
72 796

NOVA SCOTIA
$18 998 000

NEW BRUNSWICK
$5 853 000

Toronto
62 985

DOMINION-PROVINCIAL WARTIME DAY
NURSERIES AGREEMENT, TORONTO, 1944

Children registered

More than 100

50–100
40–49
30–39
10-29

After-school
day care

Day nursery

Percentage of mothers
in war industries

Type of firm

Industrial firms to which women
were referred by the Campaign for
Women War Workers, September 1943

● Electrical apparatus
■ Iron and steel products
♦ Other manufacturing
▲ Other industry

SELECTED NON-TRADITIONAL FEMALE
OCCUPATIONS, 1939 AND 1944

Thousands of employees

Total iron and steel products
Aircraft
Total non-ferrous metals
Electrical apparatus
Total chemicals and allied products

1939 1944 1939 1944 1939 1944 1939 1944 1939 1944

Male
Female

Eglinton
Dufferin
Bathurst
Spadina
St Clair
Avenue
Yonge
Danforth
Woodbine
Greenwood
Kingston
Jane
Scarlett
Bloor
Don
Logan
College
Dundas
Queen
Humber
King

TORONTO

LAKE ONTARIO

0   2 miles
0   2 kilometres
Scale 1:128 000

During the war women were urged to work, particularly in war
industries, and the participation of women in all sectors of the
paid work-force increased dramatically, almost doubling in the
war years to approximately 1.1 million in 1944. The National
Selective Service, established in 1942 to mobilize labour for the
war effort, targeted single women at first, but, as the labour
shortage grew, married women were encouraged to join the
work-force through incentives such as part-time work, income-
tax concessions, and day nurseries. When the war ended, these
incentives were withdrawn; married women were expected to
leave available jobs to men and return home to their children,
while single women were directed to traditional female jobs.

Under the Dominion-Provincial Wartime
Day Nurseries Agreement each government
was to pay 50% of costs for day nurseries and
before-and-after-school day-care facilities.
Only Ontario and Québec implemented the
agreement, with most of the facilities being
established in Ontario. Priority was given to
those children whose mothers were involved
in war industry.

FARMING AND FISHING

Authors: Gerald Bloomfield, Philip D. Keddie, Eric W. Sager

Canadian farmland underwent a period of adjustment in the post-war years. In the east there was a net decline of about 6.3 million acres of improved farmland, some abandoned, notably on the Shield margins and in the Maritimes, and some lost to urbanization. However there were important additions in the Québec clay belt and in counties of southwestern Ontario where the introduction of hybrid corn helped encourage the conversion of permanent pasture and sandy scrubland into cropland. In the four western provinces there was a net gain of 15.2 million acres, mostly along the 'pioneer fringe,' in part facilitated by government assistance for clearing the land and post-war settlement schemes. Improved agricultural practices prompted the expansion of arable farming on more marginal lands while in southeast Saskatchewan and southwest Manitoba 'pothole' filling and drainage schemes also contributed to the increase. Notwithstanding the east/west patterns of change in improved farmland acreage, the value of farm output generally increased in both regions, and Ontario especially remained an important agricultural producer.

VALUE OF CATCH BY SPECIES, 1961

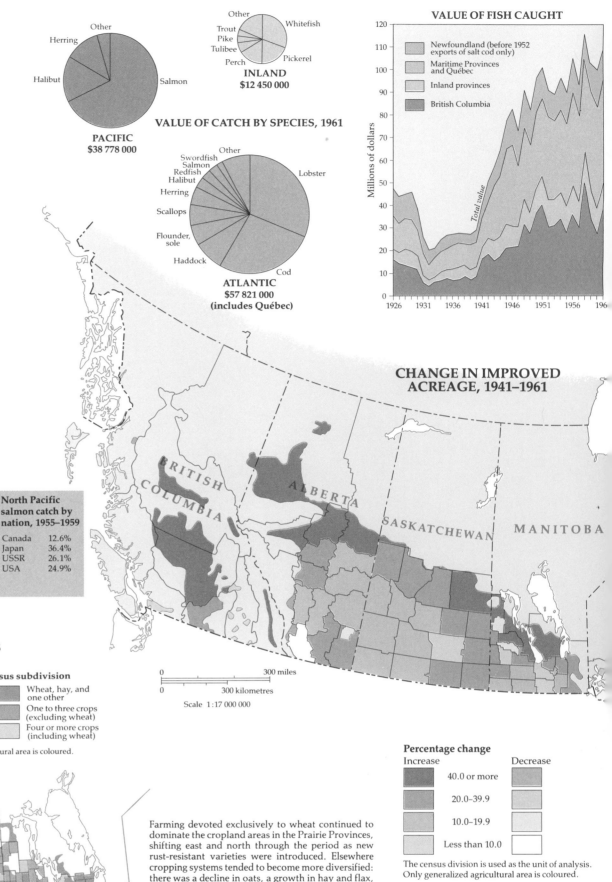

PACIFIC
$38 778 000

INLAND
$12 450 000

ATLANTIC
$57 821 000
(includes Québec)

VALUE OF FISH CAUGHT

Newfoundland (before 1952 exports of salt cod only)
Maritime Provinces and Québec
Inland provinces
British Columbia

CHANGE IN IMPROVED ACREAGE, 1941–1961

0   300 miles
0   300 kilometres

Scale 1:17 000 000

Percentage change

Increase	Decrease
40.0 or more	
20.0–39.9	
10.0–19.9	
Less than 10.0	

The census division is used as the unit of analysis. Only generalized agricultural area is coloured.

NET FARMING INCOME

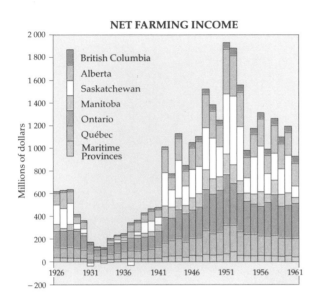

British Columbia
Alberta
Saskatchewan
Manitoba
Ontario
Québec
Maritime Provinces

North Pacific salmon catch by nation, 1955–1959	
Canada	12.6%
Japan	36.4%
USSR	26.1%
USA	24.9%

CROP COMBINATIONS IN THE PRAIRIES

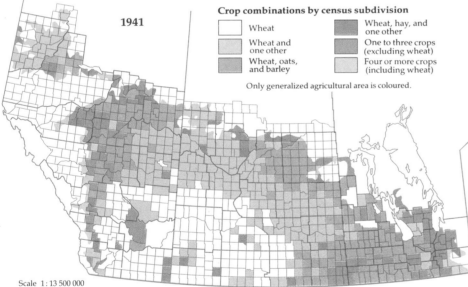

1941

Crop combinations by census subdivision

- Wheat
- Wheat and one other
- Wheat, oats, and barley
- Wheat, hay, and one other
- One to three crops (excluding wheat)
- Four or more crops (including wheat)

Only generalized agricultural area is coloured.

Scale 1:13 500 000

Farming devoted exclusively to wheat continued to dominate the cropland areas in the Prairie Provinces, shifting east and north through the period as new rust-resistant varieties were introduced. Elsewhere cropping systems tended to become more diversified: there was a decline in oats, a growth in hay and flax, and the appearance of rapeseed as a locally important crop. Large areas of rangeland in southwest Saskatchewan and southeast Alberta sustained cow-calf enterprises, with wheat dominating the limited cropland in those areas.

1961

VARIETIES OF PRAIRIE BREAD WHEAT

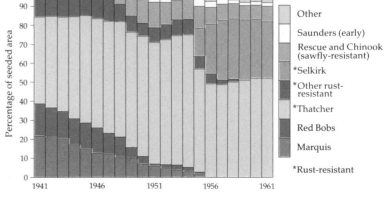

- Other
- Saunders (early)
- Rescue and Chinook (sawfly-resistant)
- *Selkirk
- *Other rust-resistant
- *Thatcher
- Red Bobs
- Marquis
- *Rust-resistant

HISTORICAL ATLAS OF CANADA

PLATE 49

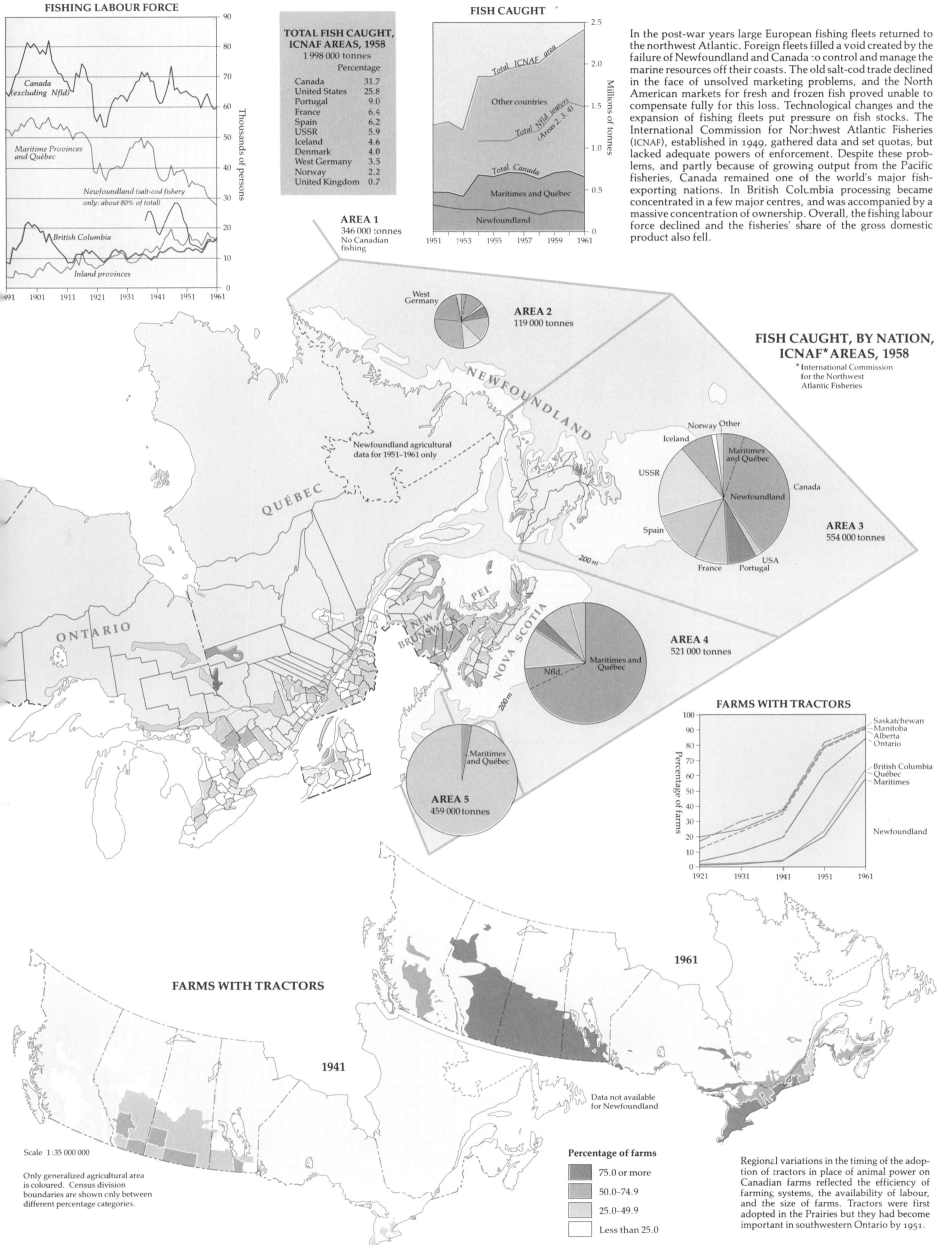

FISHING LABOUR FORCE

Canada (excluding Nfld)

Maritime Provinces and Québec

Newfoundland (salt-cod fishery only; about 80% of total)

British Columbia

Inland provinces

Thousands of persons

TOTAL FISH CAUGHT, ICNAF AREAS, 1958

1 998 000 tonnes

	Percentage
Canada	31.7
United States	25.8
Portugal	9.0
France	6.4
Spain	6.2
USSR	5.9
Iceland	4.6
Denmark	4.0
West Germany	3.5
Norway	2.2
United Kingdom	0.7

FISH CAUGHT

Total ICNAF area

Other countries

Total Nfld waters (Areas 2, 3, 4)

Total Canada

Maritimes and Québec

Newfoundland

Millions of tonnes

In the post-war years large European fishing fleets returned to the northwest Atlantic. Foreign fleets filled a void created by the failure of Newfoundland and Canada to control and manage the marine resources off their coasts. The old salt-cod trade declined in the face of unsolved marketing problems, and the North American markets for fresh and frozen fish proved unable to compensate fully for this loss. Technological changes and the expansion of fishing fleets put pressure on fish stocks. The International Commission for Northwest Atlantic Fisheries (ICNAF), established in 1949, gathered data and set quotas, but lacked adequate powers of enforcement. Despite these problems, and partly because of growing output from the Pacific fisheries, Canada remained one of the world's major fish-exporting nations. In British Columbia processing became concentrated in a few major centres, and was accompanied by a massive concentration of ownership. Overall, the fishing labour force declined and the fisheries' share of the gross domestic product also fell.

AREA 1
346 000 tonnes
No Canadian fishing

West Germany

AREA 2
119 000 tonnes

FISH CAUGHT, BY NATION, ICNAF* AREAS, 1958

* International Commission for the Northwest Atlantic Fisheries

Norway   Other

Iceland

USSR

Maritimes and Québec

Newfoundland

Canada

Spain

France   Portugal   USA

AREA 3
554 000 tonnes

Newfoundland agricultural data for 1951–1961 only

Nfld

Maritimes and Québec

AREA 4
521 000 tonnes

Maritimes and Québec

AREA 5
459 000 tonnes

FARMS WITH TRACTORS

Saskatchewan
Manitoba
Alberta
Ontario

British Columbia
Québec
Maritimes

Newfoundland

Percentage of farms

FARMS WITH TRACTORS

1961

1941

Data not available for Newfoundland

Scale 1:35 000 000

Only generalized agricultural area is coloured. Census division boundaries are shown only between different percentage categories.

Percentage of farms

- 75.0 or more
- 50.0–74.9
- 25.0–49.9
- Less than 25.0

Regional variations in the timing of the adoption of tractors in place of animal power on Canadian farms reflected the efficiency of farming systems, the availability of labour, and the size of farms. Tractors were first adopted in the Prairies but they had become important in southwestern Ontario by 1951.

RESOURCES FOR INDUSTRIAL ECONOMIES

Author: Donald Kerr

The increasing demand for resources for industrial economies, in the United States and western Europe as well as in Canada, precipitated a new round of investment, development of infrastructure, and resource extraction during the late 1940s and 1950s. The export market for newsprint, nickel, copper, and iron ore, mainly in the United States, was strong, as was demand within Canada for the newly discovered energy sources of oil and gas. Increased participation of American investors in this resource economy came as a result of partial depletion of American resources, the expansion of the American war machine during the Cold War that necessitated a search for strategic metals, and, above all, a favourable investment climate promoted by the Canadian government. Through the 1950s at least two-thirds of all Canadian exports were made up of raw or semi-processed materials, most of which were destined for the United States.

THE PULP AND PAPER INDUSTRY, 1961

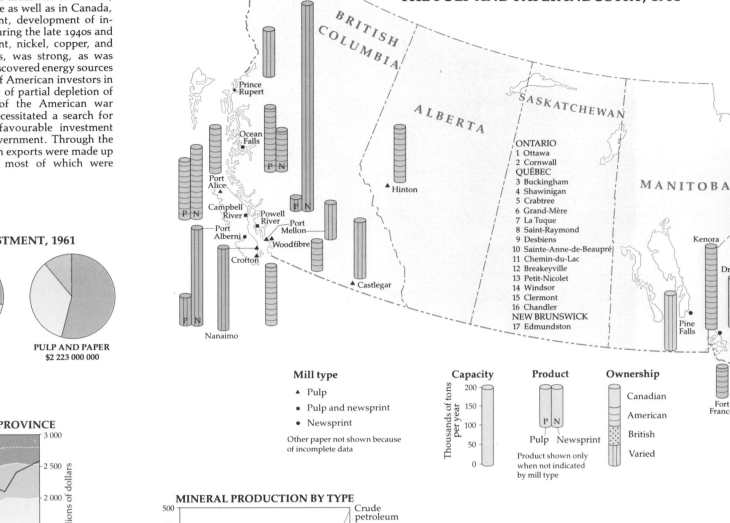

ONTARIO
1 Ottawa
2 Cornwall
QUÉBEC
3 Buckingham
4 Shawinigan
5 Crabtree
6 Grand-Mère
7 La Tuque
8 Saint-Raymond
9 Desbiens
10 Sainte-Anne-de-Beaupré
11 Chemin-du-Lac
12 Breakeyville
13 Petit-Nicolet
14 Windsor
15 Clermont
16 Chandler
NEW BRUNSWICK
17 Edmundston

Mill type
▲ Pulp
■ Pulp and newsprint
● Newsprint

Other paper not shown because of incomplete data

Capacity
Thousands of tons per year
200
150
100
50
0

Product
P N
Pulp Newsprint
Product shown only when not indicated by mill type

Ownership
Canadian
American
British
Varied

ORIGIN OF CAPITAL INVESTMENT, 1961

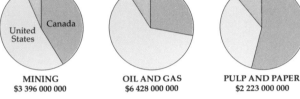

Other
United States
Canada

MINING
$3 396 000 000

OIL AND GAS
$6 428 000 000

PULP AND PAPER
$2 223 000 000

MINERAL PRODUCTION BY PROVINCE

Atlantic Provinces
British Columbia, NWT, Yukon
Québec
Total production
Prairie Provinces
Ontario

Percentage of total value (left axis): 0–100
Total value in millions of dollars (right axis): 0–3 000
Years: 1946, 1950, 1955, 1960

MINERAL PRODUCTION BY TYPE

Value in millions of dollars: 0–500

Crude petroleum
Nickel
Copper
Uranium
Iron ore
Coal

Years: 1946, 1950, 1955, 1960

In the post-war period the value of mining production increased significantly. The Shield remained the great storehouse for metallic minerals, its mines continuing to produce large amounts of nickel and copper as well as gold and silver. New production of iron ore from the Labrador trough and Atikokan, Ont, of uranium from Elliot Lake, Ont, and of nickel from Thompson, Man, added considerably to the value of mineral production.

Of great additional importance were the discovery and development of oil and gas fields in central Alberta. During the 1950s the production of oil more than quadrupled and natural gas increased eightfold. Beginning in the late 1940s the Inter-Provincial oil pipeline was built eastward to southern Ontario through the American midwest and the Trans-Mountain oil pipeline was built westward to the Pacific coast. Most of the production was directed to fill the needs of Canadians from the Pacific coast to the Ottawa valley; just over one-quarter was exported to the United States. Oil from the Middle East and Venezuela continued to feed Canadian refineries in Montréal and Atlantic Canada. The main natural-gas pipeline was routed entirely within Canada and reached Montréal in 1958.

MINERAL PRODUCTION 1961

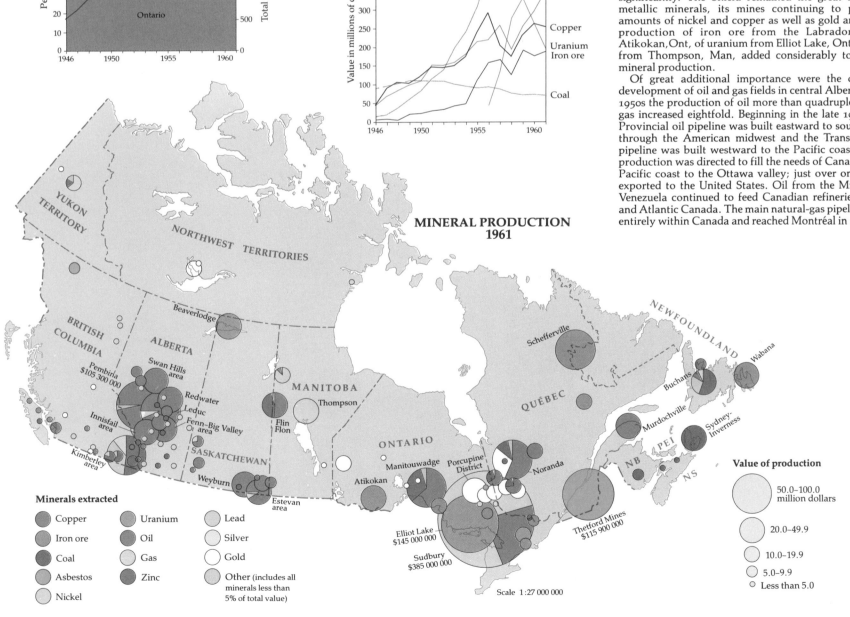

Minerals extracted
- Copper
- Iron ore
- Coal
- Asbestos
- Nickel
- Uranium
- Oil
- Gas
- Zinc
- Lead
- Silver
- Gold
- Other (includes all minerals less than 5% of total value)

Value of production
- 50.0–100.0 million dollars
- 20.0–49.9
- 10.0–19.9
- 5.0–9.9
- Less than 5.0

Scale 1:27 000 000

Pembina $105 300 000
Elliot Lake $145 000 000
Sudbury $385 000 000
Thetford Mines $115 900 000

HISTORICAL ATLAS OF CANADA

PLATE 50

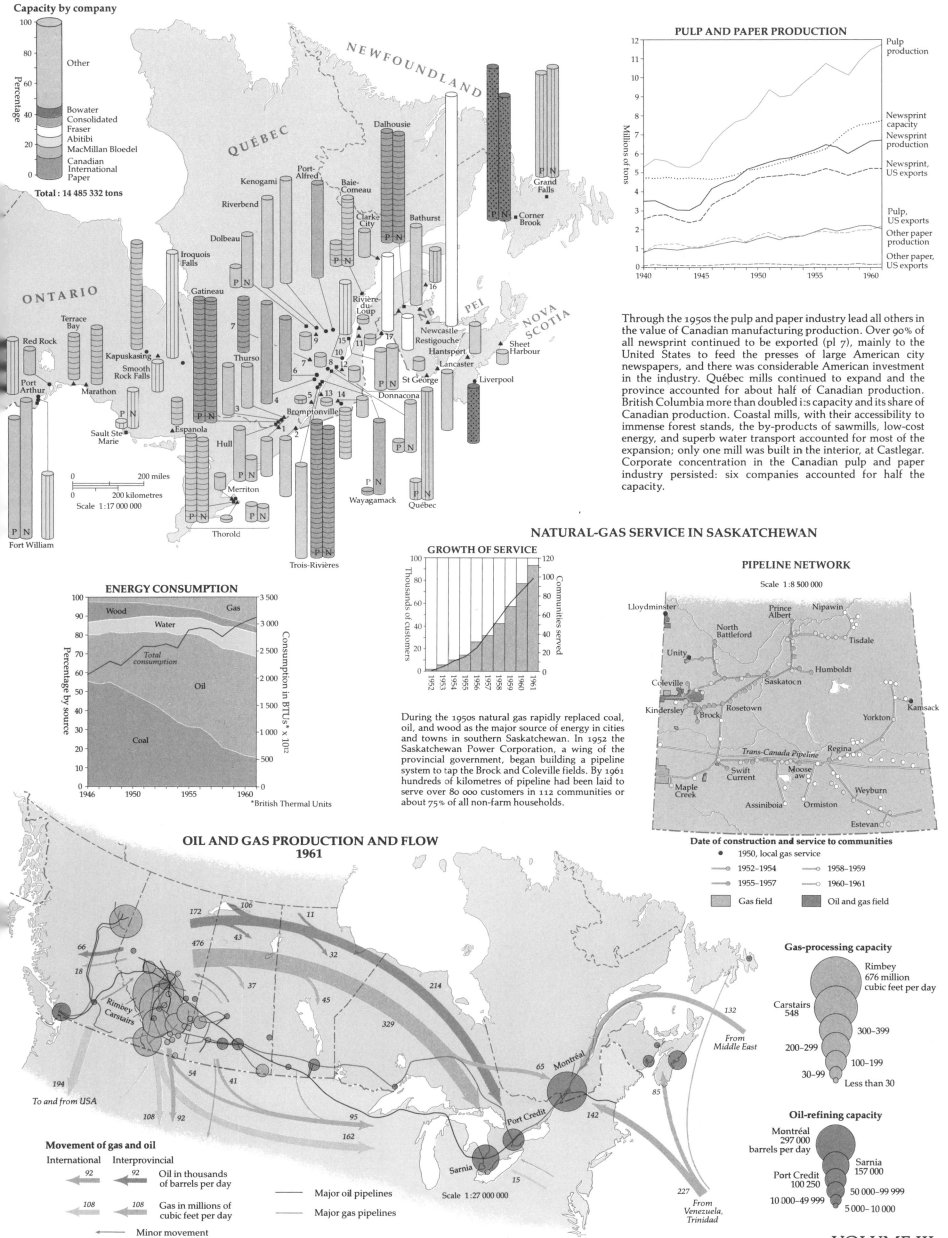

Capacity by company

Percentage

- Other
- Bowater
- Consolidated
- Fraser
- Abitibi
- MacMillan Bloedel
- Canadian International Paper

Total : 14 485 332 tons

Scale 1:17 000 000

0 200 miles
0 200 kilometres

PULP AND PAPER PRODUCTION

Millions of tons

- Pulp production
- Newsprint capacity
- Newsprint production
- Newsprint, US exports
- Pulp, US exports
- Other paper production
- Other paper, US exports

Through the 1950s the pulp and paper industry lead all others in the value of Canadian manufacturing production. Over 90% of all newsprint continued to be exported (pl 7), mainly to the United States to feed the presses of large American city newspapers, and there was considerable American investment in the industry. Québec mills continued to expand and the province accounted for about half of Canadian production. British Columbia more than doubled its capacity and its share of Canadian production. Coastal mills, with their accessibility to immense forest stands, the by-products of sawmills, low-cost energy, and superb water transport accounted for most of the expansion; only one mill was built in the interior, at Castlegar. Corporate concentration in the Canadian pulp and paper industry persisted: six companies accounted for half the capacity.

NATURAL-GAS SERVICE IN SASKATCHEWAN

GROWTH OF SERVICE

Thousands of customers / Communities served

PIPELINE NETWORK

Scale 1:8 500 000

During the 1950s natural gas rapidly replaced coal, oil, and wood as the major source of energy in cities and towns in southern Saskatchewan. In 1952 the Saskatchewan Power Corporation, a wing of the provincial government, began building a pipeline system to tap the Brock and Coleville fields. By 1961 hundreds of kilometres of pipeline had been laid to serve over 80 000 customers in 112 communities or about 75% of all non-farm households.

Date of construction and service to communities
- 1950, local gas service
- 1952–1954
- 1955–1957
- 1958–1959
- 1960–1961
- Gas field
- Oil and gas field

ENERGY CONSUMPTION

Percentage by source / Consumption in BTUs* × 10¹²

- Wood
- Gas
- Water
- Total consumption
- Oil
- Coal

*British Thermal Units

OIL AND GAS PRODUCTION AND FLOW 1961

Gas-processing capacity
- Rimbey 676 million cubic feet per day
- Carstairs 548
- 300–399
- 200–299
- 100–199
- 30–99
- Less than 30

Oil-refining capacity
- Montréal 297 000 barrels per day
- Sarnia 157 000
- Port Credit 100 250
- 50 000–99 999
- 10 000–49 999
- 5 000–10 000

Movement of gas and oil

International	Interprovincial	
92	92	Oil in thousands of barrels per day
108	108	Gas in millions of cubic feet per day

Minor movement

— Major oil pipelines
— Major gas pipelines

Scale 1:27 000 000

To and from USA

From Middle East

From Venezuela, Trinidad

THE PERSISTENCE OF MANUFACTURING PATTERNS
Authors: Donald Kerr, Gerald Bloomfield

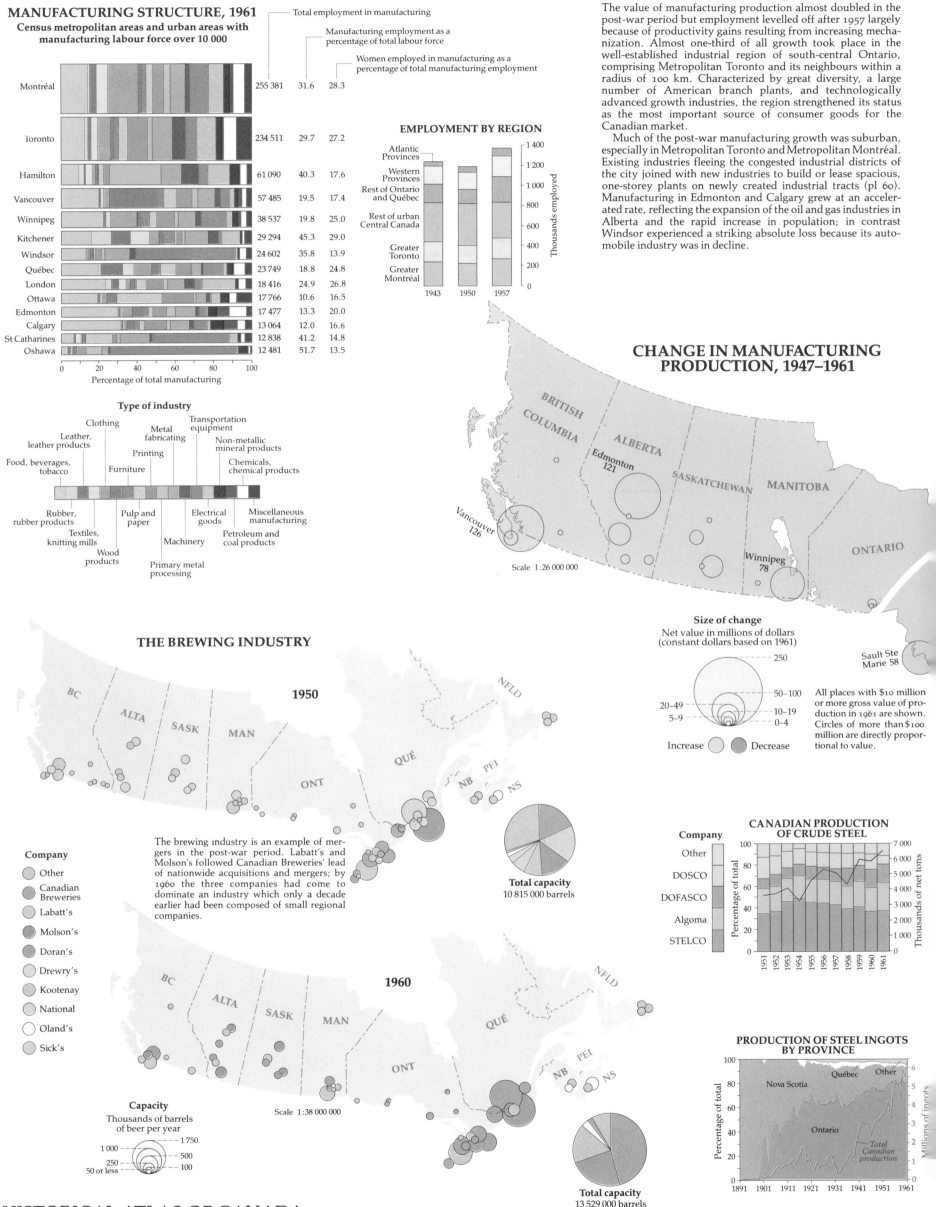

MANUFACTURING STRUCTURE, 1961
Census metropolitan areas and urban areas with manufacturing labour force over 10 000

Total employment in manufacturing

Manufacturing employment as a percentage of total labour force

Women employed in manufacturing as a percentage of total manufacturing employment

	Total	%	Women %
Montréal	255 381	31.6	28.3
Toronto	234 511	29.7	27.2
Hamilton	61 090	40.3	17.6
Vancouver	57 485	19.5	17.4
Winnipeg	38 537	19.8	25.0
Kitchener	29 294	45.3	29.0
Windsor	24 602	35.8	13.9
Québec	23 749	18.8	24.8
London	18 416	24.9	26.8
Ottawa	17 766	10.6	16.5
Edmonton	17 477	13.3	20.0
Calgary	13 064	12.0	16.6
St Catharines	12 838	41.2	14.8
Oshawa	12 481	51.7	13.5

Percentage of total manufacturing

Type of industry

Food, beverages, tobacco
Leather, leather products
Clothing
Metal fabricating
Printing
Furniture
Transportation equipment
Non-metallic mineral products
Chemicals, chemical products
Rubber, rubber products
Textiles, knitting mills
Pulp and paper
Electrical goods
Machinery
Petroleum and coal products
Miscellaneous manufacturing
Wood products
Primary metal processing

EMPLOYMENT BY REGION

Atlantic Provinces
Western Provinces
Rest of Ontario and Québec
Rest of urban Central Canada
Greater Toronto
Greater Montréal

Thousands employed

1943   1950   1957

The value of manufacturing production almost doubled in the post-war period but employment levelled off after 1957 largely because of productivity gains resulting from increasing mechanization. Almost one-third of all growth took place in the well-established industrial region of south-central Ontario, comprising Metropolitan Toronto and its neighbours within a radius of 100 km. Characterized by great diversity, a large number of American branch plants, and technologically advanced growth industries, the region strengthened its status as the most important source of consumer goods for the Canadian market.

Much of the post-war manufacturing growth was suburban, especially in Metropolitan Toronto and Metropolitan Montréal. Existing industries fleeing the congested industrial districts of the city joined with new industries to build or lease spacious, one-storey plants on newly created industrial tracts (pl 60). Manufacturing in Edmonton and Calgary grew at an accelerated rate, reflecting the expansion of the oil and gas industries in Alberta and the rapid increase in population; in contrast Windsor experienced a striking absolute loss because its automobile industry was in decline.

CHANGE IN MANUFACTURING PRODUCTION, 1947–1961

BRITISH COLUMBIA
ALBERTA
SASKATCHEWAN
MANITOBA
ONTARIO

Edmonton 121
Vancouver 126
Winnipeg 78
Sault Ste Marie 58

Scale 1:26 000 000

Size of change
Net value in millions of dollars (constant dollars based on 1961)

250
50–100
10–19
20–49
5–9
0–4

Increase   Decrease

All places with $10 million or more gross value of production in 1961 are shown. Circles of more than $100 million are directly proportional to value.

THE BREWING INDUSTRY

1950

BC   ALTA   SASK   MAN   ONT   QUÉ   NFLD   NB   PEI   NS

The brewing industry is an example of mergers in the post-war period. Labatt's and Molson's followed Canadian Breweries' lead of nationwide acquisitions and mergers; by 1960 the three companies had come to dominate an industry which only a decade earlier had been composed of small regional companies.

Total capacity
10 815 000 barrels

Company
- Other
- Canadian Breweries
- Labatt's
- Molson's
- Doran's
- Drewry's
- Kootenay
- National
- Oland's
- Sick's

1960

BC   ALTA   SASK   MAN   ONT   QUÉ   NFLD   NB   PEI   NS

Scale 1:38 000 000

Capacity
Thousands of barrels of beer per year

1 750
1 000
500
250
100
50 or less

Total capacity
13 529 000 barrels

CANADIAN PRODUCTION OF CRUDE STEEL

Company
- Other
- DOSCO
- DOFASCO
- Algoma
- STELCO

Percentage of total / Thousands of net tons

1951 1952 1953 1954 1955 1956 1957 1958 1959 1960 1961

PRODUCTION OF STEEL INGOTS BY PROVINCE

Percentage of total / Millions of ingots

Québec   Other
Nova Scotia
Ontario
Total Canadian production

1891 1901 1911 1921 1931 1941 1951 1961

HISTORICAL ATLAS OF CANADA

PLATE 51

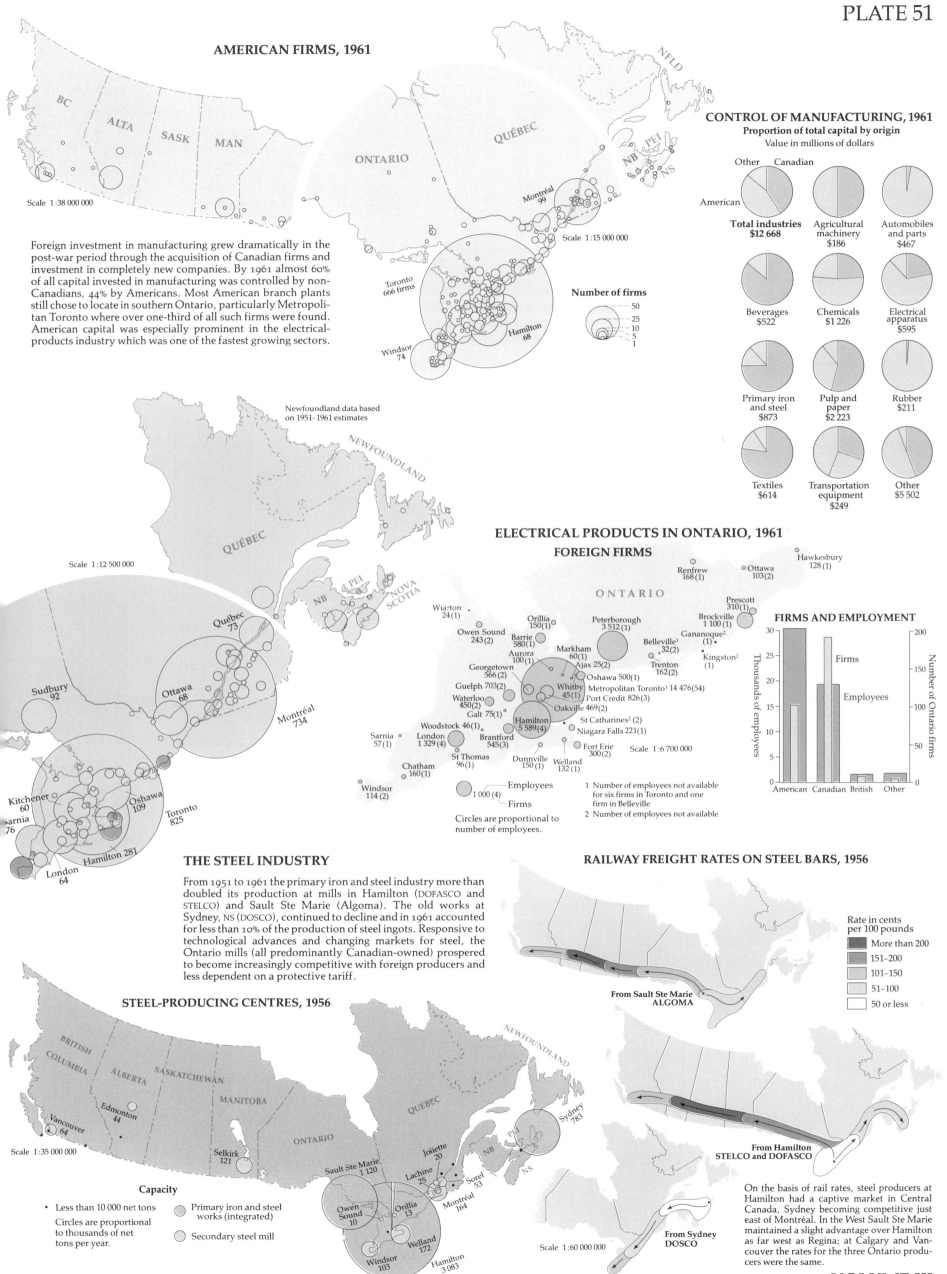

AMERICAN FIRMS, 1961

Scale 1:38 000 000

Foreign investment in manufacturing grew dramatically in the post-war period through the acquisition of Canadian firms and investment in completely new companies. By 1961 almost 60% of all capital invested in manufacturing was controlled by non-Canadians, 44% by Americans. Most American branch plants still chose to locate in southern Ontario, particularly Metropolitan Toronto where over one-third of all such firms were found. American capital was especially prominent in the electrical-products industry which was one of the fastest growing sectors.

Scale 1:15 000 000

Toronto 666 firms

Montréal 99

Windsor 74

Hamilton 68

Number of firms
50
25
10
5
1

CONTROL OF MANUFACTURING, 1961
Proportion of total capital by origin
Value in millions of dollars

Other — Canadian
American

Total industries $12 668 | Agricultural machinery $186 | Automobiles and parts $467
Beverages $522 | Chemicals $1 226 | Electrical apparatus $595
Primary iron and steel $873 | Pulp and paper $2 223 | Rubber $211
Textiles $614 | Transportation equipment $249 | Other $5 502

Newfoundland data based on 1951–1961 estimates

Scale 1:12 500 000

Québec 73
Sudbury 92
Ottawa 68
Montréal 734
Kitchener 60
Oshawa 109
Sarnia 76
Toronto 825
Hamilton 281
London 64

ELECTRICAL PRODUCTS IN ONTARIO, 1961
FOREIGN FIRMS

Hawkesbury 128 (1)
Renfrew 168 (1)
Ottawa 103 (2)
Wiarton 24 (1)
Owen Sound 243 (2)
Orillia 150 (1)
Peterborough 3 512 (1)
Brockville 1 100 (1)
Prescott 310 (1)
Barrie 580 (1)
Markham 60 (1)
Belleville[1] 32 (2)
Gananoque[2] (1)
Aurora 100 (1)
Ajax 25 (2)
Kingston[2] (1)
Georgetown 566 (2)
Oshawa 500 (1)
Guelph 703 (2)
Whitby 45 (1)
Metropolitan Toronto[1] 14 476 (54)
Waterloo 450 (2)
Port Credit 826 (3)
Galt 75 (1)
Oakville 469 (2)
St Catharines[2] (2)
Sarnia 57 (1)
Woodstock 46 (1)
Hamilton 5 589 (4)
Niagara Falls 221 (1)
London 1 329 (4)
Brantford 545 (3)
Fort Erie 300 (2)
Chatham 160 (1)
St Thomas 96 (1)
Dunnville 150 (1)
Welland 132 (1)
Windsor 114 (2)

Scale 1:6 700 000

1 000 (4)
Employees
Firms

Circles are proportional to number of employees.

1 Number of employees not available for six firms in Toronto and one firm in Belleville
2 Number of employees not available

FIRMS AND EMPLOYMENT

Thousands of employees / Number of Ontario firms

Firms
Employees

American | Canadian | British | Other

THE STEEL INDUSTRY

From 1951 to 1961 the primary iron and steel industry more than doubled its production at mills in Hamilton (DOFASCO and STELCO) and Sault Ste Marie (Algoma). The old works at Sydney, NS (DOSCO), continued to decline and in 1961 accounted for less than 10% of the production of steel ingots. Responsive to technological advances and changing markets for steel, the Ontario mills (all predominantly Canadian-owned) prospered to become increasingly competitive with foreign producers and less dependent on a protective tariff.

RAILWAY FREIGHT RATES ON STEEL BARS, 1956

Rate in cents per 100 pounds
More than 200
151–200
101–150
51–100
50 or less

From Sault Ste Marie
ALGOMA

From Hamilton
STELCO and DOFASCO

From Sydney
DOSCO

STEEL-PRODUCING CENTRES, 1956

Scale 1:35 000 000

Vancouver 64
Edmonton 44
Selkirk 121
Sydney 783
Joliette 20
Lachine 25
Montréal 164
Sorel 53
Sault Ste Marie 1 120
Owen Sound 10
Orillia 13
Welland 172
Windsor 103
Hamilton 3 083

Scale 1:60 000 000

Capacity
• Less than 10 000 net tons
Circles are proportional to thousands of net tons per year.
Primary iron and steel works (integrated)
Secondary steel mill

On the basis of rail rates, steel producers at Hamilton had a captive market in Central Canada, Sydney becoming competitive just east of Montréal. In the West Sault Ste Marie maintained a slight advantage over Hamilton as far west as Regina; at Calgary and Vancouver the rates for the three Ontario producers were the same.

RETAILING

Authors: Gerald Bloomfield, Donald Kerr

In the post-war years retailing in Canada grew dramatically both in total sales and in purchases per capita. Employment in the retail sector also increased, but at a rate which was much greater in small and medium-sized cities than in metropolitan centres. The increasingly ubiquitous automobile profoundly affected sales. From the 1930s sales in automobiles, auto parts and accessories, and gasoline rose at a phenomenal rate to account for more than a fifth of all retail sales in 1961. Increased consumer mobility and the continuing structural changes in merchandizing influenced the directions of retailing. The retail sales of independent operators declined in importance from over 67% in 1931 to 41% in 1961; by contrast, chain stores along with voluntary chains, co-operatives, and franchise dealers grew to account for half of all sales. Food groceterias and supermarkets and firms offering clothing, drugs, and hardware were especially prevalent examples of 'chains,' and national firms began to appear on many main streets. Department stores, which had enjoyed a period of growth in the 1920s, continued to expand their networks, but were responsible for a smaller proportion of retail trade.

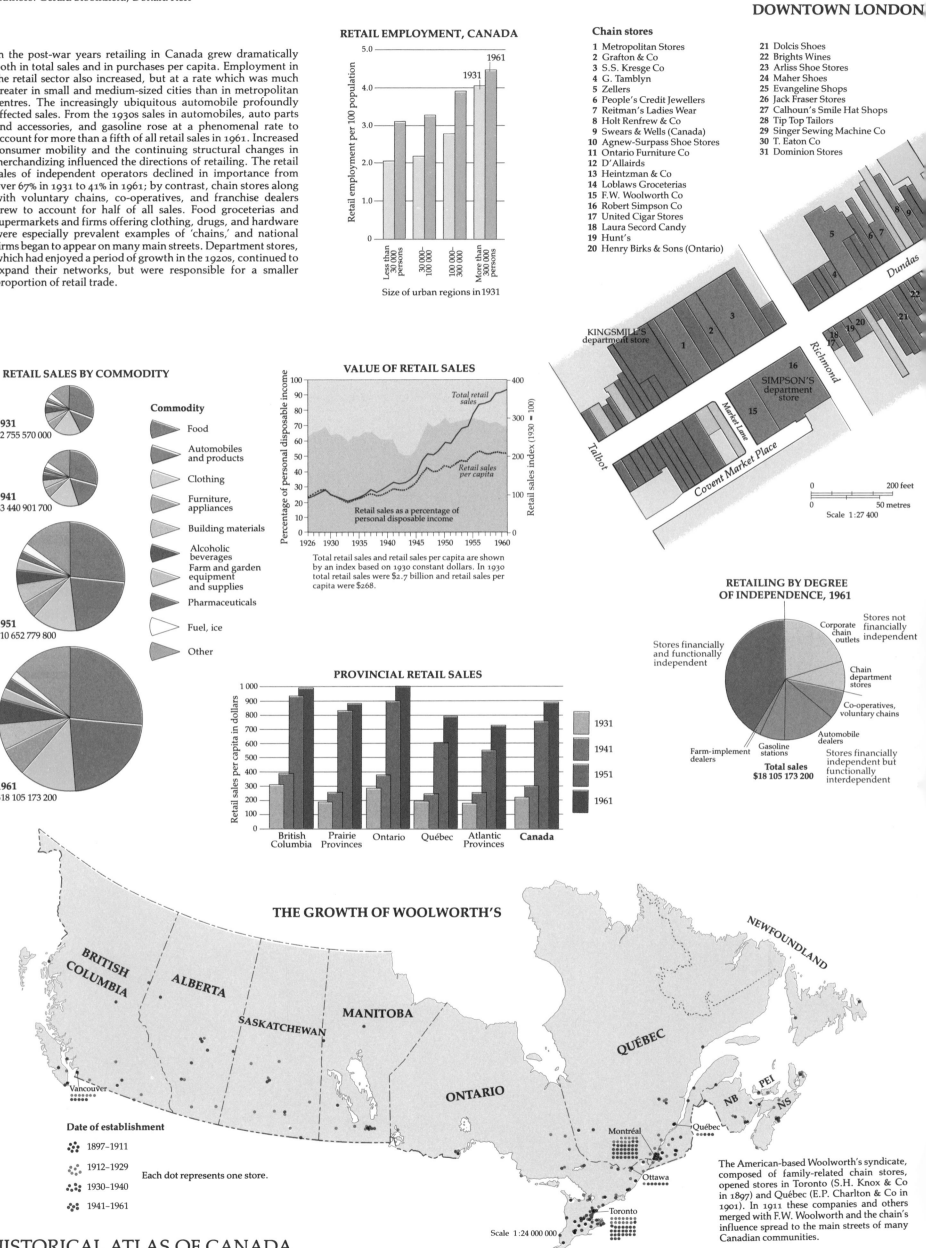

RETAIL EMPLOYMENT, CANADA

Retail employment per 100 population

Size of urban regions in 1931

Chain stores

1 Metropolitan Stores
2 Grafton & Co
3 S.S. Kresge Co
4 G. Tamblyn
5 Zellers
6 People's Credit Jewellers
7 Reitman's Ladies Wear
8 Holt Renfrew & Co
9 Swears & Wells (Canada)
10 Agnew-Surpass Shoe Stores
11 Ontario Furniture Co
12 D'Allairds
13 Heintzman & Co
14 Loblaws Groceterias
15 F.W. Woolworth Co
16 Robert Simpson Co
17 United Cigar Stores
18 Laura Secord Candy
19 Hunt's
20 Henry Birks & Sons (Ontario)
21 Dolcis Shoes
22 Brights Wines
23 Arliss Shoe Stores
24 Maher Shoes
25 Evangeline Shops
26 Jack Fraser Stores
27 Calhoun's Smile Hat Shops
28 Tip Top Tailors
29 Singer Sewing Machine Co
30 T. Eaton Co
31 Dominion Stores

RETAIL SALES BY COMMODITY

1931
$2 755 570 000

1941
$3 440 901 700

1951
$10 652 779 800

1961
$18 105 173 200

Commodity

Food
Automobiles and products
Clothing
Furniture, appliances
Building materials
Alcoholic beverages
Farm and garden equipment and supplies
Pharmaceuticals
Fuel, ice
Other

VALUE OF RETAIL SALES

Percentage of personal disposable income

Retail sales index (1930 = 100)

Total retail sales

Retail sales per capita

Retail sales as a percentage of personal disposable income

Total retail sales and retail sales per capita are shown by an index based on 1930 constant dollars. In 1930 total retail sales were $2.7 billion and retail sales per capita were $268.

PROVINCIAL RETAIL SALES

Retail sales per capita in dollars

British Columbia | Prairie Provinces | Ontario | Québec | Atlantic Provinces | **Canada**

1931
1941
1951
1961

RETAILING BY DEGREE OF INDEPENDENCE, 1961

Stores not financially independent
Corporate chain outlets
Chain department stores
Co-operatives, voluntary chains
Automobile dealers
Stores financially independent but functionally interdependent
Gasoline stations
Farm-implement dealers
Stores financially and functionally independent

Total sales
$18 105 173 200

KINGSMILL'S department store
SIMPSON'S department store
Dundas
Richmond
Market Lane
Talbot
Covent Market Place

0   200 feet
0   50 metres
Scale 1:27 400

THE GROWTH OF WOOLWORTH'S

BRITISH COLUMBIA
ALBERTA
SASKATCHEWAN
MANITOBA
ONTARIO
QUÉBEC
NEWFOUNDLAND
NB
PEI
NS

Vancouver
Montréal
Québec
Ottawa
Toronto

Date of establishment

1897–1911
1912–1929
1930–1940
1941–1961

Each dot represents one store.

Scale 1:24 000 000

The American-based Woolworth's syndicate, composed of family-related chain stores, opened stores in Toronto (S.H. Knox & Co in 1897) and Québec (E.P. Charlton & Co in 1901). In 1911 these companies and others merged with F.W. Woolworth and the chain's influence spread to the main streets of many Canadian communities.

HISTORICAL ATLAS OF CANADA

PLATE 52

ONTARIO, 1960

Park Royal Shopping Centre, West Vancouver, BC

Canada's first suburban shopping centre shortly after opening on 1 Sept 1950

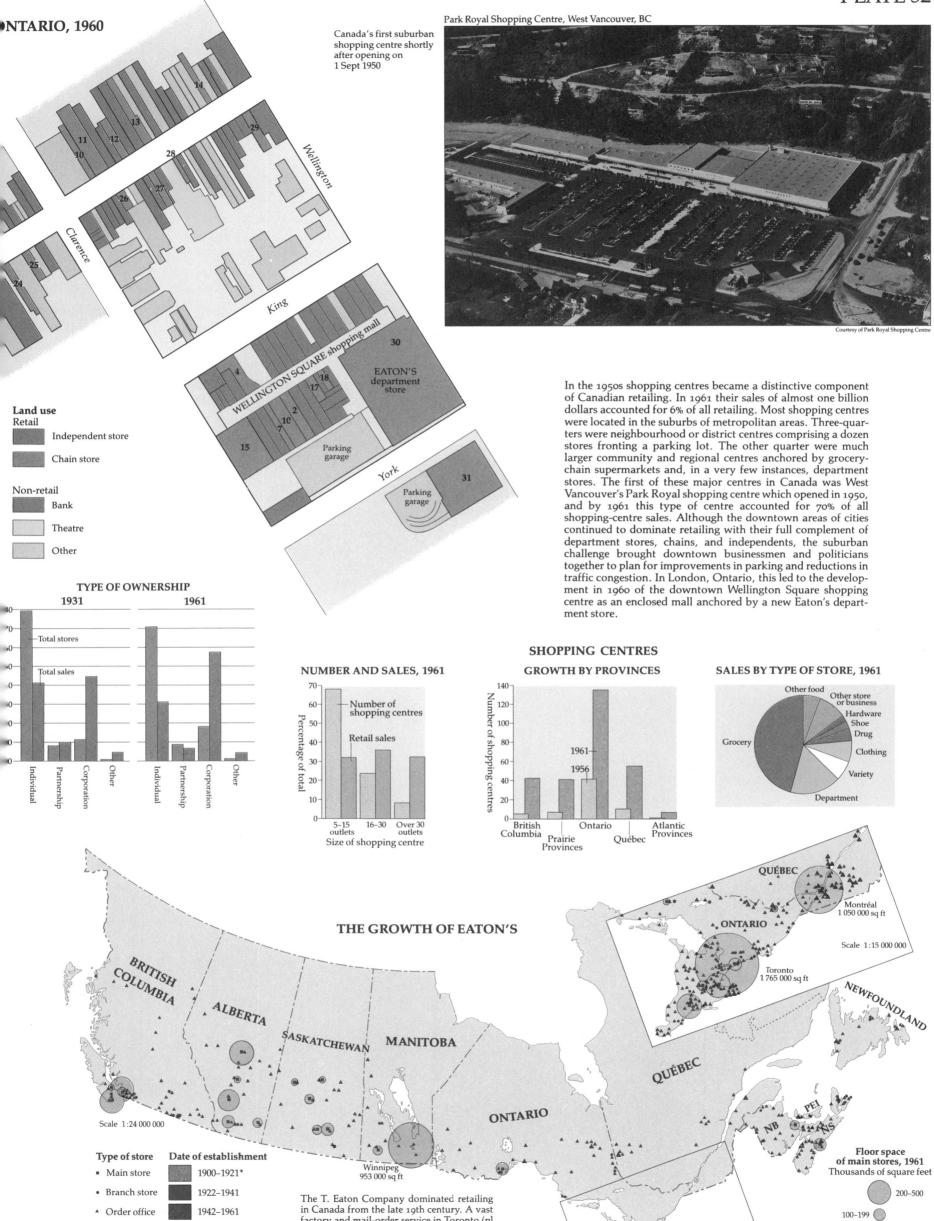

Courtesy of Park Royal Shopping Centre

Wellington

Clarence

King

14
13
11 12
10
29
28
26 27
25
24

WELLINGTON SQUARE shopping mall
4
18
17
10 2
7
15

EATON'S department store
30

Parking garage

York

Parking garage
31

Land use
Retail
Independent store
Chain store

Non-retail
Bank
Theatre
Other

In the 1950s shopping centres became a distinctive component of Canadian retailing. In 1961 their sales of almost one billion dollars accounted for 6% of all retailing. Most shopping centres were located in the suburbs of metropolitan areas. Three-quarters were neighbourhood or district centres comprising a dozen stores fronting a parking lot. The other quarter were much larger community and regional centres anchored by grocery-chain supermarkets and, in a very few instances, department stores. The first of these major centres in Canada was West Vancouver's Park Royal shopping centre which opened in 1950, and by 1961 this type of centre accounted for 70% of all shopping-centre sales. Although the downtown areas of cities continued to dominate retailing with their full complement of department stores, chains, and independents, the suburban challenge brought downtown businessmen and politicians together to plan for improvements in parking and reductions in traffic congestion. In London, Ontario, this led to the development in 1960 of the downtown Wellington Square shopping centre as an enclosed mall anchored by a new Eaton's department store.

TYPE OF OWNERSHIP

1931

Total stores
Total sales

Individual Partnership Corporation Other

1961

Individual Partnership Corporation Other

SHOPPING CENTRES

NUMBER AND SALES, 1961

Percentage of total

Number of shopping centres
Retail sales

5–15 outlets 16–30 Over 30 outlets
Size of shopping centre

GROWTH BY PROVINCES

Number of shopping centres

1961
1956

British Columbia Prairie Provinces Ontario Québec Atlantic Provinces

SALES BY TYPE OF STORE, 1961

Other food
Other store or business
Hardware
Shoe
Drug
Clothing
Variety
Grocery
Department

THE GROWTH OF EATON'S

QUÉBEC

ONTARIO

Montréal
1 050 000 sq ft

Scale 1:15 000 000

Toronto
1 765 000 sq ft

NEWFOUNDLAND

BRITISH COLUMBIA

ALBERTA

SASKATCHEWAN

MANITOBA

ONTARIO

QUÉBEC

NB PEI NS

Scale 1:24 000 000

Winnipeg
953 000 sq ft

Type of store
▪ Main store
▪ Branch store
▴ Order office

Date of establishment
1900–1921*
1922–1941
1942–1961

*Original Toronto store opened 1869
Symbols outlined in black indicate stores or offices closed by 1961.

The T. Eaton Company dominated retailing in Canada from the late 19th century. A vast factory and mail-order service in Toronto (pl 15) and then in Winnipeg were the basis of a national chain of main stores, branch stores, and order offices.

Floor space of main stores, 1961
Thousands of square feet

200–500
100–199
50–99
Less than 50

See detail.

THE GROWTH OF ROAD AND AIR TRANSPORT

Authors: Gerald Bloomfield, Murdo MacPherson, David Neufeld

CANADIAN AIRLINES, 1937

MOVEMENT OF PASSENGERS

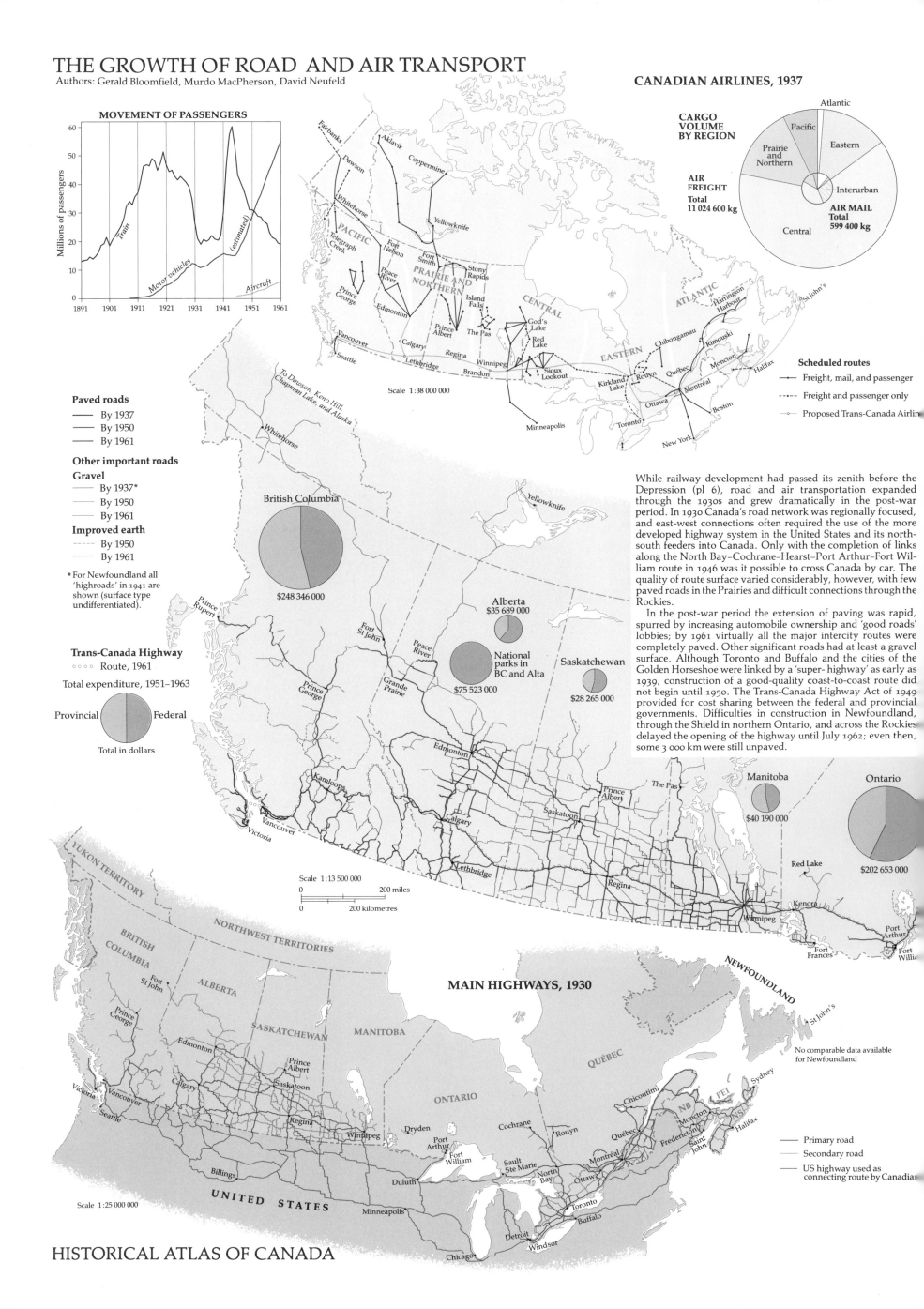

Millions of passengers

1891 1901 1911 1921 1931 1941 1951 1961

Train

Motor vehicles

(estimated)

Aircraft

CARGO VOLUME BY REGION

Atlantic
Pacific
Prairie and Northern
Eastern
Interurban
Central

AIR FREIGHT Total 11 024 600 kg

AIR MAIL Total 599 400 kg

Scale 1:38 000 000

Scheduled routes

—— Freight, mail, and passenger

--- Freight and passenger only

○○○ Proposed Trans-Canada Airlines

Paved roads
—— By 1937
—— By 1950
—— By 1961

Other important roads
Gravel
—— By 1937*
—— By 1950
—— By 1961

Improved earth
--- By 1950
--- By 1961

*For Newfoundland all 'highroads' in 1941 are shown (surface type undifferentiated).

Trans-Canada Highway
○○○○ Route, 1961

Total expenditure, 1951–1963

Provincial | Federal

Total in dollars

British Columbia
$248 346 000

Alberta
$35 689 000

National parks in BC and Alta
$75 523 000

Saskatchewan
$28 265 000

Manitoba
$40 190 000

Ontario
$202 653 000

While railway development had passed its zenith before the Depression (pl 6), road and air transportation expanded through the 1930s and grew dramatically in the post-war period. In 1930 Canada's road network was regionally focused, and east-west connections often required the use of the more developed highway system in the United States and its north-south feeders into Canada. Only with the completion of links along the North Bay–Cochrane–Hearst–Port Arthur–Fort William route in 1946 was it possible to cross Canada by car. The quality of route surface varied considerably, however, with few paved roads in the Prairies and difficult connections through the Rockies.

In the post-war period the extension of paving was rapid, spurred by increasing automobile ownership and 'good roads' lobbies; by 1961 virtually all the major intercity routes were completely paved. Other significant roads had at least a gravel surface. Although Toronto and Buffalo and the cities of the Golden Horseshoe were linked by a 'super-highway' as early as 1939, construction of a good-quality coast-to-coast route did not begin until 1950. The Trans-Canada Highway Act of 1949 provided for cost sharing between the federal and provincial governments. Difficulties in construction in Newfoundland, through the Shield in northern Ontario, and across the Rockies delayed the opening of the highway until July 1962; even then, some 3 000 km were still unpaved.

Scale 1:13 500 000

0 ————— 200 miles

0 ————— 200 kilometres

MAIN HIGHWAYS, 1930

No comparable data available for Newfoundland

Scale 1:25 000 000

UNITED STATES

Primary road
Secondary road
US highway used as connecting route by Canadians

HISTORICAL ATLAS OF CANADA

PLATE 53

ORIGINS OF THE MAJOR AIRLINES

Regional origin of constituent airlines

.... Maritime Provinces
-------- Québec and N Ontario
-- -- -- NW Ontario and N Manitoba
------- Prairie Provinces
--+--+-- N Alberta, Yukon, NWT
--+--+-- British Columbia
━━━━━ Multiple regions
↑ Subsidiary relationship

EASTERN PROVINCIAL AIRWAYS

NORDAIR

QUEBECAIR

TRANSAIR

PACIFIC WESTERN AIRLINES

CANADIAN PACIFIC AIRLINES

TRANS-CANADA AIRLINES

1921   1931   1941   1951   1961 1964

CANADIAN AIRLINES, 1963

National
——— Trans-Canada
——— Canadian Pacific

Regional
——— Pacific Western
——— Transair
——— Quebecair
——— Eastern Provincial

Resolute Bay
Aklavik Inuvik Cape Perry Cambridge Bay Hall Point Cape Dyer
Dawson Normal Wells
Whitehorse Yellowknife
Fort Smith Churchill Netherlands → UK
Fort St John Schefferville Goose Bay Gander → UK
Prince George Edmonton God's Lake Wabush St John's → UK
Japan, Hong Kong Vancouver Calgary The Pas Saskatoon Sydney
Seattle Regina Red Lake Rouyn Québec Moncton Halifax → UK
Winnipeg Timmins Montréal
Hawaii, Fiji, Australia, New Zealand Mexico, South America Ottawa → UK → France → Portugal, Spain
Toronto → Portugal, Spain, Italy
Lines represent airline connections and may not show actual routes. Chicago Cleveland New York UK
Scale 1:35 000 000 Mexico, South America Florida Bermuda, Antigua, Barbados, Bahama Islands, Jamaica, Barbados, Trinidad

Prior to the Depression there was little development of airline services. However, with the expansion of gold mining through the 1930s and the exploitation of metallic minerals after the mid-1930s, a north-south pattern in scheduled airline services into remote areas developed. Air freight, especially to north-western Ontario gold fields, drew much traffic but air mail was also an important cargo to isolated settlements and northern resource communities. The late 1930s saw the heyday of Canadian bush flying.

The development of east-west interurban links for passenger service transformed the organization of the airline industry. In the face of increasingly important regional private carriers the federal government created Trans-Canada Airlines (TCA) in April 1937 as the national carrier and through strict regulation after the Second World War thwarted Canadian Pacific's national airline aspirations. Fiercely independent operators were gradually absorbed into larger regional companies, but TCA did not have a rival until 1960 when Canadian Pacific services into Winnipeg, Toronto, and Montréal were licensed. By then the feeder pattern of regional airlines had been rationalized considerably.

PASSENGER MILES AND COMMERCIAL PILOTS

— Commercial pilots
— Passenger miles

Millions of passenger miles
25 20 15 10 5 0
1921 1931 1939

4 000 3 000 2 000 1 000 0 Thousands of pilots
4 3 2 1 0
1921 1931 1941 1951 1961

MOTOR-VEHICLE REGISTRATIONS, 1938, 1951, 1961

Vehicles per thousand persons

More than 300
200–300
100–199.9
Less than 100

Millions of vehicles
2.0 1.5 1.0 0.5 0

1961
1951
1938

PEI NFLD NB NS MAN SASK ALTA BC QUE ONT

EVOLUTION OF THE ROAD NETWORK

St John's
Sept-Îles
Québec $102 832 000
Port aux Basques
Newfoundland $61 796 000
Chibougamau
Chicoutimi
Rivière-du-Loup PEI $10 414 000 Sydney
Charlottetown
Cochrane Moncton Truro
Kirkland Lake Rouyn Québec Fredericton Halifax
Sudbury Sherbrooke Saint John Nova Scotia $27 049 000
Sault Ste Marie North Bay Ottawa Montréal New Brunswick $66 352 000
Toronto Hamilton
London
Windsor

While Ontario had an extensive network of paved roads by the 1930s, it was not until the post-war period that Québec and the Maritimes expanded their systems. The Prairies and British Columbia lagged behind; in the former the need for paved roads on prairie land was not pressing whereas in the latter problems of construction over mountainous terrain were acute.

The considerable interprovincial variation in the registration of automobiles was the result of many interrelated factors, including levels of urbanization, rural population density, economic prosperity, the quality and extent of road networks, and recreational use.

PAVED ROADS

Thousands of kilometres
100 90 80 70 60 50 40 30 20 10
No data
Total length BC Prairie Provinces Ontario Québec Maritimes
1921 1931 1941 1951 1961
Thousands of miles
60 50 40 30 20 10 0

SURFACED ROADS

Thousands of kilometres
500 400 300 200 100
No data
Total length Gravel, crushed stone Paved
1921 1931 1941 1951 1961
Thousands of miles
300 200 100 0

MOTOR-VEHICLE REGISTRATIONS

— Total vehicles
— Passenger cars
---- Commercial vehicles

Millions of vehicles
5 4 3 2 1
1901 1911 1921 1931 1941 1951 1961

INTEGRATION OF THE URBAN SYSTEM
Authors: James W. Simmons, Michael Conzen (railways)

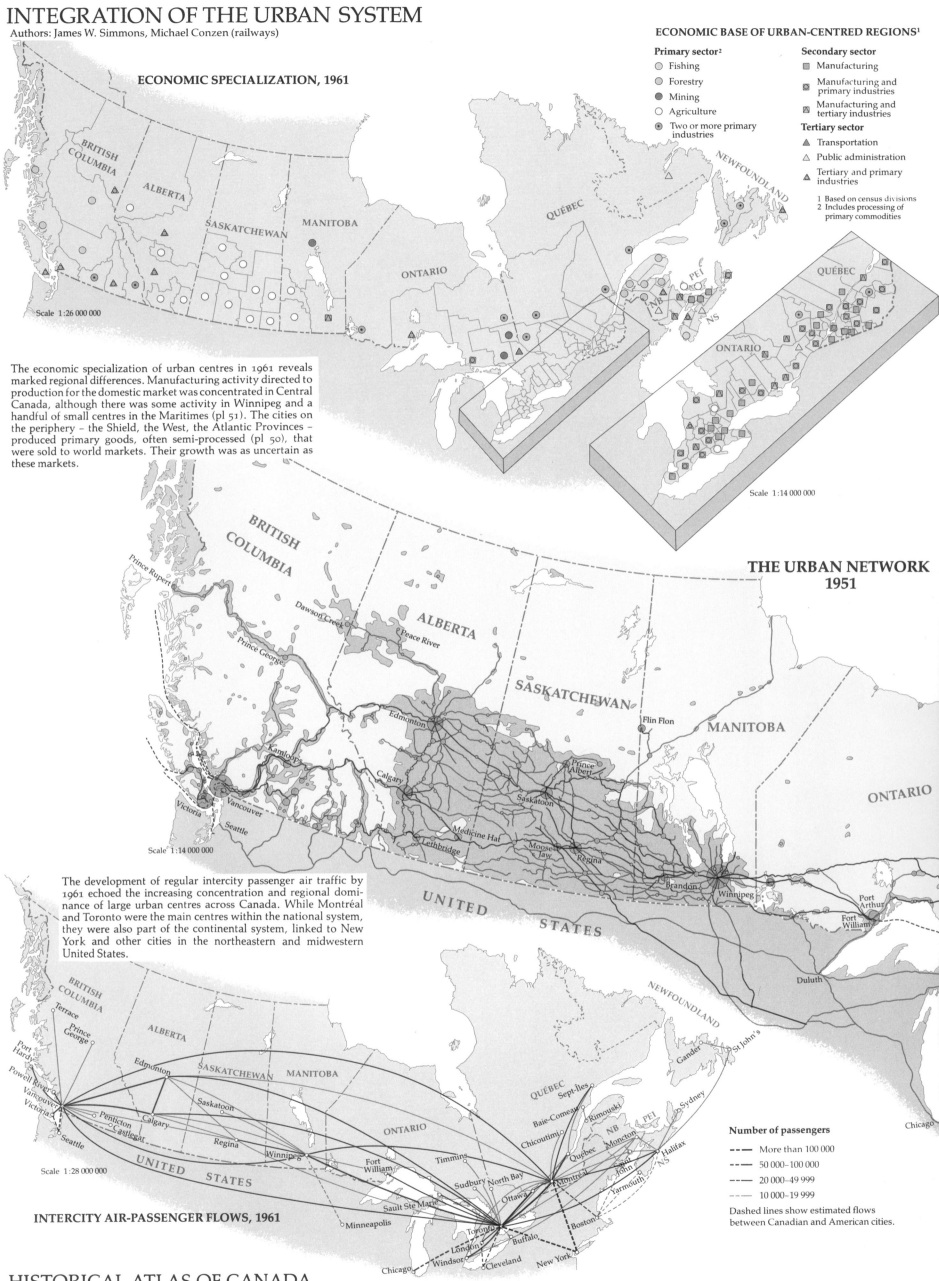

ECONOMIC SPECIALIZATION, 1961

ECONOMIC BASE OF URBAN-CENTRED REGIONS[1]

Primary sector[2]
- ◐ Fishing
- ◑ Forestry
- ● Mining
- ○ Agriculture
- ◉ Two or more primary industries

Secondary sector
- ▣ Manufacturing
- ▨ Manufacturing and primary industries
- ▧ Manufacturing and tertiary industries

Tertiary sector
- ▲ Transportation
- △ Public administration
- ◮ Tertiary and primary industries

1 Based on census divisions
2 Includes processing of primary commodities

Scale 1:26 000 000

Scale 1:14 000 000

The economic specialization of urban centres in 1961 reveals marked regional differences. Manufacturing activity directed to production for the domestic market was concentrated in Central Canada, although there was some activity in Winnipeg and a handful of small centres in the Maritimes (pl 51). The cities on the periphery – the Shield, the West, the Atlantic Provinces – produced primary goods, often semi-processed (pl 50), that were sold to world markets. Their growth was as uncertain as these markets.

THE URBAN NETWORK 1951

Scale 1:14 000 000

The development of regular intercity passenger air traffic by 1961 echoed the increasing concentration and regional dominance of large urban centres across Canada. While Montréal and Toronto were the main centres within the national system, they were also part of the continental system, linked to New York and other cities in the northeastern and midwestern United States.

Scale 1:28 000 000

INTERCITY AIR-PASSENGER FLOWS, 1961

Number of passengers
- –·–· More than 100 000
- – – – 50 000–100 000
- – – – 20 000–49 999
- – – – 10 000–19 999

Dashed lines show estimated flows between Canadian and American cities.

HISTORICAL ATLAS OF CANADA

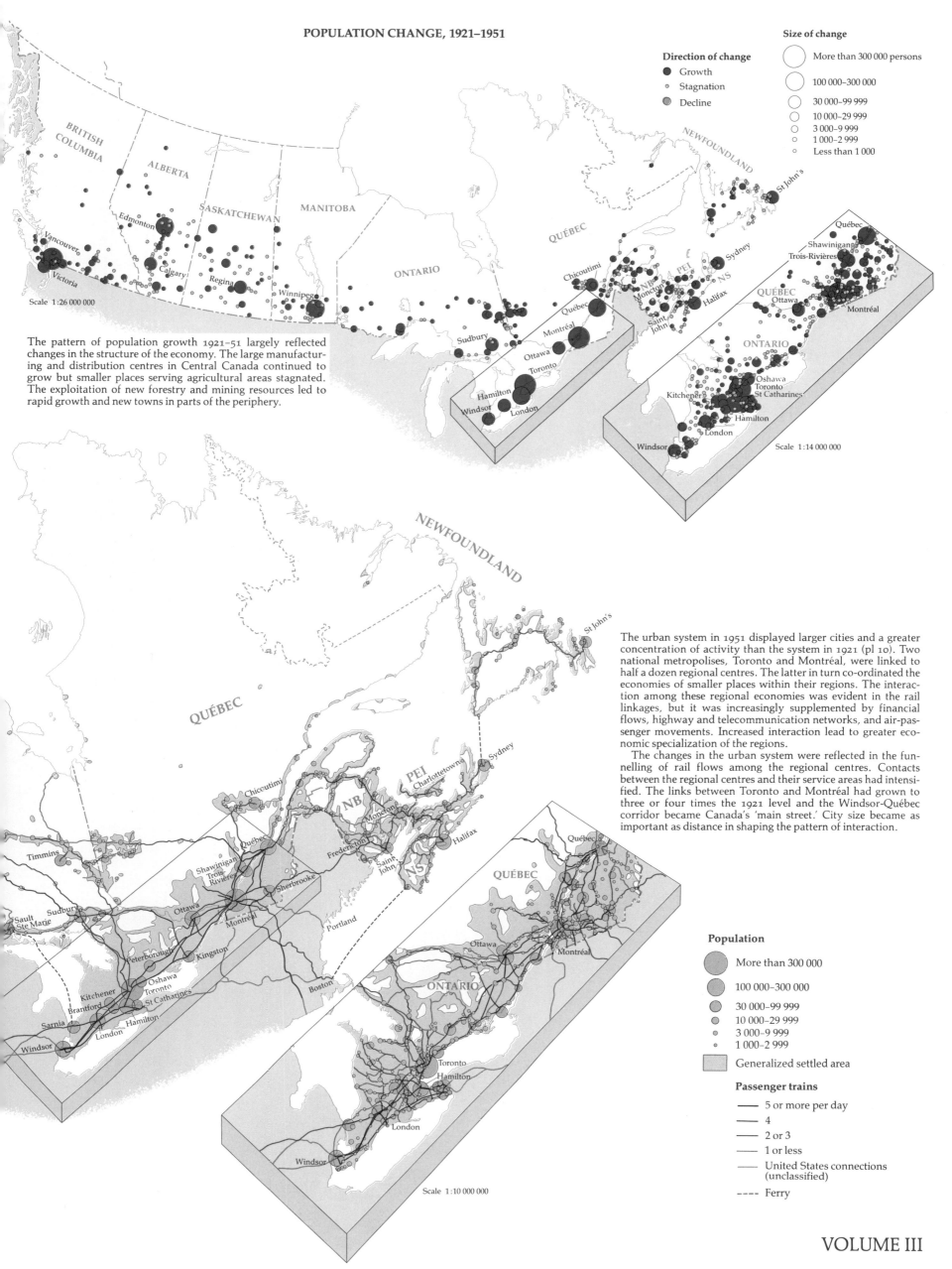

PLATE 54

POPULATION CHANGE, 1921–1951

Direction of change
- ● Growth
- · Stagnation
- ● Decline

Size of change
- ○ More than 300 000 persons
- ○ 100 000–300 000
- ○ 30 000–99 999
- ○ 10 000–29 999
- ○ 3 000–9 999
- ○ 1 000–2 999
- ○ Less than 1 000

The pattern of population growth 1921–51 largely reflected changes in the structure of the economy. The large manufacturing and distribution centres in Central Canada continued to grow but smaller places serving agricultural areas stagnated. The exploitation of new forestry and mining resources led to rapid growth and new towns in parts of the periphery.

Scale 1:26 000 000

Scale 1:14 000 000

The urban system in 1951 displayed larger cities and a greater concentration of activity than the system in 1921 (pl 10). Two national metropolises, Toronto and Montréal, were linked to half a dozen regional centres. The latter in turn co-ordinated the economies of smaller places within their regions. The interaction among these regional economies was evident in the rail linkages, but it was increasingly supplemented by financial flows, highway and telecommunication networks, and air-passenger movements. Increased interaction lead to greater economic specialization of the regions.

The changes in the urban system were reflected in the funnelling of rail flows among the regional centres. Contacts between the regional centres and their service areas had intensified. The links between Toronto and Montréal had grown to three or four times the 1921 level and the Windsor-Québec corridor became Canada's 'main street.' City size became as important as distance in shaping the pattern of interaction.

Population
- ● More than 300 000
- ● 100 000–300 000
- ● 30 000–99 999
- · 10 000–29 999
- · 3 000–9 999
- · 1 000–2 999
- ▭ Generalized settled area

Passenger trains
- ——— 5 or more per day
- ——— 4
- ——— 2 or 3
- ——— 1 or less
- ——— United States connections (unclassified)
- - - - Ferry

Scale 1:10 000 000

METROPOLITAN DOMINANCE

Author: Gunter Gad

The overriding importance of Montréal and Toronto as control centres for a whole range of economic activities persisted in the post-war period, when new developments in transportation (pll 53, 54) and communications (pl 65) reinforced the dominance of the two cities. Although Montréal had the image of Canada's leading centre especially in international circles, both cities shared a wide range of corporate functions. Differences emerged as the century progressed, with Toronto gradually becoming the nation's primary business centre.

While Montréal developed as a strong base for trust companies and maintained a slight lead over Toronto as banking centre, its insurance industry did not match the expansionary momentum of Toronto's. By 1951 insurance companies based in Toronto controlled more assets than those in Montréal, and by 1961 a substantial gap between the two had emerged. Toronto insurance companies grew faster, Toronto added more new companies, and many companies, mostly American ones, moved from Montréal to Toronto.

A wave of mergers in the 1920s and after the Second World War in all sectors of the economy ensured that corporations with increasingly diversified interests and of national scope ran complex operations from Canada's two metropolises. Few head offices of major companies were based in other Canadian cities – wood-products, resource-transportation, and utility-related enterprises being the leading exceptions. The principal offices of legal, accounting, and advertising firms providing business services to major corporations were also concentrated in Montréal and Toronto.

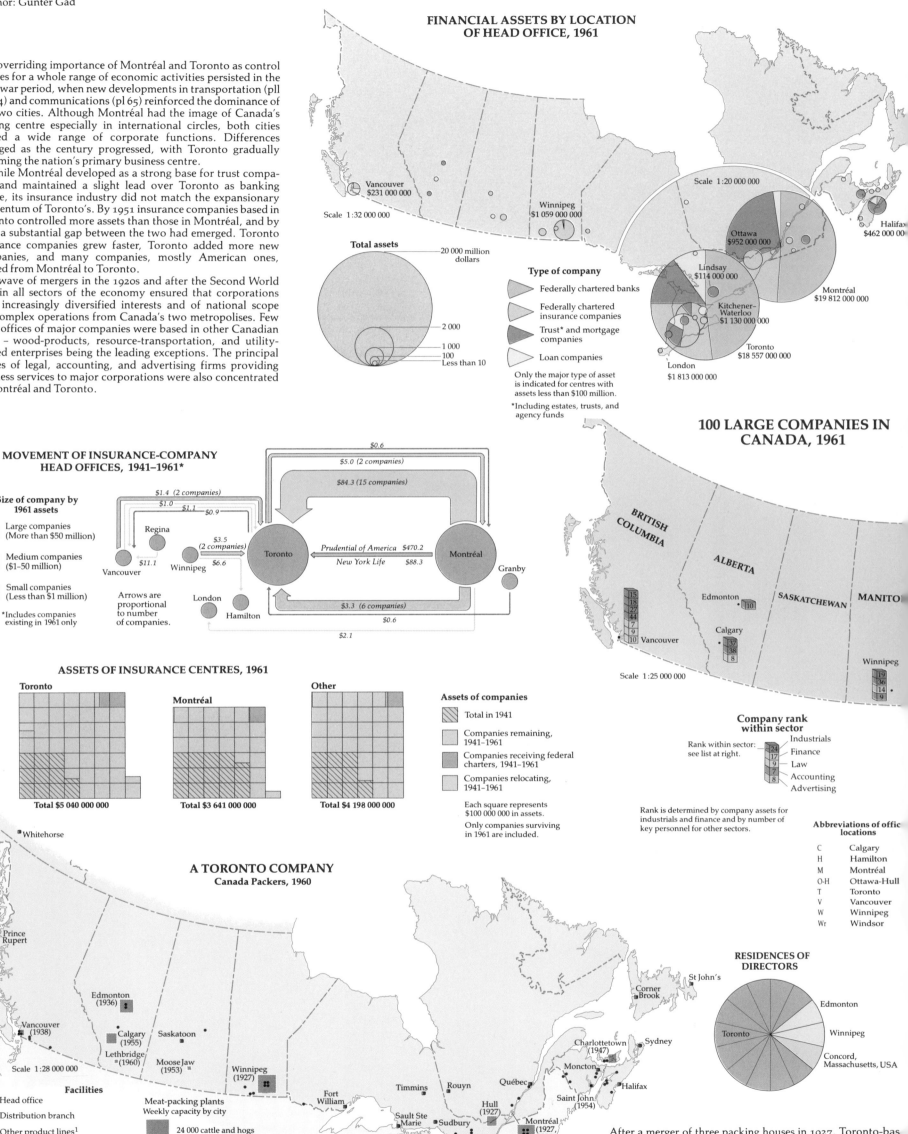

FINANCIAL ASSETS BY LOCATION OF HEAD OFFICE, 1961

Scale 1:20 000 000
Scale 1:32 000 000

Vancouver $231 000 000
Winnipeg $1 059 000 000
Ottawa $952 000 000
Lindsay $114 000 000
Kitchener-Waterloo $1 130 000 000
Toronto $18 557 000 000
London $1 813 000 000
Montréal $19 812 000 000
Halifax $462 000 000

Total assets
20 000 million dollars
2 000
1 000
100
Less than 10

Type of company
Federally chartered banks
Federally chartered insurance companies
Trust* and mortgage companies
Loan companies

Only the major type of asset is indicated for centres with assets less than $100 million.

*Including estates, trusts, and agency funds

MOVEMENT OF INSURANCE-COMPANY HEAD OFFICES, 1941–1961*

Size of company by 1961 assets
Large companies (More than $50 million)
Medium companies ($1–50 million)
Small companies (Less than $1 million)

*Includes companies existing in 1961 only

Arrows are proportional to number of companies.

Vancouver $11.1
Regina
Winnipeg $6.6
$1.4 (2 companies)
$1.0
$1.1
$0.9
$3.5 (2 companies)
Toronto
$0.6
$5.0 (2 companies)
$84.3 (15 companies)
Prudential of America $470.2
New York Life $88.3
Montréal
Granby
London
Hamilton
$3.3 (6 companies)
$0.6
$2.1

ASSETS OF INSURANCE CENTRES, 1961

Toronto — Total $5 040 000 000
Montréal — Total $3 641 000 000
Other — Total $4 198 000 000

Assets of companies
Total in 1941
Companies remaining, 1941–1961
Companies receiving federal charters, 1941–1961
Companies relocating, 1941–1961

Each square represents $100 000 000 in assets.
Only companies surviving in 1961 are included.

100 LARGE COMPANIES IN CANADA, 1961

BRITISH COLUMBIA
ALBERTA
SASKATCHEWAN
MANITOBA

Edmonton 110
Calgary 37 38 8
Vancouver 15 18 27 44 7 9 10
Winnipeg 19 36 14 9

Scale 1:25 000 000

Company rank within sector
Rank within sector: see list at right.
24 Industrials
17 Finance
9 Law
7 Accounting
8 Advertising

Rank is determined by company assets for industrials and finance and by number of key personnel for other sectors.

Abbreviations of office locations
C Calgary
H Hamilton
M Montréal
O-H Ottawa-Hull
T Toronto
V Vancouver
W Winnipeg
Wr Windsor

A TORONTO COMPANY
Canada Packers, 1960

Whitehorse
Prince Rupert
Edmonton (1936)
Vancouver (1938)
Calgary (1955)
Saskatoon
Lethbridge (1960)
Moose Jaw (1953)
Winnipeg (1927)
Fort William
Timmins
Rouyn
Sault Ste Marie
Sudbury
Hull (1927)
Québec
Montréal (1927, 1955)
Corner Brook
St John's
Charlottetown (1947)
Sydney
Moncton
Saint John (1954)
Halifax
Peterborough (1927)
Windsor
Toronto (1927)
New York
Chicago[2] (1927)
Danville[2] (1949)

Scale 1:28 000 000

Facilities
★ Head office
Distribution branch
Other product lines[1]

[1] Largely food-processing, feed, and fertilizer plants, but also includes cold-storage, tanneries, soap, jute-bag, and feather plants

Meat-packing plants
Weekly capacity by city
24 000 cattle and hogs
17 000
10 000
5 000
(1953) Year when plant was acquired or leased
[2] Capacities not available

RESIDENCES OF DIRECTORS

Toronto
Edmonton
Winnipeg
Concord, Massachusetts, USA

After a merger of three packing houses in 1927, Toronto-based Canada Packers became a diversified business with interests in fertilizer production, feed milling, and egg production, as well as meat packing. Most of the company's directors were Toronto residents. By contrast, Montréal-based Aluminium Limited had a larger number of American directors, indicating the American origin of this company. Smelter sites in Québec and BC and fabricating plants in Central Canada were but a portion of the company's world-wide operations in electricity-generation, mining, smelting, and manufacturing.

HISTORICAL ATLAS OF CANADA

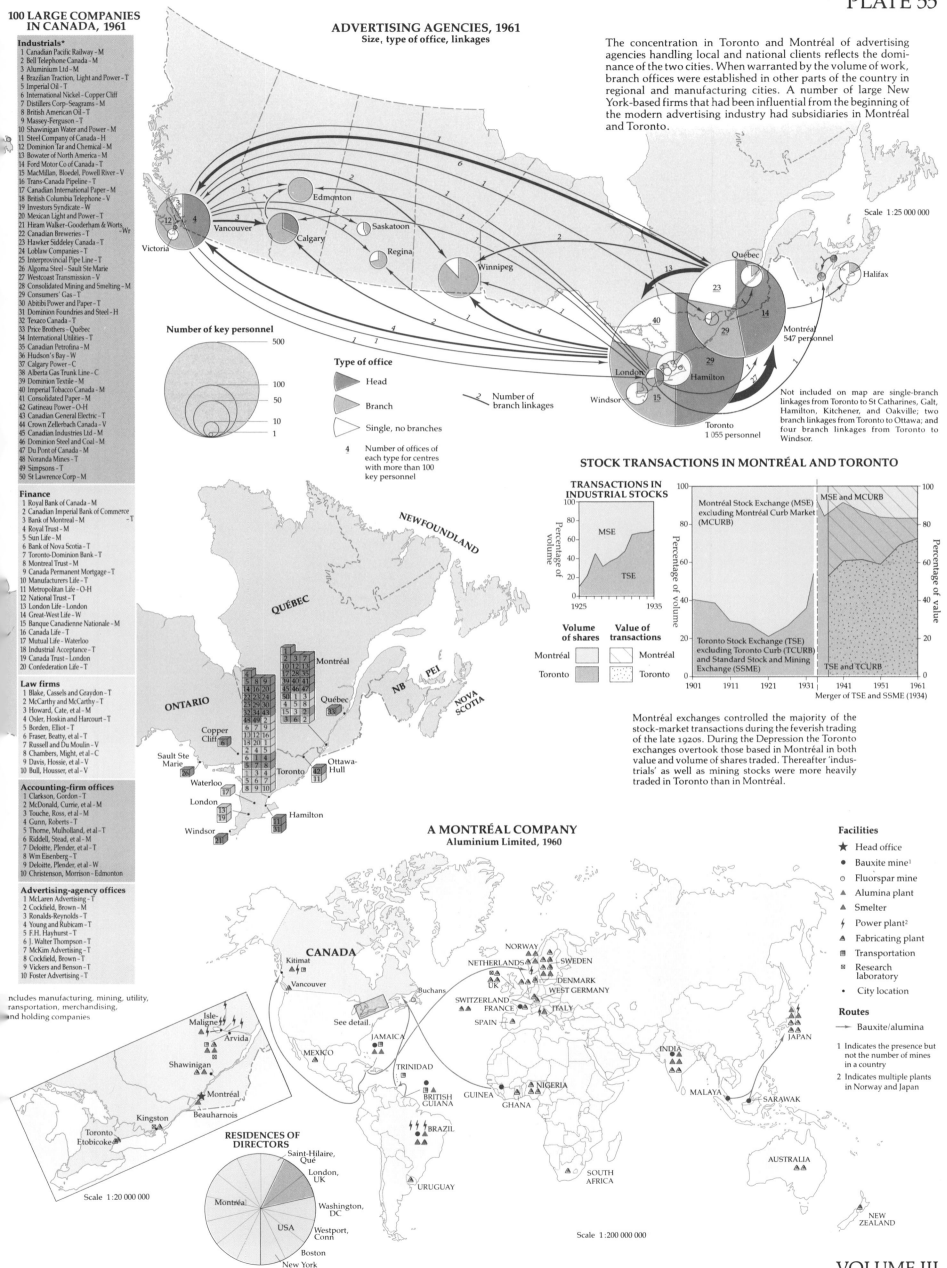

PLATE 55

100 LARGE COMPANIES IN CANADA, 1961

Industrials*
1 Canadian Pacific Railway - M
2 Bell Telephone Canada - M
3 Aluminium Ltd - M
4 Brazilian Traction, Light and Power - T
5 Imperial Oil - T
6 International Nickel - Copper Cliff
7 Distillers Corp-Seagrams - M
8 British American Oil - T
9 Massey-Ferguson - T
10 Shawinigan Water and Power - M
11 Steel Company of Canada - H
12 Dominion Tar and Chemical - M
13 Bowater of North America - M
14 Ford Motor Co of Canada - T
15 MacMillan, Bloedel, Powell River - V
16 Trans-Canada Pipeline - T
17 Canadian International Paper - M
18 British Columbia Telephone - V
19 Investors Syndicate - W
20 Mexican Light and Power - T
21 Hiram Walker-Gooderham & Worts - Wr
22 Canadian Breweries - T
23 Hawker Siddeley Canada - T
24 Loblaw Companies - T
25 Interprovincial Pipe Line - T
26 Algoma Steel - Sault Ste Marie
27 Westcoast Transmission - V
28 Consolidated Mining and Smelting - M
29 Consumers' Gas - T
30 Abitibi Power and Paper - T
31 Dominion Foundries and Steel - H
32 Texaco Canada - T
33 Price Brothers - Québec
34 International Utilities - T
35 Canadian Petrofina - M
36 Hudson's Bay - W
37 Calgary Power - C
38 Alberta Gas Trunk Line - C
39 Dominion Textile - M
40 Imperial Tobacco Canada - M
41 Consolidated Paper - M
42 Gatineau Power - O-H
43 Canadian General Electric - T
44 Crown Zellerbach Canada - V
45 Canadian Industries Ltd - M
46 Dominion Steel and Coal - M
47 Du Pont of Canada - M
48 Noranda Mines - T
49 Simpsons - T
50 St Lawrence Corp - M

Finance
1 Royal Bank of Canada - M
2 Canadian Imperial Bank of Commerce - T
3 Bank of Montreal - M
4 Royal Trust - M
5 Sun Life - M
6 Bank of Nova Scotia - T
7 Toronto-Dominion Bank - T
8 Montreal Trust - M
9 Canada Permanent Mortgage - T
10 Manufacturers Life - T
11 Metropolitan Life - O-H
12 National Trust - T
13 London Life - London
14 Great-West Life - W
15 Banque Canadienne Nationale - M
16 Canada Life - T
17 Mutual Life - Waterloo
18 Industrial Acceptance - M
19 Canada Trust - London
20 Confederation Life - T

Law firms
1 Blake, Cassels and Graydon - T
2 McCarthy and McCarthy - T
3 Howard, Cate, et al - M
4 Osler, Hoskin and Harcourt - T
5 Borden, Elliot - T
6 Fraser, Beatty, et al - T
7 Russell and Du Moulin - V
8 Chambers, Might, et al - C
9 Davis, Hossie, et al - V
10 Bull, Housser, et al - V

Accounting-firm offices
1 Clarkson, Gordon - T
2 McDonald, Currie, et al - M
3 Touche, Ross, et al - M
4 Gunn, Roberts - T
5 Thorne, Mulholland, et al - T
6 Riddell, Stead, et al - M
7 Deloitte, Plender, et al - T
8 Wm Eisenberg - T
9 Deloitte, Plender, et al - W
10 Christenson, Morrison - Edmonton

Advertising-agency offices
1 McLaren Advertising - T
2 Cockfield, Brown - M
3 Ronalds-Reynolds - T
4 Young and Rubicam - T
5 F.H. Hayhurst - T
6 J. Walter Thompson - T
7 McKim Advertising - T
8 Cockfield, Brown - T
9 Vickers and Benson - T
10 Foster Advertising - T

*Includes manufacturing, mining, utility, transportation, merchandising, and holding companies

ADVERTISING AGENCIES, 1961
Size, type of office, linkages

The concentration in Toronto and Montréal of advertising agencies handling local and national clients reflects the dominance of the two cities. When warranted by the volume of work, branch offices were established in other parts of the country in regional and manufacturing cities. A number of large New York-based firms that had been influential from the beginning of the modern advertising industry had subsidiaries in Montréal and Toronto.

Scale 1:25 000 000

Number of key personnel
500
100
50
10
1

Type of office
Head
Branch
Single, no branches

2 Number of branch linkages

4 Number of offices of each type for centres with more than 100 key personnel

Not included on map are single-branch linkages from Toronto to St Catharines, Galt, Hamilton, Kitchener, and Oakville; two branch linkages from Toronto to Ottawa; and four branch linkages from Toronto to Windsor.

STOCK TRANSACTIONS IN MONTRÉAL AND TORONTO

TRANSACTIONS IN INDUSTRIAL STOCKS

MSE
TSE
1925   1935

Volume of shares
Montréal
Toronto

Value of transactions
Montréal
Toronto

Montréal Stock Exchange (MSE) excluding Montréal Curb Market (MCURB)
MSE and MCURB
Toronto Stock Exchange (TSE) excluding Toronto Curb (TCURB) and Standard Stock and Mining Exchange (SSME)
TSE and TCURB
1901 1911 1921 1931 1941 1951 1961
Merger of TSE and SSME (1934)

Montréal exchanges controlled the majority of the stock-market transactions during the feverish trading of the late 1920s. During the Depression the Toronto exchanges overtook those based in Montréal in both value and volume of shares traded. Thereafter 'industrials' as well as mining stocks were more heavily traded in Toronto than in Montréal.

A MONTRÉAL COMPANY
Aluminium Limited, 1960

Facilities
★ Head office
● Bauxite mine[1]
○ Fluorspar mine
▲ Alumina plant
▲ Smelter
⚡ Power plant[2]
▲ Fabricating plant
⊡ Transportation
⊠ Research laboratory
• City location

Routes
→ Bauxite/alumina

1 Indicates the presence but not the number of mines in a country

2 Indicates multiple plants in Norway and Japan

RESIDENCES OF DIRECTORS

Saint-Hilaire, Qué
London, UK
Montréal
Washington, DC
USA
Westport, Conn
Boston
New York

Scale 1:20 000 000

Scale 1:200 000 000

OTTAWA: THE EMERGING CAPITAL
Author: John Taylor

On the eve of the 20th century official Ottawa huddled in its few magnificent 'piles of stone' on Parliament Hill and in the nearby Langevin Block, linked by muddy streets to Government House a few kilometres distant. Some offices were rented. The rest was commercial city: the lumber and hydroelectric capital of the Dominion. But lumber declined and the government grew as it assumed a greater management role in an increasingly complex society. Numbers in the civil service climbed steadily to 1939 and dramatically in the Second World War.

Buildings were constructed to house the new government activities and employees but also, through their location and style, to assert a national presence. Confined by the commercial city, government expanded outward from Parliament Hill mainly along the city's water courses: legislature, executive, and administration were in time linked in a riverine web. The style of the new architecture, which was dominated by a preference for European and mainly British forms, was largely settled in the office of the Chief Dominion Architect, which until the 1930s designed all capital buildings.

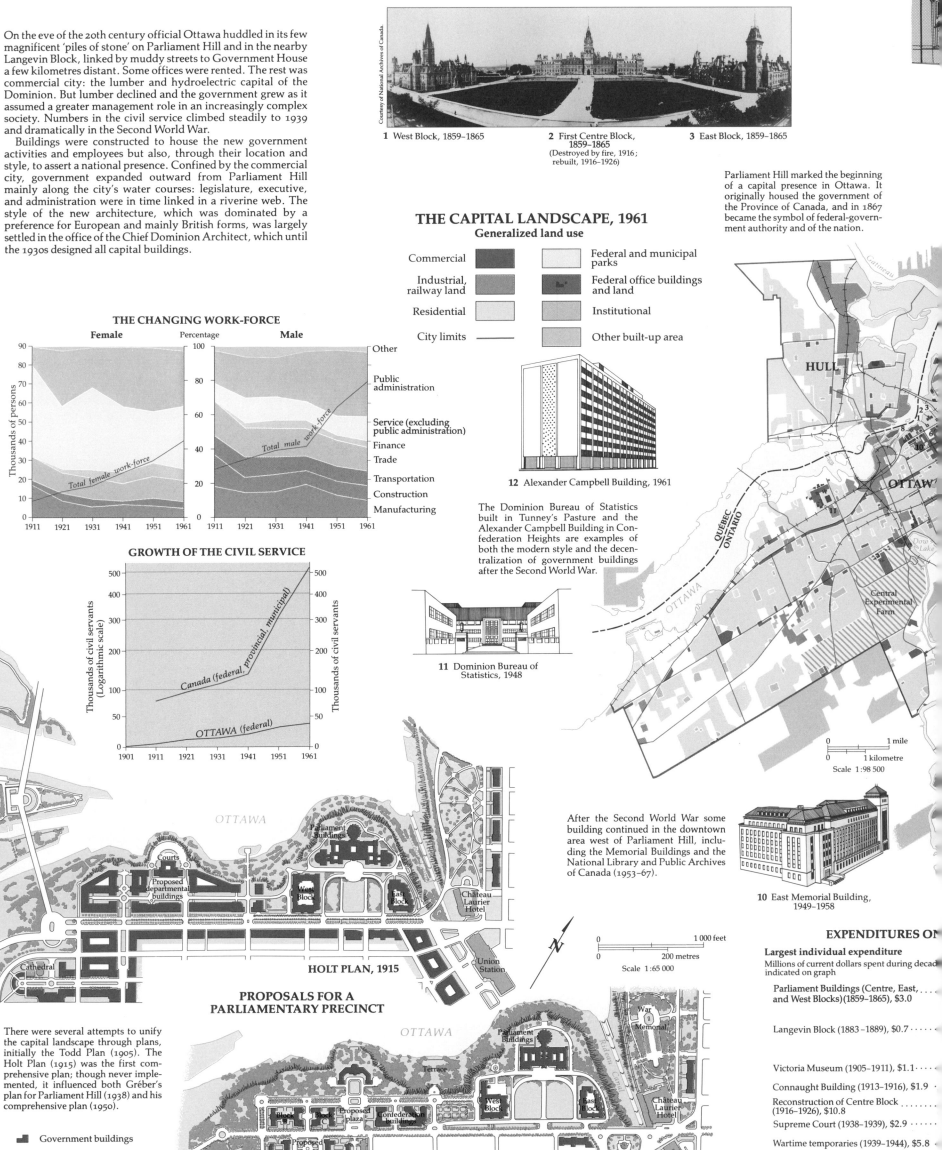

PARLIAMENT HILL

Courtesy of National Archives of Canada.

1 West Block, 1859–1865

2 First Centre Block, 1859–1865
(Destroyed by fire, 1916; rebuilt, 1916–1926)

3 East Block, 1859–1865

Parliament Hill marked the beginning of a capital presence in Ottawa. It originally housed the government of the Province of Canada, and in 1867 became the symbol of federal-government authority and of the nation.

THE CAPITAL LANDSCAPE, 1961
Generalized land use

Commercial

Industrial, railway land

Residential

City limits

Federal and municipal parks

Federal office buildings and land

Institutional

Other built-up area

12 Alexander Campbell Building, 1961

The Dominion Bureau of Statistics built in Tunney's Pasture and the Alexander Campbell Building in Confederation Heights are examples of both the modern style and the decentralization of government buildings after the Second World War.

11 Dominion Bureau of Statistics, 1948

THE CHANGING WORK-FORCE

Female | Percentage | **Male**

Thousands of persons

Total female work-force

Total male work-force

Other

Public administration

Service (excluding public administration)

Finance

Trade

Transportation

Construction

Manufacturing

GROWTH OF THE CIVIL SERVICE

Thousands of civil servants (Logarithmic scale)

Thousands of civil servants

Canada (federal, provincial, municipal)

OTTAWA (federal)

PROPOSALS FOR A PARLIAMENTARY PRECINCT

There were several attempts to unify the capital landscape through plans, initially the Todd Plan (1905). The Holt Plan (1915) was the first comprehensive plan; though never implemented, it influenced both Gréber's plan for Parliament Hill (1938) and his comprehensive plan (1950).

Government buildings

Other buildings

Treed area

HOLT PLAN, 1915

GRÉBER PLAN, 1938

After the Second World War some building continued in the downtown area west of Parliament Hill, including the Memorial Buildings and the National Library and Public Archives of Canada (1953–67).

10 East Memorial Building, 1949–1958

Scale 1:98 500

Scale 1:65 000

EXPENDITURES ON

Largest individual expenditure

Millions of current dollars spent during decade indicated on graph

Parliament Buildings (Centre, East, and West Blocks)(1859–1865), $3.0

Langevin Block (1883–1889), $0.7

Victoria Museum (1905–1911), $1.1

Connaught Building (1913–1916), $1.9

Reconstruction of Centre Block (1916–1926), $10.8

Supreme Court (1938–1939), $2.9

Wartime temporaries (1939–1944), $5.8

Tunney's Pasture (1948–1954), $18.7

Confederation Heights (1956–1965), $21.8

4 Government House
(Rideau Hall)

5 Prime Minister's Residence
(24 Sussex Drive)

Both Government House and the Prime Minister's Residence were originally private houses, later purchased by the government. The former, built in 1838, became the residence of the governor-general in 1864 and was purchased in 1868. The latter, built in 1867–8, was expropriated in 1943 and became the residence of the prime minister in 1949 after it was reconstructed.

Although the government had rented accommodation off Parliament Hill, the Langevin Block was the first government building to penetrate the vernacular city.

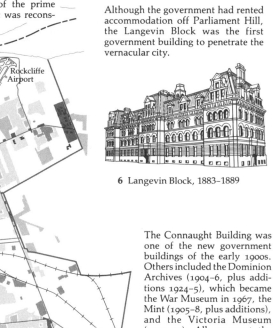

6 Langevin Block, 1883–1889

The Connaught Building was one of the new government buildings of the early 1900s. Others included the Dominion Archives (1904–6, plus additions 1924–5), which became the War Museum in 1967, the Mint (1905–8, plus additions), and the Victoria Museum (1905–11). All represent the major influence of the Chief Dominion Architect, David Ewart (1897–1914).

7 Connaught Building, 1913–1916

The Supreme Court Building marked the end both of a building boom and of in-house design. It was preceded in the 1920s and 1930s by the Confederation Building (1927–31) and the Justice Building (1934) to the west of Parliament Hill, and the National Research Council (1930–2) to the east. The Supreme Court Building was also the first major capital edifice designed in the private sector.

8 Supreme Court of Canada, 1938–1939

Throughout the 20th century government building booms followed an increase in personnel by a decade or more; temporary accommodation was thus always required, though it was generally rented. During the Second World War the dramatic growth in the civil service necessitated the construction of temporary buildings.

9 Wartime temporary buildings
(Many locations, not shown on map)

GOVERNMENT BUILDINGS, OTTAWA

Total expenditure

Current dollars

1913 constant dollars

Major capital funds were obtained first in 1927 to purchase land for the War Memorial and Confederation Park. Comprehensive planning and funding were firmly linked only when the Gréber Plan (1950) was implemented.

- 1860–1869
- 1870–1879
- 1880–1889
- 1890–1899
- 1900–1909
- 1910–1919
- 1920–1929
- 1930–1939
- 1940–1949
- 1950–1959
- 1960–1967

0 10 20 30 40 50 60 70 80 90 100
Millions of dollars

IMPROVING THE CAPITAL REGION

Changing jurisdictions

Ottawa Improvement Commission, 1899

Federal District Commission, 1927

Federal District Commission, 1945

National Capital Commission, 1958

Gatineau Park, 1961

Green Belt, 1961

City limits, 1961

QUÉBEC

ONTARIO

HULL

OTTAWA

0   10 miles
0   10 kilometres
Scale 1:715 000

A capital presence in Ottawa began to be expressed through the planning and design of the landscape. The original agency for capital design was the Ottawa Improvement Commission (OIC, 1899). It developed parks, largely piecemeal along the Rideau Canal and the Ottawa River. In 1927 the OIC was transformed into the more invasive and powerful Federal District Commission (FDC), especially to create a war memorial and park adjacent to Parliament Hill. A conscious penetration of capital functions into the commercial core of the city was thus begun. The FDC also extended its activities outside Ottawa proper. In the 1930s it acquired land in Québec that would become Gatineau Park. Guided by the proposals of French planner Jacques Gréber, the FDC made changes to the post-war national capital region including the purchase of the green belt ringing the city and the decentralization of government offices into clusters of modern buildings on the periphery of the city, notably Tunney's Pasture, Dow's Lake, and Confederation Heights. The FDC's initiatives were assumed in 1958 by its successor, the National Capital Commisssion. By 1960 Ottawa – with major parts of its commercial heritage purchased by the federal authority and either destroyed or preserved for national purposes – had been transformed into a capital city.

CITY CENTRE TO NATIONAL CENTRE

The major funding of 1927 led to the first significant reshaping of the commercial city for capital purposes. On the west bank of the canal shipping and warehousing operations were removed. Along Elgin Street the city's post office, a hotel, City Hall Square, and other properties were appropriated by the federal authorities.

Generalized land use

Government

Industrial, railway land

Commercial

Institutional

Residential

Park

Vacant

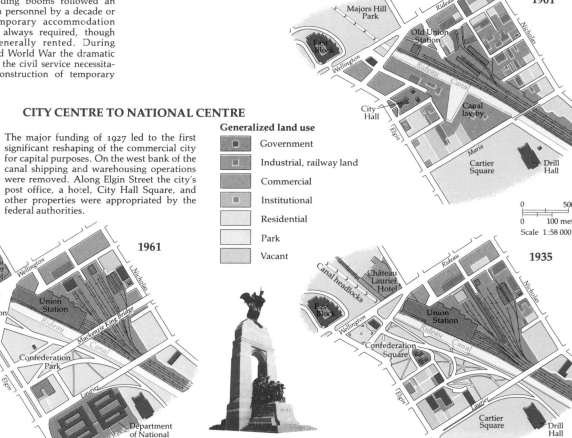

1901

1961

1935

0   500 feet
0   100 metres
Scale 1:58 000

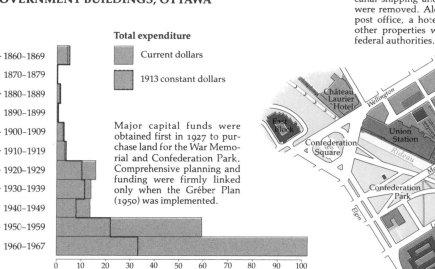

War Memorial, 1939
Confederation Square
Photo by J. Roaf, from H. Kalman and J. Roaf, *Exploring Ottawa*

PLATE 56

Authors: Norman Hillmer, Murdo MacPherson (missionaries), Neil Quigley (finance)

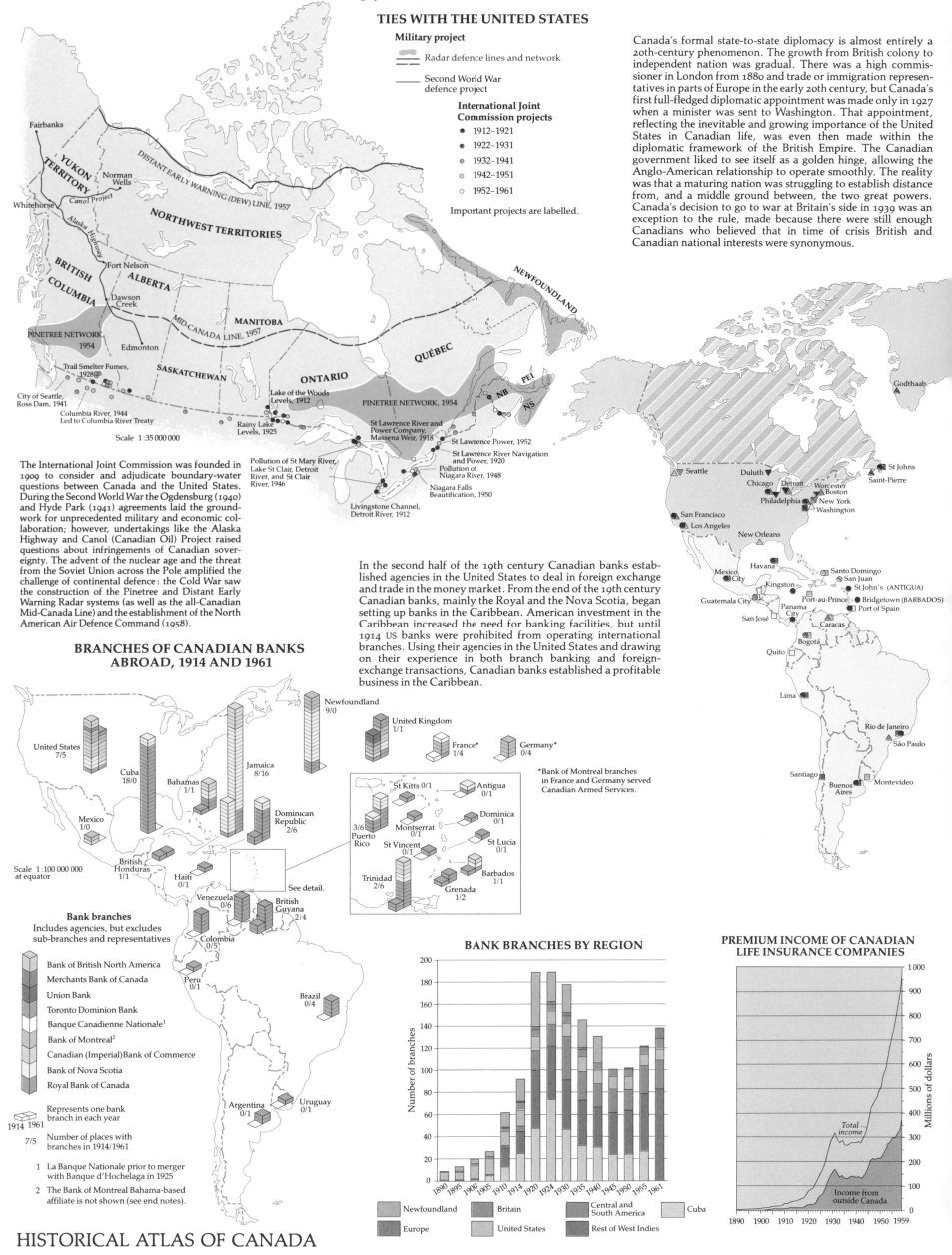

TIES WITH THE UNITED STATES

Military project

Radar defence lines and network

Second World War
defence project

**International Joint
Commission projects**
- 1912–1921
- 1922–1931
- 1932–1941
- 1942–1951
- 1952–1961

Important projects are labelled.

Canada's formal state-to-state diplomacy is almost entirely a 20th-century phenomenon. The growth from British colony to independent nation was gradual. There was a high commissioner in London from 1880 and trade or immigration representatives in parts of Europe in the early 20th century, but Canada's first full-fledged diplomatic appointment was made only in 1927 when a minister was sent to Washington. That appointment, reflecting the inevitable and growing importance of the United States in Canadian life, was even then made within the diplomatic framework of the British Empire. The Canadian government liked to see itself as a golden hinge, allowing the Anglo-American relationship to operate smoothly. The reality was that a maturing nation was struggling to establish distance from, and a middle ground between, the two great powers. Canada's decision to go to war at Britain's side in 1939 was an exception to the rule, made because there were still enough Canadians who believed that in time of crisis British and Canadian national interests were synonymous.

The International Joint Commission was founded in 1909 to consider and adjudicate boundary-water questions between Canada and the United States. During the Second World War the Ogdensburg (1940) and Hyde Park (1941) agreements laid the groundwork for unprecedented military and economic collaboration; however, undertakings like the Alaska Highway and Canol (Canadian Oil) Project raised questions about infringements of Canadian sovereignty. The advent of the nuclear age and the threat from the Soviet Union across the Pole amplified the challenge of continental defence: the Cold War saw the construction of the Pinetree and Distant Early Warning Radar systems (as well as the all-Canadian Mid-Canada Line) and the establishment of the North American Air Defence Command (1958).

In the second half of the 19th century Canadian banks established agencies in the United States to deal in foreign exchange and trade in the money market. From the end of the 19th century Canadian banks, mainly the Royal and the Nova Scotia, began setting up banks in the Caribbean. American investment in the Caribbean increased the need for banking facilities, but until 1914 US banks were prohibited from operating international branches. Using their agencies in the United States and drawing on their experience in both branch banking and foreign-exchange transactions, Canadian banks established a profitable business in the Caribbean.

BRANCHES OF CANADIAN BANKS ABROAD, 1914 AND 1961

Scale 1:100 000 000 at equator

Bank branches
Includes agencies, but excludes sub-branches and representatives

- Bank of British North America
- Merchants Bank of Canada
- Union Bank
- Toronto Dominion Bank
- Banque Canadienne Nationale[1]
- Bank of Montreal[2]
- Canadian (Imperial) Bank of Commerce
- Bank of Nova Scotia
- Royal Bank of Canada

Represents one bank branch in each year
1914 1961

7/5 Number of places with branches in 1914/1961

1 La Banque Nationale prior to merger with Banque d'Hochelaga in 1925

2 The Bank of Montreal Bahama-based affiliate is not shown (see end notes).

*Bank of Montreal branches in France and Germany served Canadian Armed Services.

BANK BRANCHES BY REGION

Number of branches

(years) 1890 1895 1900 1905 1910 1914 1920 1924 1930 1935 1940 1945 1950 1955 1961

- Newfoundland
- Europe
- Britain
- United States
- Central and South America
- Rest of West Indies
- Cuba

PREMIUM INCOME OF CANADIAN LIFE INSURANCE COMPANIES

Millions of dollars

Total income

Income from outside Canada

1890 1900 1910 1920 1930 1940 1950 1959

PLATE 57

OTTAWA'S REPRESENTATION ABROAD

Period of first establishment

Pre-1940
1940–1945
1946–1950
1951–1955
1956–1961

Establishment closed by 1961

Independent Commonwealth countries, 1961

Other dependent parts of the Commonwealth, 1961

North Atlantic Treaty Organization countries

* Participation in United Nations operations

Boundaries ca 1961

Type of establishment

□ Diplomatic post (embassy, high commission, legation, mission, or delegation)
△ Consulate
○ Trade commission
▽ Immigration office (where not part of consulate or diplomatic post)
⊡ Diplomatic post upgraded from trade commission
⊿ Consulate upgraded from trade commisssion
Embassy upgraded from consulate

TOTAL POSTS ABROAD

The Second World War changed Canada and Canadian diplomacy. The post-war Department of External Affairs had a firm commitment to international order and stability; the strong anti-Communist stance of its diplomats, deeply influenced by the Cold War, was reflected in their determination not to allow Communism the free rein that Hitler's Nazism had had in the 1930s. They gloried in their role as 'middlepowermen,' believing themselves to be representatives of a country that had emerged from the war with new prestige, power, and influence. Canada was a founding member of the United Nations (1945) and a strong supporter of the organization's programs and peacekeeping efforts, including the 'police action' in Korea. Ottawa was also a driving force in the creation of the North Atlantic Treaty Organization (NATO) in 1949 and the transformation of the British Empire into a multiracial commonwealth of independent nations.

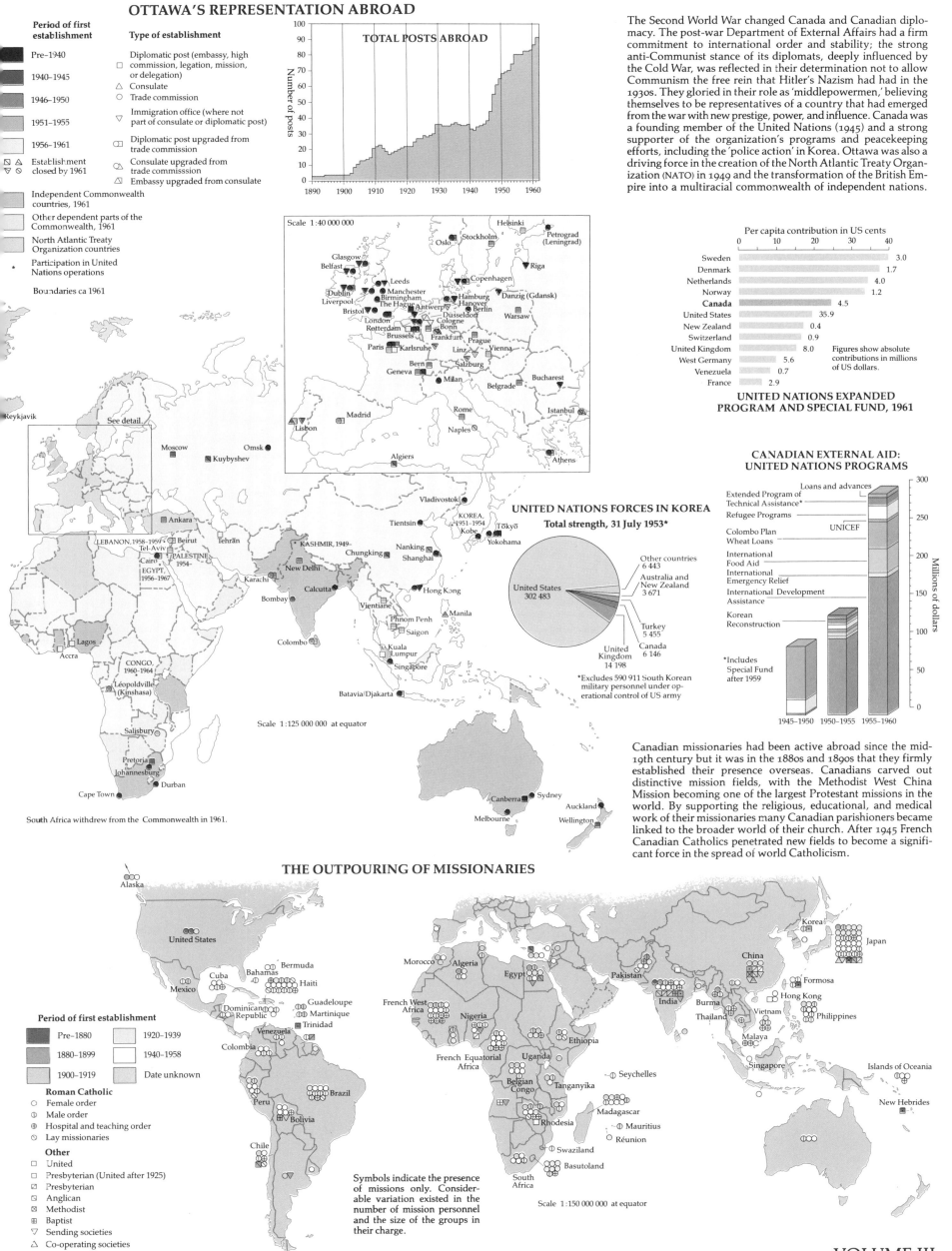

Scale 1:40 000 000

Scale 1:125 000 000 at equator

Per capita contribution in US cents

Sweden 3.0
Denmark 1.7
Netherlands 4.0
Norway 1.2
Canada 4.5
United States 35.9
New Zealand 0.4
Switzerland 0.9
United Kingdom 8.0
West Germany 5.6
Venezuela 0.7
France 2.9

Figures show absolute contributions in millions of US dollars.

UNITED NATIONS EXPANDED PROGRAM AND SPECIAL FUND, 1961

UNITED NATIONS FORCES IN KOREA
Total strength, 31 July 1953*

United States 302 483
Other countries 6 443
Australia and New Zealand 3 671
Turkey 5 455
Canada 6 146
United Kingdom 14 198

*Excludes 590 911 South Korean military personnel under operational control of US army

CANADIAN EXTERNAL AID: UNITED NATIONS PROGRAMS

Loans and advances
Extended Program of Technical Assistance*
Refugee Programs
UNICEF
Colombo Plan Wheat Loans
International Food Aid
International Emergency Relief
International Development Assistance
Korean Reconstruction

*Includes Special Fund after 1959

1945–1950 1950–1955 1955–1960

South Africa withdrew from the Commonwealth in 1961.

Canadian missionaries had been active abroad since the mid-19th century but it was in the 1880s and 1890s that they firmly established their presence overseas. Canadians carved out distinctive mission fields, with the Methodist West China Mission becoming one of the largest Protestant missions in the world. By supporting the religious, educational, and medical work of their missionaries many Canadian parishioners became linked to the broader world of their church. After 1945 French Canadian Catholics penetrated new fields to become a significant force in the spread of world Catholicism.

THE OUTPOURING OF MISSIONARIES

Period of first establishment
Pre–1880
1880–1899
1900–1919
1920–1939
1940–1958
Date unknown

Roman Catholic
○ Female order
◑ Male order
⊕ Hospital and teaching order
⊘ Lay missionaries

Other
□ United
◫ Presbyterian (United after 1925)
◨ Presbyterian
◩ Anglican
⊠ Methodist
⊕ Baptist
▽ Sending societies
△ Co-operating societies

Symbols indicate the presence of missions only. Considerable variation existed in the number of mission personnel and the size of the groups in their charge.

Scale 1:150 000 000 at equator

SOCIETIES AND ECONOMIES IN THE NORTH
Author: Peter J. Usher

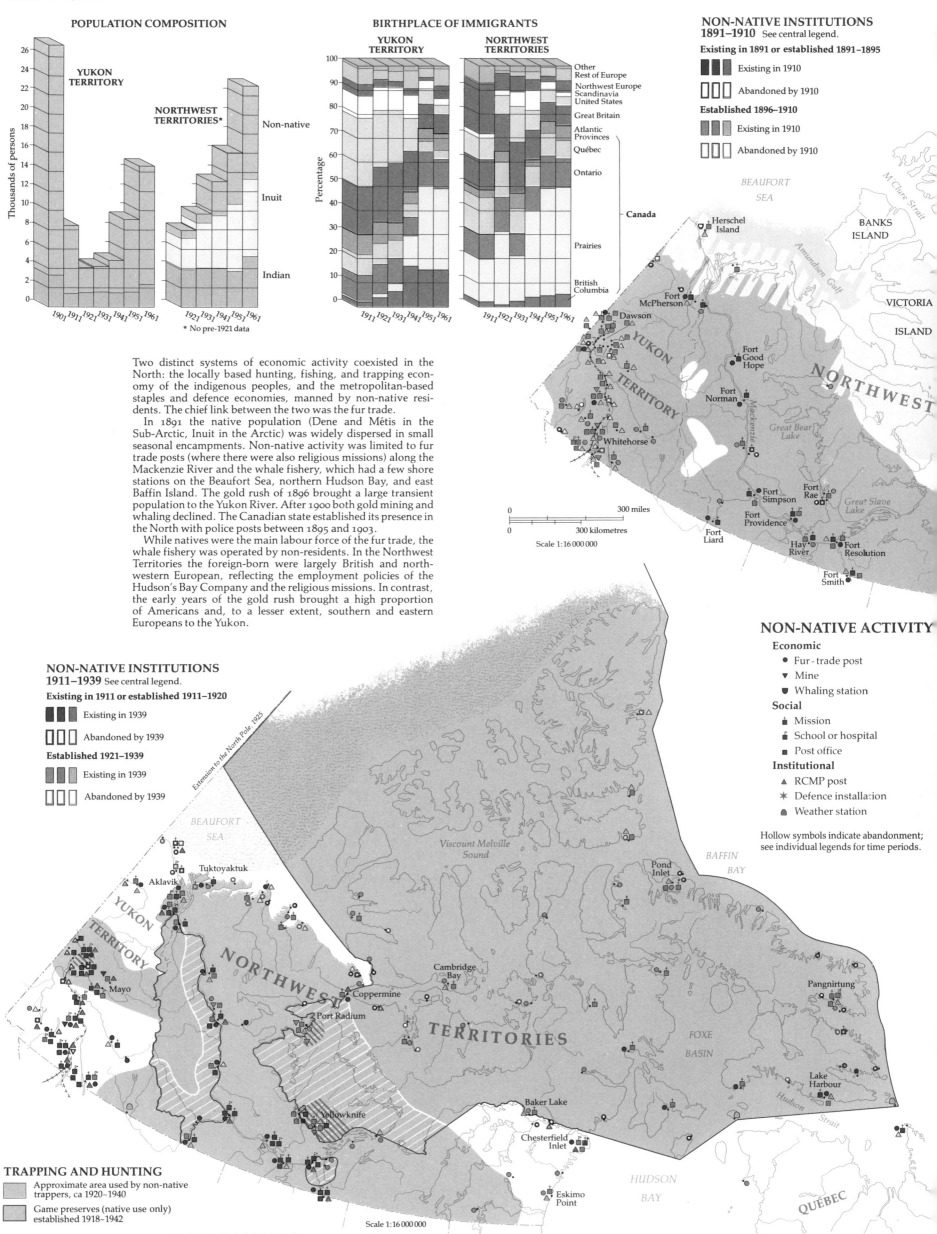

POPULATION COMPOSITION

YUKON TERRITORY

NORTHWEST TERRITORIES*

Non-native

Inuit

Indian

Thousands of persons

1901 1911 1921 1931 1941 1951 1961

1921 1931 1941 1951 1961

* No pre-1921 data

BIRTHPLACE OF IMMIGRANTS

YUKON TERRITORY

NORTHWEST TERRITORIES

Percentage

Other
Rest of Europe
Northwest Europe
Scandinavia
United States
Great Britain
Atlantic Provinces
Québec
Ontario
Prairies
British Columbia

Canada

1911 1921 1931 1941 1951 1961

1911 1921 1931 1941 1951 1961

NON-NATIVE INSTITUTIONS
1891–1910 See central legend.
Existing in 1891 or established 1891–1895

Existing in 1910

Abandoned by 1910

Established 1896–1910

Existing in 1910

Abandoned by 1910

Two distinct systems of economic activity coexisted in the North: the locally based hunting, fishing, and trapping economy of the indigenous peoples, and the metropolitan-based staples and defence economies, manned by non-native residents. The chief link between the two was the fur trade.

In 1891 the native population (Dene and Métis in the Sub-Arctic, Inuit in the Arctic) was widely dispersed in small seasonal encampments. Non-native activity was limited to fur trade posts (where there were also religious missions) along the Mackenzie River and the whale fishery, which had a few shore stations on the Beaufort Sea, northern Hudson Bay, and east Baffin Island. The gold rush of 1896 brought a large transient population to the Yukon River. After 1900 both gold mining and whaling declined. The Canadian state established its presence in the North with police posts between 1895 and 1903.

While natives were the main labour force of the fur trade, the whale fishery was operated by non-residents. In the Northwest Territories the foreign-born were largely British and northwestern European, reflecting the employment policies of the Hudson's Bay Company and the religious missions. In contrast, the early years of the gold rush brought a high proportion of Americans and, to a lesser extent, southern and eastern Europeans to the Yukon.

0   300 miles

0   300 kilometres

Scale 1:16 000 000

NON-NATIVE INSTITUTIONS
1911–1939 See central legend.
Existing in 1911 or established 1911–1920

Existing in 1939

Abandoned by 1939

Established 1921–1939

Existing in 1939

Abandoned by 1939

NON-NATIVE ACTIVITY
Economic
● Fur-trade post
▼ Mine
⬤ Whaling station
Social
🮲 Mission
🮳 School or hospital
■ Post office
Institutional
▲ RCMP post
✳ Defence installation
⬠ Weather station

Hollow symbols indicate abandonment; see individual legends for time periods.

TRAPPING AND HUNTING
Approximate area used by non-native trappers, ca 1920–1940

Game preserves (native use only) established 1918–1942

Scale 1:16 000 000

HISTORICAL ATLAS OF CANADA

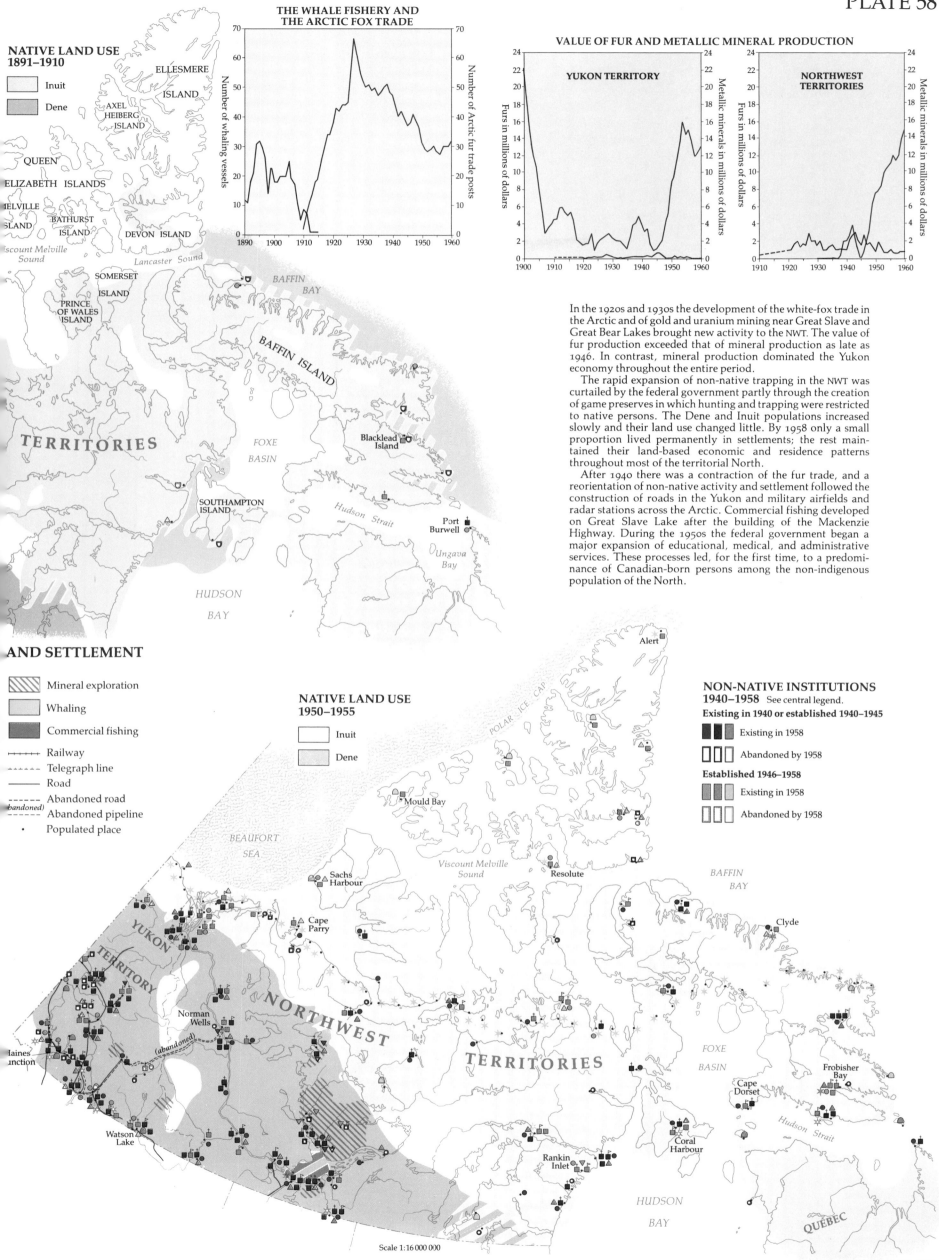

PLATE 58

THE WHALE FISHERY AND THE ARCTIC FOX TRADE

VALUE OF FUR AND METALLIC MINERAL PRODUCTION

NATIVE LAND USE 1891–1910

Inuit

Dene

AND SETTLEMENT

Mineral exploration

Whaling

Commercial fishing

Railway

Telegraph line

Road

Abandoned road

Abandoned pipeline

Populated place

NATIVE LAND USE 1950–1955

Inuit

Dene

NON-NATIVE INSTITUTIONS
1940–1958 See central legend.

Existing in 1940 or established 1940–1945

Existing in 1958

Abandoned by 1958

Established 1946–1958

Existing in 1958

Abandoned by 1958

In the 1920s and 1930s the development of the white-fox trade in the Arctic and of gold and uranium mining near Great Slave and Great Bear Lakes brought new activity to the NWT. The value of fur production exceeded that of mineral production as late as 1946. In contrast, mineral production dominated the Yukon economy throughout the entire period.

The rapid expansion of non-native trapping in the NWT was curtailed by the federal government partly through the creation of game preserves in which hunting and trapping were restricted to native persons. The Dene and Inuit populations increased slowly and their land use changed little. By 1958 only a small proportion lived permanently in settlements; the rest maintained their land-based economic and residence patterns throughout most of the territorial North.

After 1940 there was a contraction of the fur trade, and a reorientation of non-native activity and settlement followed the construction of roads in the Yukon and military airfields and radar stations across the Arctic. Commercial fishing developed on Great Slave Lake after the building of the Mackenzie Highway. During the 1950s the federal government began a major expansion of educational, medical, and administrative services. These processes led, for the first time, to a predominance of Canadian-born persons among the non-indigenous population of the North.

Scale 1:16 000 000

POPULATION CHANGES

Authors: Marvin McInnis, Warren Kalbach, Donald Kerr

From 1946 to 1961 Canada's population grew remarkably from 12 to 18 million. The union of Newfoundland with Canada added 360 000 people, but the main reason for rapid growth was that a great upswing in immigration coincided with a dramatic rise in the birth rate. The 'baby boom' was unexpected and involved a significant and sustained increase in the average size of family. It was an experience shared with the United States and a few other countries although the rise in fertility was greatest in Canada. By the end of the 1950s the birth rate had reached its peak. Immigration surged after the Second World War (pl 27) as Canada accepted many people from Europe displaced by the war and its immediate aftermath. The prosperity of the Canadian economy also attracted large numbers from a Europe still struggling to recover from the war. The immigrants came at a time when the natural growth of Canada's labour force, reflecting the low birth rate of the 1930s, was unusually small. Rapidly growing urban Ontario was the favoured destination of immigrants. By 1961 the great wave of immigration had passed and the inflow had dropped to a modest level.

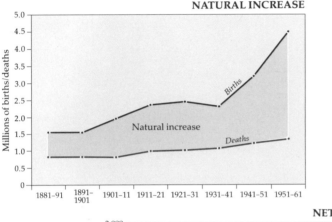

NATURAL INCREASE

y-axis: Millions of births/deaths (0 to 5.0)
x-axis: 1881–91, 1891–1901, 1901–11, 1911–21, 1921–31, 1931–41, 1941–51, 1951–61

Labels: Births, Natural increase, Deaths

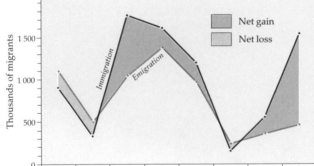

NET MIGRATION

y-axis: Thousands of migrants (0 to 2 000)
x-axis: 1881–91, 1891–1901, 1901–11, 1911–21, 1921–31, 1931–41, 1941–51, 1951–61

Legend:
- Net gain
- Net loss

Labels: Immigration, Emigration

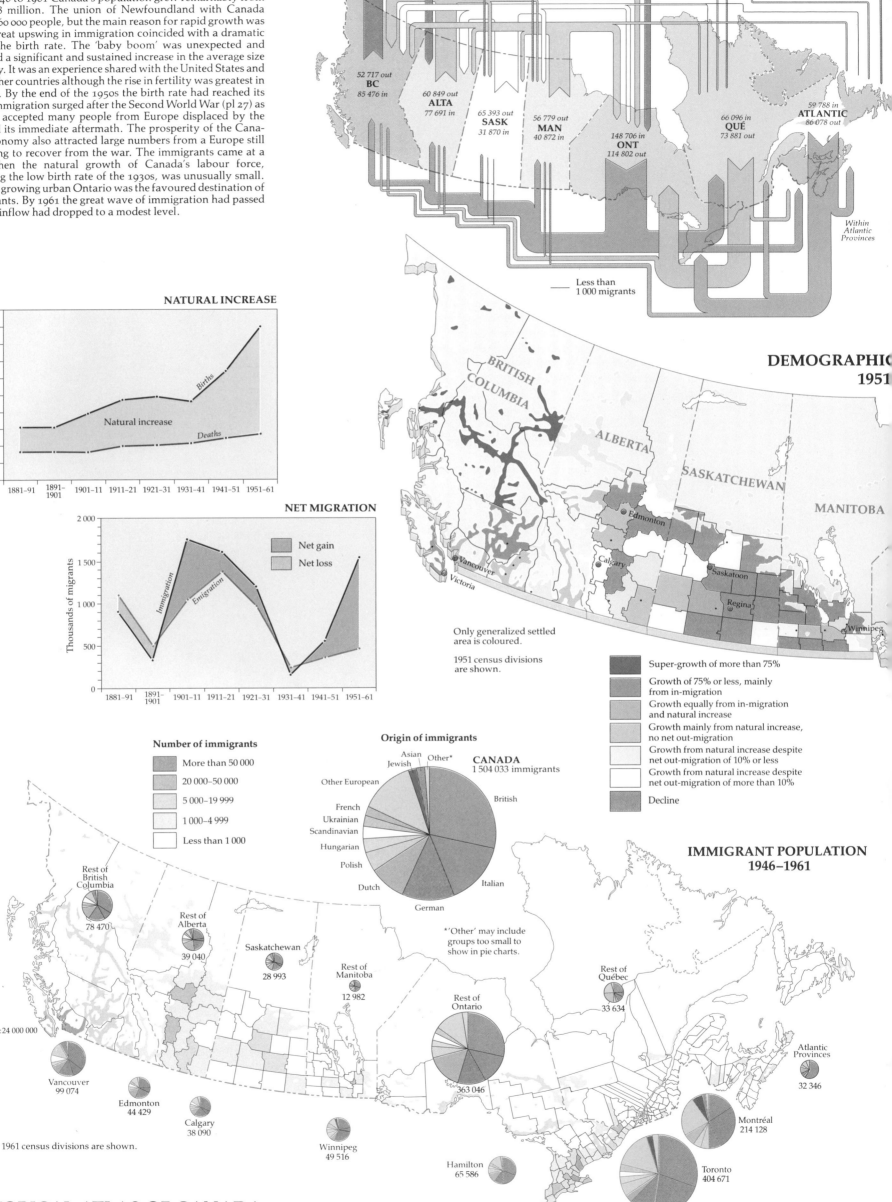

INTERPROVINCIAL MIGRATION 1956–1961

- BC: 52 717 out, 85 476 in
- ALTA: 60 849 out, 77 691 in
- SASK: 65 393 out, 31 870 in
- MAN: 56 779 out, 40 872 in
- ONT: 148 706 in, 114 802 out
- QUÉ: 66 096 in, 73 881 out
- ATLANTIC: 59 788 in, 86 078 out
- Within Atlantic Provinces

—— Less than 1 000 migrants

DEMOGRAPHIC 1951

BRITISH COLUMBIA, ALBERTA, SASKATCHEWAN, MANITOBA

Vancouver, Victoria, Edmonton, Calgary, Saskatoon, Regina, Winnipeg

Only generalized settled area is coloured.

1951 census divisions are shown.

Legend:
- Super-growth of more than 75%
- Growth of 75% or less, mainly from in-migration
- Growth equally from in-migration and natural increase
- Growth mainly from natural increase, no net out-migration
- Growth from natural increase despite net out-migration of 10% or less
- Growth from natural increase despite net out-migration of more than 10%
- Decline

Number of immigrants
- More than 50 000
- 20 000–50 000
- 5 000–19 999
- 1 000–4 999
- Less than 1 000

Origin of immigrants

CANADA 1 504 033 immigrants

Asian, Other*, Jewish, Other European, French, Ukrainian, Scandinavian, Hungarian, Polish, Dutch, German, Italian, British

*'Other' may include groups too small to show in pie charts.

IMMIGRANT POPULATION 1946–1961

- Rest of British Columbia 78 470
- Rest of Alberta 39 040
- Saskatchewan 28 993
- Rest of Manitoba 12 982
- Rest of Québec 33 634
- Rest of Ontario 363 046
- Atlantic Provinces 32 346
- Vancouver 99 074
- Edmonton 44 429
- Calgary 38 090
- Winnipeg 49 516
- Hamilton 65 586
- Montréal 214 128
- Toronto 404 671

Scale 1:24 000 000

1961 census divisions are shown.

HISTORICAL ATLAS OF CANADA

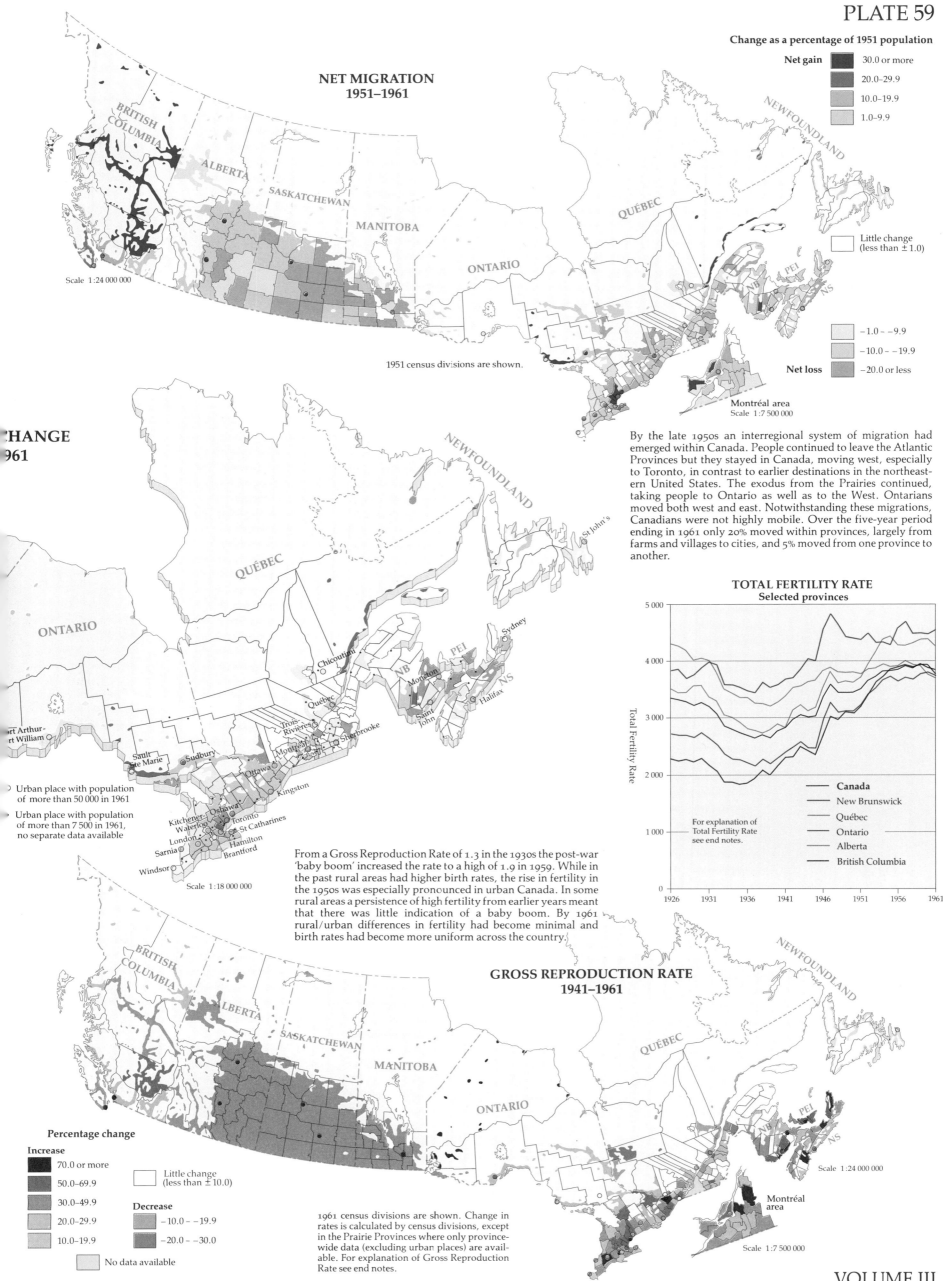

PLATE 59

Change as a percentage of 1951 population

Net gain
30.0 or more
20.0–29.9
10.0–19.9
1.0–9.9

NET MIGRATION
1951–1961

Scale 1:24 000 000

1951 census divisions are shown.

BRITISH COLUMBIA

ALBERTA

SASKATCHEWAN

MANITOBA

ONTARIO

QUÉBEC

NEWFOUNDLAND

PEI

NB

NS

Little change
(less than ± 1.0)

−1.0 − −9.9
−10.0 − −19.9
Net loss
−20.0 or less

Montréal area
Scale 1:7 500 000

By the late 1950s an interregional system of migration had emerged within Canada. People continued to leave the Atlantic Provinces but they stayed in Canada, moving west, especially to Toronto, in contrast to earlier destinations in the northeastern United States. The exodus from the Prairies continued, taking people to Ontario as well as to the West. Ontarians moved both west and east. Notwithstanding these migrations, Canadians were not highly mobile. Over the five-year period ending in 1961 only 20% moved within provinces, largely from farms and villages to cities, and 5% moved from one province to another.

CHANGE
961

QUÉBEC

NEWFOUNDLAND

ONTARIO

St John's

Chicoutimi

Sydney

NB
PEI
NS

Moncton

Québec

Saint John

Halifax

Trois-Rivières

Montréal

Sherbrooke

rt Arthur
rt William

Sault
te Marie

Sudbury

Ottawa

Kingston

Urban place with population
of more than 50 000 in 1961

Urban place with population
of more than 7 500 in 1961,
no separate data available

Kitchener-
Waterloo

London

Sarnia

Windsor

Oshawa

Toronto

St Catharines

Hamilton

Brantford

Scale 1:18 000 000

TOTAL FERTILITY RATE
Selected provinces

Canada	
New Brunswick	
Québec	
Ontario	
Alberta	
British Columbia	

For explanation of
Total Fertility Rate
see end notes.

Total Fertility Rate

5 000
4 000
3 000
2 000
1 000
0

1926 1931 1936 1941 1946 1951 1956 1961

From a Gross Reproduction Rate of 1.3 in the 1930s the post-war 'baby boom' increased the rate to a high of 1.9 in 1959. While in the past rural areas had higher birth rates, the rise in fertility in the 1950s was especially pronounced in urban Canada. In some rural areas a persistence of high fertility from earlier years meant that there was little indication of a baby boom. By 1961 rural/urban differences in fertility had become minimal and birth rates had become more uniform across the country.

BRITISH COLUMBIA

ALBERTA

SASKATCHEWAN

MANITOBA

ONTARIO

QUÉBEC

NEWFOUNDLAND

GROSS REPRODUCTION RATE
1941–1961

PEI
NS

Scale 1:24 000 000

Montréal
area

Scale 1:7 500 000

Percentage change

Increase
70.0 or more
50.0–69.9
30.0–49.9
20.0–29.9
10.0–19.9
No data available

Little change
(less than ± 10.0)

Decrease
−10.0 − −19.9
−20.0 − −30.0

1961 census divisions are shown. Change in rates is calculated by census divisions, except in the Prairie Provinces where only province-wide data (excluding urban places) are available. For explanation of Gross Reproduction Rate see end notes.

METROPOLITAN TORONTO

Author: Deryck W. Holdsworth

METROPOLITAN TORONTO
Shown at incorporation, 1953

Township of North York 1922
Township of Scarborough 1850
Town of Weston 1881
Village of Forest Hill 1923
Town of Leaside 1913
Township of East York 1924
Township of Etobicoke 1850
Township of York 1850
City of Toronto 1834
Village of Swansea 1925
Town of Mimico 1911
Village of Long Branch 1930
Town of New Toronto 1913

Scale 1:465 000

Population

1941 1951 1961

Thousands of persons

1930 Date of original incorporation of each constituent municipality

As Toronto rose to national prominence in the post-war period through the growth of industry, its continued development as a head-office city (pl 55), and its role as the primary destination of post-war immigrants (pl 59), the built-up area underwent dramatic expansion. A considerable number of peripheral industrial tracts were created, suitable for light and clean industries accessible by truck rather than on the rail lines (pl 15). While the population of the City of Toronto remained fairly constant at about 670 000 between 1941 and 1961, the populations in the municipalities around the city (which became part of Metropolitan Toronto) increased from 242 000 in 1941 to 442 000 in 1951, and then to 946 000 in 1961. The suburban governments could barely cope with the new demands for infrastructure, services, and transportation, and Canada's first metropolitan government was formed in 1953.

In an attempt to make this new sprawling metropolis work a round of infrastructure development was initiated. The Yonge Street subway, planned even earlier, was built as far north as Eglinton Avenue, arterial roads were pushed through, expressways were planned and some built. Gradually a new sewer and water system caught up with suburban growth.

Distinctive ethnic neighbourhoods developed, especially along the northwest axis of the City of Toronto and suburban York Township. Inexpensive older houses were renovated and retail strips transformed to reflect the particular ethnic character of a neighbourhood. The once emphatically Protestant city became far more Catholic and multicultural.

POST-WAR EXPANSION

RICHMOND HILL
Expressway bypass
WOODBRIDGE
Metropolitan Toronto boundary
Highway 407
Highway 400
Don Valley Parkway
See detail
Finch
Yonge
Spadina
Expressway
Warden
MALTON
Malton Airport
Humber
Cross-Town
Expressway
Lawrence
Eglinton
Danforth
Etobicoke
Highway 427
Bloor
STREETSVILLE
Toronto-Hamilton Expressway
Highway 401
F.G. Gardiner Expressway
Queen Elizabeth Way
Highway 403
Credit
PORT CREDIT

Residential and other built-up areas
- By 1945
- By 1958

Industrial areas
- By 1945
- By 1958

Transportation
- Expressway 1958
- Proposed expressway
- Subway
- Proposed subway
- Railway
- Main road

0   2 miles
0   2 kilometres
Scale 1:210 000

ETHNIC ORIGIN
City of Toronto

Percentage of total population

British
1941 1951 1961

Non-British
1941 1951 1961

Other*
Chinese
Dutch
Hungarian
Jewish
Ukrainian
Polish
French
German
Italian

*'Other' may include origins specified on graph if less than 1%.

RELIGIOUS AFFILIATION
City of Toronto

1941   1951   1961

667 457   675 754   672 407 persons

- Roman Catholic
- Anglican
- United Church
- Presbyterian
- Lutheran
- Baptist
- Jewish
- Other

ETHNIC MOSAIC, 1961
Metropolitan Toronto

Ethnic group by census tract

British
- More than 70%
- 40–70%
- Less than 40%

Other concentrations
- Italian, more than 30%
- Italian, more than 10%
- Polish, more than 10%
- Ukrainian, more than 10%
- German, more than 10%

0   4 miles
0   4 kilometres
Scale 1:320 000

HISTORICAL ATLAS OF CANADA

PLATE 60

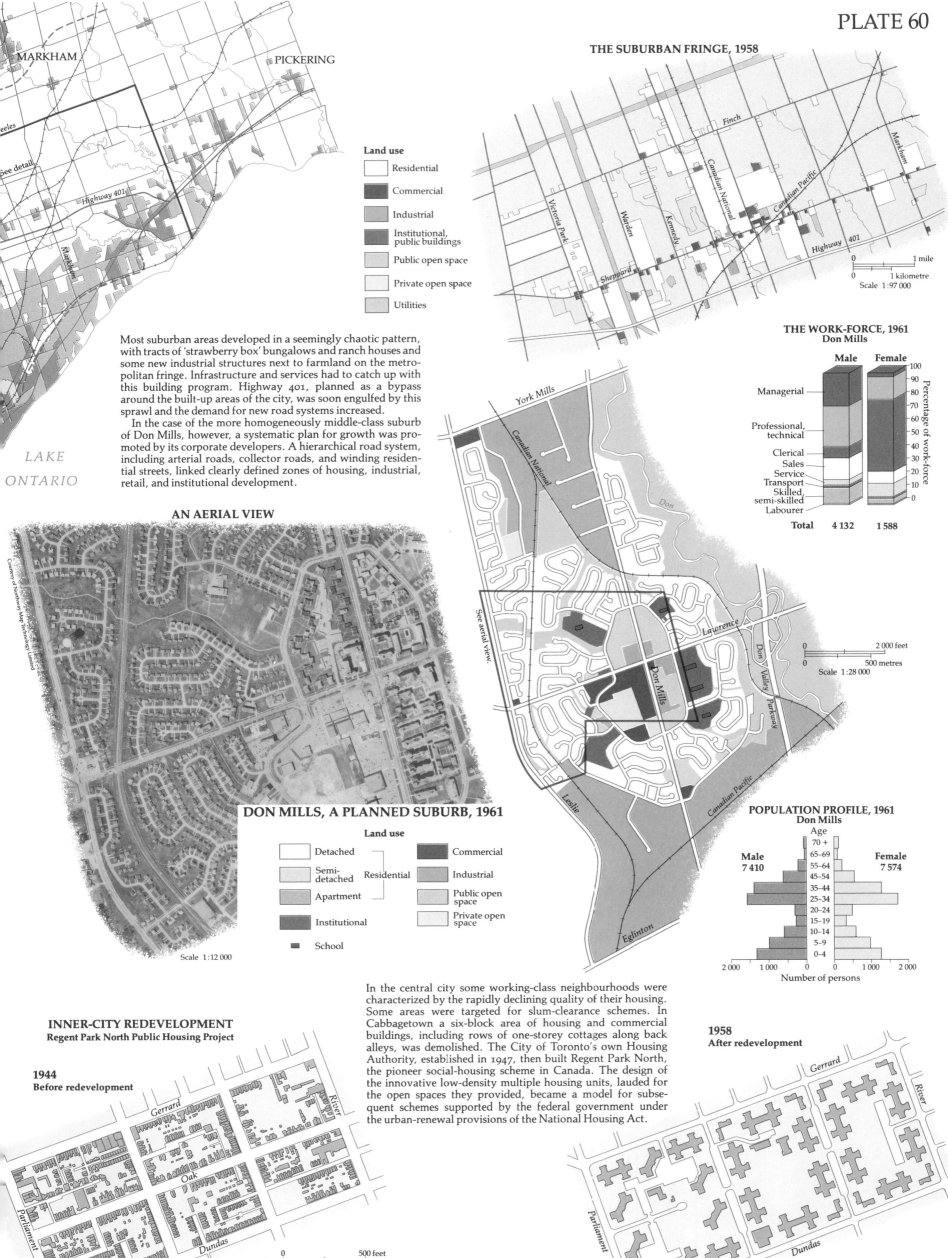

MARKHAM

PICKERING

LAKE
ONTARIO

Land use

Residential

Commercial

Industrial

Institutional,
public buildings

Public open space

Private open space

Utilities

Most suburban areas developed in a seemingly chaotic pattern,
with tracts of 'strawberry box' bungalows and ranch houses and
some new industrial structures next to farmland on the metropolitan fringe. Infrastructure and services had to catch up with
this building program. Highway 401, planned as a bypass
around the built-up areas of the city, was soon engulfed by this
sprawl and the demand for new road systems increased.

In the case of the more homogeneously middle-class suburb
of Don Mills, however, a systematic plan for growth was promoted by its corporate developers. A hierarchical road system,
including arterial roads, collector roads, and winding residential streets, linked clearly defined zones of housing, industrial,
retail, and institutional development.

THE SUBURBAN FRINGE, 1958

0   1 mile
0   1 kilometre
Scale 1:97 000

THE WORK-FORCE, 1961
Don Mills

Male   Female

Managerial

Professional,
technical

Clerical

Sales

Service

Transport

Skilled,
semi-skilled

Labourer

Percentage of work-force

Total   4 132   1 588

AN AERIAL VIEW

DON MILLS, A PLANNED SUBURB, 1961

Land use

Detached

Semi-
detached   Residential

Apartment

Institutional

School

Commercial

Industrial

Public open
space

Private open
space

Scale 1:12 000

0   2 000 feet
0   500 metres
Scale 1:28 000

POPULATION PROFILE, 1961
Don Mills

Age
70 +
65–69
55–64
45–54
35–44
25–34
20–24
15–19
10–14
5–9
0–4

**Male
7 410**   **Female
7 574**

2 000   1 000   0   1 000   2 000
Number of persons

INNER-CITY REDEVELOPMENT
Regent Park North Public Housing Project

1944
Before redevelopment

In the central city some working-class neighbourhoods were
characterized by the rapidly declining quality of their housing.
Some areas were targeted for slum-clearance schemes. In
Cabbagetown a six-block area of housing and commercial
buildings, including rows of one-storey cottages along back
alleys, was demolished. The City of Toronto's own Housing
Authority, established in 1947, then built Regent Park North,
the pioneer social-housing scheme in Canada. The design of
the innovative low-density multiple housing units, lauded for
the open spaces they provided, became a model for subsequent schemes supported by the federal government under
the urban-renewal provisions of the National Housing Act.

1958
After redevelopment

0   500 feet
0   100 metres
Scale 1:7 000

THE CHANGING WORK-FORCE
Author: Lynne Marks

Significant growth occurred within Canada's manufacturing and resource sectors in the post-war era; the adoption of new technology, however, limited the demand for new workers while transforming the nature of work for those employed. In agriculture mechanization actually contributed to a reduction in employment.

Labour-force statistics exclude the essential but unpaid work of Canadian women both on the farm and in the home. Domestic work was being transformed in this period; new domestic appliances, which were increasingly the norm at least in urban households, made housework less arduous but also led to the development of more exacting standards of housework and child care. This technology may also have made it more feasible for married women to attempt to juggle the 'double day' of housework and paid work, as they did in steadily increasing numbers in the 1950s. Women workers, both married and single, continued to be employed in a narrow range of occupations, with clerical work taking on increasing importance. The feminization of clerical work was hastened by the growing size of corporations and the expansion of government services which led to an increased emphasis on management and administration. This in turn necessitated a massive growth in the office work-force, primarily in low-paying, routine, dead-end jobs; such jobs were considered suitable for women who were viewed as temporary or secondary wage-earners.

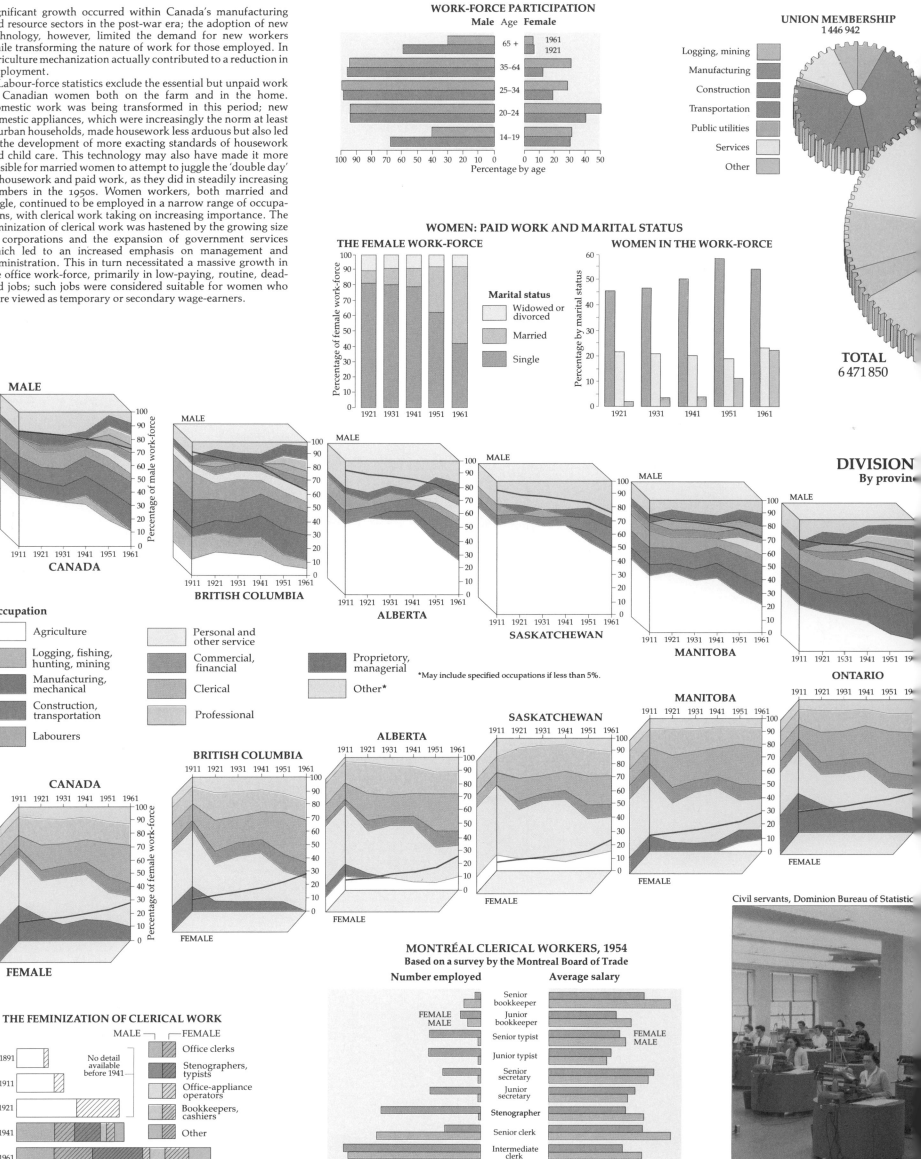

HISTORICAL ATLAS OF CANADA

PLATE 61

POST-WAR IMMIGRANTS AND EMPLOYMENT

THE WORK-FORCE, 1961

FEMALE
1 766 332

MALE
4 705 518

Total work-force comprises men and women, both union and non-union workers. Union members as shown are a subset of total work-force, classified separately according to type of union.

Industrial sector

- Agriculture
- Logging, fishing, hunting, mining
- Manufacturing
- Construction
- Transportation
- Trade
- Finance, insurance, real estate
- Personal service
- Other services
- Public administration
- Other

EMPLOYMENT BY INDUSTRY, 1961

Male   **Female**

Percentage of work-force

Native-born Canadians 3 685 694
Post-war immigrants 569 151
Native-born Canadians 1 400 871
Post-war immigrants 234 757

WORK-FORCE PARTICIPATION, 1959

Male   Age   Female

Native-born Canadians
Post-war immigrants

65 +
55–64
45–54
35–44
25–34
20–24
14–19

Percentage by age

OCCUPATIONAL INEQUALITY AMONG MALES IN QUÉBEC

1931   British origin   French origin   **1961**

- Other
- Agricultural
- Primary unskilled
- Personal service
- Clerical
- Professional, financial

%   Percentage
Under-representation   Over-representation   Under-representation   Over-representation

OF LABOUR
and gender

MALE — QUÉBEC

MALE — NEW BRUNSWICK

MALE — NOVA SCOTIA

MALE — PRINCE EDWARD ISLAND

MALE — NFLD
1951 1961

1911 1921 1931 1941 1951 1961

FEMALE — QUÉBEC

FEMALE — NEW BRUNSWICK

FEMALE — NOVA SCOTIA

FEMALE — PRINCE EDWARD ISLAND

FEMALE — NFLD
1951 1961

—— Percentage of males/females in total work-force

Ottawa, 1952

The work-force was divided not only by occupation and gender but also by language and birthplace. In Québec anglophones continued to predominate in professional and managerial jobs. This situation fuelled the anger of an emerging francophone middle class which, with the onset of the Quiet Revolution in 1960, sought to become 'Maître chez nous.'

The economic boom in the post-war years led to a strong demand for immigrants who performed the jobs Canadians were unwilling to do or lacked the skills for. The majority of immigrants went to and in many cases helped to build Canada's growing cities. Such was the case with Toronto's Italians, who predominated in the construction of that city's subway system. Married immigrant women were more likely to seek paid employment than Canadian-born women since their wages were often essential to the survival of their families and to efforts to attain some security through the purchase of a home.

INDUSTRIES WITH COMPUTERS, 1960

- Utilities
- Trade
- Transportation
- Finance, insurance
- Manufacturing
- Public administration, defence
- Community services, business

Total 89

EMERGENCE OF THE COMPUTER AGE
Electronic digital computers, 1960

Courtesy of the National Archives of Canada, PA-133212

The labour-intensive nature of clerical work led to the adoption by employers of labour-saving devices, from typewriters in the late 19th century to electronic computers which large employers began to acquire in the 1950s.

BRITISH COLUMBIA
ALBERTA
SASKATCHEWAN
MANITOBA
ONTARIO
QUÉBEC
NEWFOUNDLAND
PEI
NB
NS

Ottawa 6
Montréal 16
Toronto 18

• One dot represents one industrial computer user.

Scale 1:38 000 000

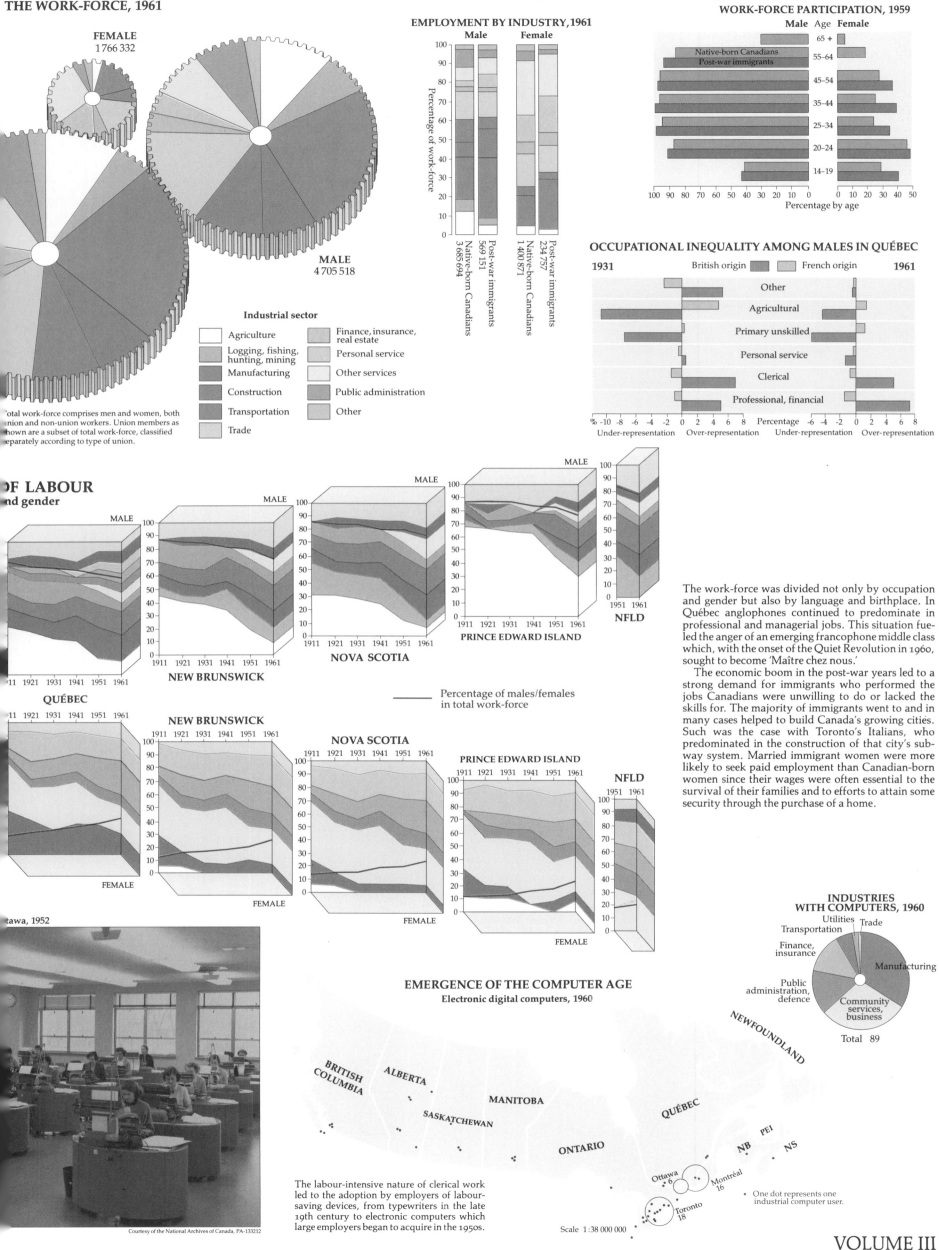

ORGANIZED LABOUR, STRIKES, AND POLITICS

Authors: Gregory S. Kealey, Douglas Cruikshank

UNION MEMBERSHIP BY PROVINCE

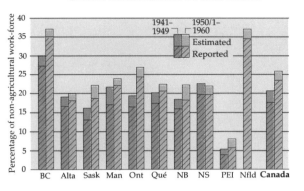

UNION MEMBERSHIP BY INDUSTRY

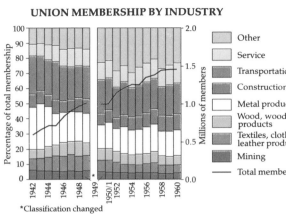
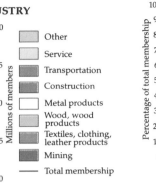

*Classification changed

UNION MEMBERSHIP BY AFFILIATION

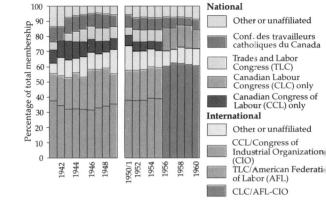

National
- Other or unaffiliated
- Conf. des travailleurs catholiques du Canada
- Trades and Labor Congress (TLC)
- Canadian Labour Congress (CLC) only
- Canadian Congress of Labour (CCL) only

International
- Other or unaffiliated
- CCL/Congress of Industrial Organization (CIO)
- TLC/American Federation of Labor (AFL)
- CLC/AFL-CIO

PROCEEDINGS UNDER THE INDUSTRIAL DISPUTES INVESTIGATION (IDI) ACT

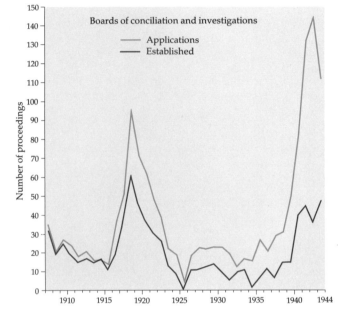

Boards of conciliation and investigations
- Applications
- Established

FREQUENCY, SIZE, AND DURATION

Type of industry
- Service
- Transportation
- Construction
- Manufacturing
- Mining

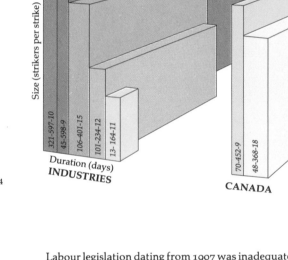

IDI ACT PROCEEDINGS BY INDUSTRY, 1907–1944

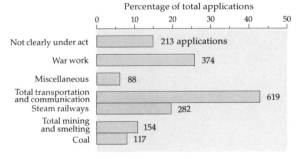

Percentage of total applications

- Not clearly under act — 213 applications
- War work — 374
- Miscellaneous — 88
- Total transportation and communication — 619
- Steam railways — 282
- Total mining and smelting — 154
- Coal — 117

Labour legislation dating from 1907 was inadequate to deal with the industrial-relations crisis of the late 1930s. However, a wave of strikes in 1943 and a surge in the political fortunes of the left finally forced the government in 1944 to pass a Privy Council Order (PC 1003) whereby employers had to bargain collectively with organized workers. Massive strikes in 1946 (including tumultuous struggles at the Ford plant in Windsor and the Stelco plant in Hamilton) compelled the government to entrench the wartime legislation. The 1948 Industrial Relations and Disputes Investigation Act set the pattern for similar provincial legislation, leading to provincial labour-relations boards and compulsory conciliation services.

During the Second World War both the Co-operative Commonwealth Federation (CCF) and the Labour Progressive Party (the renamed Communist Party of Canada) enjoyed provincial successes and victories in federal by-elections. However, 1945 saw labour's greatest federal electoral success: post-war prosperity and the exigencies of the Cold War diminished support for the left.

LABOUR POLITICS, 1941–1960

FEDERAL ELECTIONS

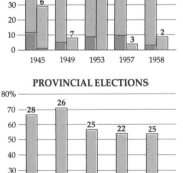

PROVINCIAL ELECTIONS

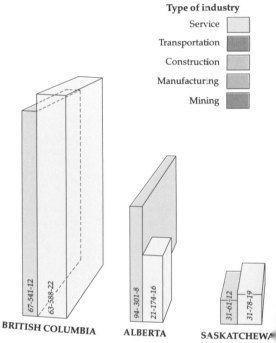

Percentage of all seats contested by Co-operative Commonwealth Federation (CCF) and other socialist or labour candidates

CONCILIATION PROCEEDINGS 1948–1960

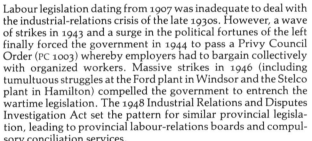

New cases / Boards of conciliation established

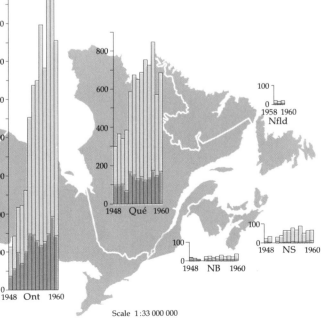

Scale 1:33 000 000

FEDERAL GOVERNMENT, 1945–1960

Wartime Labour Relations Regulations

Industrial Relations and Disputes Investigation Act

For terminology of specific provincial legislation and fiscal years see end notes.

PROVINCIAL ELECTIONS BY PROVINCE, 1941–1960

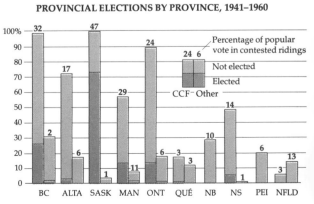

- Percentage of popular vote in contested ridings
- Not elected
- Elected

CCF / Other

PLATE 62

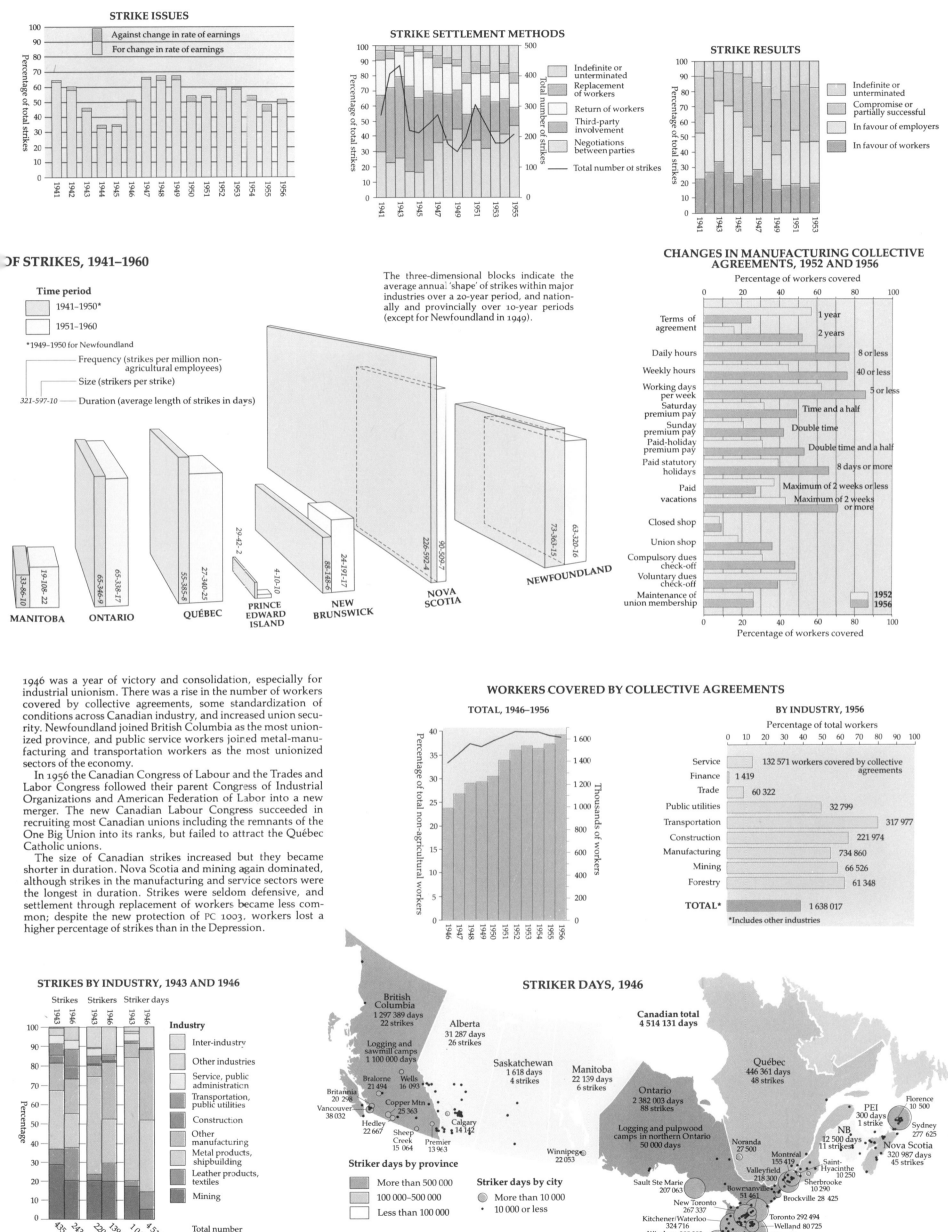

STRIKE ISSUES

- Against change in rate of earnings
- For change in rate of earnings

Percentage of total strikes

1941 1942 1943 1944 1945 1946 1947 1948 1949 1950 1951 1952 1953 1954 1955 1956

STRIKE SETTLEMENT METHODS

Percentage of total strikes / Total number of strikes

- Indefinite or unterminated
- Replacement of workers
- Return of workers
- Third-party involvement
- Negotiations between parties
- Total number of strikes

1941 1943 1945 1947 1949 1951 1953 1955

STRIKE RESULTS

Percentage of total strikes

- Indefinite or unterminated
- Compromise or partially successful
- In favour of employers
- In favour of workers

1941 1943 1945 1947 1949 1951 1953

OF STRIKES, 1941–1960

Time period
- 1941–1950*
- 1951–1960

*1949–1950 for Newfoundland

- Frequency (strikes per million non-agricultural employees)
- Size (strikers per strike)

321-597-10 — Duration (average length of strikes in days)

The three-dimensional blocks indicate the average annual 'shape' of strikes within major industries over a 20-year period, and nationally and provincially over 10-year periods (except for Newfoundland in 1949).

MANITOBA 33-86-10 / 19-108-22
ONTARIO 65-346-9 / 65-338-17
QUÉBEC 55-385-8 / 27-340-25
PRINCE EDWARD ISLAND 29-42-2 / 4-10-10
NEW BRUNSWICK 88-148-6 / 24-191-17
NOVA SCOTIA 226-592-4 / 90-509-7
NEWFOUNDLAND 73-363-15 / 63-320-16

CHANGES IN MANUFACTURING COLLECTIVE AGREEMENTS, 1952 AND 1956

Percentage of workers covered

- Terms of agreement — 1 year / 2 years
- Daily hours — 8 or less
- Weekly hours — 40 or less
- Working days per week — 5 or less
- Saturday premium pay — Time and a half
- Sunday premium pay — Double time
- Paid-holiday premium pay — Double time and a half
- Paid statutory holidays — 8 days or more
- Paid vacations — Maximum of 2 weeks or less / Maximum of 2 weeks or more
- Closed shop
- Union shop
- Compulsory dues check-off
- Voluntary dues check-off
- Maintenance of union membership

1952 / 1956

Percentage of workers covered

1946 was a year of victory and consolidation, especially for industrial unionism. There was a rise in the number of workers covered by collective agreements, some standardization of conditions across Canadian industry, and increased union security. Newfoundland joined British Columbia as the most unionized province, and public service workers joined metal-manufacturing and transportation workers as the most unionized sectors of the economy.

In 1956 the Canadian Congress of Labour and the Trades and Labor Congress followed their parent Congress of Industrial Organizations and American Federation of Labor into a new merger. The new Canadian Labour Congress succeeded in recruiting most Canadian unions including the remnants of the One Big Union into its ranks, but failed to attract the Québec Catholic unions.

The size of Canadian strikes increased but they became shorter in duration. Nova Scotia and mining again dominated, although strikes in the manufacturing and service sectors were the longest in duration. Strikes were seldom defensive, and settlement through replacement of workers became less common; despite the new protection of PC 1003, workers lost a higher percentage of strikes than in the Depression.

WORKERS COVERED BY COLLECTIVE AGREEMENTS

TOTAL, 1946–1956

Percentage of total non-agricultural workers / Thousands of workers

1946 1947 1948 1949 1950 1951 1952 1953 1954 1955 1956

BY INDUSTRY, 1956

Percentage of total workers

Service	132 571 workers covered by collective agreements
Finance	1 419
Trade	60 322
Public utilities	32 799
Transportation	317 977
Construction	221 974
Manufacturing	734 860
Mining	66 526
Forestry	61 348
TOTAL*	1 638 017

*Includes other industries

STRIKES BY INDUSTRY, 1943 AND 1946

Strikes 1943 1946 / Strikers 1943 1946 / Striker days 1943 1946

Industry
- Inter-industry
- Other industries
- Service, public administration
- Transportation, public utilities
- Construction
- Other manufacturing
- Metal products, shipbuilding
- Leather products, textiles
- Mining

Total number: 435 243 / 220 102 139 673 / 1 042 171 4 516 444

STRIKER DAYS, 1946

Canadian total 4 514 131 days

British Columbia 1 297 389 days 22 strikes
Logging and sawmill camps 1 100 000 days
Bralorne 21 494
Wells 16 093
Britannia 20 298
Vancouver 38 032
Copper Mtn 25 363
Hedley 22 667
Sheep Creek 15 064
Premier 13 963

Alberta 31 287 days 26 strikes
Calgary 14 142

Saskatchewan 1 618 days 4 strikes

Manitoba 22 139 days 6 strikes
Winnipeg 22 053

Ontario 2 382 003 days 88 strikes
Logging and pulpwood camps in northern Ontario 50 000 days
Sault Ste Marie 207 804
New Toronto 267 337
Kitchener/Waterloo 324 716
Windsor 300 392
Amherstburg 28 000
Noranda 27 500
Toronto 292 494
Welland 80 725
Hamilton 660 146
Chatham 18 773
Brockville 28 425

Québec 446 361 days 48 strikes
Montréal 155 419
Valleyfield 218 300
Sherbrooke 10 290
Saint-Hyacinthe 10 250

PEI 300 days 1 strike

NB 12 500 days 11 strikes

Nova Scotia 320 987 days 45 strikes
Florence 10 500
Sydney 277 625

Striker days by province
- More than 500 000
- 100 000–500 000
- Less than 100 000

Striker days by city
- More than 10 000
- 10 000 or less

THE EMERGENCE OF SOCIAL INSURANCE

Author: Lynne Marks

Until the Second World War Canadians were largely unprotected by the state against universal risks such as illness, injury, and unemployment. Coping with these misfortunes was considered the responsibility of each individual. The only source of public relief had been local programs, which usually required means tests and provided inadequate, short-term support because of limited local funds and the belief that charity would undermine the incentive to work. Limited health and welfare insurance was provided by mutual benefit societies, and by 1945 a minority of Canadians was covered by private and non-profit health insurance plans.

Prior to the First World War those injured at work were forced to sue their employer to receive compensation. If the workers were proven negligent, they received nothing. Provincial workers' compensation legislation during and after the war removed the issue of responsibility for injury and protected employers from high court awards to victims.

The 1940 Unemployment Insurance Act moved away from earlier beliefs in personal responsibility for unemployment. However, previous concerns regarding work incentives remained, making payments, at half of wages, inadequate for most recipients. The popularity of the CCF party, which advocated social welfare, and memories of Depression hardships pushed the government to pass the 1944 Family Allowances Act. Both unemployment insurance and family allowances were viewed as economic stabilizers through their roles in sustaining purchasing power.

No federal/provincial accord on health insurance could be reached in the immediate post-war period. Some provinces developed either full or partial hospital insurance schemes independently, while others awaited federal government initiatives in the late 1950s.

PASSAGE OF SOCIAL-WELFARE LEGISLATION

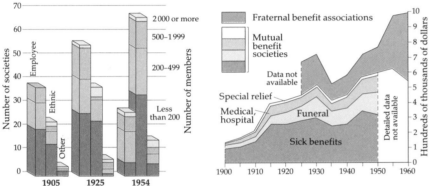

Under the British North America Act responsibility for health and welfare lay with the provinces. When the federal government wished to create certain health and welfare programs for all Canadians, it could only pass enabling legislation. Each province then had to pass its own legislation. In order to encourage provincial participation these programs involved federal/provincial cost sharing.

Year in which legislation came into effect is indicated in parentheses only if it was more than a year after legislation was passed.

Numbers relate federal acts to corresponding provincial legislation.

FEDERAL AND PROVINCIAL EXPENDITURES ON HEALTH AND WELFARE PROGRAMS, 1958–1959

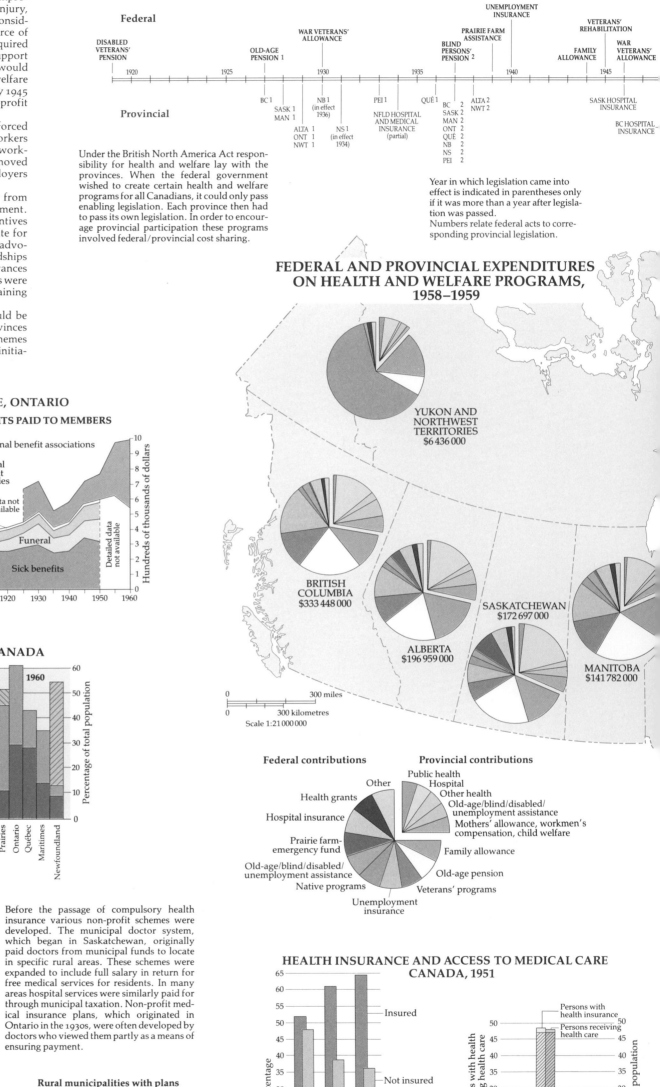

YUKON AND NORTHWEST TERRITORIES $6 436 000

BRITISH COLUMBIA $333 448 000

ALBERTA $196 959 000

SASKATCHEWAN $172 697 000

MANITOBA $141 782 000

Scale 1:21 000 000

Federal contributions

- Other
- Health grants
- Hospital insurance
- Prairie farm-emergency fund
- Old-age/blind/disabled/unemployment assistance
- Native programs
- Unemployment insurance

Provincial contributions

- Public health
- Hospital
- Other health
- Old-age/blind/disabled/unemployment assistance
- Mothers' allowance, workmen's compensation, child welfare
- Family allowance
- Old-age pension
- Veterans' programs

EARLY FORMS OF SOCIAL INSURANCE, ONTARIO

MUTUAL BENEFIT SOCIETIES

Number of societies / Number of members

2 000 or more
500–1999
200–499
Less than 200

Employee / Ethnic / Other

1905 1925 1954

BENEFITS PAID TO MEMBERS

Hundreds of thousands of dollars

- Fraternal benefit associations
- Mutual benefit societies
- Special relief
- Medical hospital
- Funeral
- Sick benefits
- Data not available
- Detailed data not available

1900 1910 1920 1930 1940 1950 1960

GROWTH OF MEDICAL INSURANCE, CANADA

- Cottage-hospital and medical plan, Nfld (data not available pre-1955)
- Municipal doctor plan, Prairies
- Non-profit
- Private

Percentage of total population

1940 1945 1950 1955 1960

Canada / Canada / British Columbia / Prairies / Ontario / Quebec / Maritimes / Newfoundland / British Columbia / Prairies / Ontario / Quebec / Maritimes / Newfoundland / British Columbia / Prairies / Ontario / Quebec / Maritimes / Newfoundland

MUNICIPAL DOCTOR PLANS, SASKATCHEWAN, 1950

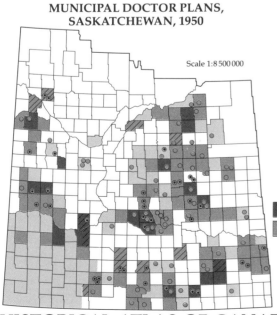

Scale 1:8 500 000

Before the passage of compulsory health insurance various non-profit schemes were developed. The municipal doctor system, which began in Saskatchewan, originally paid doctors from municipal funds to locate in specific rural areas. These schemes were expanded to include full salary in return for free medical services for residents. In many areas hospital services were similarly paid for through municipal taxation. Non-profit medical insurance plans, which originated in Ontario in the 1930s, were often developed by doctors who viewed them partly as a means of ensuring payment.

Rural municipalities with plans

- Existing in 1930
- Created 1931–1940
- Created 1941–1950
- Terminated by 1950

Towns and villages with plans

- Existing in 1940
- Created 1941–1950
- Terminated by 1950

HISTORICAL ATLAS OF CANADA

HEALTH INSURANCE AND ACCESS TO MEDICAL CARE CANADA, 1951

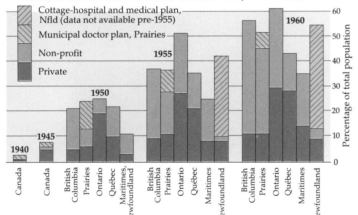

Percentage

Insured
Not insured

Total population / Receiving physician's care / Hospitalized persons

Percentage of persons with health insurance or receiving health care

Persons with health insurance
Persons receiving health care

Percentage of total population

Low / Middle / High (lower) / High (upper)
Income level

PLATE 63

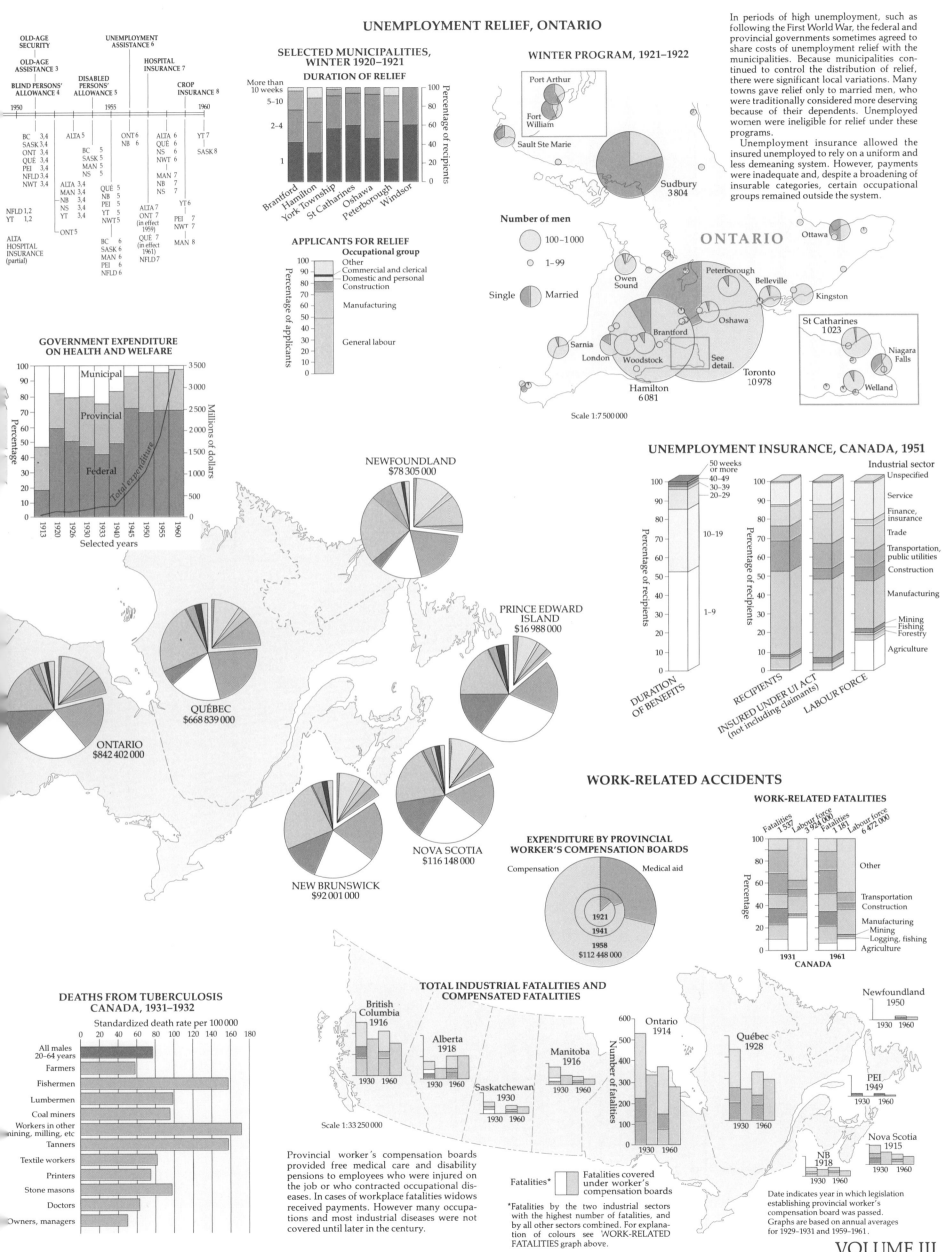

UNEMPLOYMENT RELIEF, ONTARIO

SELECTED MUNICIPALITIES, WINTER 1920–1921
DURATION OF RELIEF

WINTER PROGRAM, 1921–1922

In periods of high unemployment, such as following the First World War, the federal and provincial governments sometimes agreed to share costs of unemployment relief with the municipalities. Because municipalities continued to control the distribution of relief, there were significant local variations. Many towns gave relief only to married men, who were traditionally considered more deserving because of their dependents. Unemployed women were ineligible for relief under these programs.

Unemployment insurance allowed the insured unemployed to rely on a uniform and less demeaning system. However, payments were inadequate and, despite a broadening of insurable categories, certain occupational groups remained outside the system.

APPLICANTS FOR RELIEF

ONTARIO

Scale 1:7 500 000

GOVERNMENT EXPENDITURE ON HEALTH AND WELFARE

NEWFOUNDLAND
$78 305 000

PRINCE EDWARD ISLAND
$16 988 000

QUÉBEC
$668 839 000

ONTARIO
$842 402 000

NOVA SCOTIA
$116 148 000

NEW BRUNSWICK
$92 001 000

UNEMPLOYMENT INSURANCE, CANADA, 1951

WORK-RELATED ACCIDENTS

WORK-RELATED FATALITIES

EXPENDITURE BY PROVINCIAL WORKER'S COMPENSATION BOARDS

DEATHS FROM TUBERCULOSIS CANADA, 1931–1932

Standardized death rate per 100 000

TOTAL INDUSTRIAL FATALITIES AND COMPENSATED FATALITIES

Scale 1:33 250 000

Provincial worker's compensation boards provided free medical care and disability pensions to employees who were injured on the job or who contracted occupational diseases. In cases of workplace fatalities widows received payments. However many occupations and most industrial diseases were not covered until later in the century.

Fatalities*

Fatalities covered under worker's compensation boards

*Fatalities by the two industrial sectors with the highest number of fatalities, and by all other sectors combined. For explanation of colours see 'WORK-RELATED FATALITIES' graph above.

Date indicates year in which legislation establishing provincial worker's compensation board was passed.
Graphs are based on annual averages for 1929–1931 and 1959–1961.

UNIVERSITY EDUCATION

Authors: Chad Gaffield, Lynne Marks

Universities have come to play major cultural, scientific, and social roles in 20th-century Canada. In the late 19th century a tiny minority of Canadians, almost exclusively male, attended university in order to pursue careers as doctors, ministers, and teachers. Attendance by both men and women grew significantly after the First World War as an increasingly complex society demanded both new skills and higher qualifications. A variety of faculties was founded to train students in newly professional occupations. Some of the new professions were female-dominated, being within suitably 'feminine' fields such as domestic science and library science. In the 1920s a growing number of Canadian universities created and developed graduate programs, although most students still looked to Europe or the United States for advanced programs.

The greatest expansion in university education occurred after the Second World War. Immediately after the war returning veterans who wished to attend university were supported by federal grants. Other federal programs had a more permanent impact on universities. University education more than ever before was seen as a direct investment in Canada's future and, as a result, the federal share of university funding became significant. More faculties were established and regional universities were expanded across the country. These new facilities combined with Canada's economic and demographic growth to bring an ever increasing proportion of young people to university.

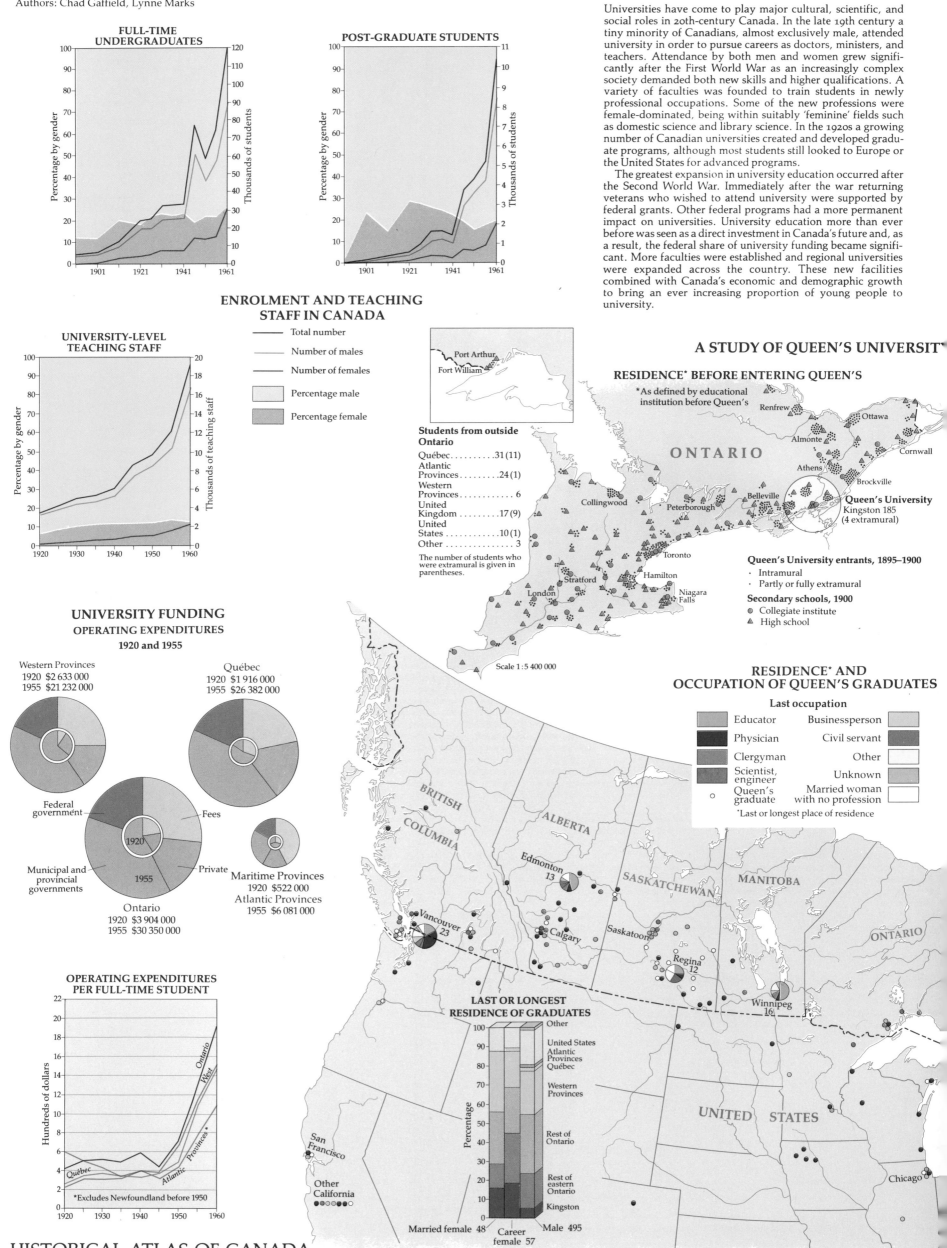

HISTORICAL ATLAS OF CANADA

PLATE 64

GEOGRAPHICAL MOBILITY OF UNIVERSITY STUDENTS

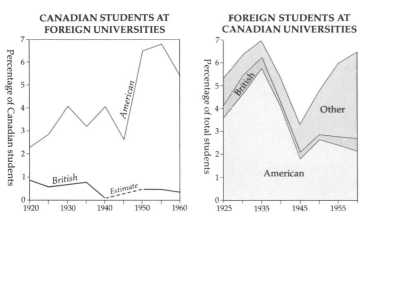

CANADIAN STUDENTS AT FOREIGN UNIVERSITIES

Percentage of Canadian students

American

British

Estimate

1920 1930 1940 1950 1960

FOREIGN STUDENTS AT CANADIAN UNIVERSITIES

Percentage of total students

British

Other

American

1925 1935 1945 1955

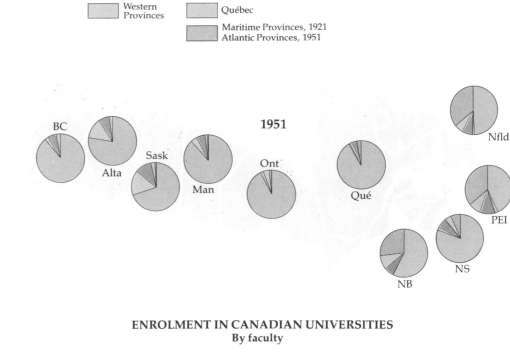

1921

BC
Alta
Sask
Man
Ont
Qué
PEI
NS
NB

Student residence before university

- Home province
- Western Provinces
- Ontario
- Québec
- Maritime Provinces, 1921 Atlantic Provinces, 1951

1951

BC
Alta
Sask
Man
Ont
Qué
Nfld
PEI
NS
NB

TUDENTS, 1895–1900

QUEEN'S UNIVERSITY ENTRANTS, 1895–1900

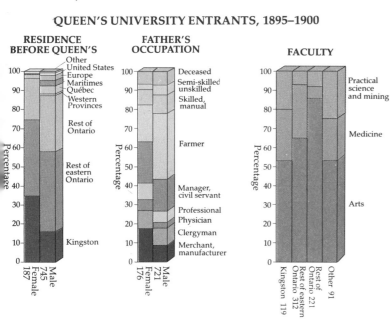

RESIDENCE BEFORE QUEEN'S

Other
United States
Europe
Maritimes
Québec
Western Provinces
Rest of Ontario
Rest of eastern Ontario
Kingston

Male 745
Female 187

FATHER'S OCCUPATION

Deceased
Semi-skilled unskilled
Skilled, manual
Farmer
Manager, civil servant
Professional
Physician
Clergyman
Merchant, manufacturer

Male 721
Female 176

FACULTY

Practical science and mining
Medicine
Arts

Kingston 119
Rest of eastern Ontario 312
Rest of Ontario 221
Other 91

Queen's University illustrates patterns of enrolment in the late 19th century and careers and destinations of graduates in the first half of the 20th century. Like most 19th-century Canadian universities Queen's began as a denominational college. Although founded in 1841 primarily to train Presbyterian ministers, by the 1890s over half of its students were non-Presbyterian. Queen's served eastern Ontario but also drew students from across the province, especially those interested in becoming ministers. Many students came from middle-class families, but some, especially males, came from farm or working-class backgrounds. Queen's was the first Ontario university to admit women (in 1878) but they remained a small minority, restricted to the Faculty of Arts, and with employment opportunities limited to high-school teaching.

Queen's graduates dispersed across the country, following the movement of Canada's population westward, helping to form an élite of teachers and ministers in the newer provinces. A high proportion of medical graduates moved south, looking to better opportunities in the United States.

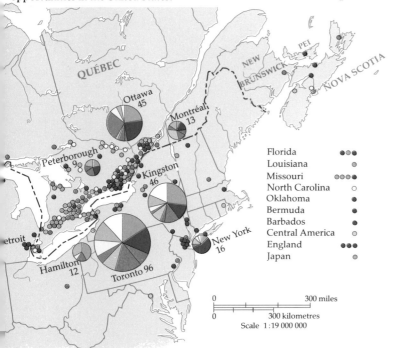

QUÉBEC
NEW BRUNSWICK
NOVA SCOTIA
NEWFOUNDLAND
Ottawa 45
Montreal 13
Peterborough 9
Kingston 46
Detroit
Hamilton 12
Toronto 96
New York 16

Florida
Louisiana
Missouri
North Carolina
Oklahoma
Bermuda
Barbados
Central America
England
Japan

0   300 miles
0   300 kilometres
Scale 1 : 19 000 000

ENROLMENT IN CANADIAN UNIVERSITIES
By faculty

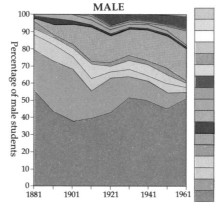

MALE

Percentage of male students

Other
Library science
Fine art
Nursing
Social work
Domestic science
Commerce
Forestry
Education
Dentistry
Veterinary medicine
Engineering
Pharmacy
Agriculture
Law
Medicine
Arts and science

1881 1901 1921 1941 1961

FEMALE

Percentage of female students

1881 1901 1921 1941 1961

FOUNDING OF UNIVERSITY FACULTIES

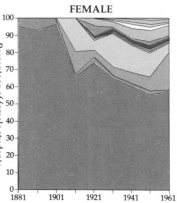

- Pre-1900 (existing in 1899)
- 1900–1920
- 1921–1940
- 1941–1960
- □ Unavailable by 1920
- • Unavailable by 1960

Selected faculty*

Library science
Fine art
Nursing
Social work
Domestic science
Commerce
Forestry
Education
Dentistry
Veterinary medicine
Engineering
Pharmacy
Agriculture
Law
Medicine
Secretarial science
Music

*For definition of faculty see end notes.

Selected urban place

Victoria, Vancouver, Calgary, Edmonton, Saskatoon, Regina, Brandon, Winnipeg, London, Waterloo, Guelph, Hamilton, Toronto, Kingston, Ottawa, Oka, Montréal, Saint-Hyacinthe, Sherbrooke, Lennoxville, Québec, Sainte-Anne-de-la-Pocatière, Fredericton, Saint John, Sackville, Wolfville, Windsor, Halifax, Antigonish, Charlottetown, St John's

NATIONAL BROADCASTING SYSTEMS

Authors: Michael J. Doucet, Margaret Hobbs

RADIOS IN CANADA

1931
1941
1949
1961

0 10 20 30 40 50 60 70 80 90 100
Percentage of households with radios

HOUSEHOLDS WITH RADIOS, 1931

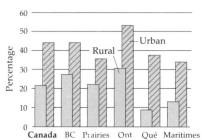

Percentage

60
50
40
30
20
10
0

Rural   Urban

Canada BC Prairies Ont Qué Maritimes

RADIO STATIONS, 1929

HIGH-POWERED RADIO STATIONS, 1929

5 000 watts or more

Number of stations

16
14
12
10
8
6
4
2
0

North-central North-east South West Canada

United States

Despite Canada's early technical leadership in wireless voice transmission, by the late 1920s Canadian radio stations were underpowered and few in number compared to their American counterparts. Public concern over the Americanization of the airwaves led to the Radio Broadcasting Act (1932) which created the Canadian Radio Broadcasting Commission (CRBC). Private as well as public radio stations were allowed under the act, though the former were to be regulated by the CRBC. The result was a compromise between British (public) and American (private) models, which signalled an acceptance of the early importance of private stations in the building of a national system.

In 1936 the CRBC was replaced by the more effectively administered and financed Canadian Broadcasting Corporation (CBC). Within three years the CBC had established four 50-kilowatt stations; the proportion of the Canadian population that could receive CBC broadcasts at some time of the day increased from 49% to almost 90%. By the 1950s the CBC was operating two English-language and one French-language national – though patchwork – radio networks. In 1958 coverage was further extended with the CBC Northern Service.

Even with the increase in public and private Canadian radio stations the level of Canadian content was quite low, especially from private stations which primarily transmitted recorded music. CBC radio programming was more original, encouraging the development of Canadian music and drama. Still, American soap operas were a regular part of CBC's typical broadcast day.

Ownership
- CNR
- Newspaper
- Institutional
- Other

Station power
- 5 000 watts
- 1 000–4 000
- Less than 1 000

Type
- With own equipment
- 'Phantom' station

A 'phantom' station owned call letters but rented equipment from another licensed broadcaster.

RADIO STATIONS AND NETWORKS, 1956

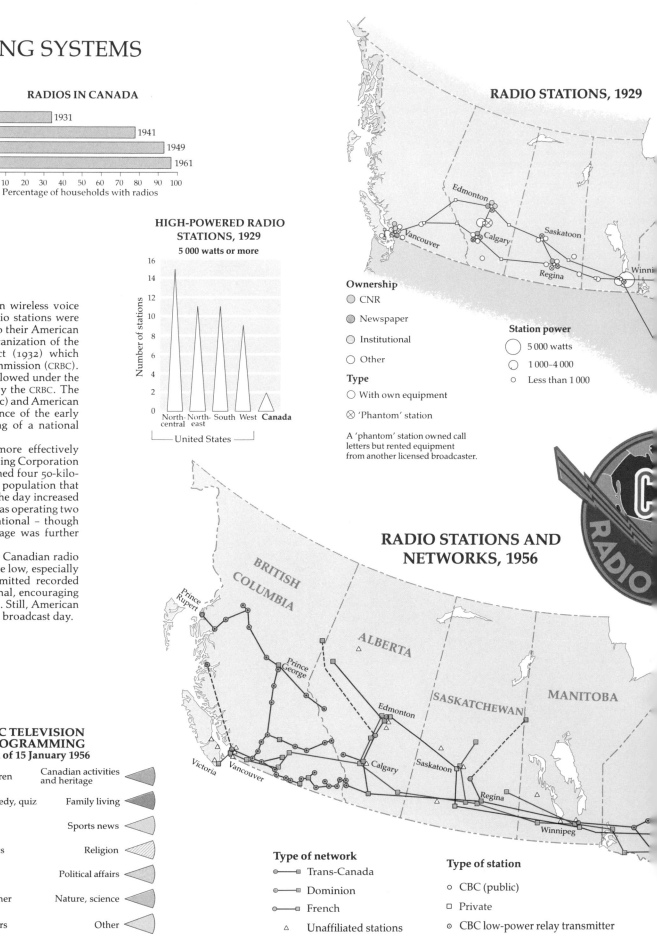

Type of network
- Trans-Canada
- Dominion
- French
- Unaffiliated stations

Type of station
- CBC (public)
- Private
- CBC low-power relay transmitter

FRENCH-LANGUAGE

CBC TELEVISION PROGRAMMING
Week of 15 January 1956

- Youth, children
- Variety, comedy, quiz
- Drama
- Sports events
- Music
- News, weather
- Foreign affairs

- Canadian activities and heritage
- Family living
- Sports news
- Religion
- Political affairs
- Nature, science
- Other

ENGLISH- LANGUAGE

TELEVISION NETWORKS, 1956

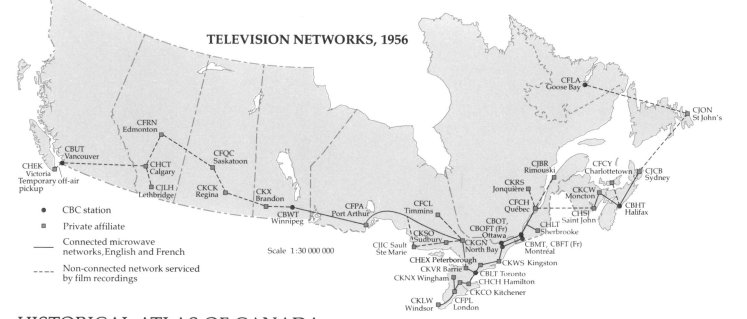

- CBC station
- Private affiliate
- Connected microwave networks, English and French
- Non-connected network serviced by film recordings

Scale 1:30 000 000

THE GROWING POPULARITY OF TELEVISION

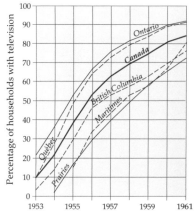

Percentage of households with television

100
90
80
70
60
50
40
30
20
10
0

Ontario
Canada
British Columbia
Maritimes
Québec
Prairies

1953 1955 1957 1959 1961

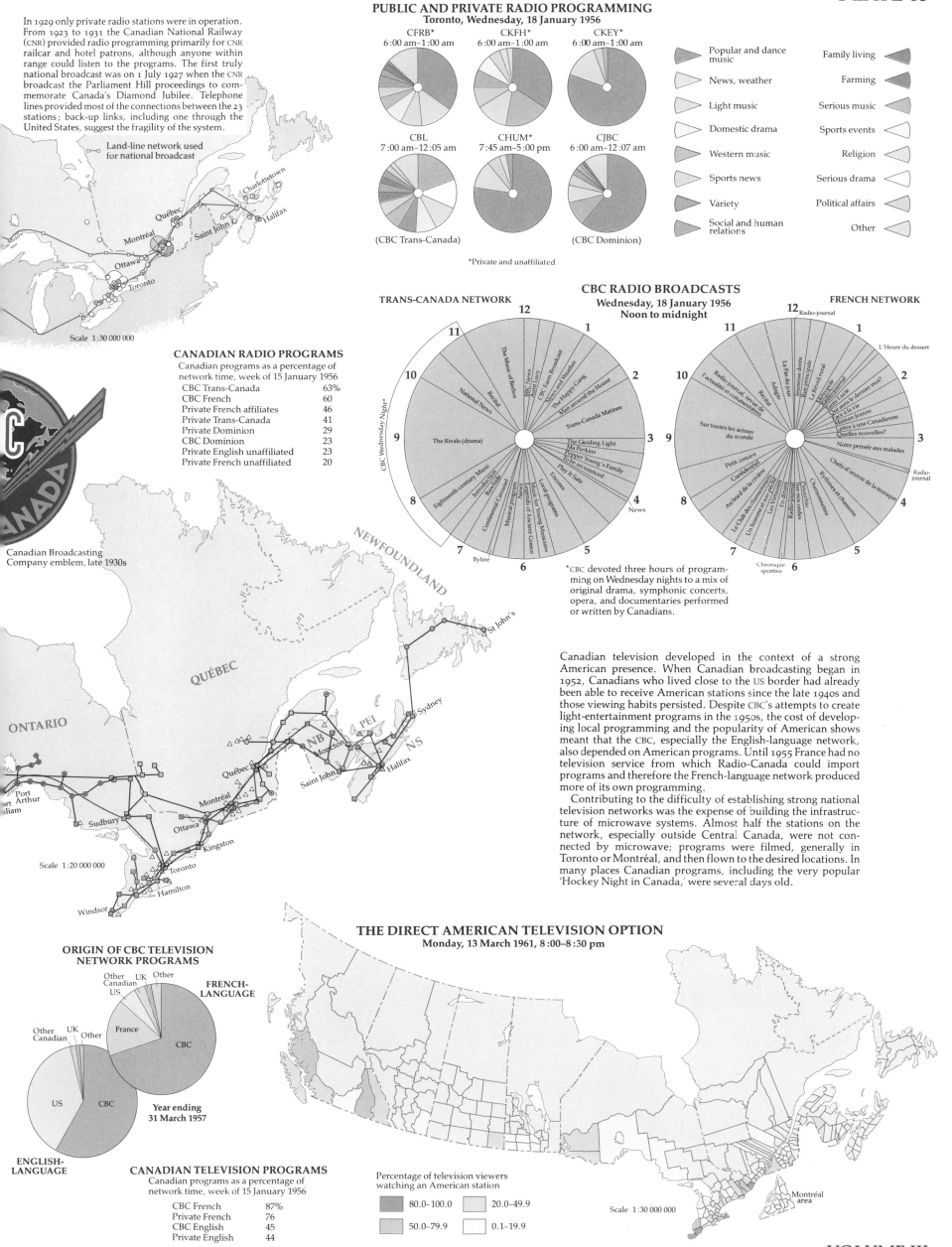

PLATE 65

PUBLIC AND PRIVATE RADIO PROGRAMMING
Toronto, Wednesday, 18 January 1956

In 1929 only private radio stations were in operation. From 1923 to 1931 the Canadian National Railway (CNR) provided radio programming primarily for CNR railcar and hotel patrons, although anyone within range could listen to the programs. The first truly national broadcast was on 1 July 1927 when the CNR broadcast the Parliament Hill proceedings to commemorate Canada's Diamond Jubilee. Telephone lines provided most of the connections between the 23 stations; back-up links, including one through the United States, suggest the fragility of the system.

Land-line network used for national broadcast

Scale 1:30 000 000

CANADIAN RADIO PROGRAMS
Canadian programs as a percentage of network time, week of 15 January 1956

CBC Trans-Canada	63%
CBC French	60
Private French affiliates	46
Private Trans-Canada	41
Private Dominion	29
CBC Dominion	23
Private English unaffiliated	23
Private French unaffiliated	20

Canadian Broadcasting Company emblem, late 1930s

CBC RADIO BROADCASTS
Wednesday, 18 January 1956
Noon to midnight

TRANS-CANADA NETWORK

FRENCH NETWORK

*CBC devoted three hours of programming on Wednesday nights to a mix of original drama, symphonic concerts, opera, and documentaries performed or written by Canadians.

Canadian television developed in the context of a strong American presence. When Canadian broadcasting began in 1952, Canadians who lived close to the US border had already been able to receive American stations since the late 1940s and those viewing habits persisted. Despite CBC's attempts to create light-entertainment programs in the 1950s, the cost of developing local programming and the popularity of American shows meant that the CBC, especially the English-language network, also depended on American programs. Until 1955 France had no television service from which Radio-Canada could import programs and therefore the French-language network produced more of its own programming.

Contributing to the difficulty of establishing strong national television networks was the expense of building the infrastructure of microwave systems. Almost half the stations on the network, especially outside Central Canada, were not connected by microwave; programs were filmed, generally in Toronto or Montréal, and then flown to the desired locations. In many places Canadian programs, including the very popular 'Hockey Night in Canada,' were several days old.

ORIGIN OF CBC TELEVISION NETWORK PROGRAMS

Year ending 31 March 1957

THE DIRECT AMERICAN TELEVISION OPTION
Monday, 13 March 1961, 8:00–8:30 pm

CANADIAN TELEVISION PROGRAMS
Canadian programs as a percentage of network time, week of 15 January 1956

CBC French	87%
Private French	76
CBC English	45
Private English	44

Percentage of television viewers watching an American station

80.0–100.0
50.0–79.9
20.0–49.9
0.1–19.9

Scale 1:30 000 000

CANADA IN 1961
Author: Marvin McInnis

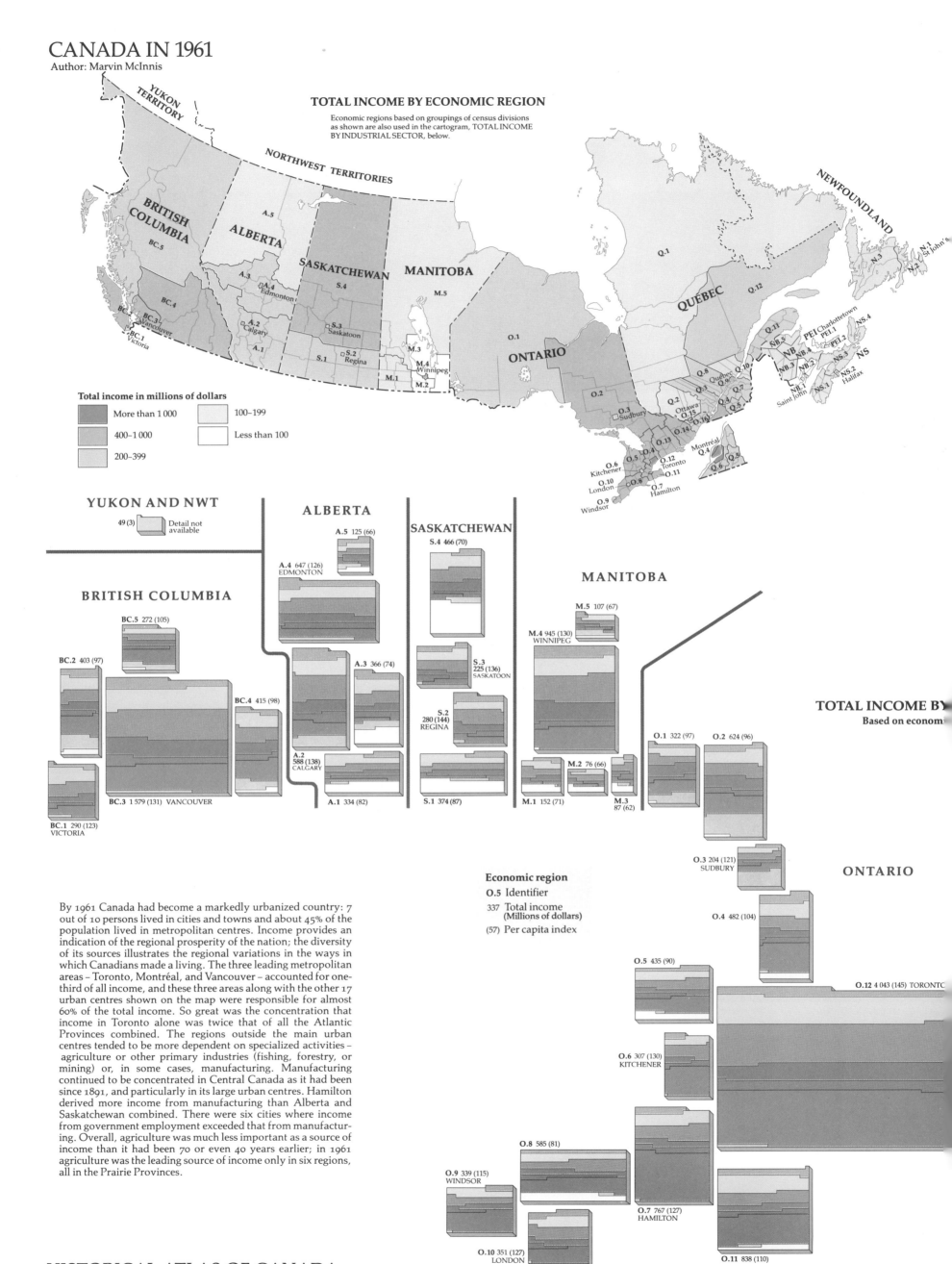

TOTAL INCOME BY ECONOMIC REGION

Economic regions based on groupings of census divisions
as shown are also used in the cartogram, TOTAL INCOME
BY INDUSTRIAL SECTOR, below.

Total income in millions of dollars

More than 1 000
400–1 000
200–399
100–199
Less than 100

YUKON AND NWT

49 (3) Detail not available

BRITISH COLUMBIA

BC.5 272 (105)
BC.2 403 (97)
BC.4 415 (98)
BC.3 1 579 (131) VANCOUVER
BC.1 290 (123) VICTORIA

ALBERTA

A.5 125 (66)
A.4 647 (126) EDMONTON
A.3 366 (74)
A.2 588 (138) CALGARY
A.1 334 (82)

SASKATCHEWAN

S.4 466 (70)
S.3 225 (136) SASKATOON
S.2 280 (144) REGINA
S.1 374 (87)

MANITOBA

M.5 107 (67)
M.4 945 (130) WINNIPEG
M.2 76 (66)
M.1 152 (71)
M.3 87 (62)

Economic region

O.5 Identifier

337 Total income (Millions of dollars)

(57) Per capita index

TOTAL INCOME BY

Based on econom

ONTARIO

O.1 322 (97)
O.2 624 (96)
O.3 204 (121) SUDBURY
O.4 482 (104)
O.5 435 (90)
O.6 307 (130) KITCHENER
O.12 4 043 (145) TORONTO
O.8 585 (81)
O.9 339 (115) WINDSOR
O.7 767 (127) HAMILTON
O.10 351 (127) LONDON
O.11 838 (110)

By 1961 Canada had become a markedly urbanized country: 7
out of 10 persons lived in cities and towns and about 45% of the
population lived in metropolitan centres. Income provides an
indication of the regional prosperity of the nation; the diversity
of its sources illustrates the regional variations in the ways in
which Canadians made a living. The three leading metropolitan
areas – Toronto, Montréal, and Vancouver – accounted for one-
third of all income, and these three areas along with the other 17
urban centres shown on the map were responsible for almost
60% of the total income. So great was the concentration that
income in Toronto alone was twice that of all the Atlantic
Provinces combined. The regions outside the main urban
centres tended to be more dependent on specialized activities –
agriculture or other primary industries (fishing, forestry, or
mining) or, in some cases, manufacturing. Manufacturing
continued to be concentrated in Central Canada as it had been
since 1891, and particularly in its large urban centres. Hamilton
derived more income from manufacturing than Alberta and
Saskatchewan combined. There were six cities where income
from government employment exceeded that from manufacturing. Overall, agriculture was much less important as a source of
income than it had been 70 or even 40 years earlier; in 1961
agriculture was the leading source of income only in six regions,
all in the Prairie Provinces.

PLATE 66

ISODEMOGRAPHIC CANADA

The isodemographic map distorts the conventional map of Canada by relating population to map space. Census divisions make up the component units and have been drawn proportional to their population. In the construction of the map attempts have been made to preserve some semblance of conventional geographic space. Metropolitan centres command most of the area, illustrating the urban reality of Canada. A comparison of the cartogram of income with the isodemographic map suggests some important variations in the levels of material well-being across the country.

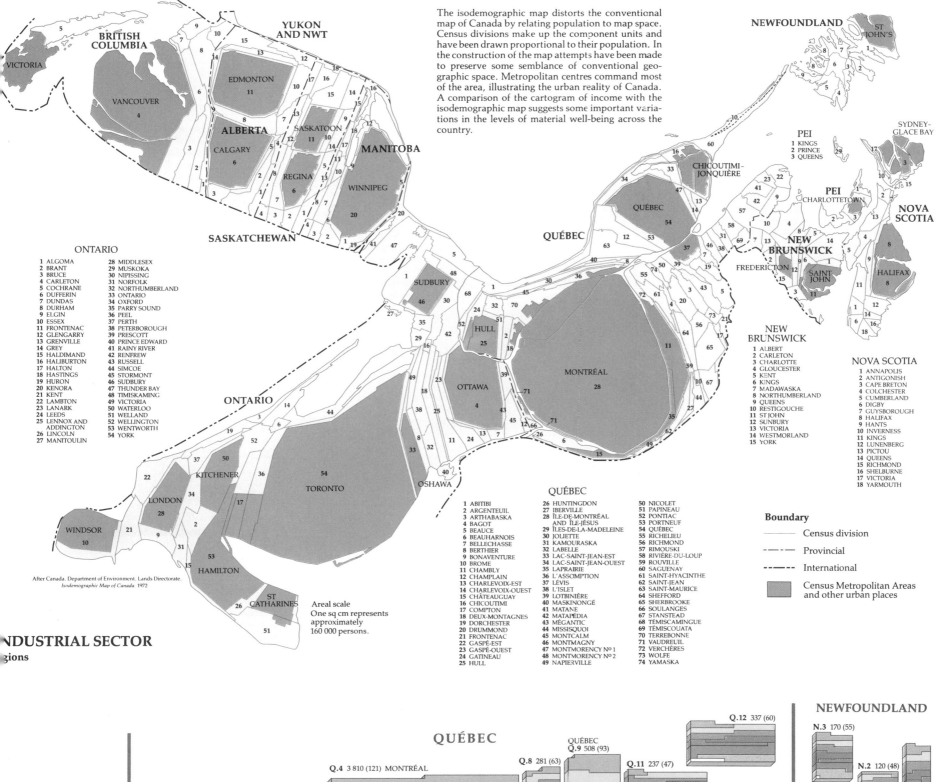

After Canada. Department of Environment. Lands Directorate. *Isodemographic Map of Canada* 1972

Areal scale
One sq cm represents approximately 160 000 persons.

ONTARIO
1 ALGOMA
2 BRANT
3 BRUCE
4 CARLETON
5 COCHRANE
6 DUFFERIN
7 DUNDAS
8 DURHAM
9 ELGIN
10 ESSEX
11 FRONTENAC
12 GLENGARRY
13 GRENVILLE
14 GREY
15 HALDIMAND
16 HALIBURTON
17 HALTON
18 HASTINGS
19 HURON
20 KENORA
21 KENT
22 LAMBTON
23 LANARK
24 LEEDS
25 LENNOX AND ADDINGTON
26 LINCOLN
27 MANITOULIN
28 MIDDLESEX
29 MUSKOKA
30 NIPISSING
31 NORFOLK
32 NORTHUMBERLAND
33 ONTARIO
34 OXFORD
35 PARRY SOUND
36 PEEL
37 PERTH
38 PETERBOROUGH
39 PRESCOTT
40 PRINCE EDWARD
41 RAINY RIVER
42 RENFREW
43 RUSSELL
44 SIMCOE
45 STORMONT
46 SUDBURY
47 THUNDER BAY
48 TIMISKAMING
49 VICTORIA
50 WATERLOO
51 WELLAND
52 WELLINGTON
53 WENTWORTH
54 YORK

QUÉBEC
1 ABITIBI
2 ARGENTEUIL
3 ARTHABASKA
4 BAGOT
5 BEAUCE
6 BEAUHARNOIS
7 BELLECHASSE
8 BERTHIER
9 BONAVENTURE
10 BROME
11 CHAMBLY
12 CHAMPLAIN
13 CHARLEVOIX-EST
14 CHARLEVOIX-OUEST
15 CHÂTEAUGUAY
16 CHICOUTIMI
17 COMPTON
18 DEUX-MONTAGNES
19 DORCHESTER
20 DRUMMOND
21 FRONTENAC
22 GASPÉ-EST
23 GASPÉ-OUEST
24 GATINEAU
25 HULL
26 HUNTINGDON
27 IBERVILLE
28 ÎLE-DE-MONTRÉAL AND ÎLE-JÉSUS
29 ÎLES-DE-LA-MADELEINE
30 JOLIETTE
31 KAMOURASKA
32 LABELLE
33 LAC-SAINT-JEAN-EST
34 LAC-SAINT-JEAN-OUEST
35 LAPRAIRIE
36 L'ASSOMPTION
37 LÉVIS
38 L'ISLET
39 LOTBINIÈRE
40 MASKINONGÉ
41 MATANE
42 MATAPÉDIA
43 MÉGANTIC
44 MISSISQUOI
45 MONTCALM
46 MONTMAGNY
47 MONTMORENCY Nº 1
48 MONTMORENCY Nº 2
49 NAPIERVILLE
50 NICOLET
51 PAPINEAU
52 PONTIAC
53 PORTNEUF
54 QUÉBEC
55 RICHELIEU
56 RICHMOND
57 RIMOUSKI
58 RIVIÈRE-DU-LOUP
59 ROUVILLE
60 SAGUENAY
61 SAINT-HYACINTHE
62 SAINT-JEAN
63 SAINT-MAURICE
64 SHEFFORD
65 SHERBROOKE
66 SOULANGES
67 STANSTEAD
68 TÉMISCAMINGUE
69 TÉMISCOUATA
70 TERREBONNE
71 VAUDREUIL
72 VERCHÈRES
73 WOLFE
74 YAMASKA

NEW BRUNSWICK
1 ALBERT
2 CARLETON
3 CHARLOTTE
4 GLOUCESTER
5 KENT
6 KINGS
7 MADAWASKA
8 NORTHUMBERLAND
9 QUEENS
10 RESTIGOUCHE
11 ST JOHN
12 SUNBURY
13 VICTORIA
14 WESTMORLAND
15 YORK

PEI
1 KINGS
2 PRINCE
3 QUEENS

NOVA SCOTIA
1 ANNAPOLIS
2 ANTIGONISH
3 CAPE BRETON
4 COLCHESTER
5 CUMBERLAND
6 DIGBY
7 GUYSBOROUGH
8 HALIFAX
9 HANTS
10 INVERNESS
11 KINGS
12 LUNENBERG
13 PICTOU
14 QUEENS
15 RICHMOND
16 SHELBURNE
17 VICTORIA
18 YARMOUTH

Boundary
— Census division
—·—·— Provincial
— — — International
▨ Census Metropolitan Areas and other urban places

INDUSTRIAL SECTOR
gions

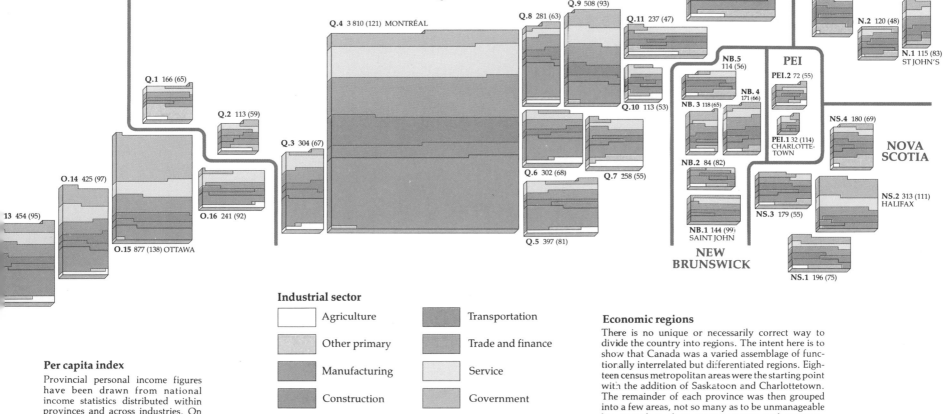

Industrial sector
□ Agriculture
▨ Other primary
▨ Manufacturing
▨ Construction
▨ Transportation
▨ Trade and finance
▨ Service
▨ Government

🍃 Represents one million dollars

Per capita index

Provincial personal income figures have been drawn from national income statistics distributed within provinces and across industries. On the basis of 1961 census data income has been related to population to derive a per capita index.

Economic regions

There is no unique or necessarily correct way to divide the country into regions. The intent here is to show that Canada was a varied assemblage of functionally interrelated but differentiated regions. Eighteen census metropolitan areas were the starting point with the addition of Saskatoon and Charlottetown. The remainder of each province was then grouped into a few areas, not so many as to be unmanageable but enough to show some variation and structure. These regional divisions were based mainly on internal structural interrelatedness as well as locational contiguity.

Notes

Canada Year Book   Canada. Department of Agriculture. *The Statistical Year-Book of Canada.* 1891–1904

Canada. Department of Agriculture. Census and Statistics Office. *The Canada Year Book.* 2nd series. 1905–10

Canada. Department of Trade and Commerce. Census and Statistics Office. *The Canada Year Book.* 2nd series. 1911–17

Canada. Department of Trade and Commerce. Dominion Bureau of Statistics. *Canada Year Book.* 1918–61

Census   Canada. Dominion Bureau of Statistics. *Census of Canada*

DBS   Canada. Dominion Bureau of Statistics

Leacy. *Historical Statistics*   Leacy, F.H., ed. *Historical Statistics of Canada.* 2nd ed. Ottawa: Statistics Canada with the Social Science Federation of Canada, 1983. This is a revision of the original compilation prepared by Urquhart and Buckley in 1965.

NAC   National Archives of Canada

SP   Canada. *Sessional Papers*

Urquhart and Buckley. *Historical Statistics*   Urquhart, M.C., and K.A.H. Buckley, eds. *Historical Statistics of Canada.* Toronto: Macmillan, 1965

Documents published by the federal government have been printed in Ottawa by the King's Printer or the Queen's Printer unless otherwise indicated.

Titles of annual reports of government documents and the names of the departments themselves may have changed over time.

PLATE 1

Canada in 1891

MARVIN McINNIS   Economics, Queen's University
PETER J. USHER   P.J. Consulting Services, Ottawa

Non-native land use: agriculture, fishing, forestry, mining
Net agricultural output by county was estimated from census data, supplemented by data on market prices, using a complex procedure involving a FORTRAN algorithm of more than 300 lines. Full details of the method will be reported in a forthcoming study by McInnis. The general form of the procedure and the motivation for its particular steps are discussed by Lewis and McInnis (1984) in the context of estimates made for Québec counties in 1851.

Manufacturing and forestry output were drawn directly from the census although it must be noted that the reported number of pine logs cut in Essex County, Ontario, is far too large when compared with related data and has been adjusted. Mineral production was based on quantities of output reported in DBS Reference Paper No. 68 (1957), converted to values in some instances and prices reported in annual reports of the provincial departments of mines.
Canada. *Census.* 1891. Vols 3, 4
– DBS. *Canadian Mineral Statistics, 70 Years, 1886–1952.* Reference Paper No. 68. 1957
– *SP.* 1892. No. 11A, App A
Lewis, Frank D., and Marvin McInnis. 'Agricultural Output and Efficiency in Lower Canada, 1851.' *Research in Economic History* 9 (1984): 45–87

Non-native land use: missions
As far as possible, the missions shown represent permanent posts.
Beech, H.P. *A Geography and Atlas of Protestant Missions.* Vol 2. New York: Student Volunteer Movement for Foreign Missions, 1903
Carrière, Gaston. *Histoire documentaire de la Congrégation des missionaires oblats de Marie-Immaculée dans l'Est du Canada.* Pt 2. Vol 9. Ottawa: Éditions de l'Université d'Ottawa, 1970
Champagne, Claude. *Les débuts de la mission dans le Nord-Ouest canadien: mission et église chez Mgr Vital Grandin, o.m.i., 1829–1902.* Ottawa: Éditions de l'Université Saint-Paul, 1983
Levasseur, Donat. *Histoire des Missionaires oblats de Marie Immaculée: essai de synthèse.* Vol 1: (1815–1898). Montréal: Maison provinciale, 1983
Musée du Québec. *Le grand héritage: l'église catholique et la société du Québec.* Vol 2. Québec, 1984

Non-native land use: fur trading posts
Many thanks to Arthur J. Ray (History, University of British Columbia) for providing the information on fur-trade posts south of 60°.
Hudson Bay Company Archives. A 74/1. 'Annual Reports, Outfit 1891 Contents'
– A 12/L 58/2 fo. 21. 'Map showing the Position of the Trading Establishments of the Hudson's Bay Company'
The National Atlas of Canada. 4th ed, rev. Ottawa: Macmillan / Department of Energy, Mines and Resources and Information Canada, 1974. Information from original research files of P.J. Usher
Ray, A.J. 'The Hudson's Bay Company and Native People.' In W.E. Washburn, ed. *History of Indian-White Relations.* Vol 4 of *Handbook of North American Indians,* ed W.C. Sturtevant. Washington: Smithsonian Institution, 1988. Pp 335–50
– *The Canadian Fur Trade in the Industrial Age.* Toronto: University of Toronto Press, 1990. Information from original research files of Arthur J. Ray

Non-native land use: whaling stations
Native land use
The National Atlas of Canada. 4th ed, rev. Information from original research files of P.J. Usher

The land: unexplored by Europeans
Adjustments to the sources below were made on the advice of Wm G. Dean, University of Toronto, Richard I. Ruggles, Queen's University, Alan Cooke, Montréal, and J. Garth Taylor, Museum of Civilization, Hull.
Harris, R. Cole, ed. *Historical Atlas of Canada.* Vol I: *From the Beginning to 1800.* Toronto: University of Toronto Press, 1987
The National Atlas of Canada. 4th ed, rev.

PLATE 2

Territorial Evolution

ROBERT GALOIS   Geography, University of British Columbia
NORMAN NICHOLSON
MICHAEL STAVELEY   Geography, Memorial University of Newfoundland

Before he died in Nov 1984 Professor Norman Nicholson had provided us with maps and other research material as well as much good advice for this plate. In his rich and varied career Norman had been Director of the Geographical Branch in Ottawa, Assistant Dean of the Graduate School, Principal of University College, and Chairman of the Geography Department at University of Western Ontario, and Editor of the *Canadian Geographer* which he helped found. Above all he was a dedicated scholar whose book, *The Boundaries of Canada, Its Provinces and Territories,* remains the definitive statement in the field.

Two views of land in British Columbia
The map of the Gitskan and Wet'suwet'en territories was compiled under the authority of the hereditary chiefs. Many thanks are due to the Tribal Council for providing the map and refining the text, and to Richard Overstall for providing liaison during this process.
British Columbia. Department of Lands. Pre-Emptor's Map. 'Bulkley Sheet,' 1922

Regional share of territory
Land area indicated as 1949 uses 1951 data; 1951 was the first time Newfoundland was included.
Canada Year Book. 1892: p 115. 1952: p 129

Canada, 1891–1961
The National Atlas of Canada 5th ed, rev. Ottawa: Energy, Mines and Resources Canada, 1985. Pl 13.5

Proposals for the Prairie Provinces, 1905
Nicholson, Norman L. *The Boundaries of Canada, Its Provinces and Territories.* Ottawa: Queen's Printer, 1954. Pp 129–38

Arctic exploration
There were other explorers who ventured into the Arctic region between 1891 and 1961. Those shown on the map were the first to travel to particular areas.
Taylor, Andrew. *Geographical Discovery and Exploration in the Queen Elizabeth Islands.* Geographical Branch Memoir No. 3. Department of Mines and Technical Surveys. Ottawa, 1955

Newfoundland joins Confederation
The Newfoundland Gazette. Aug 1948

PLATE 3

Economic Growth

MARVIN McINNIS   Economics, Queen's University

National work-force
Leacy. *Historical Statistics*. Series D8–85
McInnis, R.M. 'Output and Productivity in Canadian Agriculture, 1870–71 to
   1926–27.' In Stanley L. Engerman and Robert E. Gallman, eds. *Long-Term
   Factors in American Economic Growth*. Vol 51. National Bureau of Economic
   Research. Studies in Income and Wealth, Vol 51. Chicago: University of
   Chicago Press, 1986. Pp 737–78

Gross domestic product per capita
'Germany' refers to the area of the Federal Republic of Germany for all years.
Maddison, Angus. *Phases of Capitalist Development*. Oxford / New York: Oxford
   University Press, 1982. App
Urquhart, M.C. 'New Estimates of Gross National Product, Canada 1870–1926:
   Some Implications for Canadian Development.' In Engerman and Gallman,
   eds. *Long-Term Factors*. 1986. Pp 9–94

Manufacturing production per capita
'Germany' refers to Federal Republic of Germany in 1957.
Maddison. *Phases of Capitalist Development*. 1982. P 537, Table E4

Share of world trade
Hilgerdt, F. *Industrialization and Foreign Trade*. Geneva: League of Nations, 1948
Lewis, W.A. 'The Rate of Growth of World Trade, 1830–1973.' In Svend Grassman
   and Erik Lundberg, eds. *The World Economic Order, Past and Prospects*. New
   York: St Martin's Press, 1979. App II
Maizels, Alfred. *Industrial Growth and World Trade*. Cambridge: Cambridge Univer-
   sity Press, 1969
United Nations. *Yearbook of Trade Statistics*. New York, 1961

Foreign investment
Leacy. *Historical Statistics*. Series G188–202, G318–40

Balance of trade
Urquhart and Buckley. *Historical Statistics*. Series F348–56

Exports and imports: destinations
Canada. Department of Trade and Commerce. *Trade of Canada*. 1925–61
– SP. 1892–1908. Tables of the Trade and Navigation of Canada
– SP. 1909–24. Report of the Department of Trade and Commerce

Exports and imports: commodities
In the absence of comparable figures for 1916 and 1917 the period 1916 to 1920
represents only three years. Electrical apparatus was removed from 'non-
ferrrous metals and products' and transferred to the machinery component of 'iron
and steel products.' 'Machinery' includes the categories of machinery, farm
implements and machinery, rolling-mill products, engines and boilers, automobiles, automobiles parts, and electrical apparatus. Sources for graphs of selected
individual commodities are those indicated for 'destinations' and 'value.'
Urquhart and Buckley. *Historical Statistics*. Series F246–69, F270–93, F360–79,
   F380–99, F316–33

Exports and imports: value
Total values of exports and imports shown on the graph are the averages for each
five-year period.
Urquhart and Buckley. *Historical Statistics*. Series F242–45
See also sources for 'commodities.'

Net value of commodity production
'Construction' was not included in 1926 and 1961 because data were unreliable for
1926. For 1926 manufacturing figures were adjusted downwards to eliminate the
estimated wood-cut used by manufacturing firms. For 1926 forestry figures were
based on the value of forest production.
Canada. DBS. *Annual Report on the Forest Industry*, 1926
– DBS. *Survey of Production*, 1962. 1965. Cat. 61–202. Tables 7–13

Gross domestic product, 1891 (map)
Using a GDP total of $858.5 million (divided into $210.9 million 'agricultural' and
$647.6 million 'non-agricultural'), based on a constant 1913 dollar, the provincial
estimates in Green (1971) were used to distribute GDP proportionally.
Green, Alan George. *Regional Aspects of Canada's Economic Growth*. Toronto:
   University of Toronto Press, 1971. Table B1
McInnis. 'Output and Productivity.' 1986

Gross domestic product: 1891; 1926; 1961 (graphs)
For each year forest products cut on farms were removed from the agriculture totals
in Urquhart (1986) and added to forestry, after McInnis (1986).
McInnis. 'Output and Productivity.' 1986
Urquhart. 'New Estimates of Gross National Product.' 1986. Table 2:1
Urquhart and Buckley. *Historical Statistics*. Series F56–75

Growth of economic production: 1891; 1926; 1961
For 1891 the national GDP total of $858.5 million was distributed on the basis of
urban and rural population; in rural areas the dots represent general districts
rather than specific places. For 1926 the national GDP total of $3 217.7 million was
distributed on the basis of net sales of retail merchandise. For 1961 the national
GDP total of $13 663.3 million was distributed on the basis of personal income.
Canada. *Census*. 1891: Vol 1, Table VI. 1931: Vol 10, Table 12. 1961: Vol 4, Bulletin
   4.1–3, Table C5
For 1891 see also sources for 'Gross domestic product, 1891.'

PLATE 4

Population Composition

DONALD CARTWRIGHT   Geography, University of Western Ontario
MURDO MacPHERSON   Historical Atlas of Canada, Toronto

Ethnic origin: 1901; 1931; 1961
Since the 1901 and 1935 censuses of Newfoundland and Labrador gave only place of
birth and not ethnic origin, Newfoundland is not included in 1891 and 1931. Graphs
of cities specify ethnic groups of 0.4% or larger; graphs of provinces specify groups
of 1.0% or more except 'other' which may be less than 1.0%.
Canada. Census. 1901: Vol 1, Table XI. 1931: Vol 2, Tables 32, 34. 1961: Vol 1, Pt 2,
   Tables 37, 38

Major ethnic groups
Canada. *Census*. 1901: Vol 1, Table XI. 1931: Vol 2, Table 31. 1961: Vol 1, Pt 2, Table 35

Population profile: 1901; 1931; 1961
Canada. *Census*. 1961. Vol 1, Pt 2, Table 20

Rural and urban population: 1901; 1931; 1961
Estimates of Newfoundland population were provided by Michael Staveley
(Geography, Memorial University of Newfoundland).
Canada. *Census*. 1901–61. Various tables
Newfoundland. *Census of Newfoundland and Labrador*. Various years

Population growth
Leacy. *Historical Statistics*. Series A67–9

The bilingual belt
With the exception of Montréal, urban areas have been incorporated with the census
subdivisions in which they are located. On the map adjacent census subdivisions
with similar values and thus of the same category are amalgamated into a single unit.
Individual subdivisions are shown only when they are of a different category from
surrounding divisions.
Canada. *Census*. 1961: Vol 1, Pt 1, Table 7; Series SP, Bulletin SP–5

Further readings
Canada. Royal Commission on Bilingualism and Biculturalism. *The Official Languages*.
   Book I. 1967
Coons, W.H., D.M. Taylor, and M.-A. Tremblay, eds. *The Individual, Language and
   Society in Canada*. Ottawa: The Canada Council, 1977
Joy, Richard J. *Languages in Conflict: The Canadian Experience*. Toronto: McClelland
   and Stewart, 1972
Lachapelle, Réjean, and Jacques Henripin. *La situation démolinguistique au Canada:
   évolution passée et pros*. Montréal: Institut de recherches politiques, 1980. Also
   issued in English as *The Demolinguistic Situation in Canada: Past Trends and Future
   Prospects* in 1982
Lieberson, Stanley. *Language and Ethnic Relations in Canada*. New York: Wiley, 1970
Maheu, Robert. *Les francophones au Canada: 1941–1991*. Montréal: Éditions Parti pris,
   1970

PLATE 5

Primary Production

MARVIN McINNIS   Economics, Queen's University

Agricultural production, 1891 and 1921
Procedures used to estimate net agricultural output in dollars by county and by
province are exceedingly complex, the estimating algorithms alone taking at
least 300 lines of FORTRAN. Production data have been drawn from the agricultural
census and price data from a wide variety of sources. The main complexity of the
estimation procedure lies in the conversion of census data on stocks of animals,
sales and production of animal products, and production of field crops into
measures of net output, to give the net amount of crops used for animal feed. The
method is an adaptation of one first developed by Lewis and McInnis (1984) in a
study of mid-19th-century Québec and later modified by McInnis (full details to be
discussed by McInnis in a forthcoming monograph).
   Three categories of agricultural commodities are shown: livestock and animal
products such as milk, butter, and wool; the net production (not counting crops
used for animal feed) of the conventional field crops such as wheat, barley, and hay
sold to the non-agricultural sectors of the economy; and an assortment of other
products such as tobacco, apples, beans, and clover seed that were typically grown
in only a few specific areas. Dots representing given amounts of each of the first
two categories of agricultural production have been distributed randomly by a
computer program within the settled area of each township. Dots for the
specialty products were located manually in locations known to have large
concentrations of those products. On the map of the whole nation in 1921
agricultural production is aggregated into a single product. This is a counterpart to
the 1891 map shown on pl 1. The agricultural detail has been mapped separately
for Central Canada in 1891 and 1921 and for the Prairie Provinces in 1921.
   The provincial and national totals of agricultural production are aggregations of
the county totals. National aggregates for 1891 and 1921 obtained in this way
agree quite closely with national estimates of GDP originating in agriculture made by
a quite different method and reported by McInnis (1986) in a study of trends in
agricultural productivity.
Canada. *Census*. 1891: Vol 3. 1921: Vol 5
Lewis, Frank D., and Marvin McInnis. 'Agricultural Output and Efficiency in Lower
   Canada, 1851.' *Research in Economic History* 9 (1984): 45–87, esp App, 'The
   estimation of net agricultural productivity'
McInnis, Marvin. 'Output and Productivity in Canadian Agriculture, 1870–71 to
   1926–27.' In Stanley L. Engerman and Robert E. Gallman, eds. *Long-Term
   Factors in American Economic Growth*. National Bureau of Economic Research.
   Studies in Income and Wealth, Vol 51. Chicago: University of Chicago Press,
   1986. Pp 737–78

Mining production

Value of mineral production has unavoidably been upwardly biased because minerals are valued at market prices. No data are available for pithead prices and consequently transport and other costs are built into the price used for conversion to value of production.

Canada. DBS. *Canadian Mineral Statistics, 70 Years, 1886–1956*. Reference Paper No. 68. 1957

Various annual reports of provincial departments of mines were also used.

Forestry production

Value of forestry production is based on national figures for GDP originating in forestry, as estimated by Urquhart (1986), allocated to provinces on the basis of the value of woods operations reported by the DBS (1926). The value of forest production includes transport to the sawmills and pulp mills. The symbols on the map representing value of forestry production do not take into account farm cut which was widely dispersed; this omission is especially noteworthy in Québec.

Canada. *Census*. 1891. Vol 6
– DBS. *Forest Industries of Canada, 1926*. 'Operations in the woods'
Urquhart, M.C. 'New Estimates of Gross National Product, Canada 1870–1926: Some Implications for Canadian Development.' In Engerman and Gallman, eds. *Long-Term Factors*. 1986. Pp 9–94

Fishing production

Canada. DBS. *Fishery Statistics of Canada*. Cat. 24–201. 1921
Urquhart. 'New Estimates of Gross National Product.' 1986. Esp Table 2:1

PLATE 6

The Expansion and Consolidation of Railways

CHRISTOPHER ANDREAE Historica Research, London

Corporate structure
Corporate connections
Expansion of the railway network

Various sources were consulted in the preparation of these illustrations. The following are the principal sources:

Bladen, M.L. 'Construction of Railways in Canada.' *Contributions to Canadian Economics* 5 (1932): 43–60; 7 (1934): 61–107
Booth, J. Derek. *Railways of Southern Quebec*. 2 vols. West Hill: Railfare, 1982, 1985
Bowman, R.F.P. *Railways in Southern Alberta*. Lethbridge: Whoop-up Country Chapter, Historical Society of Alberta, 1973
Canada. DBS. *Railway Statistics* (various titles). 1919–60
– DBS. *Railway Transport in Canada*. 1919–60
– Department of Railways and Canals. *Annual Report*. 1879–1936
– Department of Railways and Canals. *Railway Statistics*. 1879–1918
Currie, Archibald W. *The Grand Trunk Railway of Canada*. Toronto: University of Toronto Press, 1957
Dorman, Robert, compiler. *A Statutory History of the Steam and Electric Railways of Canada, 1836–1937*. Ottawa: Department of Transport, 1938
Due, John F. *The Intercity Electric Railway Industry in Canada*. Toronto: University of Toronto Press, 1966
Glazebrook, G.P. de T. *A History of Transportation in Canada*. Toronto: Ryerson, 1938. Repr Toronto: McClelland and Stewart, 1964
Helm, Norman. *In the Shadow of Giants: The Story of the Toronto, Hamilton & Buffalo Railway*. Cheltenham, Ont: Boston Mills, 1978
Innis, Harold A. *A History of the Canadian Pacific Railway*. Toronto: University of Toronto Press, 1923. Repr 1971
Jackson, John N., and John Burtniak. *Railways in the Niagara Peninsula*. Belleville: Mika, 1978
Lamb, W. Kaye. *History of the Canadian Pacific Railway*. New York: Macmillan, 1977
Lavallée, Omer S.A. *Narrow Gauge Railways of Canada*. Montréal: Railfare, 1972
Legget, Robert F. *Railroads of Canada*. Vancouver: Douglas, David & Charles, 1973
McLean, S.J. 'National Highways Overland.' In A. Shortt and A.G. Doughty, eds. *Canada and Its Provinces*. Toronto: Glasgow, Brook, 1914. Vol 10, pp 359–472
Moody's Investors Service. *Moody's Transportation Manual: Railroads, Airlines, Shipping, Traction, Bus and Truck Lines* (various titles). New York: Moody's Investor Service, 1900–60
Nock, Oswald. *Algoma Central Railway*. London: Black, 1975
– *Railways of Canada*. London: Black, 1973
Penney, Alfred R. 'The Newfoundland Railway: Newfoundland Epic.' In J.R. Smallwood, ed. *The Book of Newfoundland*. St John's: Nfld Book Pub, 1967. Pp 473–502
Poor, H.V., and H.W. Poor. *Poor's Manual of Railroads* (various titles). New York: Poor, 1868–1941
Ramsay, Bruce. *PGE – Railway to the North*. Vancouver: Mitchell, 1962
Regehr, T.D. *The Canadian Northern Railway*. Toronto: Macmillan, 1976
Stephens, David E. *Iron Roads, Railways of Nova Scotia*. Windsor, NS: Lancelot, 1972
Stevens, G.R. *Canadian National Railways*. 2 vols. Toronto: Clarke Irwin, 1960, 1962
– *History of the Canadian National Railways*. New York: Macmillan, 1973
Tucker, Albert. *Steam into Wilderness: Ontario Northland Railway, 1902–1962*. Toronto: Fitzhenry and Whiteside, 1978
Turner, Robert. *Vancouver Island Railroads*. San Marino, Calif: Golden West, 1973
Wilgus, William T. *The Railway Interrelations of the United States and Canada*. New York, 1937. Repr New York: Russell and Russell, 1970

Freight traffic

Canada. Royal Commission on Railways and Transportation in Canada. *Report*. 1931–2

Gross revenue and trackage

Canada. DBS. *Railway Statistics* (various titles). 1919–60
– Department of Railways and Canals. *Railway Statistics*. 1897, 1917

Construction of the first main track

Urquhart and Buckley. *Historical Statistics*. Series S120–8

Freight rates by territory

Darling, Howard. *The Politics of Freight Rates: The Railway Freight Rate Issue in Canada*. Toronto: McClelland and Stewart, 1980. Fig 1, p 12

Grain and flour rates

Henry, R.A.C., and Associates. 'Railway Freight Rates in Canada. Royal Commission on Dominion-Provincial Relations. Ottawa, 1939. Schedule 33, p 282

Evolution of corporate emblems

Canadian Pacific Railway Corporate Archives, Montréal
Clegg, Anthony, and Ray Corley. *Canadian National Steam Power*. Montréal: Railfare, 1969. P 16
Lavallée, Omer. 'Sir William Would Have Approved.' *Spanner* 7, no. 5 (July–Aug 1968): 12

PLATE 7

The Changing Structure of Manufacturing

GERALD BLOOMFIELD Geography, University of Guelph
MICHAEL HINTON Montréal
T.D. REGEHR History, University of Saskatchewan, Saskatoon
GLEN WILLIAMS Political Science, Carleton University

We wish to acknowledge the help of Stephen Bellinger in the preparation of this plate.

Manufacturing production and employment

All the primary sources of manufacturing statistics suffer from three major problems – classification, coverage, and comparability. Classifications of manufacturing in the earlier censuses include many activities which are no longer regarded as manufacturing (eg, electric-power generation, dyeing and cleaning, blacksmithing). Until the 1920s when classification systems based primarily on materials were adopted, there was little attempt to group manufacturing activities. All the census reports merely present an alphabetical listing of industries (the 1911 census has 228 separate categories from 'abrasive goods' to 'wool pulling'). The coverage of industrial activity is variable over time. Prior to 1901 all industrial establishments regardless of size were included in the census. From 1901 to 1911 establishments with fewer than five employees were excluded although some activities such as cheese making were included even if they had fewer than five employees. The 1916 *Postal Census of Manufactures* covered only establishments with an annual output of $2 500 or more.

Comparability is, then, a major problem in using the primary published materials. It has been difficult to revise the data to make them comparable because in earlier periods an activity may have been insufficiently defined and, to avoid disclosure of an individual establishment, the data were sometimes included under 'all other industries.' The problems of disclosure are greatest at the subprovincial level and it is virtually impossible to construct data for small areas by industrial group.

For the most part the various sectors or subdivisions of Canadian manufacturing are well covered in the primary sources. Indeed it would seem that the greatest original interest in and use of the statistics was by sector of manufacturing. Until the 1920s there was little attempt to develop higher-order aggregations of statistics. The 1907 and 1913 *Canada Year Books* had a 15-group classification for contemporary statistics and retrospective summaries. The schemes developed in the 1920s were based on similarity of materials and therefore included some curious groups of industries.

The introduction of a Standard Industrial Classification by the DBS in 1948 reorganized the classification of manufacturing activities. This 1948 classification was used by Bertram (1964) and Urquhart and Buckley (1965) to develop a comparable series of statistics from 1870 to the 1950s. Bertram's (1964) compilations of sectors by provinces have made it possible to prepare data to show production by industry by province for 1890, 1910, and 1929.

Bertram, G.W. 'Historical Statistics on Growth and Structure of Manufacturing in Canada 1870–1957.' In J. Henripin and A. Asimakopulos, eds. *Conferences on Statistics 1962 and 1963, Papers*. Canadian Political Studies Association. Toronto: University of Toronto Press, 1964. Pp 93–151
Bloomfield, G.T. 'General Statistics on Canadian Manufacturing to 1929.' Unpublished report submitted to the Historical Atlas of Canada project, Vol III, 1982
Canada. *Census*. 1891: Vol 3. 1911: Vol 3
– DBS. *Annual Survey of Manufactures*. 1929. Series 31–D–20–7
Canada Year Book. 1932. Pp 305–35
Drummond, Ian M. *Progress without Planning: The Economic History of Ontario from Confederation to the Second World War*. Ontario Historical Studies Series. Toronto: University of Toronto Press, 1987. App B, pp 353–9
Urquhart and Buckley. *Historical Statistics*. Section Q, pp 455–92

American branch plants

Field (1914) provides the only early listing of American firms operating in Canada. Although Field's estimates of the dollar value of foreign capital investments in Canada have been criticized, his compilation of American firms is generally accepted. However, Hooper (1983) revealed a few flaws in Field's list of American firms operating in Hamilton in 1913.

Bellinger, S.L. 'American Firms in Canada: Data Sources and Review.' Unpublished report submitted to the Historical Atlas of Canada project, Vol III, 1984
Field, Frederick William. *Capital Investments in Canada*. Montréal: Monetary Times, 1914
Hooper, Diana. 'Foreign Ownership and the Evolution of Canada's Industrial Structure: A Case Study of Hamilton, Ontario.' MA thesis, University of Toronto, 1983

The motor-vehicle industry

Data on companies are drawn from company files.

Bloomfield, G.T. 'Elements of the Canadian Motor Vehicle Industry to 1929.' Unpublished report submitted to the Historical Atlas of Canada project, Vol III, 1982
Canada. DBS. *Automobile Statistics for Canada*. Cat. 42–209. 1930

The newsprint industry
Comprehensive statistical data are available on capacity of mills but data on production are fragmentary and in some cases unreliable.
Financial Post. 4 Sep 1925. 26 Sep 1931. Supplemented by other statistical data published in various issues of the *Financial Post, Financial Times, Pulp and Paper Directory of Canada, Pulp and Paper Business Directory of Canada, Pulp and Paper Canada, National Directory of the Canadian Pulp and Paper Industries*
Urquhart and Buckley. *Historical Statistics*. Series k156–68

The cotton industry
Manuscript material from Michael Hinton (Montréal)

Origin of capital investment of growth industries
Williams, Glen. *Not for Export*. Toronto: McClelland and Stewart, 1983. Ch 2, Table 2, p 29

Further readings
Acheson, T.W. 'The National Policy and the Industrialization of the Maritimes, 1880–1910.' *Acadiensis* 1, no. 1 (Spring 1972): 3–28
Bertram, Gordon W. 'Economic Growth in Canadian Industry, 1870–1915: The Staple Model and the Take-off Hypothesis.' *Canadian Journal of Economics and Political Science* 29, no. 2 (May 1963): 162–84. Repr in W.T. Easterbrook and Mel Watkins, eds. *Approaches to Canadian Economic History*. Toronto: McClelland and Stewart, 1967. Pp 74–98
Bloomfield, Gerald. *The World Automotive Industry*. Newton Abbot: David Charles, 1987
Gilmour, James M., and Kenneth Murricane. 'Structural Divergence in Canada's Manufacturing Belt.' *Canadian Geographer* 17, no. 1 (Spring 1973): 1–18
Guthrie, John Alexander. *The Newsprint Paper Industry*. Cambridge, Mass: Harvard University Press, 1941
Kerr, Donald. 'The Emergence of the Industrial Heartland c. 1750–1950.' In L.D. McCann, ed. *Heartland and Hinterland: A Geography of Canada*. Scarborough: Prentice-Hall, 1982. Pp 64–99
Linteau, Paul-André, René Durocher, and Jean-Claude Robert. *Quebec: A History 1867–1929*, transl Robert Chodos. Toronto: Lorimer, 1983
Marshall, Herbert, Frank Southard, and Kenneth Wiffen Taylor. *Canadian-American Industry: A Study of International Investment*. New York: Russel & Russel, 1970. Repr Toronto: McClelland and Stewart, 1976
Piedalue, Gilles. 'Les Groupes Financiers et la Guerre du Papier au Canada 1920–1930.' *Revue d'histoire de l'Amérique française* 30, no. 2 (Sep 1976): 223–58
Rae, John B. *The American Automotive Industry*. Boston: Twayne, 1984
Rouillard, Jacques. *Les travailleurs du coton au Québec 1900–1915*. Montréal: Les Presses de l'Université du Québec, 1974
Weldon, J.C. 'Consolidations in Canadian Industry 1900–1948.' In Lawrence Alexander Skeoch, ed. *Restrictive Trade Practices in Canada*. Toronto: McClelland and Stewart, 1966. Pp 228–79

PLATE 8
Wholesale Trade

GERALD BLOOMFIELD   Geography, University of Guelph
DONALD KERR   Geography, University of Toronto
G.E. MILLS   Canadian Parks Service, Victoria

We would like to acknowledge the help of Ian Drummond (Economics, University of Toronto) in the preparation of this plate.

Wholesaling, 1930
The first comprehensive census of wholesale trade in Canada was not taken until 1930 and was published in the census of 1931. There was a small incomplete census of wholesale and retail trade in 1924 which has only limited value. From 1891 to 1961, as the population increased and the economy expanded, the volume, diversity, and sale of consumer goods increased. However, any quantitative measure of change is difficult before 1931. Drummond (1987) marshalled statistical and other evidence on retailing and wholesaling for Ontario for the 1870s, 1880s, and 1890s to compare with censuses of 1931 and 1941 in order to measure change, but he has declined to put his data in tabular form, arguing that the evidence could be very misleading. Reynolds (1938) discusses in detail procedures for making estimates. He broadens the definition of trade somewhat and uses the term 'marketing' to include the activities of wholesale and retail establishments as well as manufacturing activities related to the selling of goods rather than physical production. As measured by employment, marketing increased almost fivefold from 1890 to 1930, in contrast to manufacturing (about 2½ times) and agriculture (about 1⅓ times). Estimates of employment in trade, both retail and wholesale, made by McInnis (1983) for the period 1911 to 1931 show an increase from 259 800 in 1911 to 425 000 in 1931.
Canada. *Census*. 1931. Vol 2, Pt 2
– *Census of Trading Establishments, 1924*. 1928
Drummond, Ian M. *Progress without Planning: The Economic History of Ontario from Confederation to the Second World War*. Ontario Historical Studies Series. Toronto: University of Toronto Press, 1987. P 300
McInnis, R.M. 'Work Force by Industrial Category.' In Leacy. *Historical Statistics*. Series D8–85, D86–106
Reynolds, Lloyd. 'Some Notes on the Distributive Trades in Canada.' *Canadian Journal of Economics and Political Science* 4, no. 4 (Nov 1938): 533–48

Dixon Brothers General Store
The Dixon brothers opened a general store in Maple Creek, Sask, in 1883. Unlike most store owners, they kept all their records and correspondence which their descendants deposited partly in the Glenbow Museum in Calgary and partly in the Saskatchewan Archives in Regina. Invoices for the purchase of goods from wholesalers for the year 1889 were examined and tabulated.
Kerr, Donald. 'Wholesale Trade on the Canadian Plains in the Late 19th Century: Winnipeg and its Competition.' In Howard Palmer, ed. *The Settlement of the West*. Calgary: University of Calgary, 1977. Pp 130–52, esp nn 60, 61, 62

Imperial Oil Company
We are grateful to Imperial Oil for giving us access to various materials in its business library in Toronto. We wish to acknowledge the help of R. Taylor-Vaizey and his staff in 1982 and Les Czarnota and Linda Scott in 1988–9.
Bloomfield, G.T. 'Development of National Marketing in Canada to 1929: The Case of Imperial Oil Ltd.' Unpublished report submitted to the Historical Atlas of Canada project, Vol III, 1982
'The Distribution of Imperial Products.' *Imperial Oil Review* 3, no. 4 (Apr 1919): 8
Ewing, J.S. 'The History of Imperial Oil.' 4 vols. 1951. Unpublished
'Increasing our Marketing Facilities.' *Imperial Oil Review* 3, no. 2 (Feb 1919): 3–12

Massey-Harris Company
Statistical and other material has been drawn from a variety of records of the Massey-Ferguson Company and its predecessors deposited in the Ontario Agricultural Museum in Milton, Ontario, by the Varity Corporation in 1987. In 1989 the material was only partly catalogued and access was somewhat difficult for the library staff. We are very grateful to Susan Bennett, Research and Reference Librarian, for her assistance in locating material.
Bloomfield, G.T. 'The Development of Manufacturer-Dominated Marketing Channels: A Case Study of Massey Harris 1890–1930.' Unpublished report submitted to the Historical Atlas of Canada project, Vol III, 1989
Ontario Agricultural Museum. Massey-Ferguson Company records

Canadian Western Lumber Company
Dominion of Canada and Newfoundland Gazetteer and Classified Business Directory. Toronto: Canadian Gazetteer Publishing Company, 1914. Esp pp 442–4, 640–2, 1589–93

Further readings
Canada. Royal Commission on Price Spreads. *Report 1935*. 1937
Dennison, Merrill. *Harvest Triumph: The Story of Massey-Harris*. Toronto: McClelland and Stewart, 1948
Porter, Glenn, and Harold C. Livesay. *Merchants and Manufacturers: Studies in the Changing Structure of Nineteenth Century Marketing*. Baltimore: The Johns Hopkins University Press, 1971
Vance, James E. *The Merchant's World: A Geography of Wholesaling*. Englewood Cliffs, NJ: Prentice-Hall, 1970

PLATE 9
Financial Institutions

WILLIAM CODE   Geography, University of Western Ontario
GUNTER GAD   Geography, University of Toronto
NEIL QUIGLEY   Economics, Victoria University of Wellington, New Zealand

With the exception of the graph showing the assets of all financial intermediaries, only federally chartered banks and insurance companies are included on this plate. Unless otherwise stated, the data shown reflect the assets and the locations of banks and insurance companies at year end.

Assets of financial intermediaries
Assets shown are Canadian assets; ie, foreign assets of Canadian financial intermediaries are excluded. The graph includes assets chartered in either Ontario or Québec only.
Neufeld, Edward P. *The Financial System of Canada. Its Growth and Development*. Toronto: Macmillan, 1972. Pp 580–603, 617–25

The ten largest banks by assets
Bank assets by location of head office
Changing location of bank head offices
The 1911 totals include the assets of Sovereign Bank. Although the bank went into liquidation in 1908, its assets were still listed in the 1911 'Returns of the chartered banks of the Dominion of Canada.' The location of the executive or general managers' offices rather than the legal seats of chartered banks are considered on this plate. In 1901 the general managers' offices of the Royal Bank were in Montréal and those of the Bank of Nova Scotia were in Toronto while the legal head offices of both companies were in Halifax. The executive offices of the short-lived Sovereign Bank were in Montréal; its legal head office was in Toronto.
The Banque Jacques-Cartier was reorganized as Banque Provinciale du Canada in 1900 and the Merchants Bank of Halifax changed its name to the Royal Bank of Canada in 1901. After absorbing the Bank Nationale in 1924/5, the Banque d'Hochelaga adopted the name Banque Canadienne Nationale.
Annual Financial Review. Various issues
Bank Canadian National 1874–1974: A Hundred Years of History. Montréal: np, nd (ca 1975). Pp 57–9
Beckhart, B.H. *The Banking System of Canada*. New York: Henry Holt, 1929. Pp 334–9
Canada. Department of Finance. *Annual Report of the Chartered Banks of Canada*. 1891, 1901, 1911, 1921, 1931. Reprinted as supplements to the *Canada Gazette*, usually in Jan or Feb of the subsequent year
Canada Year Book. 1932. Pp 779–80
Code, William Robert. 'The Spatial Dynamics of Financial Intermediaries: An Interpretation of the Distribution of Financial Decision Making in Canada.' PH D thesis, University of California, Berkeley, 1971
Monetary Times. 5 and 12 Jan 1900; 4 and 11 Jan 1924
Royal Bank of Canada. *Fiftieth Anniversary of the Royal Bank of Canada*. Montréal: Royal Bank of Canada, 1920. Pp 17–20, 23
Schull, J., and J.D. Gibson. *The Scotiabank Story: A History of the Bank of Nova Scotia 1832–1982*. Toronto: Macmillan, 1982. Pp 79–81

Structure of banking
Branch data for 1921, 1926, and 1931 include 'subagencies,' ie, deposit-receiving agencies. These were particularly numerous in Québec. Until 1918 data sources on bank branches do not separate full branches and subagencies. Bank branches outside Canada in 1931 are excluded.
Beckhart. *The Banking System*. Pp 860–3

Breckenridge, R.M. *The History of Banking in Canada*. Washington: Government
Printing Office, 1910. P 310
Canada. Department of Finance. *Annual Report of the Chartered Banks of Canada*. 1891,
1901, 1911, 1921, 1931
Canada Year Book. 1916–17: p 555. 1921: p 720. 1926: p 828. 1932: p 776

Development of the national branch system of banks
Branch data for 1890 include the main branch of each bank, usually attached to the
head office. The number of branches shown for 1890 apply to the mid-1890s.
Branch data do not include 'subagencies.' Figures for British Columbia include two
branches each of the Canadian Bank of Commerce and the Bank of Montreal.
Garland, N.S. *Garland's Banks, Bankers and Banking in Canada*. Ottawa: Mortimer,
1890. Pp 22, 29, 30
Canada Year Book. 1932. P 776

Loans and deposits of the Bank of Nova Scotia
In order to avoid the portrayal of unusual events, three-year averages were used:
1900, 1901, 1902 for 1901; 1910, 1911, 1912 for 1911; and 1925, 1926, 1927 for 1926.
The 1926 average for Saskatchewan excludes two Saskatoon branches (Main and
West Side) and the 1926 average for Newfoundland excludes the branch at Fogo.
Data for these branches were not available.
We gratefully acknowledge the assistance of Jane Nokes, Laura Power, and
Garron Wells at the archives of the Bank of Nova Scotia.
Bank of Nova Scotia Archives. Head-office ledgers
Quigley, Neil C. 'Bank Credit and the Structure of the Canadian Space Economy c.
1890–1935.' PH D thesis, University of Toronto, 1986. Pp 301–77

The ten largest insurance companies by assets
Insurance-company assets by location of head office
The insurance industry, 1921
Nationality of insurance companies
All assets, Canadian and those in foreign countries held by Canadian companies,
are included. Totals are derived by adding the assets of individual companies
and include assets arising from the accident business of life-insurance companies.
The assets included and the methods used to arrive at totals result in figures for
totals different from those published in other places. The head-office locations of
foreign companies are those of the 'chief agency in Canada.'
The breakdown by nationality excludes one non-American or non-British foreign
company in 1911, six in 1921, and fourteen in 1931.
Canada. Department of Insurance. *Annual Report*. 1891, 1901, 1911, 1921, 1931

Mortgage loans of life-insurance companies
Figures on mortgage loans are for mortgages outstanding at the end of each year
and do not indicate the amount of money spent on mortgages in that year.
Canada. Department of Insurance. *Annual Report*. 1928. Vol 2, p xxxv

PLATE 10

The Emergence of the Urban System

MICHAEL P. CONZEN   Committee on Geographical Studies,
University of Chicago
DONALD KERR   Geography, University of Toronto
JAMES W. SIMMONS   Geography, University of Toronto

The urban network: 1891; 1921
Population change
In the measurement and mapping of urbanization there are problems of definition:
what is the threshold size below which places are not considered to be urban;
and what is the areal demarcation used to separate an urban place from its rural
surroundings? In Canada there is no alternative to using population data as
compiled in decennial censuses. Prior to 1951, the DBS defined the urban population
as those persons residing within *incorporated* cities, towns, and villages of
whatever population. Between 1941 and 1951 the rapid expansion of suburban
populations within rural municipalities led to a redefinition. In 1951 the
definition of urban population was modified to include all persons living in cities,
towns, and villages with populations of 1 000 and over, *incorporated or not*, as
well as the residents of *metropolitan areas*. This latter concept included municipalities
and parts of townships adjacent to major centres with populations of over
100 000.
A decision was made to adopt the 1951 definition to identify urban centres in 1891
and 1921 on these maps. Unincorporated places were considered, closely linked
urban centres were aggregated together, and the urbanized parts of rural
municipalities were assigned to the appropriate urban place.
Allen, E.S., compiler. *The Official Guide of the Railways and Steam Navigation Lines of
the United States, Puerto Rico, Canada, Mexico, and Cuba*. New York: National
Railway Publication Company, 1921
Allen, W.F., compiler. *Travellers' Official Railway Guide for the United States and
Canada*. New York: National Railway Publications Company, 1891
Canada. *Census*. 1891. 1921. Various tables, data modified by author
Simmons, J.W., and G. Dobilas. 'Population Nodes, 1871–1951.' Unpublished
report submitted to the Historical Atlas of Canada project, Vol III, 1984

The long-distance telephone network
Telephone connections from Montréal
From the early 20th century on, Canadian telephone facilities were greatly
decentralized, being controlled by eight major companies and several smaller
ones: each province in western Canada and Nova Scotia, New Brunswick, and
Newfoundland had its own telephone company; the Bell Telephone Company
controlled facilities in Ontario and Québec. The variable quality and general lack of
comparability of the historical records make research difficult. Without question
the archives and historical section of Bell Canada in Montréal are the largest and
most valuable source of information. Very few records are available in provincial
or federal archives.
Using maps as sources of information had limitations. The existence of a line
between two points on a map did not necessarily mean that there was a reliable
long-distance service between the two points. Further research is needed to establish

more precisely the spread of the service in terms of reliability and frequency of calls.
A special acknowledgment is made to the staff of the Bell Canada Archives in
Montréal and especially Stephanie Sykes, Director of the Historical and
Information Resource Centre, and Catherine Lowe, Manager of the Historical
Research Division, for providing maps and other source material as well as
answering countless questions. Without their help it would have been impossible to
prepare the maps.
Dick Priest and later Robert Lewis of the American Telephone and Telegraph
Company in New York were extremely helpful. Research commissioned under
their supervision to answer our questions is gratefully acknowledged. Additional
invaluable assistance was received from across Canada: Tony Cashman of
Edmonton, retired historian of the Alberta Telephone Company; R. Cole Harris,
Department of Geography, University of British Columbia; Ted Chown of
Saskatchewan Telephone; and L.D. McCann, Department of Geography, Mount
Allison University.
American Telephone and Telegraph Company Archives. New York. 'Growth of the
Long Lines Plant 1881–1941.' 21 June 1946. Map
Archives Bell Canada, Montréal. Reference No. 1544, 'Bell Telephone Company of
Canada: Long Distance Lines and Connections, October 1891' and 'United
States Connections.' Reference No. 14258, 'Bell Telephone Company of Canada:
Wire Map Long Distance Lines, 1909.' Reference No. 14258, 'Bell Telephone
Company of Canada: Wire Map Long Distance Lines, 1909. Maps
'British Columbia Telephone Company Ltd.: Toll Circuit and Route Map.' *Telephone
Talk* (Dec 1919): 13
Kee, C.A. *History of Telephone Service in New Brunswick*. 1920 (unpublished). Maps 1
and 2, 'New Brunswick Toll Lines, August 1906', pp 71A, 71B. A copy of the
manuscript has been deposited in the NAC.
NAC. National Map Collection. 'Route of Trans-Canada Telephone System.' 1932
Saskatchewan Telephone and Telegraph Company, Regina. Historical Records.
'Saskatchewan Government: Long Distance Telephone System and Connec-
tions.' 1913, 1920, 1924. Maps
United States. Federal Communications Commission Special Investigation. Docket
No.1, 'Telephone and Telegraph Trunk Routes of the American Telephone
and Telegraph Company Long Lines Department, 1935.' Exhibit 134, Report on
American Telephone and Telegraph Company, Washington, Apr 15, 1936. Map

Further readings
Abler, Ronald. 'The Telephone and the Evolution of the American Metropolitan
System.' In Itheil de Sola Pool, ed. *The Social Impact of the Telephone*.
Cambridge, Mass: Massachussetts Institute of Technology Press, 1977. Pp 318–41
Armstrong, Christopher, and H.V. Nelles. *Monopoly's Moment: The Organization and
Regulation of Canadian Utilities*. Philadelphia: Temple University Press, 1986 /
Toronto: University of Toronto Press, 1987
Cashman, Anthony W. *Singing Wires – The Telephone in Alberta*. Edmonton: Alberta
Government Telephones Commission, 1972
George, M.V. 'Population Growth In Canada.' Profile Study. 1971 Census
Monograph. Bulletin 5.1–1. Cat. 99–701. Ottawa: Statistics Canada, 1976
Langdale, John V. 'The Growth of Long Distance Telephony in the Bell System:
1875–1907.' *Journal of Historical Geography* 4, no. 2 (1978): 145–59
Ogle, Edmond B. *Long Distance Please: The Story of the TransCanada Telephone System*.
Don Mills: Collins, 1979
Patten, William. 'Pioneering the Telephone in Canada.' Montréal, 1926 (privately
printed)
Simmons, James W. 'The Growth of the Canadian Urban System.' Centre for Urban
and Community Studies, University of Toronto, Research Paper No. 65. 1974
Simmons, J.W., and Bourne, L.S. 'Defining Urban Places: Differing Concepts of the
Urban System.' In L.S. Bourne and J.W. Simmons, eds. *System of Cities:
Readings on Structure, Growth and Policy*. New York: Oxford University Press,
1978. Pp 28–41
Stone, Leroy O. *Urban Development in Canada*. 1961 Census Monograph. Ottawa:
DBS, 1967
Trotier, Louis. 'La genèse du réseau urbain du Québec.' *Recherches sociographiques* 9,
no. 1 (Jan 1968): 23–32
Wasserman, Neil H. *From Invention to Innovation: Long Distance Telephone Transmis-
sion at the Turn of the Century*. Baltimore: The Johns Hopkins University Press,
1985

PLATE 11

Resource Industries Based in Central Canada

MARVIN McINNIS   Economics, Queen's University

It is difficult to define resource-processing industries: should they be restricted to
industries that do the first-stage processing of local resources (eg, cheese
factories, vegetable-canning plants) or can they include the processing of imported
resources (eg, sugar refineries, cotton-spinning plants, meat packing in 1891)?
Industries change in nature and orientation over time. In 1891 Central Canada had a
large number of leather tanneries located close to supplies of tanning bark; by
1926 leather tanning had been freed from its orientation to supplies of tanning bark
and the smaller number of large tanneries reflected instead an orientation to the
market represented by boot- and shoe-manufacturing plants. The industries
selected for this plate are the most important during the period, in terms of value
of production. Graphs are used to depict the overall magnitude of output, the
extent of its concentration in Québec and Ontario, and the degree of orientation
to export.

1891
Unless otherwise indicated the information for 1891 came from the census of 1891.

SAWMILLS
Census data on sawmills are given for the following groups of census divisions:
Grenville North and Leeds, Muskoka and Parry Sound, Arthabaska and Drummond,
Chicoutimi and Saguenay; Lincoln includes Niagara; Ottawa includes Papineau,
Hull, and Labelle. On the map the combined data were spread within the grouped
census divisions but the individual census division boundaries were kept.

Figures shown in the census for Essex County must be in error (see notes for pl 1). Scattered information from the trade literature has permitted identification of the leading large mills.

FLOUR MILLS
Scattered information from the trade literature has permitted identification of the largest plants. For the two largest categories the specific plants and their locations are shown. The large number of small plants is mapped in an approximate way in accordance with the distribution of small villages.

PULP MILLS
The 1891 census data are difficult to use because paper mills (many still using rag input) and pulp mills that produced wood pulp are not clearly separated. In the census several of the largest pulp mills were grouped with paper mills because they were integrated wood pulp/newsprint mills. *Lockwood's Directory* is helpful in sorting this out.
Lockwood's Directory of Paper, Stationery and Allied Trades, 1892–93. New York: Howard Lockwood and Co

DAIRY FACTORIES
The census of manufactures lists 1 510 cheese factories in Ontario and Québec in 1891. They tended to be of fairly uniform size so little would be achieved by trying to locate them all. The wide dispersion through the countryside is shown in the inset map of Leeds and Grenville counties. Locations of factories are from the Bureau of Industries report. Data on the production of butter and cheese in factories are from the census. The data on butter and cheese production are given for groups of counties: Lennox and Addington, Victoria and Haliburton, Arthabaska and Drummond, Beauce and Frontenac, Chicoutimi and Lac-Saint-Jean, Richmond and Wolfe.
Ontario. *Sessional Papers.* 1891. No. 67. 'Report of the Bureau of Industries of Ontario, 1891.' Data on factories and creameries in Ontario

MILK COWS
Areas of concentration of milk cows are townships with more than 6.0 milk cows per 100 acres of farmland.

1926
SAWMILLS
Total production is available only by province. Locational details are available only for plants categorized by capacity.
Canada. DBS. *Census of Industry, 1926.* 'The Lumber Industry.' Appendix

FLOUR MILLS
Only information on the capacity of individual mills is available.
Canada. DBS. *The Grain Trade of Canada, 1926.* P 34

PULP MILLS
The manufacture of wood pulp – the first stage in the utilization of forests for paper production – is shown rather than the distribution of newsprint manufacturing. Much newsprint was manufactured at the same location as wood pulp; however, there were considerable exports of wood pulp for manufacture elsewhere so the two products differ in some important respects. Data for pulp mills are for 1924.
Lockwood's Directory, 1924. 'Paper and Pulp Mills in the Dominion of Canada'

DAIRY FACTORIES
This is an industry which continued to be pursued in many small factories. Since it would be too difficult at the scale of this map to represent the more than 1 000 plants in operation in 1926, production by county, divided between cheese and butter, is shown as in 1891. Many of the factories produced both butter and cheese.
Canada. DBS. *The Manufacturing Industries of Canada, 1926.* 'Dairy Factories'

MEAT PACKING
Country abbatoirs are not included.
Canada. DBS. *The Manufacturing Industries of Canada, 1926.* 'Slaughtering and Meat Packing'

FRUIT AND VEGETABLE CANNERIES
These are primarily vegetable canneries since little fruit was canned in Central Canada. The earliest available report on the food-canning industry is for 1928 and its data are used on the map. Locations of individual plants were derived from business directories, advertisements in the *Canadian Grocer*, and the list of plants given in the report of the Royal Commission on Price Spreads.
Canada. DBS. *The Manufacturing Industries of Canada, 1928.* 'Food Canning Industry'
– Royal Commission on Price Spreads. *Report 1935.* 1937
Canadian Grocer

MILK CONDENSERIES
This industry appears for the first time on the map for 1926. In 1891 there was only one condensed-milk factory in Canada and that was located in Nova Scotia. In the 20th century the industry developed substantially in Ontario.
Canada. DBS. *The Manufacturing Industries of Canada, 1926.* 'Dairy Factories'

MILK COWS
Areas of concentration of milk cows are townships with more than 7.5 cows per 100 acres of farmland.

PLATE 12

Electricity and Industrial Development in Central Canada

GERALD BLOOMFIELD Geography, University of Guelph
RENÉ HARDY Sciences humaines, Université du Québec à Trois-Rivières
PIERRE LANTHIER Sciences humaines, Université du Québec à Trois-Rivières
NORMAND SÉGUIN Sciences humaines, Université du Québec à Trois-Rivières

We would like to acknowledge the help of D.S. Laker, Local History Development, Earl Brydges Public Library, Niagara Falls, NY, and researchers Stephen Bellinger and Alain Gamelin in preparing this plate.

Major electricity transmission systems: 1906; 1911; 1918; 1928
Canada. Department of Agriculture. Census and Statistics Office. *Postal Census of Manufactures.* 1906
– Department of the Interior. 'Dominion Water Power and Reclamation Service, Central Electric Stations in Canada.' 1929
– Department of Trade and Commerce. Census and Statistics Office. *Postal Census of Manufactures.* 1916
– *SP.* 1906. No. 13
Dennis, Leo G. *Electric Generation and Distribution in Canada.* Ottawa: Commission of Conservation, 1911
– *Electric Generation and Distribution in Canada.* Ottawa: Commission of Conservation, 1918
Ontario. *Sessional Papers.* 1932. No. 26, Ontario Hydro Annual Report 1931. P 503

Industrial generating capacity
Canada. *Census.* 1901: Vol 3, Table VI. 1911: Vol 3, Table VI
Canada Year Book. 1924: p 416. 1932: p 366

HEPCO domestic-service rates, southern Ontario
Hydro-Electric Power Company of Ontario. *Annual Report.* 1925. Statement D
Plewman, W.R. *Adam Beck and Ontario Hydro.* Toronto: Ryerson Press, 1947. P 482

The Niagara region
Canada. DBS. *Census of Manufacturing.* 1918
– Department of Inland Revenue. *Annual Report.*1929. App K

Hydroelectric generating capacity by region
Canada. Department of the Interior. *Dominion Water Power.* 1929
Dennis. *Electric Generation.* 1918
Dennis, Leo G., and A.V. White. *Water Power of Canada.* Ottawa: Commission of Conservation, 1911

Power and industry in the Saint-Maurice valley
Lanthier, Pierre, and Alain Gamelin. *L'Industrialisation de la Mauricie: dossier statistique et chronologique 1870–1975.* Trois-Rivières: Université du Québec à Trois-Rivières, 1981
Shawinigan Water and Power Company. *Rapport annuel.* 1929, 1949

Further readings
Adams, Edward Dean. *Niagara Power, History of the Niagara Falls Power Company 1886–1918.* 2 vols. Niagara Falls, NY: Niagara Falls Power Company, 1927
Bellavance, Claude, Normand Brouillette, and Pierre Lanthier. 'Financement et industrie en Mauricie, 1900–1950.' *Revue d'histoire de l'Amérique française* 40, no. 1 (June 1986): 29–50
Bloomfield, G.T. 'Electricity Generation and Transmission in Central Canada 1896–1928.' Unpublished report submitted to the Historical Atlas of Canada project, Vol III, 1982
– 'Electric Power Rates in Canada to 1929.' Unpublished report submitted to Historical Atlas of Canada project, Vol III, 1983
– 'Hydro Electricity and Industrialization in the Niagara Region to 1929.' Unpublished report submitted to Historical Atlas of Canada project, Vol III, 1983
– 'Energy and Manufacturing Industry in Canada to 1929.' Unpublished report submitted to Historical Atlas of Canada project, Vol III, 1983
Dales, John Harkness. *Hydro-Electricity and Industrial Development in Quebec 1898–1940.* Cambridge, Mass: Harvard University Press, 1957
Dow, Charles Mason. *Anthology and Bibliography of Niagara Falls.* Vol 2. Albany, NY, 1921. Pp 929–1056
Hardy, René, and Normand Séguin. *Forêt et société en Mauricie: la formation de la région de Trois-Rivières.* Montréal: Boréal Express / Musée national de l'Homme, 1984
Hogue, C., A. Bolduc, and D. Larouche. *Québec: un siècle d'électricité.* Montréal: Libre expression, 1979
Jackson, J.N., and C. White. *Industrial Structure of the Niagara Peninsula.* St Catharines, 1971
Lanthier, Pierre. 'L'industrie électrique entre l'entreprise privée et le secteur public: le cas de deux provinces canadiennes: 1890–1930.' In F. Cardot, ed. *Un siècle d'électricité dans le monde, 1880–1980.* Colloque international d'histoire de l'électricité. Paris: Les Presses universitaires de France, 1987. Pp 23–36
– 'Stratégie industrielle et développement régional: le cas de la Mauricie au xxᵉ siècle.' *Revue d'histoire de l'Amérique française* 37, no. 1 (June 1983): 3–20
McKay, Paul. *Electric Empire: The Inside Story of Ontario Hydro.* Toronto: Between the Lines, 1983
Nelles, H.V. *The Politics of Development: Forests, Mines, and Hydro-Electric Power in Ontario 1849–1941.* Toronto: Macmillan, 1974

PLATE 13

Urban Industrial Development in Central Canada

ELIZABETH BLOOMFIELD History, University of Guelph
GERALD BLOOMFIELD Geography, University of Guelph
MARC VALLIÈRES Histoire, Université Laval

For a discussion of manufacturing data see notes for pl 7. Many thanks to Stephen
Bellinger, Pierre Poulin, and Alain Gelly for their assistance in the preparation
of this plate.

Regional share of manufacturing
Greater Montréal includes, in addition to the City of Montréal, the following
municipalities in the years specified: Lachine in each year; Saint-Louis,
Saint-Henri, and Sainte-Cunegonde in 1890, 1900, and 1905; Maisonneuve in 1900,
1905, 1910, 1915, and 1920; Westmount in 1900, 1905, 1920, and 1929;
Saint-Lambert, Saint-Laurent, Longueuil, Verdun, and Outremont in 1910, 1915,
1920, and 1929; La Salle, Saint-Pierre, and Montréal East in 1929 only.

Greater Toronto includes, in addition to the City of Toronto, the following
municipalities in the years specified: Toronto Junction (West Toronto) in 1890,
1900, and 1905; North Toronto in 1910; Weston in 1910, 1915, 1920, and 1929; New
Toronto in 1920 and 1929; Mimico and Leaside in 1929 only.

For the graph the term 'rest of Central Canada urban centres' is defined as all
other urban centres with a minimum population of 1 500 in Central Canada, and
these places are included on the three maps, 'Manufacturing: distribution and
change.' The 'rest of Ontario and Quebec' is the remainder of the two provinces
outside the area defined as Central Canada (ie, northern Ontario and northeastern
and northern Québec) as well as rural and small urban centres within Central
Canada. The 'rest of Canada' is all provinces except Ontario and Québec.
Canada. *Census*. 1891. Vol 3
– DBS. *Annual Survey of Manufactures*. 1929
– Department of Agriculture. Census and Statistics Office. *Postal Census of
  Manufactures*. 1906
– Department of Trade and Commerce. Census and Statistics Office. *Postal Census
  of Manufactures*. 1916

Manufacturing structure of the 15 largest centres
Urban centres with a population over 15 000 were included. Occupations were
reclassified according to 1970 standard industrial-classification groupings.
Canada. *Census*. 1911. Vol 6, Table VI

Manufacturing: distribution and change
Changes in definitions and confidentiality rules limit the comparability of industrial
data for urban centres over the 40-year period considered. To reduce such
problems and to include as many urban centres as possible it was decided to make
use of data for urban centres with a population of at least 1 500 in the years 1890,
1905, 1915, and 1929. This selection produced data for over 100 urban centres in
Central Canada, but the exact numbers varied over the period.

For data sources see above, 'Regional share of manufacturing.'

Berlin/Kitchener-Waterloo
Berlin changed its name to Kitchener in 1916. In order to construct the map on
workplace and residence, lists of workers in each of the selected firms were compiled
from the alphabetical section of *Vernon's Directory* for the years 1897 and 1927.
The precise location of each worker's home was checked in the street-directory
section. Locations were plotted on detailed base maps derived from contemporary
fire-insurance plans; this helped overcome problems of changed street names.
From other evidence the work-force seems to have been under-represented in the
directory. Hibner's furniture factory was claimed to employ 60–70 men in 1896–7,
but only 20 were listed in the directory. The Williams, Greene and Rome shirt factory
had only 78 workers in the directory, but contemporary accounts mention figures
of between 350 and 500 at this time. It may be that the directory did not specify the
workplace of casual workers, general labourers, apprentices, and other very young
workers. Figures from the 1927 directory also seem lower than the quoted
work-forces: Canadian Goodrich, for example, probably employed at least twice the
number of 384 given in the directory. Two categories of workers were distinguished:
'white collar' workers were those in clerical, managerial, and supervisory positions;
'blue collar' were skilled, semi-skilled, or unskilled workers and also those whose
jobs were not specified in the directories.
Bloomfield, Elizabeth. 'Home-Workplace Distributions of Factory Workers in
  Berlin/Kitchener-Waterloo 1897–1929.' Unpublished report submitted to the
  Historical Atlas of Canada project, Vol III, 1983
– 'Industrial Development in Berlin/Kitchener-Waterloo to 1929.' Unpublished
  report submitted to the Historical Atlas of Canada project, Vol III, 1983
– Urban-industrial data base
Vernon's Berlin, Waterloo and Bridgeport Directory for 1897. Hamilton: Henry Vernon
  and Son, 1897
Vernon's Kitchener, Waterloo and Bridgeport Directory 1927. Hamilton: Henry Vernon
  and Son, 1927

The Windsor Area
For a discussion of the methodology for the map of workplace and residence of
employees of the Ford Motor Company see above 'Berlin/Kitchener-Waterloo.'
Bellinger, S., and G.T. Bloomfield. 'Workplace and Residence in the Border Cities,
  1905 and 1926–7.' Unpublished report submitted to the Historical Atlas of
  Canada project, Vol III, 1983
Bloomfield, Elizabeth. Urban-industrial data base
Bloomfield, G.T. 'Industrial Development in the Border Cities to 1929.' Unpublished
  report submitted to the Historical Atlas of Canada project, Vol III, 1983
*Vernon's City of Windsor, Ojibway, Sandwich, Walkerville, Ford and Riverside Directory
  1926–7*. 14th edition. Hamilton: Henry Vernon and Son, 1927

Québec
For a discussion of problems of methodology see above, 'Berlin/
Kitchener-Waterloo.'
Bluteau, Marc-André. 'L'industrie de la chaussure à Québec (1896–1940).' MA
  thesis, Université Laval, 1979
– et al. *Les cordonniers, artisans du cuir*. Montréal: Boréal Express / Musée national de
  l'Homme, 1980
Bradstreet Co. *Bradstreet's Commercial Ratings*. July 1912
Gelly, Alain. 'Importance et incidence de l'industrie des munitions sur la structure
  industrielle de Québec, 1879–1946.' MA thesis, Université Laval, 1989
Poulin, Pierre. 'Déclin portuaire et industrialisation: l'évolution de la bourgeoisie
  d'affaires de Québec à la fin du XIXe siècle et au début du XXe siècle.' MA thesis,
  Université Laval, 1985
Publicity Bureau. *Quebec, Canada*. Québec: Commercial Magazine Co, 1912
Quebec and Levis Directory 1912. Québec: Boulanger et Marcotte

Further readings
Bloomfield, Elizabeth. 'Building Industrial Communities, Berlin and Waterloo to
  1915.' In David Walker, ed. *Manufacturing in Kitchener-Waterloo, A Long-Term
  Perspective*. Department of Geography Publication Series No. 26. Waterloo:
  University of Waterloo Press, 1987. Pp 5–33
– 'The Maturing Industrial Economy, Kitchener-Waterloo 1915–1945.' In Walker,
  ed. *Manufacturing in Kitchener-Waterloo*. 1987. Pp 35–59
Drummond, Ian M. *Progress without Planning: The Economic History of Ontario from
  Confederation to the Second World War*. Ontario Historical Studies Series.
  Toronto: University of Toronto Press, 1987
Harvey, Fernand. *Révolution industrielle et travailleurs: une enquête sur les rapports entre
  le capital et le travail au Québec à la fin du 19e siècle*. Montréal: Boréal Express,
  1978
Kerr, Donald. 'The Emergence of the Industrial Heartland c. 1750–1950.' In L.D.
  McCann, ed. *Heartland and Hinterland: A Geography of of Canada*. Scarborough:
  Prentice-Hall, 1982. Pp 64–99
Linteau, Paul-André, René Durocher, and Jean-Claude Robert. *Quebec: A History
  1867–1929*, transl Robert Chodos. Toronto: Lorimer, 1983
Raynauld, André. *Croissance et structure économique de la province de Québec*. Québec:
  Ministère de l'Industrie et du Commerce, 1961
Robinson, J.L. 'Windsor, Ontario: A Study in Urban Geography.' *Canadian
  Geographical Journal* 27, no. 3 (Sep 1943): 106–21
Ryan, W.F. *The Clergy and Economic Growth in Quebec (1816–1914)*. Québec: Les
  Presses de l'université Laval, 1966
Spelt, Jacob. *Urban Development in South Central Ontario*. Carleton Library Series No.
  57. Toronto: McClelland and Stewart, 1972
Vance, James E., Jr. 'Labor-Shed, Employment Field and Dynamic Analysis in
  Urban Geography.' *Economic Geography* 36, no. 3 (July 1960): 189–220

PLATE 14

Industrial Development in Montréal

PAUL-ANDRÉ LINTEAU Histoire, Université du Québec à Montréal
SYLVIE TASCHEREAU PHD candidate, histoire, Université du Québec à
  Montréal

The process of annexation
Ville de Montréal. Service d'urbanisme. *Toponymie*. 'Bulletin d'information.' No. 4.
June 1966. 'Annexions-Annexations' (map)

Population and the building cycle
Population figures for the City of Montréal are those of the official territory of the
city at the time of the census. Because of the annexation movement city limits in
1891, 1901, 1911, and 1921 were different from those in the preceding census.
Population figures for the city and its suburbs from 1861 to 1921 have been
computed by adding those for the city and those for the suburban towns
surrounding it on the Island of Montréal; figures for 1931 are for the urban
population of the entire Island of Montréal.

The number of building permits is for the City of Montréal and does not include
the figures for the independent suburbs; the territory covered was gradually
extended as suburban towns or villages were annexed and became wards of the
city. A single building permit was issued for each building even if it had many
dwellings. Thus the figures do not reflect perfectly the expansion of the housing
stock. In the last decades of the 19th century most houses were either
single-family homes or two-storey buildings with two or three dwellings (often
called the Montréal duplex), whereas in the first decades of the 20th century
three-storey buildings with usually five dwellings (often called triplexes) became
much more common.
Canada. *Census*. 1891–31
Data on building permits were collected by David Hanna from the annual reports of
  the departments of the City of Montréal, Montréal Municipal Archives.

Major industrial sites and built-up area, 1879
In 1880 Montréal had 1 467 manufacturing establishments and the suburbs had
144. Only the most important ones are plotted on the map for 1879.
Hopkins, Henry W. *Atlas of the City and Island of Montreal including the Counties of
  Jacques Cartier and Hochelaga: From Actual Surveys, Based upon the Cadastral Plans
  Deposited in the Office of the Department of Crown Lands*. Montréal: Provincial
  Surveying and Publishing Co, 1879
Montreal Directory. Montréal: John Lovell, 1879–80

Major industrial sites and built-up areas, 1915

Montréal recorded 1 104 manufacturing establishments in 1910 (1 147 with the suburbs) and 2 823 in 1920 (2 936 with the suburbs). Only the most important ones are plotted on the map for 1915.

Canada. Department of Militia and Defence. 'Laval Sheet.' Canada 1 inch to 1 mile, Topographic Map No. 22 (31H/12) 1909, repr with corrections, 1915
Goad, Charles E. *Atlas of the City of Montreal and Vicinity in Four Volumes; From Official Plans & Special Surveys, Showing Cadastral Numbers, Buildings & Lots*. 4 vols. Montréal, 1912–14
Goad, Chas E., Co. *Insurance Plan of the City of Montreal, Quebec, Canada*. Montréal, 1909–15. Vols 1, 2, 3, 5, 6
Montreal Directory. Montréal: John Lovell, 1914–15
Montreal Street Railway Company. *Annual Report*. 1910. 'Montreal Street Railway Company's Local and Suburban Lines'

Land use in the central area

Many of the buildings in the downtown area were multi-purpose. Only the dominant function is indicated on the map.

Goad. *Insurance Plan of the City of Montreal*. 1909–15

Growth of manufacturing

For sources see notes for pl 7.

Montréal, 1921

Canada. *Census*. 1921. Vol 4, Table 3

Montréal, 1889

NAC. National Map Collection. Montreal Photo (R) H1/340/Montreal 1889 UMC 11075

Further readings

Blanchard, Raoul. *L'ouest du Canada français. Montréal et sa région*. Montréal: Beauchemin, 1953
Copp, Terry. *The Anatomy of Poverty: The Condition of the Working Class in Montreal 1897–1929*. Toronto: McClelland and Stewart, 1974
Linteau, Paul-André. *The Promoters' City: Building the Industrial Town of Maisonneuve 1883–1918*, transl Robert Chodos. Toronto: Lorimer, 1985
– 'Le développement du port de Montréal au début du 20e siècle.' Canadian Historical Association, *Historical Papers* (1972): 181–205

PLATE 15

The Emergence of Corporate Toronto

GUNTER GAD Geography, University of Toronto
DERYCK W. HOLDSWORTH Geography, Pennsylvania State University

Expansion of built-up and industrial areas

In the case of conflicting information the 1891 and 1923 directories were used as the ultimate data source. Under 'industrial areas' an attempt was made to show only manufacturing establishments. Warehousing, sales, and administrative facilities of manufacturing companies are excluded whenever available information permitted. Political boundaries, major streets, and railways reflect their status in 1923.

Goad, Chas E. *Atlas of the City of Toronto and Vicinity*. 2nd ed. Toronto and Montréal, 1890
Goad's Atlas and Plan Co. *Atlas of the City of Toronto and Suburbs*. 3rd ed, rev. 3 vols. Toronto, 1910, rev to July 1923 (Vol 1), Oct 1923 (Vol 2), Feb 1924 (Vol 3)
Toronto Harbour Commission. *Waterfront Development Progress Plan 1914–1921*. Toronto, May 1925
Toronto City Directory. 1891, 1924

Investment in industrial buildings

Only building permits of a value equal to or greater than $100 are included. If several permits were issued for one address in 1912, one circle shows the total value of permits issued. Workshops and production facilities combined with retail establishments (eg, tinsmiths, bakers, tailors) are excluded. All dairies are excluded. Also excluded are utilities, coal yards, ice houses, stockyards, and similar facilities. It was not always possible to exclude separately located non-production facilities (warehouses, service buildings, offices) of manufacturing companies. The 'clothing, textile' category includes several multi-tenant buildings. Although these buildings were erected for clothing companies, they were usually occupied by a range of tenants, including printing, jewellery, and other kinds of manufacturing companies.

No systematic attempt was made to check which permits did not lead to construction; however the authors' familiarity with data on Toronto in 1914 leads to the conclusion that most permits were 'taken up.'

City of Toronto Archives. Building Permits. Vols 169–98. 1912
Goad, Chas E. *Atlas of the City of Toronto and Suburbs*. 3rd ed. rev. 3 vols. Toronto and Montréal, 1910, rev to 1912
Toronto Harbour Commission. *Waterfront Development Progress Plan*
Toronto City Directory. 1913

Central-area land use

The directories and assessment rolls were used to override insurance-plan information in the case of conflicting data. Although vol 1 of the 1909 insurance plan was revised in 1915, several of the plates used for the 1914 central-area land-use map include revision labels with 1917 dates.

The 'mixed commercial' category is very important in the central area. A large number of buildings housed a variety of office, retail, wholesale, and manufacturing activities. The non-production activities of manufacturing companies are shown in this category whenever sufficient information was available.

City of Toronto. *Assessment Rolls*. 1890, 1913
Goad, Chas E. *Insurance Plan for the City of Toronto*. Rev. Vol 1. Toronto and Montréal, 1880, rev to 1889
– *Insurance Plan of the City of Toronto*. Rev. Vol 1. Toronto, 1909, rev to 1915
Toronto City Directory. 1891, 1915

Expansion of Eaton's and Simpson's

The map shows the first occupancy of a parcel of land by Eaton's or Simpson's and the dates do not indicate either ownership or construction. Sometimes land and buildings owned by these companies were not yet occupied. In other cases Eaton's rented property for store expansions. Sometimes buildings were bought and occupied by Eaton's and later redeveloped.

We gratefully acknowledge the assistance of Elizabeth Buchanan in extracting data from the City of Toronto assessment rolls and Judith Hudson Beattie at the Hudson's Bay Company Archives. Thanks are also due to Daniel Hiebert, Department of Geography, University of British Columbia, for his work in the T. Eaton Company archives. When that research was undertaken the archives were held in Eaton's Yorkdale, Toronto; in 1988 they were moved to the Archives of Ontario.

Archives of Ontario. T. Eaton Company records
City of Toronto. *Assessment Rolls*. 1890, 1900, 1910, 1920, 1930
City of Toronto Archives. Photograph collection
Ditchett, S.H. *Eaton's of Canada. A Unique Institution of Extraordinary Magnitude*. New York: Dry Goods Economist, 1923
Goad. *Atlas*. 2nd ed. 1890
– *Atlas*. 2nd ed, rev. 1890, rev to 1903
– *Atlas*. 3rd ed. Vol 1. 1910
– *Atlas*. 3rd ed, rev. Vol 1. 1910, rev to 1912
– *Insurance Plan*. Rev. Vol 1. 1909, rev to 1915
Goad's Atlas and Plan Co. *Atlas*. 3rd ed, rev. Vol 1. 1910, rev to 1923
Hudson's Bay Company Archives, Winnipeg. Various news releases and unpublished histories of the Robert Simpson Company
Metropolitan Toronto Reference Library, Baldwin Room. Photograph collection
T. Eaton Company. *Golden Jubilee 1869–1919. A Book to Commemorate the Fiftieth Anniversary of the T. Eaton Co Limited*. Toronto and Winnipeg: T. Eaton Co, 1919
Toronto City Directory. 1891, 1901, 1911, 1921, 1931
Santink, Joy L. *Timothy Eaton and the Rise of His Department Store*. Toronto: University of Toronto Press, 1990
Stephenson, William. *The Store that Timothy Built, 1869–1919*. Toronto: McClelland and Stewart, 1969
Underwriters' Survey Bureau Ltd. *Insurance Plan of the City of Toronto*. Vol 1. Toronto, 1954

Toronto 'plutocrats'

In the issue for 25 June 1913 the *Grain Growers' Guide*, a weekly Winnipeg-based publication, identified 42 'plutocrats,' men who 'control more than one-third of the wealth of the nation' (p 11). Of these 42 men 19 were residents of Toronto. There were other wealthy and powerful Torontonians, but they were omitted for three major reasons. First, the authors of the article presumably could not get information on assets or capital for privately held companies (ie, those not obliged to make their financial affairs public). Secondly, since there was a bias in the type of companies that were traded on stock exchanges at the time (transportation, utility, and financial companies), a number of wealthy men heavily involved in manufacturing companies were not included. Finally, manufacturing companies are less capital-intensive than transportation and utility companies and therefore it was much harder for industrialists to be considered 'wealthy' when measured in terms of their control of assets.

In the list of leading companies of the Toronto plutocrats, only the largest companies from each sector were included. Figures for assets, taken from the *Grain Growers' Guide*, are in agreement with those reported in the 1912 volume of the *Annual Financial Review* and reflect company assets in 1911 (except in the case of financial companies for which the assets given appear to be 1912 assets). Missing information on assets was supplemented by the *Annual Financial Review* and in some cases had to be estimated. Information on head offices from the *Annual Financial Review* was used. In some cases legal head offices and executive offices were in different cities.

The diagram of interlocking directorships includes plutocrats from the *Grain Growers' Guide* who were company presidents and who shared board memberships with other Toronto plutocrats. Although J.S. Moore was president of several companies, none of the other Toronto plutocrats served on the boards presided over by him, nor did Moore sit on the boards presided over by the other Toronto plutocrats. He therefore does not appear on the diagram. However there were many companies where Moore and other plutocrats were jointly directors.

For the map of offices of company presidents the office location was taken to be the business address listed under the name of the plutocrat in the directory. In a few cases only the name of a company was provided and it was assumed that this address was the office location.

Annual Financial Review. 1912. Toronto: Houston's Standard Publications, May 1912
Toronto City Directory. 1913, 1914
'Who Owns Canada?' *The Grain Growers' Guide*. 25 June 1913. Pp 11–34

Offices of banks and law firms

Annual Financial Review. 1915. Toronto: Houston's Standard Publications, May 1915
Canada. Department of Finance. *Report of the Chartered Banks of the Dominion of Canada*. 1890, 1914
Toronto City Directory. 1891, 1915

Dominion Bank: national employment

Toronto Dominion Bank Archives, Toronto. Dominion Bank, General Bonus to Staff, 1 June 1911

Building occupancy along King Street, south side

Estimates of floor space are based on floor outlines measured from the insurance plans and the number of rooms or floors occupied by individual businesses according to directories and assessment rolls. Many additional sources such as bank histories and construction journals provided further valuable information.

City of Toronto. *Assessment Rolls*. 1890, 1914
Goad. *Insurance Plan*. Rev. Vol 1. 1880, rev to 1889
– *Insurance Plan*. Rev. Vol 1. 1909, rev to 1915
Toronto City Directory. 1891, 1915

King Street, south side: building elevations

The elevation drawings rely on measured drawings of a few buildings, a number of key heights provided in articles in construction magazines, and field measurements of one building. Also of great help was a composite drawing showing eight buildings in existence in 1914. This panorama was drawn by Darling and Pearson in the context of preliminary designs for the Canadian Bank of Commerce Building of 1929–31. None of the architectural drawings, least of all the Darling and Pearson panorama could be trusted, and the final drawings rely on a great deal of cross-checking of many sources, especially photographs.

The extraordinary assistance offered by archivists and other officers of the Toronto Dominion Bank, the Bank of Nova Scotia, and the Canadian Imperial Bank of Commerce is gratefully acknowledged; Mildred Pulleyblank, Toronto Dominion Bank Archives, is owed special thanks.

Field measurements of no. 7 King Street West (formerly Michie and Co) were taken by Gunter Gad in Aug 1984. The drawings for publication were done by Jane Davie.

In the preparation of the drawings, many photographs, bank histories, books on Toronto, and construction magazines were consulted. Of particular importance was *Canadian Illustrated News* as well as the following photograph collections:
Bank of Nova Scotia Archives
Canadian Imperial Bank of Commerce. Architect's Office
City of Toronto Archives
Metropolitan Toronto Reference Library. Baldwin Room
NAC
Royal Bank of Canada Archives
Toronto Dominion Bank Archives
The architectural drawings that were used are listed below:

No. 1–5 King Street West – Dominion Bank Building
Darling and Pearson, Architects. King Street Elevation. Drawing No. 16, 31 May 1913. Toronto-Dominion Bank Archives
Giffels Associates Ltd, Consulting Engineers and Architects. Toronto Dominion Bank. Renovations to 68 Yonge Street. Building Elevations – North and South, Drawing No. A031, c 1988

No. 21–25 King Street West – Canadian Bank of Commerce Building
Darling and Pearson, Architects, York and Sawyer, Consulting Architects. Canadian Bank of Commerce. Head Office Building, Toronto. King Street Elevation, Drawings No. 18 and 19, 26 Sep 1929. Canadian Imperial Bank of Commerce, Architect's Office

No. 35–37 King Street West – Quebec Bank
Front elevation in *Construction* 5, no. 8 (July 1912): 57

No. 39–41 King Street West – Bank of Nova Scotia
J. Dominik, School of Architecture, University of Toronto, Aug 1962. Library, School of Architecture and Landscape Architecture, University of Toronto

No. 55–57 King Street West – Bank of Toronto
Carrere and Hastings. Bank of Toronto Head Office, King Street Elevation. Drawing No. 211–10, c 1911. Toronto Dominion Bank Archives

No. 1–5 King Street East – No. 55–57 King Street West – streetscape elevation drawing
Darling and Pearson, Architects, c 1925. Canadian Imperial Bank of Commerce, Architect's Office

Further readings
Gad, Gunter, and Holdsworth, Deryck W. 'Building for City, Region, and Nation: Office Development in Toronto 1834–1984.' In Victor L. Russell, ed. *Forging a Consensus: Historical Essays on Toronto*. Toronto: University of Toronto Press, 1984. Pp 272–322
– 'Streetscape and Society: The Changing Built Environment of King Street, Toronto.' In Roger Hall, William Westfall, and Laurel Sefton MacDowell, eds. *Patterns of the Past: Interpreting Ontario's History*. Toronto: Dundurn Press, 1988. Pp 174–205

PLATE 16

Resource Development on the Shield

SUSAN L. LASKIN   Historical Atlas of Canada, Toronto

The assistance of Patricia M. Orr in preparing this plate is gratefully acknowledged.

Silver shipments
Value is for silver contents of shipments reported by the operators at the mines. Figures were given in troy ounces and were converted to value using the average (New York) price in cents per ounce.
Ontario. Department of Mines. *Annual Report*. 1904–29

A Northern Silver Mine
This work was painted by Franklin Carmichael after a sketching trip to the Cobalt area of northern Ontario in 1930.
McMichael Canadian Art Collection, gift of Mrs. A.J. Latner, 1971.9

Gold production
The value of gold is calculated at $20.67 per fine ounce (or $1 = 0.048375 ounce).
Ontario. Department of Mines. *Annual Report*. 1929
Robinson, A.H.A. *Gold in Canada 1935*. Department of Mines. Mines Branch Report No. 769. Ottawa, 1935. Tables III, XXIV, XXXV

Head-office locations of mining companies
Only those companies which owned property on the Shield are included. The *Financial Post* report lists companies by the province in which they were registered, but for the purpose of the graphs a company was included in the province in which it held property; there were some Ontario companies that held property both in Québec and Ontario and they were counted for both provinces. Companies that were no longer in business but were listed in the report were not included. There are approximately twenty companies for which head-office locations were not given. The author would like to thank Donald Kerr for recommending that this study be undertaken.
Financial Post Survey of Mines, 1926. Toronto: Maclean, 1926
McBride, Norine. 'The Role of the Mining Industry in Metropolitan Development: Toronto and Montreal.' Unpublished paper submitted to Donald Kerr, Department of Geography, University of Toronto, 1984

Resource development
The value of mineral production at Sudbury includes the value derived from refining the nickel-copper ores (the value of the smelted ore without refining could not be determined). Refining was done by the International Nickel Company at Port Colborne, Ontario, and in the United States, and by the Mond Company in Wales. During refining platinum, gold, silver, and a small amount of cobalt are produced. The value of mineral production at Cobalt includes the value of cobalt produced from the ores and refined at Deloro, Ontario. The value of mineral production at Noranda was determined by the amount of copper, gold, and silver produced at the smelter (Robinson, 1935) multiplied by the average price (DBS, 1928). The amounts of gold ($11 000) and silver ($108 000) were too small to show. The remaining gold ($1 229 000) and silver ($421 000) produced in Québec comes from the lead-zinc ores of Portneuf County and the copper-sulphur ores of the Eastern Townships but the proportion produced by each could not be determined.

For pulp and paper production the value of 'other paper' for Hull and Jonquière includes newsprint; the value of 'newsprint' for Kenogami includes other paper. Not shown on the map is production of 30 000 pounds per day (St Andrews East, Saint-Basile, and Saint-Jerome).

The road and railway connections shown on the map are based primarily on the 1926 Department of Interior maps. Important additional linkages (eg between Rouyn and the Ontario-Quebec border) that were known to have been completed between 1926 and 1928 have been included.
Canada. DBS. *Mineral Production of Canada*. Cat. 26–D–28. 1928
– Department of the Interior. Dominion Water Power and Reclamation Service. *Central Electric Stations in Canada*. Water Resources Paper No. 55. Ottawa, 1929. Part II, Directory, 1 May 1928
– Department of the Interior. Natural Resources Intelligence Service. 'Map of Central Canada Showing Transportation and Commercial Development.' Jan 1927
– Department of the Interior. Natural Resources Intelligence Service. 'Map Indicating Main Automobile Roads between Canada and United States 1926'
Lockwood's Directory of the Paper and Allied Trades 1928. New York: Lockwood Trade Journal, 1928
Ontario. Department of Mines. *Annual Report*. 1929
Québec. Bureau of Mines. *Annual Report*. 1929
Robinson. *Gold in Canada 1935*

Plan of the model townsite of Kapuskasing
Saarinen, O.W. 'Provincial Land Use Planning Initiatives in the Town of Kapuskasing.' *Urban History Review* 10, no. 1 (June 1981): 5

Sudbury region
Canada. *Central Electric Stations in Canada*. 1929
– 'Map of Central Canada showing Transportation and Commercial Development.' 1927
Ontario. Department of Mines. *Annual Report*. 1929

Smelting in the Sudbury region
Ontario. Department of Mines. *Annual Report*. 1893–1929

Copper Cliff and Sudbury, 1931
Canada. *Census*. 1931. Vol 7, Table 43
Stelter, Gilbert A. 'Community Development in Toronto's Commercial Empire: The Industrial Towns of the Nickel Belt, 1883–1931.' *Laurentian University Review* 6, no. 3 (June 1974): 3–54

Provincial wood-pulp production
Provincial paper production
For wood pulp, the value of pulp consumed in pulp mills is the cost price whereas the value of pulp sold in Canada and elsewhere is the sale price. Value of paper is according to sale price. Value of Québec paper 1924–6 includes that of New Brunswick.
Canada. DBS. *Census of Industry*. 'Pulp and Paper.' 1917, 1919, 1926–8
Québec. Bureau of Statistics. *Statistical Year Book*. 1921–9

Further readings
Beach, Noel. 'Nickel Capital: Sudbury and the Nickel Industry, 1905–25.' *Laurentian University Review* 6, no. 3 (June 1974): 55–74
Dales, John H. *Hydro-Electricity and Industrial Development in Quebec 1898–1940*. Cambridge, Mass: Harvard University Press, 1957
Hall, A.V. 'Considerations in the Lay-Out of the Town of Kapuskasing.' *Journal of the Town Planning Institute of Canada* 1 (1922): 5–12
Nelles, H.V. *The Politics of Development: Forests, Mines and Hydro-Electric Power in Ontario, 1849–1941*. Toronto: Macmillan, 1974
Tucker, Albert. *Steam into Wilderness: Ontario Northland Railway, 1902–1962*. Toronto: Fitzhenry and Whiteside, 1978
Wallace, Iain. 'The Canadian Shield: The Development of a Resource Frontier.' In L.D. McCann, ed. *Heartland and Hinterland: A Geography of Canada*. Scarborough: Prentice-Hall, 1982. Pp 372–409

PLATE 17
Peopling the Prairies

WILLIAM J. CARLYLE Geography, University of Winnipeg
JOHN C. LEHR Geography, University of Winnipeg
G.E. MILLS Canadian Park Service, Victoria

Urban and rural population
For Saskatchewan and Alberta in 1891 population for the Territories was used.
Canada. *Census*. 1891: Vol 1, Table 1. 1931: Vol 1, Table 5

Ethnic origin
Canada. *Census*. 1931. Vol 1, Table 35

Population of the 'North West,' 1904
Canada. Department of Interior. 'Map of the North West of Canada, showing the distribution of population in 1904, and the racial origin of the immigrants'

Ukrainian settlement in southern Manitoba
Field interviews by John C. Lehr, 1974–6
Kaye, V.J. *Dictionary of Ukrainian Canadian Biography. Pioneer Settlers of Manitoba 1891–1900*. Toronto: Ukrainian Canadian Research Foundation, 1975
Manitoba. Records of homestead entry.
Panchuk, John. *Bukowinian Settlements in Southern Manitoba (Gardenton Area)*. Battle Creek, Mich: John Panchuk, 1971

Progress of Prairie settlement
The total population of a township was obtained by adding the population of incorporated urban centres, if any, to the rural population of a township. Population densities were calculated by dividing the total population of a township by its area. Most townships have a land area of about 36 square miles. Others are smaller in size because of the land survey or dimunition by lakes or wide rivers.
Canada. *Census of the Prairie Provinces*. 1936. Vol 1, pp 5–29, 360–431, 833–95

Disposition of land: Township 2, range 3, west 2, Saskatchewan
All the railway land in this township was assigned to the Manitoba Southwestern Colonization Railway, which was controlled by the Canadian Pacific Railway Company (CPR). Most of its land in the township was sold to American land companies, notably the Northwest Colonization Company and the Canada Land and Colonization Company. In some instances, settlers were already on the railway land before its sale to American land companies, in which case the settlers continued their time payments but to the land company instead of the railway. Such railway land and land unoccupied at the time of sale by the railway to the land companies are both mapped as being sold to land companies. In other instances, railway land was sold directly to individuals. Substantial grants of land were made to the Canada Northwest Land Company which, by the early 1900s, was a subsidiary of the CPR. Most of the Americans, both land companies and individuals, had headquarters in or were from North Dakota and Minnesota.
Glenbow Archives. Calgary. Information on the sale of railway lands
Saskatchewan Land Branch. Regina. Information on the original disposition of land

Ukrainian settlers' houses
Field surveys in Alberta and Manitoba conducted by John C. Lehr

A range of shelter for homesteaders
Thanks are due to Hedy Later for drawing the houses.
Provincial Archives of Manitoba. Boissevain Community Archives Coll. N123
Saskatchewan Archives Board. 'Homestead of Archie Roberge at Plunkett, Sask, 1913.' Photograph R–A2306
T. Eaton Co. *Plan Book of Ideal Homes*. Winnipeg, 1919. 'Earlsfield,' E–35

Further readings
Dawson, Carl. *Group Settlement: Ethnic Communities in Western Canada*. Vol 7 of W.A. MacIntosh and W.L.G. Joerg, eds. *Canadian Frontiers of Settlement*. Toronto: Macmillan, 1936
Dawson, Carl, and Eva R. Younge. *Pioneering in the Prairie Provinces: The Social Side of the Settlement Process*. Vol 8 of MacIntosh and Joerg, eds. *Canadian Frontiers of Settlement*. Toronto: Macmillan, 1940
Hedges, James B. *Building the Canadian West*. New York: Macmillan, 1939
Hill, Douglas. *The Opening of the Canadian West*. Don Mills: Longman, 1967
Martin, Chester. *Dominion Lands Policy*. Toronto: Macmillan, 1934. Reprinted in Carleton Library Series. Toronto: McClelland and Stewart, 1973
Schlichtman, Hansgeorg. 'Ethnic Themes in Geographical Research in Western Canada.' *Canadian Ethnic Studies* 9, no. 2 (1977): 9–41
Warkentin, John. 'Manitoba Settlement Patterns.' *Transactions. Historical and Scientific Society of Manitoba* series III, no. 16 (1961): 62–77

PLATE 18
Prairie Agriculture

PHILIP D. KEDDIE Geography, University of Guelph
SIMON M. EVANS Geography, Sir Wilfred Grenfell College, Memorial University of Newfoundland

The wheat belt
Canada. *Census*. 1931. Vol 3, Table 38

Improved land
Canada. *Census*. 1931. Vol 3, Table 37

Expansion of farmland, 1881–1931
Canada. *Census*. 1931. Vol 8, Table I, p xxviii

Expansion of the agricultural frontier, 1906–1931
Data for townships in 1906, municipalities, local improvement districts, and unorganized territorial units in 1916, and municipalities and subdivisions in 1931 were aggregated to form the statistical units used for mapping purposes.
Canada. *Census*. 1931. Vol 8, Table 38
– *Census of Population and Agriculture of the Northwest Provinces*. 1906. Table XXVII
– *Census of Prairies Provinces, Population and Agriculture*. 1916. Part II, Table XXV

Southeastern Saskatchewan, 1906
Canada. *Census of Population and Agriculture of the Northwest Provinces*. 1906. Tables IX, XXVII
Richards, J.H., and K.I. Fung. *Atlas of Saskatchewan*. Saskatoon: University of Saskatchewan, 1969

The ranching frontier: origins of leaseholders
Canada. Department of the Interior. *Orders in Council*. 1882–6

The ranching frontier: railways and the open range
Canada. Department of the Interior. 'Disposition of Lands.' 1906, 1909, 1914. Maps
Glenbow-Alberta Institute. Calgary. Various railway maps published by railway companies

Cattle shipments
Cattle shipments include both exports and local shipments.
Alberta. Department of Agriculture. *Annual Report*. 1910. Pp 26–8
Saskatchewan. Department of Agriculture. *Annual Report*. 1910. P 17

Further readings
Artibise, A.F.J. *Western Canada Since 1870, A Select Bibliography and Guide*. Vancouver: University of British Columbia Press, 1978
Brado, Edward. *Cattle Kingdom: Early Ranching in Alberta*. Vancouver: Douglas and McIntyre, 1984
Breen, David H. *The Canadian Prairie West and the Ranching Frontier 1874–1927*. Toronto: University of Toronto Press, 1983
Dunae, Patrick A. *Gentlemen Emigrants: From the British Public Schools to the Canadian Frontier*. Vancouver: Douglas and McIntyre, 1981
– ed. *Ranchers' Legacy: Alberta Essays by Lewis G. Thomas*. Edmonton: University of Alberta Press, 1986
Evans, Simon M. 'The End of the Open Range in Western Canada.' *Prairie Forum* 8, no. 1 (Spring 1983): 71–88
– 'The Origins of Ranching in Western Canada: American Diffusion or Victorian Transplant?' *Great Plains Quarterly* 3, no. 2 (Spring 1983): 79–91
Fowke, Vernon C. *The National Policy and the Wheat Economy*. Toronto: University of Toronto Press, 1957
Hedges, James Blaine. *Building the Canadian West: The Land and Colonization Policies of the Canadian Pacific Railway*. New York: Macmillan, 1939
MacEwan, Grant. *Between the Red and the Rockies*. Toronto: University of Toronto Press, 1952
Mackintosh, W.A. *Prairie Settlement, The Geographical Setting*. Toronto: Macmillan, 1934
Morton, Arthur Silver, and Chester M. Martin. *History of Prairie Settlement and 'Dominion Lands' Policy*. Toronto: Macmillan, 1938
Sharp, Paul F. *Whoop-Up Country: The Canadian American West, 1865–1885*. Minneapolis: University of Minnesota Press, 1955
Strange, Henry George Latimer. *A Short History of Prairie Agriculture*. Winnipeg: Searle Grain Co Ltd, 1954

PLATE 19
The Prairie Grain-Handling System

DONNA SHIMAMURA EVERITT Brandon
JOHN C. EVERITT Geography, Brandon University
SUSAN L. LASKIN Historical Atlas of Canada, Toronto

We would like to acknowledge the assistance of the Canadian Plains Research Center, Manitoba Heritage Federation, and Brandon University Research Committee.

The cost of moving a bushel of wheat from Saskatchewan to Liverpool, UK, 1925
Food Research Institute. *Wheat Studies of the Food Research Institute, 1925*. Vol 2. Stanford: Stanford University Press, Nov 1925–Sep 1926. P 139

Monthly wheat prices
Canada. DBS. Agricultural Branch. *Report on the Grain Trade of Canada, For the Crop Year ended July 31 and to the close of Navigation, 1929*. Table 112.

Export destination of wheat
'Europe' includes the Netherlands, Belgium, Italy, Germany, France, Greece, Portugal, Spain, Denmark, and Sweden. 'Asia' includes Japan and China. 'Others' are unspecified.
Canada. DBS. Agricultural Branch. *Report on the Grain Trade 1929*. Table 98.

Movement of wheat, 1928–1929
'On hand, 1 Aug 1928' refers to that wheat which was available to be distributed at the beginning of the new season (1 Aug 1928). 'In store, 31 July 1929' refers to that wheat which had not been disposed of and, therefore, was still in the system at the end of the season (31 July 1929). On 1 Aug 1929 this wheat would be considered 'on hand' for the 1929–30 season. The wheat 'on hand' or 'in store' could have been still in farmers' hands, in country, private, manufacturing, or internal terminal elevators, in four mills, or in transit.
Canada. DBS. Agricultural Branch. *Report on the Grain Trade 1929*. 'Movement of Canadian wheat crop 1928–1929.' Map, with modifications by the authors

The major elevator companies

All companies with nine or more elevators are shown. Only the eleven companies with the largest total number of elevators for all seven time periods are numbered along with seven additional predecessor companies. Companies are distinguished by ownership except in the case of the 'other' category where multiple companies may differ in ownership.
Canada. Board of Grain Commissioners. *List of Licensed Elevators and Warehouses in the Western Grain Inspection Division*. 1911–33
United Grain Growers Ltd Archives. Winnipeg
Wilson, C.F. *A Century of Canadian Grain*. Saskatoon: Western Producer Prairie Books, 1978. P 15

Growth of the elevator network

Report year ends 1 Aug.
Canada. Board of Grain Commissioners. *Grain Elevators in Canada*. Various years

Waskada, Manitoba, 1916

Western Canada Fire Underwriters' Association Atlas, 1916

Waskada branch line

Elevator ownership is based on total capacity in bushels for the licence years 1916–17 and 1928–9 for each company operating during those two periods in the seven communities studied. Companies with capacity of less than 50 000 bushels in the 'other' category include Imperial Elevator and Lumber Co Ltd, Province Elevator Co Ltd, United Grain Growers Ltd, and Ogilvie Flour Mills Co.
Canada. Board of Grain Commissioners. *Grain Elevators in Canada*. 1916–17, 1928–9

The Lakehead

Canada. Board of Grain Commissioners. *Annual Report*. 1911–30. 'Report of scale inspection in elevators at Fort William and Port Arthur'
'City of Port Arthur, Ontario.' 1929. Map
Felker, Capt J.A. *Canadian Shipmaster's and Mate's Guide, 1939*. Toronto, 1939. Foldout map, 'Lakehead harbours'

PLATE 20

Land Development in Edmonton

P.J. SMITH   Geography, University of Alberta

Subdivided and developed lands
Central development

'Driscoll & Knight's Map of the City of Edmonton, Province of Alberta.' 7th ed. 1912–13. Updated to 1914 from later street maps
Goad, Charles E., and Co. Fire-insurance maps of Edmonton. 1913. Rev to 1914
Graham, W. Mark. 'Construction of Large-Scale Structural Base Maps of Central Edmonton for 1907, 1911 and 1914.' MA thesis, University of Alberta, 1984
Henderson's Directory of Edmonton. 1914
Numerous other maps, photographs, books, theses, reports, and unpublished documents were consulted to verify details of the development pattern.

Subdivisions in the Greater Edmonton area

City of Edmonton. *Special Report on Assessment and Taxation*. Presented to the aldermen by D.M. Duggan, Mayor, and C.J. Yorath, Commissioner, August 1921
'Mundy's Map of the City of Edmonton and Suburbs.' Edmonton: Mundy's Map Co., Apr 1913. Updated from records in the Edmonton City Archives

First survey, Edmonton Settlement

Canada. Department of the Interior. Dominion Lands Office. Plan of Edmonton Settlement as surveyed by M. Deane, DLS. 1882

Edmonton building permits

Graph begins 1 Mar 1905. Data for the period 1905–12 do not include building permits issued by the City of Strathcona, prior to its amalgamation with Edmonton; these records are not available.
Edmonton City Archives. Building permits

Municipal boundary changes

The Alberta Gazette. 1905–17
Statutes, city charters, and contemporary maps were also used.

The streetcar network

Hatcher, Colin K., and Schwartzkopf, Tom. *Edmonton's Electric Transit: The Story of Edmonton's Streetcars and Trolley Buses*. Toronto: Railfare Enterprises Ltd, 1983. Pp 4–93

Development in Garneau neighbourhood

Windsor, Robert F. 'The Campus Fringe of the University of Alberta.' MA thesis, University of Alberta, 1964. Fig 16

Land forfeited to the city

Developable land excludes streets and lanes.
Dale, Edmund H. 'The Role of Successive Town and City Councils in the Evolution of Edmonton, Alberta, 1892 to 1966.' PH D dissertation, University of Alberta, 1969. Fig 15b

Further readings

Betke, Carl. 'The Original City of Edmonton: A Derivative Prairie Urban Community.' In Gilbert A. Stelter and Alan F.J. Artibise, eds. *The Canadian City: Essays in Urban and Social History*. Ottawa: Carleton University Press, 1984. Pp 392–430
Gilpin, John. *Edmonton: Gateway to the North*. Woodlands Hills, CA: Windsor Publications, 1984
– 'Failed Metropolis: The City of Strathcona, 1891–1912.' In Alan F.J. Artibise, ed. *Town and City: Aspects of Western Canadian Urban Development*. Canadian Plains Studies 10. Regina: Canadian Plains Research Center, 1981. Pp 259–88

– 'The Land Development Process in Edmonton, Alberta, 1881–1917.' In Gilbert A. Stelter and Alan F.J. Artibise, eds. *Power and Place: Canadian Urban Development in the North American Context*. Vancouver: University of British Columbia Press, 1986. Pp 151–72
– 'Urban Land Speculation in the Development of Strathcona (South Edmonton), 1891–1912.' In John E. Foster, ed. *The Developing West: Essays on Canadian History in Honor of Lewis H. Thomas*. Edmonton: University of Alberta Press, 1983. Pp 181–99
MacGregor, J.G. *Edmonton: A History*. Edmonton: Hurtig, 1967
Selwood, H.J., and Evelyn Baril. 'The Hudson's Bay Company and Prairie Town Development, 1870–1888.' In Artibise, ed. *Town and City*. 1981. p 61–94
Weaver, John C. 'Edmonton's Perilous Course, 1904–1929.' *Urban History Review* 2 (Oct 77): 20–32

PLATE 21

British Columbia Resources

ROBERT GALOIS   Geography, University of British Columbia

I would like to thank R. Cole Harris for his encouragement and his warnings.

Resource activity: 1891; 1912; 1928

Placer-mining sites have been included on the 1891 map only. This form of gold mining was of greater relative importance in 1891 but dwindled to insignificance in the 20th century; in addition, data for 1912 and 1928 are problematic.

Data on the location and size of individual sawmills and shingle mills are difficult to obtain. Even official data, when available, are of uncertain reliability: many smaller mills operated for short periods only. In 1891 the timber inspectors' reports list 57 operating mills; unofficial sources indicate a further 21 operating mills. In 1912 no official data are available but a small-scale map (Forest Branch, *Annual Report*, 1913) shows 309 mills; information on 276 of these, obtained from other sources, is mapped. In 1928 official aggregate data indicate 370 mills were operating in the province; information on 305 of these, obtained from other sources, is mapped. Shingle production is converted to board feet per diem to correspond to the data on the capacity of sawmills; the conversion factor used is 10 shingles per board foot. All data on sawmill capacity are approximate.

The mapping of pulp and paper mills, coal mines, and salmon canneries is relatively complete. For salmon canneries no official data on individual canneries were published in 1928 and the data are incomplete for 1912; manuscript sources fills these gaps. Metal mines producing less than 100 tons of ore have not been mapped; in most instances such undertakings were 'prospects' rather than producing mines.
The 'ABC' Lumber Trade Directory and Year Book. Vancouver: Progress Publishing Co, 1927–9
Bella Coola Courier. 1912
British Columbia. Commissioner of Fisheries. *Annual Report*. 1902–28
– Department of Agriculture. *Annual Report*. 1891
– Department of Lands (title varies). *Annual Report*. 1891–1911. Annual report of timber inspectors
– Forest Branch. *Annual Report*. 1912–28. For 1912 this report is included in Department of Lands, *Annual Report*.
– Minister of Mines. *Annual Report*. 1891–1928
British Columbia Lumberman. Vancouver. 1927–9
British Columbian. New Westminster, 1912
Canada. DBS. *Census of Industry: Lumber, Lath, Shingles*. 1928, 1929
– Department of Indian Affairs. *Annual Report*. 1912–13
– SP. 1892. No. 13, Annual Report of Department of the Interior, 1891
– SP. 1914. No. 25, Annual Report of the Department of the Crown Timber Agent
Canada Lumberman. Toronto. 1891–2
Chilliwack Progress. 1912
Ft George Herald. 1912
Golden Star. 1912
Grand Forks Gazette. 1912
Henderson's Greater Vancouver, New Westminister and Fraser Valley Directory. 1912. Vancouver: Henderson's Publishing Co
Higginbottom, Edward N. 'The Changing Geography of Salmon Canning in British Columbia 1870–1931.' MA thesis, Simon Fraser University, 1988
Kamloops Sentinel. 1891
Leynard, A. 'The Coal Mines of Nanaimo.' Nanaimo: Nanaimo Museum, 1982
Lumberman's Atlas of British Columbia: Mills and Camps at a Glance. Vancouver: Gordon Black Publications, 1930
NAC. Canada. Department of Fisheries. 1928 Statistics. General and General Supplemental Schedules. GR 23, Box 500510, 500496, 500497
Provincial Archives of British Columbia. British Columbia. Forest Branch. Timber Investigations and Inspections. GR 946, Box 1, file 8
– Forest Branch. Timber Inspectors' Reports. 1912. GR 949, files 4/10, 8/10
Reid, D.J. *The Development of the Fraser River Salmon Canning Industry, 1885–1913*. Vancouver, 1973
Ross, W.M. 'Salmon Cannery Distribution on the Nass and Skeena Rivers of British Columbia, 1877–1926.' Honours essay, University of British Columbia, 1967
University of British Columbia. Canada. Department of Fisheries. Inspection Reports. District 1 Fraser River. 1912. Microfilm reel 5474:70
– H. Bell-Irving Diaries, 1912, 1913, 1928. Microfilm reel 4560
– Special Collections. C.D. Orchard Papers. Box 6, file 2, MSS, M492
Vancouver Daily News Advertiser. 1912
Vancouver Public Archives. H. Bell-Irving. Cannery Statistics. 1928. Add. MSS. 485
Vernon News. 1891, 1912
Western Lumberman. Vancouver and Winnipeg, 1911–13
Williams, R.T. *Williams Illustrated Official British Columbia Directory, 1892*. Victoria
Wrigley's British Columbia Directory 1928. Vancouver
Wrigley's British Columbia Directory 1929. Vancouver

Value of resources
No direct revenue was derived from fisheries until 1910; between 1910 and 1928 the maximum contribution of this resource industry was 0.8% (1911). From 1922 to 1928 percentage calculations exclude capital account. The data are for fiscal years and not calendar years: from 1891 to 1908 the fiscal year ended on 30 June; from 1909 to 1928 the fiscal year ended on 31 Mar.
British Columbia. Forest Branch. *Annual Report*. 1912–28. For 1912 this report was included in Department of Lands, *Annual Report*
– *Public Accounts*. 1891–1928

Type of fishery
Water-bone salmon shipments
Salmon canning by region
Categories contributing less than 1% not shown. Fur seals include hair seals.
Canada. DBS. *Fisheries Statistics of British Columbia*. 1918–28
– Department of Fisheries. *Annual Report*. 1891–1917

Water-borne lumber shipments
Data in 1891 are based on all timber exports; percentages are calculated on the basis of value and not volume. Hawaii is included under south and east Asia.
British Columbia. Forest Branch. *Annual Report*. 1912–28. For 1912 this report was included in Department of Lands, *Annual Report*.
Canada. *SP*. 1892. No. 5, 'Tables of Trade and Navigation of the Dominion of Canada, Annual Returns'
Gosnell, R.E. *The Year Book of British Columbia and Manual of Provincial Information*. Victoria, 1903, 1911
Whitford, H.N., and Craig, R.D. 'Forests of British Columbia.' Ottawa: Commission of Conservation, 1918

Coal and coke markets
1891 and 1928 data are based on exports; 1912 and 1928 data are based on sales. 1912 data include coke sales. Coast colleries include those in the Bulkley valley and the Nicola and Merrit districts.
British Columbia. Minister of Mines. *Annual Report*. 1891–1928

Mining by region
Percentages between 1891 and 1899 are estimates only.
British Columbia. Minster of Mines. *Annual Report*. 1891–1928

Further readings
Carrothers, W.A. 'Forest Industries of British Columbia.' In A.R.M. Lower, ed. *The North American Assault on the Canadian Forest: A History of the Lumber Trade Between Canada and the United States*. Toronto: Ryerson Press, 1938. Pp 227–344. Facsimile edition published New York: Greenwood Press, 1968
Falconer, Dickson, M., ed. *British Columbia: Patterns in Economic, Political and Cultural Development*. Victoria: Camosun College, 1982
Friesen, J., and H.K. Ralston. *Historical Essays on British Columbia*. Toronto: McClelland and Stewart, 1976
Hardwick, Walter G. *Geography of the Forest Industry of Coastal British Columbia*. Vancouver: Tantalus, 1963
Kent, D. *British Columbia: A Bibliography of Industry, Labour, Resources and Regions for the Social Sciences*. Vancouver: University of British Columbia Press, 1978
Lawrence, Joseph Collins. 'Markets and Capital: A History of the Lumber Industry of British Columbia, 1778–1952.' MA thesis, University of British Columbia, 1957
Lyons, Cicley. *Salmon: Our Heritage: the Story of a Province and an Industry*. Vancouver: Mitchell Press, 1969
Mulholland, F.D. *The Forest Resources of British Columbia*. Victoria: King's Printer, 1937
Prouty, Andrew Mason. *More Deadly than War: Pacific Coast Logging 1827–1981*. New York: Garland, 1985
Roy, Patricia E. *A History of British Columbia: Selected Readings*. Toronto: Copp Clark Pitman, 1989
Taylor, Geoffrey W. *Timber: History of the Forest Industry in B.C.* Vancouver: J.J. Douglas, 1975
Ward, W. Peter, and Robert A.J. McDonald. *British Columbia: Historical Readings*. Vancouver: Douglas and McIntyre, 1981

PLATE 22

Resource Communities in British Columbia

ROBERT GALOIS   Geography, University of British Columbia

I would like to thank R. Cole Harris for his encouragement and his warnings.

Fish processing, Nass River
Canada. Department of Indian Affairs. *Annual Report*. 1901, 'Schedule of Indian Reserves, Northwest Coast Agency, British Columbia'
– *Report of the Royal Commission on Indian Affairs for the Province of British Columbia*. 4 vols. Victoria, 1916
University of British Columbia. Special Collections. H. Doyle Notebook No. 6–8 (1911–13). Doyle Papers 1864–1958, Mss. M205
– 'Mill Bay Cannery.' In British Columbia Insurance Underwriters Association. Plan Department. *British Columbia Canneries*. 113 sheets. Vancouver, 1924
– 'Mill Bay Cannery.' In *Northern Canneries*. Toronto and Montréal: C.E. Goad and Co, 1915

Provincial salmon canning
Wallace Fisheries was taken over by BC Packers in 1926. Official reports do not include data on the production of individual companies for 1924. Data taken from the Pacific Fisherman's yearbook have been used for that year; the aggregate production for all companies from this source slightly exceeds the aggregate in the official data.
British Columbia. Commissioner of Fisheries. *Annual Report*. 1902–28
Canada. DBS. *Fisheries Statistics of British Columbia*. 1918–28
– Department of Fisheries. *Annual Report*. 1891–1917
Pacific Fisherman. *Annual Statistical Number*. Seattle, Jan 1925

Salmon catch by ethnic group
Seasonal activity, Mill Bay cannery
Data are for the 1913 season up to 25 Aug. There may have been a small amount of fishing after this date.
University of British Columbia. H. Doyle Notebook No. 6–8 (1911–13)

The Nanaimo coal field
Before 1907 data on the Western Fuel Company (title varies) are not listed by individual mine; operating mines during this period include Esplanade No. 1 and Protection, 1891–1906; Northfield, 1891–5; Northfield No. 4, 1904–6; Southfield No. 5, 1891–1902; Southfield Nos. 1 and 2, 1891–3; Southfield No. 4, 1891; Chase River No. 3, 1891–3; Harewood, 1900–4. In 1928 the ownership of the Reserve and Wakesiah mines changed from the Western Fuel Company to Canadian Collieries; they are shown on the map as belonging to the Western Fuel Company.
British Columbia. Minister of Mines. *Annual Report*. 1891–1928
Clapp, C.H. *Geology of the Nanaimo Map-Area*. Geological Survey of Canada Memoir No. 51. Ottawa, 1914
– 'Nanaimo Sheet.' Geological Survey of Canada. Map No. 160A, to accompany Memoir No. 51. Ottawa, 1916
Leynard, A. *The Coal Mines of Nanaimo*. Nanaimo: Nanaimo Museum, 1982
Tuner, Robert D. *Vancouver Island Railroads*. San Marino, CA: Olden West Books, 1973

Fatal accidents
Fatalities per 1 000 employees, excluding clerical and supervisory employees. A small number of native Indian employees have been included in the Chinese and Japanese category.
British Columbia. Minister of Mines. *Annual Report*. 1891–1928

Provincial coal production
No official data are available for Canadian Colleries (Dunsmuir) and the Western Fuel Coal Corporation for the years 1903–5. Estimates for 1904 and 1905 are based on unofficial sources, prorated to conform with official aggregate data. Estimates for 1903 are based upon the sum of unoffical returns; these differ somewhat from official regional totals.
In 1928 Western Fuel Corporation had the same directorate as Canadian Colleries (Dunsmuir) although it was still listed as a separate company.
British Columbia. Minister of Mines. *Annual Report*. 1891–1928

Canadian Western Lumber Company, Fraser Mills
The total Caucasian work-force numbered 502: employee numbers in the three graphs vary according to the availability of the data and the variables represented.
University of British Columbia. Special Collections. British Columbia Insurance Underwriters Association. Plan Department. 'Fraser Mills.' Vancouver, 1922
Williams, M. Jeanne Meyers. 'Ethnicity and Class Conflict in Fraser Mills/Maillardville: The Strike of 1931.' MA thesis, Simon Fraser University, 1982

Phoenix
The fire-insurance maps do not cover the entire built-up area of Phoenix in 1911. Details of land use beyond the area of the insurance maps are uncertain; they have been designated as unknown.
British Columbia Archives and Records Service. HP18382
British Columbia. Minister of Mines. *Annual Report*. 1911
Canada. *Census*. 1911. Vol 1, Table II; Vol 2, Table VII
LeRoy, O.E. *The Geology and Ore Deposits of Phoenix British Columbia*. Geological Survey of Canada Memoir No. 21. Ottawa, 1912
– 'Phoenix, British Columbia.' Geological Survey of Canada Map No. 15A, to accompany Memoir No. 21. Ottawa, 1911
NAC. National Map Collection. No. 0010461, 'Phoenix.' Toronto and Montréal: C.E. Goad and Co, 1912–14

Further readings
Bowen, Lynne. *Boss Whistle: The Coal Miners of Vancouver Island Remember*. Lantzville: Oolichan Books, 1982
Knight, Rolph. *Indians at Work: An Informal History of Native Indian Labour in British Columbia, 1858–1930*. Vancouver: New Star Books, 1978
Latham, Barbara K., and R.J. Pazdro. *Not Just Pin Money: Selected Essays on the History of Women's Work in British Columbia*. Victoria: Camosun College, 1984
Norris, John. *Strangers Entertained: A History of Ethnic Groups of British Columbia*. Vancouver: British Columbia Centennial '71 Committee, 1971
Prouty, Andrew Mason. *More Deadly than War: Pacific Coast Logging, 1827–1981*. New York: Garland, 1988
Ward, W. Peter. *White Canada Forever: Popular Attitudes and Public Policy toward Orientalism in British Columbia*. Montréal: McGill-Queen's University Press, 1978

See also further readings for pl 21.

PLATE 23

Sea and Livelihood in Atlantic Canada

JOHN J. MANNION   Geography, Memorial University of Newfoundland
ERIC W. SAGER   History, University of Victoria

We would like to acknowledge the assistance of Garry Penner in the preparation of this plate.

Fishermen and their catch
For Newfoundland the value of catch by species was estimated from the value of fish-products exports. Data on value by species were not available but most fish landed in Newfoundland were for export.
Canada. Department of Marine and Fisheries. *Annual Report*. 1890, 1900
Newfoundland. *Census of Newfoundland*. 1891, 1901
– *Customs Returns*. 1900. Printed separately
– *Journals of the House of Assembly*. 'Customs Returns.' 1890

Fish exports from the Maritimes

Total Maritime exports is the value of shipments from Maritime ports. For the period after 1900 data on commodity exports by province of origin are not available but data on fish exports by species are available. The values for cod, haddock, hake, pollock, redfish, herring, lobster (fresh and canned), fish oil, and half of all other fish except halibut and salmon were added to estimate the total value of fish exported from the Maritimes. When the totals by this method were compared with total exports of fish prior to 1900, the figures closely approximate one another.

Canada. DBS. *The Maritime Provinces Since Confederation*. Ottawa, 1927. P 83
– Department of Marine and Fisheries. *Annual Report*. 1890, 1900

Newfoundland salt-cod exports
Newfoundland seal-products exports

The official totals for salt-cod exports found in Newfoundland, *Historical Statistics of Newfoundland*, for the years 1893, 1896, and 1918 were lower than those calculated by adding separate figures for exports to each country given in Newfoundland's *Customs Returns*, because the totals in *Historical Statistics* sometimes omit exports going directly from Labrador. In these years the calculated totals were used.

Government of Newfoundland. *Historical Statistics of Newfoundland*. St John's, 1970. Table A–11
Newfoundland. *Custom Returns*. Printed separately, 1897–1909, 1930–42
– *Journals of the House of Assembly*. 'Customs Returns.' 1890–6, 1910–29, 1942–9

Sealing disasters

The number of men lost in sealing disasters shown on the map is less than the actual total; more men died than were reported at the time.

Evening Telegram. St John's, Newfoundland. 28 Mar 1898. 3, 4 Apr 1914

The Fishermen's Protective Union

Coaker, Sir William Ford. compiler. *Twenty Years of the Fishermen's Protective Union of Newfoundland from 1901–1929*. St John's: Advocate, 1930

Fishermen as a percentage of total work-force

The number of fishermen is the number of men engaged in catching and curing fish. Total labour-force figures include women engaged in curing fish.

Canada. *Census*. 1931. Vol 2, Tables 1, 44
– Department of Marine and Fisheries. *Annual Report*. 1891–1931
Green, Alan George. *Regional Aspects of Canada's Economic Growth*. Toronto: University of Toronto Press, 1971. Table C–1
Newfoundland. *Census of Newfoundland*. 1891: Table I. 1901: Table I. 1911: Table I. 1921: Table I. 1935: Table IV

Nets and lobster traps
Boats and vessels

Canada. Department of Marine and Fisheries. *Annual Report*. 1900
Newfoundland. *Census of Newfoundland*. 1901. Table II

Point Lance

Tilts were summer homes of the fishermen, each one housing a crew. The stage comprised a wharf and a shed for processing fish. Behind these, sometimes part of the wharf complex, sometimes in a separate structure, were the stores for supplies, salt, fishing gear, and for storing the fish.

Mannion, John J. *Point Lance in Transition: The Transformation of a Newfoundland Outport*. Toronto: McClelland and Stewart, 1976. Figs 2–5, 3–4

Illustrations of fishing vessels

Thanks to Ralph Getson, Fisheries Museum of the Atlantic, Lunenburg, for information on the dory and to Ada Cheung for drawing the illustrations.

Canadian Fisheries Annual. 1942. P 35
Nicholson, F.W. 'The Dory.' *Maritime Museum of Canada Occasional Papers*. No. 7 (June 1960)

Further readings

Alexander, David. *The Decay of Trade: An Economic History of the Newfoundland Saltfish Trade, 1935–1965*. St John's: Institute of Social and Economic Research, 1977
Bates, Stewart. *Report on the Canadian Atlantic Sea Fishery*. Halifax: Department of Trade and Industry, 1944
Innis, Harold A. *The Cod Fisheries: The History of an International Economy*. Toronto: University of Toronto Press, 1954
Nova Scotia. Department of Fisheries. *Sea, Salt and Sweat: A Story of Nova Scotia and the Vast Atlantic Fisheries*. Halifax, 1977
Ryan, Shannon. *Fish Out of Water: The Newfoundland Saltfish Trade, 1814–1914*. St John's: Breakwater Books, 1986
Sinclair, Peter R., ed. *A Question of Survival: The Fisheries and Newfoundland Society*. St John's: Institute of Social and Economic Research, 1988

PLATE 24

Industrialization and the Maritimes

L.D. McCANN   Geography, Mount Allison University

The labour force

Green, Alan. *Regional Aspects of Canada's Economic Growth*. Toronto: University of Toronto Press, 1971. Pp 104–6, Tables C1–3

New Brunswick forest industry

Assets of sawmills are based on 'pecuniary strength' of the sawmills as defined by Dun and Company.

Canada. *Census*. 1891: Vol 3, Table I. 1911: Vol 3, Table XI
Canada Year Book. 1933. Pp 441–2
Dun, R.G., and Company. *The Mercantile Agency Reference Book for the Dominion of Canada*. 1891, 1911, 1931

Major corporate changes in the iron and steel industry

Dalhousie University Archives. Hawker Siddeley Papers. MS 4–106, 'Letters Patent Incorporation the Nova Scotia Company, Limited, 1882'
Donald, W.J.A. *The Canadian Iron and Steel Industry*. Boston, 1915
Eldon, W.D.R. 'American Influence in the Canadian Iron and Steel Industry.' PH D thesis, Harvard University, 1952. P 557
Nova Scotia Steel and Coal Company. *Scotia: How Canada's Pioneer Steel Corporation was Evolved from a Country Forge*. New Glasgow, 1912
Nova Scotia Steel Company Limited. *Report of the Board of Directors and Financial Statements*. 1883–1910
Public Archives of Nova Scotia. G.F. Mackay MSS File. 'Articles of Copartnership (1874)'

Nova Scotia Steel and the structure of manufacturing

Canada. *Census*. 1911. Vol 3, Tables IX, XII, XIII
Nova Scotia. Department of Mines. *Annual Report*. 1910
Nova Scotia Steel Company Limited. *Report of the General Manager 1910*. New Glasgow, 1911
Public Archives of Nova Scotia. Nova Scotia Steel and Coal Company Papers. MG 3, No. 395–1016

Metal manufacturers in Pictou County

Assets of manufacturers are based on 'pecuniary strength' of the manufacturing firms as defined by Dun and Company.

Dun. *The Mercantile Agency Reference Book*. 1911, 1931

Decline in industrial Cape Breton

Value of industries is based on 'pecuniary strength' of the industries as defined by Dun and Company. Sydney Mines was not shown in 1931; the value of its industries was only $750. Value of coal was derived from the production of coal in tons and an estimated value of coal per ton; the estimated value was determined by Canadian figures on total value and total production: $2.34 per ton in 1911 and $3.37 per ton in 1931.

Dun. *Mercantile Agency Reference Book*. 1911, 1932
Nova Scotia. Department of Mines. *Annual Report*. 1911
Urquhart and Buckley. *Historical Statistics*. Series N170–1

Change in manufacturing employment, 1920–1929

Urban places with 200 or more manufacturing employees in 1920 are included.
Canada Year Book. 1920, 1929.

Metropolitan outreach

Branch outlets include both a business with branches and branch businesses of a company. The number of metropolitan branches indicates the number of branch outlets in a metropolitan centre.

Dun. *Mercantile Agency Reference Book*. 1881, 1911, 1931

Further readings

Acheson, T.W. 'The National Policy and the Industrialization of the Maritimes, 1880–1910.' *Acadiensis* 1, no. 2 (Spring 1972): 3–28
Alexander, David. 'Economic Growth in the Atlantic Region, 1880 to 1940.' *Acadiensis* 8, no. 1 (Autumn 1978): 47–76
Forbes, Ernest R. 'Misguided Symmetry: The Destruction of Regional Transportation Policy for the Maritimes.' In David Jay Bercuson, ed. *Canada and the Burden of Unity*. Toronto: Macmillan, 1977. Pp 60–86
Frank, David. 'The Cape Breton Coal Industry and the Rise and Fall of the British Empire Steel Corporation.' *Acadiensis* 7, no. 1 (Autumn 1977): 3–34
McCann, L.D. 'The Mercantile-Industrial Transition in the Metal Towns of Pictou County, 1857–1931.' *Acadiensis* 10, no. 2 (Spring 1981): 29–64
– 'Metropolitanism and Branch Businesses in the Maritimes, 1881–1931.' *Acadiensis* 13, no. 1 (Autumn 1983): 112–25
Wynn, Graeme. 'The Maritimes: The Geography of Fragmentation and Underdevelopment.' In L.D. McCann, ed. *Heartland and Hinterland: A Geography of Canada*. 2nd ed. Scarborough: Prentice-Hall, 1987. Pp 175–245

PLATE 25

Port Development in Halifax

L.D. McCANN   Geography, Mount Allison University

Halifax: 1896; 1912; 1926

City of Halifax. *City of Halifax Assessment Plan for 1925*. Halifax, 1925
Goad, Charles. *Insurance Plan of Halifax for 1895*. Montréal: Lovell, 1896
– *Insurance Plan of Halifax for 1914*. Montréal: Lovell, 1914
Hopkins, H.W. *City Atlas of Halifax*. Halifax: Provincial Surveying and Publishing Company, 1878
McAlpine, David. *McAlpine's Halifax City Directory for 1878–79*. Halifax, 1878
McAlpine Directory Company. *McAlpine's Halifax City Directory for 1896–97*. Halifax, 1896
McAlpine Publishing Company. *McAlpine's Halifax City Directory for 1912*. Halifax, 1912
Royal Print and Litho Ltd. *McAlpine's Halifax City Directory, 1926*. Halifax, 1926

Labour force: 1881; 1911; 1931

Canada. *Census*. 1881: Vol 2, Table XV. 1911: Vol 6, Table II. 1931: Vol 7, Table 41

Proposed harbour development

Canada. Department of Railways and Canals. *Report on Halifax Harbour, 1913*

Ship traffic in Halifax harbour

The graph is based on a complete sample of ships arrived and cleared in the Port of Halifax for the first five days of every month for the years 1878, 1896, 1912, and 1926.

Halifax Herald
Halifax Morning Herald

The Halifax explosion
Public Archives of Nova Scotia. v6/240, 1917, 'Plan showing the Devastated Area of
the City of Halifax'

Cargo movement through major ports
We wish to acknowledge the help of Lewis Fischer (History, Memorial University of
Newfoundland), in tracking down comparable data for St John's and in discussing
the topic through correspondence. Thanks are also due to Charles Baker for
researching the port data.
Canada. DBS. Cat. 54–202–4. 1938–40, 1952–61
– Department of National Revenue (Customs). 'Shipping Report.' 1925–37
– SP. 'Annual Report of Trade and Navigation.' 1891–1924. 'Statement of vessels,
British, Canada and Foreign entered inwards from the sea (entered outwards
to the sea) at each port and outport during the fiscal year ending June 30'
Kerr, Donald. 'Problems of Measuring Cargo Movement at Canadian Ports.'
Unpublished report submitted to the Historical Atlas of Canada project, Vol III,
1987

Further readings
Bird, Michael J. *The Town That Died: The True Story of the Greatest Man-Made Explosion
before Hiroshima.* New York: Putnam, 1963
Lane, Frederic C. 'Tonnages, Medieval and Modern.' *Economic History Review* 2nd
series 17, no. 2 (Dec 1964): 213–33
McCann, L.D. 'Staples and the New Industrialism in the Growth of Post-
Confederation Halifax.' *Acadiensis* 8, no. 2 (Spring 1979): 47–79
Raddall, Thomas Head. *Halifax: Warden of the North.* Rev ed. Toronto:
McClelland and Stewart, 1971
Sutherland, D.A. 'The Personnel and Policies of the Halifax Board of Trade,
1890–1914.' In Lewis R. Fischer and Eric W. Sager, eds. *The Enterprising Canadians:
Entrepreneurs and Economic Development in Eastern Canada, 1820–1914.* St John's:
Memorial University, 1979. Pp 203–29
Weaver, John C. 'Reconstruction of the Richmond District in Halifax: A Canadian
Episode in Public Housing and Town Planning, 1918–1921.' *Plan Canada* 16,
no. 1 (Mar 1976): 36–47

PLATE 26

The Great War

CHRISTOPHER A. SHARPE   Geography, Memorial University of
Newfoundland

Enlistment and military installations
The data for Canadian Expeditionary Force (CEF) training camps and winter
camps are combined; when they occur at the same place, only one camp is
indicated. CEF includes 124 588 male recruits raised by the Military Service Act; it
does not include 2 854 women who volunteered as nursing sisters. Eligible
population is that of 1911.
    Enlistment is shown by place of enlistment and does not include those who
enlisted in the CEF in the United States (6 986) or the United Kingdom (3 079).
Newfoundland enlistment was in the Royal Newfoundland Regiment, not the CEF.
    There were 8 579 'aliens' interned in the camps, 5 417 of whom were civilians: 5
954 were Austro-Hungarian, 2 009 German, and 616 of other nationalities.
Canada. *Census.* 1911. Unpublished folio CXXXVI, Table 4
– SP. 1919. No. 246, Department of Justice, 'Report of the Military Service Branch of
the Ministry of Justice on the operation of the Military Service Act, 1917'
Carter, David J. *Behind Canadian Barbed Wire: Alien, Refugee and Prisoner of War Camps
in Canada.* Calgary: Tumbleweed Press, 1980. P 308
Duguid, Col. A.F. *Official History of the Canadian Forces in the Great War, 1914–1919.*
Vol 1. Ottawa: King's Printer, 1938
NAC. Militia Defence Records. RG 24. Vol 1842, Files GAQ 10–42, GAQ 10–44, GAQ
10–47, Vol 1. Vol 1843, File GAQ 10–47E. Vol 1892, No. 109

Victory-loan campaigns
Data for per capita contributions for 1917 and 1918, combined, were graphed
because these were the only years for which a provincial breakdown is available.
Prior to the campaigns to enlist small investors (with subscriptions as low as $50),
there were loans in 1915, 1916, and 1917 to attract large-scale investment. These
loans were supplemented by additional funds from New York but when the United
States entered the war in Apr 1917, it became increasingly difficult for foreign
nations to enter the New York market. Canada therefore had to rely on its own
internal resources.
Canada. SP. 1919. No. 181. Not published
Canada Year Book. 1920
Hunt, M.S. *Nova Scotia's Part in the Great War.* Halifax, 1920
Hopkins, J. Castell. *The Province of Ontario in the War: A Record of Government and
People.* Toronto: Warwick and Rutter, 1919
NAC. Department of Finance Records. RG 19. Vol 588, File 155–1D. Vol 607, File
155–87–6. Vol 608, File 155–88–6

Canadian patriotic fund
Graph includes money paid into the Canadian Fund between Aug 1914 and 31 Mar
1919. Manitoba had a separate provincial fund which raised $6 315 209, of which
$2 405 126 came from voluntary subscriptions. It disbursed $6 282 331. Newfoundland had its own patriotic fund which took in $122 706. There were also local
funds in Ontario – Toronto and York, Lincoln County, Fort William, Preston,
Kenora, Orillia – and one in Cumberland County, BC. There is some ambiguity
about the patriotic fund in Vancouver and Victoria; these organizations refused to
affiliate with the provincial organizations and it is unclear whether these two
cities are included in the BC total.
Bray, R.M. 'Canadian Patriotic Response to the Great War.' PH D thesis, York
University, 1977
Canada Year Book. 1920
Hopkins. *The Province of Ontario in the War.* 1919
Morris, Philip, ed. 'Canadian Patriotic Fund. A Record of Its Activities from
1914–1919.' nd
Newfoundland. *Journals of the House of Assembly.* 1920. 'Report of the Patriotic Fund'

Imperial Munitions Boards contracts, 1915–1919
Not included are investments made in munitions contracts in the United States
($130 123 000), the United Kingdom ($7 726 000), and Newfoundland ($261 000).
Carnegie, David. *History of Munitions Supply in Canada 1914–1918.* Toronto:
Longmans, 1925
NAC. G 30. B4, Vol 36, 'Imperial Munitions Board Report'

Provincial share of manufacturing and war trade
The data are taken from the 1916 *Postal Census of Manufactures* which for 1915 'asked
each manufacturer to report on such products of his establishment as he had
reason to believe were destined for war purposes, whether supplied directly or
indirectly.'
Canada. Department of Trade and Commerce. Census and Statistics Office. *Postal
Census of Manufactures.* 1916

Casualty rates of selected battalions
Fetherstonhaugh, R.C. *The 24th Battalion, C.E.F., Victoria Rifles of Canada, 1914–
1919.* Montréal: Gazette Printing Company, 1930
An Historical Sketch of the Seventy-Seventh Battalion Canadian Expeditionary Force.
Ottawa: War Publications Ltd, 1926
McEvoy, Bernard, and Capt. A.H. Finley. *A History of the 62nd Canadian Infantry
Battalion: Seaforth Highlanders of Canada.* Vancouver: Cowan and Brookhouse,
1920
McWilliams, James L., and R. James Steel. *The Suicide Battalion.* Edmonton: Hurtig,
1978
Murray, Col. W.W. *The History of the 2nd Canadian Battalion (East. Ontario Regiment),
Canadian Expeditionary Force in the Great War, 1914–1918.* Ottawa: The
Historical Committee, 2nd Battalion, CEF, 1947
NAC. *Reports of the Militia Department.* 1919–20
Stevens, George Roy. *A City Goes to War: 49th Infantry Battalion (Loyal Edmonton
Regiment).* Brampton: Charters, 1964

The Royal Newfoundland Regiment, final tally, St John's enlistment
Newfoundland. Department of Militia. *Report.* 1919, 1920
Provincial Archives of Newfoundland. *Regimental Rolls.* 'Royal Newfoundland
Regiment'
'St John's, Nfld Plan.' 1914. Repr Oct 1925. Toronto and Montréal: Underwriters
Survey Bureau

Military Service Act
The graph includes registration, call-up, and exemption from military service of all
male British subjects, unmarried or widowed without children, aged 20–32 years.
For Manitoba and Ontario the sum of the agricultural, medical, and occupational
exemptions did not equal the total number of exemptions granted. Kenora
District of Ontario had been included in the three Manitoba exemption categories
but in the Ontario totals. The discrepancy was 1 997 and it was divided equally
among the three categories; for the graph the data were subtracted from those of
Manitoba and added to those of Ontario.
Canada. SP. 1919. No. 246. 'Report of the Director on the operation of the Military
Service Act, 1919'
NAC. RG 24. Vol 1824. File GAQ 10–44, GAQ 10–47, Vol 1
– Department of Militia and Defence. European War Memorandum No. 6. 1919

Revenue and public debt
Taxes
Canada Year Book. 1940

Canadian military hospitals and cemeteries in Europe
Casualties and medical-care facilities
The Canadian General Hospital (CGH) category includes eight stationary hospitals,
smaller than general hospitals and originally set up as resting places on the line for
casualties on their way back to base. Given the short lines of communications, they
became small general hospitals. Some hospitals operated at various locations; in
these cases the maximum capacity at the location where that maximum occurred
was mapped. There are three exceptions where the maximum capacity was at
Salonica, but the hospitals appear on the map in locations in England (Basingstoke,
Hastings, and Liverpool) to which they were transferred in 1917 and 1918. Hospitals
in Europe outside the map area: in Britain, Buxton (2 special), Kirkdale (1 CGH),
Liverpool (1 CGH), Matlock Bath (1 convalescent); in France, Joinville (1 CGH),
Champagnoles (1 Forestry Corps Hospital, FCH), La Joux/Jura (1 FCH), Gerardmen/
Vosges (1 FCH).
Canada. *Report of the Ministry: Overseas Military Forces of Canada.* London, 1918
– SP. 1917. No. 158. Not published
NAC. G 24. Vol 1843, File GAQ 10–47E. Vol 1844, File GAQ 11–10
Nicholson, G.W.L. *Seventy Years of Service: A History of the Royal Canadian Army
Medical Corps.* Ottawa: Borealis Press, 1977
Statistics of the Military Effort of the British Empire during the Great War. London:
HMSO, 1922
Wood, Herbert Farlie, and John Swettenham. *Silent Witnesses.* Toronto: Hakkert,
1974

PLATE 27

Migration

MARVIN McINNIS   Economics, Queen's University

Special acknowledgment should be made to the important contribution of Michael
Percy (Economics, University of Alberta) in the study of the Ontario origin of
Prairie settlers.

The move to the West
This map is based on two separate bodies of evidence. The interprovincial
movement of Canadian-born people was estimated directly from census data on
province of birth, cross-tabulated with province of residence. For the Prairie
Provinces the 1916 total of those born out of the province was derived from the
census of that year. For other provinces the 1914 numbers were interpolated from
the 1911 and 1921 censuses. The number of persons in each province of

destination from each province of origin was compared with the 1891 number adjusted for survival over the 25-year period; the survival rates used were those from Bourbeau and Légaré (1982). Variations in the concentrations of Ontario-born settlers in the Prairie Provinces can be drawn directly from the 1916 census. Data on districts of origin within Ontario were based on a sample of Prairie newspaper obituaries (McInnis and Percy, 1989). For the calculations some Ontario counties/districts were grouped: Muskoka and Parry Sound, Peterborough and Haliburton, Frontenac and Addington, Leeds and Grenville, Brant and Wentworth.

Bourbeau, Robert, and Jacques Légaré. *Évolution de la mortalité au Canada et au Québec 1831–1931*. Montréal: Les Presses de l'Université de Montréal, 1982
Canada. *Census*. 1891: Vol 2, Table v. 1921: Vol 2, Table LIII
– *Census of the Prairie Provinces*. 1916. Table XXII
McInnis, Marvin, and Michael Percy. 'Dead Men Can Tell Tales: The Ontario Origins of Canadian Settlers on the Canadian Plains.' Unpublished report submitted to the Historical Atlas of Canada project, Vol III, 1989

Immigration, 1896–1914
Immigration to the Prairies, 1896–1914
The migration flows are based on changes in the numbers of foreign-born in Canada over the period between 1891 and 1914. The immigrant population in the 1921 census is tabulated by period of arrival so that post-1914 immigrants can be netted out. By covering the whole period in a net fashion a lower figure for immigration to Canada is derived, well below the cumulated annual inflow (graph of 'Immigration to Canada'). Survival rates from the model life tables given in Bourbeau and Légaré (1982) for the twenty-five-year interval are applied to the number of foreign-born in 1891. For some areas the numbers shown on the flow lines do not correspond to the totals on the pie graphs because no specific flow lines are shown for the Asian population moving beyond British Columbia.

Bourbeau and Légaré. *Évolution de la mortalité*. 1982
Canada. *Census*. 1891: Vol 1, Table v. 1921: Vol 2, Table XLII
– *Census of the Prairie Provinces*. 1916. Table XLII

Immigration to Canada
Urquhart and Buckley. *Historical Statistics*. Series A254

Asian immigration
Urquhart and Buckley. *Historical Statistics*. Series A333, A334, A335

Distribution of immigrant population
Canada. *Census*. 1921. Vol 2, Table XLI

Canadians moving to the United States
Canadians living in the United States
Truesdell, Leon E. *The Canadian Born in the United States*. New Haven: Yale University Press, 1943. Table 40, Fig 8

Origins of American homesteaders on the Prairies
Canada. Department of the Interior. *Annual Report of the Deputy Minister*. 1890–1914. Data for the plate compiled by Michael Percy
Percy, Michael B., and Tamara Woroby. 'American Homesteaders and the Canadian Prairies, 1899 and 1909.' *Explorations in Economic History* 24, no. 1 (Jan 1987): 77–100

PLATE 28
Elements of Population Change

MARVIN McINNIS   Economics, Queen's University

Thanks are due to Richard Tillman for his assistance in preparing the material for this plate.

Cities and districts change population through the processes of natural increase and migration. Migration can be either inward, increasing population, or outward, reducing population, and thus it is the net balance of migration that brings about an overall change in population. The dimensions of population change over each decade and the sources of those changes as shown on all four maps of this plate were produced by the same method of calculation. For the calculations some counties/districts were combined. In New Brunswick: Victoria and Madawaska. In Ontario: Algoma and Manitoulin; Frontenac, Lennox, and Addington; Muskoka and Parry Sound. In Québec: Beauce and Frontenac; Chicoutimi, Saguenay, and Lac-Saint-Jean; Drummond and Arthabaska; Hull Labelle, and Papineau; Rimouski and Matane; Richmond and Wolfe.

Migration was estimated, as a residual after subtracting from overall population change the growth of population due to natural increase. Natural increase was estimated by using an estimated decadal rate of natural increase that was the difference between an estimated birth rate and an estimated death rate. Birth-rate estimates for each city and census district were derived directly from the fertility-rate calculations used in pl 29.

District death rates were estimated in two parts. Deaths were calculated as a sum of deaths of infants under one year of age, directly drawn from the estimates of infant mortality described in the notes for pl 29, and what might be described as an indirectly standardized death calculation for all other ages. The latter was carried out by using provincial age-specific rates of mortality applied to district populations in each age group. In effect this assumes that underlying mortality rates for adults did not vary across cities and districts, an assumption that is manifestly wrong but which does not result in enough error to make a significant difference. By far the greater part of geographic variation in mortality is the consequence of geographic variation in the age compositions of populations.

Estimates of birth rates and death rates were thus made for cities and districts at each census date from 1891 through 1931. These were averaged over the decade to provide an estimate of the decadal average rate of natural increase. That was applied to the mean of the terminal census measures of population to estimate the growth of population due to natural increase.

A major impediment to the estimation of net migration, or even to the calculation of the change in population over a decade, is the need for population numbers for geographically comparable areas, yet there were frequent changes in census districts. The DBS has over the years provided total populations for comparable sets of districts but these lack the details on sex and age necessary for the estimation of migration. The solution was to use different sets of districts for each decade. For every set of census districts there is a total population for the previous decennial census year that is adequate to produce an approximate estimate of intercensal population change due to net migration.

Canada. *Census*. 1891: Vol 2. 1901: Vols 1, 2. 1911: Vol 1, unpublished Folio CXXXIII. 1921: Vol 1. 1931: Vol 2

Further readings
Beaujot, Roderick, and Kevin McQuillan. *Growth and Dualism*. Toronto: Gage, 1982. Ch 6, pp 137–67
Buckley, K.A.H. 'Historical Estimates of Internal Migration in Canada.' In Canadian Political Science Association. *Conference on Statistics, 1960*. Toronto: University of Toronto Press, 1962
George, M.V. *Internal Migration in Canada*. 1961 Census Monograph. Ottawa, 1970
Keyfitz, Nathan. 'The Growth of Canadian Population.' *Population Studies* 4, pt 1 (June 1950): 47–63
McInnis, R. Marvin. 'Census Survival Ratio Estimates of Net Migration for Canadian Regions.' *Canadian Studies in Population* 1 (1974): 93–116

PLATE 29
The Demographic Transition

MARVIN McINNIS   Economics, Queen's University

For the calculations on this plate some counties/districts were combined. See pl 28 for specific combinations.

Marital fertility
The index of the fertility of 15–49-year-old married women (I_g) was developed by the Office of Population Research of Princeton University and reported by Coale and Watkins (1986) for use in the European Fertility Project. I_g can be interpreted as the ratio of observed marital fertility to the maximum attainable fertility that married women in a district could experience, given their age distribution. Fertility estimates for 1891 for this plate were based on the stock of young children enumerated in the census of 1891, adjusted to take account of infant mortality (discussed below). Estimates could be made for only a few of the largest cities. No comparable measure could be estimated for Newfoundland.

Changes in marital fertility 1891–1931 were calculated from the 1891 index of marital fertility and estimates of similar indexes for counties and major cities for 1931. In order to estimate I_g for 1931 the number of married women of childbearing age had to be estimated on a county basis. The number of births in the three years 1930, 1931, and 1932 were taken directly from vital registration data. The regularly reported birth registrations at that time were for places (counties and cities) of occurrence. Fortunately, however, a special retabulation of births by place of residence of the mother was made in connection with the analytical monographs of the 1931 census. The birth tabulation was separately published in 1935. In the census of 1931 there is no tabulation of age by marital status for counties and census divisions. It was necessary to resort to an indirect estimation. A direct calculation could be made for provinces and larger cities, however, and that could be used to gauge the reliability of the estimating procedure. It was assumed first that the age-specific proportions of married and widowed women 50 years of age and over did not vary across census divisions. An estimate of married women aged 50 years or more derived in that manner was subtracted from the reported total of married women of all ages. The percentage change in I_g, the index of marital fertility between 1891 and 1931, was, in all but two instances, negative. There was a slight rise in marital fertility in the districts of Sudbury-Nippising in Ontario and Chicoutimi–Saguenay–Lac-Saint-Jean in Québec but that is treated on the map as no different from slight decline.

Canada. *Census*. 1891: Vol 2. 1931: Vol 2
– DBS. *Special Report on Births in Canada According to Place of Residence of Mother 1930–32*. 1935
Coale, Ansley J., and Susan Cotts Watkins, eds. *The Decline of Fertility in Europe*. Princeton: Princeton University Press, 1986
McInnis, Marvin. 'The Geographic Pattern of Fertility Decline in Canada: 1891–1931.' Unpublished report submitted to the Historical Atlas of Canada project, Vol III, 1987

Infant mortality
Good registration data for infant deaths do not exist for Canada in 1891. Synthetic estimates had to be made based on a blend of several bodies of data including death registrations for the period 1890–1906 in Québec and Ontario, census reports of deaths in the first year of life for 1891 and 1901, census reports of deaths by cause, and census data on children by single years of age. The most intensive investigation was made for 1901. By that year the provincial vital registration data had improved considerably and the census data are better for 1901 than for other years. The systematic element of the ratios of children under one year to children between one and two years, and of the next two intervals, is survivorship, although there are other influences at work on the observed ratios. Preston (1976) has shown that levels of mortality rates are closely related to the causes of mortality. Deaths from gastroenteric infections are very largely deaths of infants and, geographically, they are the most variable component of infant mortality. A statistical regression relationship was estimated for 1901 for a subset of counties of Québec and Ontario for which the infant morality rate calculated from vital registrations were judged not to be manifestly deficient. The regression relationship was then used in combination with the census data referred to above to obtain synthetic estimates of rates of infant mortality for cities and counties in 1891. The estimates for the Maritime Provinces are on a much weaker footing than those for districts in Québec and Ontario; the underlying census data are clearly more aberrant. The county variations shown for the Maritimes rely to a much greater degree on just the ratios of children of single years of age.

Rates of infant mortality for 1931 are much more readily and directly derived. Vital registration was fairly well developed in all provinces. The main problem was that the regular reports were by place of occurrence rather than by place of

residence. That obstacle was overcome by special tabulations for 1930–32 made
by the DBS. Those data are combined with the 1891 estimates to produce the
percentage changes.
Canada. *Census.* 1891: Vol 2, Tables I, CII, XI. 1901: Vol 4, Tables I, V, VI, VIII
– DBS. *Special Report on Births*
– DBS. *Special Report on Mortality in Canada According to Place of Residence, 1930–32.*
     1934
Kuczynski, Robert René. *Birth Registration and Birth Statistics in Canada.* Washington:
     Brookings Institution, 1930
Ontario. *Report Relating to the Registration of Births, Marriages and Deaths in the
     Province of Ontario.* Annual reports
Preston, Samuel H. *Mortality Patterns in National Population: with Special Reference to
     Recorded Causes of Death.* New York: Academic Press, 1976
Québec. *Report of the Secretary and Registrar of the Province of Quebec.* Annual reports

International decline in fertility, 1890–1930
European figures for the index of marital fertility are from Coale and Watkins (1986).
The indices for the United States are calculated from birth data in Coale and
Zelnick (1963) and census statistics on married women by age groups. The graph
shows the levels of I_g in 1891 and 1931 respectively, with the percentage change
highlighted. The lower percentage decline for Canada than for other countries is not
solely a consequence of the small reduction for Québec but also reflects the fact
that Canada, like France, had experienced a substantial decline in marital fertility
prior to 1891, whereas for most European countries the decline was concentrated
entirely in the 1891–1931 period.
Coale and Watkins, eds. *The Decline of Fertility in Europe.* 1986
Coale, Ansley J., and M. Zelnick. *New Estimates of Fertility and Population in the
     United States.* Princeton: Princeton University Press, 1963

International decline in infant mortality, 1890–1930
Van de Walle, Francine. 'Infant Mortality and the European Demographic
     Transition.' In Coale and Watkins, eds. *The Decline of Fertility in Europe.* 1986.
     Pp 212–13

PLATE 30

The Social Landscape of Montréal, 1901

DAVID HANNA   Géographie, Université du Québec à Montréal
SHERRY OLSON   Geography, McGill University

We would like to thank Robert Lewis for his research assistance, Diane Hanna and
Lourdes Meana for preparing the base maps, and Paul-André Linteau for first
suggesting the tax rolls as a source.
     Data for all the illustrations, unless otherwise indicated, were taken from the
rental valuations in the City of Montréal tax roll, 'feuilles de route,' for 1901.
Each occupation was represented by a 100% sample of household heads who
reported that occupation in June 1901.

Concentration of skilled workers
For a discussion of the ecology of work and the class position of skilled workers see
Lewis (1985) and Hoskins (1989).

Median rent by street
Methods for compiling data and segmenting streets are discussed in Hanna and
Olson (1983). Rental values are manipulated in logarithmic transformation and
grouped by multiples. Segments average 100 households, with a minimum of 30.
In addition to the present-day municipalities of Westmount and Outremont, the
65 000 households include suburbs which were independent in 1901 but were soon
after annexed to Montréal: Saint-Louis du Mile End, Saint-Henri, Sainte-
Cunégonde, and Maisonneuve.

Linguistic origin
Canada. *Census.* 1901

A scale of living space
Thanks are due to Carmen Jensen for drawing the houses.

Further readings
Hanna, David, and Sherry Olson. 'Métiers, loyers et bouts de rue: l'armature de la
     société montréalaise, 1881 à 1901.' *Cahiers de géographie du Québec* 27, no. 71
     (1983): 255–76
Hanna, David. 'Montreal, A City Built by Small Builders: 1867–1880.' PH D thesis,
     McGill University, 1986
Hoskins, Ralph. 'Workers at the Grand Trunk Railway Shops.' *Cahiers de géographie
     du Québec* 33, no. 90 (1989): 323–44
Lewis, Robert. 'The Segregated City: Residential Differentiation, Rent and Income
     in Montreal, 1861–1901.' MA thesis, McGill University, 1985
Olson, Sherry. 'Occupations and Residential Spaces in Nineteenth-Century Mon-
     treal.' *Historical Methods* 22, no. 3 (1989): 81–96
Pfautz, W., ed. *Charles Booth on the City: Physical Pattern and Social Structure.* Chicago:
     University of Chicago Press, 1967

PLATE 31

Winnipeg: A Divided City

DANIEL HIEBERT   Geography, University of British Columbia

The valuable assistance of Natalie Crook in gathering the sample data and the list of
ethnic institutions is gratefully appreciated.

Population by ethnic origin and place of residence
Data were derived from a 5% sample of households listed in the directories. The
street address for each household was provided by the directory but ethnic
origin had to be inferred on the basis of the name of the head of the household.
Afro-American, Chinese, and native Indian groups were not included on the
maps because of their small number in the sample.

Henderson's Directories Ltd. *Henderson's Directory of Winnipeg.* Winnipeg, 1891,
     1901, 1911, 1921

Ethnic institutions
Henderson's Directory of Winnipeg. 1921

Population of Winnipeg and St Boniface
Data for place of birth in 1891 and 1901 are for Winnipeg only.
Canada. *Census.* 1891: Vol 1, Table 5. 1901: Vol 1, Tables XI, XIV. 1921: Vol 1, Table
     27; Vol 2, Table 54
– DBS. *Census of the Prairie Provinces.* 1916. Tables VII, XXIII
– Department of Agriculture. *Census of the Province of Manitoba.* 1885–6. Tables III, IV

Infant mortality rates by section
City of Winnipeg. Health Department. *Report of the City Health Department for the
     Year Ending 31st December 1921.* P 86

Deaths from pneumonia and influenza
City of Winnipeg. Health Department. *Annual Report of the Department of Health for
     the Year Ending 31st December 1918.* P 10

Occupation and income
This map utilizes the same 5% sample collected for the 1921 map of ethnic origins.
Heads of households were classified in three general occupational groups:
white-collar workers, self-employed workers (eg, owners of small businesses,
building contractors), and blue-collar workers. The white-collar and blue-collar
categories were each divided into two subgroups on the basis of income. Income
estimates for each occupation were taken from the census.
Canada. *Census.* 1921. Vol 4, Table 40
Henderson's Directory of Winnipeg. 1921

Socio-economic distribution by ethnic origin
This diagram is the result of a crosstabulation between ethnic origin and
occupational category using the 5% sample of household heads drawn from the
1921 directory. The numbers on the diagram indicating the population of each
ethnic group by area were based on the census.
Canada. *Census.* 1921. Vol 1, Table 26
Henderson's Directory of Winnipeg. 1921

Urban growth and land use
Weir, Thomas R. *Atlas of Winnipeg.* Toronto: University of Toronto Press, 1978. Pp
     5–6

Further readings
Artibise, Alan F.J. *Winnipeg: A Social History of Urban Growth, 1874–1914.* Montréal:
     McGill-Queen's University Press, 1975
Bellan, Ruben Carl. *Winnipeg's First Century: An Economic History.* Winnipeg:
     Queenstone House Publishing, 1978
Hiebert, Daniel. 'Class, Ethnicity and Residential Structure: The Social Geography
     of Winnipeg, 1901–1921.' *Journal of Historical Geography* (forthcoming, 1991)
Penner, Norman, ed. *Winnipeg 1919: The Strikers' Own History of the Winnipeg General
     Strike.* Toronto: James Lewis and Samuel, 1973
Woodsworth, J.S. *Strangers Within Our Gates, or Coming Canadians.* 1911. Repr
     Toronto: University of Toronto Press, 1972

PLATE 32

New Approaches to Disease and Dependency

LYNNE MARKS   PH D candidate, History, York University

I would like to thank Peter Hajnal and his staff at Government Documents, Robarts
Library, University of Toronto, for their assistance.

Infant mortality
The figures into the 1920s cannot be considered totally accurate because of the
problems in reporting births and deaths. Deaths under one year of age per 1 000
live births do not include stillbirths. In 1916 statistics for the Maritimes include Nova
Scotia only and statistics for the Prairies do not include Manitoba. In 1921 rural
figures do not include Québec. In 1926 Québec entered into the national system for
reporting vital statistics but this system does not appear to be responsible for the
decrease in infant mortality in Québec from 1921; in 1925 under the old system the
rate was 115 and in 1927 under the new system it was 118. In 1956 and 1961
figures for native Canadians are for registered Indians and Inuit; prior to 1956
figures include Métis, Indians, and Inuit of the Yukon Territory and Northwest
Territories. Data for native Canadians graphed for 1961 are in fact 1960 figures.
Canada. DBS. *Vital Statistics.* 1921–61
– Health and Welfare Canada. Medical Health Services. Correspondence with
     author 27 June 1984
European Historical Statistics 1750–1975. Series B7. Pp 138–42
Historical Statistics of the United States from Colonial Times to 1970. Washington: United
     States Bureau of the Census, 1975. Series B136–47
Leacy. *Historical Statistics.* Series B51–8
Québec. Bureau of Statistics. *Statistical Year Book.* 1913, 1918, 1923
Annual reports of provincial departments of health for Alberta, British Columbia,
     Nova Scotia, and Ontario for 1912 and 1917 were also used.

Impact of sanitation and pasteurization, Toronto
Ontario. *Sessional Papers.* 1900–35. 'Report of the Registrar General of Births,
     Marriages, and Deaths'
Toronto. *Report of the Local Board of Health.* 1923

The decline of tuberculosis
All forms of tuberculosis are included. Prior to 1921 when a system to standardize
the reporting of vital statistics was established, data were taken from provincial
reports where possible and tallied to arrive at a Canadian total. The 1911 and 1916
figures do not include New Brunswick, Prince Edward Island, and Manitoba.
Yukon Territory and the Northwest Territories are not included until 1931.
Newfoundland data are not included until 1951. The Canadian totals include

native Indians. Until 1956 the native Indian death rate and population base also include Métis. Especially in the 1920s and 1930s the native Indian death rate appears to be less accurate than the non-native death rates. For 1956 and 1961 the death rates are for registered Indians and Inuit only; the 1961 data are in fact 1960 figures. The intercensal total population figures are from the DBS population estimates whereas the intercensal Indian population figures are averages of the two nearest censuses.

Data on expenditures on sanatoria were not available for Prince Edward Island, Québec, Manitoba, Saskatchewan, or Alberta in 1921 or for Prince Edward Island in 1926. Data graphed for 1941 are in fact 1943 figures. In some provinces, particularly Saskatchewan and Manitoba, the municipalities paid more than the provincial government for sanatoria and this is not reflected in the figures; moreover, figures do not include federal sanatoria. Some provinces also spent considerable sums on the prevention of tuberculosis, and these are not included.

Canada. DBS *Annual Reports of Tuberculosis Institutions.* 1937–52
– DBS. *Population Estimates.* 1921–52, 1952–6
– DBS. *Statistics on Provincial Finance.* 1921. Tables 9, 11
– DBS. *Vital Statistics.* 1921–61
– Department of National Health and Welfare. *Annual Report.* 1955, 1957, 1961
Canada. Statistics Canada. *Tuberculosis Statistics, Morbidity, and Mortality.* 1973
Grauer, A.E. *Public Health: A Report Prepared for the Royal Commission on Dominion–Provincial Relations.* Ottawa, 1939
Leacy. *Historical Statistics.* Series A125–63
Nova Scotia. Department of Public Health. *Annual Report.* 1912–18
Ontario. Department of Health. *Annual Report.* 1912–18
Québec. Bureau of Statistics. *Statistical Year Book.* 1914–22
Wherrett, G.L. *The Miracle of the Empty Beds: A History of Tuberculosis in Canada.* Toronto: University of Toronto Press, 1977

Public health programs, New Brunswick
New Brunswick. Department of Health. *Annual Report.* 1928, 1929

Sterilization of the mentally 'unfit,' Alberta
The Sexual Sterilization Act in Alberta was passed in 1928 and went into operation in 1929. Both those designated as 'mentally defective' and those designated as 'psychotic' could be subject to sterilization. British Columbia also passed similar legislation in 1933.
Alberta. Department of Public Health. *Annual Report of the Eugenics Board.* 1931–60

The Mandate of the Juvenile Court, Halifax, 1912–3
The Halifax Juvenile Court was created in 1911. Of the 106 juveniles brought before the court as being neglected, 48 were female; of the 373 up for other offences, 18 were female. Various misdemeanors included coasting on a public street on Sunday, causing a disturbance, setting fires, 'indecent' acts, throwing stones, and smoking on the street.
Nova Scotia. *Sessional Papers.* 'Report of the Superintendent of Neglected and Dependent Children.' 1914?

Neighbourhood Workers' Association, Toronto
The Neighbourhood Workers' Association (NWA) was fully organized with a staff of its own in 1918 although its origins date from 1912 when social-service personnel in Toronto began to organize and co-ordinate their work. The NWA both granted relief and other assistance through its central office and its nine local associations throughout the city and also acted as a referral agency, directing families to other social-service agencies. Of the 773 cases in 1919, 'advice and direction' only was given in 153 cases and 263 families were referred to other agencies. The number of problems graphed total 1 126 because the categories for the problems are not mutually exclusive. The graph refers to the social casework done from 1 Sep 1918 to 30 Apr 1919. It does not include the influenza relief work in which 1 876 families were assisted during that period although it does include 181 cases where influenza was cited as the main problem requiring assistance.
Toronto. Neighbourhood Workers' Association. *Annual Report.* 1919

Established institutions and new initiatives, Toronto and Montréal, 1928
Private non-government-funded institutions are under-represented because information concerning these institutions was difficult to find. It was also sometimes difficult to categorize institutions. The institutions noted as receiving government funding could be receiving widely varying amounts of financial support. The extent of government control/administration was often unclear.

The maps are selective and do not include all established institutions and new initiatives. For example, homes for unwed mothers, a very old institution, are not included. Baby clinics are not included on the map; they were often located in churches, schools, hospitals, and settlement houses and their locations changed frequently. Montréal's pure-milk depots, intended to combat infant deaths caused by unpasteurized milk, were similarly difficult to map. It was not possible to map the activities of public health nurses; in Toronto these nurses were primarily employed by the municipal government while in Montréal about three-quarters were employed by other organizations, both religious and lay. The medical and dental inspection of school children, another important public health initiative in the 1920s, could not be illustrated here.
Canada. *Census.* 1931. Vol 9, Tables 1, 23, and 'Directory of charitable and benevolent institutions,' pp 304–12
– DBS. *Directory of Hospitals.* 1931–45
Canadian Medical Association. *Directory of the Hospitals of Canada.* 1929
City of Toronto. *City Council Minutes.* 1929. App A, Estimates
Lovell's Montreal Directory. 1928–9
Might's Toronto City Directory. 1929
Montréal. Bureau of Health. *Annual Report.* 1928
– Health Survey Committee. *Survey of Public Health Activities.* Montréal, 1928
National Sanitarium Association. *Annual Report.* 1926–9
Neighbourhood Workers' Association. *Social Services Directory of Toronto.* 1928
Ontario. Inspector of Prisons and Public Charities. *Annual Report.* 1928
– *Public Accounts.* 1928
Public Health Journal. Various issues in the 1920s
Québec. Bureau of Statistics. *Statistical Year Book.* 1929
– *Public Accounts.* 1928
– *Report of Hospitals and Benevolent Institutions.* 1929
Quebec Gazette. 1929
Toronto. Department of Public Health. *Annual Report.* 1920–9

Mothers' allowance and old-age pension
Recipients of mothers' allowance
Recipients of old-age pension
For mothers' allowance in Nova Scotia in 1939 the figure given is the average monthly payment per family; the amount for a mother and two children was not available but is probably somewhat lower since the average number of children is 3.3. Although mothers' allowance in Québec in 1939 was $40, in 1940 it was reduced to $27.50 and in 1942 it became $30. In Ontario the sum of $40 was given to mothers in cities; the amount for mothers in towns was $5 less and for mothers in rural areas $10 less. In Manitoba the $50 indicated does not include $10 a year for winter fuel allowance. In British Columbia, although $47.50 was given, more was allowed by law; if a family owned its own home $5 less was given.

The standard of living was adapted from the Toronto Welfare Council which gives estimates of food and clothing allowances for individual members of a family by age and sex; it was particularly useful for determining the costs for a mother with two children under ten and for an aged person. In addition to food and clothing allowances, rent, expenses, and additional moneys were added to determine minimum standards. The rent allowed for a mother with two children was for a two- to three-room house, somewhat below standard, while the rent allowed for the older person was for one room. The Welfare Council study allowed $5.12 a week for expenses of operation, such as gas, coal, light, and car fare for a family with two parents and three children; $4.00 was allowed for a mother with two children and $2.56 for an older person. Although the Welfare Council study allowed $4.96 a week for recreation, health, and life insurance and savings, in the calculations for the map only $1 for a mother with two children and only $0.50 for an older person were added to make it clear how minimal a standard of living is being defined. The standard for Toronto was translated into provincial standards using the Department of Labour's Canada-wide price indices for a family budget.
Canada. *Census.* 1961. Vol 7–1, Pt 4, Table 2
– Department of National Health and Welfare. *Report on the Administration of Old Age Pensions in Canada.* 1937–51
– DBS. 'Population Estimates.' 1926–52
– Parliament. Joint Committee on Old Age Security. *Minutes.* 1950
Labour Gazette. 1939
Leacy. *Historical Statistics.* Series C508–20
Strong-Boag, Veronica. 'Wages for Housework: Mothers' Allowances and the Beginnings of Social Security in Canada.' *Journal of Canadian Studies* 14, no. 1 (Spring, 1979): 24–34
Toronto Welfare Council. *The Cost of Living: A Study of the Cost of a Standard of Living in Toronto which Should Maintain Health and Self-Respect.* Toronto, 1939

Children under public care, 1941
Canada. *Census.* 1941. Vol 1, Table 17
– DBS. *Census of Charitable and Benevolent Institutions.* 1941, 1946. Tables 14, 17
– DBS. *Survey of Elementary and Secondary Education in Canada.* 1940–2. Table 32
Jones, Andrew, and Leonard Rutman. *In the Children's Aid: J.J. Kelso and Child Welfare in Ontario.* Toronto: University of Toronto Press, 1981

Further readings
Bator, Paul A. 'Public Health Reform in Canada and Urban History: A Critical Survey.' *Urban History Review* 9, no. 2 (October 1980): 87–102
Cassels, Jay. *The Secret Plague: Venereal Disease in Canada, 1838–1939.* Toronto: University of Toronto Press, 1987
Copp, Terry. *The Anatomy of Poverty: The Condition of the Working Class in Montreal 1897–1929.* Toronto: McClelland and Stewart, 1974
'Dependency and Social Welfare.' *Journal of Canadian Studies* 14, no. 1 (Spring 1979)
Guest, Dennis. *The Emergence of Social Security in Canada.* Vancouver: University of British Columbia Press, 1980
McLaren, Angus. *Our Own Master Race: The Eugenics Crusade in Canada.* Toronto: McClelland and Stewart, forthcoming 1990
Mitchinson, Wendy, and Janice McGinnis, eds. *Essays in the History of Canadian Medicine.* Toronto: McClelland and Stewart, 1988
Sutherland, Neil. *Children in English-Canadian Society: Framing the Twentieth-Century Consensus.* Toronto: University of Toronto Press, 1976

PLATE 33

Schooling and Social Structure

CHAD GAFFIELD   Histoire, Université d'Ottawa
LYNNE MARKS   PH D candidate, History, York University

We would like to thank Peter Hajnal and his staff at Government Documents, Robarts Library, University of Toronto, for their assistance.

Secondary-school attendance, 1921 and 1951
The graph on secondary-school attendance classifies students based on place of residence; as a result students living in rural areas attending urban schools are classified as rural.
Canada. *Census.* 1921: Vol 2, Table CVIII. 1951: Vol 2, Table 24

Enrolment in secondary grades, Saskatchewan
Saskatchewan. Department of Education. *Annual Report.* 1931

Saskatchewan schools
Canada. DBS. *Comparative Efficiency of Consolidated and Rural Schools in Canada.* 1931. P xliv

Indian schooling
Day school: small school on reserve
Boarding school: fairly small school, may be on reserve; student's contact with parents discouraged
Industrial school: large boarding school away from reserve where some technical education is provided
On the graph on Indian enrolment by type of school for 1960, day pupils in residential schools are included with students in day schools.

Canada. DBS. *Annual Survey of Education in Canada.* 1921, 1936
- DBS. *Survey of Elementary and Secondary Education.* 1936, 1957
- Department of Citizenship and Immigration. Indian Affairs Branch. *Annual Report.* 1957, 1960
- Department of Indian Affairs. *Annual Report.* 1890, 1901, 1912, 1920, 1935
Canada Year Book. 1962. P 150

Secondary schooling
On the regional graph 'Maritimes' includes only Nova Scotia and New Brunswick until 1906; in 1906 'Prairies' includes only Manitoba. Students in secondary grades include students in continuation schools, vocational schools, and secondary grades in elementary schools. Until the 1930s New Brunswick students in secondary grades in ungraded schools were not distinguished from other students in these schools; since they could not be included, it is possible that up to one-third of all students in secondary grades in that province are not represented until the 1930s. This problem also exists prior to 1926 in Prince Edward Island. Québec does not appear on the graph because the classical colleges, which provided much of the secondary schooling in that province, also provided higher education and students at the two different levels could not be distinguished. Enrolment data are for June in the year specified whenever possible; there are, however, variations over time and among the provinces in the manner in which enrolment is calculated. For example, in Ontario all students on the register at some point in the school year are counted until 1933.
On the graph on gender, in 1911 and 1921 for Saskatchewan and in 1911 for Ontario, only students in high schools are included. The 1921 figures for Ontario and New Brunswick exclude secondary students in ungraded country schools.
Canada. DBS. *Historical Statistical Survey of Education in Canada.* 1921
- DBS. *Survey of Elementary and Secondary Education.* 1962
- Statistics Canada. *Historical Compendium of Educational Statistics from Confederation to 1975.* Ottawa, 1978
Annual reports of the provincial departments of education for the various provinces between 1891 and 1926 were also used.

School enrolment to 1961
Census data for school attendance were used for these graphs rather than data from provincial departments of education since the latter were often collected differently, both among the provinces and over time. While some changes were made in the way that data on school enrolment were collected in the census over time, there is more comparability, particularly between provinces. In 1901, and in 1921 for Newfoundland, enrolment includes all students rather than only those aged 5–19 years; this however does not change the figures substantially since in Canada in 1911 only 1% of 20–24-year-olds were in school.
Canada. *Census.* 1901: Vol 4, Table XII. 1911: Bulletin XIX. 1921: Vol 2, Table CV. 1931: Vol 4, Table 80. 1941: Vol 3, Table 45. 1951: Vol 2, Table 25. 1961: Vol 1, Pt 3, Table 99
Newfoundland. *Census of Newfoundland and Labrador, Interim Report.* 1935. Table 24
- *Census of Newfoundland and Labrador.* 1945. Vol 1

Development of technical and commercial schools
The definition of technical education varied over time and among provinces. This map focuses primarily on more advanced, ie, secondary or post-secondary, forms of publicly funded technical/commercial education, as well as on more long-term programs. Several provinces included technical/commercial options within many of their secondary schools; these 'composite' schools were too numerous to be included. Veterans' training centres and youth training programs, which by their nature were fairly short-lived, were not included unless they were transformed into more long-term technical schools/institutes. The extensive network of arts and crafts schools in Québec were not included unless they evolved into fully fledged secondary technical institutes. Publicly funded trade schools, which offered courses to school-leavers, unemployed adults, and apprentices and institutes providing a wide range of post-secondary technical or commercial education were included.
Canada. DBS. *List of Secondary Schools in Canada.* 1937, 1942, 1950
- DBS. *Survey of Elementary and Secondary Education.* 1930–50
- Department of Labour. *Canadian Vocational Training.* 1946–61
- Department of Labour. *Technical Education.* 1920–45
- Department of Labour. *Vocational Educational Bulletin.* 1920–8
- Department of Labour. *Vocational Education in Canada.* 1949
- Department of Labour. *Vocational Training Programs in Canada.* 1956
Annual reports of the provincial departments of education and labour for the various provinces between 1919 and 1961 were also used.

Ontario high-school students
On the graph on occupation for all Ontario men (ie, not just those whose children are high-school students) 'commerce' includes clerical, proprietary, managerial, commercial, and financial occupations. 'Labourers and trades' includes those in fishing, hunting, trapping, logging, mining and quarrying, manufacturing, construction, and transportation.
Canada. *Census.* 1961. Vol 3, Pt 1, Table 3
- *Annual Survey of Education.* 1934. Table 48
Ontario. Department of Education. *Annual Report.* 1890–1920

Classical education in Québec
There were women in classical colleges prior to 1941 but very few prior to the 1930s. From 1941 women in convents receiving the first half of the classical course are included as classical-college students. For 1956 male and female students taking the classical course in modern secondary colleges are included; the number of such female students may be underestimated. Until 1941 domestic-science students may include some primary students. Domestic-science students always include those at one Protestant school (Sainte-Anne-de-Bellevue).
The proportion of graduates of the Seminaire de Nicolet who became clergy, doctors, or lawyers changed very little over time but the proportion who became administrators and scientists did increase. The data concerning the Seminaire de Nicolet may not be representative of classical colleges within the Montréal area.
The map of classical colleges includes all colleges defined as such by Galarneau (1978). It includes religious seminaries but does not include classical sections in what were basically primary schools.

Galarneau, Claude. *Les collèges classiques au Canada français 1620–1970.* Montréal: Fides, 1978
Lessard, Claude. *Le séminaire de Nicolet 1803–1969.* Trois-Rivières: Éditions du Bien Public, 1980
Québec. Bureau of Statistics. *Statistical Year Book.* 1914–62
- Department of Agriculture. *Annual Report.* 1891–1961
- Department of Education. *Annual Report.* 1891–1961
- Statistics of Education. *Annual Yearbook.* 1914–62

Further readings
Barman, Jean, Yvonne Herbert, and Don McCaskill. *Indian Education in Canada.* I: *The Legacy.* Vancouver: University of British Columbia Press, 1986
Gaffield, Chad. 'Back to School: Towards a Fresh Agenda for the History of Education.' *Acadiensis* 15, no. 2 (Spring 1986): 169–90
Jones, David C., Nancy M. Sheehan, and Robert A. Stamp, eds. *Shaping the Schools of the Canadian West.* Calgary: Detselig, 1979
Stamp, Robert M. *The Schools of Ontario 1876–1976.* Toronto: University of Toronto Press, 1982
Thivièrge, Nicole. *Histoire de l'enseignement menager-familial au Québec, 1882–1970.* Québec: Institut québécois de recherche sur la culture, 1982
Wilson, J. Donald. *An Imperfect Past: Education and Society in Canadian History.* London: Althouse Press, 1984
Wilson, J. Donald , Robert M. Stamp, and Louis-Philippe Audet, eds. *Canadian Education: A History.* Toronto: Prentice-Hall, 1970

PLATE 34
Religious Adherence

MURDO MacPHERSON   Historical Atlas of Canada, Toronto

The author is indebted to Neil Semple for help and advice on the process of church union and the Presbyterian vote on the church union.

Religious adherence, 1921
Canada. *Census.* 1921. Vol 1, Table 38
Newfoundland. *Census of Newfoundland.* 1921. Pp 502–3

Religious diversity, Canada
Leacy. *Historical Statistics.* Series A164–84

Religious diversity, Saskatchewan
Canada. *Census.* 1921. Vol 1, Table 38

The road to church union
To approximate the number of adherents in each church both census figures and the annual reports of each church were used. For Methodist and Congregational churches differences in figures between the two sources was relatively minor, but for Presbyterian churches the differences were sufficiently great that Synod/ General Assembly figures have been factored upwards to achieve greater comparability with the census.
For all Presbyterian churches prior to 1869 the annual *Minutes of the Synod* were used. For the Presbyterian Church of Canada (Church of Scotland) the *Minutes* were succeeded in 1870–4 by the *General Assembly, Acts and Proceedings.* For the Presbyterian Church in Canada the *Acts and Proceedings of the General Assembly* from 1875 to 1926 were used.
For the Methodist Church and the Methodist Church of Canada the annual *Journal of the General Conference* (1884–1925 and 1874–83 respectively) was used. For all other Methodist churches the *Minutes of the Annual Conference* were used. For all Congregational churches *The Canadian Congregational Year Book* (annually 1871/2–1925) was used.
Canada. *Census.* 1850–1: Vol 1, App 2, 4. 1860–1: Vol 1, App 3, 4. 1870–1: Vol 1, Table II. 1880–1: Vol 1, Table II. 1891: Vol 1, Table IV. 1901: Vol 1, Table VIII. 1911: Vol 2, Table III. 1921: Vol 1, Table 34. 1931: Vol 2, Table 38
United Church Archives. Chart prepared by Rev. W.T. Gunn. 'Union of Churches in Canada leading toward The United Church.' In *Research Tool 15: United Church of Canada.* This chart, while visually useful, contains inaccuracies.
The United Church of Canada. *Year Book.* 1926

Presbyterian vote on church union
Prior to union there were 174 Congregationalist, 4 797 Methodist, and 4 512 Presbyterian congregations. Union brought 8 691 of these congregations into the United Church, with 8 Congregationalist and 784 Presbyterian congregations not taking part in union (the continuing Presbyterians claimed that 814 congregations did not take part).
The presbytery boundaries shown on the map are generalized and are based on the pastoral charges or mission fields within each presbytery.
United Church Archives. 'The Act and Proceeding of the 51st General Assembly of the Presbyterian Church in Canada.' 1925
- Church Union Collection. Box 8–13, 'Presbyterian Church.' Box 27, files 625–6, and Box 28, files 634–5, 'Bureau of Literature and Information'

Vote of congregations, Pictou and Truro presbyteries
Only 'communicants' were allowed to vote; 'adherents' were not. However, some returns include adherent votes in the total (often a source of dispute) giving some inconsistency to the figures. For the map the votes entered on the official returns, whether including or excluding adherents, have been used.
United Church Archives. Church Union Collection. Box 8, files 175–6, 178–9, 'Presbyterian Church.' Box 28, file 634, 'Bureau of Literature and Information'

Workers from religious orders
'Québec' excludes dioceses where the bulk of the population and the ecclesiastical centre are outside Québec, ie, Ottawa, Pembroke, Timmins, and James Bay. These four dioceses are included in 'rest of Canada.'
Bilan du monde. 2nd ed. Publié par le Centre Église vivante (Louvain). Tournai: Casterman, 1964

Further readings
Grant, J.W. *The Canadian Experience of Church Union.* London: Lutterworth Press, 1967
– *The Church in the Canadian Era: The First Century of Confederation.* Toronto: McGraw-Hill Ryerson, 1972
Silcox, Claris Edwin. *Church Union in Canada: Its Causes and Consequences.* New York: Institute of Social and Religious Research, 1933

PLATE 35

Organized Sport

WILLIAM HUMBER   Continuing Studies, Seneca College
LYNNE MARKS   PH D candidate, History, York University
ALAN METCALFE   Human Kinetics, University of Windsor

Victoria, British Columbia
Each line represents one link between Victoria and another location for each sporting activity, but does not indicate the volume of intercity play, the number of teams or individuals involved, nor where the competition took place. In the case of lacrosse, where there were two leagues, each league is represented by a line even when the two linkages are to the same city.
Victoria Daily Times. 1895

Peterborough, Ontario, 1890–1892
Each line represents one linkage by sporting activity, but does not indicate the volume of intercity play by sport, the number of teams involved in play, nor where the play took place.
Canada. Manuscript Census. 1891. City of Peterborough
Peterborough Examiner. 1890–2

Sponsorship of league sport, Peterborough, 1929
Peterborough Examiner. 1929

Edmonton Grads women's basketball team
Macdonald, Cathy. 'The Edmonton Grads: Canada's Most Successful Team, A History and Analysis of Their Success.' MA thesis, University of Windsor, 1976. Fig II, 'Type of Competition during Five Eras of the Grads' History'

The development of sporting leagues in selected cities
All issues for the years 1889, 1895, 1905, 1915, 1925, and 1929 of the following newspapers were examined:
Brandon Daily Star
L'Étoile (Joliette)
Halifax Herald
Peterborough Examiner
Regina Leader Post
Le Soleil (Québec)
Victoria Daily Times

American influences on Canadian football
We would like to acknowledge the assistance of Frank Cosentino in preparing this chart.
Cosentino, Frank. *Canadian Football, The Grey Cup Years.* Toronto: Musson, 1969
Humber, William. 'Hardrocking and Uproar.' *The Idler* 18 (July/Aug 1988): 31–7

Early hockey challenges, 1893–1926
Early competition for the Stanley Cup was of an *ad hoc* nature, based loosely upon an ever evolving range of leagues and challengers, but always dependent upon the board of trustees for approval. This factor, coupled with the unpredictable playing season and the difficulties of travel often resulted in challenges that were accepted in one season being played in the next or in multiple challenges leading to more than one Stanley Cup holder within a given year. Yearly winners, therefore, are not shown. The total number of Stanley Cup challenges played are shown as well as the number of times a challenge or defence of the cup was won or lost.
Between 1915 and 1926 an annual east-west play-off series was considered to be the challenge for the Stanley Cup and recognized as such by the trustees (in 1914 a series played without the trustees' permission was not formally recognized as a challenge). By 1917 the Stanley Cup was no longer considered a challenge trophy but rather an east-west competition. However, the period 1915–26 has been included on this map of hockey challenges; it is considered as a transition period between the early, *ad hoc* competitions and the later quest for the Stanley Cup which involved only the National Hockey League.
It should be noted that the locations of teams have been shown rather than individual teams since teams changed greatly not only over the years, but sometimes within a single season, and because more than one team often resided in the same city.
Coleman, Charles L. *The Trail of the Stanley Cup.* Vols 1, 2. Montréal: National Hockey League, 1966, 1969

The National Hockey League, 1927–1961
From 1927 to 1961 the Stanley Cup was the exclusive property of the National Hockey League (NHL) and was awarded to the league champion at the end of the season.
Coleman. *The Trail of the Stanley Cup.* Vols 2, 3. 1969, 1976

Birthplace of NHL players
The birthplace of every player was tabulated every second year beginning in 1927 and a final tabulation was made to derive a sample for 1927–61. Because an aggregate profile of birthplaces for any given year was desired, players were counted each and every year they appeared in the sample years.
We would like to acknowledge the assistance of Joseph A. May.
Coleman. *The Trail of the Stanley Cup.* Vols 2, 3. 1969, 1976

Minor-league baseball
Cities having teams in the same league have been linked arbitrarily. It should be noted that the locations of all the teams that engaged in play within a given league are shown only for years in which at least one Canadian team was involved and for the whole time period within which the league was in operation. Some teams, therefore, may not have been members of a given league at the same time and so may not have played against one another. The purpose of the map is to show the wide-ranging network of leagues that involved diverse Canadian and American teams.
Clifton, Merritt. *Disorganized Baseball, The Provincial League from LaRogue to Les Expos.* Proceedings of the 5th Canadian symposium on the history of sport and physical education. Toronto, 1982. Pp 116–21
Obojski, Robert. *Bush League: A History of Minor League Baseball.* New York: Macmillan, 1975. Appendix, 'Rosters of the minor leagues since 1902'

Further readings
Cochrane, Jean, Abby Hoffman, and Pat Kincaid. *Women in Canadian Sports.* Toronto: Fitzhenry and Whiteside, 1977
Metcalfe, Alan. *Canada Learns to Play: The Emergence of Organized Sport, 1807–1914.* Toronto: McClelland and Stewart, 1987
Morrow, Don, Mary Keyes, Wayne Simpson, Frank Cosentino, and Ron Laffage. *A Concise History of Sport in Canada.* Toronto: Oxford University Press, 1989
Mott, Morris, ed. *Sports in Canada, Historical Readings.* Toronto: Clopp Clark Pitman, 1989

PLATE 36

Recreational Lands

GEOFFREY WALL   Geography, University of Waterloo

Rocky Mountains National Park
Byrne, A.R. *Man and Landscape Change in Banff National Park Area Before 1911.* Studies in Land Use History and Landscape Change, National Park Series No. 1. Calgary: University of Calgary, 1968
Scace, R.C. 'Banff Townsite: An Historical-Geographical View of Urban Development in a Canadian National Park.' In J.G. Nelson and R.C. Scace, eds. *The Canadian National Parks: Today and Tomorrow.* Studies in Land Use History and Landscape Change, National Park Series No. 3. Calgary: National and Provincial Parks Association of Canada / The University of Calgary, 1968. Pp 770–93

Banff Springs Hotel, Alberta, ca 1928
Thanks are due to Joan Schwartz, Chief, Photography Acquisition and Research Section, Documentary Art and Photography Division, NAC, for her assistance in locating an appropriate photograph.
NAC. PA–804067

Muskoka District, Ontario
For the map on cottages and hotels the category 'other' includes all of Canada except Ontario and residents outside Canada and the United States.
Adam, G.M. *Muskoka Illustrated with Descriptive Narrative of this Picturesque Region.* Toronto: Bryce, 1888
Wall, Geoffrey. 'An Historical Perspective on Water-Based Recreation.' In J. Marsh, ed. *Water-Based Recreation: Problems and Prospects.* Department of Geography Occasional Paper No. 8. Peterborough: Trent University, 1979. Pp 7–26
Wall, Geoffrey. 'Recreational Land Use in Muskoka.' *Ontario Geography* 11 (1977): 11–28

National and provincial parks
Coleman, J.R.B. 'The National Parks of Canada.' Paper prepared for submission to the First World Conference on National Parks, Seattle, Wash. Apr 1962
Provincial reports on parks and various maps for provincial parks of greater than 50 000 hectares in the provinces of New Brunswick, Québec, Ontario, Saskatchewan, and British Columbia

National-park attendance
The graph is based on operations figures by fiscal year 1 Apr–31 Mar, assigned to the first date for graphing purposes. 'Other' includes: Georgian Bay Islands (1930–61); Glacier (1930–61); Mount Revelstoke (1930–61); Prince Albert (1930–61); St Lawrence Islands (1930–61); Buffalo (1930–40); Neomiskan (1930–45); and Terra Nova (1960–1)
Canada. Canadian Park Service. Socio-Economic Branch. Hull, Qué

Vancouver Island, British Columbia
'Number of facilities' refers to the number of establishments providing overnight accommodation rather than the number of rooms or campsites. If an establishment had more than one type of facility, each facility was counted. 'Other' includes motor courts, cottages, lodges, apartments, cabins, and bungalows.
British Columbia. Bureau of Provincial Information. *Highways, Motor Camps and Stopping Places.* 1929
– Department of Recreation and Conservation. British Columbia Travel Bureau. *British Columbia Tourist Accommodations.* 1959

Public recreational facilities, Toronto
In a survey by the Welfare Council of Toronto (the main source of information for this map) private recreation, which falls under the category of 'recreation centre operated by private agency,' included 'voluntary supported organizations with a constitution, program service and a full time staff' but 'did not include many types of groups which, though engaging in recreation, are not in an organizational program' (p xx).
Armstrong, Frederick H. *Toronto, The Place of Meeting.* Toronto: Windsor Publications, produced in cooperation with the Ontario Historical Society, 1983
Boyer, Barbaranne. *The Boardwalk Album: Memories of the Beach.* Erin, Ont: Boston Mills Press, 1985
City of Toronto. The Welfare Council of Toronto and District. *The Recreation Survey of Metropolitan Toronto: An Inventory of Facilities and Programs in Relation to Population Data.* 1956

City of Toronto Archives. Parks and Recreation. RG12

Filey, Mike. *Trillium and Toronto Island*. Toronto: Peter Martin Associates, 1976

Goad, Chas E. *Map of the City of Toronto and Vicinity*. Toronto: Quebec Bank Chambers, 1890

Penson, S.R.G. *Plan of the City of Toronto and Suburbs*. Toronto: S.R.G. Penson, 1891

Hunting and sport fishing, New Brunswick
In the graph of hunting licences 'resident' refers to residents of New Brunswick, while 'non-resident' refers to all others. The graphs of Restigouche River licences use data which include the address of the person/club leasing an area of the river and the term of the lease; totals were tabulated for the period 1883–1927 by calculating totals for each location, for each year, and then a final total. Individuals or fishing clubs that held leases for more than one year were counted for each year in which they held a lease.

For the map on sport fishing totals were derived from tabulating the total rent paid and whether or not the lease was to an individual or a club for each year between 1883 and 1927. A grand total for each river or river portion was then calculated.

Brown, C.J.A. 'An Evaluation of the Salmon River Leasing System of New Brunswick 1869–1927.' MA thesis, University of Waterloo, 1982

Guyer, C.F. 'Big Game Management in New Brunswick 1889–1971.' MA thesis, University of Waterloo, 1982

New Brunswick. Department of Lands and Mines (name changed from Crown Lands Department in 1926). *Annual Report*. 1863–1961

Further readings
Bella, Leslie. *Parks for Profit*. Montréal: Harvest House, 1987

McFarlane, Elsie Marie. *The Development of Public Recreation in Canada*. Ottawa: Canadian Parks and Recreation Association, 1970

Nelson, J.Gordon, ed. *Canadian Parks in Perspective*. Montréal: Harvest House, 1969

Wall, Geoffrey, ed. *Outdoor Recreation in Canada*. Toronto: Wiley, 1989

Wall, Geoffrey, and John Marsh, eds. *Recreational Land Use: Perspectives on Its Evolution in Canada*. Ottawa: Carleton University Press, 1982

PLATE 37

Working Worlds

LYNNE MARKS   PHD candidate, History, York University
DEBRA McNABB   Nova Scotia Museum of Industry

Earnings of selected occupations
Farm-help wages
Average weekly earnings were calculated for a selection of occupations based on samples of wage rates obtained by the federal Department of Labour from a variety of sources across the country. The Department of Labour relied primarily on employers or on trade-union agreements for information. Since workers in union shops would generally be paid better than those in non-union workplaces and since some employers may have reported paying the higher wages than they actually paid, these wage rates are probably higher than average rates. However the data still provide useful information regarding wage differentials between occupations and between men and women in the same occupation.

The data were recorded on a weekly, daily, or hourly basis but also included hours worked so that average weekly wages could be calculated. No fewer than six sample wage rates were used to calculate the average. Only for occupational categories of garment workers were gender distinctions provided.

For the table on farm-help, although board is given a dollar value, there would no doubt have been no exchange of monies; rather there was an agreement that part of an employee's farm labour would be performed for board in lieu of wages.
Canada. Department of Labour. *Wages and Hours of Labour in Canada, 1920–1928*. Wages and Hours of Labour Report No. 12. Tables X, N, and App A

Provincial minimum-wage legislation
McCallum, Margaret E. 'Keeping Women in Their Place: The Minimum Wage in Canada, 1910–25.' *Labour/Le Travail* 17 (Spring 1986): 29–56

The factory system, Eaton's, Toronto
The illustration was clearly aimed at the public, but it does give some sense of the scale and division of labour found in large factories of the period. While Eaton's had cleaner and healthier working conditions than many other factories, Eaton's employees, like most garment workers, faced low wages, as well as long hours in peak season and layoffs in slack season. As a 1912 strike at Eaton's Toronto factory made clear, Eaton's workers also had to deal with a virulently anti-union employer.
Eaton's Spring and Summer Catalogue. No. 114. 1915. P 1

Selected land use, Glace Bay, Nova Scotia
Residential land use by occupation is based on the occupation of the head of the household. Occupation is divided into three categories: miner; other coal company employee, which includes all surface and underground employees of the coal company not listed as miner in the directory; and other, which includes all other occupations, including heads of households who are widowed females.

Generalized residential areas have been coloured according to the three occupational categories but may represent anything from one household to a densely populated block of households, where the heads of the households all fall into the same occupational group. Within these broad areas heads of households whose occupations differ from the generalized category are represented by a coloured dot. The category 'other land use' does not list all other land uses within the study area but only mines and the downtown commercial core. Other land uses and commercial activities outside the downtown area have been excluded.
Beaton Institute. University College of Cape Breton. Map No. 45, 'Insurance Plan of the Town & District of Glace Bay, March 1959.' Montréal: Underwriter's Survey Bureau Ltd, 1959

– Map No. 467, 'Glace Bay & Morien.' Ottawa: Department of Militia and Defence, 1919

Cadegan, P.L. 'Town of Glace Bay, Nova Scotia, Canada.' Glace Bay: Town of Glace Bay, nd. Map

Might, J.M. *Town of Glace Bay Street Directory*. and *Glace Bay City Directory*. Halifax: Atlantic Ltd, 1928

A family budget, Cape Breton
'Other food and household' includes rolled outs, kerosene oil, and soap. 'Other expenditures' include doctor's fees, hospital fees, patriotic fund, church, taxes, and luxury food and household items such as salt, ginger, utensils, furnishings, and linens. This information originally appeared in a letter to the *Canadian Labor Leader* 15, 29 Dec 1917 in response to a 'Wage Earner's Contest' held by the Amalgamated Mine Workers of Nova Scotia. The contest asked women how they would allocate funds in a family budget based on a yearly income of $1 071.
Frank, David. 'The Miner's Financier: Women in the Cape Breton Coal Town, 1917.' *Atlantis* 8, no. 2 (1983): 137–43

Family economy, Campbellford, Ontario
In 1891 Campbellford had two woolen mills: the Trent Valley Woolen Mill with over 120 workers and the Campbellford Woolen Mill with 40 workers. The table includes all households within the census boundary of Campbellford with at least one member employed by either woolen mill. Excluded from this table are children of lodgers who are less than 15 years of age, and persons residing in hotels. Sons-in-law and daughters-in-law appear as children. Very few children under 15 years are listed as being employed but some may have lied about their age to avoid child-labour legislation.
Canada. Manuscript Census. 1891. Village of Campellford

The work-force, 1921
Excluded are the Yukon Territory, Northwest Territories, and Newfoundland. 'Mining' includes quarrying; 'other manufacturing' includes food, leather and furs, chemicals and allied products, non-ferrous metals, non-metallic industries, printing and book-binding and unspecified; 'wood and paper' includes pulp; and 'other' includes unspecified.
For the data source for union members see pl 38.
Canada. *Census*. 1921. Vol 4, Tables XX, XXI, XXII, XIV

Work, birthplace, and gender, 1921
Categories of occupations are the same as those used for the graphs on the work-force.
Canada. *Census*. 1921. Vol 4, Tables L, LIII

Further readings
Avery, Donald. *'Dangerous Foreigners': European Immigrant Workers and Labour Radicalism in Canada 1896–1932*. Toronto: McClelland and Stewart, 1979

Bradbury, Bettina. 'The Family Economy and Work in an Industrializing City, Montreal, 1871.' *Historical Papers* (1979): 71–96

– 'Women's History and Working-Class History.' *Labour/Le Travail* 19 (Spring 1987): 23–43

Brandt, Gail Cuthbert. 'Weaving It Together: Life Cycle and the Industrial Experience of Female Cotton Workers in Quebec, 1910–1950.' *Labour/Le Travail* 7 (Spring 1981): 113–26

Bullen, John. 'Hidden Workers: Child Labour and the Family Economy in Late Nineteenth Century Urban Ontario.' *Labour/Le Travail* 18 (Fall 1986): 163–87

Frager, Ruth. 'No Proper Deal: Women Workers and the Canadian Labour Movement, 1870–1940.' In Linda Briskin and Lynda Yanz, eds. *Union Sisters: Women in the Labour Movement*. Toronto: Women's Press, 1983. Pp 44–64

Frank, David. 'Tradition and Culture in the Cape Breton Mining Community in the Early Twentieth Century.' In Kenneth Donovan, ed. *Cape Breton at 200. Historical Essays in Honour of the Island's Bicentennial 1785–1985*. Sydney: University College of Cape Breton Press, 1985. Pp 203–18

Heron, Craig. *Working in Steel*. Toronto: McClelland and Stewart, 1988

Heron, Craig, and Robert Storey, eds. *On the Job: Confronting the Labour Process in Canada*. Montréal: McGill-Queen's University Press, 1986

Mellor, John. *The Company Store. James Bryson McLachlan and the Cape Breton Coal Miners 1900–1925*. Toronto: Doubleday, 1983

Muise, D.A. 'The Making of an Industrial Community: Cape Breton Coal Towns 1867–1900.' In Don Macgillvray and Brian Tennyson, eds. *Cape Breton Historical Essays*. Sydney: College of Cape Breton Press, 1980. Pp 76–94

Radforth, Ian. *Bushworkers and Bosses: Logging in Northern Ontario 1900–1980*. Toronto: University of Toronto Press, 1987

Ramirez, Bruce. 'Brief Encounters: Italian Immigrant Workers and the CPR.' *Labour/Le Travail* 17 (Spring 1986): 9–27

Strong-Boag, Veronica. 'The Girl of the New Day: Canadian Working Women in the 1920s.' *Labour/Le Travail* 4, no. 4 (1979): 131–64

PLATE 38

Organized Labour

DOUGLAS CRUIKSHANK   PHD candidate, History, Simon Fraser University
GREGORY S. KEALEY   History, Memorial University of Newfoundland

We are grateful for the research and archivist aid of Peter DeLottinville and John Smart, Department of Labour Records, NAC.

Union membership by province, industry, and affiliation
The Department of Labour's estimates of provincial union membership were based solely on reports submitted by union locals. Since many locals failed to return reports, the provincial graph includes estimates of total membership based on the average size, nationally, of non-reporting locals.

The department began estimating membership by industry and trade groups in 1914. Until 1949 it considered all the members of a union to be employed in the same industry as the majority of its members. The inter-industrial branches of the One Big Union (OBU) and the Confédération des travailleurs catholiques du Canada were apparently classed as 'other.'

Statistics on union affiliation were calculated using the Department of Labour's estimates for individual unions. The Trades and Labor Congress (TLC) only (international), American Federation of Labor only, and Industrial Workers of the

World were counted as 'otherwise or unaffiliated internationals' if their membership did not reach 5% of the total membership during the period 1911–30. Similarly, TLC only (national), national and Catholic, OBU, and Canadian Federation of Labour (CFL) were sometimes classed as 'otherwise or unaffiliated nationals.'

For a detailed explanation of the provincial and industrial statistics see Canada, Department of Labour, Economics and Research Branch, *Union Growth in Canada, 1921–1967* (Ottawa: Information Canada, 1970), pp 56–7.
Canada. Department of Labour. *Labour Organizations in Canada.* 1911–30

Trades and Labor Congress of Canada and alternate union centres
Figures for 1891–4 were estimated from per capita tax revenues. Similar estimates for 1895–1900 were not possible because of a more complex taxing system.
Trades and Labor Congress of Canada. *Convention Proceedings.* 1891–1930

Bricklayers' and Masons' International Union of America
Bricklayers' and Masons' International Union of America. *Convention Proceedings.* 1890–1906

Development of mining unions
The category 'other regional or local' includes the following:
British Columbia: Miners' and Mine Laborers' Protective Association, 1890–1902; Nicola Valley Mine Workers' Association (Merritt), 1919–22; and British Columbia Miners' Association, 1924–9
Alberta: Canada West Employees' Union (Taber), 1919–22; Workmen's Club (Pocahontas), 1919–22; Monarch Employees' Union (Drumheller), 1920–2; Edmonton and District Miners' Federation, 1923–1925/6; Canadian Federation of Miners (Blairmore and Bellevue), 1925–1925/6; Lethbridge Miners' Federation, 1925–1925/26; Red Deer Valley District of the Mine Workers' Union of Canada, 1925–6; Wayne Mine Workers' Union, 1925–6; Luscar Miners' Union, 1925–6; and Cadomin Miners' Union, 1927–30
Ontario: Porcupine Mine Workers' Union (Timmins), 1922–5
New Brunswick: Minto Miners' Union, 1918–19
Nova Scotia: Federal Labor Union, AFL-TLC (Westville), 1916–19; United Mine Workers of Nova Scotia, 1916–17; and Amalgamated Mine Workers of Nova Scotia, 1917–19
Labour Gazette. 1900–10
Labour Organizations in Canada. 1911–30
United Mine Workers of America. *Convention Proceedings.* 1892–1930
Western Federation of Miners/International Union of Mine, Mill and Smelter Workers. *Convention Proceedings.* 1893–1930

Units of the One Big Union
'Other' includes textiles, clothing, footwear (8% of total units), metal products and shipbuilding (6%), building trades (9%), transportation (18%), public employees and service (4%), general (17%) and miscellaneous (10%).
British Columbia Federationist. 26 Dec 1919
Labour Organizations in Canada. 1919
One Big Union Bulletin. 17 and 31 Jan 1920

National and catholic unions, Québec
The Department of Labour estimated the number of unions in each locality as of 31 Dec 1921 and the Bureau of Statistics as of 1 Apr 1922. When the two figures differed, an average was calculated.
Membership was taken from the Department of Labour estimates and is considered to be exaggerated (Rouillard, 1979).
Labour Organizations in Canada. 1913–30
Québec. Bureau of Statistics. *Statistical Year Book.* 1920–30
Rouillard, Jacques. *Les syndicats nationaux au Québec de 1900 à 1930.* Québec: Les Presses de l'université Laval, 1979. Esp pp 232–6

Metal-trades councils
Labour Organizations in Canada. 1911–27

Railway unions
A local of the Brotherhood of Railway and Steamship Clerks, Freight Handlers, Express and Station Employees was reported in St Thomas in 1913 and 1914, but membership figures are not available.
Greening, W.E., and M.M. Maclean. *It Was Never Easy 1908–1958: A History of the Canadian Brotherhood of Railway, Transport and General Workers.* Ottawa: Canadian Brotherhood of Railway, Transport and General Workers, 1961. Pp 67–93
Labour Organizations in Canada. 1911–29

Affiliates of the All-Canadian Congress of Labour
Former CFL affiliates included the Amalgamated Carpenters of Canada (3.66% of total members), the Canadian Electrical Trades Union (2.39%), and the Canadian Federation of Bricklayers, Masons and Plasterers (1.18%). 'Other' includes the Electrical Communications Workers of Canada (2.32%), the Canadian Association of Railway Enginemen (1.32%), the National Union of Painters, Decorators and Paperhangers of Canada (0.43%), and sixteen directly chartered locals (1.88%).
Labour Organizations in Canada. 1927

Labour politics
The percentage of contested votes gained by labour and socialist candidates is not strictly comparable between periods and provinces because of differences in and changes in the electoral systems. Because of difficulties in identifying exact party affiliations during this period, the term 'labour and socialist' was broadly defined to include: candidates either having or claiming to have the endorsement of one of the various labour, socialist, or communist parties and/or organizations; independent labour or socialist candidates; government or opposition labour candidates (on the grounds that support for the government or opposition did not necessarily mean support for the governing or opposing party); and labour or socialist candidates also endorsed by farmer or soldier parties and/or groups. Excluded were Liberal-labour or Conservative-labour candidates (even though these candidates were sometimes difficult to distinguish from straight labour, independent labour, government labour, and opposition labour candidates) and farmer and soldier candidates also endorsed by labour or socialist parties and/or organizations.

Alberta. Chief Electoral Officer. *A Report on Alberta Elections 1905–1982.* Edmonton, 1983
British Columbia. Department of Provincial Secretary. *Statement of Votes*
Canada. Chief Electoral Officer. *Reports*
– Parliament. Clerk of the Crown in Chancery. *Resumé of General Elections of 1896, 1900, 1904, 1908 and 1911 and of By-Elections Held between 1896 and 1916.* Ottawa, 1916
Canadian Parliamentary Guide
Lewis, Roderick. *Centennial Edition of a History of the Electoral Districts, Legislatures and Ministries of the Province of Ontario 1867–1968.* Toronto, nd
Manitoba. Chief Electoral Officer. *Thirty-First General Election.* 1977
New Brunswick. Legislative Assembly. *Journals*
Nova Scotia. Legislature. *Election Returns*
Québec. Bibliothèque de la Législature. Service de documentation. *Répertoire des parlementaires Québécois 1867–1978.* Québec, 1980
Saskatchewan. Archives Board. *Directory of Saskatchewan Ministries, Members of the Legislative Assembly and Elections 1905–1953.* Regina and Saskatoon, 1954
Scarrow, Howard. *Canada Votes: A Handbook of Federal and Provincial Election Data.* New Orleans: The Hauser Press, 1962
In order to identify political affiliations many newspapers, labour journals, and secondary works were consulted.

PLATE 39
Strikes

DOUGLAS CRUIKSHANK PH D, History, Simon Fraser University
GREGORY S. KEALEY   History, Memorial University of Newfoundland

We are grateful for the research and archivist aid of Peter DeLottinville and John Smart, Department of Labour Records, NAC.

Frequency, size, and duration of strikes
This method of portraying strike activity was first suggested by Shorter and Tilly (1971). The dimensions of the cubes for the 1890s are based on an entirely new series of strike statistics. In compiling these statistics a preliminary list of strikes was prepared after surveying the *Globe*, 1891–1900, Ian McKay's notes from the *Acadian Recorder*, 1891–1900, labour newspapers, union proceedings, and relevant secondary literature, including Hamelin, Larocque, and Rouillard (1970). Local newspapers were then checked in an attempt to round out the data and additional strikes discovered during this second search were added to the list. The statistics are still very tentative and so comparisons with the later decades should be made cautiously. Estimates for the Northwest Territories (Alberta and Saskatchewan) were not included because of insufficient information.

The data for 1901–30 were obtained primarily from a set of 'Trade Dispute Record' summary sheets and statistical tables found in the *Labour Gazette* and at the NAC which had been prepared by the Department of Labour in the late 1920s. Before the cube dimensions were calculated, the department's estimates were revised in the following ways: (1) a large number of strikes which the Department of Labour knew about but did not count either because they were considered too small or because of a lack of information were reincorporated into the statistics; (2) several major tabulation errors were corrected; (3) interprovincial coal-mining strikes were disaggregated by province; and (4) a number of strikes found by Ian McKay in his research on strikes in the Maritime provinces between 1901 and 1914 were added to the totals.

The dimensions showing average size and duration are based solely on strikes for which information on both the number of workers involved and the duration of the strike in working days was available. Work-force figures were calculated using the censuses of 1891 and 1951, and standardized estimates for the census years 1911–31 from Marvin McInnis (Economics, Queen's University). They assume constant growth between census years.
Cruikshank, Douglas G., and Gregory S. Kealey. 'Strikes in Canada, 1891–1950.' *Labour/Le Travail* 20 (Fall 1987): 85–145
Globe. Toronto. 1891–1900
Hamelin, Jean, Paul Larocque, and Jacques Rouillard. *Répertoire des grèves dans la province de Québec au XIXe siècle.* Montréal: Les Presses de l'École des hautes études commerciales, 1970
Labour Gazette 31 (Feb 1931): 133–41
McKay, Ian. 'Strikes in the Maritimes.' *Acadiensis* 13, no. 1 (Autumn 1983): 3–46
NAC. Records of the Department of Labour. RG 27, Vols 2332–40, 2342–3
Shorter, Edward, and Charles Tilly. 'The Shape of Strikes in France, 1830–1960.' *Comparative Studies in Society and History* 13 (1971): 60–86
Strikes and Lockouts in Canada During 1950. Supplement to the *Labour Gazette* 51 (Apr 1951): 8–23

Strike issues, methods of settlement, and results
The graph on issues shows the percentage of strikes fought over changes in the rate of wages, supplementary pay, and benefits. It does not include disputes over changes in the method of payment or over the calculation of wages. The totals differ from those tabulated by the Department of Labour because they include all strikes over earnings rather than just strikes principally over earnings, and because, like the graphs on settlement and results, they include the additional strikes described above.
For data sources see 'Frequency, size, and duration of strikes.'

Strikes in May, June, and July 1919
The data on the graph and map are for strikes in progress during the three-month period. The Department of Labour calculated 'man days lost' (striker days) for each dispute by multiplying the total number of strikers (periodically adjusted to account for strikers returning to work before the end of the strike) and the duration in working days (adjusted to account for days not normally worked).
Kealey, Gregory S. '1919: The Canadian Labour Revolt.' *Labour/Le Travail* 13 (1984): 11–44
NAC. Records of the Department of Labour. Strikes and Lockouts. RG 27, Vols 2337–8

Strikes with collective violence

The map shows the location of strikes in which 50 or more persons acted together and attempted to seize or damage persons or objects not belonging to themselves. This definition of collective violence was adapted from Tilly (1975, p 313).

Labour Gazette. 1900–30
NAC. Records of the Department of Labour. Strikes and Lockouts. RG 27, Vols 294–346, 557–61
Tilly, Charles, Louise Tilly, and Richard Tilly. *The Rebellious Century 1830–1930*. Cambridge, Mass: Harvard University Press, 1975

Strikes with military intervention

Pariseau, J.J.B. 'Forces armées et maintien de l'ordre au Canada 1867–1967: un siècle d'aide au pouvoir civil.' PH D thesis, Université Paul Valéry III, Montpelier, 1981

PLATE 40

Economic Crisis

ELIZABETH BLOOMFIELD   History, University of Guelph
GERALD BLOOMFIELD   Geography, University of Guelph
DERYCK W. HOLDSWORTH   Geography, Pennsylvania State University
MURDO MacPHERSON   Historical Atlas of Canada, Toronto

Index of international incomes

Canada. DBS. *National Accounts Income and Expenditure*. Cat. 13–502. 1926–50. Table 20
League of Nations. Economic Intelligence Service. *World Economic Survey*. New York, 1938–9. P 84

National income

Canada. DBS. *National Accounts*. 1926–50

Selected exports

Canada Year Book. 1930, 1932, 1936, 1940. 'Detailed Exports of Canadian Produce' (table)

Employment index

Index of 1926 = 100 was converted to 1929 = 100.
Canada Year Book. 1938: p 773. 1940: pp 753, 755–6

Money supply

Leacy. *Historical Statistics*. Series J10, J181–92

Gross domestic investment

Canada. DBS. *National Accounts*. 1926–50. Table 19

Manufacturing employment

The Gibb index, which expresses change as an annual rate, was used as the method of calculating changes in industrial employment. The index is designed to compare trends in units of very different size, from the few hundreds employed in small urban centres to the hundreds of thousands in Montréal and Toronto. Such a measure is also appropriate for the widespread incidence of declining numbers employed, in contrast to the prevailing upward trend in the period before 1929.
Canada. DBS. *A General Review of the Manufacturing Industries of Canada*. Cat. 31–201. 1929–37
Gibbs, Jack P. 'The Measurement of Change in the Population Size of an Urban Unit.' In *Urban Research Methods*. Princeton: Van Nostrand, 1961. Pp 107–13

Motor-vehicle and railway-car production

Thanks are due to Brian Hickey and James Dykes of the Motor Vehicle Manufacturer's Association, Toronto, and Jacques Eves of the Motor Vehicle Manufacturers Association of the United States, Detroit.
Canada. DBS. *Motor Vehicle Manufacturers*. Cat. 42–209. 1927–40
Canada Year Book. 1939. P 663
Canadian Automobile Chamber of Commerce. *Facts and Figures of the Automobile Industry*. Toronto, 1934–41
Leacy. *Historical Statistics*. Series R716–29

Abitbi Power and Paper Company

Bladen, Vincent W. *An Introduction to Political Economy*. Toronto: University of Toronto Press, 1941. Pp 184–9
Canada. DBS. *Sawmills and Planing Mills and Shingle Mills*. Cat. 36–204. 1927–39

Canadian newsprint

Ankli, R.E. 'The Canadian Newsprint Industry, 1900–1940.' In Bruce R. Dalgaard and Richard K. Vedder, eds. *Variations in Business and Economic History: Essays in Honor of Donald L. Kemmerer*. Research in Economic History, suppl. 2. Greenwich, Conn: AIJAI Press, 1982. Pp 1–30
Bladen. *An Introduction to Political Economy*. 1941. P 159
Urquhart and Buckley. *Historical Statistics*. P 483

The gold-mining boom

Canada. DBS. *Summary of the Gold Mining Industries in Canada*. 1935: pp 10–1. 1940: pp 6–8. 1945: p 7
Ontario. Department of Mines. *Annual Report*. 1940. Inserts facing pp 12, 24
Robinson, A.H.A. *Gold in Canada, 1935*. Department of Mines. Mines Branch Report No. 769. Ottawa, 1935. Pp 55–6, map facing p 66, p 114

Mineral production

Leacy. *Historical Statistics*. Series P1–26, Q6–12

Further readings

Bloomfield, G.T. 'Canadian Manufacturing in the Depression.' Unpublished paper submitted to the Historical Atlas of Canada project, Vol III, 1984
– 'The Canadian Motor Vehicle Industry in the Depression.' Unpublished paper submitted to the Historical Atlas of Canada project, Vol III, 1984
– 'Industrial Trends in Central Canada 1929–57.'Unpublished paper submitted to the Historical Atlas of Canada project, Vol III, 1984

– 'An Industry in the Depression: The Canadian Newsprint Industry and Abitibi 1928–1936.' Unpublished paper submitted to the Historical Atlas of Canada project, Vol III, 1984
Brecher, Irving. *Monetary and Fiscal Thought and Policy in Canada*. Toronto: University of Toronto Press, 1957
Drummond, Ian M. *Imperial Economic Policy, 1917–1939: Studies in Expansion and Protection*. London: Allen and Unwin, 1974
Guthrie, John Alexander. *The Newsprint Paper Industry*. Cambridge, Mass: Harvard University Press, 1941
Marcus, Edward. *Canada and the International Business Cycle 1927–1939*. New York: Bookman Associates, 1954
Saafarian, Albert Edward. *The Canadian Economy in the Great Depression*. Toronto: University of Toronto Press, 1959
Shearer, R.A., J.F. Chant, and D.E. Bond. *The Economics of The Canadian Financial System*. 2nd ed. Scarborough: Prentice-Hall, 1984

PLATE 41

The Impact of the Depression on People

DERYCK W. HOLDSWORTH   Geography, Pennsylvania State University
MURDO MacPHERSON   Historical Atlas of Canada, Toronto

The unemployed and relief

Reliable data on unemployment during the Depression are available only at the national level. The provincial situation can only be displayed indirectly through the distribution of relief (see 'Relief recipients by province').
Canada. *Census*. 1931. Vol 13, monograph on unemployment, pp 274–6
– DBS. *Statistics Relating to Labour Supply Under War Conditions*. Cat. 71–D–52. 1941. P 14
– Department of Labour. *Annual Report of the Dominion Commissioner of Unemployment Relief*. 1932–41
Marsh, Leonard C. *Canadians In and Out of Work: A Survey of Economic Classes and Their Relation to the Labour Market*. Toronto: Oxford University Press, 1940. P 364

Relief recipients by province

The yearly average number on relief shown on all provincial graphs was calculated from the monthly totals given in the Department of Labour's annual reports.
Cape Breton cities include Sydney, Glace Bay, Sydney Mines, and North Sydney.
Canada. Department of Labour. *Annual Reports of the Dominion Commissioner of Unemployment Relief*. 1930–41
Goldenberg, H. Carl. *Municipal Finance in Canada*. A Study Prepared for the Royal Commission on Dominion-Provincial Relations. Ottawa, 1939. P 70
Provincial Archives of Newfoundland. Records of the Department of Public Health and Welfare, Newfoundland Commission of Government
Newfoundland. *Census of Newfoundland and Labrador*. 1935

Occupational classification of workers on relief

'Other manual' includes longshoremen, miners, fishermen, and seamen. Number of persons included in the regional totals: Western Provinces 27 904; Ontario 53 251; Québec 60 897; Maritime Provinces 5 575.
Marsh. *Canadians In and Out of Work*. 1940. P 472

'Riding the rails'

Glenbow Archives, Calgary. NC6–12955(b)

The trek in search of work

Johnstone, Bill. *'Coal Dust in My Blood': The Autobiography of a Coal Miner*. British Columbia Provincial Museum, Heritage Record No. 9. Victoria, 1980
Knight, Rolf. *A Very Ordinary Life*. Vancouver: New Star Books, 1974
Thibault, Nelson. Interview conducted by Deryck W. Holdsworth. Winnipeg, 10 Apr 1985

Monthly relief budgets

Marsh, Leonard, A. Grant Fleming, and C.F. Blackler. *Health and Unemployment: Some Studies of Their Relationships*. Toronto: Oxford University Press, 1938. P 163

Monthly food allowances

The 'low cost restricted emergency diet' was a minimum-level food budget drawn up by the United States Department of Agriculture, Bureau of Home Economics. Marsh, Fleming, and Blackler (1938) adapted this budget for Canadian prices (pp 160–72). This diet was not recommended for prolonged use.
Marsh, Fleming, and Blackler. *Health and Unemployment*. 1938. P 169

Relief budget

Horn, Michael Steven Daniel, ed. *The Dirty Thirties: Canadians in the Great Depression*. Toronto: Copp Clark, 1972. P 284

Deportations

Urquhart and Buckley. *Historical Statistics*. Series A342–7

Price and wage indices
Wage rate and purchasing power

For the retail indices, 1940 figures from the 1940 *Canada Year Book*, which were represented on a 1935–9 base, had to be converted to a 1926 base. 'Purchasing power,' or 'real' wages, was calculated by dividing the wage-rate index by the cost-of-living index.
Bank of Canada. *Statistical Summary*. Ottawa, 1941. P 34
Canada Year Book. 1939: p 860–1. 1941: p 717

Further readings

Cassidy, Harry Morris. *Unemployment and Relief in Ontario, 1929–1932*. Toronto: Dent, 1932
Drystek, Henry F. 'The Simplest and Cheapest Mode of Dealing With Them: Deportation from Canada before World War II.' *Histoire sociale/Social History* 15, no. 30 (Nov 1982): 407–41
Richter, Lothar, ed. *Canada's Unemployment Problem*. Toronto: Macmillan, 1939

Sautter, Udo. 'Measuring Unemployment in Canada: Federal Efforts Before World War II.' *Histoire sociale/Social History* 15, no. 30 (Nov 1982): 475–87
Struthers, James. *No Fault of Their Own: Unemployment and the Canadian Welfare State, 1914–1941.* Toronto: University of Toronto Press, 1983

PLATE 42

Managing the Relief Burden

MURDO MacPHERSON Historical Atlas of Canada, Toronto

Government relief

Direct relief, formerly a public charity granted to the chronically poor, was extended in the Depression to those whose distress was caused solely by unemployment. Relief works were deliberately labour-intensive and mainly concerned with municipal projects such as the construction of water mains, sewers, and roads. Agricultural aid provided seed, feed, and fodder and sought to re-establish farmers. Although most dominion funds were administered through provincial-municipal agencies, federal departments, especially Defence and Agriculture, directly funded programs such as work camps and projects under the Prairie Farm Rehabilitation Act (see pl 43).

For Newfoundland there was difficulty in identifying government expenditures specifically directed at the relief problem. As far as possible, types of relief comparable to those in Canada were identified; no data could be found for 1930 and 1929 information was used instead.
Canada. Department of Labour. *Annual Report of the Dominion Commissioner of Unemployment Relief.* 1938–40
– Department of Labour. *Comparative Statistics of Public Finance, 1936–1940.* Ottawa, 1941. Tables 39–43
– Department of Labour. *Report of the Royal Commission on Dominion-Provincial Relations, 1937.* Book III. Ottawa, 1939. Tables 33–42
Newfoundland. *Annual Report of the Comptroller and Auditor General.* St John's, 1929, 1932, 1934–40
– *Newfoundland Royal Commission Report, 1933.* St John's

Dominion relief loans

Canada. Department of Labour. *Annual Report of the Dominion Commissioner of Unemployment Relief.* 1938–40
– *Report of the Royal Commission on Dominion-Provincial Relations.* 1939. Book II, p 20

Unemployment relief work camps

Thanks to Douglas Cruikshank for help with sources on relief camps.
Canada. Department of the Interior. National Parks Branch. *Annual Report.* 1932–6
Labour Gazette. Ottawa, Mar 1933. P 300
NAC. McNaughton Papers. MG 30 E 133, Vol 98. Final Report on the Unemployment Relief Scheme for the Care of Single Homeless Men, Administered by the Department of National Defence, 1932–1936. App 4–26

The municipal relief burden

Bradshaw, Thomas. 'The Maintenance of Public Credit.' *Canadian Chartered Accountant* 26 (1935): 123–4
City of Toronto. *Municipal Finance: A Report Prepared by the Civic Advisory Council of Toronto.* Toronto: University of Toronto Press, 1950. Tables XII, XIII, XIX
– Treasury Department. *Annual Report of the Commissioner of Finance.* 1939. P 9

United Church relief shipments

Gray, James Henry. *The Winter Years: The Depression on the Prairies.* Toronto: Macmillan, 1972. P 165
United Church Archives. National Emergency Relief Committee. File 1, National Emergency Relief, 'United Church of Canada, National Emergency Relief Committee'

Further readings

Riendeau, Roger E. 'A Clash of Interests: Dependency and the Municipal Problem in the Great Depression.' *Journal of Canadian Studies* 14, no. 1 (1979): 50–8
Schultz, Patricia V. *The East York Workers Association: A Response to the Great Depression.* Toronto: New Hogtown Press, 1975
Struthers, James. *No Fault of Their Own: Unemployment and the Canadian Welfare State, 1914–1941.* Toronto: University of Toronto Press, 1983

PLATE 43

Drought and Depression on the Prairies

MURDO MacPHERSON Historical Atlas of Canada, Toronto

Wheat returns by area

Canada. Department of Agriculture. *P.F.R.A.: A Record of Achievement.* 1943. Pp 4, 15

Market value of wheat

Britnell, George Edwin. *The Wheat Economy.* Toronto: University of Toronto Press, 1939. Pp 71–2
Urquhart and Buckley. *Historical Statistics.* Series L98–113

Index of net farm income

Canada. DBS. *National Accounts, Income and Expenditure.* Cat. 13–502. 1926–50. Table 32

Wheat yields

The author is indebted to G D.V. Williams, formerly Atmospheric Environment Service, Environment Canada, Downsview, Ont, for data and advice on Prairie wheat yields during the Depression.

Total relief expenditure, Saskatchewan

Provincial Archives of Saskatchewan, Regina. Collection 266. Vol 8. 'Agricultural Statistics, Relief Advances'

Government-assisted settlers, Saskatchewan

In all but 100 cases destination data indicated the section of land taken up by the settler. For the exceptions only a rural municipality containing the railway destination was given; although the settlers may have taken up land further afield, their destinations had to be plotted in that rural municipality. Precise figures on the process of farm abandonment in the drought area are difficult to obtain. However, within the general area of Palliser's Triangle, the 1936 census shows 8 500 abandoned farms in Saskatchewan, almost 5 000 in Alberta, and 500 in Manitoba – a total of over 3 million acres of farmland.
Canada. *Census of the Prairie Provinces.* 1936. Vol 1, Table 112, pp 272, 276, 1174
Provincial Archives of Saskatchewan, Regina. Collection 266. File III/10, 'Re-Establishment Assistance, Agricultural Statistics'

Rural population change, Saskatchewan

Canada. *Census.* 1941. Vol 2, Table 10

Migration from the Prairie Provinces Interprovincial migration, Canada

Canada. *Census.* 1941. Vol 1, Table 9

The work of the Prairie Farm Rehabilitation Administration

The map of small water projects is based on a synthesis of the maps in Stapleford (1939). By Jan 1938, 2 541 dugouts, 1 414 stockwater dams, and 330 small irrigation works had been constructed with $289 790 of financial assistance. The post–1940 reports of the Prairie Farm Rehabilitation Administration (PFRA) are at slight variance with Stapleford, however, and show that by Mar 1938 2 410 dugouts, 1 343 stockwater dams, and 321 small irrigation works had been constructed with $329 486 of financial assistance. To more effectively display the data the large rural municipalities created in Alberta by 1936 have been disaggregated into their 1931 divisions. Using information from Stapleford and later PFRA annual reports the small water projects were allocated to these smaller 1931 rural municipalities.

In the 1940 fiscal year $580 519 was spent constructing the large water projects, compared to $761 163 for the small water projects (25% and 33% of PFRA expenditure respectively). Following the Second World War there was a dramatic increase in expenditure on large water projects (including major irrigation and reclamation schemes) and the $8 069 627 spent in 1950 represented 66% of PFRA expenditure. This proportion of expenditure continued throughout the decade.

Between 1938 and Mar 1940 612 300 acres of land were put into operation as community pasture at a cost of $663 472; this acreage doubled by Mar 1943, at which time two-thirds of the pasture acreage up to 1961 had been established.
Canada. Department of Agriculture. *Annual Report on Activities Conducted Under the Prairie Farm Rehabilitation Act.* 1940–1: Tables 1, 2, 3, 5, pp 26–34, Map II. 1950–1: App VII. 1959–60, App VIII. 1960–1: App V, VIII
Stapleford, E. William. *Report on Rural Relief Due to Drought Conditions and Crop Failures in Western Canada, 1930–1937.* Ottawa: King's Printer, 1939. Maps XIX, XX, XXI, pp 104–12

Further readings

Charnetski, John. 'A Study of Settlers' Progress in Northern Saskatchewan for the Period 1935 to 1939.' M SC thesis, University of Saskatchewan, 1940
Davidson, Alex T. 'Forest Versus Agricultural Land Use Along the Pioneer Fringe in Saskatchewan.' MA thesis, University of Toronto, 1952
Fitzgerald, Dennis Patrick. 'Pioneer Settlement in Northern Saskatchewan.' PH D thesis, University of Minnesota, 1965
Gray, James Henry. *Men Against the Desert.* Saskatoon: Western Producer Prairie Books, 1967
– *The Winter Years: The Depression on the Prairies.* Toronto: Macmillan, 1966
Neatby, Blair. 'The Saskatchewan Relief Commission, 1931–1934.' *Saskatchewan History* 3, no. 2 (Spring 1950): 41–56
Powell, T.J.D. 'Northern Settlement 1929–35.' *Saskatchewan History* 30 (1977): 81–98

PLATE 44

Colonization and Co-Operation

SERGE COURVILLE Géographie, Université Laval
DANIEL MacINNES Sociology, St Francis Xavier University
MURDO MacPHERSON Historical Atlas of Canada, Toronto

Thanks are due to Normand Séguin and Luc Bureau for their assistance with the work on colonization in Québec.

Destinations under colonization plans

Québec. *Rapport du Ministre de la Colonisation de la Province de Québec.* 1932–41

Colonization in Québec: Vautrin Plan

Hamelin, Jean, Jacques Letarte, and Marcel Hamelin. 'Les élections provinciales dans le Québec.' *Cahiers de géographie de Québec* 4, no. 7 (Oct 1959–Mar 1960): 44
Québec. *Rapport du Ministre de la Colonisation de la Province de Québec.* 1936–7

Colonization in Québec: new parishes

The research assistance of Andrée Héroux is gratefully acknowledged.
Bureaux d'archives de l'État civil de la Province de Québec
Le Canada ecclésiastique
Magnan, Hormidas. *Dictionnaire historique et géographique des paroisses, missions et municipalités du Québec.* Arthabaska: Imprimerie de l'Arthabaska, 1925
– *Monographies paroissiales. Esquisses des paroisses de colonisation de la Province de Québec.* Québec: Département de la Colonisation, des Mines et des Pêcheries, 1923

Dominion relief settlement plan

Canada. Department of Labour. *Report of the Dominion Commissioner of Unemployment Relief, 1939–1940.* Table 1, p 78

Colonization in Abitibi region

Canada. Department of the Interior. *Standard Topographical Map, 1:500 000.* 'Ontario and Quebec – Harricanaw Sheet.' 1936
Imperial Oil Limited. 'Imperial Oil Map Number 3: Quebec.' 1946
McDermott, George L. 'Advancing and Retreating Frontiers of Agricultural Settlement in the Great Clay Belt of Ontario and Quebec.' PH D thesis, University of Wisconsin, 1959. Pp 114, 116
'La Province de Québec, Carte routière et touristique.' Province de Québec, Office de tourisme, 1943

Settlers' houses

Thanks are due to Hedy Later for drawings of the houses based on photographs.
Noiseux, Donat-C. *Dix années de colonisation a Ste-Anne de Roquemaure, 1933–1943.* Province de Québec, Ministère de la Colonisation, 1943

The caisses populaires Desjardins

Thanks are due to Sherry Olson for providing the information on caisses populaires.
Archives of the Desjardins Movement, Lévis, Québec
Répertoire des caisses d'épargnes et de crédit du Québec. 1974

The Antigonish Movement

Credit Union Charters Granted and Cancelled. Halifax: Credit Union League, nd
MacSween, R.J. *Report of Co-operative Associations in Nova Scotia.* Nova Scotia, Department of Marketing, 1940
St Francis Xavier University Archives. RG 30–3/12/1–29, Mailing lists of study clubs. RG 30–3/2/1039–60 and RG 30–3/4/572, Lists of Antigonish co-operatives. Various co-operative, credit union, and study club reports. Various reports and letters regarding work and liaison with St Francis Xavier University Extension Department

Further readings

'Agriculture et colonisation.' *Annuaire du Québec 1962.* Division 1, Section 5, pp 235–44
Barrette, R. 'Le plan de colonization Vautrin.' MA thesis, Université d'Ottawa, 1972
Blanchard, Raoul. 'L'Abitibi-Témiscamingue.' *Revue de géographie alpine* 37 (1949): 421–552
– *Le Canada Français, Province de Québec.* Montréal: Arthème Fayard, 1960
Caron, Ivanhoe. *La colonisation de la province de Québec.* Québec, 1923
Chagnon, Vincent-F. 'Historique et situation présente de la colonisation.' *Annuaire du Québec 1964–1965.* Pp 372–7
'Domaine et colonisation.' *Annuaire du Québec 1944.* Pp 67–76
Garon, J.E. *Historique de la colonisation dans la province de Québec de 1825 à 1940.* Québec: Ministère de la Colonisation, 1940
Linteau, Paul-André, René Durocher, and Jean-Claude Robert. *Quebec: A History 1867–1929,* transl Robert Chodos. Toronto: Lorimer, 1983
Magnan, Hormidas. *Les régions de colonisation de la province de Québec.* Québec: Ministère de la Colonisation, des Mines et des Pecheries, 1922
Minville, Esdras. *L'agriculture.* Montréal: Fides, 1943
Séguin, Normand. *Agriculture et colonisation au Québec, aspects historiques.* Montréal: Boréal Express, 1980

PLATE 45

Workers' Responses

DOUGLAS CRUIKSHANK   PH D candidate, History, Simon Fraser University
GREGORY S. KEALEY   History, Memorial University of Newfoundland

We are grateful for the research and archivist aid of Peter DeLottinville and John Smart, Department of Labour records, NAC.

Union membership by province, industry, and affiliation

On the graph showing membership by affiliation the Canadian Congress of Labour (CCL) only (international), Congress of Industrial Organizations (CIO) only, American Federation of Labor (AFL) only, Trades and Labour Congress (TLC) only (international), and Industrial Workers of the World were included under 'otherwise or unaffiliated international,' and the TLC only, Workers' Unity League (WUL), One Big Union (OBL), and Canadian Federation of Labour (CFL) under 'otherwise or unaffiliated national,' unless their memberships exceeded 5% of the total between the period 1931 and 1940. The data required to calculate membership by affiliation for 1939 were not available. For further explanation of calculations see pl 38.
Canada. Department of Labour. *Labour Organizations in Canada.* 1931–40

Workers' Unity League and Congress of Industrial Organizations Unions

This chart shows the lineage of the main WUL and CIO unions between 1930 and 1942. It does not include unions directly chartered by the WUL, TLC, or CCL. Unions of this type preceeded many of the WUL unions and followed some of the CIO unions shown on the chart.
Labour Organizations in Canada. 1930–42
Manley, John. 'Communism and the Canadian Working Class During the Great Depression: The Workers' Unity League, 1930–1936.' PH D thesis, Dalhousie University, 1984

Labour politics

The category 'other labour and socialist' includes independent Co-operative Commonwealth Federation (CCF) candidates. 'CCF' includes Farmer-Labour Party candidates in Saskatchewan in 1934 and Independent Labour Party candidates in Manitoba in 1936. For sources and further explanation of calculations see pl 38.

Frequency, size, and duration of strikes

The Department of Labour's statistics were revised to exclude relief strikes in 1931–3. For a description of other revisions and also an explanation of the cubes see pl 39.
Labour Gazette. 1932–41

NAC. Records of the Department of Labour. Strikes and Lockouts. RG 27, Vols 2340–1
Strikes and Lockouts in Canada During 1950. Supplement to *Labour Gazette* 51 (Apr 1951): 8–23

Strike issues, methods of settlement, and results

See 'Frequency, size, and duration of strikes' above and pl 39.

Strikes with collective violence and sit-downs

Strikes were counted as 'sit-downs' or 'stay-downs' if they were defined as such by observers or participants and if the strikers occupied their workplace against the wishes of their employer. For the definition of collective violence see pl 39. Although it could be argued that all sit-down strikes involving 50 persons or more were collectively violent, only forcible occupations were also counted here as acts of collective violence.
Labour Gazette. 1931–40
NAC. Records of the Department of Labour. Strikes and Lockouts. RG 27, Vols 347–408
Selected newspapers, labour journals, and secondary works

Relief strikes

The figures include all cases in which more than one relief recipient ceased work or refused to commence work in an attempt to redress grievances. They do not include numerous protests and demonstrations involving non-recipients or recipients not immediately required to work for their relief. In twelve cases a number of stoppages were counted as single 'general' strikes. These strikes occurred in British Columbia in 1932, 1933, 1934, 1935, and 1938; in Alberta in 1935 and 1936; in Manitoba and northwestern Ontario in 1935; and in Ontario in 1936 and 1939.
Brown, Lorne A. 'The Bennett Government, Political Stability and the Politics of the Unemployed Relief Camps, 1930–1935.' PH D thesis, Queen's University, 1979
NAC. Records of the Department of Labour. Strikes and Lockouts. RG 27, Vols 346–94, 2278–9
– Records of the House of Commons. RG 14, D2, Vol 348, 'Final Report on the Unemployment Relief Scheme for the Care of Single, Homeless Men, administered by the Department of National Defence, 1932–1936.' Canada. *SP.* No. 225, 18th Parliament, 2nd session. Tabled 16 Mar 1937. App 22, pp 140–82

The On-to-Ottawa Trek and relief strikes

Canadian Security Intelligence Service. RCMP. Security Bulletins. 1935
Howard, Victor. *'We were the Salt of the Earth': The On-to-Ottawa Trek and the Regina Riot.* Regina: Canadian Plains Research Center, 1985
Liversedge, Ronald. *Recollections of the On to Ottawa Trek.* Toronto: McClelland and Stewart, 1973
Various newspaper clippings held by the federal Department of Labour

PLATE 46

Political Responses

MURDO MacPHERSON   Historical Atlas of Canada, Toronto
MARY MAGWOOD   National Atlas Information Service, Energy, Mines and Resources Canada, Ottawa

Federal elections

Canadian Parliamentary Guide. 1936
NAC. AT/1100–1933. Canada. Department of the Interior. *Federal Electoral Districts: Representation Act 1933*
Scarrow, H.A. *Canada Votes: A Handbook of Federal and Provincial Election Data.* New Orleans: Hauser Press, 1962

The rise to power of the Union nationale

Hamelin, Jean, Jacques Letarte, and Marcel Hamelin. 'Les élections provinciales dans le Québec.' *Cahiers de géographie de Québec* 4, no. 7 (Oct 1959–Mar 1960): 5–207
Statistiques Électorales du Québec, 1867–1985. Bibliographie et documentation 10. Québec: Bibliothèque de l'Assemblée nationale, 1986. Pp 21–286

Circulation of the daily and weekly *Clarion*

The *Daily Clarion* and the *Clarion Weekly* succeeded the *Worker* (a bi-weekly) and were published in Toronto by the Communist Party of Canada between May 1936 and June 1939. The weekly version contained a summary of the main news and articles appearing in the daily and was circulated largely in remote areas or those outside 24-hour distribution from Toronto. Between June and Oct 1939 only a weekly tabloid, the *Clarion,* was published until it was banned (along with the French-language *Clarté*) under Article 39a of the Defence of Canada regulations. In 1940 the *Canadian Tribune,* which presented itself as an 'independent' newspaper to avoid the regulations, appeared in its place. All issues of the *Daily Clarion* (as well as the *Worker, Clarion,* and *Canadian Tribune*) are held on microfilm in the offices of the *Canadian Tribune,* 290A Danforth Avenue, Toronto.
Clarté, published in Montréal by the Communist Party of Canada twice a month from 1935 to 1939, reached peak print runs of 3 000 issues, yet never had more than 300 subscribers, most of whom were in Montréal (Fournier, 1979).
In Canada the number of members of the Communist Party of Canada (CPC) are estimated at 4 000 in 1930, 5 500 in 1934, 10 000 in 1936, 15 000 in 1938, and 16 000 in 1939 (Avakumovic, 1975; Olssen-Lévesque, 1973). In Montréal, where the bulk of the Québec CPC members were, 20 out of 80 party members were French Canadian in 1930, 40 out of 140 in 1932, 100 out of 500 in 1936, and 200 out of 1 000 in 1939 (Olssen-Lévesque, 1973).
The circulation of the daily and weekly *Clarion* was used to estimate the distribution of CPC membership across Canada. Provincial data on circulation were available for every month for the period May 1936 to Sep 1937; for urban places data were available only for May 1936, May 1937, and Sep 1937. On the map provincial circulation was shown as the greatest monthly readership over the 17 months, while circulation figures for urban places was the greatest number among the three months. The figures for Val d'Or and Rouyn have been removed from the northern Ontario figures and added to those for Québec (for May 1936 in all cases).

Avakumovic, Ivan. *The Communist Party in Canada: A History*. Toronto: McClelland and Stewart, 1975. P 115

Fournier, Marcel. *Communisme et anti-communisme au Québec 1920–1950*. Montréal: Les Éditions coopératives, Albert Saint-Martin, 1979. App 2, pp 133–4

Olssen-Lévesque, A. 'The Canadian Left in Quebec During the Great Depression: The Communist Party of Canada and the Co-operative Commonwealth Federation in Quebec, 1929–1939.' PH D thesis, Duke University, 1973. P 82

Thomas Fisher Rare Book Library, University of Toronto. Robert Kenney Collection. Box 9, Ref 179, 'Financial Report of the Clarion Publishing Association, submitted to the Eighth National Convention, Communist Party of Canada, Oct 8, 1937, Toronto'

The Mackenzie-Papineau Battalion

Hoar, Victor. *The Mackenzie-Papineau Battalion*. Toronto: Copp Clark, 1969. Pp 31, 238

NAC. MG 30 E 173. File 20, Mackenzie-Papineau Collection

Rosenstone, Robert A. 'The Men of the Abraham Lincoln Battalion.' *Journal of American History* 54 (Sep 1967): 327–38

Thomas, Hugh. *The Spanish Civil War*. 3rd rev ed. New York: Harper and Row, 1977. App 7, pp 982–3

Further readings

Osborne, S. *Social Credit for Beginners: An Armchair Guide*. Vancouver: Pulp Press, 1986

Penner, Norman. *Canadian Communism: The Stalin Years and Beyond*. Toronto: Methuen, 1988

Quinn, Herbert F. *The Union Nationale: Quebec Nationalism from Duplessis to Lévesque*. Toronto: University of Toronto Press, 1979

Young, Walter D. *The Anatomy of a Party: The National CCF 1932–61*. Toronto: University of Toronto Press, 1969

PLATE 47

Military Activity in the Second World War

CHRISTOPHER A. SHARPE Geography, Memorial University of Newfoundland

This plate benefited enormously from the expertise of Norman Hillmer, Ben Greenhaus, and Roger Sarty of the Directorate of History, National Defence Headquarters, Ottawa. Thanks also are due to Michael Hadley for his advice.

Military mobilization
Enlistment of women

Canada. *Census*. 1941. Vol 1, Tables 18, 35, 37

– National Personnel Records Centre. 'Canadian Army Statistics, War 1939–45,' 'Royal Canadian Air Force Statistics, War 1939–45,' 'Canadian Navy Statistics, War 1939–45'

Douglas, W.A.B. *The Creation of a National Air Force*. Vol 2 of *The Official History of the Royal Canadian Air Force*, ed Norman Hillmer. Toronto: University of Toronto Press, 1986. 'British Commonwealth Air Training Plan' (foldout maps)

NAC. RG 24. G3 Files 133.008 (D103), 133.009 (D131)

'Report on the operations of military mobilization in Canada during World War Two.' Prepared by the Associate Director of National Selection Service (Mobilization Division) in collaboration with the Research and Statistics Branch, Department of Labour. 10 Feb 1947. Typescript held at National Defence Headquarters, Historical Division

Stacey, C.P. *Six Years of War: The Army in Canada, Britain and the Pacific*. Ottawa: Queen's Printer, 1955. App D

Tucker, G.N. *Naval Service of Canada*. Ottawa: King's Printer, 1952

Canadian fatalities in two world wars
Military fatalities in the Second World War

Canada. Department of Veteran's Affairs, Newfoundland District Office. 'Service Ledger, Royal Navy Enlistments (Newfoundland)'

– National Personnel Records Centre. *Canadian Medical Service 1939–45*

Canada Year Book. 1947. Pp 1120–30

Dupuy, R. Ernest, and Trevor N. Dupuy. *The Encyclopedia of Military History*. 2nd rev ed. New York: Harper and Row, 1986

Singer, J. David, and M. Small. *The Wages of War*. New York: Wiley, 1972

Stacey, C.P. *Arms, Men and Government: The War Policies of Canada 1939–1945*. Ottawa: Queen's Printer, 1970

Ill-Fated Trio

Rikki Cameron of the Canadian War Museum assisted in the search for an appropriate war painting and Douglas Champion generously displayed his works for the editors.

Douglas Champion, a resident of Toronto known for his marine art under the name of Alfred Leete, enlisted in the Royal Navy in the spring of 1940 and saw service in the Arctic, the North Atlantic, and the Mediterranean. His painting *Ill-Fated Trio* (North Atlantic Convoys ONS18 and ON202 combined, Sep 1943) shows HMCS *St Croix* and HMS *Itchen* of support group EG9 AND HMS *Polyanthus* of C2 escort group. All three were lost to acoustic torpedo attack by U-boats in a fierce battle to protect the big combined convoy. *St Croix* and *Polyanthus* were sunk on 20 Sep. Survivors from both ships were picked up by *Itchen*. On 22 Sep *Itchen* was hit and sank, taking all but three survivors from the combined ships' companies with her.

Canadian War Museum. Ottawa. Cat. 87061

Canadian war graves

Wood, Herbert Farlie, and John Swettenham. *Silent Witnesses*. Toronto: Hakkert, 1974

Canadian forces in Europe and the North Atlantic

Roger Sarty, Directorate of History, National Defence Hedquarters, made available recently released material from the British Navy Historical Branch which made it possible to refine information concerning military ship losses. The data from the secondary sources listed below were updated using these sources, as well as books by Douglas (1986) and Rohwer (1983).

Barraclough, Geoffrey, ed. *The Times Atlas of World History*. London: Times Books, 1978. P 273

Britain. Historical Section Admiralty. Naval Staff History Second World War. 'Defeat of the Enemy Attack on Shipping 1939–1945: A Study of Policy and Operations.' Vols 1A, 1B. 1957

Coppock, R.M. 'Reassessments concerning the destruction of *FAA Di Bruno*, U-163, U-756, U-311.' Written for Britain. Ministry of Defence Dec 1982–Sep 1987. Not published. Copies held at Directorate of History, National Defence Headquarters, Ottawa

Douglas. *The Creation of a National Air Force*. 1986

Douglas, W.A.B., and B. Greenhaus. *Out of the Shadows: Canada in the Second World War*. Toronto: Oxford University Press, 1977

Goodspeed, D.J. *The Armed Forces of Canada, 1867–1967, A Century of Achievement*. Ottawa: Directorate of History, Canadian Forces Headquarters, 1967

Hadley, M. *U-Boats Against Canada: German Submarines on Canadian Waters*. Montréal: McGill-Queen's University Press, 1977

Kostenuk, Samuel, and John Griffen. *R.C.A.F. Squadron Histories and Aircraft, 1924–1968*. Toronto / Sarasota: Hakkert / Samuel Stevens, 1977

Rohwer, Jurgen. *Axis Submarine Successes, 1939–1945*. Annapolis, Md: Naval Institute Press, 1983

Schull, Joseph. *The Far Distant Ships, An Official Account of Canadian Naval Operation*. Ottawa: King's Printer, 1950

Stacey. *Six Years of War*. 1955

Tucker. *Naval Service of Canada*. 1952

Further readings

Granatstein, J.L. *Canada's War: Policies of the MacKenzie King Government 1939–1945*. Toronto: Oxford University Press, 1975

Morton, Desmond. *Canada and War: A Political and Military History*. Toronto: Butterworths, 1981

PLATE 48

The Home Front in the Second World War

LYNNE MARKS PH D candidate, History, York University
CHRISTOPHER A. SHARPE Geography, Memorial University of Newfoundland

Cost of the war

Canada. Department of External Affairs. Canadian Information Service. *Reference Paper 4*. 15 May 1946. 'Canadian War Data'

Canada Year Book. 1950

Stacey, C.P. *Arms, Men and Government: The War Policies of Canada 1939–1945*. Ottawa: Queen's Printer, 1970. App B

Victory-loan campaigns

Provincial and national populations in 1941 were used for all per capita calculations.

Canada. *Census*. 1941. Vol 1, p 5

– *SP*. No. 176 (a). 1945. Unpublished

The 1942 conscription plebiscite

Canada Gazette. 27 June 1942

Federal government involvement in war industry
Exports of principal commodities
Convoys

'Exports of vehicles and parts' includes gun carriers and tanks; 'chemicals and products' includes explosives. Under the Department of Munitions and Supply some 28 Crown companies were incorporated, 11 to operate plants and the remainder to carry out supervisory, administrative, and purchasing functions. All the issued share capital of the companies was held by the minister in trust for His Majesty the King in Right of Canada. The directors were appointed by the minister for their knowledge of the operation to be carried out and generally received no remuneration. The financial arrangements of the companies were approved by the Privy Council and the accounts audited by the Auditor-General of Canada.

Canada. *Auditor General's Reports*. 1939–45

– Canadian Information Service. *Reference Paper 4*. 15 May 1946. Table 78

– *SP*. No. 87B. 1945. No. 199. 1947

Elliott, Peter. *Allied Escort Ships of World War II: A Complete Survey*. London: MacDonald and Jane's, 1977

Gregg, W.A. *Blueprint for Victory: The Story of Military Vehicle Design and Production in Canada from 1937–45*. Rockwood, Ont: Canadian Military Historical Society, 1981

– *Canadian Fighting Vehicles: Europe 1943–45*. Rockwood, Ont: Canadian Military Historical Society, 1980

Hall, Hessel Duncan. *North American Supply*. London: HMSO / Longmans, 1955

Hall, Hessel Duncan, and C.C. Wrigley. *Studies of Overseas Supply*. London: HMSO / Longmans, 1956

Kennedy, John de Navarre. *History of the Department of Munitions and Supply, Canada in the Second World War*. Ottawa: King's Printer, 1950

NAC. RG 28B. B2-B8, Vol 264. 'Canada's Industrial War Effort 1939–45,' 'Wartime Shipbuilding Limited: Ship Cost Report'

Tucker, G.N. *Naval Service of Canada*. Ottawa: King's Printer, 1952

Employment structure

Data were based on a federal Department of Labour Survey of 1 827 establishments. Work-force figures for 1941 include persons on active service in 1941 in their normal peacetime industries; estimates were provided by Marvin McInnis (Economics, Queen's University).

NAC. RG 28, Vol 261. Sec I, Table 4

Japanese and Japanese Canadians
Prisoner-of-war and internment camps
The 'protected zone' in British Columbia where Japanese Canadians were prohibited from living during the war was a strip 100 miles wide running the length of the Pacific coast from Alaska to the United States border.

Adachi, Ken. *The Enemy That Never Was: A History of the Japanese Canadians.* Toronto: McClelland and Stewart, 1976. Tables 3, 5, 7, 9, 10
Carter, David J. *Behind Canadian Barbed Wire: Alien, Refugee and Prisoner of War Camps in Canada.* Calgary: Tumbleweed Press, 1980. Pp 308–12
NAC. RG 27. Vol 654, File 23–2–7–2

Selected non-traditional female occupations
Occupations include both salaried and wage workers.
Canada. DBS. *General Review of the Manufacturing Industries of Canada.* 1939, 1944

Dominion-Provincial Day Nurseries Agreement, Toronto, 1944
NAC. RG 27. Vol 605, File 6–24–1, Pt 2
– RG 27. Vol 611, File 6–52–6–1, Vol 2

Further readings
Granatstein, J.L. *Canada's War: Policies of the MacKenzie King Government 1939–1945.* Toronto: Oxford University Press, 1975
Pierson, Ruth. *'They're Still Women After All': The Second World War and Canadian Womenhood.* Toronto: McClelland and Stewart, 1986
Sunahara, Ann. *The Politics of Racism.* Toronto: Lorimer, 1981
Ward, Peter. *White Canada Forever: Popular Attitudes and Public Policy Towards Orientals in British Columbia.* Montréal: McGill-Queen's University Press, 1978

PLATE 49

Farming and Fishing

GERALD BLOOMFIELD   Geography, University of Guelph
PHILIP D. KEDDIE   Geography, University of Guelph
ERIC W. SAGER   History, University of Victoria

The research assistance of Garry Penner in assembling the information on fishing is gratefully acknowledged. For data on fishing the value of the fish caught is the value at the boat's landing, based on sale to first buyer. Inland provinces include Ontario, Manitoba, Saskatchewan, and Alberta.

Value of catch by species
Canada. DBS. *Fisheries Statistics of Canada.* 1961. Table 2

Value of fish caught
Prior to 1952 annual figures for value of all fish landed are not available for Newfoundland. The nearest equivalent is total export value of salt cod and this was used for 1926 to 1952. The British Columbia figure in 1961 includes halibut landed in US ports and fish caught in the Yukon Territory.
Government of Newfoundland and Labrador. *Historical Statistics of Newfoundland.* St John's, 1970. Table K-7
Leacy. *Historical Statistics.* Series N1–11
Newfoundland. *Journals of the House of Assembly.* 'Customs Returns'

Fishing labour force
Statistics for Newfoundland are for number of fishermen in the cod fishery only; for other regions the number of persons engaged in primary fishing operations was used.
Canada. DBS. *Fisheries Statistics of Canada.* 1917–62
– Department of Marine and Fisheries. *Annual Report.* 1891–1917
Canadian Fisheries Annual. 1952–61
Leacy. *Historical Statistics.* Series N38–48, N139–42

Fish caught, ICNAF areas, 1958: total and by region
International Commission for the Northwest Atlantic Fisheries (ICNAF). *Statistical Bulletin.* 1958. Vol 8, Pt 1, p 7; Pt 2, pp 12–13

Fish caught, ICNAF areas, 1951–61
Alexander, David. *Decay of Trade, An Economic History of the Newfoundland Saltfish Trade, 1935–1965.* St John's: Institute of Social and Economic Research, 1977. P 151
ICNAF. *Statistical Bulletin.* 1958. Vols 1–11
Leacy. *Historical Statistics.* N125–7

North Pacific salmon catch
International North Pacific Fisheries Commission. *Bulletin.* Vol 39. 1978

Net farming income
Net returns from farming operations were used as net farm income.
Leacy. *Historical Statistics.* Series M119–28

Change in improved acreage
Canada. *Census.* 1941: Vol 8, Table 52. 1961: Vol 5, Table 28

Crop combinations in the Prairies
When wheat is designated as the only crop, at least 75% and more commonly over 80% of the cropland is devoted to wheat. When wheat is combined with one other crop, it is generally the more important of the two dominant crops. In the combination of wheat, hay, and one other the third crop is generally either oats or barley, though flax is popular in Manitoba. The combination of four or more crops, including wheat, generally includes oats, barley, and hay; other crops appearing in these combinations are rye, flax, and rapeseed (in 1961). The most prominent crops grown singly or in combination not including wheat are hay and oats; barley is generally added to these in a three-crop combination.
Canada. *Census.* 1941: Vol 8, Table 54. 1961: Vol 5, Table 30

Varieties of Prairie bread wheat
Data on varietal compositon are based on information from Line Elevator Farm Service (see below) provided by J.R. Rogalsky, Chief, Crops Section, Agriculture Manitoba at the Agriculture Canada Research Station, Winnipeg.
  'Other rust-resistant' varieties include Apex (first licensed in 1937), Renown (1937), Regent (1939), Redman (1946), and Lee (1950). Marquis was first distributed to farmers in 1909. Red Bobs was first licensed in 1926, Thatcher in 1935, Rescue in 1946, Chinook in 1952, Selkirk in 1953.
Bushuk, W. 'Development, Licensing and Distribution of New Varieties of Grain in Canada.' *Grains and Oilseeds, Handling, Marketing, Processing.* 3rd rev ed. Winnipeg: Canadian International Grains Institute, 1982. Pp 443–62
Greaney, F.J., and J. Barnes. *Distribution of Wheat Varieties in the Prairie Provinces, 1941 to 1950.* Circular No. 15. Winnipeg: Line Elevator Farm Service, 1953
Line Elevator Farm Service. Winnipeg. Distribution of wheat varieties for the crop districts of Manitoba, Saskatchewan, and Alberta, 1955–61. Untitled and unpublished annual tables
Line Elevator Farm Service. Winnipeg. 'Distribution of Wheat Varieties in the Prairie Provinces (1951 to 1955).' Unpublished table

Farms with tractors
Canada. *Census.* 1921: Vol 5, Table 38. 1931: Vol 8, Table XXIX. 1941: Vol 8, Tables 28, 48. 1951: Vol 6, Table 24. 1961: Vol 5, Table 29

Further readings
Bennett, John W. *Northern Plainsmen: Adaptive Strategy and Agrarian Life.* Chicago: Aldine, 1969
Canada. *Navigating Troubled Waters: A New Policy for the Atlantic Fisheries.* Ottawa: Supply and Services Canada, 1983
MacEwan, G. *Harvest of Bread.* Saskatoon: Western Producer, 1969
Marchak, Patricia, N. Guppy, and J. McMullan, eds. *Uncommon Property: The Fishing and Fish Processing Industries in British Columbia.* Toronto: Methuen, 1987
Sinclair, Peter R. *From Traps to Draggers: Domestic Commodity Production in Northwest Newfoundland, 1850–1982.* St John's: Institute of Social and Economic Research, 1985
– ed. *A Question of Survival: The Fisheries and Newfoundland Society.* St John's: Institute of Social and Economic Research, 1988

PLATE 50

Resources for Industrial Economies

DONALD KERR   Geography, University of Toronto

Origin of capital investment
Leacy. *Historical Statistics.* Series G303–17

The pulp and paper industry, 1961
Financial Post Survey of Industries, 1962. Pulp and Paper and Lumber Securities
National Directory of Canadian Pulp and Paper Industries. Gardenvale, Qué: National Business Publications, 1962
Reader, W.J. *Bowater: A History.* Cambridge: Cambridge University Press, 1981

Pulp and paper production
Canadian Pulp and Paper Association. Reference tables. June 1962

Mineral production by province
Canada. DBS. *General Review of the Mining Industry.* Cat. 26–201. 1961. Table 5

Mineral production by type
Canada. DBS. *General Review of the Mining Industry.* Cat. 26–201. 1949–61
– DBS. *Mineral Statistics.* Cat. 26–D–28. 1946–9

Mineral production, 1961
Data on value of production by individual mines or mining districts are not generally available and consequently an estimated value of production for mines and mining regions was calculated. Production data for minerals from individual mines were converted to value figures using the average price of the minerals in a particular market. For example, Manitouwadge, Ontario, produced 1 526 976 ounces of silver in 1961. The average quoted price for silver in 1961 was 94.3 cents per ounce. By multiplying 1 526 976 by 94.3 an estimated value for the mine of $1 439 938 was obtained. Where appropriate, values for individual mines were aggregated into mining districts.
Canada. Department of Mines and Technical Surveys. Mineral Resources Division. *Canadian Minerals Yearbook.* 1961
Canadian Mines Handbook, 1961. Toronto: Northern Miner Press, 1962

Oil and gas production and flow
Camu, Pierre, E.P. Weeks, and Z.W. Sametz. *Economic Geography of Canada.* Toronto: Macmillan, 1964. Figs 5.4, 5.5, p 133
Canada. DBS. *Crude Petroleum and Natural Gas Industry.* Cat. 26–213. 1961
– Department of Mines and Technical Surveys. Mineral Resources Division. *Canadian Minerals Yearbook.* 1961
– Department of Mines and Technical Surveys. Mineral Resources Division. 'Natural Gas Processing Plants in Canada, Operators List No. 7.' Jan 1962
– Department of Mines and Technical Surveys. Mineral Resources Division. 'Petroleum Refineries in Canada, Operators List No. 5.' Jan 1962

Natural-gas service in Saskatchewan
Saskatchewan. Saskatchewan Power Corporation. *Annual Report.* 1951–61. Financial statements

Energy consumption
For the years 1956 and 1957 estimated consumption was calculated from a variety of sources and converted to BTUs $\times$ 10^{12} according to conversion tables used by Davis (1957).
Canada. DBS. *Detailed Energy Supply and Demand in Canada.* Cat. 57–505. 1958–61
Davis, John. *Canadian Energy Prospects.* Monograph for Royal Commission on Canada's Economic Prospects. Ottawa, 1957. App F, Table 1

Further readings

Barr, Brenton M. 'Reorganization of the Economy.' In Peter J. Smith, ed. *The Prairie Provinces*. Toronto: University of Toronto Press, 1972. Pp 65–82

Burton, Thomas L. *Natural Resource Policy in Canada: Issues and Perspectives*. Toronto: McClelland and Stewart, 1972

Hare, F. Kenneth. 'New Light from Labrador Ungava.' *Annals of the Association of American Geographers* 54 (1964): 459–76

Hunter, W.D.G. 'The Development of the Canadian Uranium Industry: An Experiment in Public Enterprise.' *Canadian Journal of Economics and Political Science* 28, no. 3 (August 1962): 329–52

McKay, D. *The MacMillan Bloedel Story*. Vancouver: Douglas and McIntyre, 1982

Pratt, Larry, and John Richards. *Prairie Capitalism: Power and Influence in the West*. Toronto: McClelland and Stewart, 1979

Robin, Martin. *Pillars of Profit: The Company Province 1932–1972*. Toronto: McClelland and Stewart, 1973

Scott, Anthony. 'The Development of the Extractive Industries.' *Canadian Journal of Economics and Political Science* 27, no. 1 (Feb 1962): 70–87

Stewart, Max Douglas. *Concentration in Canadian Manufacturing and Mining Industries; Background Study to the Interim Report on Competition Policy*. Ottawa: Economic Council of Canada, 1970

Wallace, Iain. *The Transportation Impact of the Canadian Mining Industry*. Kingston: Queen's University Centre for Resource Studies, 1977

PLATE 51

The Persistence of Manufacturing Patterns

GERALD BLOOMFIELD Geography, University of Guelph
DONALD KERR Geography, University of Toronto

The research assistance of Steven Bellinger and Charles Baker is gratefully acknowledged. For a discussion of manufacturing statistics see pl 7.

Manufacturing structure
Canada. *Census*. 1961. Vol 3, Pt 2, Tables 3.2–2, 3.2–3

Control of manufacturing
Leacy. *Historical Statistics*. Series G303–17

Changes in manufacturing production, 1947–61
Data were collected for cities and towns with a gross value of production of $10 million in 1961. By adding cost of materials to cost of fuel and electricity and subtracting the total from gross value of production (in 1961 the selling value of factory shipments) for each town and city a figure for net value of production was obtained. To make the 1947 data comparable with those of 1961, values were multiplied by 1.51, thereby achieving 1961 constant dollars. To gain a measure of growth or decline (1947–61) 1947 values for net value of production adjusted to 1961 constant dollars were subtracted from 1961 figures. To measure change in metropolitan centres 1961 boundaries were selected and estimates were made for 1947 value of production according to those boundaries.

No data were available for Newfoundland for 1947 and a comparison of 1951 and 1961 data was made. 1951 dollars were converted into 1961 constant dollars by multiplying by 1.02.

Canada. DBS. *Geographical Distribution of Industries of Canada*. Cat. 31–209. 1961
– *Manufacturing Industries of Canada*. Cat. 31–201. 1947

American firms
The basic source used was the *Directory of American Firms Operating in Foreign Countries* (DAFOFC) compiled by Angel. Since only American names of the firms are listed, some American-controlled firms with Canadian names have been omitted. Moreover the list provides no information on location, number of employees, or products, and it was necessary to consult a variety of sources to determine these variables. Among the most important were *Scotts Ontario Industrial Directory*, which was used to identify the location of some 800 of the 1 308 firms listed in DAFOFC and Blackbourn's thesis, and the Ontario government's unpublished list of 'Ontario Companies Controlled by or Subsidiaries of American Companies,' which made possible the confirmation of over 200 firms listed in DAFOFC. In addition the Ontario government's list provided corrections to firms previously identified incorrectly. At the time of this research the Ontario government's list was not in any public repository and we are grateful to Anthony Blackbourn for making it available to us. Copies should now be available from the Ontario Ministry of Industry, Trade, and Technology. This compilation is the best source for Ontario since it documents the Canadian company name, the parent company name, the products of each firm, and the address of each firm. In total, of the 1 308 firms listed in DAFOFC, 1 069 were identified and form the statistical basis of the map.

Angel, J.L., compiler. *Directory of American Firms Operating in Foreign Countries*. New York: World Trade Academy Press, 1962

Bellinger, Steven. 'American Branch Plants.' Unpublished report submitted to the Historical Atlas of Canada project, Vol III, 1983

Blackbourn, Anthony. 'Locational Patterns of American-Owned Industry in Southern Ontario.' PH D thesis, University of Toronto, 1968

'Canadian American Concerns.' *Agricultural and Industrial Progress in Canada* 12, no. 10 (Oct 1930): 188–99

Canadian Trade Index, 1961. Toronto: Canadian Manufacturers Association, 1962

Dun and Bradstreet's Municipal Reference Handbook 1961. Toronto: Dun and Bradstreet, 1962

Ontario. Department of Economics and Development. Trade and Government Branch. 'Ontario Companies Controlled by or Subsidiaries of American Companies.' 1961. Unpublished

Scotts Ontario Industrial Directory, 1961. Oakville: Penstock Publications, 1962

Electrical-products industry in Ontario
Included under 'electrical apparatus and supplies' are batteries, heavy electrical machinery, telecommunications equipment, refrigerators and appliances, wires and cables, and miscellaneous electrical products. In a few cases where data on employment were not available in *Scotts Directory* most information was obtained by direct mail or by contacting Chambers of Commerce in the relevant cities. Thanks are due to John Jackson (Geography, Brock University) for providing data for two firms in the Niagara area.

Canada. DBS. *The Electrical Apparatus and Supplies Industry*. Cat. 43–201. 1962
Ontario. Department of Economics and Development. 'Ontario Companies Controlled by or Subsidiaries of American Companies.' 1961
Scotts Ontario Industrial Directory, 1961

The brewing industry
Canada. DBS. *The Brewing Industry*. Cat. 32–205. 1950–60
– Restrictive Trade Practices Commission. *Report Concerning an Alleged Combine in the Manufacture, Distribution and Sale of Beer in Canada*. Ottawa, 1955
– Royal Commission on Corporate Concentration. *Argus*. Study No. 1. Ottawa: Supply and Services, 1977
– Royal Commission on Corporate Concentration. *Brascan Limited*. Study No. 2. Ottawa: Supply and Services, 1977
– Royal Commission on Corporate Concentration. *The Molson Companies Ltd*. Study No. 8. Ottawa: Supply and Services, 1976
Roseman, Frank. 'The Canadian Brewing Industry.' PH D thesis, Northwestern University, 1968

Production of steel ingots by province
Data on steel production 1891–1939 have been compiled by Kris Inwood and we are grateful for his assistance.

Canada. DBS. *Iron and Steel*. Cat. 41–203. 1939–60
Dominion Iron and Steel Corporation. *Annual Report*. 1905–6
Geological Survey of Canada. *Report of Progress*. 1894–1900. Statistical section
Lake Superior Corporation. *Annual Report*. 1905–6
NAC. G 87. Vols 18, 19
Nova Scotia. Department of Mines. *Annual Report*. 1921–2
Ontario. Department of Mines. *Annual Report*. 1921–2
Public Archives of Nova Scotia. Manuscript Group 3, Vol 1873, n 52

Canadian production of crude steel
Correspondence with companies
Kilbourn, William. *Elements Combined*. Toronto: Clarke Irwin, 1960. App, Statistical summary, 1910–59
Prior, Leonard. 'Sault Ste. Marie and Algoma Steel Corporation.' MA thesis, University of Toronto, 1956. Fig 25
Wittur, G.E. *Primary Iron and Steel in Canada*. Mineral Information Bulletin, MR 92, Mineral Resources Branch, Department of Energy, Mines and Resources, Ottawa, 1968. Table 10

Steel-producing centres
Primary iron and steel works by definition require the delivery of iron ore, coal, limestone, and other raw materials at the mill site. Pig iron, coke, and crude steel are produced and at some mills galvanized and tinplate steel as well. Secondary steel mills produce steel in electric furnaces mainly from scrap.

Canada. DBS. *Primary Iron and Steel Industry*. Cat. 41–203. 1957

Railway freight rates on steel bars
Canada. The Tariff Board. *Basic Iron and Steel Products*. Ref. 118. Ottawa, 1957. P 280
Morgan, Lucy. 'The Canadian Primary Iron and Steel Industry.' Royal Commission on Canada's Economic Prospects. Ottawa, 1956. P 82

Further readings

Barber, Clarence C. 'The Canadian Electrical Manufacturing Industry.' Royal Commission on Canada's Economic Prospects. Ottawa, 1956

Baron, Stanley Wade. *Brewed in America: A History of Beer and Ale in the United States*. Boston: Little, Brown, 1962

Bloomfield, G.T. 'Consolidation in the Canadian Brewing Industry 1940–1960.' Unpublished report submitted to the Historical Atlas of Canada project, Vol III, 1984

– 'Industrial Reorganization in the Depression: The Ontario Brewing Industry 1930–1940.' Unpublished report submitted to the Historical Atlas of Canada project, Vol III, 1984

Bright, Arthur Aaron. *The Electric-Lamp Industry: Technological Change and Economic Development 1800–1947*. New York: Macmillan, 1949

Inwood, Kris. 'The Iron and Steel Industry.' In Ian Drummond, ed. *Progress Without Planning: The Economic History of Ontario from Confederation to the Second World War*. Toronto: University of Toronto Press, 1987. Pp 185–207

Kerr, Donald P. 'The Location of the Iron and Steel Industry in Canada.' In R. Louis Gentilcore, ed. *Geographical Approaches to Canadian Problems*. Scarborough: Prentice Hall, 1971. Pp 59–68

MacDowall, Duncan. *Steel at the Sault: Francis H. Clergue, Sir James Dunn and the Algoma Steel Corporation 1901–1956*. Toronto: University of Toronto Press, 1984

Ray, David Michael. *Market Potential and Economic Shadow: A Quantitative Analysis of Industrial Location in Southern Ontario*. Department of Geography Research Paper No. 101. Chicago: University of Chicago, 1965

Reuber, Grant L., and Frank Roseman. *The Take-Over of Canadian Firms 1945–61: An Empirical Analysis*. Economic Council of Canada Special Study No. 10. Ottawa, 1969

Rohmer, Richard H. *E.P. Taylor: The Biography of Edward Plunkett Taylor*. Toronto: McClelland and Stewart, 1978

Rosenbluth, Gideon. *Concentration in Canadian Manufacturing Industries*. Princeton: Princeton University Press, 1957

Woods, Shirley E. *The Molson Saga 1763–1983*. Toronto: Doubleday, 1983

PLATE 52

Retailing

GERALD BLOOMFIELD Geography, University of Guelph
DONALD KERR Geography, University of Toronto

Retail employment
Canada. *Census*. 1931: Vol 10, Tables 18, 20, 21. 1961: Vol 6, Pt 1, Table 2

Value of retail sales
Moyer, M.S., and G. Snyder. *Trends in Canadian Marketing*. DBS. 1961 Census
  Monograph. Ottawa, 1967. Table 3.1

Retail sales by commodity
The data from Moyer and Snyder were modified by the authors.
Moyer and Snyder. *Trends in Canadian Marketing*. 1967. Table 3.3

Provincial retail sales
Canada. *Census*. 1931: Vol 10, Table 1B. 1951: Vol 7, Table 1. 1961: Vol 6, Pt 1, Table 1

Retailing by degree of independence
Moyer and Snyder. *Trends in Canadian Marketing*. 1967. Table 7.13

Type of ownership
Moyer and Snyder. *Trends in Canadian Marketing*. 1967. Table 3.8

Shopping centres
Canada. DBS. *Shopping Centres in Canada, 1961–1963*. Cat. 63–214. 1965
Moyer and Snyder. *Trends in Canadian Marketing*. 1967. Tables 8.10, 8.11

Downtown London, Ontario
Bloomfield, G.T. 'Structural and Spatial Changes in Retailing: A Case Study of
  London, Ontario, 1919–1959.' Unpublished report submitted to the Historical
  Atlas of Canada project, Vol III, 1989
Vernon's City of London Directory. Various years

The growth of Eaton's
We would like to acknowledge the assistance of Judith McErvel, Archivist, Eaton's
Yorkdale, Toronto, 1985, and E.C. Hawkinson, Corporate Architect, T. Eaton
Company, Toronto. Most of the research for this map was undertaken in 1985 at the
Eaton's archives at Eaton's Yorkdale. The historical records of the T. Eaton
Company were transferred to the Archives of Ontario in 1988.
Archives of Ontario. T. Eaton Company records
Hawkinson, E.C. Corporate Architect, T. Eaton Company. Correspondence, Feb
  1989

The Growth of Woolworth's
Woolworth, F.W., Co. *Annual Reports*
– 100th Anniversary, 1879–1979. New York, 1979

Park Royal Shopping Centre, West Vancouver, BC
We would like to acknowledge the assistance of Daniel Hiebert (Geography,
University of British Columbia), and Per Danielson, Park Royal Shopping
Centre, for locating an appropriate photograph.

Further readings
Armstrong, F.H. *The Forest City: An Illustrated History of London, Canada*. Burlington:
  Windsor Publications, 1986
Bloomfield, G.T. 'The Growth of Woolworth's in Canada.' Unpublished report
  submitted to the Historical Atlas of Canada project, Vol III, 1987
– 'The Impact of the Automobile on Cities: A London Case Study.' Unpublished
  report submitted to the Historical Atlas of Canada project, Vol III, 1983
Canada. Royal Commission on Price Spreads. *Report*. Ottawa, 1937
Cheasley, C.H. *The Chain Store Movement in Canada*. McGill Economics Studies No.
  17. Montréal, 1929
Drummond, Ian M. *Progress without Planning: The Economic History of Ontario from
  Confederation to the Second World War*. Toronto: University of Toronto Press,
  1987. Pp 274–308
Huston, B.T. 'The Chain Store.' *Queen's Quarterly* 36 (1929): 313–25
Jones, Ken, and Jim Simmons. *Location, Location, Location: Analysing the Retail
  Environment*. Toronto: Nelson, 1987
Nichols, John P. *Skyline Queen and the Merchant Prince: The Woolworth Story*. New
  York: Trident Press, 1973
Stephenson, William. *The Store That Timothy Built, 1869–1919*. Toronto: McClelland
  and Stewart, 1969
Winkler, John K. *Five and Ten: The Fabulous Life of F.W. Woolworth*. London: Robert
  Hale, 1941

PLATE 53

The Growth of Road and Air Transport

GERALD BLOOMFIELD Geography, University of Guelph
MURDO MacPHERSON Historical Atlas of Canada, Toronto
DAVID NEUFELD Canadian Parks Service, Winnipeg

Canadian airlines, 1937
NAC. RG 12. Department of Transport files. Vol 2154, f. 5562–18, pt 2
Winnipeg Evening Tribune. 8 Dec 1937. P 63, map, 'Canadian Air Lines,' amended by
  author

AIR CARGO
Canada. Department of Transport. 'Quarterly Civil Air Liaison Letter.' no. 38, 39,
  40, 41

AIR FREIGHT
Canada. Department of Trade and Commerce. Transportation and Public Utilities
  Branch. *Civil Aviation in Canada 1937*. 1938
– *Aviation in Canada 1971: A Statistical Handbook of Canadian Civil Aviation*. Aviation
  Statistics Centre, 1972
Canadian Aviation. Various issues, Oct 1936–Mar 1938
Cunningham, H. *Development of Commercial Air Services in Canada 1919–1944*.
  Directorate of Air Development, Department of Reconstruction and Supply,
  1946
NAC. G 12. Department of Transport files
Provincial Archives of Manitoba. MG 11A 34. Canadian Airways Collection
University of Saskatchewan Archives. Tweddell Papers. 'The Bulletin,' Canadian
  Airways Newsletter

Origins of the major airlines
Canada. Department of Industry, Trade, and Commerce. *Aviation in Canada, 1971*.
  Fig 1.2
Fuller, G.A., J.A. Griffin, and K.M. Molson. *125 Years of Canadian Aeronautics:
  A Chronology 1840–1965*. Willowdale, Ont: Canadian Aviation Historical
  Society, 1983

Canadian airlines, 1963
Canada Year Book. 1962. P 823
*A Comparative Economic Analysis of EPA and Its Role in the Development of the Atlantic
  Provinces*. Aug 1965. P 48, map, amended by author
Davies, R.E.G. *A History of the Worlds' Airlines*. London: Oxford University Press,
  1964. P 373 Pacific Western Airlines. 17th Annual Report. 1963
Quebecair. *Financial Report*. 1963
– *Wings in Space*. Oct 1964
Transair. *Annual Report*. 1962
Trans-Canada Airlines. *Annual Report*. 1963
Wagner, U. Stan, Senior Operations Manager for Transair from the 1950s to 1974.
  Interview 2, Jan 1988

Passenger miles and commercial pilots
Canada. DBS. Cat. 51–202. 1936–69
– Department of Industry, Trade, and Commerce. *Aviation in Canada, 1971*
– Department of Marine. Civil Aviation Branch. *Annual Report*. 1923–36

Evolution of the road network
Canada. Department of Mines and Technical Surveys. Geographical Branch. 'Major
  Roads.' Ottawa, 1962. Map
– Department of Resources and Development. Canadian Government Travel
  Bureau. 'Highway map of Canada and Northern United States.' Ottawa, 1961
– Department of Resources and Development. Canadian Government Travel
  Bureau. 'Main Automobile Roads Between United States and Canada.'
  Ottawa, 1950. Map
Imperial Oil Ltd. 'Imperial Oil Map of Eastern Canada.' 1937. Maps 1–3
– 'Imperial Oil Map of Western Canada.' 1937. Maps 4, 5
Newfoundland. Department of Natural Resources. Crown Land and Surveys
  Branch. 'Ten Mile Map of Newfoundland.' St John's, 1941

The Trans-Canada Highway: total expenditure
Canada. DBS. Cat. 53–201. 1963

Main highways, 1930
Fragmentary evidence points to some errors on the firestone map (1930). More
  research is needed to confirm its accuracy.
Canada. Department of the Interior. 'Map Indicating Main Automobile Roads
  Between Canada and the United States.' Ottawa, 1930
Firestone's Road Maps of Canada and Northern United States. Preston, Ont: Peerless
  Vulcanizing Co, 1930

Motor-vehicle registrations
Canada. DBS. Cat. 53–201. 1938, 1951, 1961
Urquhart and Buckley. *Historical Statistics*. Series s222–35

Surfaced roads
Canada Year Book. 1962. P 771
Urquhart and Buckley. *Historical Statistics*. Series s215–21

Paved roads
Canada. DBS. Cat. 53–201. 1945–57, 1959–75
Canada Year Book. 1956: p 834. 1958: p 793. 1960: pp 798–9. 1962: p 771

Movement of passengers
For motor vehicles, estimate was based on total number of registrations multiplied
by ten.
Leacy. *Historical Statistics*. Series T39–46, T147–94, T 195–8
Urquhart and Buckley. *Historical Statistics*. Series s39–52, s112–19, s236–9

Further readings
Bloomfield, G.T. 'Canadian Highways and the Automobile.' Unpublished report
  submitted to the Historical Atlas of Canada project, Vol III, 1983
Guillet, E.C. *The Story of Canadian Roads*. Toronto: University of Toronto Press, 1966
Main, J.R.K. *Voyageurs of the Air: Canadian Civil Aviation, 1858–1967*. Ottawa:
  Queen's Printer, 1967
Molson, K.M. *Pioneering in Canadian Air Transport*. Winnipeg: James Richardson &
  Sons, 1974
Neufeld, D. 'Canada: Air Transport in 1939.' Manuscript map and supporting
  documents prepared for *The National Atlas of Canada*, 1989

PLATE 54

The Integration of the Urban System

MICHAEL P. CONZEN   Committee on Geographical Studies, University of
   Chicago
JAMES W. SIMMONS   Geography, University of Toronto

We would like to acknowledge the assistance of Charles Baker and Michael Bloor in preparing material for this plate. For a discussion of the definition of 'urban' see pl 10.

Population change
The urban network
Material was drawn from various tables in the census and carefully synthesized by the authors.
Canada. Census. 1921–51

Railways
Burns, A.J., compiler. *The Official Guide of the Railways and Steam Navigation Lines of the United States, Puerto Rico, Canada, Mexico and Cuba.* New York: National Railway Publication Company, 1951

Economic specialization
This map was constructed by: (1) grouping the counties and census divisions of Canada around urban places with populations of approximately 10 000, except in BC where the census divisions were used as given; (2) examining the labour force by industry as given in the 1961 census; (3) modifying the breakdown into sectors by re-allocating the resource processing part of manufacturing, such as pulp making, into the appropriate primary activity; and (4) examining more closely those sectors contributing more than 10% of the labour force. Four individual primary specializations were indicated with provision for a multiple primary role (fish/forest, mine/forest, etc). Manufacturing could occur alone or in combination with a primary activity, always agriculture except for the Sydney (mining) and Sault Ste Marie (forest) regions, or a tertiary activity, often transportation. Tertiary specializations were limited to transportation or public administration, because each of the cities contains a high proportion of retail, finance, and service jobs.
Canada. *Census.* 1961
– DBS. *Geographical Distribution of Manufacturing Industries of Canada.* Cat. 31–209. 1961

Intercity air-passenger flows
The help of Flemming Leicht, Statistical Officer, Air Transport Bureau, International Civil Aviation Organization, Montréal, in providing data on trans-border flights is gratefully acknowledged. It was not until 1966 that the Canadian Air Transport Board published data on trans-border flights for carriers other than Canadian. The International Civil Aviation Organization (ICAO) published data on a quarterly basis for all carriers. The Canadian data are not precisely comparable with ICAO data because they derive from a continuous statistical sample for the whole year whereas the ICAO data derive from four specific months.
Canada. Department of Transportation. Statistics Section. *Origin and Destination Statistics, Mainline Revenue Passengers Domestic Survey, 1960–61.* Ottawa, 1962
International Civil Aviation Organization. *Digest of Statistics of the Traffic by Flight Stage.* Montréal, 1961 (Mar, June, Sep, Dec issues)

Further readings
See pl 10.

PLATE 55

Metropolitan Dominance

GUNTER GAD   Geography, University of Toronto

Unless otherwise stated, all data refer to 1961. Data for banks and insurance companies reflect their status as of 31 Dec 1961.

100 large companies in Canada, 1961
'Industrials' includes manufacturing, mining, utility, transportation, merchandising, and holding companies. Their rank is based on assets, since sales or revenue figures are frequently not available for 1961. Some large companies did not publish asset figures in 1961 (eg, General Motors of Canada and Eaton's) and are therefore not on the list. If a company listed an 'executive office,' its location was considerd the company's base, rather than the city where the legal head office was located. The executive office of the Dominion Steel and Coal Corporation Ltd was in Ville Saint-Pierre, a local government unit which in 1961 was part of the Montréal Census Metropolitan Area. Ford of Canada, based in Oakville, has been allocated to the Toronto Census Metropolitan Area.
   Finance-company ranking is based on assets. Only banks and insurance companies with federal charters are included. Trust-company assets include estates, trusts, and agency funds. The assets of the Canada Permanent Mortgage Corporation include those of its subsidiary, the Canada Permanent Toronto General Trust Company.
   The ranking of law firms is based on the number of lawyers in a firm. Three law firms were tied for tenth place: one from Toronto, one from Vancouver, and one from Edmonton. Since Toronto was already well represented on the list and since Vancouver rather than Edmonton had the next largest law firm, the Vancouver firm was chosen for inclusion.
   The ranking of accountants is based on the number of accountants in an office. Offices rather than firms are considered and thus the same firm may appear in several cities. Two Toronto offices, one in Vancouver, and one in Edmonton tied for tenth place. The Toronto offices were not considered because Toronto was already well represented on the list. The Edmonton office was chosen for inclusion because the next largest office was in Edmonton rather than in Vancouver. The list of offices was compiled for 1962; 1961 data are not available.
   The ranking of advertising-agency offices is by number of key personnel, including presidents, managers, department directors, lawyers, and others.

Offices rather than firms were considered. If firms had been considered, the distribution would have been: Toronto 4, Montréal 4, London 1, Vancouver 1.
Canada. Department of Insurance. *Annual Report.* 3 vols. 1961
Canada Gazette. Supplement. 3 Feb 1962
Canada Legal Directory 1962. Toronto: J.H. Wharton, 1962
Canadian Advertising. Nov–Dec 1961. Pp 4–8
Directory of Canadian Chartered Accountants 1962. Toronto: Canadian Institute of Chartered Accountants, 1962
Financial Post Survey of Industrials, 1962. Toronto: MacLean-Hunter, 1962
Financial Post Survey of Mines, 1964. Toronto: MacLean-Hunter, 1964
Ontario. Department of Insurance. Registrar of Loan and Trust Corporations. *Loan and Trust Corporations' Statements being Abstracts from Financial Statements made by Loan Corporations and Trust Companies for the Year Ended December 31, 1961.* 1962

Financial assets by location of head office
Only federally chartered banks, federally chartered insurance companies, and federally and provincially chartered trust and mortgage-loan companies are included. Trust-company assets include estates, trusts, and agency funds. For a few companies 1961 figures were unavailable and 1960 assets were used.
Canada. Department of Insurance. *Annual Report.* 3 vols. 1961
Canada Gazette. Supplement. 3 Feb 1962
Financial Post Survey of Industrials, 1962
Ontario. Department of Insurance. *Loan and Trust Corporations' Statements.* 1962

Movement of insurance-company head offices
Assets of insurance centres
The map showing the movement of head offices includes head offices of Canadian companies and 'chief agencies in Canada' of British and foreign, mostly US, companies. The data base consists of three cross-sections: 1941, 1951, and 1961. Only companies still in existence in 1961 were included. Excluded are, for instance, companies which moved between 1941 and 1960 but did not exist in 1961, or companies which moved after 1951.
   The graph on assets of insurance centres is also based on 1941, 1951, and 1961 cross-sectional data. 'Relocating' companies are for the purpose of the diagram only those which moved between Toronto, Montréal, and the aggregate of all the other cities. Thus one company moving from Regina to Vancouver and another moving from Winnipeg to Hamilton are included in the 'remaining' category. 'Companies receiving federal charters' includes five which existed already under provincial charters; all five of these stayed in the 'other' than Toronto and Montréal group of cities.
Canada. Department of Insurance. *Annual Report.* 1941, 1951, 1961

Advertising agencies
Since employment figures are not available, the 'key personnel' in advertising-agency offices was used to determine the size of the advertising industry in each urban centre (see '100 large companies' above for definition of key personnel).
Canadian Advertising. Nov–Dec 1961. Pp 4–8
National List of Advertisers. 1962. Pp 365–424

Stock transactions in Montréal and Toronto
Data on the volume of shares traded on markets other than the official Toronto and Montréal stock exchanges are inconsistent before 1934 and therefore excluded. Data on the value of stock transactions are available only from 1937 onwards. 'Industrial stocks' are those of manufacturing companies only.
Annual Financial Review. 1926–37
Monetary Times 78 (7 Jan 1927): 131
Toronto Stock Exchange. Statistical Service. Unpublished tables for 1941, 1946, 1951, 1956, 1961

Canada Packers
Facilities are aggregated by urban centres. In some cases the symbol used for 'other product lines' may denote separate plants or warehouses; in other cases two or more product lines may be located in the same plant but two or more symbols are used. Other product lines include: feed mills; fertilizer plants; feed concentrating plants; tanneries; soap, jute, bag, and feather plants; edible-oil processing and margarine production; poultry processing; creameries; cheese processing; ice-cream production; fruit and vegetable canning; hatcheries; egg, cheese, and fruit wholesaling. The map does not show 11 hatcheries in Saskatchewan and Manitoba, 5 creameries in Manitoba, and 7 creameries in Ontario since location details could not be found.
   Thanks are due to the Corporate Information Department, Canada Packers Ltd, Toronto, for making available the company's annual reports, *Mapleleaf* and *Maple Leaflet*.
Canada. Department of Justice. Restrictive Trade Practices' Commission. *Report Concerning the Meat Packing Industry and the Acquisition of Wilsil Limited and Calgary Packers Limited by Canada Packers Limited.* Ottawa, 1961
Canada Packers Limited. *Annual Report.* 1961
– *Mapleleaf. A Special Anniversary Edition, 1977*
– *Maple Leaflet.* 1960–1. Various issues

Aluminium Limited
Arvida-area facilities include: alumina plant, smelter, fabricating plant, and research lab at Arvida; wharf at Port Alfred and railway from Port Alfred to Arvida; power plant and smelter at Isle-Maligne; power plants at Chute-à-Caron, Shipshaw, Chute-du-Diable; Chute-à-la-Savane, and Chute-des-Passes. Thanks are due to Information Services, Alcan Ltd, Montréal, for making available annual reports of Aluminium Limited and various pamphlets and unpublished material.
Aluminium Limited. *Aluminium Panorama.* Montréal, 1953
– *Annual Report.* 1958–61
'Aluminium Limited.' New York: Smith, Barney and Co, 1959
'Aluminium Ltd. A Time for Re-Assessment.' Montréal: C.J. Hodgson, 1965
Campbell, D.C. *Global Mission, The Story of Alcan.* Vol 1: *To 1950.* np: Ontario Publishing Company, 1985
Canada. Royal Commission on Corporate Concentration. *Alcan Aluminium Ltd. – A Case Study.* Study No. 13. Ottawa, 1977
McGuire, B.J. 'Aluminum, The Story of Fifty Years of Growth by the Canadian Industry.' *Canadian Geographical Journal* 43, no. 4 (Oct 1951): 144–63

PLATE 56

Ottawa: The Emerging Capital

JOHN TAYLOR History, Carleton University

Invaluable information and comment were provided by the following: members of Architectural History, Parks Canada, notably Sally Coutts; Public Works Canada; the planning, policy, and engineering departments, the library, and the chief photographer of the National Capital Commission, notably Michael Newton and William DeGrace; the planning branch of the City of Ottawa; the map divisions of the NAC and Statistics Canada.

The capital landscape
Thanks to John Roaf for permission to use the photographs of the National War Memorial, Langevin Block, Supreme Court of Canada, Dominion Bureau of Statistics, and Sir Alexander Campbell Building, previously published in *Exploring Ottawa* (1983), and to Harold D. Kalman for negotiating that permission. Thanks to Joan Schwartz, Chief, Photography Acquisition and Research Section, Documentary Art and Photography Division, NAC, for searching out photographs of the early Parliament Buildings, Rideau Hall, the Connaught Building, the East Memorial Building, and the wartime temporary buildings. The drawings for publication were based on these photographs and were done by the cartographic staff of the Historical Atlas of Canada project.
City of Ottawa. Planning Branch. 'Generalized Existing Land Use.' Official Plan of the Ottawa Planning Area. Rev May 1961
Kalman, Harold D., and John Roaf. *Exploring Ottawa*. Toronto: University of Toronto Press, 1983. Pp 4, 8, 13, 150, 183
NAC. C 4961, 10010. PA 9280, 43766, 138609, 166791
National Atlas of Canada. 3rd ed, rev. Ottawa, 1957. Pl 10
National Capital Commission. 'Ottawa and Environs.' 1961. Map
'Pathfinder Map of Ottawa.' 1965

The changing work-force
'Service' does not include public administration, which has been designated as a separate category. 'Other' includes agriculture, logging, fishing, trapping, mining, quarrying, and unspecified.
Canada. *Census*. 1911: Vol 6, Table VI. 1921: Vol 4, Table 5. 1931, Vol 7, Table 41. 1941, Vol 7, Table 22. 1951: Vol 4, Table 17. 1961: Vol 3, Pt 1, Table 7

Growth of the civil service
Canada figures represent all civil servants in municipal, provincial, and federal governments across Canada except those on active service in 1941. Ottawa figures represent only those civil servants employed by the federal government, except in 1921 and 1931 when provincial government employees were included. (The number of provincial government employees in Ottawa numbered only 75 in 1941.) Ottawa figures are based on place of residence rather than place of employment.
Leacy. *Historical Statistics*. Series D8-85
Taylor, John H. *Ottawa: An Illustrated History*. Toronto: Lorimer, 1986. P 212

Proposals for a parliamentary precinct: Holt Plan, Gréber Plan
National Capital Commission, Planning Branch, and Public Works Canada. *Parliamentary Precinct: Previous Studies*. Ottawa, 1985. Pp 10–11, 14–15

Expenditure on government buildings
The largest individual expenditures indicate the portion spent during the decade specified; they do not indicate the total amount spent on the building if part of that amount was expended in the previous or following decade. Decadal average deflators were used in calculating the 1913 constant-dollar figures. Total expenditures for 1960–7 exclude buildings started, but not finished in this period. The dates of building construction used on the graph were those provided by Parks Canada. The graph excludes Department of National Defence construction and crown corporations.
Canada. Department of Public Works. 'Inventory of Expenditures on Buildings under the Jurisdiction of the Department of Public Works, 1859–1967.' Ottawa, nd

Improving the capital region
National Capital Commission. 'The National Capital Commission: Its History, Mandate and Organization.' Ottawa, nd

City centre to national centre
Goad's Atlas and Plan Co. 'Fire Insurance Plans of the City of Ottawa.' 1901: Sheets 31–4. 1922: Sheets 31–4. 1956–63: Vol 1, Sheets 113–5, 123–3, 124–1,2
Might's Directory of the City of Ottawa. 1935

Further readings
Taylor, John H. 'City Form and Capital Culture: Remaking Ottawa.' *Planning Perspectives* 4 (1989): 79–105

PLATE 57

Canadians Abroad

NORMAN HILLMER Directorate of History, Department of National Defence, Ottawa
MURDO MacPHERSON Historical Atlas of Canada, Toronto
NEIL QUIGLEY Economics, Victoria University, Wellington, New Zealand

Ties with the United States
For data on the Distant Early Warning (DEW) line see pl 58.
Air Plotting Charts, Canada 1/3 m
Canada. Department of National Defence. Directorate of History. Correspondence from Directorate of Ground Environmental Control, Royal Canadian Air Force Headquarters. Ottawa. 7 Feb 1959
Coates, P. *The Alaska Highway: Papers of the 40th Annual Anniversary Symposium*. Vancouver: University of British Columbia Press, 1985
International Joint Commission. *Annual Report* 1975

Ottawa's representation abroad
Canada. *Royal Commission on Conditions of Foreign Service*. 1981. Pp 95–105
Taylor, Alastair MacDonald, David Cox, and J.L. Granatstein. *Peacekeeping: International Challenge and Canadian Response*. Toronto: Canadian Institute of International Affairs, 1968. Pp 194–6, App B

Total posts abroad
The graph shows the total number of posts existing each year. This total reflects the addition of new posts and the removal of closed ones.
Canada. *Royal Commission on Conditions of Foreign Service*. 1981. Pp 95–105

United Nations Expanded Program and Special Fund
Canada Year Book. 1963–4. Pp 192–7
United Nations Yearbook. 1960. Pp 239–40, 247

Canadian external aid: United Nations programs
Spicer, James Keith. *A Samaritan State: External Aid in Canada's Foreign Policy*. Toronto: University of Toronto Press, 1966. Pp 252–3, App B

United Nations forces in Korea
Wood, Herbert Farlie. *Strange Battleground: The Operations in Korea and Their Effects on the Defence Policy in Canada*. Ottawa: Queen's Printer, 1966. Pp 12–13

Branches of Canadian banks abroad
Bank of Montreal. *Annual Report*. 1914, 1961
Bank of Montreal Archives. Montréal
Bank of Nova Scotia. *Annual Report*. 1914, 1961
Banque Canadienne Nationale. 1874, 1974: Banque Canadian Nationale. Montréal, 1974
Canada Year Book. 1917, 1961
Canadian Annual Review of Public Affairs. 1911–14
Canadian Imperial Bank of Commerce. *Annual Report*. 1914, 1961
Denison, Merrill. *Canada's First Bank: A History of the Bank of Montreal*. Vol 2. Toronto: McClelland and Stewart, 1967
Dominion Bank / Toronto Dominion Bank. *Annual Report*. 1914, 1961
Merchants Bank. *Annual Report*. 1914
Royal Bank of Canada. *Annual Report*. 1914, 1961
Royal Bank of Canada Archives. Montréal

Bank branches by region
Bank of Montreal Archives. Montréal
Bank of Nova Scotia. *Annual Report*. 1905, 1910, 1914
Banque Canadian Nationale. 1874, 1974: Banque Canadian Nationale. 1974
Canada Year Book. 1917, 1921–62. Table, 'Canadian Chartered Banks in Other Countries' (variously titled)
Canadian Annual Review of Public Affairs. 1911–14
Canadian Imperial Bank of Commerce. *Annual Report*. 1890, 1895, 1900, 1905, 1914
Denison. *Canada's First Bank*. 1967
Garland, N.S. *Garland's Banks, Bankers and Banking in Canada*. Ottawa: Mortimer, 1890
Royal Bank of Canada. *Annual Report*. 1902, 1905, 1910, 1914, 1919
Royal Bank of Canada Archives. Montréal
Schull, Joseph, and J. Douglas Gibson. *The Scotiabank Story: A History of the Bank of Nova Scotia, 1832–1982*. Toronto: Macmillan, 1982

Premium income of Canadian life-insurance companies
Canada. Department of Insurance. *Annual Report*. 1890–1959

The outpouring of missionaries
The map shows the initial period of mission establishment only. Not all missions remained in operation in 1958, especially in China where missionaries were forced to withdraw following the establishment of the People's Republic of China.
'Co-operating societies' include Congregational and Lutheran missionaries. All the Methodist and Congregational (Co-operating Society, Angola) missions and specific Presbyterian missions, indicated in the legend, went to the United Church after 1925.
Bartholomew, John, Harlan Pase Beach, and Charles Harvey Fahs, eds. *World Missionary Atlas: Containing a Directory of Missionary Societies*. New York: Institute of Social and Religious Research, 1925
Dayton, E.R., ed. *Mission Handbook: North American Protestant Missionaries Overseas*. Monrovia, Ca: Missions Advanced Research and Communications Centre, 1976
Goddard, Burton L., ed. *Encyclopedia of Modern Christian Missions*. Camden, NJ: Thomas Nelson, 1967
Prêtre et Missions. *Esquimaux: Études sur les missions Esquimaux Canadiennes*. Vol 12. Union Missionnaire du Clergé. July–Sep 1953
Union Missionnaire du Clergé. *Bulletin* 2 (Apr 1933): 398–405
Union Pontificale Missionnaire du Clergé. *Messages* 15 (Jan–June 1959): 59–93

PLATE 58

Economies and Societies in the North

PETER J. USHER P.J. Usher Consulting Services, Ottawa

Thanks to Michael Asch and Tom Andrews, Dene Mapping Project (Anthropology, University of Alberta), for providing data on Dene land use, and to the Dene Nation, Yellowknife, NWT, for permission to publish it. Thanks also to Dan Mackay, Geographical Services Directorate, Energy, Mines and Resources, Ottawa, for providing access to research files on the 'Northern Settlements' plate, *The National Atlas of Canada*, 4th ed (1974).
For this plate the North includes all territorial land in Canada north of the 60th parallel but not settlement south of 60° in the Northwest Territories (Belcher and other islands offshore in Hudson Bay) or settlements in Québec north of the 60th parallel. Posts and sites are mapped only if they were in operation for at least one year and involved the stationing of personnel; white trapper routes and areas are not mapped.

Population composition
Birthplace of immigrants
Population data were derived from the census except in the following cases: (1) In the Northwest Terrritories ethnic breakdowns in 1931 came from Fumoleau (1975) and in 1951 from *Arctic Circular* (1953), revised figures. (2) In the Northwest Territories in 1931 the numbers of those born in Québec were estimated at 100. The census gives the anomalous figure of 881; it would seem that a large part of the eastern Arctic Inuit population was recorded as having been born in Arctic Québec. In no other cases does the census appear to do this as virtually all native people are recorded as having been born in the North (even where this is not, in fact, the case). To all intents and purposes, therefore, the graph of the birthplace of immigrant population does not include native people; rather it is intended to portray the geographic origins of the adult non-native populations of the two territories.

The Indian population does not include Métis. Only the 1941 census identifies Métis separately, and in that year there were 193 in the Yukon Territory and 282 in the Northwest Territories. It would appear that in all other years Métis are included in the non-native ethnic groups, based on paternal lineage.

Early censuses may underestimate Indian and especially Inuit populations. The censuses of 1951 and 1961 are considered accurate. In the Yukon Territory Indian totals include 30 Inuit in 1951 and 40 Inuit in 1961.

Canada. *Census.* 1921, 1931, 1941, 1951, 1961
Fumoleau, René. *As Long as This Land Shall Last: A History of Treaty 8 and Treaty 11, 1870–1939.* Toronto: McClelland and Stewart, 1975
'The 1951 Census in the Northwest Territories.' *Arctic Circular* 6, no. 4 (1953): 37–43

The whale fishery and the arctic fox trade
The number of whaling vessels includes vessels in Davis Strait, Hudson Bay, and the Beaufort Sea. The number of Arctic fur-trade posts include posts in the Arctic portions of the Northwest Territories where white fox was the sole item of trade. During these years there were 10 to 15 additional fur-trade posts in Arctic Québec dependent on the white fox trade.

Ross, W. Gillies. 'The Annual Catch of Greenland (Bowhead) Whales in Waters North of Canada 1719–1915: A Preliminary Compilation.' *Arctic* 32, no. 2 (June 1979): 91–121, esp Tables 3, 4, 5
Usher, P.J. *Fur Trade Posts of the Northwest Territories 1870–1970.* NSRG–71–4. Ottawa: Department of Indian Affairs and Northern Development, Northern Science Research Group, 1971

Value of fur and metallic-mineral production
Rea, K.J. *The Political Economy of the Canadian North.* Toronto: University of Toronto Press, 1968. Tables 3.1, 4.4, 4.5

Non-native institutions
Native land use
Freeman, M.M.R., ed. *Report, Inuit Land Use and Occupancy Project.* Ottawa: Department of Indian Affairs and Northern Development, 1976
Hunt, Constance. 'The Development and Decline of Northern Conservation Reserves.' *Contact* 8, no. 4 (Nov 1976): 30–75
The National Atlas of Canada. 4th ed, rev. Ottawa: Macmillan / Department of Energy, Mines and Resources and Information Canada, 1974. Original research files of P.J. Usher for 'Northern Settlements,' pp 87–8
Smith, James G.E., and Ernest S. Burch, Jr. 'Chipewyan amd Inuit in the Central Canadian Subarctic, 1613–1977.' *Arctic Anthroplogy* 16, no. 2 (1979): 76–101

Further readings
Coates, Kenneth. *Canada's Colonies: A History of the Yukon and Northwest Territories.* Toronto: Lorimer, 1985
Cooke, Alan, and Clive Holland. *The Exploration of Northern Canada, 500 to 1920.* Toronto: Arctic History Press, 1978
Usher, Peter J. 'The North: One Land, Two Ways of Life.' In L.D. McCann, ed. *Heartland and Hinterland: A Geography of Canada.* 2nd ed. Scarborough: Prentice-Hall, 1987. Pp 483–529
Zaslow, Morris. *The Northwest Expansion of Canada, 1914–1967.* Toronto: McClelland and Stewart, 1988
– *The Opening of the Canadian North, 1870–1914.* Toronto: McClelland and Stewart, 1971

PLATE 59

Population Changes

WARREN KALBACH   Sociology, University of Toronto
DONALD KERR   Geography, University of Toronto
MARVIN McINNIS   Economics, Queen's University

Interprovincial migration
Canada. *Census.* 1961. Vol 4, Pt 1 (Bull 4.1–9), Table 14
George, M.V. *Internal Migration in Canada: Demographic Analyses.* DBS. 1961 Census Monograph. Ottawa, 1970. Ch 6, Appendix (various tables)
Stone, Leroy O. *Migration in Canada: Some Regional Aspects.* DBS. 1961 Census Monograph. Ottawa, 1969. Section 2.2, Appendix (various tables)

Demographic change
For non-metropolitan urban areas and for rural sectors of counties and census divisions containing metropolitan urbanized areas, estimates have been made by McInnis based on the census.
Canada. *Census.* 1961. Vol 7, Pt 1 (Bull 7.1–2), Table x

Immigration population
Canada. *Census.* 1961. Vol 1, Pt 1 (Bull 1.3–11), Tables 125–6

Net migration
Canada. *Census.* 1961. Vol 7, Pt 1, Table 2

Gross reproduction rate
The Gross Reproduction Rate (GRR) is a widely used measure of fertility that is free from the influence of age composition. For that reason it is better suited than crude birth rates for comparison across geographic areas. The GRR is usually interpreted in a cohort sense, that is, if age-specific fertility rates continued at their given level, the GRR would measure the number of female children women would bear, on average, over their span of reproductive years. A GRR value of 1.00 would indicate a population that is just reproducing itself. No adjustment is made for survival (hence the *gross* rate). Another way of describing the GRR is as the sum of age-specific fertility rates, multiplied by the fraction of births that is female children. The age weights are taken to be equal (a rectangular distribution).

The choice of GRR is, in part, dictated by the availability of those rates for counties, cities, and towns of more than 5 000 population for 1940–2. Those are found in the 1941 census monograph on fertility by Charles (1948). They are the only properly constructed measures of fertility available for subprovincial areas in Canada for that date. In most parts of the nation fertility in 1941 was still very close to the all-time low reached in the mid–1930s. Nationally the GRR reached its Baby Boom peak in 1959, but it fell slowly at first and by 1961 was down only 2½% from the peak. The period shown thus spans the full extent of the Baby Boom. A tabulation of births by place of residence of mother is readily available for the 1960–2 births period. The problem is that there are no age-specific fertility rates for counties and towns. The GRR for 1960–2 is approximated by factoring the GRR into two component indices that can be separately calculated and recombined. The procedure ignores a small, indeterminate interaction term. An index of births to women 15–49 years of age as a whole could be directly calculated. It was then modified by an index of the deviation of local from national age composition of women (where women in each age group are weighted by the national average age-specific fertility rates). A comparison of this estimated GRR with values directly calculated for provinces and large cities (for which the requisite data are available) shows a close match. See McInnis (1988).
Canada. DBS. *Vital Statistics.* 1900, 1961, 1962. Tables s6, s7
Charles, Enid. *The Changing Size of the Family in Canada.* 1941 Census Monograph No 1. Ottawa, 1948
McInnis, Marvin. 'Geographic Dimensions of the Baby Boom in Canada.' Unpublished report submitted to the Historical Atlas of Canada project, Vol III, 1988

Total fertility rate
Canada. Statistics Canada. *Vital Statistics.* Cats. 84–204, 84–206. 1971

Natural increase
Net migration
Canada. Statistics Canada. *Vital Statistics.* Cats. 84–204, 84–206. 1971
Urquhart and Buckley. *Historical Statistics.* Series A233–43, A244–53

Further readings
Beaujot, Roderic, and Kevin McQuillan. *Canadian Dualism, The Demographic Development of Canadian Society.* Toronto: Gage, 1982
Butz, William, and Michael P. Ward. 'Will U.S. Fertility Remain Low? A New Economic Interpretation.' *Population and Development Review* 5 (1979): 663–88
Easterlin, Richard. *Birth and Fortune.* New York: Basic Books, 1980
Kalbach, W.E. *The Impact of Immigration on Canada's Population.* DBS. 1961 Census Monograph. Ottawa, 1970
Kalbach W.E., and W.E. McVey. *Demographic Basis of Canadian Society.* 2nd ed. Toronto: McGraw Hill Ryerson, Toronto, 1979

PLATE 60

Growth of Metropolitan Toronto

DERYCK W. HOLDSWORTH   Geography, Pennsylvania State University

The assistance of Gunter Gad (Geography, University of Toronto) in the preparation of this plate is gratefully acknowledged. Thanks are also due to Rachel Pitch, head of the Urban Affairs Branch of the North York Library System, for her help in securing publications and maps on the Don Mills study.

Metropolitan Toronto
Goldenberg, J. Carl. *Report of the Ontario Royal Commission on Metropolitan Toronto.* Toronto: Queen's Printer, 1965
Lemon, James T. *Toronto Since 1918 – An Illustrated History.* Toronto: Lorimer, 1985. App, Tables I, II

Ethnic mosaic
Dean, W.G., and G. Matthews. *Economic Atlas of Ontario.* Toronto: University of Toronto Press, 1969. Pl 22, Map No. 5

Ethnic origin
Lemon. *Toronto Since 1918.* 1985. App, Table VIII

Religious affiliation
Lemon. *Toronto Since 1918.* 1985. App, Table IX

Post-war expansion
Built-up area includes parks, recreation areas, cemeteries, and golf courses where they are a contiguous part of the urban area.
Canada. Department of National Defence. Topographic Survey Sheets R 3400.63, 1929. Revisions 1936 to 1943. Bolton, Markham, Brampton, and Toronto sheets
Hooper, N.A. 'Toronto – A Study in Urban Geography.' MA thesis, University of Toronto, 1941 (with modifications)
Metropolitan Toronto Planning Board. *The Official Plan of Metropolitan Toronto Planning Area.* Draft. Toronto, 1959. Pp 24, 42

The suburban fringe
Metropolitan Toronto Planning Board. *The Official Plan.* 1959. Pl 24, 'General Land Use 1958'

Don Mills

LAND USE
Borough of North York. North York Planning Board. District 4–5 Plan. Apr 1971. Land Use Map A (modified by author)

AN AERIAL VIEW
Northway Map Technology Limited, Toronto

OCCUPATIONS
POPULATION PROFILE
Data are for census tracts 191 and 290.
Canada. *Census.* Cat. 95–530. 1961. Tables 1, 3

Regent Park North Housing Project

City of Toronto Archives. MT00925. City of Toronto Planning Board, Drawing No. 12C. Dec 1957
City of Toronto Planning Board. *Third Annual Report.* 30 Dec 1944

Further readings

Bourne, Larry S. *Private Redevelopment of the Central City: Spatial Processes of Structural Change in the City of Toronto.* Geography Research Paper No. 112. Chicago: University of Chicago Press, 1967
City of Toronto Planning Board. *Report on the Ethnic Origins of the Population of Toronto.* Toronto, 1961
Kaplan, Harold. *Urban Political Systems, A Functional Analysis in Metropolitan Toronto.* New York: Columbia University Press, 1967
Rose, Albert. *Governing Metropolitan Toronto: A Social and Political Analysis, 1953–1971.* Berkeley: University of California Press, 1972
– *Regent Park: A Study in Slum Clearance.* Toronto: University of Toronto Press, 1958
Sewell, John. 'Don Mills, E.P. Taylor and Canada's First Suburb.' *City Magazine* 2 (Jan 1977): 28–38
Spelt, Jacob. *Toronto.* Toronto: Collier Macmillan, 1973

PLATE 61

The Changing Work-Force

LYNNE MARKS   PHD candidate, History, York University

Work-force participation

Leacy. *Historical Statistics.* Series D107–22

Women: paid work and marital status

For 1921, 1931, and 1961 the work-force is based on persons 15 years and over as is the number of persons by marital status. For the years 1941 and 1951 the work-force includes persons 14 years and older while the figures by marital status are based on persons 15 years and over. Note that for 1921, 1931, and 1941 the concept of gainfully occupied rather than labour force was used. 'Labour force' is defined as that portion of the civilian population employed or unemployed (but seeking work) whereas 'gainfully occupied' is defined as those who regularly engage in an occupation whether or not they are working or seeking work on census date. This definition tended to underestimate the proportion of women, especially married women, and particularly if they are working part-time (since their main occupation may be seen as homemaker).
Canada. *Census.* 1931: Vol 7, Table 26. 1941: Vol 1, Table 63, Vol 3, Table 7. 1951: Vol 4, Table 11. 1961: Vol 3, Pt 1, Table 17
Leacy. *Historical Statistics.* Series A110–24

The work-force, 1961

Totals exclude the Yukon and Northwest Territories. The category 'forestry, fishing, trapping, mining' includes quarries, oil wells, and milling associated with mining.
Canada. *Census.* 1961. Vol 3, Pt 2, Table 1A
– Department of Labour. *Labour Organizations in Canada.* 1961

Post-war immigrants and employment

'Post-war immigrants' refers to those persons who immigrated to Canada between 1946 and 1961, although figures used for 1961 are for the first five months only. Totals also exclude the Yukon and Northwest Territories. The industrial sectors used are the same as for 'The work-force, 1961.'
Canada. *Census.* 1961. Vol 3, Pt 2, Table 11
Davis, N.H.W., and Gupta, M.L. *Labour Force Characteristics of Post-War Immigrants and Native-Born Canadians 1956–67.* DBS. Special Labour Force Studies No. 6. Ottawa, 1968. Table D8

Occupational inequality among males in Québec

Porter, John. *The Vertical Mosaic: An Analysis of Social Class and Power in Canada.* Toronto: University of Toronto Press, 1965. P 94, Table III

Divisions of labour

Canadian totals exclude Yukon and the Northwest Territories and include Newfoundland in 1951 and 1961 only. The figures for 1941 exclude persons on active service on 2 June 1941. In 1921 'clerical' includes proofreaders, shippers, weighmen, and postmen, classified elsewhere in other years. 'Logging, fishing, hunting, mining' includes trapping and quarrying for all years and almost all mine and smelter employees, except clerical workers in 1911. Totals for Indians living on reserves were excluded for the years 1921 and 1951. 'Logging' includes pulp-mill employees in 1911. 'Manufacturing and mechanical' includes stationary enginemen and occupations associated with electric-power production. 'Construction and transportation' includes communication. The category 'labourers' includes all labourers in all industries except those engaged in agriculture, fishing, logging, or mining.
Canada. *Census.* 1961. Vol 3, Pt 1, Table 3

The feminization of clerical work

For 1961 the information on office clerks was derived from the census category 'clerical, not elsewhere specified.'
Canada. *Census.* 1941: Vol 7, Table 4. 1961: Vol 3, Pt 1, Table 6
Lowe, Graham S. *Women in the Administrative Revolution: The Feminization of Clerical Work.* Toronto: University of Toronto Press, 1987. Table 3.1
Meltz, Noah M. *Manpower in Canada 1931 to 1961: Historical Statistics of the Canadian Labour Force.* Ottawa: Department of Manpower and Immigration Canada, 1969

Montréal clerical workers

Montreal Board of Trade. Employee Relations Section. 'Annual Survey of Clerical Salaries, 1954'

Civil servants, Federal Bureau of Statistics, Ottawa, 1952

NAC. PA–133212. The photograph appears in Linteau, Durocher, Robert, and Richard (1986), p 351 (see 'Further readings').

Emergence of the computer age

Although the graph lists a total of 89 industrial firms using computers, the addresses of only 81 were available for mapping.
Canada. Department of Labour. *The Current Status of Electronic Data Processing.* 1960

Further readings

Armstrong, Pat, and Hugh Armstrong. *The Double Ghetto: Canadian Women and Their Segregated Work.* Toronto: McClelland and Stewart, 1978
Burnet, Jean R., with Howard Palmer. *'Coming Canadians': An Introduction to a History of Canada's Peoples.* Toronto: McClelland and Stewart, 1988
Danys, Milda. *DP: Lithuanian Immigration to Canada After the Second World War.* Toronto: Multicultural History Society of Ontario, 1986
Heron, Craig, and Robert Storey. *On the Job: Confronting the Labour Process in Canada.* Montréal: McGill-Queen's University Press, 1986
Iacovetta, Franca. 'From Contadina to Worker: Southern Italian Immigrant Working Women in Toronto, 1947–1962.' In Jean Burnet, ed. *Looking into My Sister's Eyes: An Exploration in Women's History.* Toronto: Multicultural History Society of Toronto, 1986
Linteau, Paul-André, René Durocher, Jean-Claude Robert, and François Richard. *Histoire du Québec contemporain: Le Québec depuis 1930.* Montréal: Boréal Press, 1986
Luxton, Meg. *More Than a Labour of Love: Three Generations of Women's Work in the Home.* Toronto: Women's Press, 1980
McRoberts, Kenneth. *Quebec: Social Change and Political Crisis.* 3rd ed. Toronto: McClelland and Stewart, 1988

PLATE 62

Organized Labour, Strikes, and Politics

DOUGLAS CRUIKSHANK   PHD candidate, History, Simon Fraser University
GREGORY S. KEALEY   History, Memorial University of Newfoundland

We are grateful for the research and archivist aid of Peter DeLottinville and John Smart, Department of Labour records, NAC.

Union membership by province, industry, and affiliation

In 1950 the Department of Labour began estimating membership as of 1 Jan rather than 31 Dec. Consequently there are no statistics for 1950. In 1942 several minor changes were made to the industrial classification system, including the addition of a category for wood and wood products. A more significant change was made in 1949 when the department began using reports submitted by union locals rather than union headquarters to calculate membership according to the Standard Industrial Classification System of 1948.
On the graph showing membership by affiliation the Canadian Congress of Labour (CCL) only (international), American Federation of Labor–Congress of Industrial Organizations (AFL-CIO) only, CIO only, Industrial Workers of the World, AFL only, and Trades and Labor Congress (TLC) only (international) were included in the 'otherwise or unaffiliated international' category unless their memberships exceeded 5% of the total in the period between 1941 and 1960. Similarly, the National Council of Canadian Labour, TLC only, One Big Union, and Canadian Federation of Labour were sometimes included in the 'otherwise or unaffiliated national' category.
See pl 39 for further explanations.
Canada. Department of Labour. *Labour Organizations in Canada.* 1941–60
'Industrial and Geographic Distribution of Union Membership in Canada.' *Labour Gazette* 60 (Aug 1960): 782–8; 61 (Apr 1961): 342–8

Labour politics

For sources and explanation see pll 38, 45.

Frequency, size, and duration of strikes

Since the Department of Labour stopped preparing Trade Dispute Record sheets in 1944, the strikes and lockouts clippings files were used to carry forward to 1956 the revisions described on pl 39. After 1956 the department stopped compiling complete strike lists, making revisions of the official statistics for 1957–60 impractical. The absence of complete lists also made the calculation of mean duration for 1957–60 impossible. Instead, for these years only, the total number of person-days lost (striker days) was divided by the total number of workers involved.
In the 1940s the department began to abandon its practice of counting each stoppage in a recurring or rotating strike separately, provided that the stoppages did not overlap. The data were revised in order to correct this inconsistency.
Canada. Department of Labour. Economics and Research Branch. *Strikes and Lockouts in Canada.* 1952–60
Labour Gazette. 1942–7
NAC. Records of the Department of Labour. Strikes and Lockouts. RG 27, Vols 443–520, 2276–8, 2290–2326, 2341–2
Strikes and Lockouts in Canada. Supplement to *Labour Gazette.* 1948–52

Strike issues, methods of settlement, and results
The Department of Labour stopped publishing complete strike lists with data on issues after 1956, statistics on settlement after 1955, and figures on results after 1953.

See pl 39 for further explanations.

For sources see 'Frequency, size, and duration of strikes' above.

Strikes by industry
On the graph for 1943 'inter-industry' includes two strikes in Nova Scotia involving workers in coal mining, salt mining, metal manufacturing, shipbuilding, and public administration. A British Columbia strike involving workers in both the logging and wood-manufacturing industries was counted as inter-industrial on the 1946 graph.

On the map all but two strikes occurring in more than one place were disaggregatd by location: it was impossible to estimate striker days by location for logging strikes in Ontario and British Columbia because of insufficient data.

Labour Gazette 44 (Mar 1944): 326–53; 47 (Mar 1947): 435–51

NAC. Records of the Department of Labour. Strikes and Lockouts. RG 27, Vols 426–34, 444–52, 2301, 2314

Proceedings under the Industrial Disputes Investigation (IDI) Act
IDI Act proceedings by industry
Data are for the years ending 31 Mar 1908–44.

Canada. Department of Labour. *Annual Report*. 1944

Conciliation proceedings
The graphs are not strictly comparable because of slightly different conciliation procedures and different fiscal years. The procedures and fiscal years for each jurisdiction are as follows:

Dominion. New conciliation-officer cases and boards of conciliation established under the Wartime Labour Relations Regulations (1944) during the 12 months ending 31 Mar 1945 to 1947 and 17 months ending 31 Aug 1948; and under the Industrial Relations and Disputes Investigation Act (1948) during 7 months ending 31 Mar 1949 and 12 months ending 31 Mar 1950 to 1960

British Columbia. New conciliation-officer cases and boards of conciliation established under the Industrial Conciliation and Arbitration Act (1947) and the Labour Relations Act (1954) during the 12 months ending 31 Dec 1948 to 1960

Alberta. New conciliation-commission cases and boards of arbitration established under the Alberta Labour Act (1947) during the 12 months ending 31 Dec 1948, 7 months ending 31 Oct 1949, and 12 months ending 31 Dec 1951 to 1960

Saskatchewan. New informal conciliations and boards of conciliation established under the Trade Union Act (1944) during the 12 months ending 31 Dec 1948 to 1951, 15 months ending 31 Mar 1953, and 12 months ending 31 Mar 1953 to 1960

Manitoba. New conciliation-officer cases and boards of conciliation established under the Manitoba Wartime Labour Relations Regulations (1944) and the Manitoba Labour Relations Act (1948) during the 12 months ending 31 Mar 1948 to 1957, and 12 months ending 31 Dec 1958 to 1960

Ontario. New conciliation-officer appointments and boards of conciliation established under the Labour Relations Board Act (1947), the Labour Relations Act (1948), and the Labour Relations Act (1950) during the 12 months ending 31 Mar 1948 to 1960

Quebec. New conciliatory interventions and councils of arbitration established under the Quebec Trade Disputes Act (1941) during the 12 months ending 31 Mar 1948 to 1960

New Brunswick. New conciliation-officer cases and boards of conciliation under the Labour Relations Act (1945) and the Labour Relations Act (1949) during the 12 months ending 31 Oct 1948 to 1950, 17 months ending 31 Mar 1952, and 12 months ending 31 Mar 1953 to 1960

Nova Scotia. New conciliation-officer cases and boards of conciliation established under the Trade Union Act (1947) during the 12 months ending 30 Nov 1948 to 1949, 16 months ending 31 Mar 1951, and 12 months ending 31 Mar 1952 to 1960

Alberta. Board of Industrial Relations. *Bulletin*. 1948–60

British Columbia. Department of Labour. *Annual Report*. 1948–60

Canada. Department of Labour. *Annual Report*. 1948–60

Manitoba. Department of Labour. *Annual Report*. 1948–60

New Brunswick. Department of Labour. *Annual Report*. 1948–60

Newfoundland. Department of Labour. *Annual Report*. 1950–60

Nova Scotia. Department of Labour. *Annual Report*. 1948–60

Ontario. Department of Labour. *Annual Report*. 1948–60

Québec. Minister of Labour. *Annual Report*. 1948–60

Changes in manufacturing collective agreements
The Department of Labour prepared this graph to illustrate the major changes occurring in collective agreements in Canadian manufacturing industries between 1952 and 1956. Out of more than 3 000 contracts on file, the department sampled 564 agreements, covering 343 100 workers, in 1952, and 458 agreements, covering 308 500 workers, in 1956.

Maintenance of union membership means that workers are required to keep up membership for the length of their contracts or else lose their jobs.

Labour Gazette 53 (Feb 1953): 221–8; 57 (Apr 1957): 454–63

Workers covered by collective agreements
Labour Gazette 57 (Dec 1957): 1473

PLATE 63

The Emergence of Social Insurance

LYNNE MARKS PH D candidate, History, York University

I would like to thank Peter Hajnal and the staff at Government Documents, Robarts Library, University of Toronto, for their assistance.

Early forms of social insurance, Ontario
The data on fraternal benefit societies include those licensed by both the federal and the provincial governments; prior to 1925 only Canada-wide data are available. The figures on mutual benefit societies prior to 1925 include only those

that did not provide life insurance (since from 1925 mutual benefit societies were defined as such by virtue of not providing life insurance). To make the figures for fraternal benefit associations comparable with those for mutual benefit societies, life-insurance benefits paid out by the former were not include in the graph. Sick benefits refer to money paid to people when they were sick and not able to work; this was not medical insurance. The medical and hospital benefits were a form of health insurance. Employee mutual benefit associations include union-, employee-, and employer-sponsored organizations because the data did not always separate them.

Ontario. Superintendent of Insurance and Registrar of Friendly Societies. *Annual Report*. 1900–60

Growth of medical insurance, Canada
Municipal Doctors Plans, Saskatchewan
The graph on medical insurance refers only to medical insurance, not to hospital insurance, when it is possible to differentiate the two. Non-profit insurance is offered by agencies not seeking to make a profit from the insurance, such as doctors' associations, trade unions, employee organizations, co-operatives, industries, or municipalities. Private insurance is offered by companies seeking to make a profit. 'Non-profit' and 'private' insurance includes both individual and group coverage. One must assume that there was some overlap in enrolment between private and non-profit plans. To eliminate this overlap the formula used by the Department of Health and Welfare in *Voluntary Medical Insurance* (1955–61) was employed. When both medical and surgical insurance were offered, by either private or non-profit plans, there would be considerable overlap; only surgical insurance, the more common form, was counted.

In the municipal doctor system in Saskatchewan municipalities would employ a physician on a contract basis. Through prepaid tax premiums people in municipalities having such plans would receive basic services of a general practitioner and a range of additional benefits which varied among municipalities. Many municipalities had similar plans for local hospital services. The other Prairie Provinces had similar plans, although they were less widespread. In the Newfoundland Cottage Hospital Plan hospital, medical, and nursing care were provided on a prepaid basis throughout much of the province (only those with nursing or medical care are shown on the graph). With the development of federal hospital insurance in 1958 the plan was limited to medical insurance. Although premiums were required for the Newfoundland plan, the program was heavily subsidized by the provincial government.

Canada. Department of National Health and Welfare. *Selected Public Hospital and Medical Plans in Canada*. Ottawa, July 1955

– Department of National Health and Welfare. *Voluntary Medical Insurance in Canada*. 1955–61

– Joint Committee on Health Insurance. *Financing Health Services in Canada*. 1956

– Royal Commission on Health Services. *Hearings*. Vol 6. 1961

Leacy. *Historical Statistics*. B514–16

Rorem, C. Rufus. *The Municipal Doctor System in Rural Saskatchewan*. Committee on the Costs of Medical Care. Publication No. 11. Chicago: University of Chicago, 1931

Saskatchewan. Commission on Medical Insurance. *Report*. 1962

– Department of Public Health. *Annual Report*. 1938–60

– Department of Public Health. 'Health Survey Report.' Vol 1. 1951

– Department of Public Health. 'Interim Report of the Advisory Planning Committee on Medical Care to the Government of Saskatchewan.' 1961

Taylor, Malcolm G. *Health Insurance and Canadian Public Policy*. Montréal: McGill-Queen's University Press, 1978

Health insurance and access to medical care
Canada. DBS. *Canadian Sickness Survey, 1950–51*. Ottawa, 1956

Deaths from tuberculosis
Canada. DBS. *Special Report on Occupational Mortality in Canada*. 1931–2. Table V

Passage of social-welfare legislation
Alberta had its own disabled persons act one year before that of the federal government but it was superseded by the federal act.

Canada. Health and Welfare Canada. *A Chronology of Social Welfare and Related Legislation 1908–1974: Selected Federal Statutes*. 1975

Guest, Dennis. *The Emergence of Social Security in Canada*. Vancouver: University of British Columbia Press, 1980

Statutes for all the provinces for the period 1919–61 were also used.

Government expenditures on health and welfare
Guest. *The Emergence of Social Security in Canada*. 1980. App, Table 1

Federal and provincial expenditures on health and welfare
Old-age assistance, disabled pensions, blind pensions, and unemployment assistance involve federal/provincial cost-sharing arrangements. Mothers' allowances, workers' compensation, and child welfare are provincially funded programs. In provincial expenditures the category of mothers' allowance, workers' compensation (non-medical), and child welfare also includes all other welfare expenditures not specified; the category of 'other health' includes general health, medical, dental, and allied services, and medical aid and hospitalization for workers' compensation. In British Columbia and Newfoundland mothers' allowances are included under unemployment assistance.

Canada. Department of National Health and Welfare. *Government Expenditures on Health and Welfare 1927–1959*. Ottawa, 1961. App 4, 5

Unemployment relief, Ontario
Ontario. Department of Labour. *Annual Report*. 1921: Tables XIV, XV. 1922: pp 33–6

Unemployment insurance, Canada
Total number of insured is that on 1 Apr 1951 based on a 10% sample. It does not include claimants.

Canada. *Census*. 1951. Vol 4, Table 16

Canada. DBS. *Annual Report on Benefit Years Established and Terminated under the Unemployment Insurance Act, Calendar Year 1951*. Tables 8, 13, 16

Work-related fatalities
Total industrial fatalities and compensated fatalities
Work-related fatalities in those industries not covered by workers' compensation boards, such as agriculture, fishing, trapping, and certain service industries, may be underestimated because the federal Department of Labour relied on newspaper reports in compiling figures for total industrial fatalities. Workers' compensation legislation does not cover the self-employed or owners. Wth regard to total industrial fatalities Ontario is overrepresented compared to other provinces because it is the only province in which at least some companies submitted reports of fatalities. Both compensated and total fatalities are averages of three years 1929–31 and 1959–61. During the period 1929–61 workers' compensation boards were known as workmen's compensation boards.
Canada. *Census.* 1931: Vol 7, Table 56. 1961: Vol 3, Pt 2, Table 1
Labour Gazette. 1930–2, 1960–2

Expenditure by provincial workers' compensation boards
For Ontario and Québec medical-aid expenditures include only those made by Schedule 1 employers since employers under Schedule 2 paid medical aid directly.
Canada Year Book. 1938, 1949
Leacy. *Historical Statistics.* Series E387–9

Further readings
Albert, Jim, and Allan Moscovitch, eds. *The 'Benevolent' State: The Growth of Welfare in Canada.* Toronto: Garamond Press, 1987
Naylor, C. David. *Private Practice, Public Payment: Canadian Medicine and the Politics of Health Insurance, 1911–1966.* Kingston and Montréal: McGill-Queen's University Press, 1986
Owram, Douglas. *The Government Generation: Canadian Intellectuals and the State 1900–1945.* Toronto: University of Toronto Press, 1986
Piva, Michael J. 'The Workmen's Compensation Movement in Ontario.' *Ontario History* 67 (1975): 39–56
Struthers, James. *No Fault of Their Own: Unemployment and the Canadian Welfare State.* Toronto: University of Toronto Press, 1983
Taylor, Malcolm G. *Health Insurance and Public Policy.* Montréal: McGill-Queen's University Press, 1978

PLATE 64
University Education

CHAD GAFFIELD   Histoire, Université d'Ottawa
LYNNE MARKS   PH D candidate, History, York University

We would like to thank Peter Hajnal and the staff at Government Documents, Robarts Library, University of Toronto, for their assistance.

Enrolment and teaching staff
Full undergraduate enrolment does not include normal-school students or nurses studying for registered nursing. Graduate enrolment does not include theology except in 1891, and includes both full-time and part-time students. Teaching staff does not include prematriculation but does include both full-time and part-time teachers and research staff at colleges and universities.
Canada. DBS. *Annual Survey of Education in Canada.* 1919–36
– DBS. *Biennial Survey of Higher Education in Canada.* 1936–52
– DBS. *Survey of Higher Education in Canada.* 1962–3. Tables 9, 14, 15, 16, 23
Canada Year Book. 1916
Harris, Robin. *A History of Higher Education in Canada, 1663–1960.* Toronto: University of Toronto Press, 1976

University funding
Operating expenditures per full-time student include graduate and undergraduate students and part-time graduate students.
Canada. DBS. *Biennial Survey of Higher Education in Canada.* 1946–8
– DBS. *Historical Compendium of Education Statistics.* 1978

Canadian students at foreign universities
Foreign students at Canadian universities
Figures for Canadian students in 1921 include Newfoundland students. Figures for 1942 (rather than 1940) were used for Canadian students in British universities. Foreign students at Canadian universities do not include Newfoundland students.
Association of Universities of the British Commonwealth. *Students from the King's Dominion Overseas and from Foreign Countries.* 1921
– *Report of the Executive Council.* 1943
Canada. DBS. *Survey of Higher Education in Canada.* 1954–61
Institute of International Education. *Annual Report.* 1931, 1946

Geographical mobility of university students
Canada. DBS. *Biennial Survey of Higher Education in Canada.* 1944: Table 14. 1950: Table 18

Enrolment in Canadian universities
Arts and science includes journalism. Fine art includes architecture and music; 1920, 1930, 1940, and 1950 figures are used instead of those for 1921, 1931, 1941, 1951.
Canada. DBS. *Annual Survey of Education in Canada.* 1922. Table 98
– DBS. *Biennial Survey of Higher Education in Canada.* 1950–2. Table 13
– DBS. *Historical Compendium of Education Statistics.* 1978. Table 23
– DBS. *Survey of Higher Education in Canada.* 1961. Table 13

Founding of university faculties
For the purposes of this study a faculty was defined as a university-level program from which a specialized diploma or degree could be obtained. It was sometimes difficult to assess the status of courses/faculties in the late 19th and early 20th centuries. Not included were programs offered at colleges which were not university-level and those that were not complete courses of study. Moreover, if a university offered a program in a particular subject for only a few years in the late 19th or early 20th centuries and then established a school, department, or

faculty in that same subject some years later, the later date was used.
Calendars for all Canadian universities from the late 19th century to 1960, and histories of all relevant universities (too numerous to name)
Harris. *A History of Higher Education in Canada, 1663–1960.* 1976

Queen's University students
This study is based on students who registered at Queen's University, Kingston, for the first time between 1895 and 1900. It includes 186 extramural students. The students' geographic origin was taken to be the address of the school they attended prior to registering at Queen's rather than their residential address. The latter was not always interpreted in the same manner by students: some students gave their parents' address, while other students gave a temporary location where they were employed rather than a home address. For this study Eastern Ontario was defined as the area east of a line connecting Port Hope, Peterborough, and Pembroke. The information on the careers of graduates, derived from alumni records, is available for most graduates (85%) but few non-graduates (12%) and reflects those students who maintained contact with the alumni office. Thanks are due to Ann MacDermaid and her colleagues at Queen's Univeristy Archives and the staff at Queen's University alumni office for their assistance.
Ontario. Department of Education. *Annual Report.* 1900. Tables I, J
Queen's University Alumni Office. Alumni files. 1900–60
Queen's University Archives. Records of students. 1895–1900

Further readings
Axelrod, Paul. 'Historical Writing and Canadian Universities: The State of the Art.' *Queen's Quarterly* 91, no. 1 (Spring 1982): 137–44
– *Scholars and Dollars: Politics, Economics, and the Universities of Ontario, 1945–1980.* Toronto: University of Toronto Press, 1982
Axelrod, Paul, and John Reid, eds. *Youth, University and Canadian Society: Essays in the Social History of Higher Education.* Montréal: McGill-Queen's University Press, 1989
Marks, Lynne, and Chad Gaffield. 'Women at Queen's University, 1895–1905: A 'Little Sphere' All Their Own?' *Ontario History* 78, no. 4 (Dec 1986): 331–50
Reid, John G. 'Some Recent Histories of Canadian Universities.' *American Review of Canadian Studies* 14, no. 4 (Fall 1984): 369–73

PLATE 65
National Broadcasting Systems

MICHAEL J. DOUCET   Geography, Ryerson Polytechnical Institute
MARGARET HOBBS   PH D candidate, History and Philosophy of Education, Ontario Institute for Studies in Education

Thanks are due to librarian Nola Brunelle, Canadian National Railway (CNR) Headquarters, Montréal, for her assistance in providing information on CNR radio; Carol White, National Map Collection, NAC, for her help in finding a map relating to the CNR's 1927 broadcast; the archives and business affairs departments of the Canadian Broadcasting Corporation (CBC) for their assistance in locating and their permission to use the CBC logo; and David Adams for his help with the Bureau of Broadcast Measurement information.

Households with radios, 1931
Canada. *Census.* 1931. Vol 5, Table 57

Radios in Canada
Figures for 1941 are based on the number of dwellings; in other years the number of households was used. Figures for 1949 and 1961 include Newfoundland.
Canada. *Census.* 1931: Vol 5, Table 57. 1941: Vol 9, Table 18
– DBS. Cat. 64–202. 1949, 1961

High-powered radio stations, 1929
Radio stations, 1929
Shown on the map are private, commercial broadcasting stations; amateur stations are not included.
Canada. Royal Commission on Radio Broadcasting. *Report.* Ottawa, 1929
NAC. National Map Collection. 27565, HI/1100/1927

Radio stations and networks, 1956
Public and private radio programming
Canadian radio programs
Canadian television programs
Television networks, 1956
CBC television programming
Figures on Canadian radio and television programs include both live and recorded programs and represent the amount of Canadian content in total programming. The illustrations showing the type of programming on radio and television are based on the number of hours rather the number of programs broadcast.
Canada. Royal Commission on Broadcasting. *Report.* Ottawa, 1957

CBC radio broadcasts
CBC Times 8, no. 27 (15–21 Jan 1956): 5, 7
La semaine à Radio-Canada 6, no. 15 (14–20 Jan 1956)

The growing popularity of television
Canada. DBS. Cat. 64–202. 1953–61

Origin of CBC television network programs
Figures were based on the total number of hours broadcast.
CBC. *Annual Report.* 1956–7. P 42

The direct American television option
Data in 1961 included for the first time all television stations in Canada, both members and non-members of the Bureau of Broadcasting Measurement. To be counted here a station had to be tuned into by at least 1% of the households in the specified area for at least 7 half-hour periods during the week specified.
Bureau of Broadcasting Measurement. *Television Area Report Spring 1961 Survey.* 13–19 Mar 1961 inclusive

Further readings

Allard, T.J. *Straight Up: Private Broadcasting in Canada, 1918–1958*. Ottawa: Canadian Communications Federation, 1975

Bird, Roger, ed. *Documents of Canadian Broadcasting*. Ottawa: Carleton University Press, 1988

Frick, Nora Alice. *Image in the Mind: CBC Radio Drama, 1944–1954*. Toronto: Canadian Stage, 1987

Maistre, Gilbert. 'L'influence de la radio et la télévision américaines au Canada.' *Recherches sociographiques* 12, no. 1 (Jan–Apr 1971): 51–72

McNeil, Bill, and Morris Wolfe. *Signing On: The Birth of Radio in Canada*. Toronto: Doubleday, 1982

Miller, Mary Jane. *Turn Up the Contrast: CBC Television Drama Since 1952*. Vancouver: University of British Columbia Press / CBC Enterprises, 1987

Peers, Frank W. *The Politics of Canadian Broadcasting 1920–51*. Toronto: University of Toronto Press, 1969

– *The Public Eye: Television and the Politics of Canadian Broadcasting, 1952–1968*. Toronto: University of Toronto Press, 1979

Prang, Margaret. 'The Origins of Public Broadcasting in Canada.' *Canadian Historical Review* 46, no. 1 (Mar 1965): 1–31

Weir, E. Austin. *The Struggle for National Broadcasting in Canada*. Toronto: McClelland and Stewart, 1965

PLATE 66

Canada in 1961

MARVIN McINNIS   Economics, Queen's University

Total income by regions
Total income by industrial sector

The starting point for these maps was the aggregate of personal income, as estimated in the *National Income and Expenditure Accounts*, by province, separated into agriculture and non-agricultural components. These aggregates were allocated within provinces to Census Metropolitan Areas (CMA) and to regions making up the remainder of the provinces. These regions are rather arbitrary groupings of counties and districts. The provincial total of farm income was allocated across regions in proportion to the total capital value of farms. Total farm revenues might have been used but would have involved a laborious aggregation of individual components over a large number of regions. Capital values provided a simple but satisfactory approximation. The provincial total of non-agricultural income was allocated to broad industry groupings within each province on the basis of aggregate earnings of wage earners in each industry group as reported in the census.

The same census data on earnings of wage earners by industry group were used to estimate the share of industry. Industry-specific provincial totals were allocated to each CMA. No such data existed for counties and smaller cities. For those the basis of allocation was shifted to an artificial industry – an aggregate of specific earnings composed of the labour force, of each sex, in each industry, weighted by provincial average wage earnings, for males and females separately, in each respective industry. One adjustment had to be made at a provincial boundary. The Ottawa CMA includes Hull and several adjacent communities in Québec. The Québec and Ontario segments of that CMA were estimated separately although it should be evident from the estimating procedure described above that the Québec segment of the CMA involves a different procedure and different data from the Ontario segment.

Canada. *Census*. 1961. Vol 5, Pt 1, Table 18; Vol 3, Pt 2, 3

– Statistics Canada. *National Income and Expenditure Accounts*. Vol 1: 1926–74. 1976

Isodemographic Canada

Since no isodemographic map exists for 1961, the map for 1966 was used; a comparison of population distribution in 1961 and 1966 revealed no differences that would appear at the scale of the map on this plate.

Skoda, L., and J.C. Robertson. *Isodemographic Map of Canada*. Department of Environment. Lands Directorate. Geographical Paper No. 50. Ottawa, 1972

Typesetting, text: University of Toronto Press

Typesetting, plates: Cooper and Beatty Limited

Photomechanical services and colour proofs: Northway Map Technology Limited

Jacket separation and film services: Colour Technologies

Printer: Ashton-Potter Limited

Case binder: Anstey Graphic Limited